Interpretable Machine Learning with Python

Learn to build interpretable high-performance models with hands-on real-world examples

Serg Masís

BIRMINGHAM—MUMBAI

Interpretable Machine Learning with Python

Group Product Manager: Kunal Parikh
Publishing Product Manager: Sunith Shetty
Acquisition Editor: Reshma Raman
Senior Editor: Roshan Kumar
Content Development Editors: Sean Lobo and Joseph Sunil
Technical Editor: Sonam Pandey
Copy Editor: Safis Editing
Project Coordinator: Aishwarya Mohan
Proofreader: Safis Editing
Indexer: Priyanka Dhadke
Production Designer: Roshan Kawale

First published: March 2021
Production reference: 1250321

Published by Packt Publishing Ltd.
Livery Place
35 Livery Street
Birmingham
B3 2PB, UK.

ISBN 978-1-80020-390-7

www.packt.com

Contributors

About the author

Serg Masís has been at the confluence of the internet, application development, and analytics for the last two decades. Currently, he's a climate and agronomic data scientist at Syngenta, a leading agribusiness company with a mission to improve global food security. Before that role, he co-founded a start-up, incubated by Harvard Innovation Labs, that combined the power of cloud computing and machine learning with principles in decision-making science to expose users to new places and events. Whether it pertains to leisure activities, plant diseases, or customer lifetime value, Serg is passionate about providing the often-missing link between data and decision-making—and machine learning interpretation helps bridge this gap robustly.

About the reviewers

Shailendra Kadre is a seasoned ML, DL, Product Development, and Digital Transformation professional with more than 20 years of industry experience with global IT products and services companies. Currently, Shailendra is Worldwide Product Analytics Lead with HP Inc, Bangalore. He is active as an advisor to universities and corporates on AI. He has authored two books on AI, published by Springer and McGraw-Hill, USA. He is also a professional photography enthusiast. He has held leadership positions in Machine Learning, Product Analytics, and Digital Transformation space with HP Inc., Citi Group/ Oracle, Satyam, and TCS. Shailendra Kadre holds a master's degree in Design Engineering from the Indian Institute of Technology (IIT), Delhi.

James Le is a Data Advocate for Superb AI, a Y Combinator-backed company that radically improves AI production workflows with an advanced training data management platform. Before that, he completed his M.S. in Computer Science from RIT, doing research at the intersection of deep learning and recommendation systems.

Muhammad Rehman Zafar is a Ph.D. candidate at Ryerson University, Toronto, Canada and affiliated with Ryerson Multimedia Research Laboratory (RML). His research focuses on designing and developing interpretable models by combining interactive visualizations and machine learning approaches that help end-users to understand the decisions made by complex models in an effective way. Rehman is also part of the Toronto-based team of Aggregate Intellect as a machine learning interpretability stream owner.

Ali El-Sharif lives in Windsor, Ontario, Canada with his wife, three children, mother, and a cat. Ali is a Ph.D. candidate at Nova Southeastern University, conducting research in Machine Learning interpretability. Ali is also part of the Toronto-based team of Aggregate Intellect as a Machine Learning Interpretability Stream Owner. Ali holds a bachelor's degree in computer engineering and an MBA from Wright State University in Dayton, Ohio. He also holds a master's degree in information security from Nova Southeastern University. Ali is currently an instructor teaching Data Analytics and Information Security as part of the Zekelman School of Business & IT at St. Clair College in Windsor, ON, Canada.

Federico Riveroll is an expert in the fields of ML and Data Science. He is the co-founder of OpenBlender.io and has 11 years of experience working with global companies like AB InBev. Federico has also worked with startups and universities on varied AI projects.

Packt is searching for authors like you

If you're interested in becoming an author for Packt, please visit `authors.packtpub.com` and apply today. We have worked with thousands of developers and tech professionals, just like you, to help them share their insight with the global tech community. You can make a general application, apply for a specific hot topic that we are recruiting an author for, or submit your own idea.

Table of Contents

3

Interpretation Challenges

Section 2: Mastering Interpretation Methods

4

Fundamentals of Feature Importance and Impact

5

Global Model-Agnostic Interpretation Methods

6

Local Model-Agnostic Interpretation Methods

7

Anchor and Counterfactual Explanations

8

Visualizing Convolutional Neural Networks

9

Interpretation Methods for Multivariate Forecasting and Sensitivity Analysis

Section 3: Tuning for Interpretability

10
Feature Selection and Engineering for Interpretability

11
Bias Mitigation and Causal Inference Methods

12

Monotonic Constraints and Model Tuning for Interpretability

13

Adversarial Robustness

14
What's Next for Machine Learning Interpretability?

Other Books You May Enjoy

Index

Preface

From this book's title, you can infer that this book is about three things: **Interpretation**, **Machine Learning**, and **Python**. And they are precisely in that order of importance!

"Why?", you might ask.

Interpretable Machine Learning, also known as **Explainable AI (XAI)**, is an ever-increasing family of methods that we can leverage to learn from models and make them safe, fair, and reliable, which is something, I hope, we all want for our models.

However, since AI is replacing software (and humans), machine learning models are seen as a more "intelligent" form of software. Yes, they are ones and zeros, but they are not software in the sense that their logic is programmed by people and does as intended, by design. So, interpretation is how we can make sense of them and their mistakes, then correct their flaws, hopefully before they cause any harm. Hence, interpretation is critical to make models trustworthy, and ethical. Also, soon enough, we won't even train models with code, but with drag-and-drop interfaces! So, while we all love Python, the skill that will stand the test of time is machine learning interpretation.

For now, it still takes ample code to prepare and explore data and then train and productionize models, so every chapter in this book involves detailed Python code examples. Yet, the book wasn't designed to be employed as a programming "cookbook" disconnected from use cases and any sense of purpose. Instead, this book is flipping this paradigm around. The reason for this is simple: For **Interpretable Machine Learning** to be effective, the "**why?**" has to precede the "**how?**". After all, interpretation is all about answering the question "why?".

For this reason, most chapters begin with a mission (the "why?") followed by an approach (the "how?"). After that, the goal is to complete the mission using the methods (more "how?") taught throughout the chapter, focusing on interpreting outcomes (more "why?"). Lastly, it will reflect on what actionable insights were learned completing the task.

The book itself is also structured. It goes from fundamentals to more advanced topics. The tools employed are all open source and built by the most advanced research labs, such as Microsoft, Google, and IBM. It's a very broad area of research, most of which hasn't even left the lab and become widely used. This book has no intention of covering absolutely all of it. Instead, the objective is to present many interpretability tools in sufficient depth to be useful for practitioners and the many professionals involved in the machine learning field.

The first section of the book is a beginner's guide to interpretability, covering its relevance in business and exploring its key aspects and challenges. The second section will get you up to speed with a comprehensive collection of interpretation methods and how to apply them to different use cases, be it for classification or regression, for tabular data, time-series, images, or text. In the third section, you'll get hands-on with tuning models and training data for interpretability by reducing complexity, mitigating bias, placing guardrails, and enhancing reliability.

By the end of this book, you will be employing interpretation methods to understand machine learning models better and improving them through interpretability tuning.

Who this book is for

This book is for the following people:

- Beginners and students of data science with a foundational knowledge of machine learning and the Python programming language.

- Data professionals with an increasingly critical responsibility to explain how the AI systems they develop and maintain work, and how to improve them.

- Machine learning engineers and data scientists who want to expand their skillset to include the latest interpretation methods and bias mitigation techniques.

- AI ethics officers, to deepen their understanding of the implementation side of their work to direct those efforts better.

- AI project managers and business leaders who want to introduce interpretable machine learning to their businesses to comply with principles of fairness, accountability, and transparency.

What this book covers

Chapter 1, Interpretation, Interpretability, and Explainability; and Why Does It All Matter?, introduces machine learning interpretation and related concepts such as interpretability, explainability, black-box models, and transparency, providing definitions for these terms to avoid ambiguity. We then underpin the value of machine learning interpretability for businesses.

Chapter 2, Key Concepts of Interpretability, uses a cardiovascular disease prediction example to introduce two fundamental concepts (**feature importance** and **decision regions**) and the most important taxonomies used to classify interpretation methods. We also detail what elements hinder machine learning interpretability as a primer for what lies ahead.

Chapter 3, Interpretation Challenges, discusses the traditional methods used for machine learning interpretation for both regression and classification with a flight delay prediction problem. We will then examine the limitations of these traditional methods and explain what makes "white-box" models intrinsically interpretable and why we cannot always use white-box models. To answer this question, we consider the trade-off between prediction performance and model interpretability. Finally, we will discover some new "glass-box" models that attempt to not compromise in this trade-off.

Chapter 4, Fundamentals of Feature Importance and Impact, employs a birth order classification example to discuss different methods to obtain feature importance such as those that use a model's intrinsic parameters, and a more reliable model-agnostic method called **Permutation Feature Importance**. Then, to convey a single feature's marginal impact on the prediction, we will study how to render and interpret **Partial Dependence Plots (PDP)** and **Individual Conditional Expectation (ICE)** plots.

Chapter 5, Global Model-Agnostic Interpretation Methods, explores game-theory-inspired **SHapley Additive exPlanations (SHAP)** in great detail with fuel efficiency regression models, then visualizes conditional marginal distribution **Accumulated Local Effects (ALE)** plots. Finally, we touch on **Global Surrogates**, which can be very accurate and efficient interpretation tools when chosen correctly.

Chapter 6, Local Model-Agnostic Interpretation Methods, covers local interpretation methods, explaining a single or a group of predictions. To this end, the chapter covers how to leverage **SHAP** and **Local Interpretable Model-agnostic Explanations (LIME)** for local interpretations with a chocolate bar rating example, with both tabular and text data.

Chapter 7, Anchor and Counterfactual Explanations, continues with local model interpretations, but only for classification problems. We use a recidivism risk prediction example to understand how we can explain unfair predictions in a human-interpretable way. This chapter covers **Anchors**, **Counterfactuals**, and the **Contrastive Explanation Method** (**CEM**), as well as the **What-If-Tool** (**WIT**).

Chapter 8, Visualizing Convolutional Neural Networks, exclusively explores interpretation methods that work with **Convolutional Neural Network** (**CNN**) models with a fruit classifier model. Once we have grasped how a CNN learns with **Activations**, we will study several gradient-based attribution methods, such as **Saliency Maps**, **Grad-CAM**, and **Integrated Gradients** to debug class attribution. Lastly, we will extend our attribution debugging know-how with perturbation-based attribution methods such as **Occlusion Sensitivity**, **LIME**, and **CEM**.

Chapter 9, Interpretation Methods for Multivariate Forecasting and Sensitivity Analysis, uses a traffic forecasting problem and **Long Short-Term Memory** (**LSTM**) models to look at how to employ **Integrated Gradients** and **SHAP** for this use case. Lastly, the chapter looks at how forecasting and uncertainty are intrinsically linked, and sensitivity analysis – a family of methods designed to measure the uncertainty of a model's output in relation to its input. We study two such methods: **Morris** for factor prioritization and **Sobol** for factor fixing.

Chapter 10, Feature Selection and Engineering for Interpretability, uses a challenging non-profit direct mailing optimization problem to review filter-based feature selection methods such as **Spearman**'s correlation and learn about embedded methods such as **Lasso**. Then, you will discover wrapper methods such as **Sequential Feature Selection** and hybrid ones such as **Recursive Feature Elimination**, as well as more advanced ones such as **Genetic Algorithms**. Lastly, even though feature engineering is typically conducted before selection, there's value in exploring **feature engineering** for many reasons after the dust has settled.

Chapter 11, Bias Mitigation and Causal Inference Methods, takes a credit card default problem to demonstrate leveraging fairness metrics and visualizations to detect undesired bias. Then, the chapter looks at how to reduce it via **pre-processing** methods such as reweighting and disparate impact remover for **in-processing** and **equalized odds** for post-processing. Then, we test treatments for lowering credit card default and leverage causal modeling to determine their **average treatment effects** (**ATE**), and **conditional average treatment effects** (**CATE**). Finally, we test causal assumptions and the robustness of estimates.

Chapter 12, Monotonic Constraints and Model Tuning for Interpretability, continues with the recidivism risk prediction problem from Chapter 7. We will learn how to place guardrails with **feature engineering** on the data side and **monotonic and interaction constraints** on the model to ensure fairness while also learning how to tune a model when there are several objectives.

Chapter 13, Adversarial Robustness, uses a face mask detection problem to cover an end-to-end adversarial solution. An adversary can purposely thwart a model in many ways, but we focus on evasion attacks such as **Carlini and Wagner Infinity-Norm** and **Adversarial Patches** and briefly explain other forms of attacks. We explain two defense methods: **spatial smoothing preprocessing** and **adversarial training**. Lastly, we demonstrate one **robustness evaluation** method and one certification method.

Chapter 14, What's Next for Machine Learning Interpretability?, summarizes what was learned in the context of the ecosystem of machine learning interpretability methods. And then speculates on what's to come next!

To get the most out of this book

You will need a Jupyter environment with Python 3.6+. You can do either of the following:

- Install one on your machine locally via **Anaconda Navigator** or from scratch with **pip.**
- Use a cloud-based one such as **Google Colaboratory**, **Kaggle Notebooks**, **Azure Notebooks**, or **Amazon Sagemaker.**

The instructions on how to get started will vary accordingly, so we strongly suggest that you search online for the latest instructions for setting them up.

For instructions on installing the many packages employed throughout the book, please go to the Git repository, which will have the updated instructions in the **readme** file. We expect these to change from time to time, given how often packages change. We also tested the code with specific versions detailed in the **readme**, so should anything fail with later versions, please install the specific version instead.

Individual chapters begin with instructions on how to install packages in this form:

```
!pip install --upgrade nltk lightgbm lime
```

But depending on the way **Jupyter** was set up, installing packages might be best done through the **command line** or using **conda**, so we suggest you adapt these installation instructions to suit your needs.

If you are using the digital version of this book, we advise you to type the code yourself or access the code via the GitHub repository (link available in the next section). Doing so will help you avoid any potential errors related to the copying and pasting of code.

If you are not a machine learning practitioner or are a beginner, the advice is to read the book sequentially since many concepts are only explained in great detail in earlier chapters. The recommendation for practitioners skilled in machine learning but not acquainted with interpretability is that they can skim the first three chapters to get the ethical context and concept definitions they need to make sense of the rest, but read in the rest in order. As for advanced practitioners that have the foundations of interpretability, reading in any order should be fine.

As for the code, you can read the book without running the code simultaneously or strictly for the theory. But if you plan to run the code, it is best to do it with the book as a guide to assist with the interpretation of outcomes, and to strengthen your understanding of the theory.

While you are reading the book, think of ways in which you could use the tools learned, and by the end of it, hopefully, you will be inspired to put this newly gained knowledge into action!

Download the example code files

You can download the example code files for this book from GitHub at `https://github.com/PacktPublishing/Interpretable-Machine-Learning-with-Python/`. In case there's an update to the code, it will be updated on the existing GitHub repository. You can also find the hardware and software list of requirements on the repository in the `README.MD` file.

We also have other code bundles from our rich catalog of books and videos available at `https://github.com/PacktPublishing/`. Check them out!

Download the color images

We also provide a PDF file that has color images of the screenshots/diagrams used in this book. You can download it here: `https://static.packt-cdn.com/downloads/9781800203907_ColorImages.pdf`.

Conventions used

There are a number of text conventions used throughout this book.

`Code in text`: Indicates code words in text, database table names, folder names, filenames, file extensions, pathnames, dummy URLs, user input, and Twitter handles. Here is an example: "Next, we can adversarially train the model by first initializing a new `KerasClassifier` with the `robust_model`."

A block of code is set as follows:

```
base_classifier = KerasClassifier(model=base_model,\
                                  clip_values=(min_, max_))
y_test_mdsample_prob = np.max(y_test_prob[sampl_md_idxs],\
                                                  axis=1)
y_test_smsample_prob = np.max(y_test_prob[sampl_sm_idxs],\
                                                  axis=1)
```

When we wish to draw your attention to a particular part of a code block, the relevant lines or items are set in bold:

```
robust_classifier = KerasClassifier(model=robust_model,\
                                    clip_values=(min_, max_))
attacks = BasicIterativeMethod(robust_classifier, eps=0.3,\
                               eps_step=0.01, max_iter=20)
trainer = AdversarialTrainer(robust_classifier, attacks,
ratio=0.5)
trainer.fit(X_train, ohe.transform(y_train), nb_epochs=30,\
            batch_size=128)
```

Any command-line input or output is written as follows:

```
$ mkdir css
$ cd css
```

Bold: Indicates a new term, an important word, or words that you see onscreen. For example, words in menus or dialog boxes appear in the text like this. Here is an example: "Select **System info** from the **Administration** panel."

> **Tips or important notes**
> Appear like this.

Get in touch

Feedback from our readers is always welcome.

General feedback: If you have questions about any aspect of this book, mention the book title in the subject of your message and email us at customercare@packtpub.com.

Errata: Although we have taken every care to ensure the accuracy of our content, mistakes do happen. If you have found a mistake in this book, we would be grateful if you would report this to us. Please visit www.packtpub.com/support/errata, selecting your book, clicking on the Errata Submission Form link, and entering the details.

Piracy: If you come across any illegal copies of our works in any form on the Internet, we would be grateful if you would provide us with the location address or website name. Please contact us at copyright@packt.com with a link to the material.

If you are interested in becoming an author: If there is a topic that you have expertise in and you are interested in either writing or contributing to a book, please visit authors.packtpub.com.

Reviews

Please leave a review. Once you have read and used this book, why not leave a review on the site that you purchased it from? Potential readers can then see and use your unbiased opinion to make purchase decisions, we at Packt can understand what you think about our products, and our authors can see your feedback on their book. Thank you!

For more information about Packt, please visit packt.com.

Section 1:
Introduction to
Machine Learning
Interpretation

In this section, you will recognize the importance of interpretability in business and understand its key aspects and challenges.

This section includes the following chapters:

- *Chapter 1, Interpretation, Interpretability and Explainability; and why does it all matter?*
- *Chapter 2, Key Concepts of Interpretability*
- *Chapter 3, Interpretation Challenges*

1
Interpretation, Interpretability, and Explainability; and Why Does It All Matter?

We live in a world whose rules and procedures are governed by data and algorithms.

For instance, there are rules as to who gets approved for credit or released on bail, and which social media posts might get censored. There are also procedures to determine which marketing tactics are most effective and which chest x-ray features might diagnose a positive case of pneumonia.

You expect this because it is nothing new!

But not so long ago, rules and procedures such as these used to be hardcoded into software, textbooks, and paper forms, and humans were the ultimate decision-makers. Often, it was entirely up to human discretion. Decisions depended on human discretion because rules and procedures were rigid and, therefore, not always applicable. There were *always* exceptions, so a human was needed to make them.

For example, if you would ask for a mortgage, your approval depended on an acceptable and reasonably lengthy credit history. This data, in turn, would produce a credit score using a scoring algorithm. Then, the bank had rules that determined what score was good enough for the mortgage you wanted. Your loan officer could follow it or override it.

These days, financial institutions train models on thousands of mortgage outcomes, with dozens of variables. These models can be used to determine the likelihood that you would default on a mortgage with a presumed high accuracy. If there is a loan officer to stamp the approval or denial, it's no longer merely a guideline but an algorithmic decision. How could it be wrong? How could it be right?

Hold on to that thought because, throughout this book, we will be learning the answers to these questions and many more!

To interpret decisions made by a machine learning model is to find meaning in it, but furthermore, you can trace it back to its source and the process that transformed it. This chapter introduces machine learning interpretation and related concepts such as interpretability, explainability, black-box models, and transparency. This chapter provides definitions for these terms to avoid ambiguity and underpins the value of machine learning interpretability. These are the main topics we are going to cover:

- What is machine learning interpretation?
- Understanding the difference between interpretation and explainability
- A business case for interpretability

Let's get started!

Technical requirements

To follow the example in this chapter, you will need Python 3, either running in a Jupyter environment or in your favorite **integrated development environment** (**IDE**) such as PyCharm, Atom, VSCode, PyDev, or Idle. The example also requires the `requests`, `bs4`, `pandas`, `sklearn`, `matplotlib`, and `scipy` Python libraries. The code for this chapter is located here: `https://github.com/PacktPublishing/Interpretable-Machine-Learning-with-Python/tree/master/Chapter01`.

What is machine learning interpretation?

To interpret something is to *explain the meaning of it*. In the context of machine learning, that something is an algorithm. More specifically, that algorithm is a mathematical one that takes input data and produces an output, much like with any formula.

Let's examine the most basic of models, simple linear regression, illustrated in the following formula:

$$\hat{y} = \beta_0 + \beta_1 x_1$$

Once fitted to the data, the meaning of this model is that $\hat{y}$ predictions are a weighted sum of the x features with the β coefficients. In this case, there's only one x **feature** or **predictor** variable, and the y variable is typically called the **response** or **target** variable. A simple linear regression formula single-handedly explains the transformation, which is performed on the input data x_1 to produce the output $\hat{y}$. The following example can illustrate this concept in further detail.

Understanding a simple weight prediction model

If you go to this web page maintained by the University of California, `http://wiki.stat.ucla.edu/socr/index.php/SOCR_Data_Dinov_020108_HeightsWeights`, you can find a link to download a dataset of 25,000 synthetic records of weights and heights of 18-year-olds. We won't use the entire dataset but only the sample table on the web page itself with 200 records. We scrape the table from the web page and fit a linear regression model to the data. The model uses the height to predict the weight.

In other words, x_1 = height and y = weight, so the formula for the linear regression model would be as follows:

$$\text{weight} = \beta_0 + \beta_1 \text{height}$$

You can find the code for this example here: `https://github.com/PacktPublishing/Interpretable-Machine-Learning-with-Python/blob/master/Chapter01/WeightPrediction.ipynb`.

To run this example, you need to install the following libraries:

- `requests` to fetch the web page
- `bs4` (Beautiful Soup) to scrape the table from the web page
- `pandas` to load the table in to a dataframe
- `sklearn` (scikit-learn) to fit the linear regression model and calculate its error

- `matplotlib` to visualize the model
- `scipy` to test the correlation

You should load all of them first, as follows:

```
Import math
import requests
from bs4 import BeautifulSoup
import pandas as pd
from sklearn import linear_model
from sklearn.metrics import mean_absolute_error
import matplotlib.pyplot as plt
from scipy.stats import pearsonr
```

Once the libraries are all loaded, you use `requests` to fetch the contents of the web page, like this:

```
url = \
'http://wiki.stat.ucla.edu/socr/index.php/SOCR_Data_
Dinov_020108_HeightsWeights'
page = requests.get(url)
```

Then, take these contents and scrape out just the contents of the table with `BeautifulSoup`, as follows:

```
soup = BeautifulSoup(page.content, 'html.parser')
tbl = soup.find("table",{"class":"wikitable"})
```

`pandas` can turn the raw **HyperText Markup Language** (**HTML**) contents of the table into a dataframe, as illustrated here:

```
height_weight_df = pd.read_html(str(tbl))[0]\
[['Height(Inches)','Weight(Pounds)']]
```

And voilà! We now have a dataframe with `Heights(Inches)` in one column and `Weights(Pounds)` in another. As a sanity check, we can then count the number of records. This should be 200. The code is shown here:

```
num_records = height_weight_df.shape[0]
print(num_records)
```

Now that we have confirmed that we have the data, we must transform it so that it conforms to the model's specifications. `sklearn` needs it as NumPy arrays with (200,1) dimensions, so we must first extract the `Height(Inches)` and `Weight(Pounds)` pandas Series. Then, we turn them into (200,) NumPy arrays, and, finally, reshape them into (200,1) dimensions. The following commands perform all the necessary transformation operations:

```
x = height_weight_df['Height(Inches)'].values.\
                                reshape(num_records, 1)
y = height_weight_df['Weight(Pounds)'].values.\
                                reshape(num_records, 1)
```

Then, you initialize the scikit-learn `LinearRegression` model and `fit` it with the training data, as follows:

```
model = linear_model.LinearRegression()
_ = model.fit(x, y)
```

To output the fitted linear regression model formula in scikit-learn, you must extract the intercept and coefficients. This is the **formula** that explains how it makes predictions:

```
print("ŷ =" + str(model.intercept_[0]) + " " + " +\
                    str(model.coef_.T[0][0]) + " x")
                                                  1
```

The following is the output:

```
ŷ = -106.02770644878132 + 3.432676129271629 x1
```

This tells us that, on average, for every additional pound, there are 3.4 inches of height.

However, *explaining how the model works* is only one way to explain this linear regression model, and this is only one side of the story. The model isn't perfect because the actual outcomes and the predicted outcomes are not the same for the training data. The difference between both is the **error** or **residuals**.

There are many ways of understanding an error in a model. You can use an error function such as `mean_absolute_error` to measure the deviation between the predicted values and the actual values, as illustrated in the following code snippet:

```
y_pred = model.predict(x)
mae = mean_absolute_error(y, y_pred)
print(mae)
```

The following is the output:

```
7.7587373803882205
```

A 7.8 mean absolute error means that, on average, the prediction is 7.8 pounds from the actual amount, but this might not be intuitive or informative. Visualizing the linear regression model can shed some light on how accurate these predictions truly are.

This can be done by using a `matplotlib` scatterplot and overlaying the linear model (in blue) and the *mean absolute error* (as two parallel bands in gray), as shown in the following code snippet:

```
plt.scatter(x, y, color='black')
plt.plot(x, y_pred, color='blue', linewidth=3)
plt.plot(x, y_pred + mae, color='lightgray')
plt.plot(x, y_pred - mae, color='lightgray')
plt.xlabel('Height(Inches)')
plt.ylabel('Weight(Pounds)')
```

If you run the preceding snippet, the plot shown here in *Figure 1.1* is what you get as the output:

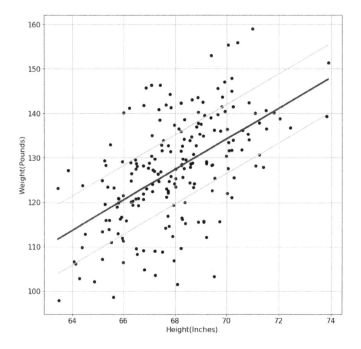

Figure 1.1 – Linear regression model to predict weight based on height

As you can appreciate from the plot in *Figure 1.1*, there are many times in which the actuals are $20 - 25$ pounds away from the prediction. Yet the mean absolute error can fool you into thinking that the error is always closer to 8. This is why it is essential to visualize the error of the model to understand its distribution. Judging from this graph, we can tell that there are no red flags that stand out about this distribution, such as residuals being more spread out for one range of heights than for others. Since it is more or less equally spread out, we say it's **homoscedastic**. In the case of linear regression, this is one of many model assumptions you should test for, along with *linearity, normality, independence*, and lack of *multicollinearity* (if there's more than one feature). These assumptions ensure that you are using the right model for the job. In other words, the height and weight *can be explained* with a linear relationship, and it is a good idea to do so, statistically speaking.

With this model, we are trying to establish a linear relationship between x height and y weight. This association is called a **linear correlation**. One way to measure this relationship's strength is with **Pearson's correlation coefficient**. This statistical method measures the association between two variables using their covariance divided by their standard deviations. It is a number between -1 and 1 whereby the closer the number it is to zero, the weaker the association is. If the number is positive, there is a positive association, and if it's negative, there is a negative one. In Python, you can compute Pearson's correlation coefficient with the `pearsonr` function from `scipy`, as illustrated here:

```
corr, pval = pearsonr(x[:,0], y[:,0])
print(corr)
```

The following is the output:

```
0.5568647346122992
```

The number is positive, which is no surprise because as height increases, weight also tends to increase, but it is also closer to 1 than to 0, denoting that it is strongly correlated. The second number produced by the `pearsonr` function is the p-value for testing non-correlation. If we test that it's less than an error level of 5%, we can say there's sufficient evidence of this correlation, as illustrated here:

```
print(pval < 0.05)
```

The following is the output:

```
True
```

Understanding how a model performs and in which circumstances can help us **explain why it makes certain predictions**, and when it cannot. Let's imagine we are asked to explain why someone who is 71 inches tall was predicted to have a weight of 134 pounds but instead weighed 18 pounds more. Judging from what we know about the model, this margin of error is not unusual even though it's not ideal. However, there are many circumstances in which we cannot expect this model to be reliable. What if we were asked to predict the weight of a person who is 56 inches tall with the help of this model? Could we assure the same level of accuracy? Definitely not, because we fit the model on the data of subjects no shorter than 63 inches. Ditto if we were asked to predict the weight of a 9-year-old, because the training data was for 18-year-olds.

Despite the acceptable results, this weight prediction model was not a realistic example. If you wanted to be more accurate but—more importantly—faithful to what can really impact the weight of an individual, you would need to add more variables. You can add—say—gender, age, diet, and activity level. This is where it gets interesting because you have to make sure **it is fair to include them, or not to include them**. For instance, if gender were included yet most of our dataset was composed of males, how could you ensure accuracy for females? This is what is called **selection bias**. And what if weight had more to do with lifestyle choices and circumstances such as poverty and pregnancy than gender? If these variables aren't included, this is called **omitted variable bias**. And then, does it make sense to include the sensitive gender variable at the risk of adding bias to the model?

Once you have multiple features that you have vetted for fairness, you can find out and *explain which features impact model performance*. We call this **feature importance**. However, as we add more variables, we increase the complexity of the model. Paradoxically, this is a problem for interpretation, and we will explore this in further detail in the following chapters. For now, the key takeaway should be that model interpretation has a lot to do with explaining the following:

1. Can we explain that predictions were made fairly?

2. Can we trace the predictions reliably back to something or someone?

3. Can we explain how predictions were made? Can we explain how the model works?

And ultimately, the question we are trying to answer is this:

Can we trust the model?

The three main concepts of interpretable machine learning directly relate to the three preceding questions and have the acronym of **FAT**, which stands for **fairness**, **accountability**, and **transparency**. If you can explain that predictions were made without discernible bias, then there is **fairness**. If you can explain why it makes certain predictions, then there's **accountability**. And if you can explain how predictions were made and how the model works, then there's **transparency**. There are many ethical concerns associated to these concepts, as shown here in *Figure 1.2*:

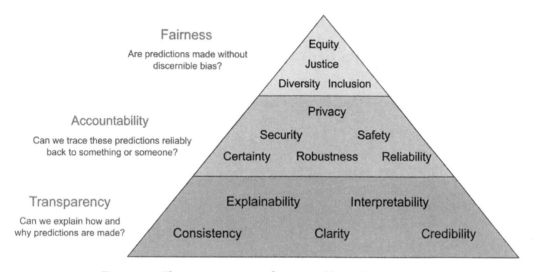

Figure 1.2 – Three main concept of Interpretable Machine Learning

Some researchers and companies have expanded FAT under a larger umbrella of ethical **artificial intelligence (AI)**, thus turning FAT into FATE. Ethical AI is part of an even larger discussion of algorithmic and data governance. However, both concepts very much overlap since interpretable machine learning is how FAT principles and ethical concerns get implemented in machine learning. In this book, we will discuss ethics in this context. For instance, *Chapter 13, Adversarial Robustness* relates to reliability, safety, and security. *Chapter 11, Mitigating Bias and Causal Inference Methods* relates to fairness. That being said, interpretable machine learning can be leveraged with no ethical aim in mind, and also for unethical reasons.

Understanding the difference between interpretability and explainability

Something you've probably noticed when reading the first few pages of this book is that the verbs *interpret* and *explain*, as well as the nouns *interpretation* and *explanation*, have been used interchangeably. This is not surprising, considering that to interpret is to explain the meaning of something. Despite that, the related terms *interpretability* and *explainability* should not be used interchangeably, even though they are often mistaken for synonyms.

What is interpretability?

Interpretability is the extent to which humans, including non-subject-matter experts, can understand the cause and effect, and input and output, of a machine learning model. To say a model has a high level of interpretability means you can describe in a human-interpretable way its inference. In other words, why does an input to a model produce a specific output? What are the requirements and constraints of the input data? What are the confidence bounds of the predictions? Or, why does one variable have a more substantial effect than another? For interpretability, detailing how a model works is only relevant to the extent that it can explain its predictions and justify that it's the right model for the use case.

In this chapter's example, you could explain that there's a linear relationship between human height and weight, so using linear regression rather than a non-linear model makes sense. You can prove this statistically because the variables involved don't violate the assumptions of linear regression. Even when statistics are on our side, you still ought to consult with the domain knowledge area involved in the use case. In this one, we rest assured, biologically speaking, because our knowledge of human physiology doesn't contradict the connection between height and weight.

Beware of complexity

Many machine learning models are inherently harder to understand simply because of the math involved in the inner workings of the model or the specific model architecture. In addition to this, many choices are made that can increase complexity and make the models less interpretable, from dataset selection to feature selection and engineering, to model training and tuning choices. This complexity makes explaining how it works a challenge. Machine learning interpretability is a very active area of research, so there's still much debate on its precise definition. The debate includes whether total transparency is needed to qualify a machine learning model as sufficiently interpretable. This book favors the understanding that the definition of interpretability shouldn't necessarily exclude opaque models, which, for the most part, are complex, as long as the choices made don't compromise their trustworthiness. This compromise is what is generally called **post-hoc interpretability**. After all, much like a complex machine learning model, we can't explain exactly how a human brain makes a choice, yet we often trust its decision because we can ask a human for their reasoning. Post-hoc machine learning interpretation is exactly the same thing, except it's a human explaining the reasoning on behalf of the model. Using this particular concept of interpretability is advantageous because we can interpret opaque models and not sacrifice the accuracy of our predictions. We will discuss this in further detail in *Chapter 3, Interpretation Challenges*.

When does interpretability matter?

Decision-making systems don't always require interpretability. There are two cases that are offered as exceptions in research, outlined here:

- When incorrect results have no significant consequences. For instance, what if a machine learning model is trained to find and read the postal code in a package, occasionally misreads it, and sends it elsewhere? There's little chance of discriminatory bias, and the cost of misclassification is relatively low. It doesn't occur often enough to magnify the cost beyond acceptable thresholds.

- When there are consequences, but these have been studied sufficiently and validated enough in the real world to make decisions without human involvement. This is the case with a **traffic-alert and collision-avoidance system (TCAS)**, which alerts the pilot of another aircraft that poses a threat of a mid-air collision.

On the other hand, interpretability is needed for these systems to have the following attributes:

- **Minable for scientific knowledge**: Meteorologists have much to learn from a climate model, but only if it's easy to interpret.

- **Reliable and safe**: The decisions made by a self-driving vehicle must be debuggable so that its developers can understand points of failure.

- **Ethical**: A translation model might use gender-biased word embeddings that result in discriminatory translations, but you must be able to find these instances easily to correct them. However, the system must be designed in such a way that you can be made aware of a problem before it is released to the public.

- **Conclusive and consistent**: Sometimes, machine learning models may have incomplete and mutually exclusive objectives—for instance, a cholesterol-control system may not consider how likely a patient is to adhere to the diet or drug regimen, or there might be a trade-off between one objective and another, such as safety and non-discrimination.

By explaining the decisions of a model, we can cover gaps in our understanding of the problem—*its incompleteness*. One of the most significant issues is that given the high accuracy of our machine learning solutions, we tend to increase our confidence level to a point where we think we fully understand the problem. Then, we are misled into thinking our solution covers *ALL OF IT*!

At the beginning of this book, we discussed how levering data to produce algorithmic rules is nothing new. However, we used to second-guess these rules, and now we don't. Therefore, a human used to be accountable, and now it's the algorithm. In this case, the algorithm is a machine learning model that is accountable for all of the ethical ramifications this entails. This switch has a lot to do with accuracy. The problem is that although a model may surpass human accuracy in aggregate, machine learning models have yet to interpret its results like a human would. Therefore, it doesn't second-guess its decisions, so as a solution it lacks a desirable level of completeness. and that's why we need to interpret models so that we can cover at least some of that gap. So, why is machine learning interpretation not already a standard part of the pipeline? In addition to our bias toward focusing on accuracy alone, one of the biggest impediments is the daunting concept of black-box models.

What are black-box models?

This is just another term for opaque models. A black box refers to a system in which only the input and outputs are observable, and you cannot see what is transforming the inputs into the outputs. In the case of machine learning, a black-box model can be opened, but its mechanisms are not easily understood.

What are white-box models?

These are the opposite of black-box models (see *Figure 1.3*). They are also known as transparent because they achieve total or near-total interpretation transparency. We call them **intrinsically interpretable** in this book, and we cover them in more detail in *Chapter 3, Interpretation Challenges*.

Have a look at a comparison between the models here:

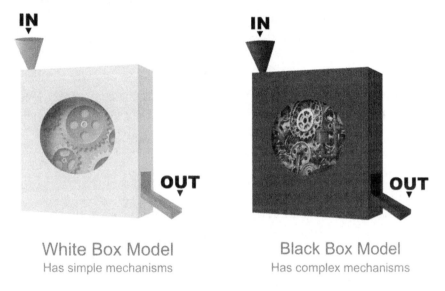

White Box Model
Has simple mechanisms

Black Box Model
Has complex mechanisms

Figure 1.3 – Visual comparison between white- and black-box models

What is explainability?

Explainability encompasses everything interpretability is. The difference is that it goes deeper on the transparency requirement than interpretability because it demands human-friendly explanations for a model's inner workings and the model training process, and not just model inference. Depending on the application, this requirement might extend to various degrees of model, design, and algorithmic transparency. There are three types of transparency, outlined here:

- **Model transparency**: Being able to explain how a model is trained step by step. In the case of our simple weight prediction model, we can explain how the optimization method called **ordinary least squares** finds the β coefficient that minimizes errors in the model.

- **Design transparency**: Being able to explain choices made, such as model architecture and hyperparameters. For instance, we could justify these choices based on the size or nature of the training data. If we were performing a sales forecast and we knew that our sales had a seasonality of 12 months, this could be a sound parameter choice. If we had doubts, we could always use some well-established statistical method to find the right seasonality.

- **Algorithmic transparency**: Being able to explain automated optimizations such as grid search for hyperparameters; but note that the ones that can't be reproduced because of their random nature—such as random search for hyperparameter optimization, early stopping, and stochastic gradient descent—make the algorithm non-transparent.

Opaque models are called *opaque* simply because they lack *model transparency*, but for many models this is unavoidable, however justified the model choice might be. In many scenarios, even if you outputted the math involved in—say—training a neural network or a random forest, it would raise more doubts than generate trust. There are at least a few reasons for this, outlined here:

- **Not "statistically grounded"**: An opaque model training process maps an input to an optimal output, leaving behind what appears to be an arbitrary trail of parameters. These parameters are optimized to a cost function but are not grounded in statistical theory.

- **Uncertainty and non-reproducibility**: When you fit a transparent model with the same data, you always get the same results. On the other hand, opaque models are not equally reproducible because they use random numbers to initialize their weights or to regularize or optimize their hyperparameters, or make use of stochastic discrimination (such is the case for Random Forest).

- **Overfitting and the curse of dimensionality**: Many of these models operate in a high-dimensional space. This doesn't elicit trust because it's harder to generalize on a larger number of dimensions. After all, there's more opportunity to overfit a model, the more dimensions you add.

- **Human cognition and the curse of dimensionality**: Transparent models are often used for smaller datasets with fewer dimensions, and even if they aren't a transparent model, never use more dimensions than necessary. They also tend to not complicate the interactions between these dimensions more than necessary. This lack of unnecessary complexity makes it easier to visualize what the model is doing and its outcomes. Humans are not very good at understanding many dimensions, so using transparent models tends to make this much easier to understand.

- **Occam's razor**: This is what is called the principle of simplicity or parsimony. It states that the simplest solution is usually the right one. Whether true or not, humans also have a bias for simplicity, and transparent models are known for— if anything—their simplicity.

Why and when does explainability matter?

Trustworthy and ethical decision-making is the main motivation for interpretability. Explainability has additional motivations such as causality, transferability, and informativeness. Therefore, there are many use cases in which total or nearly total transparency is valued, and rightly so. Some of these are outlined here:

- **Scientific research**: Reproducibility is essential to the scientific method. Also, using statistically grounded optimization methods is especially desirable when causality needs to be proven.

- **Clinical trials**: These must also produce reproducible findings and be statistically grounded. In addition to this, given the potential gravity of overfitting, they must use the fewest dimensions possible and models that don't complicate them.

- **Consumer product safety testing**: Much as with clinical trials, when life-and-death safety is a concern, simplicity is preferred whenever possible.

- **Public policy and law**: This is a more nuanced discussion, as part of what is called by law scholars **algorithmic governance**, and they have distinguished between **fishbowl transparency** and **reasoned transparency**. The former is closer to the rigor required for consumer product safety testing, and the latter is one where post-hoc interpretability would suffice. One day, the government could be entirely run by algorithms. When that happens, it's hard to tell which policies will align with which form of transparency, but there are many areas of public policy, such as criminal justice, where absolute transparency is necessary. However, whenever total transparency contradicts privacy or security objectives, a less rigorous form of transparency would have to make do.

- **Criminal investigation and regulatory compliance audits**: If something goes wrong, such as an accident at a chemical factory caused by a robot malfunction or a crash by an autonomous vehicle, an investigator needs to trace the **decision trail**. This is to "facilitate the assignment of accountability and legal liability". Even when no accident has happened, this kind of auditing can be performed when mandated by authorities. Compliance auditing applies to industries that are regulated, such as financial services, utilities, transportation, and healthcare. In many cases, fishbowl transparency is preferred.

A business case for interpretability

This section describes several practical business benefits for machine learning interpretability, such as better decisions, as well as being more trusted, ethical, and profitable.

Better decisions

Typically, machine learning models are trained and then evaluated against the desired metrics. If they pass quality control against a hold-out dataset, they are deployed. However, once tested in the real world, that's when things can get wild, as in the following hypothetical scenarios:

- A high-frequency trading algorithm could single-handedly crash the stock market.

- Hundreds of smart home devices might inexplicably burst into unprompted laughter, terrifying their users.

- License-plate recognition systems could incorrectly read a new kind of license plate and fine the wrong drivers.

- A racially biased surveillance system could incorrectly detect an intruder, and because of this guards shoot an innocent office worker.

- A self-driving car could mistake snow for a pavement, crash into a cliff, and injure passengers.

Any system is prone to error, so this is not to say that interpretability is a cure-all. However, focusing on just optimizing metrics can be a recipe for disaster. In the lab, the model might generalize well, but if you don't know why the model is making the decisions, then you can miss on an opportunity for improvement. For instance, knowing *what* the self-driving car thinks is a road is not enough, but knowing *why* could help improve the model. If, say, one of the reasons was that road is light-colored like the snow, this could be dangerous. Checking the model's assumptions and conclusions can lead to an improvement in the model by introducing winter road images into the dataset or feeding real-time weather data into the model. Also, if this doesn't work, maybe an algorithmic fail-safe can stop it from acting on a decision that it's not entirely confident about.

One of the main reasons why a focus on machine learning interpretability leads to better decision-making was mentioned earlier when we talked about completeness. If you think a model is complete, what is the point of making it better? Furthermore, if you don't question the model's reasoning, then your understanding of the problem must be complete. If this is the case, perhaps you shouldn't be using machine learning to solve the problem in the first place! Machine learning creates an algorithm that would otherwise be too complicated to program in *if-else* statements, precisely to be used for cases where our understanding of the problem is incomplete!

It turns out that when we predict or estimate something, especially with a high level of accuracy, we think we control it. This is what is called the **illusion of control bias**. We can't underestimate the complexity of a problem just because, in aggregate, the model gets it right almost all the time. Even for a human, the difference between snow and concrete pavement can be blurry and difficult to explain. How would you even begin to describe this difference in such a way that it is always accurate? A model can learn these differences, but it doesn't make it any less complex. Examining a model for points of failure and continuously being vigilant for outliers requires a different outlook, whereby we admit that we can't control the model but we can try to understand it through interpretation.

The following are some additional decision biases that can adversely impact a model, and serve as reasons why interpretability can lead to better decision-making:

- **Conservatism bias**: When we get new information, we don't change our prior beliefs. With this bias, entrenched pre-existing information trumps new information, but models ought to evolve. Hence, an attitude that values questioning prior assumptions is a healthy one to have.

- **Salience bias**: Some prominent or more visible things may stand out more than others, but statistically speaking, they should get equal attention to others. This bias could inform our choice of features, so an interpretability mindset can expand our understanding of a problem to include other less perceived features.

- **Fundamental attribution error**: This bias causes us to attribute outcomes to behavior rather than circumstances, character rather than situations, nature rather than nurture. Interpretability asks us to explore deeper and look for the less obvious relationships between our variables or those that could be missing.

One crucial benefit of model interpretation is locating *outliers*. These outliers could be a potential new source of revenue or a liability waiting to happen. Knowing this can help us to prepare and strategize accordingly.

More trusted brands

Trust is defined as a belief in the reliability, ability, or credibility of something or someone. In the context of organizations, trust is their reputation; and in the unforgiving court of public opinion, all it takes is one accident, controversy, or fiasco to lose substantial amounts of public confidence. This, in turn, can cause investor confidence to wane.

Let's consider what happened to Boeing after the 737 MAX debacle or Facebook after the 2016 presidential election scandal. In both cases, there were short-sighted decisions solely made to optimize a single metric, be it forecasted plane sales or digital ad sales. These underestimated known potential points of failure and missed out entirely on very big ones. From there, it can often get worse when organizations resort to fallacies to justify their reasoning, confuse the public, or distract the media narrative. This behavior might result in additional public relations blunders. Not only do they lose credibility with *what they do* with their first mistake but they attempt to fool people, losing credibility with *what they say*.

And these were examples of, for the most part, decisions made by people. With decisions made exclusively by machine learning models, this could get worse because it is easy to drop the ball and keep the accountability in the model's corner. For instance, if you started to see offensive material in your Facebook feed, Facebook could say it's because its model was trained with *your data* such as your comments and likes, so it's really a reflection of *what you want to see*. Not their fault—your fault. If the police targeted your neighborhood for aggressive policing because it uses PredPol, an algorithm that predicts where and when crimes will occur, it could blame the algorithm. On the other hand, the makers of this algorithm could blame the police because the software is trained on their police reports. This generates a potentially troubling feedback loop, not to mention an accountability gap. And if some pranksters or hackers eliminate lane markings, this could cause a Tesla self-driving car to veer into the wrong lane. Is this Tesla's fault that they didn't anticipate this possibility, or the hackers', for throwing a monkey wrench into their model? This is what is called an **adversarial attack**, and we discuss this in *Chapter 13, Adversarial Robustness*.

It is undoubtedly one of the goals of machine learning interpretability to make models better at making decisions. But even when they fail, you can show that you tried. Trust is not lost entirely because of the failure itself but because of the lack of accountability, and even in cases where it is not fair to accept all the blame, some accountability is better than none. For instance, in the previous set of examples, Facebook could look for clues as to why offensive material is shown more often, then commit to finding ways to make it happen less even if this means making less money. PredPol could find other sources of crime-rate datasets that are potentially less biased, even if they are smaller. They could also use techniques to mitigate bias in existing datasets (these are covered in *Chapter 11, Bias Mitigation and Causal Inference Methods*). And Tesla could audit its systems for adversarial attacks, even if this delays shipment of its cars. All of these are interpretability solutions. Once a common practice, they can lead to an increase in not only public trust—be it from users and customers, but also internal stakeholders such as employees and investors.

The following screenshot shows some public relation AI blunders that have occurred over the past couple of years:

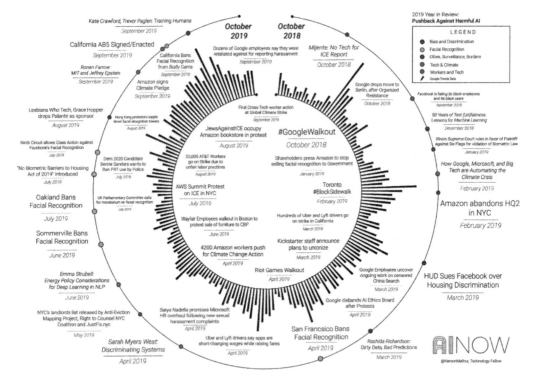

Figure 1.4 – AI Now Institute's infographic with AI's public relation blunders for 2019

Due to trust issues, many AI-driven technologies are losing public support, to the detriment of both companies that monetize AI and users that could benefit from them (see *Figure 1.4*). This, in part, requires a legal framework at a national or global level and, at the organizational end, for those that deploy these technologies, more accountability.

More ethical

There are three schools of thought for ethics: utilitarians focus on consequences, deontologists are concerned with duty, and teleologicalists are more interested in overall moral character. So, this means that there are different ways to examine ethical problems. For instance, they are useful lessons to draw from all of them. There are cases in which you want to produce the greatest amount of "good", despite some harm being produced in the process. Other times, ethical boundaries must be treated as lines in the sand you mustn't cross. And at other times, it's about developing a righteous disposition, much like many religions aspire to do. Regardless of the school of ethics we align with, our notion of what it is evolves with time because it mirrors our current values. At this moment, in Western cultures, these values include the following:

- Human welfare
- Ownership and property
- Privacy
- Freedom from bias
- Universal usability
- Trust
- Autonomy
- Informed consent
- Accountability
- Courtesy
- Environmental sustainability

Ethical transgressions are cases whereby you cross the moral boundaries that these values seek to uphold, be it by discriminating against someone or polluting their environment, whether it's against the law or not. Ethical dilemmas occur when you have a choice between options that lead to transgressions, so you have to choose between one and another.

The first reason machine learning is related to ethics is because technologies and ethical dilemmas have an intrinsically linked history.

Since the first widely adopted tool made by humans, it brought progress but also caused harm, such as accidents, war, and job losses. This is not to say that technology is always bad but that we lack the foresight to measure and control its consequences over time. In AI's case, it is not clear what the harmful long-term effects are. What we can anticipate is that there will be a major loss of jobs and an immense demand for energy to power our data centers, which could put stress on the environment. There's speculation that AI could create an "algocratic" surveillance state run by algorithms, infringing on values such as privacy, autonomy, and ownership.

The second reason is even more consequential than the first. It's that machine learning is a technological first for humanity: machine learning is a technology that can make decisions for us, and these decisions can produce individual ethical transgressions that are hard to trace. The problem with this is that accountability is essential to morality because you have to know who to blame for human dignity, atonement, closure, or criminal prosecution. However, many technologies have accountability issues to begin with, because moral responsibility is often shared in any case. For instance, maybe the reason for a car crash was partly due to the driver and mechanic and car manufacturer. The same can happen with a machine learning model, except it gets trickier. After all, a model's programming has no programmer because the "programming" was learned from data, and there are things a model can learn from data that can result in ethical transgressions. Top among them are biases such as the following:

- **Sample bias**: When your data, the sample, doesn't represent the environment accurately, also known as the population

- **Exclusion bias**: When you omit features or groups that could otherwise explain a critical phenomenon with the data

- **Prejudice bias**: When stereotypes influence your data, either directly or indirectly

- **Measurement bias**: When faulty measurements distort your data

Interpretability comes in handy to mitigate bias, as seen in *Chapter 11, Bias Mitigation and Causal Inference Methods*, or even place guardrails on the right features, which may be a source of bias. This is covered in *Chapter 12, Monotonic Constraints and Model Tuning for Interpretability*. As explained in this chapter, explanations go a long way in establishing accountability, which is a moral imperative. Also, by explaining the reasoning behind models, you can find ethical issues before they cause any harm. But there are even more ways in which models' potentially worrisome ethical ramifications can be controlled for, and this has less to do with interpretability and more to do with design. There are frameworks such as **human-centered design, value-sensitive design**, and **techno moral virtue ethics** that can be used to incorporate ethical considerations into every technological design choice. An article by Kirsten Martin (`https://doi.org/10.1007/s10551-018-3921-3`) also proposes a specific framework for algorithms. This book won't delve into algorithm design aspects too much, but for those readers interested in the larger umbrella of ethical AI, this article is an excellent place to start. You can see Martin's algorithm morality model in *Figure 1.5* here:

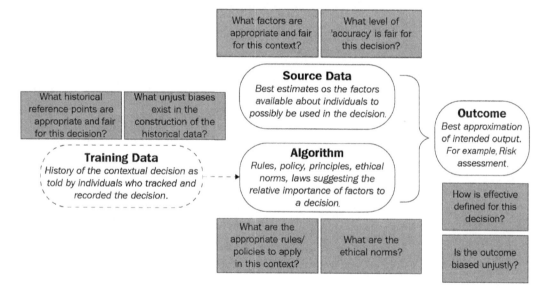

Figure 1.5 – Martin's algorithm morality model

Organizations should take the ethics of algorithmic decision-making seriously because ethical transgressions have monetary and reputation costs. But also, AI left to its own devices could undermine the very values that sustain democracy and the economy that allows businesses to thrive.

More profitable

As seen already in this section, interpretability improves algorithmic decisions, boosting trust and mitigating ethical transgressions.

When you leverage previously unknown opportunities and mitigate threats such as accidental failures through better decision-making, you can only improve the bottom line; and if you increase trust in an AI-powered technology, you can only increase its use and enhance overall brand reputation, which also has a beneficial impact on profits. On the other hand, as for ethical transgressions, they can be there by design or by accident, but when they are discovered, they adversely impact both profits and reputation.

When businesses incorporate interpretability into their machine learning workflows, it's a virtuous cycle, and it results in higher profitability. In the case of a non-profit or governments, profits might not be a motive. Still, finances are undoubtedly involved because lawsuits, lousy decision-making, and tarnished reputations are expensive. Ultimately, technological progress is contingent not only on the engineering and scientific skills and materials that make it possible but its voluntary adoption by the general public.

Summary

Upon reading this chapter, you should now have a clear understanding of what machine learning interpretation is and isn't, and recognize the importance of interpretability. In the next chapter, we will learn what can make machine learning models so challenging to interpret, and how you would classify interpretation methods in both category and scope.

Image sources

- Mathur, Varoon (2019). *AI in 2019: A Year in Review - The Growing Pushback Against Harmful AI*. AI Now Institute via Medium.

- Martin, K. (2019). *Ethical Implications and Accountability of Algorithms*. Journal of Business Ethics 160. 835–850. https://doi.org/10.1007/s10551-018-3921-3

Further reading

- Microsoft (2019). *Responsible AI principles from Microsoft*. Retrieved from https://www.microsoft.com/en-us/ai/responsible-ai

- Lipton, Zachary (2017). *The Mythos of Model Interpretability*. _ICML 2016 Human Interpretability in Machine Learning Workshop_ https://doi.org/10.1145/3236386.3241340

- Doshi-Velez, F. & Kim, B. (2017). *Towards A Rigorous Science of Interpretable Machine Learning.* http://arxiv.org/abs/1702.08608

- Roscher, R., Bohn, B., Duarte, M.F. & Garcke, J. (2020). *Explainable Machine Learning for Scientific Insights and Discoveries.* IEEE Access, 8, 42200-42216. https://dx.doi.org/10.1109/ACCESS.2020.2976199

- Coglianese, C. & Lehr, D. (2019). *Transparency and algorithmic governance.* Administrative Law Review, 71, 1-4. https://ssrn.com/abstract=3293008

- Weller, Adrian. (2019) "*Transparency: Motivations and Challenges*". arXiv:1708.01870 [Cs]. http://arxiv.org/abs/1708.01870

2
Key Concepts of Interpretability

This book covers many model interpretation methods: some produce metrics, other visuals, and some both; some depict your model broadly and others granularly. In this chapter, we will learn about two methods, feature importance and decision regions, as well as the taxonomies used to describe these methods. We will also detail what elements hinder machine learning interpretability as a primer to what lies ahead.

The following are the main topics we are going to cover in this chapter:

- Learning about interpretation method types and scopes
- Appreciating what hinders machine learning interpretability

Technical requirements

Although we began the book with a "toy example," we will be leveraging real datasets throughout this book to be used in specific interpretation use cases. These come from many different sources and are often used only once.

To avoid that, readers spend a lot of time downloading, loading, and preparing datasets for single examples; there's a library called `mldatasets` that takes care of most of this. Instructions on how to install this library are located in the *preface*. In addition to `mldatasets`, this chapter's examples also use the `pandas`, `numpy`, `statsmodel`, `sklearn`, and `matplotlib` libraries. The code for this chapter is located here: `https://github.com/PacktPublishing/Interpretable-Machine-Learning-with-Python/tree/master/Chapter02`.

The mission

Imagine you are an analyst for a national health ministry, and there's a **Cardiovascular Diseases** (**CVDs**) epidemic. The minister has made it a priority to reverse the growth and reduce the case load to a 20-year low. To this end, a task force has been created to find clues in the data to ascertain the following:

1. What risk factors can be addressed.

2. If future cases can be predicted, interpret predictions on a case-by-case basis.

You are part of this task force!

Details about CVD

Before we dive into the data, we must gather some important details about CVD in order to do the following:

- Understand the problem's context and relevance.

- Extract domain knowledge information that can inform our data analysis and model interpretation.

- Relate an expert-informed background to a dataset's features.

CVDs are a group of disorders, the most common of which is coronary heart disease (also known as *Ischaemic Heart Disease*). According to the World Health Organization, CVD is the leading cause of death globally, killing close to 18 million people annually. Coronary heart disease and strokes (which are, for the most part, a byproduct of CVD) are the most significant contributors to that. It is estimated that 80% of CVD is made up of modifiable risk factors. In other words, some of the preventable factors that cause CVD include the following:

- Poor diet

- Smoking and alcohol consumption habits

- Obesity

- Lack of physical activity

- Poor sleep

Also, many of the risk factors are non-modifiable, and therefore known to be unavoidable, including the following:

- Genetic predisposition

- Old age

- Male (varies with age)

We won't go into more domain-specific details about CVD because it is not required to make sense of the example. However, *it can't be stressed enough how central domain knowledge is to model interpretation.* So, if this example was your job and many lives depended on your analysis, it would be advisable to read the latest scientific research on the subject or consult with domain experts to inform your interpretations.

The approach

Logistic regression is one common way to rank risk factors in medical use cases. Unlike linear regression, it doesn't try to predict a continuous value for each of your observations, but it predicts a probability score that an observation belongs to a particular class. In this case, what we are trying to predict is, given x data for each patient, what is the y probability, from 0 to 1, that they have cardiovascular disease?

Preparations

You will find the code for this example here: `https://github.com/PacktPublishing/Interpretable-Machine-Learning-with-Python/blob/master/Chapter02/CVD.ipynb`.

Loading the libraries

To run this example, you need to install the following libraries:

- `mldatasets` to load the dataset
- `pandas` and `numpy` to manipulate it
- `statsmodels` to fit the logistic regression model
- `sklearn` (scikit-learn) to split the data
- `matplotlib` to visualize the interpretations

You should load all of them first:

```
Import math
import mldatasets
import pandas as pd
import numpy as np
import statsmodels.api as sm
from sklearn.model_selection import train_test_split
import matplotlib.pyplot as plt
```

Understanding and preparing the data

The data to be used in this example should then be loaded into a DataFrame we call `cvd_df`:

```
cvd_df = mldatasets.load("cardiovascular-disease")
```

From this, you should be getting 70,000 records and 12 columns. We can take a peek at what was loaded with `info()`:

```
cvd_df.info()
```

The preceding command will output the names of each column with its type and how many non-null records it contains:

```
<class 'pandas.core.frame.DataFrame'>
RangeIndex: 70000 entries, 0 to 69999
Data columns (total 12 columns):
age            70000 non-null int64
gender         70000 non-null int64
```

```
height           70000 non-null int64
weight           70000 non-null float64
ap_hi            70000 non-null int64
ap_lo            70000 non-null int64
cholesterol      70000 non-null int64
gluc             70000 non-null int64
smoke            70000 non-null int64
alco             70000 non-null int64
active           70000 non-null int64
cardio           70000 non-null int64
dtypes: float64(1), int64(11)
memory usage: 6.4 MB
```

The data dictionary

To understand what was loaded, the following is the data dictionary, as described in the source:

- age: Of the patient in days (Objective Feature)

- height: In centimeters (Objective Feature)

- weight: In kg (Objective Feature)

- gender: A binary where 1: female, 2: male (Objective Feature)

- ap_hi: Systolic blood pressure, which is the arterial pressure exerted when blood is ejected during ventricular contraction. Normal value: < 120 mmHg (Examination Feature)

- ap_lo: Diastolic blood pressure, which is the arterial pressure in between heartbeats. Normal value: < 80 mmHg (Examination Feature)

- cholesterol: An ordinal where 1: normal, 2: above normal, 3: well above normal (Examination Feature)

- gluc: An ordinal where 1: normal, 2: above normal, 3: well above normal (Examination Feature)

- smoke: A binary where 0: non-smoker, 1: smoker (Subjective Feature)

- alco: A binary where 0: non-drinker, 1: drinker (Subjective Feature)

- active: A binary where 0: non-active, 1: active (Subjective Feature)

- cardio: A binary where 0: no CVD, 1: has CVD (Target Feature)

Data preparation

For the sake of interpretability and model performance, there are several data preparation tasks that we can take care of, but the one that stands out right now is age. Age is not something we usually measure in days. In fact, for health-related predictions like this one, we might even want to bucket them into **age groups** since people tend to age differently. For now, we will convert all ages into years:

```
cvd_df['age'] = cvd_df['age'] / 365.24
```

The result is a more understandable column because we expect age values to be between 0 and 120. We took existing data and transformed it. This is an example of **feature engineering**, which is when you use domain knowledge of your data to create features that better represent your problem, thereby improving your models. We will discuss this further in *Chapter 10, Feature Selection and Engineering for Interpretability*, and *Chapter 12, Monotonic Constraints and Model Tuning for Interpretability*. There's value in performing feature engineering simply to make model outcomes more *interpretable* as long as this doesn't hurt model performance. As regards the age column, it can't hurt it because we haven't degraded the data. This is because you still have the decimal points for the years that represent the days.

Now we are going to take a peak at what the summary statistics are for each one of our features using the describe() method:

```
cvd_df.describe().transpose()
```

Figure 2.1 shows the summary statistics outputted by the preceding code. In *Figure 2.1*, age is looking good because it ranges between 29 and 65 years, which is not out of the ordinary, but there are some anomalous outliers for ap_hi and ap_lo. Blood pressure can't be negative, and the highest ever recorded was 370. These records will have to be dropped because they could lead to poor model performance and interpretability:

	count	mean	std	min	25%	50%	75%	max
age	70000.0	53.304309	6.755152	29.564122	48.36272	53.945351	58.391742	64.924433
gender	70000.0	1.349571	0.476838	1.000000	1.00000	1.000000	2.000000	2.000000
height	70000.0	164.359229	8.210126	55.000000	159.00000	165.000000	170.000000	250.000000
weight	70000.0	74.205690	14.395757	10.000000	65.00000	72.000000	82.000000	200.000000
ap_hi	70000.0	128.817286	154.011419	-150.000000	120.00000	120.000000	140.000000	16020.000000
ap_lo	70000.0	96.630414	188.472530	-70.000000	80.00000	80.000000	90.000000	11000.000000
cholesterol	70000.0	1.366871	0.680250	1.000000	1.00000	1.000000	2.000000	3.000000
gluc	70000.0	1.226457	0.572270	1.000000	1.00000	1.000000	1.000000	3.000000
smoke	70000.0	0.088129	0.283484	0.000000	0.00000	0.000000	0.000000	1.000000
alco	70000.0	0.053771	0.225568	0.000000	0.00000	0.000000	0.000000	1.000000
active	70000.0	0.803729	0.397179	0.000000	1.00000	1.000000	1.000000	1.000000
cardio	70000.0	0.499700	0.500003	0.000000	0.00000	0.000000	1.000000	1.000000

Figure 2.1 – Summary statistics for the dataset

For good measure, we ought to make sure that ap_hi is always higher than ap_lo, so any record with that discrepancy should also be dropped:

```
cvd_df = cvd_df[(cvd_df['ap_lo'] <= 370) &\
                (cvd_df['ap_lo'] > 0)].reset_
index(drop=True)
cvd_df = cvd_df[(cvd_df['ap_hi'] <= 370) &\
                (cvd_df['ap_hi'] > 0)].reset_
index(drop=True)
cvd_df = cvd_df[cvd_df['ap_hi'] >=\
                cvd_df['ap_lo']].reset_
index(drop=True)
```

Now, in order to fit a logistic regression model, we must put all objective, examination, and subjective features together as X and the target feature alone as y. After this, you split the X and y into training and test datasets, but make sure to include `random_state` for reproducibility:

```
y = cvd_df['cardio']
X = cvd_df.drop(['cardio'], axis=1).copy()
X_train, X_test, y_train, y_test =\
            train_test_split(X, y, test_size=0.15, random_
state=9)
```

Learning about interpretation method types and scopes

Now that we have prepared our data and split it into training/test datasets, we can fit the model using the training data and print a summary of the results:

```
log_model = sm.Logit(y_train, sm.add_constant(X_train))
log_result = log_model.fit()
print(log_result.summary2())
```

Printing `summary2` on the fitted model produces the following output:

```
Optimization terminated successfully.
         Current function value: 0.561557
         Iterations 6
                        Results: Logit
========================================================================
===
```

Model:	Logit	Pseudo R-squared:	0.190
Dependent Variable:	cardio	AIC:	65618.3485
Date:	2020-06-10 09:10	BIC:	65726.0502
No. Observations:	58404	Log-Likelihood:	-32797.
Df Model:	11	LL-Null:	-40481.
Df Residuals:	58392	LLR p-value:	0.0000
Converged:	1.0000	Scale:	1.0000
No. Iterations:	6.0000		

```
----------------------------------------------------------------
---
                 Coef.     Std.Err.      z      P>|z|      [0.025
0.975]
----------------------------------------------------------------
---
const          -11.1730    0.2504  -44.6182  0.0000  -11.6638
-10.6822
age              0.0510    0.0015   34.7971  0.0000    0.0482
0.0539
gender          -0.0227    0.0238   -0.9568  0.3387   -0.0693
0.0238
height          -0.0036    0.0014   -2.6028  0.0092   -0.0063
-0.0009
weight           0.0111    0.0007   14.8567  0.0000    0.0096
0.0125
ap_hi            0.0561    0.0010   56.2824  0.0000    0.0541
0.0580
ap_lo            0.0105    0.0016    6.7670  0.0000    0.0075
0.0136
cholesterol      0.4931    0.0169   29.1612  0.0000    0.4600
0.5262
gluc            -0.1155    0.0192   -6.0138  0.0000   -0.1532
-0.0779
smoke           -0.1306    0.0376   -3.4717  0.0005   -0.2043
-0.0569
alco            -0.2050    0.0457   -4.4907  0.0000   -0.2945
-0.1155
active          -0.2151    0.0237   -9.0574  0.0000   -0.2616
-0.1685
================================================================
===
```

The preceding summary helps us to understand which X features contributed the most to the y CVD diagnosis using the model coefficients (labeled Coef. in the table). Much like with linear regression, they are like a weight applied to every predictor. However, the linear combination exponent is a **logistic function**. This makes the interpretation more difficult. We explain this function further in *Chapter 3, Interpretation Challenges*.

You can only tell by looking at it that the features with the absolute highest values are `cholesterol` and `active`, but it's not very intuitive in terms of what this means. A more interpretable way of looking at these values is revealed once you calculate the exponential of these coefficients:

```
np.exp(log_result.params).sort_values(ascending=False)
```

The preceding code outputs the following:

cholesterol	1.637374
ap_hi	1.057676
age	1.052357
weight	1.011129
ap_lo	1.010573
height	0.996389
gender	0.977519
gluc	0.890913
smoke	0.877576
alco	0.814627
active	0.806471
const	0.000014
dtype: float64	

Why the exponential? The coefficients are the **log odds**, which are the logarithms of the *odds*. Also, *odds* are the probability of a positive case over the probability of a negative case, where the **positive case** is the phenomenon we are trying to predict. It doesn't necessarily indicate what is favored by anyone. For instance, if we are trying to predict the odds of rain today, the positive case would be that it rained, regardless of whether you predicted rain or not. Odds are often expressed as a ratio. The news could say the probability of rain today is 60% or say the odds of rain are 3:2 or 3/2 = 1.5. In log odds form, this would be 0.176, which is the logarithm of 1.5. They are basically the same thing, but expressed differently. An exponential function is the inverse of a logarithm, so it can take any *log odds* and return the *odds*.

Back to our CVD case. Now that we have the odds, we can interpret what it means. For example, what do the odds mean in the case of cholesterol? It means that the odds of CVD increase by a factor of 1.64 for each additional unit of cholesterol, provided every other feature stays unchanged. Being able to explain the impact of a feature on the model in such tangible terms is one of the advantages of an *intrinsically interpretable* model such as logistic regression.

Although the *odds* provide us with useful information, they don't tell us what matters the most and, therefore, by themselves, cannot be used to measure feature importance. But how could that be? If something has higher odds, then it must matter more, right? Well, for starters, they all have different scales, so that makes a huge difference. This is because if you are to measure the odds of how much something increases, you have to know by how much it typically increases because that provides context. For example, we could say that the odds of a specific species of butterfly living one day more are 0.66 after their first eggs hatch. This statement is meaningless to you unless you know the lifespan and reproductive cycle of this species.

To provide context to our odds, we can easily calculate the standard deviation of our features using the `np.std` function:

```
np.std(X_train, 0)
```

The following series is what is outputted by the `np.std` function:

```
age            6.757537
gender         0.476697
height         8.186987
weight        14.335173
ap_hi         16.703572
ap_lo          9.547583
cholesterol    0.678878
gluc           0.571231
smoke          0.283629
alco           0.225483
active         0.397215
dtype: float64
```

As you can tell by the output, binary and ordinal features only typically vary by one at most, but continuous features, such as `weight` or `ap_hi`, can vary 10 – 20 times more, as evidenced by the standard deviation of the features.

Another reason why *odds* cannot be used to measure feature importance is because despite favorable odds, sometimes features are not statistically significant. They are entangled with other features in such a way they might appear to be significant, but we can prove that they aren't. This can be seen in the summary table for the model, under the P>|z| column. This value is called the **p-value**, and when it's less than 0.05, hypothesis testing determines that there's strong evidence that it is significant. However, when it's above this number, especially by a large margin, there's no statistical evidence that it affects the predicted score. Such is the case with gender, at least in this dataset.

If we are trying to obtain what features matters most, one way to approximate this is to multiply the coefficients by the standard deviations of the features. Incorporating the standard deviations accounts for differences in variances between features. Hence, it is better if we get gender out of the way too while we are at it:

```
coefs = log_result.params.drop(labels=['const','gender'])
stdv = np.std(X_train, 0).drop(labels='gender')abs(coefs *
stdv).sort_values(ascending=False)
```

The preceding code produced this output:

ap_hi	0.936632
age	0.344855
cholesterol	0.334750
weight	0.158651
ap_lo	0.100419
active	0.085436
gluc	0.065982
alco	0.046230
smoke	0.037040
height	0.029620
dtype: float64	

The preceding table can be interpreted as an **approximation of risk factors** from high to low according to the model. It is also a **model-specific** feature importance method, in other words, a **global model (modular) interpretation method**. There's a lot of new concepts to unpack here so let's break them down.

Model interpretability method types

There are two model interpretability method types:

- **Model-specific**: When the method can only be used for a specific model class, then it's model-specific. The method detailed in the previous example can only work with logistic regression because it uses its coefficients.

- **Model-agnostic**: These are methods that can work with any model class. We cover these in *Chapter 4, Fundamentals of Feature Importance and Impact*, onward.

Model interpretability scopes

There are several model interpretability scopes:

- **Global holistic interpretation**: You can explain how a model makes predictions simply because you can comprehend the entire model at once with a complete understanding of the data, and it's a trained model. For instance, the simple linear regression example in *Chapter 1, Interpretation, Interpretability, and Explainability; and Why Does It All Matter?*, can be visualized in a two-dimensional graph. You can conceptualize this in memory, but this is only possible because the simplicity of the model allows you to do so, and it's not very common nor expected.

- **Global modular interpretation**: In the same way that you can explain the role of *parts* of an internal combustion engine in the *whole* process of turning fuel into movement, you can also do so with a model. For instance, in the CVD risk factor example, our feature importance method tells us that ap_hi (systolic blood pressure), age, cholesterol, and weight are the *parts* that impact the *whole* the most. Feature importance is only one of many global modular interpretation methods but arguably the most important one. *Chapter 4, Fundamentals of Feature Importance and Impact*, goes into more detail on feature importance.

- **Local single-prediction interpretation**: You can explain why a single prediction was made. The next example will illustrate this concept.

- **Local group-prediction interpretation**: The same as single-prediction, except that it applies to groups of predictions.

Congratulations! You've already determined the risk factors with a **global model interpretation method**, but the health minister also wants to know whether the model can be used to interpret individual cases. So, let's look into that.

Interpreting individual predictions with logistic regression

What if you used the model to predict CVD for the entire test dataset? You could do so like this:

```
y_pred = log_result.predict(sm.add_constant(X_test)).to_numpy()
print(y_pred)
```

The resulting array is the probabilities that each test case is positive for CVD:

```
[0.40629892 0.17003609 0.13405939 ... 0.95575283 0.94095239
0.91455717]
```

Let's take one of the positive cases; test case #2872:

```
print(y_pred[2872])
```

We know that it predicted positive for CVD because the score exceeds 0.5:

```
0.5746680418975686
```

And these are the details for test case #2872:

```
print(X_test.iloc[2872])
```

The following is the output:

```
age              60.521849
gender            1.000000
height          158.000000
weight           62.000000
ap_hi           130.000000
ap_lo            80.000000
cholesterol       1.000000
gluc              1.000000
smoke             0.000000
alco              0.000000
active            1.000000
Name: 46965, dtype: float64
```

So, by the looks of the preceding series, we know that the following applies to this individual:

- A borderline high `ap_hi` (systolic blood pressure).
- Normal `ap_lo` (diastolic blood pressure). Having high systolic blood pressure and normal diastolic blood pressure is what is known as *isolated systolic hypertension*. It could be causing a positive prediction, but `ap_hi` is borderline (130 mmHg being the border), so therefore the condition of *isolated systolic hypertension* is borderline.
- `age` is not too old, but among the oldest in the dataset.
- `cholesterol` is normal.
- `weight` also appears to be in the healthy range.

There are also no other risk factors: glucose is normal, no smoking, no alcohol, and no sedentarism, since the individual is active. It is not clear exactly why it's positive. Is the age and borderline *isolated systolic hypertension* enough to tip the scales? It's tough to understand the reasons for the prediction without putting all the predictions into context, so let's try to do that!

But how do we put everything in context at the same time? We can't possibly visualize how one prediction compares with the other ten thousand for every single feature and their respective predicted CVD diagnosis. Unfortunately, humans can't process that level of dimensionality, even if it were possible to visualize a ten-dimensional hyperplane!

However, we can do it for two features at a time, resulting in a graph that conveys where the decision boundary for the model lies for those features. On top of that, we can overlay what the predictions were for the test dataset based on all the features. This is to visualize the discrepancy between the effect of two features and all eleven features.

This graphical interpretation method is what is termed a **decision boundary**. It draws boundaries for the classes, leaving areas that belong to one class or another. Such areas are called **decision regions**. In this case, we have two classes, so we will see a graph with a single boundary between `cardio=0` and `cardio=1`, only concerning the two features we are comparing.

We have managed to visualize the two decision-based features at a time, with one big assumption that if all the other features are held constant, we can observe only two in isolation. This is also known as the **ceteris paribus** assumption and is critical in a scientific inquiry, allowing us to *control* some variables in order to *observe* others. One way to do this is to fill them with a value that won't affect the outcome. Using the table of odds we produced, we can tell whether a feature increases as it will increase the odds of CVD. So, in aggregate, a lower value is less risky for CVD.

For instance, `age=30` is the least risky value of those present in the dataset for `age`. It can also go in the opposite direction, so `active=1` is known to be less risky than `active=0`. We can come up with optimal values for the remainder of the features:

- `height=165`.

- `weight=57` (optimal for that `height`).

- `ap_hi=110`.

- `ap_lo=70`.

- `smoke=0`.

- `cholesterol=1` (this means normal).

- `gender` can be coded for male or female, which doesn't matter because the odds for gender (`0.977519`) are so close to 1.

The following `filler_feature_values` dictionary exemplifies what should be done with the features matching their index to their least risky values:

```
filler_feature_values = {0: 1, 1: 30, 2: 1, 3: 165, 4: 57, 5:
110, 6: 70, 7: 1, 8: 1, 9: 0, 10:0, 11:1 }
```

In the dictionary, the features are numbered and not named because the function we will use to plot the decision regions only takes in NumPy arrays. Also, since, in `statsmodels`, you must explicitly define the **constant** (also known as the **intercept**), the logistic model has an additional 0 feature, which always equals 1.

We also intend to plot the actual predictions for the test dataset. To do this, we must define another dictionary like `filler_feature_values`, but with a range so that, for example, the `filler_feature_value` for `height` is 165. We can then make this range 120, so it includes all cases with heights 165 ± 110, so this means a range of [55 – 275], which contains all possible heights in the test dataset:

```
filler_feature_ranges = {0: 1, 1: 35, 2: 2, 3: 110, 4: 150, 5:
140, 6: 70, 7: 3, 8: 3, 9: 2, 10:2, 11:2 }
```

The next thing to do is to create a (1,12) shaped NumPy array with test case #2872 so that the plotting function can highlight it. To this end, we first convert it to NumPy and then prepend the *constant* of 1, which must be the first feature, and then reshape it so that it meets the (1,12) dimensions:

```
X_highlight = np.reshape(\
        np.concatenate(([1], X_test.iloc[2872].to_numpy())), (1,
12))
print(X_highlight)
```

The following is the output:

```
[[   1.         60.52184865    1.           158.          62.
    130.        80.           1.             1.            0.
      0.         1.          ]]
```

We are good to go now! Let's visualize some decision region plots! We will compare the feature that is thought to be the highest *risk factor*, ap_hi, with the following four most important risk factors: age, cholesterol, weight, and ap_lo.

The following code will generate the plots in *Figure 2.2*:

```
plt.rcParams.update({'font.size': 14})
fig, axarr = plt.subplots(2, 2, figsize=(12,8), sharex=True,\
                sharey=False)
mldatasets.create_decision_plot(X_test, y_test, log_result, [5,
1],\
        ['ap_hi [mmHg]', 'age [years]'], X_highlight,\
        filler_feature_values, filler_feature_ranges,\
        ax=axarr.flat[0])
mldatasets.create_decision_plot(X_test, y_test, log_result, [5,
7], ['ap_hi [mmHg]', 'cholesterol [1-3]'], X_highlight,\
        filler_feature_values, filler_feature_ranges,\
        ax=axarr.flat[1])
mldatasets.create_decision_plot(X_test, y_test, log_result, [5,
6], ['ap_hi [mmHg]', 'ap_lo [mmHg]'], X_highlight,\
        filler_feature_values, filler_feature_ranges,\
        ax=axarr.flat[2])
```

```
mldatasets.create_decision_plot(X_test, y_test, log_result, [5,
4], ['ap_hi [mmHg]', 'weight [kg]'], X_highlight,\
       filler_feature_values, filler_feature_ranges,\
       ax=axarr.flat[3])
plt.subplots_adjust(top = 1, bottom=0, hspace=0.2, wspace=0.2)
plt.show()
```

In the plot in *Figure 2.2*, the circle represents test case #2872. In all the plots bar one, this test case is on the negative (left-side) decision region, representing `cardio=0` classification. The borderline high `ap_hi` (systolic blood pressure) and the relatively high `age` is barely enough for a positive prediction in the top-left chart. Still, in any case, for test case #2872, we have predicted a 57% score for CVD, so this could very well explain most of it.

Not surprisingly, by themselves, `ap_hi` and a healthy `cholesterol` are not enough to tip the scales in favor of a definitive CVD diagnosis according to the model because it's decidedly in the negative decision region, and neither is a normal `ap_lo` (diastolic blood pressure). You can tell from these three charts that although there's some overlap in the distribution of squares and triangles, there is a tendency for more triangles to gravitate toward the positive side as the *y*-axis increases, while fewer squares populate this region:

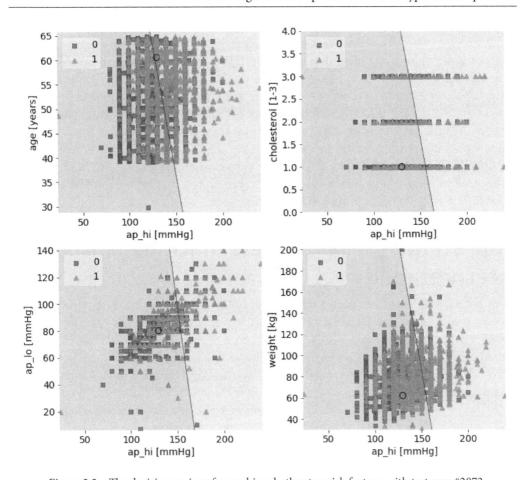

Figure 2.2 – The decision regions for ap_hi and other top risk factors, with test case #2872

The overlap across the decision boundary is expected because, after all, these squares and triangles are based on the effects of **all** features. Still, you expect to find a somewhat consistent pattern. The chart with ap_hi versus weight doesn't have this pattern vertically as weight increases, which suggests something is missing in this story... Hold that thought because we are going to investigate that in the next section!

Congratulations! You have completed the second part of the minister's request.

Decision region plotting, a **local model interpretation method**, provided the health ministry with a tool to interpret individual case predictions. You could now extend this to explain several cases at a time, or plot all-important feature combinations to find the ones where the circle is decidedly in the positive decision region. You can also change some of the filler variables one at a time to see how they make a difference. For instance, what if you increase the filler age to the median age of 54 or even to the age of test case #2872. Would a borderline high `ap_hi` and healthy `cholesterol` now be enough to tip the scales? We will answer this question later, but first let's understand what can make machine learning interpretation so difficult.

Appreciating what hinders machine learning interpretability

In the last section, we were wondering why the chart with `ap_hi` versus `weight` didn't have a conclusive pattern. It could very well be that although `weight` is a risk factor, there are other critical *mediating variables* that could explain the increased risk of CVD. A **mediating variable** is one that influences the strength between the independent and target (*dependent*) variable. We probably don't have to think too hard to find what is missing. In *Chapter 1, Interpretation, Interpretability, and Explainability; and Why Does It All Matter?*, we performed linear regression on `weight` and `height` because there's a linear relationship between these variables. In the context of human health, `weight` is not nearly as *meaningful* without `height`, so you need to look at both.

Perhaps if we plot the decision regions for these two variables, we will get some clues. We can plot them with the following code:

```
fig, ax = plt.subplots(1,1, figsize=(12,8))
mldatasets.create_decision_plot(X_test, y_test, log_result, [3,
4], ['height [cm]', 'weight [kg]'], X_highlight,\
    filler_feature_values, filler_feature_ranges, ax=ax)
plt.show()
```

The preceding snippet will generate the plot in *Figure 2.3*:

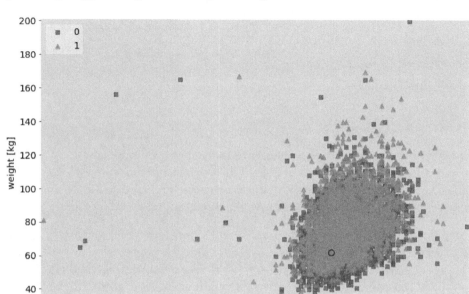

Figure 2.3 – The decision regions for weight and height, with test case #2872

No decision boundary was ascertained in *Figure 2.3* because if all other variables are held constant (at a less risky value), no `height` and `weight` combination is enough to predict CVD. However, we can tell that there is a pattern for the orange triangles, mostly located in one ovular area. This provides exciting insight that even though we expect `weight` to increase when `height` increases, the concept of an inherently unhealthy `weight` is not one that increases linearly with `height`.

In fact, for almost two centuries, this relationship has been mathematically understood by the name **body mass index (BMI)**:

$$\mathrm{BMI} = \frac{\mathrm{weight}_{kg}}{\mathrm{height}_m^2}$$

Before we discuss BMI further, you must consider complexity. Dimensionality aside, there are chiefly three things that introduce complexity that makes interpretation difficult:

1. Non-linearity

2. Interactivity

3. Non-monotonicity

Non-linearity

Linear equations such as y = a + bx are easy to understand. They are additive, so it is easy to separate and quantify the effects of each of its terms (*a* and *bx*) from the outcome of the model (*y*). Many model classes have linear equations incorporated in the math. These equations can both be used to fit the data to the model and describe the model.

However, there are model classes that are inherently non-linear because they introduce non-linearity in their training. Such is the case for *deep learning* models because they have non-linear activation functions such as *sigmoid*. However, logistic regression is considered a **generalized linear model (GLM)** because it's additive. In other words, the outcome is a sum of weighted inputs and parameters. We will discuss GLMs further in *Chapter 3, Challenges of Interpretability.*

However, even if your model is linear, the relationships between the variables may not be linear, which can lead to poor performance and interpretability. What you can do in these cases is adopt either of the following approaches:

*   *Use a non-linear model class*, which will fit these non-linear feature relationships much better, possibly improving model performance. Nevertheless, as we will explore in more detail in the next chapter, this can make it less interpretable.

*   *Use domain knowledge to engineer a feature that can help "linearize" it*. For instance, if you had a feature that increased exponentially against another, you can engineer a new variable with the logarithm of that feature. In the case of our CVD prediction, we know BMI is a better way to understand weight in the company of height. Best of all, it's not an *arbitrary* made-up feature, so it's easier to interpret. We can prove this point by making a copy of the dataset, engineering the BMI feature in it, training the model with this extra feature, and performing local model interpretation. The following code snippet does just that:

```
X2 = cvd_df.drop(['cardio'], axis=1).copy()
X2["bmi"] = X2["weight"] / (X2["height"]/100)**2
X2_train, X2_test,__,_ = train_test_split(X2, y,\
                              test_size=0.15, random_state=9)
```

To illustrate this new feature, let's plot BMI against both weight and height using the following code:

```
fig, axs = plt.subplots(1,3, figsize=(15,4))
axs[0].scatter(X2["weight"], X2["bmi"], color='black',
s=2) axs[0].set_xlabel('weight [kg]')
axs[0].set_ylabel('bmi')
axs[1].scatter(X2["height"], X2["weight"], color='black',
s=2)
axs[1].set_xlabel('height [cm]')
axs[1].set_ylabel('weight [kg]')
axs[2].scatter(X2["bmi"], X2["height"], color='black',
s=2) axs[2].set_xlabel('bmi')
axs[2].set_ylabel('height [cm]')
plt.subplots_adjust(top = 1, bottom=0, hspace=0.2,
wspace=0.3) plt.show()
```

Figure 2.4 is produced with the preceding code:

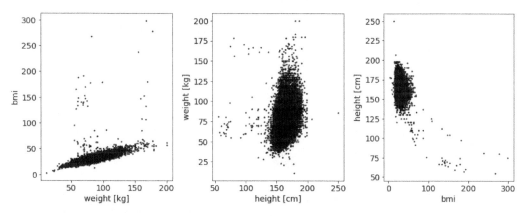

Figure 2.4 – Bivariate comparison between weight, height, and bmi

As you can appreciate by the plots in *Figure 2.4*, there is a more definite linear relationship between bmi and weight than between height and weight and, even, between bmi and height.

Let's fit the new model with the extra feature using the following code snippet:

```
log_model2 = sm.Logit(y_train, sm.add_constant(X2_train))
log_result2 = log_model2.fit()
```

Now, let's see whether test case #2872 is on the positive decision region when comparing ap_hi to bmi:

```
filler_feature_values2 = {0: 1, 1: 60, 2: 1, 3: 165, 4:
57, 5: 110, 6: 70, 7: 1, 8: 1, 9: 0, 10:0, 11:1, 12:20
       }
filler_feature_ranges2 = {0: 1, 1: 35, 2: 2, 3: 120, 4:
150, 5: 140, 6: 70, 7: 3, 8: 3, 9: 2, 10:2, 11:2, 12:250
       }
X2_highlight = np.reshape(\
 np.concatenate(([1],X2_test.iloc[2872].to_numpy())), (1,
13))
fig, ax = plt.subplots(1,1, figsize=(12,8))
mldatasets.create_decision_plot(X2_test, y_test, log_
result2, [5, 12], ['ap_hi [mmHg]', 'bmi'],\ X2_highlight,
filler_feature_values2,\
                    filler_feature_ranges2, ax=ax)
plt.show()
```

The preceding code plots decision regions in the following *Figure 2.5*:

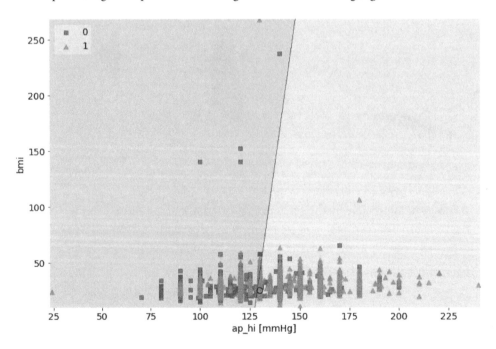

Figure 2.5 – The decision regions for ap_hi and bmi, with test case #2872

Figure 2.5 shows that `ap_hi` and `bmi` can help explain the positive prediction for CVD because the circle is in the positive decision region. Please note that there are some likely anomalous `bmi` outliers (the highest BMI ever recorded was 204), so there are probably some incorrect weights or heights in the dataset.

What's the problem with outliers?

Outliers can be **influential** or **high leverage** and therefore affect the model when trained with these. Even if they don't, they can make interpretation more difficult. If they are **anomalous**, then you should remove them, as we did with blood pressure at the beginning of this chapter. And sometimes, they can hide in plain sight because they are only perceived as *anomalous* in the context of other features. In any case, there are practical reasons why outliers are problematic, such as making plots like the preceding one "zoom out" to be able to fit them while not letting you appreciate the decision boundary where it matters. And there are also more profound reasons, such as losing trust in the data, thereby tainting trust in the models that were trained on that data. This sort of problem is to be expected with real-world data. Even though we haven't done it in this chapter for the sake of expediency, it's essential to begin every project by thoroughly exploring the data, treating missing values and outliers, and other data housekeeping tasks.

Interactivity

When we created `bmi`, we didn't only linearize a non-linear relationship, but we also created interactions between two features. `bmi` is, therefore, an **interaction feature**, but this was informed by domain knowledge. However, many model classes do this automatically by permutating all kinds of operations between features. After all, features have *latent* relationships between one another, much like `height` and `width`, and `ap_hi` and `ap_lo`. Therefore, automating the process of looking for them is not always a bad thing. In fact, it can even be absolutely necessary. This is the case for many deep learning problems where the data is unstructured and, therefore, part of the task of training the model is looking for the latent relationships to make sense of it.

However, for structured data, even though interactions can be significant for model performance, they can hurt interpretability by adding potentially unnecessary complexity to the model and also finding latent relationships that **don't mean anything** (which is called a **spurious relationship or correlation**).

Non-monotonicity

Often, a variable has a meaningful and consistent relationship between a feature and the target variable. So, we know that as `age` increases, the risk of CVD (`cardio`) must increase. There is no point at which you reach a certain age and this risk drops. Maybe the risk slows down, but it does not drop. We call this **monotonicity**, and functions that are *monotonic* are either always increasing or decreasing throughout their entire domain.

Please note that **all** linear relationships are monotonic, but not all monotonic relationships are necessarily linear. This is because they don't have to be a straight line. A common problem in machine learning is that a model doesn't know about a monotonic relationship that we expect because of our domain expertise. Then, because of noise and omissions in the data, the model is trained in such a way in which there are ups and downs where you don't expect them.

Let's propose a hypothetical example. Let's imagine that due to a lack of availability of data for 57-60-year-olds, and because the few cases we did have for this range were negative for CVD, the model could learn that this is where you would expect a drop in CVD risk. Some model classes are inherently monotonic, such as logistic regression, so they can't have this problem, but many others do. We will examine this in more detail in *Chapter 12, Monotonic Constraints and Model Tuning for Interpretability*:

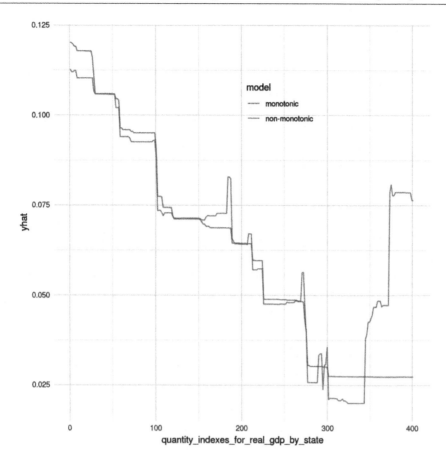

Figure 2.6 – A partial dependence plot between a target variable (yhat) and a predictor with monotonic and non-monotonic models

Figure 2.6 is what is called a **Partial Dependence Plot (PDP)**, from an unrelated example. PDPs are a concept we will study in further detail in *Chapter 4, Fundamentals of Feature Importance and Impact*, but what is important to grasp from it is that the prediction yhat is supposed to decrease as the feature quantity_indexes_for_real_gdp_by_state increases. As you can tell by the lines, in the monotonic model, it consistently decreases, but in the non-monotonic one, it has jagged peaks as it decreases, and then increases at the very end.

Mission accomplished

The first part of the mission was to understand risk factors for cardiovascular disease, and you've determined that the top four risk factors are systolic blood pressure (`ap_hi`), `age`, `cholesterol`, and `weight` according to the logistic regression model, of which only `age` is non-modifiable. However, you also realized that systolic blood pressure (`ap_hi`) is not as meaningful on its own since it relies on diastolic blood pressure (`ap_lo`) for interpretation. The same goes for `weight` and `height`. We learned that the interaction of features plays a crucial role in interpretation, and so does their relationship with each other and the target variable, whether linear or monotonic. Furthermore, the data is only a representation of the truth, which can be wrong. After all, we found *anomalies* that, left unchecked, can bias our model.

Another source of bias is how the data was collected. After all, you can wonder why the model's top features were all objective and examination features. Why isn't smoking nor drinking a larger factor? To verify whether there was *sample bias* involved, you would have to compare with other more trustworthy datasets to check whether your dataset is under-representing drinkers and smokers. Or maybe the bias was introduced by the question that asked whether they smoked now, and not whether they had ever smoked for an extended period.

Another type of bias that we could address is *exclusion bias* — our data might be missing information that explains the truth that the model is trying to depict. For instance, we know through medical research that blood pressure issues such as isolated systolic hypertension, which increases CVD risk, are caused by underlying conditions such as diabetes, hyperthyroidism, arterial stiffness, and obesity, to name a few. The only one of these conditions that we can derive from the data is obesity, and not the other ones. If we want to be able to interpret a model's predictions well, we need to have all relevant features. Otherwise, there will be gaps we cannot explain. Maybe once we add them, they won't make much of a difference, but that's what the methods we will learn in *Chapter 10, Feature Selection and Engineering for Interpretability*, are for.

The second part of the mission was to be able to interpret individual model predictions. We can do this well enough by plotting decision regions. It's a simple method, but it has many limitations, especially in situations where there are more than a handful of features, and they tend to interact a lot with each other. *Chapter 6, Local Model-Agnostic Interpretation Methods*, and *Chapter 7, Anchor and Counterfactual Explanations*, will cover better local interpretation methods. However, the decision region plot method helps illustrate many of the concepts surrounding decision boundaries we will discuss in those chapters.

Summary

After reading this chapter, you should know about two model interpretation methods: feature importance and decision boundaries. You also learned about model interpretation method types and scopes and the three elements that impact interpretability in machine learning. We will keep mentioning these fundamental concepts in subsequent chapters. For a machine learning practitioner, it is paramount to be able to spot them so you can know what tools to leverage to overcome interpretation challenges. In the next chapter, we will dive deeper into this topic.

Further reading

- Molnar, Christoph. *Interpretable Machine Learning. A Guide for Making Black Box Models Explainable*, 2019: `https://christophm.github.io/interpretable-ml-book/`.

- *Mlextend Documentation. Plotting Decision Regions.* `http://rasbt.github.io/mlxtend/user_guide/plotting/plot_decision_regions/`.

3
Interpretation Challenges

In this chapter, we will discuss the traditional methods used for machine learning interpretation for both regression and classification. This includes model performance evaluation methods such as RMSE, R-squared, AUC, ROC curves, and the many metrics derived from confusion matrices. We will also explore several dimensionality reduction visualization techniques that can be leveraged for interpretation purposes. We will then examine the limitations of these traditional methods and explain what exactly makes "white-box" models intrinsically interpretable and why we cannot always use white-box models. To answer this question, we'll consider the trade-off between prediction performance and model interpretability. Finally, we will discover some new "glass-box" models such as EBM and skope-rules that attempt to not compromise in this trade-off.

The following are the main topics that will be covered in this chapter:

- Reviewing traditional model interpretation methods
- Understanding the limitations of traditional model interpretation methods
- Studying intrinsically interpretable (white-box) models
- Recognizing the trade-off between performance and interpretability
- Discovering newer interpretable (glass-box) models

Technical requirements

From *Chapter 2*, *Key Concepts of Interpretability*, onward, we are using a custom `mldatasets` library to load our datasets. Instructions on how to install this library are located in the Preface. In addition to `mldatasets`, this chapter's examples also use the `pandas`, `numpy`, `sklearn`, `rulefit`, `cvae`, `interpret`, `statsmodels`, `matplotlib`, and `skope-rules` libraries. The code for this chapter is located here: `https://github.com/PacktPublishing/Interpretable-Machine-Learning-with-Python/tree/master/Chapter03`.

The mission

Picture yourself, a data science consultant, in a conference room in Forth Worth, Texas, during early January 2019. In this conference room, executives for one of the world's largest airlines, **American Airlines (AA)**, are briefing you on their **on-time performance (OTP)**. OTP is a widely accepted key performance indicator for flight punctuality. It is measured as the percentage of flights that arrived within 15 minutes of the scheduled arrival. It turns out that AA has achieved an OTP of just over 80% for 3 years in a row, which is already acceptable, and much better than before, but they are still ninth in the world and fifth in North America. To brag about it next year in their advertising, they aspire to achieve, at least, number one in North America for 2019, besting their biggest rivals.

On the financial front, it is estimated that delays cost the airline close to $2 billion, so reducing this by even 25-35% to be on parity with their competitors could produce sizable savings. And it is estimated that it costs passengers just as much due to tens of millions of lost hours. A reduction in delays would produce happier customers, which could lead to an increase in ticket sales.

Your task is to create models that can predict delays for domestic flights only. What they hope to gain from the models is the following:

- To understand what factors impacted domestic arrival delays the most in 2018

- To anticipate a delay caused by the airline in midair with enough accuracy to mitigate some of these factors in 2019

But not all delays are made equal. The **International Air Transport Association (IATA)** has over 80 delay codes ranging from 14 (*oversales, booking errors*) to 75 (*de-icing of aircraft, removal of ice/snow, frost prevention*). Some are preventable, and others unavoidable.

The airline executives told you that the airline is not, for now, interested in predicting delays caused by events out of their control, such as extreme weather, security events, and air traffic control issues. They are also not interested in delays caused by late arrivals from previous flights using the same aircraft because this was not the root cause. Nevertheless, they would like to know the effect of a busy hub on avoidable delays even if this has to do with congestion because, after all, perhaps there's something they can do with flight scheduling or flight speed, or even gate selection. And while they understand that international flights occasionally impact domestic flights, they hope to tackle the sizeable local market first.

Executives have provided you with a dataset from the United States Department of Transportation *Bureau of Transportation Statistics* with all 2018 AA domestic flights.

The approach

Upon careful consideration, you have decided to approach this both as a regression problem and a classification problem. Therefore, you will produce models that predict minutes delayed as well as models that classify whether flights were delayed by more than 15 minutes or not. For interpretation, using both will enable you to use a wider variety of methods, and expand your interpretation accordingly. Also, dimensionality reduction can only further enrich interpretation possibilities. So we will approach this example by taking the following steps:

1. Predicting minutes delayed with various regression methods

2. Classifying flights as delayed or not delayed with various classification methods

3. Visualizing delayed flights with dimensionality reduction methods

These steps in the *Reviewing traditional model interpretation methods* section are followed by conclusions spread out in the rest of the sections of this chapter.

The preparations

You will find the code for this example here: `https://github.com/ PacktPublishing/Interpretable-Machine-Learning-with-Python/ blob/master/Chapter03/FlightDelays.ipynb`.

Loading the libraries

To run this example, you need to install the following libraries:

- `mldatasets` to load the dataset

- `pandas` and `numpy` to manipulate it

- `sklearn` (scikit-learn), `rulefit`, `cvae`, `statsmodels`, `interpret`, and `skope-rules` to fit models and calculate performance metrics

- `matplotlib` and `seaborn` to create visualizations

Load these libraries as seen in the following snippet:

```
import math
import mldatasets
import pandas as pd
import numpy as np
from sklearn.pipeline import make_pipeline
from sklearn.preprocessing import PolynomialFeatures,
StandardScaler
from sklearn.model_selection import train_test_split
from sklearn import metrics, linear_model, tree, naive_bayes,\
  neighbors, ensemble, neural_network, svm, decomposition,
manifold
from rulefit import RuleFit
import statsmodels.api as sm
from interpret.glassbox import ExplainableBoostingClassifier
from interpret import show
from interpret.perf import ROC
import matplotlib.pyplot as plt
import seaborn as sns
from cvae import cvae
from skrules import SkopeRules
```

Understanding and preparing the data

We then load the data as shown:

```
aad18_df = mldatasets.load("aa-domestic-delays-2018")
```

There should be nearly 900,000 records and 23 columns. We can take a peek at what was loaded like this:

```
aad18_df.info()
```

The following is the output:

```
<class 'pandas.core.frame.DataFrame'>
RangeIndex: 899527 entries, 0 to 899526
Data columns (total 23 columns):
FL_NUM                899527 non-null int64
ORIGIN                899527 non-null object
DEST                  899527 non-null object
PLANNED_DEP_DATETIME  899527 non-null object
CRS_DEP_TIME          899527 non-null int64
DEP_TIME              899527 non-null float64
DEP_DELAY             899527 non-null float64
DEP_AFPH              899527 non-null float64
DEP_RFPH              899527 non-null float64
TAXI_OUT              899527 non-null float64
WHEELS_OFF            899527 non-null float64
    :           :   :    :
WEATHER_DELAY         899527 non-null float64
NAS_DELAY             899527 non-null float64
SECURITY_DELAY        899527 non-null float64
LATE_AIRCRAFT_DELAY   899527 non-null float64
dtypes: float64(17), int64(3), object(3)
memory usage: 157.8+ MB
```

Everything seems to be in order because all columns are there and there are no null values.

The data dictionary

Let's examine the data dictionary.

General features are as follows:

- `FL_NUM`: Flight number
- `ORIGIN`: Starting airport code (IATA)
- `DEST`: Destination airport code (IATA)

Departure features are as follows:

- `PLANNED_DEP_DATETIME`: The planned date and time of the flight.
- `CRS_DEP_TIME`: The planned departure time.
- `DEP_TIME`: The actual departure time.
- `DEP_AFPH`: The number of actual flights per hour occurring during the interval in between the planned and actual departure from the origin airport (factoring in 30 minutes of padding). The feature tells you how busy the origin airport was during takeoff.
- `DEP_RFPH`: The departure relative flights per hour is the ratio of actual flights per hour over the median amount of flights per hour that occur at the origin airport at that time of day, day of the week, and month of the year. The feature tells you how *relatively* busy the origin airport was during takeoff.
- `TAXI_OUT`: The time duration elapsed between the departure from the origin airport gate and wheels off.
- `WHEELS_OFF`: point in time that the aircraft's wheels leave the ground.

In-flight features are as follows:

- `CRS_ELAPSED_TIME`: The planned amount of time needed for the flight trip.
- `PCT_ELAPSED_TIME`: The ratio of actual flight time over planned flight time to gauge the plane's relative speed.
- `DISTANCE`: The distance between two airports.

Arrival features:

- CRS_ARR_TIME: The planned arrival time.

- ARR_AFPH: The number of actual flights per hour occurring during the interval between the planned and actual arrival time at the destination airport (factoring in 30 minutes of padding). The feature tells you how busy the destination airport was during landing.

- ARR_RFPH: The arrival relative flights per hour is the ratio of actual flights per hour over the median amount of flights per hour that occur at the destination airport at that time of day, day of the week, and month of the year. The feature tells you how *relatively* busy the destination airport was during landing.

Delay features:

- DEP_DELAY: The total delay on departure in minutes.

- ARR_DELAY: The total delay on arrival in minutes can be subdivided into any or all of the following:

  a) CARRIER_DELAY: The delay in minutes caused by circumstances within the airline's control (for example, maintenance or crew problems, aircraft cleaning, baggage loading, fueling, and so on).

  b) WEATHER_DELAY: The delay in minutes caused by significant meteorological conditions (actual or forecasted).

  c) NAS_DELAY: The delay in minutes mandated by a national aviation system such as non-extreme weather conditions, airport operations, heavy traffic volume, and air traffic control.

  d) SECURITY_DELAY: The delay in minutes caused by the evacuation of a terminal or concourse, re-boarding of an aircraft because of a security breach, faulty screening equipment, or long lines above 29 minutes in screening areas.

  e) LATE_AIRCRAFT_DELAY: The delay in minutes caused by a previous flight with the same aircraft that arrived late.

Data preparation

For starters, PLANNED_DEP_DATETIME must be of datetime data type:

```
aad18_df['PLANNED_DEP_DATETIME'] =\
            pd.to_datetime(aad18_df['PLANNED_DEP_DATETIME'])
```

The exact day and time of a flight don't matter, but maybe the month and day of the week do because of weather and seasonal patterns that can only be appreciated at this level of granularity. Also, the executives mentioned weekends and winters being especially bad for delays. Therefore, we will create features for the month and day of the week:

```
aad18_df['DEP_MONTH'] = aad18_df['PLANNED_DEP_DATETIME'].
dt.month
```

```
aad18_df['DEP_DOW'] = aad18_df['PLANNED_DEP_DATETIME'].
dt.dayofweek
```

We don't need the PLANNED_DEP_DATETIME column so let's drop it like this:

```
aad18_df = aad18_df.drop(['PLANNED_DEP_DATETIME'], axis=1)
```

It is essential to record whether the arrival or destination airport is a hub. AA, in 2019, had 10 hubs: Charlotte, Chicago–O'Hare, Dallas/Fort Worth, Los Angeles, Miami, New York–JFK, New York–LaGuardia, Philadelphia, Phoenix–Sky Harbor, and Washington–National. Therefore, we can encode which ORIGIN and DEST airports are AA hubs using their IATA codes, and get rid of columns with codes since they are too specific (FL_NUM, ORIGIN, and DEST):

```
#Create list with 10 hubs (with their IATA codes)
hubs = ['CLT', 'ORD', 'DFW', 'LAX', 'MIA', 'JFK', 'LGA',
'PHL',\
        'PHX', 'DCA']
#Boolean series for if ORIGIN or DEST are hubs
is_origin_hub = aad18_df['ORIGIN'].isin(hubs)
is_dest_hub = aad18_df['DEST'].isin(hubs)
#Use boolean series to set ORIGIN_HUB and DEST_HUB
aad18_df['ORIGIN_HUB'] = 0
aad18_df.loc[is_origin_hub, 'ORIGIN_HUB'] = 1
aad18_df['DEST_HUB'] = 0
aad18_df.loc[is_dest_hub, 'DEST_HUB'] = 1
#Drop columns with codes
aad18_df = aad18_df.drop(['FL_NUM', 'ORIGIN', 'DEST'], axis=1)
```

After all these operations, we have a fair number of useful features, but we are yet to determine the target feature. There are two columns that could serve this purpose. We have ARR_DELAY, which is the total amount of minutes delayed regardless of the reason, and then there's CARRIER_DELAY, which is just the total amount of those minutes that can be attributed to the airline. For instance, look at the following sample of flights delayed over 15 minutes (which is considered late according to the airline's definition):

```
aad18_df.loc[aad18_df['ARR_DELAY'] > 15,\
                ['ARR_DELAY','CARRIER_DELAY']].head(10)
```

The preceding code outputs *Figure 3.1*:

	ARR_DELAY	CARRIER_DELAY
8	168	136
16	20	5
18	242	242
19	62	62
22	19	19
26	26	0
29	77	77
32	19	19
33	18	1
40	36	16

Figure 3.1 – Sample observations with arrival delays over 15 minutes

Of all the delays in *Figure 3.1*, one of them (#26) wasn't at all the responsibility of the airline. Four of them were partially the responsibility of the airline (#8, #16, #33, #40), two of which were over 15 minutes late due to the airline (#8, #40). The rest of them were entirely the airline's fault. We can tell that although the total delay is useful information, the airline executives were only interested in delays caused by the airline so ARR_DELAY can be discarded. Furthermore, there's another more important reason it should be discarded, and it's that if the task at hand is to predict a delay, we cannot use pretty much the very same delay (minus the portions not due to the airline) to predict it. This would be *like using today's newspaper slightly redacted to predict today's news*. For this very same reason, it is best to remove ARR_DELAY:

```
aad18_df = aad18_df.drop(['ARR_DELAY'], axis=1)
```

Finally, we can put the target feature alone as y and all the rest as X. After this, we split y and X into train and test datasets. Please note that the target feature (y) stays the same for regression so we split it into `y_train_reg` and `y_test_reg`. However, for classification, we must make binary versions of these labels denoting whether it's more than 15 minutes late or not, called `y_train_class` and `y_test_class`. Please note that we are setting a fixed `random_state` for reproducibility:

```
rand = 9
y = aad18_df['CARRIER_DELAY']
X = aad18_df.drop(['CARRIER_DELAY'], axis=1).copy()
X_train, X_test, y_train_reg, y_test_reg = train_test_split(X,\
y, test_size=0.15, random_state=rand)
y_train_class = y_train_reg.apply(lambda x: 1 if x > 15 else 0)
y_test_class = y_test_reg.apply(lambda x: 1 if x > 15 else 0)
```

To examine how linearly correlated the features are to the target CARRIER_DELAY, we compute *Pearson's correlation coefficient*, turn coefficients to absolute values (because we aren't interested in whether they are positively or negatively correlated), and sort them in descending order:

```
corr = aad18_df.corr()
abs(corr['CARRIER_DELAY']).sort_values(ascending=False)
```

As you can tell from the output, only one feature (DEP_DELAY) is highly correlated. The others aren't:

```
CARRIER_DELAY           1.000000
DEP_DELAY               0.703935
ARR_RFPH                0.101742
LATE_AIRCRAFT_DELAY     0.083166
DEP_RFPH                0.058659
ARR_AFPH                0.035135
DEP_TIME                0.030941
NAS_DELAY               0.026792
    :         :
WEATHER_DELAY           0.003002
SECURITY_DELAY          0.000460
Name: CARRIER_DELAY, dtype: float64
```

However, this is only *linearly* correlated and on a one-by-one basis. It doesn't mean that they don't have a non-linear relationship, or that several features interacting together wouldn't impact the target. In the next section, we will discuss this further.

Reviewing traditional model interpretation methods

To explore as many model classes and interpretation methods as possible, we will fit the data to regression and classification models as well as to dimensionality reduction methods.

Predicting minutes delayed with various regression methods

To compare and contrast regression methods, we will first create a dictionary named `reg_models`. Each model is its own dictionary and the function that creates it in the `model` attribute. This structure will be used later to store the fitted model neatly and its metrics. Model classes in this dictionary have been chosen to represent several model families and to illustrate important concepts that we will discuss later:

```
Reg_models = {
  #Generalized Linear Models (GLMs)
  'linear':{'model': linear_model.LinearRegression()},
  'linear_poly':{'model':
              make_pipeline(PolynomialFeatures(degree=2),
              linear_model.LinearRegression(fit_intercept=False))
  'linear_interact':{'model':
              make_pipeline(PolynomialFeatures(interaction_
only=True),
        linear_model.LinearRegression(fit_intercept=False)) },
  'ridge':{'model': linear_model.\
                    RidgeCV(alphas=[1e-3, 1e-2, 1e-1, 1]) },
  #Trees
  'decision_tree':{'model': tree.\
            DecisionTreeRegressor(max_depth=7, random_
state=rand)},
  #RuleFit
  'rulefit':{'model': RuleFit(max_rules=150, rfmode='regress',\
```

```
                              random_state=rand)},
  #Nearest Neighbors
  'knn':{'model': neighbors.KNeighborsRegressor(n_
neighbors=7)},
  #Ensemble Methods
  'random_forest':{'model':ensmble.\
            RandomForestRegressor(max_depth=7, random_
state=rand)},
  #Neural Networks
  'mlp':{'model':neural_network.\
            MLPRegressor(hidden_layer_sizes=(21,),\
                      max_iter=500, \
                      early_stopping=True,\
                      random_state=rand)}
}
```

Before we start fitting the data to these models, we will briefly explain them one by one:

- linear: **Linear regression** was the first model class we discussed. For better or for worse, it makes several assumptions about the data. Chief among them is the assumption that the y prediction must be a linear combination of X features. This, naturally, limits the capacity to discover non-linear relationships and interactions among the features.

- linear_poly: **Polynomial regression** extends linear regression by adding polynomial features. In this case, as indicated by degree=2, the polynomial degree is two, so it's quadratic. This means, in addition to having all features in their monomial form (for example, DEP_FPH), it also has them in a quadratic form (for example, DEP_FPH2), plus the many interaction terms for all of the 21 features. In other words, for DEP_FPH, there would be interaction terms such as DEP_FPH ´ DISTANCE, DEP_FPH ´ DELAY, and so on for the rest of the features.

- linear_interact: This is just like the **polynomial regression** model but without the quadratic terms. In other words, only the interactions, as interaction_only=True would suggest. It's useful because there is no reason to believe any of our features have a relationship that is better fitted with quadratic terms. Still, perhaps it's the interaction with other features that makes an impact.

- `ridge`: **Ridge regression** is a variation of linear regression. However, even though the method behind linear regression, called **Ordinary Least Squares (OLS)**, does a pretty good job in reducing the error, fitting the model to the features, it does it without considering **overfitting**. The problem here is that OLS treats all features equally, so the model becomes more complex as each variable is added. As the word *overfitting* suggests, the resulting model fits the training data too well, resulting in the lowest bias but the highest variance. There's a sweet spot in this **trade-off between bias and variance**, and one way of getting to this spot is reducing the complexity added by the introduction of too many features. Linear regression is not equipped to do so on its own. This is where ridge regression comes along, with our friend **regularization**. It does this by shrinking coefficients that don't contribute to the outcome with a penalty term called the **L2 norm**. In this example, we use a cross-validated version of ridge (`RidgeCV`) that tests several regularization strengths (`alphas`).

- `decision_tree`: A **decision tree** is precisely as the name suggests. Imagine a tree-like structure where at every point where branches subdivide to form more branches, there is a "test" performed on a feature partitioning the datasets into each branch. When branches stop subdividing, they become leaves, and at every leaf, there's *a decision*, be it to assign a *class* for classification or a fixed value for regression. We are limiting this tree to `max_depth=7` to prevent overfitting because the larger the tree, the better it will fit our training data.

- `rule_fit`: **RuleFit** is a regularized linear regression expanded to include feature interactions in the form of rules. The rules are formed by traversing a decision tree, except it discards the leaves and keeps the feature interactions found traversing the branches toward these leaves. It uses **Lasso Regression**, which like ridge, uses regularization, but instead of using the **L2 norm**, it uses the **L1 norm**. The result is that useless features end up with a coefficient of zero and do not just converge to zero, as they do with L2. We are limiting the rules to 150 (`max_rules=150`) and the attribute `rfmode='regress'` tells RuleFit that this is a regression problem, since it can also be used for classification. Unlike all other models used here, this isn't a scikit-learn one but was created by Christoph Molnar adapting a paper.

- knn: **k-Nearest Neighbors (kNN)** is a simple method based on the *locality* assumption, which is that data points that are close to each other are similar. In other words, they must have similar predicted values, and, in practice, this isn't a bad guess, so it takes k data points nearest to the point you want to predict and derives a prediction based on that. In this case, n_neighbors=7 so $k = 7$. It's an **instance-based machine learning model**, also known as a **lazy learner** because it simply stores the training data. During inference, it employs training data to calculate the similarity with points and generate a prediction based on that. This is opposed to what model-based machine learning techniques, or **eager learners**, do, which is to use training data to learn formulas, parameters, coefficients, or bias/weights, which it then leverages to make a prediction during inference.

- random_forest: Imagine not one but hundreds of decision trees trained on random combinations of the features and random samples of the data. **random forest** takes an average of these randomly generated decision trees to create the best tree. This concept of training less effective models in parallel and combining them using an averaging process is called **bagging**. It is an **ensemble** method because it combines more than one model (usually called **weak learners**) into a **strong learner**. In addition to *bagging*, there are two other ensemble techniques, called **boosting** and **stacking**. For bagging deeper, trees are better because they reduce variance, so this is why we are using max_depth=7.

- mlp: **A multi-layer perceptron** is a "vanilla" feed-forward (sequential) neural network, so it uses non-linear activation functions (MLPRegressor uses *ReLU* by default), stochastic gradient descent, and backpropagation. In this case, we are using 21 neurons in the first and only hidden layer, hence hidden_layer_sizes=(21,), running training for 500 epochs (max_iter=500), and terminating training when the validation score is not improving (early_stopping=True).

If you are unfamiliar with some of these models, don't fret! We will cover them in more detail either later in this chapter or later in the book. Also, please note that some of these models have a random process somewhere. To ensure reproducibility, we have set random_state. It would be best if you strived to always set this, otherwise, it will randomly set it every single time, which will make your results hard to reproduce.

Now, let's iterate over our dictionary of models (`reg_models`), fit them to the training data, and predict and compute two metrics based on the quality of these predictions. We'll then save the fitted model, test predictions, and metrics in the dictionary for later use. Note that `rulefit` only accepts `numpy` arrays, so we can't `fit` it in the same way. Also, note `rulefit` and `mlp` take longer than the rest to train, so this can take a few minutes to run:

```
For model_name in reg_models.keys():
  if model_name != 'rulefit':
   fitted_model = reg_models[model_name]['model'].\
                                        fit(X_train, y_
train_reg)
  else:
   fitted_model = reg_models[model_name]['model'].\
             fit(X_train.values, y_train_reg.values, X_test.
columns)
  y_train_pred = fitted_model.predict(X_train.values)
  y_test_pred = fitted_model.predict(X_test.values)
  reg_models[model_name]['fitted'] = fitted_model
  reg_models[model_name]['preds'] = y_test_pred
  reg_models[model_name]['RMSE_train'] =\
     math.sqrt(metrics.mean_squared_error(y_train_reg, y_train_
pred))
  reg_models[model_name]['RMSE_test'] =\
    math.sqrt(metrics.mean_squared_error(y_test_reg, y_test_
pred))
  reg_models[model_name]['R2_test'] =\
    metrics.r2_score(y_test_reg, y_test_pred)
```

We can now convert the dictionary to a `DataFrame` and display the metrics in a sorted and color-coded fashion:

```
reg_metrics = pd.DataFrame.from_dict(reg_models,\
                  'index')[['RMSE_train', 'RMSE_test', 'R2_
test']]
reg_metrics.sort_values(by='RMSE_test').style.\
  background_gradient(cmap='viridis', low=1, high=0.3,
                  subset=['RMSE_train', 'RMSE_test']).\
```

```
background_gradient(cmap='plasma', low=0.3, high=1,
                    subset=['R2_test'])
```

The preceding code outputs *Figure 3.2*. Please note that color-coding doesn't work in all Jupyter Notebook implementations:

	RMSE_train	RMSE_test	R2_test
mlp	3.18388	3.23262	0.987614
linear_poly	6.21339	6.33494	0.952433
random_forest	5.37769	6.35627	0.952112
linear_interact	6.45271	6.55931	0.949004
decision_tree	6.54292	7.53014	0.932791
linear	7.81963	7.88287	0.926347
ridge	7.92769	7.98758	0.924377
rulefit	8.8205	9.015	0.903672
knn	7.36014	9.26012	0.898362

Figure 3.2 – Regression metrics for our models

To interpret the metrics in *Figure 3.2*, we ought to first understand what they mean, both in general and in the context of this regression exercise:

- **RMSE: Root Mean Square Error** is defined as the standard deviation of the residuals. It's the square root of the squared residuals divided by the number of observations, in this case, flights. It tells you, on average, how far apart the predictions are from the actuals, and as you can probably tell from the color-coding, less is better because you want your predictions to be as close as possible to the actuals in the *test* (**hold-out**) dataset. We have also included this metric for the **train** dataset to see how well it's generalizing. You expect the test error to be higher than the training error, but not by much. If it is, like it is for `random_forest`, you need to tune some of the parameters. In this case, reducing the trees' maximum depth, increasing the number of trees (also called **estimators**), and reducing the maximum number of features to use should do the trick. On the other hand, with `knn`, you can adjust the k, but it is expected, because of its **lazy learner** nature, to overperform on the training data.

- In any case, these numbers are pretty good because even our worst performing model is below a test RMSE of 10, and about half of them have a test RMSE of less than 7.5, quite possibly predicting a delay effectively, on average, since the threshold for a delay is 15 minutes.

Note that `linear_poly` is the second and `linear_interact` is the fourth most performant model, significantly ahead of `linear`, suggesting that non-linearity and interactivity are important factors to produce better predictive performance.

- **R2**: **R-squared** is also known as the **coefficient of determination**. It's defined as the proportion of the variance in the *y* (outcome) target that can be explained by the *X* (predictors) features in the model. It answers the question of what is the variability explained by the model as a proportion of all of it? And as you can probably tell from the color-coding, more is better. And our models appear to include significant X features, as evidenced by our *Pearson's correlation coefficients*. So if this *R2* value was low, perhaps adding additional features would help, such as flight logs, terminal conditions, and even those things airline executives said they weren't interested in exploring right now, such as *knock-off* effects and international flights. These could fill in the gaps in the unexplained variance.

Let's see if we can get good metrics with classification.

Classifying flights as delayed or not delayed with various classification methods

Just as we did with regression, to compare and contrast classification methods, we will first create a dictionary for them named `class_models`. Each model is its own dictionary and the function that creates it in the `model` attribute. This structure will be used later to store the fitted model neatly, and its metrics. Model classes in this dictionary have been chosen to represent several model families and to illustrate important concepts that we will discuss later. Some of these will look familiar because they are the same methods used in regression but applied to classification:

```
Class_models = {
    #Generalized Linear Models (GLMs)
    'logistic':{'model': linear_model.LogisticRegression()},
    'ridge':{'model': linear_model.\
                        RidgeClassifierCV(cv=5,\
                                    alphas=[1e-3, 1e-2,
1e-1, 1],\
                                    class_weight='balanced')},|
    #Tree
    'decision_tree':{'model': tree.\
                        DecisionTreeClassifier(max_depth=7,\
                                    random_state=rand)},
```

```
#Nearest Neighbors
'knn':{'model': neighbors.KNeighborsClassifier(n_
neighbors=7)},
#Naive Bayes
'naive_bayes':{'model': naive_bayes.GaussianNB()},
#Ensemble Methods
'gradient_boosting':{'model':ensemble.\
        GradientBoostingClassifier(n_estimators=210)},
'random_forest':{'model':ensemble.\
              RandomForestClassifier(max_depth=11,\
        class_weight='balanced', random_state=rand)},
#Neural Networks
'mlp':{'model': make_pipeline(StandardScaler(), neural_
network.MLPClassifier(hidden_layer_sizes=(7,),\
                     max_iter=500, early_
                     stopping=True,\
                     random_state=rand))}
}
```

Before we start fitting the data to these models, we will briefly explain them one by one:

- logistic: **logistic regression** was introduced in *Chapter 2, Key Concepts of Interpretability*. It has many of the same pros and cons as **linear regression**. For instance, feature interactions must be added manually. Like other classification models, it returns a probability between 0 and 1, which, when closer to 1 denotes a probable match to a **positive class** while when closer to 0, it denotes an improbable match to the **positive class**, and therefore a probable match to the **negative class**. Naturally, 0.5 is the threshold used to decide between classes, but it doesn't have to be. As we will examine later in the book, there are interpretation and performance reasons to adjust the threshold. Note that this is a binary classification problem, so we are only choosing between delayed (positive) and not delayed (negative), but this method could be extended to multi-class classification. It would then be called **multinomial classification**.

- `ridge`: **Ridge classification** leverages the same regularization technique used in **ridge regression** but applied to classification. It does this by converting the target values to -1 (for a negative class) and keeping 1 for a positive class and then performing ridge regression. At its heart, its regression in disguise will predict values between -1 and 1, and then convert them back to a 0-1 scale. Like with `RidgeCV` for regression, `RidgeClassifierCV` uses leave-one-out cross-validation, which means it first splits the data into different equal-size sets – in this case, we are using five sets (`cv=5`) – and then removes features one at a time to see how well the model performs without them, on average in all the five sets. Those features that don't make much of a difference are penalized testing several regularization strengths (`alphas`) to find the optimal strength. As with all *regularization* techniques, the point is to discourage learning from unnecessary complexity, minimizing the impact of less salient features.

- `decision_tree`: A **"vanilla" decision Tree**, such as this one, is also known as a **CART (Classification And Regression Tree)** because it can be used for regression or classification tasks. It has the same architecture for both tasks but functions slightly differently, like the algorithm used to decide where to "split" a branch. In this case, we are only allowing our trees to have a depth of 7.

- `knn`: **kNN** can also be applied to classification tasks, except instead of averaging what the nearest neighbors' target features (or labels) are, it chooses the most frequent one (also known as the **mode**). We are also using a k of 7 for classification (`n_neighbors`).

- `naive_bayes`: **Gaussian Naïve Bayes** is part of the family of *Naïve Bayes* classifiers, which are called naïve because they make some assumptions that the features are independent of each other, which is usually not the case. This dramatically impedes its capacity to predict unless the assumption is correct. It's called *Bayes* because it's based on **Bayes' theorem of conditional probabilities**, which is that the conditional probability of a class is the class probability times the feature probability given the class. *Gaussian Naïve Bayes* makes an additional assumption, which is that continuous values have a normal distribution, also known as a **Gaussian distribution**.

- `gradient_boosting`: Like **random forest, gradient boosted trees** are also an ensemble method, but that leverages **boosting** instead of **bagging. Boosting** doesn't work in parallel but in sequence, iteratively training weak learners and incorporating their strengths into a stronger learner, while adapting another weak learner to tackle their weaknesses. Although ensembles and boosting, in particular, can be done with a model class, this one uses decision trees. We have limited the number of trees to 210 (`n_estimators=210`).

- `random_forest`: The same **random forest** as with regression except it uses classification decision trees and not regression trees.

- `mlp`: The same **multi-layer perceptron** as with regression, but the output layer, by default, uses a **logistic** function in the output layer to yield probabilities, which it then converts to 1 or 0, based on the 0.5 threshold. Another difference is that we are using seven neurons in the first and only hidden layer (`hidden_layer_sizes=(7,)`) because binary classification tends to require fewer of them to achieve an optimal result.

Please note that some of these models use balanced weights for the classes (`class_weight='balanced'`), which is very important because this happens to be an **imbalanced classification** task. By that, we mean that negative classes vastly outnumber positive classes. You can find out what this looks like for our training data:

```
y_train_class[y_train_class==1].shape[0] / y_train_class.
shape[0]
```

The following is the output:

```
0.061283264255549
```

As you can see, the output in our training data's positive classes represents only 6% of the total. Models that account for this will achieve *fairer* results. There are different ways for accounting for *class imbalance*, which we will discuss in further detail in *Chapter 11, Bias Mitigation and Causal Inference Methods*, but `class_weight='balanced'` applies a weight inversely proportional to class frequencies, giving the outnumbered *positive* class a leg up.

Training and evaluating the classification models

Now, let's iterate over our dictionary of models (`class_models`), fit them to the training data, and predict both probabilities and the class except for `ridge`, which doesn't output probabilities. We'll then compute five metrics based on the quality of these predictions. Lastly, we'll save the fitted model, test predictions, and metrics in the dictionary for later use. You can go get a coffee while you run the next snippet of code because `gradient_boosting` of `sklearn` takes longer than the rest to train, so this can take a few minutes to run:

```
For model_name in class_models.keys():
 fitted_model = class_models[model_name]['model'].\
                             fit(X_train, y_train_class)
 y_train_pred = fitted_model.predict(X_train.values)
 if model_name == 'ridge':
  y_test_pred = fitted_model.predict(X_test.values)
 else:
  y_test_prob = fitted_model.predict_proba(X_test.values)[:,1]
  y_test_pred = np.where(y_test_prob > 0.5, 1, 0)
 class_models[model_name]['fitted'] = fitted_model
 class_models[model_name]['probs'] = y_test_prob
 class_models[model_name]['preds'] = y_test_pred
 class_models[model_name]['Accuracy_train'] =\
            metrics.accuracy_score(y_train_class, y_train_pred)
 class_models[model_name]['Accuracy_test'] =\
            metrics.accuracy_score(y_test_class, y_test_pred)
 class_models[model_name]['Recall_train'] =\
            metrics.recall_score(y_train_class, y_train_pred)
 class_models[model_name]['Recall_test'] =\
            metrics.recall_score(y_test_class, y_test_pred)
 if model_name != 'ridge':
  class_models[model_name]['ROC_AUC_test'] =\
            metrics.roc_auc_score(y_test_class, y_test_prob)
 else:
  class_models[model_name]['ROC_AUC_test'] = 0
 class_models[model_name]['F1_test'] =\
            metrics.f1_score(y_test_class, y_test_pred)
 class_models[model_name]['MCC_test'] =\
```

```
metrics.matthews_corrcoef(y_test_class, y_test_pred)
```

We can now convert the dictionary to a `DataFrame` and display the metrics in a sorted and color-coded fashion:

```
class_metrics = pd.DataFrame.from_dict(class_models,\
                'index')[['Accuracy_train', 'Accuracy_test',\
                'Recall_train', 'Recall_test',\
                'ROC_AUC_test', 'F1_test', 'MCC_test']]
class_metrics.sort_values(by='ROC_AUC_test', ascending=False).\
 style.background_gradient(cmap='plasma', low=0.3, high=1,
                subset=['Accuracy_train', 'Accuracy_
test']).\
 background_gradient(cmap='viridis', low=1, high=0.3,\
                subset=['Recall_train', 'Recall_test',\
                'ROC_AUC_test', 'F1_test', 'MCC_test'])
```

The preceding code outputs *Figure 3.3*:

	Accuracy_train	Accuracy_test	Recall_train	Recall_test	ROC_AUC_test	F1_test	MCC_test
mlp	0.998364	0.99851	0.984826	0.986444	0.999909	0.987819	0.987027
gradient_boosting	0.991725	0.991662	0.89293	0.893851	0.998885	0.929223	0.925619
decision_tree	0.983297	0.982895	0.856969	0.852215	0.994932	0.859182	0.85011
random_forest	0.938783	0.937879	0.997546	0.990559	0.992844	0.661333	0.677145
logistic	0.9786	0.978381	0.743923	0.742677	0.971935	0.807953	0.800067
knn	0.97289	0.965123	0.680667	0.607722	0.948387	0.680906	0.668176
naive_bayes	0.925115	0.925561	0.279126	0.274268	0.811872	0.310922	0.275073
ridge	0.890447	0.891255	0.777002	0.77802	0	0.466998	0.463706

Figure 3.3 – Classification metrics for our models

To interpret the metrics in *Figure 3.3*, we ought to first understand what they mean, both in general and in the context of this classification exercise:

- **Accuracy**: Accuracy is the simplest way to measure the effectiveness of a classification task, and it's the percentage of correct predictions over all predictions. In other words, in a binary classification task, you can calculate this by adding the number of **True Positives (TPs)** and **True Negatives (TNs)** and dividing them by a tally of all predictions made. As with regression metrics, you can measure accuracy for both train and test to gauge overfitting.

- **Recall**: Even though accuracy sounds like a great metric, recall is much better in this case and the reason is you could have an accuracy of 94%, which sounds pretty good, but it turns out you are always predicting no delay! In other words, even if you get high accuracy, it is meaningless unless you are predicting accurately for the least represented class, delays. We can find this number with recall (also known as **sensitivity** or **true positive rate**), which is $TP / TP + FN$ and it can be interpreted as how much of the relevant results were returned. In other words, in this case, what percentage of the actual delays were predicted. Another good measure involving true positives is **precision**, which is how much our predicted samples are relevant, which is $TP / TP + FP$. In this case, that would be what percentage of predicted delays were actual delays. For imbalanced classes, it is recommended to use both, but depending on your preference for FN over FP, you will prefer recall over precision or vice versa.

- **ROC-AUC**: ROC is an acronym for **Receiver Operating Characteristic** and was designed to separate signal from noise. What it does is plot the proportion of **true positive rate** (**Recall**) on the x axis and the false positive rate on the y axis. **AUC** stands for **area under the curve**, which is a number between 0 and 1 that assesses the prediction ability of the classifier 1 being perfect, 0.5 being as good as a coin toss, and anything lower meaning that if we inverted the results of our prediction, we would have a better prediction. To illustrate this, let's generate a ROC curve for our worse-performing model, Naïve Bayes, according to the AUC metric:

```
plt.tick_params(axis = 'both', which = 'major',\
                labelsize = 12)
fpr, tpr, _ = metrics.roc_curve(y_test_class,
              class_models['naive_bayes']['probs'])
plt.plot(fpr, tpr, label='ROC curve (area = %0.2f)' %\
              class_models['naive_bayes']['ROC_AUC_test'])
plt.plot([0, 1], [0, 1], 'k-') #coin toss line
plt.xlabel('False Positive Rate', fontsize = 14)
```

```
plt.ylabel('True Positive Rate', fontsize = 14)
plt.xlim([0.0, 1.0])
plt.ylim([0.0, 1.0])
plt.legend(loc="lower right")
```

The preceding code outputs *Figure 3.4*. Note that the diagonal line signifies half the area. In other words, the point where it has coin-toss-like prediction qualities:

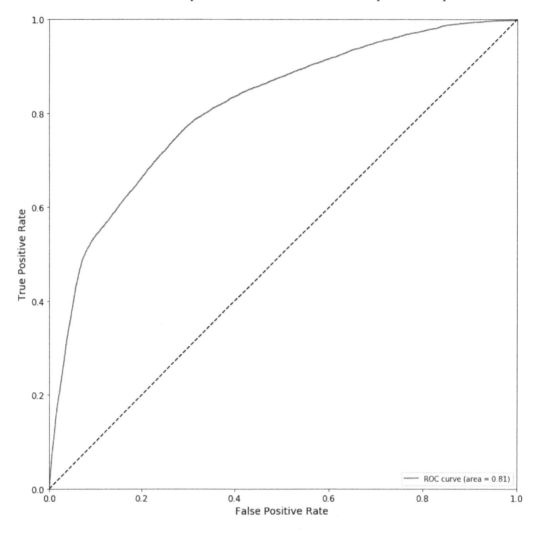

Figure 3.4 – ROC curve for Naïve Bayes

- **F1**: The **F1-score** is also called the harmonic average of precision and recall because it's calculated like this: 2TP / 2TP + FP + FN. Since it includes both precision and recall metrics, which pertain to the proportion of true positives, it's a good metric choice to use when your dataset is imbalanced, and you don't prefer either precision or recall.

- **MCC**: The **Matthews correlation coefficient** is a metric drawn from biostatistics. It's gaining popularity in the broader data science community because it has the ability to produce high scores considering *TP*, *FN*, *TN*, and *FP* fairly because it takes into account proportions of classes. This makes it optimal for imbalanced classification tasks. Unlike all other metrics used so far, it doesn't range from 0 to 1 but -1, complete disagreement, to 1, a total agreement between predictions and actuals. The mid-point, 0, is equivalent to a random prediction.

Our classification metrics are mostly very good, exceeding 96% accuracy and 75% recall. However, even recall isn't everything. For instance, RandomForest, due to its class balancing with weights, got the highest recall but did poorly in F1 and MCC, which suggests that precision is not very good.

Ridge classification also had the same setting and had such a poor F1 score, precision must have been dismal. This doesn't mean this weighting technique is inherently wrong, but it often requires more control. This book will cover techniques to achieve the right balance between fairness and accuracy, accuracy and reliability, reliability and validity, and so on. This is a balancing act that requires many metrics and visualizations. A key takeaway from this exercise should be that a **single metric will not tell you the whole story**, and interpretation is about **telling the most relevant and sufficiently complete story**.

Now, to complete this story, we are going to try a few dimensionality reduction methods.

Visualizing delayed flights with dimensionality reduction methods

Visualization, and interpretation for that matter, do not always deal with tangibles. With machine learning, we are often dealing with latent relationships between features that, given their complexity, are hard to find and even harder to describe or visualize. And one effective way of reducing this complexity in visualizing them is through dimensionality reduction methods, which help extract representations that, although lacking a discernable name, might have some identifiable insights we can derive meaning from.

To compare and contrast dimensionality reduction methods, we will first create a dictionary for them named `dimred_methods`. Each method is its own dictionary and the function that creates it in the `method` attribute. This structure will be used later to store the data once reduced neatly or, in the case of `cvae`, the fitted model. Methods in this dictionary have been chosen to represent several families of methods to illustrate the important concepts that we will discuss later.

Given the potentially resource-intensive nature of some of these methods, we are using an abbreviated nine-column version of our dataset for both train (`X_train_abbrev`), and test (`X_test_abbrev`). And we are also sampling only 10% of the test dataset using a randomly generated index (`sample_idx`). This is just a `numpy` array of numbers that tell us which observations were randomly selected. If you have more resources to work with, feel free to change the `sample_size` to a more significant percentage:

```
X_train_abbrev = X_train.iloc[:,[0, 1, 2, 4, 8, 9, 11, 17, 20]]
X_test_abbrev = X_test.iloc[:,[0, 1, 2, 4, 8, 9, 11, 17, 20]]
np.random.seed(rand)
sample_size = 0.1
sample_idx = np.random.choice(X_test.shape[0],\
        math.ceil(X_test.shape[0]*sample_size), replace=False)
dimred_methods = {
    #Decomposition
    'pca':{'method': decomposition.PCA(n_components=3,\
                                    random_
state=rand)},
    #Manifold Learning
    't-sne':{'method': manifold.TSNE(n_components=3,\
                                    random_state=rand)},
    #Variational Autoencoders
    'vae':{'method': cvae.CompressionVAE(X_train_abbrev.values,\
                        dim_latent=3, tb_logging=False)}
}
```

Before we begin to apply these methods to our data, we will briefly explain them one by one:

- `pca`: **Principal Component Analysis (PCA)** is one of the oldest techniques of dimensionality reduction, and it's usually done by performing **eigenvalue decomposition** of the covariance matrix of the data. Unlike the others we are exploring here, it's computationally speedy. The process of eigenvalue decomposition finds orthogonal vectors, which means that geometrically they are far apart. This is so that PCA can reduce dimensions to ones that are uncorrelated to each other. Its name refers to principal components because eigenvectors are also called **principal directions**. This makes sense because data is reduced by projecting data to fewer dimensions while trying not to lose information, so it assumes directions with the greatest variances are the most important.

- `t-sne`: **T-distributed Stochastic Neighbor Embedding (t-SNE)** is one of the newer methods of dimensionality reduction, and unlike PCA, it is non-linear, so it's good at capturing non-linearities. Also unlike PCA, the mathematical theory behind t-SNE is not linear algebra but probability. It minimizes the difference between pairwise distribution similarities between high-dimensional (our input data) and the lower-dimensional representation using **Kullback-Leibler divergence** (which is a distance measurement). Unlike PCA, which focuses on putting dissimilar points as far apart as possible, **t-SNE is about placing similar points close together**.

- `vae`: **Variational Autoencoders (VAEs)** are a deep learning method that learns how to best encode data from a high dimension and then decode it back from a low to a high dimension. Since it uses linear algebra for the neural network and measures **Kullback-Leibler divergence** between probability distributions, it has elements from both PCA and t-SNE. Of course, it's different in many ways. While VAE minimizes the reconstruction error between the original and reconstructed data, it doesn't preserve distances between similar points on a granular level like t-SNE does. Unlike both PCA and t-SNE, VAE provides reversibility between low dimensions and higher dimensions and can even generate new data.

Please note that for all of the methods, we are reducing data to three **components** (`n_components=3`) or **dimensions** (`dim_latent=3`). Also, `vae` is not just a dimensionality reduction method but a machine learning model class, so it will train on data first. So, unlike the others, we will use the abbreviated training data `X_train_abbrev` to this effect.

Now, let's iterate over our dictionary of methods (`dimred_methods`) and perform the dimensionality reduction with each method. In the case of `vae`, there will be a fitted model too. Lastly, we save the reduced data and fitted model for `vae`, in the dictionary for later use. Two of these methods take a few minutes each, so don't worry if it takes a while:

```
For method_name in dimred_methods.keys():
  if method_name != 'vae':
    lowdim_data = dimred_methods[method_name]['method'].\
                   fit_transform(X_test_abbrev.values[sample_idx])
  else:
    fitted_model = dimred_methods[method_name]['method'].train()
    lowdim_data = fitted_model.\
                   embed(X_test_abbrev.values[sample_idx])
  dimred_methods[method_name]['fitted'] = fitted_model
  dimred_methods[method_name]['lowdim'] = lowdim_data
```

So what can we do with the low-dimensional data we now have? For starters, we can visualize it!

So, one neat visualization we can do is plot the three dimensions – let's call them x, y, and z – as two dimensions at a time, while we show our classifications in different colors. This will be like seeing the three dimensions from different angles (top, side, and front). To do this, we will leverage a plotting function called `plot_3dim_decomposition`, which takes our low-dimensional data z and plots its three dimensions while color-coding `y_labels`. Initially, our labels can be our actual y's (coding 0 for not delayed and 1 for delayed), but so that it can display a legend, we will also include `y_names`, which is a dictionary that helps translate these in the plot legend:

```
Y_names = {0:'Not Delayed', 1:'Delayed'}
```

Now let's plot PCA's low-dimensional data against the sampled `y_test_class`:

```
mldatasets.plot_3dim_decomposition(dimred_methods['pca']
['lowdim'], y_test_class.values[sample_idx], y_names)
```

In *Figure 3.5*, you can tell **Delayed** is separable, in some parts, from not delayed, and this is clearer when comparing some dimensions than others:

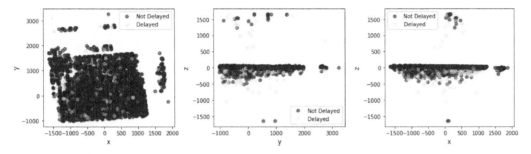

Figure 3.5 – PCA with three components plotted in two dimensions at a time and color-coded for labels

How about we do the same for t-SNE and VAE?

```
mldatasets.\
        plot_3dim_decomposition(dimred_methods['t-sne']
['lowdim'], y_test_class.values[sample_idx], y_names)
mldatasets.plot_3dim_decomposition(dimred_methods['vae']
['lowdim'], y_test_class.values[sample_idx], y_names)
```

The preceding code outputs *Figure 3.6* and *Figure 3.7* for t-SNE and VAE respectively:

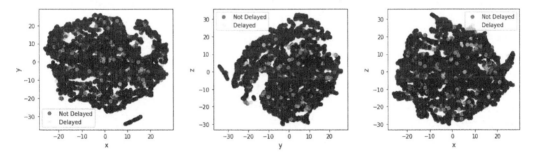

Figure 3.6 – t-SNE with three components plotted in two dimensions at a time
and color-coded for labels

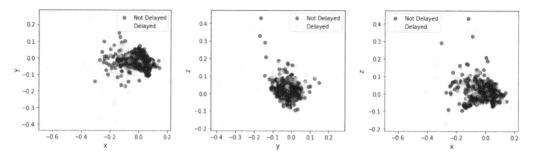

Figure 3.7 – VAE with three dimensions plotted in two dimensions at a time and color-coded for labels

t-SNE (*Figure 3.6*) is very dense, but you still find clusters in which delays are prevalent, and with VAE (*Figure 3.7*), it's harder to identify the clusters, especially in the area where most of the purple is concentrated. As you can tell from these initial steps, these techniques can be used to identify areas where your classes are most concentrated. But is that all there is to it?

There are many ways in which dimensionality reduction can be leveraged. Some are entirely visual, and others can be extended to enhance feature selection and engineering, anomaly detection, and even the modeling where you can use it to make sense of intermediate steps.

But sticking to the visualizations, for now, you can even use it to debug models. For instance, if instead of the actual binary classes, you displayed the classification errors (*FP, FN*), or lack thereof (*TP, TN*), for each of your observations, you could visualize where most of your errors for a particular model are located. To that end, we will use a function called encode_classification_error_vector, which takes our actuals and model predictions and returns the array of classification errors (error_vector). Also, its corresponding dictionary for the plot legend error_labels. We can then plug this into the very same plot_3dim_decomposition function. We can use this to visualize the classification errors for the ridge classifier we fitted earlier, one of our worst-performing classifiers:

```
Y_test_class_samp = y_test_class.values[sample_idx]
y_test_pred_samp = class_models['ridge']['preds'][sample_idx]
error_vector, error_labels =\
        encode_classification_error_vector(y_test_class_samp,\
                                        y_test_pred_samp)
```

Now we can visualize these classification errors using all three dimensionality reduction methods:

```
mldatasets.plot_3dim_decomposition(dimred_methods['pca']
['lowdim'], error_vector, error_labels)
```
```
mldatasets.\
    plot_3dim_decomposition(dimred_methods['t-sne']['lowdim'],\
                    error_vector, error_labels)
```
```
mldatasets.plot_3dim_decomposition(dimred_methods['vae']
['lowdim'], error_vector, error_labels)
```

The preceding code outputs *Figure 3.8*:

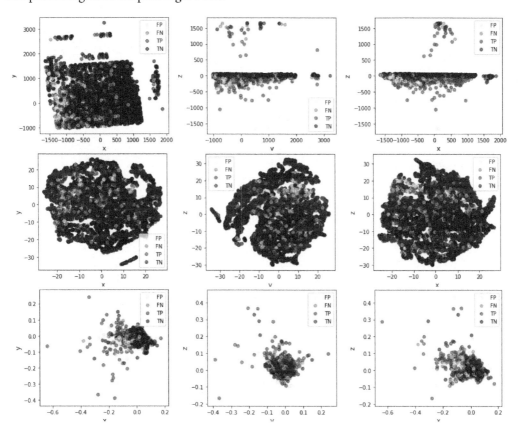

Figure 3.8 – PCA, t-SNE, and VAE, each with three components plotted in two dimensions at a time and color-coded for classification errors

In *Figure 3.8*, for all three dimensionality reduction techniques, you can identify "weak" areas where FPs and FNs are prevalent. You can dig deeper into these areas and try different combinations of features on dimensionality reduction to see if it makes a difference, or even perform some transformations on your features. If you find three dimensions lack the **expressiveness** to represent patterns, try more dimensions. There's a lot to explore here.

If dimensionality reduction techniques capture the essence of your datasets, why not train on them? In some cases, it makes sense to do so, but x, y, and z lack inherent meaning, and **meaning is indispensable for interpretation**. But you can find meaning in clusters where your models are misclassifying, and this could be extended to all your models. In fact, you could ask and answer the question: where do all my models consistently have FPs or FNs? You could find clusters where this happens and incorporate these insights into your models.

When using visualization to examine models, decisions aren't limited to dimensionality reduction methods. Some model classes are easy to visualize, as we'll cover later in this chapter.

Now, let's examine some limitations of the traditional methods we've been practicing.

Understanding limitations of traditional model interpretation methods

In a nutshell, traditional interpretation methods *only cover surface-level questions about your models* such as the following:

- In aggregate, do they perform well?
- *What* changes in hyperparameters may impact predictive performance?
- *What* latent patterns can you find between the features and their predictive performance?

These questions are very limiting if you are trying to understand not only whether your model works but *why* and *how*?

This gap in understanding can lead to unexpected issues with your model that won't necessarily be immediately apparent. Let's consider that models, once deployed, are not static but dynamic. They face different challenges than they did in the "lab" when you were training them. They may face not only performance issues but issues with bias such as imbalance with underrepresented classes, or security with adversarial attacks. Realizing that the features have changed in the real-world environment, we might have to add new features instead of merely retraining with the same feature set. And if there are some troubling assumptions made by your model, you might have to re-examine the whole pipeline. But how do you recognize that these problems exist in the first place? That's when you will need a whole new set of interpretation tools that can help you dig deeper and answer more specific questions about your model. These tools provide interpretations that can truly account for **Fairness, Accountability, and Transparency (FAT)**, which we discussed in *Chapter 1, Interpretation, Interpretability, and Explainability; and Why Does It All Matter?*

Studying intrinsically interpretable (white-box) models

So far, in this chapter, we have already fitted our training data to model classes representing each of these "white-box" model families. The purpose of this section is to show you exactly why they are *intrinsically interpretable*. We'll do so by employing the models that were previously fitted.

Generalized Linear Models (GLMs)

GLMs are a large family of model classes that have a model for every statistical distribution. Just like **linear regression** assumes your target feature and residuals have a normal distribution, **logistic regression** assumes the Bernoulli distribution. There are GLMs for every distribution, such as **Poisson regression** for Poisson distribution and **multinomial response** for multinomial distribution. You choose which GLM to use based on the distribution of your target variable and whether your data meets the other assumptions of the GLM (they vary). In addition to an underlying distribution, what ties GLMs together into a single family is the fact that they all have a linear predictor. In other words, the $\hat{y}$ target variable (or predictor) can be expressed mathematically as a weighted sum of X features, where weights are called b coefficients. This is the simple formula, the linear predictor function, that all GLMs share:

$$\hat{y} = \beta X$$

However, although they share this same formula, they each have a different link function, which provides a link between the linear predictor function and the mean of the statistical distribution of the GLM. This can add some non-linearity to the resulting model formula while retaining the linear combination between the *b* coefficients and the *X* input data, which can be a source of confusion. Still, it's linear because of the linear combination.

There are also many variations for specific GLMs. For instance, **Polynomial regression** is *linear regression* with polynomials of its features, and **ridge regression** is *linear regression* with L2 regularization. We won't cover all GLMs in this section because they aren't needed for the example in this chapter, but all have plausible use cases.

Incidentally, there's also a similar concept called **Generalized Additive Models (GAMs)**, which are GLMs that don't require linear combinations of features and coefficients and instead retain the addition part, but of arbitrary functions applied on the features. GAMs are also interpretable, but they are not as common, and usually tailored to specific use cases *ad hoc*.

Linear regression

In *Chapter 1, Interpretation, Interpretability, and Explainability, and Why Does It All Matter?*, we covered the formula of simple linear regression, which only has a single *X* feature. Multiple linear regression extends this to have any number of features, so instead of being:

$$\hat{y} = \beta_0 + \beta_1 X_1$$

it can be:

$\hat{y} = \beta_0 + \beta_1 X_1 + \beta_2 X_2 \ldots + \beta_n X_n$ with n features, and where β_0 is the intercept,

and thanks to linear algebra, this can be a simple matrix multiplication, if $X_0 = 1$:

$$\hat{y} = \beta X$$

The method used to arrive at the optimal *b* coefficients, **OLS**, is well-studied and understood. Also, in addition to the coefficients, you can extract confidence intervals for each. The model's correctness depends on whether the input data meets the assumptions: **linearity**, normality, independence, (mostly) a lack of multicollinearity, and homoscedasticity. We've discussed linearity, so far, quite a bit so we will briefly explain the rest:

- **Normality** is the property that that each feature is normally distributed. This can be tested with a **Q-Q plot**, histogram, or **Kolmogorov-Smirnov** test, and non-normality can be corrected with non-linear transformations. If a feature isn't normally distributed, it will make its coefficient confidence intervals invalid.

- **Independence** is when your *observations* (the rows in your dataset) are independent of each other, like different and unrelated events. If your *observations* aren't independent, it could affect your interpretation of the results. In this chapter's example, if you had multiple rows about the same flight, that could violate this assumption and make results hard to understand. This can be tested by looking for duplicate flight numbers.

- **Lack of multicollinearity** is desirable because, otherwise, you'd have inaccurate coefficients. Multicollinearity occurs when the features are highly correlated with each other. This can be tested with a **correlation matrix**, **tolerance measure**, or **Variance Inflation Factor** (**VIF**), and it can be fixed by removing one of each highly correlated feature.

- **Homoscedasticity** was briefly discussed in *Chapter 1, Interpretation, Interpretability, and Explainability; and Why Does It All Matter?* and it's when the residuals (the errors) are more or less equal across the regression line. This can be tested with the **Goldfeld-Quandt test**, and heteroscedasticity (the lack of homoscedasticity) can be corrected with non-linear transformations. This assumption is often violated in practice.

Even though we haven't done it for this chapter's example, if you are going to rely on linear regression heavily, it's always good to test these assumptions before you even begin to fit your data to a linear regression model. This book won't detail how this is done because it's more about model-agnostic and deep-learning interpretation methods than delving into how to meet the assumptions of a specific class of models such as **normality** and **homoscedasticity**. However, we covered the characteristics that trump interpretation the most in *Chapter 2, Key Concepts of Interpretability*, and we will continue to look for these characteristics: **non-linearity**, **non-monotonicity**, and **interactivity**. We will do this, mainly, because the linearity and correlation of and between features are still relevant, regardless of the modeling class used to make predictions. And these are characteristics that can be easily tested for in the methods used for linear regression.

Interpretation

So how do we interpret a linear regression model? Easy! Just get the coefficients and the intercept. Our *scikit-learn* models have these attributes embedded in the fitted model:

```
coefs_lm = reg_models['linear']['fitted'].coef_
intercept_lm = reg_models['linear']['fitted'].intercept_
print('coefficients:%s' % coefs_lm)
print('intercept:%s' % intercept_lm)
```

The preceding code outputs the following:

```
coefficients:   [ 4.54955677e-03 -5.25032459e-03   8.94123625e-
01   1.25274473e-01 -6.46799581e-04 ...]
intercept:   -37.860211953237275
```

So now you know the formula, which looks something like this:

$$\hat{y} = -37.86 + 0.0045X_1 + -0.0053X_2 + 0.894X_3 + \ldots$$

This formula should provide some intuition on how the model can be interpreted globally. Interpreting each coefficient in the model can be done for multiple linear regression, just as we did with the simple linear regression example in *Chapter 1, Interpretation, Interpretability, and Explainability; and Why Does It All Matter?*. The coefficients act as weights, but they also tell a story that varies depending on the kind of feature. To make interpretation more manageable, let's put our coefficients in a DataFrame alongside the names of each feature:

```
coef_df = pd.DataFrame({'feature':X_train.columns.values.
tolist(), 'coef': coefs_lm})
coef_df
```

The preceding code produces the data frame in *Figure 3.9*:

	feature	coef
0	CRS_DEP_TIME	0.00454956
1	DEP_TIME	-0.00525032
2	DEP_DELAY	0.894124
3	TAXI_OUT	0.125274
4	WHEELS_OFF	-0.0006468
5	CRS_ARR_TIME	-0.000369914
6	CRS_ELAPSED_TIME	-0.0126273
7	DISTANCE	0.000676793
8	WEATHER_DELAY	-0.906354
9	NAS_DELAY	-0.674053
10	SECURITY_DELAY	-0.917398
11	LATE_AIRCRAFT_DELAY	-0.929841
12	DEP_AFPH	-0.0152963
13	ARR_AFPH	0.000548174
14	DEP_MONTH	-0.039835
15	DEP_DOW	-0.0182132
16	DEP_RFPH	-0.469474
17	ARR_RFPH	0.373844
18	ORIGIN_HUB	-1.02909
19	DEST_HUB	-0.394899
20	PCT_ELAPSED_TIME	45.0116

Figure 3.9 – Coefficients of linear regression features

Here's how to interpret a feature using the coefficients in *Figure 3.9*:

- **Continuous**: Like ARR_RFPH, you know that for every one-unit increase (relative flights per hour), it increases the predicted delay by 0.373844 minutes, if all other features stay the same.

- **Binary**: Like ORIGIN_HUB, you know the difference between the origin airport being a hub or not is expressed by the coefficient -1.029088. In other words, since it's a negative number, the origin airport is a hub. It reduces the delay by just over 1 minute if all other features stay the same.

- **Categorical**: We don't have categorical features, but we have ordinal features that could have been, and **actually should have been**, categorical features. For instance, DEP_MONTH and DEP_DOW are integers from 1-12 and 0-6, respectively. If they are treated as ordinals, we are assuming because of the linear nature of linear regression that an increase or decrease in months has an impact on the outcome. It's the same with the day of the week. But the impact is tiny. Had we treated them as dummy or one-hot encoded features, we could measure whether Fridays are more prone to carrier delays than Saturdays and Wednesdays, or Julys than Octobers and Junes. This couldn't possibly be modeled with them in order, because they have no relation to this order (yep – it's non-linear!).

- So, say, we had a feature called DEP_FRIDAY and another called DEP_JULY. They are treated like binary features and can tell you precisely what effect a departure being on a Friday or in July has on the model. Some features were kept as ordinal or continuous on purpose, despite being good candidates for being categorical, to demonstrate how not making the right adjustments to your features can impact the **expressive power** of model interpretation. It would have been good to tell airline executives more about how the day and time of a departure impacted delays. Also, in some cases – not in this one – an oversight like this can grossly affect a linear regression model's performance.

The intercept (-37.86) is not a feature, but it does have a meaning, which is if all features were at 0, what would the prediction be? In practice, this doesn't happen unless your features happen to all have a plausible reason to be 0. Just as in *Chapter 1, Interpretation, Interpretability, and Explainability; and Why Does It All Matter?* you wouldn't have expected anyone to have a height of 0, in this example, you wouldn't expect a flight to have a distance of 0. However, if you standardized the features so that they had a mean of 0, then you would change the interpretation of the intercept to be the prediction you expect if all features are their mean value.

Feature importance

The coefficients can also be leveraged to calculate feature importance. Unfortunately, scikit-learn's linear regressor is ill-equipped to do this because it doesn't output the standard error of the β coefficients. According to their importance, all it takes to rank features is to divide the βs by their corresponding standard errors. This result is something called the t-statistic:

$$t_{\beta_i} = \frac{\beta_i}{SE(\beta_i)}$$

And then you take an absolute value of this and sort them from high to low. It's easy enough to calculate, but you need the standard error. You could reverse engineer the linear algebra involved to retrieve it using the intercept, and the coefficients returned by scikit-learn. However, it's probably a lot easier to fit the linear regression model again, but this time using the `statsmodels` library, which has a summary with all the statistics, including t! By the way, `statsmodels` names its linear regressor `OLS`, which makes sense because OLS is the name of the mathematical method that fits the data:

```
linreg_mdl = sm.OLS(y_train_reg, sm.add_constant(X_train))
linreg_mdl = linreg_mdl.fit()
linreg_mdl.summary()
```

The preceding code yields *Figure 3.10*:

OLS Regression Results

Dep. Variable:	CARRIER_DELAY	R-squared:	0.921
Model:	OLS	Adj. R-squared:	0.921
Method:	Least Squares	F-statistic:	4.251e+05
Date:	Wed, 02 Sep 2020	Prob (F-statistic):	0.00
Time:	13:32:20	Log-Likelihood:	-2.6574e+06
No. Observations:	764597	AIC:	5.315e+06
Df Residuals:	764575	BIC:	5.315e+06
Df Model:	21		
Covariance Type:	nonrobust		

	coef	std err	t	P>|t|	[0.025	0.975]
const	-37.8618	0.125	-301.763	0.000	-38.108	-37.616
CRS_DEP_TIME	0.0045	7.24e-05	62.872	0.000	0.004	0.005
DEP_TIME	-0.0053	9.19e-05	-57.116	0.000	-0.005	-0.005
DEP_DELAY	0.8941	0.000	2951.056	0.000	0.894	0.895
DEP_AFPH	-0.0153	0.000	-47.725	0.000	-0.016	-0.015
DEP_RFPH	-0.4696	0.017	-27.353	0.000	-0.503	-0.436
TAXI_OUT	0.1253	0.001	104.120	0.000	0.123	0.128
WHEELS_OFF	-0.0006	6.7e-05	-9.646	0.000	-0.001	-0.001
CRS_ELAPSED_TIME	-0.0126	0.001	-19.132	0.000	-0.014	-0.011
PCT_ELAPSED_TIME	45.0113	0.117	384.073	0.000	44.782	45.241
DISTANCE	0.0007	8.02e-05	8.429	0.000	0.001	0.001
CRS_ARR_TIME	-0.0004	2.18e-05	-16.939	0.000	-0.000	-0.000
ARR_AFPH	0.0005	0.000	1.651	0.099	-0.000	0.001
ARR_RFPH	0.3739	0.013	28.386	0.000	0.348	0.400
WEATHER_DELAY	-0.9064	0.001	-995.366	0.000	-0.908	-0.905
NAS_DELAY	-0.6741	0.001	-829.129	0.000	-0.676	-0.672
SECURITY_DELAY	-0.9174	0.005	-167.857	0.000	-0.928	-0.907
LATE_AIRCRAFT_DELAY	-0.9298	0.001	-1827.018	0.000	-0.931	-0.929
DEP_MONTH	-0.0397	0.003	-15.019	0.000	-0.045	-0.034
DEP_DOW	-0.0180	0.004	-4.005	0.000	-0.027	-0.009
ORIGIN_HUB	-1.0291	0.027	-38.589	0.000	-1.081	-0.977
DEST_HUB	-0.3949	0.026	-15.041	0.000	-0.446	-0.343

Omnibus:	211121.387	Durbin-Watson:	2.001
Prob(Omnibus):	0.000	Jarque-Bera (JB):	24359701.834
Skew:	0.098	Prob(JB):	0.00
Kurtosis:	30.651	Cond. No.	5.69e+04

Figure 3.10 – The statsmodels linear regression summary

As you can tell by the summary in *Figure 3.10*, there's quite a bit to unpack. This book won't address everything here except that the **t-statistic** can tell you how important features are in relation to each other. There's another more pertinent statistical interpretation, which is that if you were to hypothesize that the b coefficient is 0, in other words, that the feature has no impact on the model, the distance of the t-statistic from 0 helps reject that null hypothesis. This is what the **p-value** to the right of the t-statistic does. It's no coincidence that the closest t to 0 (for ARR_AFPH) has the only p-value above 0.05. This puts this feature at a level of insignificance since everything below 0.05 is statistically significant according to this method of hypothesis testing.

So to rank our features, let's extract the data frame from the statsmodels summary. Then, we drop the const (the intercept) because this is not a feature. We need the names of the features to make sense of it, so we turn this array of features into its dataframe. Then, we concat the names dataframe with the summary dataframe. Finally, we make a new column with the absolute value of the t-statistic and sort it accordingly. To demonstrate how the absolute value of the t-statistic and p-value are inversely related, we are also color-coding these columns:

```
summary_df = linreg_mdl.summary2().tables[1]
summary_df = summary_df.drop(['const']).reset_index().\
rename(columns={'index':'feature'})
summary_df['t_abs'] = abs(summary_df['t'])
summary_df.sort_values(by='t_abs', ascending=False).style.\
  background_gradient(cmap='plasma_r', low=0, high=0.1,\
                      subset=['P>|t|']).\
  background_gradient(cmap='plasma_r', low=0, high=0.1,\
                      subset=['t_abs'])
```

The preceding code outputs *Figure 3.11*:

	feature	Coef.	Std.Err.	t	P>|t|	[0.025	0.975]	t_abs
2	DEP_DELAY	0.894124	0.000302981	2951.09	0	0.89353	0.894717	2951.09
11	LATE_AIRCRAFT_DELAY	-0.929841	0.000508937	-1827.03	0	-0.930839	-0.928844	1827.03
8	WEATHER_DELAY	-0.906354	0.000910567	-995.373	0	-0.908138	-0.904569	995.373
9	NAS_DELAY	-0.674053	0.000812964	-829.13	0	-0.675646	-0.67246	829.13
20	PCT_ELAPSED_TIME	45.0116	0.117195	384.076	0	44.7819	45.2413	384.076
10	SECURITY_DELAY	-0.917398	0.00546544	-167.855	0	-0.928111	-0.906686	167.855
3	TAXI_OUT	0.125274	0.00120321	104.117	0	0.122916	0.127633	104.117
0	CRS_DEP_TIME	0.00454956	7.23674e-05	62.8675	0	0.00440772	0.00469139	62.8675
1	DEP_TIME	-0.00525032	9.19302e-05	-57.1121	0	-0.0054305	-0.00507014	57.1121
12	DEP_AFPH	-0.0152963	0.000320506	-47.7256	0	-0.0159245	-0.0146681	47.7256
18	ORIGIN_HUB	-1.02909	0.0266686	-38.5879	0	-1.08136	-0.976818	38.5879
17	ARR_RFPH	0.373844	0.0131708	28.3844	3.89612e-177	0.34803	0.399658	28.3844
16	DEP_RFPH	-0.469474	0.0171688	-27.3446	1.50325e-164	-0.503124	-0.435824	27.3446
6	CRS_ELAPSED_TIME	-0.0126273	0.000659852	-19.1366	1.3093e-81	-0.0139206	-0.011334	19.1366
5	CRS_ARR_TIME	-0.000369914	2.18388e-05	-16.9384	2.4083e-64	-0.000412717	-0.00032711	16.9384
14	DEP_MONTH	-0.039835	0.00264082	-15.0844	2.08773e-51	-0.045011	-0.0346591	15.0844
19	DEST_HUB	-0.394899	0.0262564	-15.0401	4.07781e-51	-0.44636	-0.343437	15.0401

Figure 3.11 – Linear regression summary table sorted by the absolute value of the t-statistic

Something particularly interesting about the feature importance in *Figure 3.11* is that different kinds of delays occupy 5 out of the top six positions. Of course, this could be because linear regression is confounding different non-linear effects these have, or perhaps there's something here we should look further into. Especially since the statsmodels summary under the "**Warnings**" section cautions:

> "[2] The condition number is large, 5.69e+04. This might indicate that there are strong multicollinearity or other numerical problems."

This is odd. Hold that thought. We will examine this further later.

Ridge regression

Ridge regression is part of a sub-family of **penalized** or **regularized** regression along with the likes of LASSO and ElasticNet because, as explained earlier in this chapter, it penalizes using the *L2 norm*. This sub-family is also called **sparse linear models** because, thanks to the regularization, it cuts out some of the noise by making irrelevant features less relevant. **Sparsity** in this context means less is more because reduced complexity will lead to lower variance and improved generalization.

To illustrate this concept, look at the feature importance table (*Figure 3.11*) we output for linear regression. Something that should be immediately apparent is how the t_abs column starts with every row a different color, and then a whole bunch of them are the same shade of yellow. Because of the variation in confidence intervals, the absolute t-value is not something you can take proportionally and say that your top feature is hundreds of times more relevant than every one of your bottom 10 features. However, it should indicate that there are significantly more important features than others to the point of irrelevance, and possibly confoundment, hence creating noise. There's ample research on how there's a tendency for a small subset of features to have the most substantial effects on the outcome of the model. This is called the **bet on sparsity principle**. Whether it's true or not for your data, it's always good to test the theory by applying regularization, especially in cases where data is very wide (many features) or exhibits multicollinearity. These regularized regression techniques can be incorporated into feature selection processes or to inform your understanding of what features are essential.

There is a technique to adapt ridge regression to classification problems. It was briefly discussed before. It converts the labels to a -1 to 1 scale for training to predict values between -1 and 1, and then turns them back to a 0-1 scale. However, it uses regularized linear regression to fit the data, and can be interpreted in the same way.

Interpretation

Ridge regression can be interpreted in the same way as linear regression, both globally and locally, because once the model has been fitted, there's no difference. The formula is the same:

$$\hat{y} = \beta^{ridge} X$$

Except β^{ridge} coefficients are different because they were penalized with a λ parameter, which controls how much **shrinkage** (also known as **penalty**) to apply.

We can quickly compare coefficients by extracting the ridge coefficients from their fitted model and placing them side by side in a DataFrame with the coefficients of the linear regression:

```
coefs_ridge = reg_models['ridge']['fitted'].coef_
coef_ridge_df =
            pd.DataFrame({'feature':X_train.columns.values.
tolist(), 'coef_linear': coefs_lm, 'coef_ridge': coefs_ridge})
coef_ridge_df.style.\
  background_gradient(cmap='viridis_r', low=0.3, high=0.2,
  axis=1)
```

As you can tell in *Figure 3.12* output by the preceding code, the coefficients are always slightly different, but sometimes they are lower and sometimes higher:

	feature	coef_linear	coef_ridge
0	CRS_DEP_TIME	0.00454956	0.00501961
1	DEP_TIME	-0.00525032	-0.00441738
2	DEP_DELAY	0.894124	0.894292
3	TAXI_OUT	0.125274	0.125165
4	WHEELS_OFF	-0.0006468	0.000232365
5	CRS_ARR_TIME	-0.000369914	-0.00189765
6	CRS_ELAPSED_TIME	-0.0126273	-0.0125826
7	DISTANCE	0.000676793	0.0021406
8	WEATHER_DELAY	-0.906354	-0.906168
9	NAS_DELAY	-0.674053	-0.67396
10	SECURITY_DELAY	-0.917398	-0.917398
11	LATE_AIRCRAFT_DELAY	-0.929841	-0.929537
12	DEP_AFPH	-0.0152963	-0.0154111
13	ARR_AFPH	0.000548174	0.000532269
14	DEP_MONTH	-0.039835	-0.0398301
15	DEP_DOW	-0.0182132	-0.018213
16	DEP_RFPH	-0.469474	-0.469473
17	ARR_RFPH	0.373844	0.373847
18	ORIGIN_HUB	-1.02909	-1.02909
19	DEST_HUB	-0.394899	-0.394898
20	PCT_ELAPSED_TIME	45.0116	45.0116

Figure 3.12 – Linear regression coefficients compared to ridge regression coefficients

We didn't save the λ parameter (which scikit-learn calls *alpha*) that the ridge regression cross-validation deemed optimal. However, we can run a little experiment of our own to figure out which parameter was the best. We do this by iterating through 100 possible alpha values between 100(1) and 1013(10,000,000,000,000), fitting the data to the ridge model which each alpha, and then appending the coefficients to an array. We exclude one coefficient in the array simply because it's so much larger than the rest and it will make it harder to visualize the effects of shrinkage:

```
num_alphas = 100
alphas = np.logspace(0, 13, num_alphas)
```

```
alphas_coefs = []
for alpha in alphas:
  ridge = linear_model.Ridge(alpha=alpha).fit(X_train, y_train_
reg)
  alphas_coefs.append(np.concatenate((ridge.coef_[:8],\
                                      ridge.coef_[9:])))
```

Now that we have an array of coefficients, we can plot the progression of coefficients:

```
plt.gca().invert_xaxis()
plt.tick_params(axis = 'both', which = 'major')
plt.plot(alphas, alphas_coefs)
plt.xscale("log")
plt.xlabel('Alpha')
plt.ylabel('Ridge coefficients')
plt.grid()
plt.show()
```

The preceding code generates *Figure 3.13*:

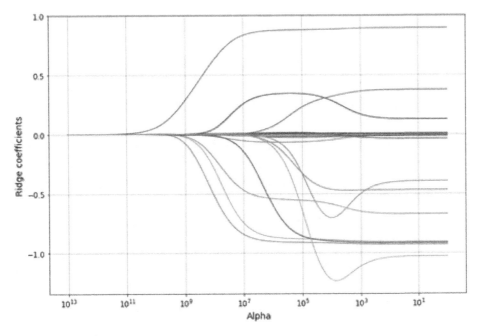

Figure 3.13 – Value of alpha hyperparameters versus the value of ridge regression coefficients

Something to note in *Figure 3.13* is that the higher the alpha, the higher the regularization. This is why when alpha is 1012, all coefficients have converged to 0, and as the alpha becomes smaller, they get to a point where they have all diverged and more or less stabilized. In this case, this point is reached at about 102. Another way of seeing it is when all coefficients are around 0, it means that the regularization is so strong that all features are irrelevant. When they have sufficiently diverged and stabilized, the regularization makes them all relevant, which defeats the purpose. Now on that note, if we go back to our code, we will find that this is what we chose for alphas in our `RidgeCV`: `alphas=[1e-3, 1e-2, 1e-1, 1]`. As you can tell from the preceding plot, by the time the alphas have reached 1 and below, the coefficients have already stabilized even though they are still fluctuating slightly. This can explain why our ridge was not better performing than linear regression. Usually, you would expect a regularized model to perform better than one that isn't – unless your hyperparameters are not right.

> **Interpretation and hyperparameters**
>
> Well-tuned regularization can help cut out the noise and thus increase interpretability but the alphas chosen for RidgeCV were selected on purpose to be able to convey this point: **Regularization can only work if you chose hyperparameters correctly**. Or, when regularization hyperparameter tuning is automatic, the method must be optimal for your dataset.

Feature importance

This is precisely the same as with linear regression, but again we need the standard error of the coefficients, which is something that cannot be extracted from the scikit-learn model. You can use the `statsmodels fit_regularized` method to this effect.

Polynomial regression

Polynomial regression is a special case of linear or logistic regression where the features have been expanded to have higher degree terms. We have only performed polynomial linear regression in this chapter's exercise, so we will only discuss this variation. However, it is applied similarly.

A two-feature multiple linear regression would look like this:

$$\hat{y} = \beta_0 + \beta_1 X_1 + \beta_2 X_2$$

But in polynomial regression, every feature is expanded to have higher degree terms and interactions between all the features. So, if this two-feature example were to be expanded to a second-degree polynomial, the linear regression formula would look like this:

$$\hat{y} = \beta_0 + \beta_1 X_1 + \beta_2 X_2 + \beta_3 X_1^2 + \beta_4 X_1 X_2 + \beta_5 X_2^2$$

It's still linear regression in every way except it has extra features, higher-degree terms, and interactions. While you can limit polynomial expansion to only one or a few features, we used `PolynomialFeatures`, which does this to all features. Therefore, 21 features were likely multiplied many times over. We can extract the coefficients from our fitted model and, using the `shape` property of the `numpy` array, return how many coefficients were generated. This amount corresponds to the number of features generated:

```
reg_models['linear_poly']['fitted'].\
            get_params()['linearregression'].coef_.shape[0]
```

It outputs 253. We can do the same with the version of polynomial regression, which was with interaction terms only:

```
reg_models['linear_interact']['fitted'].\
            get_params()['linearregression'].coef_.shape[0]
The above code outputs 232. The reality is that most terms in a
polynomial generated like this are interactions between all the
features.Interpretation and Feature Importance
```

Polynomial regression can be interpreted, both globally and locally, in precisely the same way as linear regression. In this case, it's not practical to understand a formula with 253 linearly combined terms, so it loses what we defined in *Chapter 2, Key Concepts of Interpretability*, as **global holistic interpretation**. However, it still can be interpreted in all other scopes and retains many of the properties of linear regression. For instance, since the model is additive, so it easy to separate the effects of the features. You can also use the same many peer-reviewed tried and tested statistical methods that are used for linear regression. For instance, you can use the t-statistic, p-value, confidence bounds, R-squared, as well as the many tests used to assess goodness or a lack of fit, residual analysis, linear correlation, and analysis of variance. This wealth of statistically proven methods to test and interpret models isn't something most model classes can count on. Unfortunately, many of them are model-specific to linear regression and its special cases.

Also, we won't do it here because there are so many terms. Still, you could undoubtedly rank features for polynomial regression in the same way we have for linear regression using the statsmodels library. The challenge is figuring out the order of the features generated by PolynomialFeatures to name them accordingly in the feature name column. Once this is done, you can tell if some second-degree terms or interactions are important. This could tell you if these features have a non-linear nature or highly depend on other features.

Logistic regression

We discussed logistic regression as well as its interpretation and feature importance in *Chapter 2, Key Concepts of Interpretability*. We will only expand on that a bit here in the context of this chapter's classification exercise and to underpin why exactly it is interpretable. The fitted logistic regression model has coefficients and intercepts just as the linear regression model does:

```
coefs_log = class_models['logistic']['fitted'].coef_
intercept_log = class_models['logistic']['fitted'].intercept_
print('coefficients:%s' % coefs_log)
print('intercept:%s' % intercept_log)
```

The preceding code outputs this:

```
coefficients:    [[-6.31114061e-04  -1.48979793e-04   2.01484473e-
01   1.32897749e-01 1.31740116e-05 -3.83761619e-04 -7.60281290e-
02   ..]]
intercept:   [-0.20139626]
```

However, the way these coefficients appear in the formula for a specific prediction $\hat{y}^{(i)}$ is entirely different:

$$P(\hat{y}^{(i)} = 1) = \frac{e^{\beta_0 + \beta_1 x_1^{(i)} + \beta_2 x_2^{(i)} \dots + \beta_n x_n^{(i)}}}{1 + e^{\beta_0 + \beta_1 x_1^{(i)} + \beta_2 x_2^{(i)} \dots + \beta_n x_n^{(i)}}}$$

In other words, the probability that $\hat{y}^{(i)} = 1$ (is a positive case) is expressed by a **logistic function** that involves exponentials of the linear combination of β coefficients and the x features. The presence of the exponentials explains why the coefficients extracted from the model are log-odds because to isolate the coefficients, and you should apply a logarithm to both sides of the equation.

Interpretation

To interpret each coefficient, you do it in precisely the same way as with linear regression, except each unit increase in the features, you increase the odds of getting the positive case by a factor expressed by the exponential of the coefficient – all things being equal (remember the **ceteris paribus** assumption discussed in *Chapter 2, Key Concepts of Interpretability*). An exponential $e\beta$ has to be applied to each coefficient because they express an increase in log-odds and not odds. Besides incorporating the log-odds into the interpretation, the same as was said about continuous, binary, and categorical in linear regression interpretation applies to logistic regression.

Feature importance

Frustrating as it is, there isn't consensus yet from the statistical community on how to best get feature importance for logistic regression. There's a standardize-all-features-first method, a pseudo *R2* method, a one-feature-at-a-time ROC AUC methods, a partial chi-squared statistic method, and then the simplest one, which is multiplying the standard deviations of each feature times the coefficients. We won't cover all these methods, but it has to be noted that computing feature importance consistently and reliably is a problem for most model classes, even white-box ones. We will dig deeper into this in *Chapter 4, Fundamentals of Feature Importance and Impact*. For logistic regression, perhaps the most popular method is achieved by standardizing all the features before training. That is, making sure they are centered at zero and divided by their standard deviation. But we didn't do this because although it has other benefits, it makes the interpretation of coefficients more difficult, so here we are using the rather crude method leveraged in *Chapter 2, Key Concepts of Interpretability* which is to multiply the standard deviations of each feature times the coefficients:

```
stdv = np.std(X_train, 0)
abs(coefs_log.reshape(21,) * stdv).sort_values(ascending=False)
```

The preceding code yields the following output:

DEP_DELAY	8.918590
CRS_ELAPSED_TIME	6.034794
DISTANCE	5.309037
LATE_AIRCRAFT_DELAY	4.985519
NAS_DELAY	2.387845
WEATHER_DELAY	2.155292
TAXI_OUT	1.311593
SECURITY_DELAY	0.383242
ARR_AFPH	0.320974

:	:	
WHEELS_OFF	0.006806	
PCT_ELAPSED_TIME	0.003410	
dtype: float64		

It can still approximate the importance of features quite well. And just like with linear regression, you can tell that delay features are ranking quite high. All five of them are among the top eight features. Indeed, it's something we should look into. We will discuss more on that as we discuss some other white-box methods.

Decision trees

Decision trees have been used for the longest time, even before they were turned into algorithms. They hardly require any mathematical abilities to understand them and this low barrier for comprehensibility makes them extremely interpretable in their simplest representations. However, in practice, there are many kinds of decision trees and most of them are not very interpretable because they use **ensemble methods** (boosting, bagging, and stacking), or even leverage PCA or some other embedder. Even non-ensembled decision trees can get extremely complicated as they become deeper. Regardless of the complexity of a decision tree, they can always be mined for important insights about your data and expected predictions, and they can be fitted to both regression and classification tasks.

CART decision trees

The **Classification and Regression Trees (CART)** algorithm is the "vanilla" no-frills decision tree of choice in most use cases. And as noted, most decision trees aren't white-box models, but this one is because it is expressed as a mathematical formula, visualized and printed as a set of rules that subdivide the tree into branches and eventually the leaves.

Here's the mathematical formula:

$$\hat{y} = \sum_{m=1}^{M} \mu_m I\{x \in R_m\}$$

And what this means is that if according to the identity function I, x is in the subset R_m, then it returns a 1, and if not a 0. This binary term is multiplied by the averages of all elements in the subset R_m denoted as μ_m. So if x_i is in the subset belonging to the leaf node R_k, then the prediction $\hat{y}_i = \mu_k$. In other words, the prediction is the average of all elements in subset R_k. This is what happens to regression tasks, and in binary classification, there is simply no μ_m to multiply times the I identify function.

At the heart of every decision tree algorithm, there's a method to generate the R_m subsets. For CART, this is achieved using something called the **Gini index**, recursively splitting on where the two branches are as different as possible.

Interpretation

A decision tree can be globally and locally interpreted visually. Here, we have established a maximum depth of 2 (max_depth=2) because we could generate all 7 layers, but the text would be too small to appreciate. One of the limitations of this method is that it can get complicated to visualize with depths above 3 or 4. However, you can always programmatically traverse through the branches of the tree and visualize only some branches at a time:

```
fig, axes = plt.subplots(nrows = 1, ncols = 1,\
                        figsize = (16,8), dpi=600)
tree.plot_tree(class_models['decision_tree']['fitted'],\
            feature_names=X_train.columns.values.tolist(),\
            filled = True, max_depth=2)
fig.show()
```

The preceding code prints out the tree in *Figure 3.14*. From the tree, you can tell that the very first branch splits the decision tree based on the value of DEP_DELAY being equal to or smaller than 20.5. It tells you the Gini index that informed that decision and the number of samples (just another way of saying observations, data points, or rows) present. You can traverse these branches till they reach a leaf. There is one leaf node in this tree, and it is on the far left. This is a classification tree, so you can tell by value= [629167, 0] that all 629,167 samples left in this node have been classified as a 0 (Not Delayed):

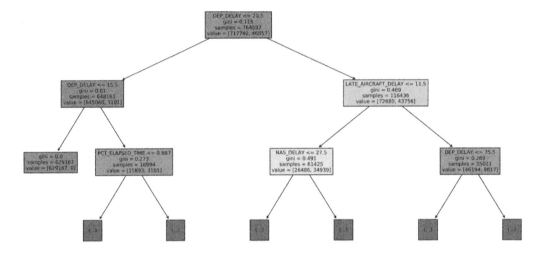

Figure 3.14 – Our models' plotted decision tree

Another way the tree can be better visualized but with fewer details such as the Gini index and sample size is by printing out the decisions made in every branch and the class in every node:

```
text_tree = tree.\
        export_text(class_models['decision_tree']
['fitted'], feature_names=X_train.columns.values.tolist())
print(text_tree)
```

And the preceding code outputs the following:

```
|--- DEP_DELAY <= 20.50
|   |--- DEP_DELAY <= 15.50
|   |   |--- class: 0
|   |--- DEP_DELAY >  15.50
|   |   |--- PCT_ELAPSED_TIME <= 0.99
|   |   |   |--- PCT_ELAPSED_TIME <= 0.98
|   |   |   |   |--- PCT_ELAPSED_TIME <= 0.96
|   |   |   |   |   |--- CRS_ELAPSED_TIME <= 65.50
|   |   |   |   |   |   |--- PCT_ELAPSED_TIME <= 0.94
|   |   |   |   |   |   |   |--- class: 0
|   |   |   |   |   |   |--- PCT_ELAPSED_TIME >  0.94
|   |   |   |   |   |   |   |--- class: 0
|   |   |   |   |   |--- CRS_ELAPSED_TIME >  65.50
|   |   |   |   |   |   |--- PCT_ELAPSED_TIME <= 0.95
|   |   |   |   |   |   |   |--- class: 0
|   |   |   |   |   |   |--- PCT_ELAPSED_TIME >  0.95
|   |   |   |   |   |   |   |--- class: 0
|   |   |   |   |--- PCT_ELAPSED_TIME >  0.96
|   |   |   |   |   |--- CRS_ELAPSED_TIME <= 140.50
|   |   |   |   |   |   |--- DEP_DELAY <= 18.50
|   |   |   |   |   |   |   |--- class: 0
|   |   |   |   |   |   |--- DEP_DELAY >  18.50
|   |   |   |   |   |   |   |--- class: 0
|   |   |   |   |   |--- CRS_ELAPSED_TIME >  140.50
|   |   |   |   |   |   |--- DEP_DELAY <= 19.50
|   |   |   |   |   |   |   |--- class: 0
|   |   |   |   |   |   |--- DEP_DELAY >  19.50
|   |   |   |   |   |   |   |--- class: 0
|   |   |   |--- PCT_ELAPSED_TIME >  0.98
|   |   |   |   |--- DEP_DELAY <= 18.50
|   |   |   |   |   |--- DISTANCE <= 326.50
|   |   |   |   |   |   |--- LATE_AIRCRAFT_DELAY <= 0.50
|   |   |   |   |   |   |   |--- class: 1
|   |   |   |   |   |   |--- LATE_AIRCRAFT_DELAY >  0.50
|   |   |   |   |   |   |   |--- class: 0
```

```
|   |   |   |   |   |--- DISTANCE >  326.50
|   |   |   |   |   |   |--- DEP_DELAY <= 17.50
|   |   |   |   |   |   |   |--- class: 0
|   |   |   |   |   |   |--- DEP_DELAY >  17.50
|   |   |   |   |   |   |   |--- class: 0
|   |   |   |   |--- DEP_DELAY >  18.50
|   |   |   |   |   |--- LATE_AIRCRAFT_DELAY <= 1.50
|   |   |   |   |   |   |--- DISTANCE <= 1358.50
|   |   |   |   |   |   |   |--- class: 1
|   |   |   |   |   |   |--- DISTANCE >  1358.50
|   |   |   |   |   |   |   |--- class: 0
|   |   |   |   |   |--- LATE_AIRCRAFT_DELAY >  1.50
|   |   |   |   |   |   |--- class: 0
|   |   |--- PCT_ELAPSED_TIME >  0.99
|   |   |   |--- LATE_AIRCRAFT_DELAY <= 1.50
|   |   |   |--- … (goes on for 6 more pages!)
```

There's a lot more that can be done with a decision tree, and scikit-learn provides an API to explore the tree.

Feature importance

Calculating feature importance in a CART decision tree is reasonably straightforward. As you can appreciate from the visualizations, some features appear more often in the decisions, but their appearances are weighted by how much they contributed to the overall reduction in the Gini index compared to the previous node. All the sum of the relative decrease in the Gini index throughout the tree is tallied, and the contribution of each feature is a percentage of this reduction:

```
dt_imp_df = pd.DataFrame({'feature':X_train.columns.values.
tolist(),
        'importance': class_models['decision_tree']['fitted'].\
                    feature_importances_}).\
        sort_values(by='importance', ascending=False)
dt_imp_df
```

The `dt_imp_df` data frame output by the preceding code can be appreciated in *Figure 3.15*.

	feature	importance
2	DEP_DELAY	0.527482
11	LATE_AIRCRAFT_DELAY	0.199153
20	PCT_ELAPSED_TIME	0.105381
8	WEATHER_DELAY	0.101649
9	NAS_DELAY	0.0627577
10	SECURITY_DELAY	0.00199756
7	DISTANCE	0.000993382
6	CRS_ELAPSED_TIME	0.000280958
3	TAXI_OUT	0.000238682
4	WHEELS_OFF	3.46469e-05
12	DEP_AFPH	3.10537e-05
5	CRS_ARR_TIME	0
1	DEP_TIME	0
13	ARR_AFPH	0
14	DEP_MONTH	0
15	DEP_DOW	0
16	DEP_RFPH	0
17	ARR_RFPH	0
18	ORIGIN_HUB	0
19	DEST_HUB	0
0	CRS_DEP_TIME	0

Figure 3.15 – Our decision tree's feature importance

This last feature importance table, *Figure 3.15*, increases suspicions about the delay features. They occupy, yet again, five of the top six positions. Is it possible that all five of them have such an outsized effect on the model?

Interpretation and domain expertise

The target `CARRIER_DELAY` is also called a dependent variable because it's dependent on all the other features, the independent variables. Even though a statistical relationship doesn't imply causation, we want to inform our feature selection based on our understanding of what independent variables could plausibly affect a dependent one. It makes sense that a departure delay (`DEPARTURE_DELAY`) affects the arrival delay (which we removed), and therefore, `CARRIER_DELAY`. Similarly, `LATE_AIRCRAFT_DELAY` makes sense as a predictor because it is known before the flight takes off if a previous aircraft was several minutes late, causing this flight to be at risk of arriving late, but not as a cause of the current flight (ruling this option out). However, even though the Bureau of Transportation Statistics website defines delays in such a way that they appear to be discrete categories, some may be determined well after a flight has departed. For instance, in predicting a delay mid-flight, could we predict based on `WEATHER_DELAY` if the bad weather hasn't yet happened? And could we predict based on `SECURITY_DELAY` if the security breach hasn't yet occurred? The answers to these questions are that we probably shouldn't because the rationale for including them is they could serve to rule out `CARRIER_DELAY` but this only works if they are discrete categories that pre-date the dependent variable! Before coming to further conclusions, what you would need to do is talk to the airline executives to determine the timeline on which each delay category gets consistently set and (hypothetically) is accessible from the cockpit or the airline's command center. Even if you are forced to remove them from the models, maybe other data can fill the void in a meaningful way, such as the first 30 minutes of flight logs and or historical weather patterns. **Interpretation is not always directly inferred from the data and the machine learning models, but by working closely with domain experts. But sometimes domain experts can mislead you too.** In fact, another insight is with all the time-based metrics and categorical features we engineered at the beginning of the chapter (`DEP_DOW`, `DEST_HUB`, `ORIGIN_HUB`, and so on). It turns out they have consistently had little to no effect on the models. Despite the airline executives hinting at the importance of days of the week, hubs, and congestion, we should have explored the data further, looking for correlations before engineering the data. But even if we do engineer some useless features, it also helps to use a white-box model to assess their impact, as we have. In data science, practitioners often will learn the same way the most performant machine learning models do – by trial and error!

RuleFit

RuleFit is one model-class family that is a hybrid between a LASSO linear regression to get regularized coefficients for every feature and merges this with decision rules, which it also uses LASSO to regularize. These **decision rules** are extracted by traversing a decision tree finding interaction effects between features and assigning coefficients to them based on their impact on the model. The implementation used in this chapter uses gradient boosted decision trees to perform this task.

We haven't covered decision rules explicitly in this chapter, but they are yet another family of **intrinsically interpretable models**. They weren't included because, at the time of writing, the only Python library that supports decision rules, called **Bayesian Rule List (BRL)** by Skater, is still at an experimental stage. In any case, the concept behind decision rules is very similar. They extract the feature interactions from a decision tree but don't discard the leaf node, and instead of assigning coefficients, they use the predictions in the leaf node to construct the rules. The last rule is a catch-all like an *ELSE* statement. Unlike RuleFit, it can only be understood sequentially because it's so similar to any *IF-THEN-ELSE* statement, but that's its main advantage.

Interpretation and feature importance

You can put everything you need to know about RuleFit into a single dataframe (`rulefit_df`). Then you remove the rules that have a coefficient of 0. It has these because in LASSO, unlike ridge, coefficient estimates converge to zero. You can sort the dataframe by importance in a descending manner to see what features or feature interactions (in the form of rules) are most important:

```
rulefit_df = reg_models['rulefit']['fitted'].get_rules()
rulefit_df = rulefit_df[rulefit_df.coef !=0].\
                    sort_values(by="importance",
ascending=False)
rulefit_df
```

The rules in the `rulefit_df` data frame can be seen in *Figure 3.16*:

	rule	type	coef	support	importance
129	LATE_AIRCRAFT_DELAY <= 222.5 & WEATHER_DELAY <= 166.0 & DEP_DELAY > 344.0	rule	207.246	0.0016835	8.49625
80	DEP_DELAY > 477.5 & LATE_AIRCRAFT_DELAY <= 333.5	rule	170.948	0.00112233	5.72377
53	WEATHER_DELAY > 255.0 & DEP_DELAY > 490.5	rule	-333.579	0.000187056	4.56188
11	LATE_AIRCRAFT_DELAY	linear	-0.383065	1	4.48841
2	DEP_DELAY	linear	0.162592	1	4.25384
46	LATE_AIRCRAFT_DELAY <= 198.0 & DEP_DELAY <= 788.0 & DEP_DELAY > 341.5	rule	-95.8115	0.00149645	3.70359
57	DEP_DELAY > 1206.0	rule	254.29	0.000187056	3.47755
84	DEP_DELAY > 300.0 & DEP_DELAY > 576.5 & LATE_AIRCRAFT_DELAY <= 158.5	rule	121.199	0.000748223	3.31401
64	DEP_DELAY > 880.5	rule	102.969	0.000748223	2.81552
147	DEP_DELAY <= 37.5 & DEP_DELAY <= 370.5	rule	-9.13357	0.898429	2.7591
52	LATE_AIRCRAFT_DELAY <= 19.5 & DEP_DELAY <= 849.0 & DEP_DELAY > 66.5 & NAS_DELAY > 43.5	rule	-41.4699	0.00430228	2.71422
63	WEATHER_DELAY <= 61.0 & DEP_DELAY <= 849.0 & LATE_AIRCRAFT_DELAY <= 19.5 & DEP_DELAY > 270.0 & NAS_DELAY <= 43.5 & DEP_DELAY > 66.5	rule	99.0067	0.000748223	2.70718
153	WEATHER_DELAY <= 61.0 & DEP_DELAY <= 849.0 & LATE_AIRCRAFT_DELAY <= 19.5 & NAS_DELAY <= 43.5 & DEP_DELAY > 109.0 & DEP_DELAY > 66.5 & DEP_DELAY <= 270.0	rule	29.733	0.00598578	2.29348
169	WEATHER_DELAY > 61.0 & DEP_DELAY <= 849.0 & LATE_AIRCRAFT_DELAY <= 19.5 & NAS_DELAY <= 43.5 & DEP_DELAY > 66.5	rule	-45.9107	0.00224467	2.17271
162	DEP_DELAY > 117.0 & WEATHER_DELAY <= 10.0 & DEP_DELAY <= 225.0 & LATE_AIRCRAFT_DELAY <= 56.5 & DEP_DELAY <= 459.0 & DEP_DELAY > 68.5 & NAS_DELAY <= 66.0	rule	28.4973	0.00467639	1.9442
38	LATE_AIRCRAFT_DELAY <= 32.5 & NAS_DELAY <= 40.5 & DEP_DELAY <= 491.5 & DEP_DELAY > 57.5 & DEP_DELAY <= 245.5 & WEATHER_DELAY <= 20.0	rule	12.1724	0.0226337	1.81044
51	DEP_DELAY <= 20.5 & DEP_DELAY <= 68.5 & DEP_DELAY <= 459.0	rule	-4.56733	0.846053	1.64834

Figure 3.16 – RuleFit's rules

There's a `type` for every RuleFit feature in *Figure 3.16*. Those that are `linear` are interpreted as you would any linear regression coefficient. Those that are `type=rule` are also to be treated like binary features in a linear regression model. For instance, if the rule `WEATHER_DELAY > 255.0 & DEP_DELAY > 490.5` is true, then the coefficient `-333.579026` is applied to the prediction. The rules capture the interaction effects, so you don't have to add interaction terms to the model manually or use some non-linear method to find them. Furthermore, it does this in an easy-to-understand manner. You can use RuleFit to guide your understanding of feature interactions even if you choose to productionize other models.

Nearest neighbors

Nearest neighbors is a family of models that even includes unsupervised methods. All of them use the closeness between data points to inform their predictions. Of all these methods, only the supervised kNN and its cousin Radius Nearest Neighbors are somewhat interpretable.

k-Nearest Neighbors

The idea behind **kNN** is straightforward. It takes the k closest points to a data point in the training data and uses their labels (y_train) to inform the predictions. If it's a classification task, it's the **mode** of all the labels, and if it's a regression task, it's the **mean**. It's a **lazy learner** because the "fitted model" is not much more than the training data and the parameters such as k and the list of classes (if it's classification). It doesn't do much till inference. That's when it leverages the training data, tapping into it directly rather than extracting parameters, weights/biases, or coefficients learned by the model as **eager learners** do.

Interpretation

kNN only has local interpretability because since there's no fitted model, you don't have global modular or global holistic interpretability. For classification tasks, you could attempt to get a sense of this using the decision boundaries and regions we studied in *Chapter 2, Key Concepts of Interpretability*. Still, it's always based on local instances.

To interpret a local point from our test dataset, we query the pandas dataframe using its index. We will be using flight #721043:

```
print(X_test.loc[721043,:])
```

The preceding code outputs the following pandas series:

CRS_DEP_TIME	655.000000
DEP_TIME	1055.000000
DEP_DELAY	240.000000
TAXI_OUT	35.000000
WHEELS_OFF	1130.000000
CRS_ARR_TIME	914.000000
CRS_ELAPSED_TIME	259.000000
DISTANCE	1660.000000
WEATHER_DELAY	0.000000
NAS_DELAY	22.000000
SECURITY_DELAY	0.000000
LATE_AIRCRAFT_DELAY	221.000000
DEP_AFPH	90.800000
ARR_AFPH	40.434783
DEP_MONTH	10.000000
DEP_DOW	4.000000

DEP_RFPH	0.890196
ARR_RFPH	1.064073
ORIGIN_HUB	1.000000
DEST_HUB	0.000000
PCT_ELAPSED_TIME	1.084942
Name: 721043, dtype: float64	

In the y_test_class labels for flight #721043, we can tell that it was delayed because this code outputs 1:

```
print(y_test_class[721043])
```

However, our kNN model predicted that it was not because this code outputs 0:

```
print(class_models['knn']['preds'][X_test.index.get_
loc(721043)])
```

Please note that the predictions are output as a NumPy array, so we can't access the prediction for flight #721043 using its pandas index (721043). We have to use the sequential location of this index in the test dataset using get_loc to retrieve it.

To find out why this was the case, we can use kneighbors on our model to find the 7 nearest neighbors of this point. To this end, we have to reshape our data because kneighbors will only accept it in the same shape found in the training set, which is $(n, 21)$ where n is the number of observations (rows). In this case, n=1 because we only want the nearest neighbors for a single data point. And as you can tell from what was output by X_test.loc[721043,:], the pandas series has a shape of $(21,1)$, so we have to reverse this shape:

```
print(class_models['knn']['fitted'].\
    kneighbors(X_test.loc[721043,:].values.reshape(1,21), 7))
```

kneighbors outputs two arrays:

```
(array([[143.3160128 , 173.90740076, 192.66705727,
211.57109221,
        243.57211853, 259.61593993, 259.77507391]]),
 array([[105172, 571912,  73409,  89450,  77474, 705972,
706911]]))
```

The first is the distance of each of the seven closest training points to our test data point. And the second is the location of these data points in the training data:

```
print(y_train_class.iloc[[105172, 571912, 73409, 89450, 77474,\
                          705972, 706911]])
```

The preceding code outputs the following pandas series:

3813	0
229062	1
283316	0
385831	0
581905	1
726784	1
179364	0
Name: CARRIER_DELAY, dtype: int64	

We can tell that the prediction reflects the **mode** because the most common class in the seven nearest points was 0 (Not delayed). You can increase or decrease the k to see if this holds. Incidentally, when using binary classification, it's recommended to choose an odd-numbered k so that there are no ties. Another important aspect is the distance metric that was used to select the closest data points. You can easily find out which one it is using:

```
print(class_models['knn']['fitted'].effective_metric_)
```

The output is Euclidean, which makes sense for this example. After all, Euclidean is optimal for a **real-valued vector space** because most features are continuous. You could also test alternative distance metrics such as minkowski, seuclidean, or mahalanobis. When most of your features are binary and categorical, you have an **integer-valued vector space**. So your distances ought to be calculated with algorithms suited for this space such as hamming or canberra.

Feature importance

Feature importance is, after all, a global model interpretation method and kNN has a hyper-local nature, so there's no way of deriving feature importance from a kNN model.

Naïve Bayes

Like GLMs, **Naïve Bayes** is a family of model classes with a model tailored to different statistical distributions. However, unlike GLMs' assumption that the target y feature has the chosen distribution, all Naïve Bayes models assume that your X features have this distribution. More importantly, they were based on **Bayes' theorem of conditional probability**, so they output a probability and are, therefore, exclusively classifiers. But they treat the probability of each feature impacting the model independently, which is a strong assumption. This is why they are called naïve. There's one for Bernouilli called **Bernouilli Naïve Bayes**, one for multinomial called **Multinomial Naïve Bayes**, and, of course, one for Gaussian, which is the most common.

Gaussian Naïve Bayes

Bayes' theorem is defined by this formula:

$$P(A|B) = \frac{P(A|B)P(A)}{P(B)}$$

In other words, to find the probability of A happening given that B is true, you take the conditional probability of B given A is true times the probability of A occurring divided by the probability of B. In the context of a machine learning classifier, this formula can be rewritten as follows:

$$P(y|X) = \frac{P(X|y) \cdot P(y)}{P(X)}$$

This is because what we want is the probability of y given X is true. But our X has more than one feature, so this can be expanded like this:

$$P(y|x_1, x_2, \ldots x_n) = \frac{P(x_1|y)P(x_2|y) \ldots P(x_n|y) \cdot P(y)}{P(x_1)P(x_2) \ldots P(x_n)}$$

To compute $\hat{y}$ predictions, we have to consider that we have to calculate and compare probabilities for each C_k class (the probability of a delay versus the probability of no delay) and choose the class with the highest probability:

$$\hat{y} = P(y|X) = \underset{C_k}{\mathrm{argmax}} P(y = C_k) \prod_{i=1}^{n} P(x_i|y = C_k)$$

Calculating the probability of each class $P(y = C_k)$ (also known as the class prior) is relatively trivial. In fact, the fitted model has stored this in an attribute called `class_prior_`:

```
print(class_models['naive_bayes']['fitted'].class_prior_)
```

This outputs the following:

```
array([0.93871674, 0.06128326])
```

Naturally, since delays caused by the carrier only occur 6% of the time, there is a marginal probability of this occurring.

Then the formula has a product $\prod_{i=1}^{n}$ of conditional probabilities that each feature belongs to a class $P(x_i|y = C_k)$. Since this is binary there's no need to calculate the probabilities of multiple classes because they are inversely proportional. Therefore, we can drop C_k and replace it with a 1 like this:

$$\hat{y} = P(y = 1|X) = P(y = 1) \prod_{i=1}^{n} P(x_i|y = 1)$$

This is because what we are trying to predict is the probability of a delay. Also, $P(x_i|y = 1)$ is its own formula, which differs according to the assumed distribution of the model, in this case, Gaussian:

$$P(x_i|y = 1) = \frac{1}{\sqrt{2\pi\sigma_i^2}} e^{-\frac{(x_i-\theta_i)^2}{2\sigma_i^2}}$$

This formula is called the probability density of the Gaussian distribution.

Interpretation and feature importance

So what are these **sigmas** (σ_i) and **thetas** (θ_i) in the formula? They are, respectively, the variance and mean of the x_i feature when y=1. The intuition behind this is that features have a different variance and mean in one class versus another, which can inform the classification. This is a binary classification task, but you could calculate σ_i and θ_i for both classes. Fortunately, the fitted model has this stored:

```
print(class_models['naive_bayes']['fitted'].sigma_)
```

There are two arrays output, the first one corresponding to the negative class and the second to the positive. The arrays contain the sigmas (variance) for each of the 21 features given the class:

```
array([[2.50123026e+05, 2.61324730e+05, ..., 1.13475535e-02],
       [2.60629652e+05, 2.96009867e+05, ..., 1.38936741e-02]])
```

You can also extract the thetas (means) from the model:

```
print(class_models['naive_bayes']['fitted'].theta_)
```

The preceding code also outputs two arrays, one for each class:

```
array([[1.30740577e+03, 1.31006271e+03, ..., 9.71131781e-01],
       [1.41305545e+03, 1.48087887e+03, ..., 9.83974416e-01]])
```

These two arrays are all you need to debug and interpret Naïve Bayes results because you can use them to compute the conditional probability that x_i feature given a positive class $P(x_i|y = 1)$. You could use this probability to rank the features by importance on a global level or interpret a specific prediction, on a local level.

Naïve Bayes is a fast algorithm with some good use cases, such as spam filtering and recommendation systems, but the independence assumption hinders its performance for most situations. Speaking of performance, let's discuss this topic in the context of interpretability.

Recognizing the trade-off between performance and interpretability

We have briefly touched on this topic before, but high performance often requires complexity, and complexity inhibits interpretability. As studied in *Chapter 2, Key Concepts of Interpretability*, this complexity comes from primarily three sources: non-linearity, non-monotonicity, and interactivity. If the model adds any complexity, it is **compounded by the number and nature of features** in your dataset, which by itself is a source of complexity.

Special model properties

These special properties can help make a model more interpretable.

The key property: explainability

In *Chapter 1, Interpretation, Interpretability, and Explainability; and Why Does It All Matter?*, we discussed why being able to look under the hood of the model and intuitively understand how all its moving parts derive its predictions in a consistent manner is, mostly, what separates *explainability* from *interpretability*. This property is also called **transparency** or **translucency.** A model can be interpretable without this, but in the same way that we can interpret a person's decisions because we can't understand what is going on "under the hood." This is often called **post-hoc interpretability** and this is the kind of interpretability this book primarily focuses on, with a few exceptions. That being said, we ought to recognize that if a model is understood by leveraging its mathematical formula (grounded in statistical and probability theory), as we've done with linear regression and Naïve Bayes, or by visualizing a human-interpretable structure, as with decision trees, or a set of rules as with RuleFit, it is much more interpretable than machine learning model classes where none of this is practically possible. White-box models will always have the upper hand in this regard, and as listed in *Chapter 1, Interpretation, Interpretability, and Explainability; and Why Does It All Matter?* there are many use cases in which a white-box model is a must-have. But even if you don't productionize white-box models, they can always serve a purpose in assisting with interpretation, if data dimensionality allows. It is a key property because it wouldn't matter if it didn't comply with the other properties as long as it had explainability; it would still be more interpretable than those without it.

The remedial property: regularization

In this chapter, we've learned that *regularization* tones down the complexity added by the introduction of too many features, and this can make the model more interpretable, not to mention more performant. Some models incorporate regularization into the training algorithm, such as RuleFit and gradient boosted trees; others have the ability to integrate it, such as multi-layer perceptron, or linear regression, and some cannot include it, such as kNN. Regularization comes in many forms. Decision trees have a method called pruning, which can help reduce complexity by removing non-significant branches. Neural networks have a technique called dropout, which randomly drops neural network nodes from layers during training. Regularization is a remedial property because it can help even the least interpretable models lessen complexity and thus improve interpretability.

Assessing performance

By now, in this chapter, you have already assessed performance on all of the white-box models reviewed in the last section as well as a few black-box models. Maybe you've already noticed that black-box models have topped most metrics, and for most use cases, this is generally the case.

Figuring out which model classes are more interpretable is not an exact science, but the following table (*Figure 3.17*) is sorted by those models with the most desirable properties. That is, they don't introduce non-linearity, non-monotonicity, and interactivity. Of course, explainability on its own is a property that is a game-changer, regardless, and regularization can help. There are also cases in which it's hard to assess properties. For instance, polynomial (linear) regression implements a linear model, but it fits nonlinear relationships, which is why it is color-coded differently. As you will learn in *Chapter 12, Monotonic Constraints and Model Tuning for Interpretability*, some libraries support adding monotonic constraints to gradient boosted trees and neural networks, which means it's possible to make these monotonic. However, the black-box methods we used in this chapter do not support monotonic constraints.

The task columns tell you whether they can be used for regression or classification. And the **Performance Rank** columns show you how well these models ranked in RMSE (for regression) and ROC AUC (for classification), where lower ranks are better. Please note that even though we have used only one metric to assess performance for this chart for simplicity's sake, the discussion about performance should be more nuanced than that. Another thing to note is that ridge regression did poorly, but this is because we used the wrong hyperparameters, as explained in the previous section.

White Box?	Model Class	Properties that Increase Interpretability					Task		Performance Rank	
		⚲ Expl.	Linear	Monotone	Non-Interactive	⚲ Regul.	Regr.	Classif.	Regr.	Classif.
✓	Linear Regression	●	●	●	●	●	✓	✗	6	
✓	Regularized Regression	●	●	●	●	●	✓	✓	7	8
✓	Logistic Regression	●	○	●	●	●	✗	✓		5
✓	Gaussian Naïve Bayes	●	●	●	●	●	✗	✓		7
✓	Polynomial Regression	○	○	●	○	●	✓	✓	2	
✓	RuleFit	●	●	●	●	●	✓	✓	8	
✓	Decision Tree	●	●	○	●	●	✓	✓	5	3
✓	k-Nearest Neighbors	○	●	●	●	●	✓	✓	9	6
✗	Random Forest	●	●	●	●	●	✓	✓	3	4
✗	Gradient Boosted Trees	●	●	●	●	●	✓	✓		2
✗	Multi-layer Perceptron	●	●	●	●	●	✓	✓	1	1

Figure 3.17 – A table assessing the interpretability and performance of several white-hat and black-box models we have explored in this chapter

Because it's compliant on all five properties, it's easy to tell why **linear regression is the gold standard for interpretability**. Also, while recognizing that this is anecdotal evidence, it should be immediately apparent that most of the best ranks are with black-box models. This is no accident! The math behind neural networks and gradient boosted trees is brutally efficient in achieving the best metrics. Still, as the red dots suggest, they have all the properties that make a model less interpretable, making their biggest strength (complexity) a potential weakness.

This is precisely why black-box models are our primary interest in this book, although many of the methods you will learn to apply to white-box models. In *Part 2*, which comprises *Chapters 4 through 9*, we will learn model-agnostic and deep-learning-specific methods that assist with interpretation. And in *Part 3*, which includes *Chapters 10 through 14*, we will learn how to tune models and datasets to increase interpretability.

Interpretation and execution speed

Predictive performance is not the only kind of performance to watch out for. When we have discussed performance so far in this book, we have not directly addressed the importance of **execution speed** (also called **computation time**). Predictive performance is, generally, inversely proportional to both interpretability and execution speed. Just as black-box models tend to predict better, white-box models are more interpretable and faster than black-box models. Often, not only in training but also in the inference. This problem used to be a significant deterrent. Even though deep learning methods have existed for over half a century, they only really took off a decade ago because of resource constraints! So why is it still relevant? Because data scientists, data engineers, and machine learning engineers are continually pushing the boundaries by increasing the complexity of their models, the size of datasets, and the use of hyperparameter tuning to improve predictive performance. They thus require more resources to train and possibly make them quick at inference. However, a model that has slow inference is not practical for many use cases because it might not be cost-effective or requires real-time inference, which it would have too much latency to achieve. Therefore, there is a trade-off between predictive performance and execution performance. And while AI researchers push the boundaries for model interpretability, there will be cases where trade-offs between all three are considered: predictive performance, execution speed performance, and interpretability (see *Figure 3.18*). Higher interpretability, while retaining high predictive performance, might come with a significant loss in execution speed performance. Such is the case for the glass-box models we review in the next section, but who knows? Someday we might have our cake and eat it too!

	White Box	Glass Box	Black Box
Interpretability	High	Mid-High	Low
Predictive Performance	Mid	High	High
Execution Speed Performance	High	Low	Mid

Figure 3.18 – A table comparing white-box, black-box, and glass-box models, or at least what is known so far about them

Discovering newer interpretable (glass-box) models

Recently, there are significant efforts in both industry and in academia to create new models that can have enough complexity to find the sweet spot between underfitting and overfitting, known as the **bias-variance trade-off**, but retain an adequate level of explainability.

Many models fit this description, but most of them are meant for specific use cases, haven't been properly tested yet, or have released a library or open-sourced the code. However, two general-purpose ones are already gaining traction, which we will look at now.

Explainable Boosting Machine (EBM)

EBM is part of Microsoft's InterpretML framework, which includes many of the model-agnostic methods we will use later in the book.

EBM leverages the **GAMs** we mentioned earlier, which are like linear models but look like this:

$$\hat{y} = g(E[y]) = \beta_0 + f_1(x_1) + f_2(x_2) + \ldots + f_j(x_j)$$

Individual functions f_1 through f_p are fitted to each feature using spline functions. Then a link function g adapts the GAM to perform different tasks such as classification or regression, or adjust predictions to different statistical distributions. GAMs are white-box models, so what makes EBM a glass-box model? It incorporates bagging and gradient boosting, which tend to make models more performant. The boosting is done one feature at a time using a low learning rate so as not to confound them. It also finds practical interaction terms automatically, which improves performance while maintaining interpretability:

$$\hat{y} = g(E[y]) = \beta_0 + \Sigma f_j(x_j) + \Sigma f_{ji}(x_j, x_i)$$

Once fitted, this formula is made up of complicated non-linear formulas, so a global holistic interpretation isn't likely feasible. However, since the effects of each feature or pairwise interaction terms are additive, they are easily separable, and global modular interpretation is entirely possible. Local interpretation is equally easy given that a mathematical formula can assist in debugging any prediction.

One drawback is that EBM can be much slower than gradient boosted trees and neural networks because of the *one feature at a time* approach, a low learning rate not impacting the feature order, and spline fitting methods. However, it is parallelizable, so in environments with ample resources and multiple cores or machines, it will be much quicker. To not have you wait for results for an hour or two, it is best to use the same technique for dimensionality reduction using the abbreviated versions of `X_train` and `X_test`. However, this time we will only use the eight features white-box models found to be most important: `DEP_DELAY`, `LATE_AIRCRAFT_DELAY`, `PCT_ELAPSED_TIME`, `WEATHER_DELAY`, `NAS_DELAY`, `SECURITY_DELAY`, `DISTANCE`, `CRS_ELAPSED_TIME`, and `TAXI_OUT`. These are placed in a `feature_samp` array, and then the `X_train` and `X_test` dataframes are subset to only include this feature. We are setting the `sample2_size` to 10%, but if you feel you have enough resources to handle it, adjust accordingly:

```
#Make new abbreviated versions of datasets
feature_samp = ['DEP_DELAY', 'LATE_AIRCRAFT_DELAY',\
                'PCT_ELAPSED_TIME', 'DISTANCE', 'WEATHER_DELAY',\
                'NAS_DELAY', 'SECURITY_DELAY', 'CRS_ELAPSED_TIME']
X_train_abbrev2 = X_train[feature_samp]
X_test_abbrev2 = X_test[feature_samp]
#For sampling among observations
np.random.seed(rand)
sample2_size = 0.1
sample2_idx = np.random.choice(X_train.shape[0],
        math.ceil(X_train.shape[0]*sample2_size), replace=False)
```

To train your EBM, all you have to do is instantiate an `ExplainableBoostingClassifier()` and then fit your model to your training data. Just as we did with dimensionality reduction, we are using `sample2_idx` to sample a portion of the data:

```
ebm_mdl = ExplainableBoostingClassifier()
ebm_mdl.fit(X_train_abbrev2.iloc[sample2_idx],
            y_train_class.iloc[sample2_idx])
```

Global interpretation

Global interpretation is dead simple. It comes with an `explain_global` dashboard you can explore. It loads with the feature importance plot first, and you can select individual features to graph what was learned from each one:

```
show(ebm_mdl.explain_global())
```

The preceding code generates a dashboard that looks like *Figure 3.19*:

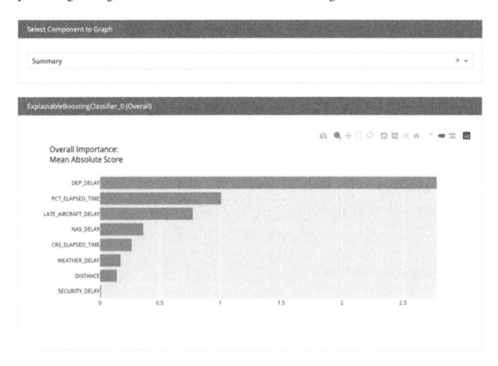

Figure 3.19 – EBM's global interpretation dashboard

Local interpretation

Local interpretation uses a dashboard like global does except you choose specific predictions to interpret with `explain_local`. In this case, we are selecting #76, which, as you can tell, was incorrectly predicted. But the LIME-like plot we will study in *Chapter 6, Local Model Agnostic Interpretation Methods*, helps make sense of it:

```
ebm_lcl = ebm_mdl.explain_local(X_test_abbrev2.iloc[76:77],\
                          y_test_class[76:77], name='EBM')
show(ebm_lcl)
```

Similar to the global dashboard, the preceding code generates another one, depicted in *Figure 3.20*:

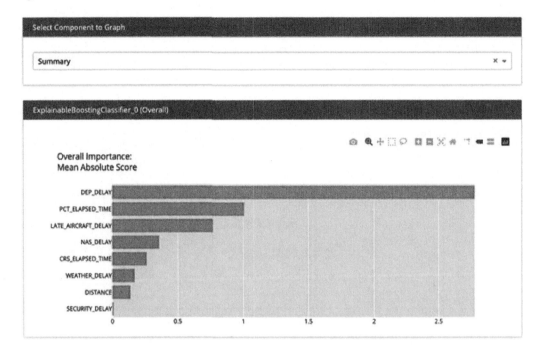

Figure 3.20 – EBM's local interpretation dashboard

Performance

Performance, at least measured with the ROC AUC, EBM is not far from what was achieved by the top 2 classification models, and we can only expect it to get better with 10 times more training and testing data!

```
ebm_perf = ROC(ebm_mdl.predict_proba).\
              explain_perf(X_test_abbrev2.iloc[sample_idx],
                  y_test_class.iloc[sample_idx], name='EBM')
show(ebm_perf)
```

You can appreciate the performance dashboard produced by the preceding code in *Figure 3.21*. The performance dashboard can also compare several models at a time since its explainers are model-agnostic. And there's even a fourth dashboard that can be used for data exploration:

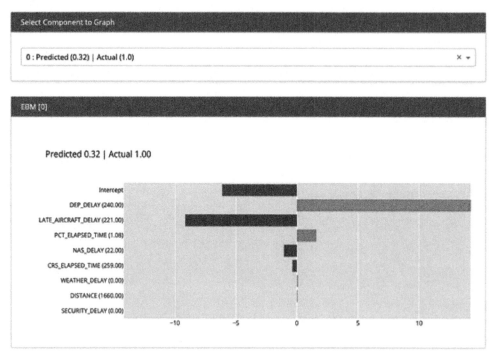

Figure 3.21 – One of EBM's performance dashboards

Skoped Rules

For **Skoped Rules**, rules are extracted from an ensemble of trees just as is done with RuleFit, and L1-regularization (*LASSO*) is also applied. However, it uses random forest instead of gradient boosted trees and doesn't incorporate linear regression coefficients. Instead, it only uses the binary rules but they are only applied if precision and recall conditions are held true, and weights are proportional to the **OOB** (**out of bag**) score used in random forest. By the way, OOB is like validation accuracy, but using a randomly selected subset of decision trees. Because of its focus on precision and recall, Skoped Rules can be great for imbalanced datasets while retaining interpretability.

To fit the model, instantiate `SkopeRules` and `fit` the model to the training data. We are using the same `sample2_idx` as was used with EBM because it can also get slow but not quite as much. Thankfully, `n_jobs=-1` tells it to leverage all your processor cores. Several parameters can impact performance: `n_estimators` is the number of decision trees, and `max_depth` is the depth of the tree. At the same time, `precision_min` and `recall_min` are the minimum amount of precision and recall for a rule to be selected. `random_state` is just for reproducibility. The same as with EBM, this model training snippet of code can take a few minutes:

```
sr_mdl = SkopeRules(n_estimators=200, precision_min=0.2,\
                recall_min=0.01, n_jobs=-1, random_state=rand,\
                max_depth=7, feature_names=X_train_abbrev2.columns)
sr_mdl.fit(X_train_abbrev2.iloc[sample2_idx],\
                y_train_class.iloc[sample2_idx])
```

In the following code, the probability of each flight being delayed is returned by `score_top_rules`, and this, in turn, can be used to create the predictions using `np.where` with the threshold set at 0.5:

```
sr_y_test_prob = sr_mdl.\
                score_top_rules(X_test_abbrev2.iloc[sample_idx])
sr_y_test_pred = np.where(sr_y_test_prob > 0.5, 1, 0)
```

Global interpretation

The `rules_` attribute has a list of tuples with each rule. We can count them as such:

```
print(len(sr_mdl.rules_))
```

As you can tell, there are 1,517 rules generated but because of the way the algorithm uses precision and recall, rules are not always considered. This makes inference slower. The rules are sorted by how well they perform. Let's look at the five highest-performing rules generated:

```
print(sr_mdl.rules_[0:5])
```

The preceding code prints the following:

```
[('DEP_DELAY > 39.5 and LATE_AIRCRAFT_DELAY <= 12.5 and
WEATHER_DELAY <= 12.0 and NAS_DELAY <= 27.5 and SECURITY_DELAY
<= 16.5', (0.9579037047855509, 0.47316836019772934, 4)),
 ('DEP_DELAY > 39.5 and LATE_AIRCRAFT_DELAY <= 11.5 and
```

```
WEATHER_DELAY <= 12.0 and NAS_DELAY <= 27.5 and SECURITY_DELAY
<= 8.5', (0.9594577495919502, 0.47085055043737395, 10)),
  ('DEP_DELAY > 39.5 and LATE_AIRCRAFT_DELAY <= 12.5 and
WEATHER_DELAY <= 12.5 and NAS_DELAY <= 27.5 and SECURITY_DELAY
<= 16.5', (0.9569012547735952, 0.4712520150456744, 2)),
  ('DEP_DELAY > 39.5 and LATE_AIRCRAFT_DELAY <= 11.5 and
WEATHER_DELAY <= 12.0 and NAS_DELAY <= 29.5 and SECURITY_DELAY
<= 16.5', (0.9564531654942614, 0.4705427055644734, 4)),
  ('DEP_DELAY > 39.5 and LATE_AIRCRAFT_DELAY <= 11.5 and
WEATHER_DELAY <= 12.0 and NAS_DELAY <= 27.5 and SECURITY_DELAY
<= 16.5', (0.9599182584158368, 0.46956357202280874, 12))]
```

As you go down the list, you can start to understand what matters the most to the model as singular IF statements, if true, indicate a positive class.

Local interpretation

Let's examine one model-specific local prediction method – the prediction for the seventy-sixth flight not being delayed even though the flight was delayed:

```
print('actual: %s, predicted: %s' %\
                    (y_test_class.iloc[76], sr_y_test_pred[76]))
```

The preceding code prints out the following:

```
actual: 1, predicted: 0
```

We can tell why leveraging the decision function that tells you the anomaly score for the input sample. This score is the weighted sum of the binary rules, where each weight is the precision of each rule. So, the lower the score, the more likely it is a positive match, and if it's null, it's a definite positive match:

```
print(sr_mdl.decision_function(X_test_abbrev2.iloc[76:77]))
```

The result is 18.23, which is not close to 0 or null.

Performance

The performance was not bad considering it was trained on 10% of the training data and evaluated on only 10% of the test data. Especially the recall score, which was among the top three places:

```
print('accuracy: %.3g, recall: %.3g, roc auc: %.3g, f1: %.3g,
mcc: %.3g' %\
```

```
   (metrics.accuracy_score(y_test_class.iloc[sample_idx],\
                              sr_y_test_pred),
   metrics.recall_score(y_test_class.iloc[sample_idx],\
                            sr_y_test_pred),
   metrics.roc_auc_score(y_test_class.iloc[sample_idx],\
                            sr_y_test_prob),
   metrics.f1_score(y_test_class.iloc[sample_idx], sr_y_test_
pred),
   metrics.matthews_corrcoef(y_test_class.iloc[sample_idx],\
                              sr_y_test_pred)))
```

The preceding code yields the following metrics:

```
accuracy: 0.969, recall: 0.981,
roc auc: 0.989, f1: 0.789, mcc: 0.787
```

Mission accomplished

The mission was to train models that could predict preventable delays with enough accuracy to be useful, and thhen, to understand the factors that impacted these delays, according to these models, to improve OTP. The resulting regression models all predicted delays, on average, well below the 15-minute threshold according to the RMSE. And most of the classification models achieved an F1 score well above 50% – one of them reached 98.8%! We also managed to find factors that impacted delays for all white-box models, some of which performed reasonably well. So, it seems like it was a resounding success!

Don't celebrate just yet! Despite the high metrics, this mission was a failure. Through interpretation methods, we realized that the models were accurate mostly for the wrong reasons. This realization helps underpin the mission-critical lesson that a model can easily be right for the wrong reasons, so **the question "why?" is not a question to be asked only when it performs poorly but always**. And using interpretation methods is how we ask that question.

But if the mission failed, why is this section called *Mission accomplished*? Good question!

It turns out there was a secret mission. Hint: it's the title of this chapter. The point of it was to learn about common interpretation challenges through the failure of the overt mission. In case you missed them, here are the interpretation challenges we stumbled upon:

- Traditional model interpretation methods only cover surface-level questions about your models. Note that we had to resort to model-specific global interpretation methods to discover that the models were right for the wrong reasons.

- Assumptions can derail any machine learning project since this is information that you suppose without evidence. Note that it is crucial to work closely with domain experts to inform decisions throughout the machine learning workflow, but sometimes they can also mislead you. Ensure you check for inconsistencies between the data and what you assume to be the truth about that data. Finding and correcting these problems is at the heart of what interpretability is about.

- Many model classes, even white-box models, have issues with computing feature importance consistently and reliably.

- Incorrect model tuning can lead to a model that performs well enough but is less interpretable. Note that a regularized model overfits less but is also more interpretable. We will cover methods to address this challenge in *Chapter 12, Monotonic Constraints and Model Tuning for Interpretability*. Feature selection and engineering can also have the same effect, which you can read about in *Chapter 10, Feature Selection and Engineering for Interpretability*.

- There's a trade-off between predictive performance and interpretability. And this trade-off extends to execution speed. For these reasons, this book primarily focuses on black-box models, which have the predictive performance we want and a reasonable execution speed but could use some help on the interpretability side.

If you learned about these challenges, then congratulations! Mission accomplished!

Summary

After reading this chapter, you should understand some traditional methods for interpretability and what their limitations are. You learned about **intrinsically interpretable models** and how to both use them and interpret them, for both regression and classification. You also studied the **performance versus interpretability trade-off** and some models that attempt not to compromise in this trade-off. You also discovered many practical interpretation challenges involving the roles of feature selection and engineering, hyperparameters, domain experts, and execution speed. In the next chapter, we will learn more about different interpretation methods to measure the effect of a feature on a model.

Dataset sources

- United States Department of Transportation Bureau of Transportation Statistics. (2018). Airline On-Time Performance Data. Originally retrieved from `https://www.transtats.bts.gov`.

Further reading

- Friedman, J., & Popescu, B. (2008). Predictive Learning via Rule Ensembles. The Annals of Applied Statistics, 2(3), 916-954. `http://doi.org/10.1214/07-AOAS148`

- Hastie, T., R. Tibshirani, and M. Wainwright. 2015. Statistical Learning with Sparsity: The Lasso and Generalizations. Chapman & Hall/Crc Monographs on Statistics & Applied Probability. Taylor & Francis

- Thomas, D.R., Hughes, E. & Zumbo, B.D. On Variable Importance in Linear Regression. Social Indicators Research 45, 253–275 (1998). `https://doi.org/10.1023/A:1006954016433`

- Nori, H., Jenkins, S., Koch, P., & Caruana, R. (2019). InterpretML: A unified framework for machine learning interpretability. arXiv preprint `https://arxiv.org/pdf/1909.09223.pdf`

- Hastie, T and Tibshirani, R. Generalized additive models: some applications. Journal of the American Statistical Association, 82(398):371–386, 1987. `http://doi.org/10.2307%2F2289439`

Section 2: Mastering Interpretation Methods

In this section, you will master how to interpret models using both model-agnostic and deep learning methods.

This section includes the following chapters:

4
Fundamentals of Feature Importance and Impact

In the first part of this book, we introduced the concepts, challenges, and purpose of machine learning interpretation. This chapter kicks off the second part, which dives into a vast array of methods that are used to diagnose models and understand their underlying data. One of the biggest questions answered by interpretation methods is: *What matters most to the model and how does it matter?* Precisely, interpretation methods can shed light on the overall importance of features and how they—individually or combined—impact a model's outcome. This chapter will provide a theoretical and practical foundation to approach these questions.

In this chapter, we will first use several scikit-learn models' intrinsic parameters to derive the most important features. Then, realizing how inconsistent these results are, we will learn how to use **Permutation Feature Importance** (**PFI**) to rank the features intuitively and dependably. Also, to convey the marginal impact of a single feature on the prediction, we will study how to render and interpret **Partial Dependence Plots** (**PDPs**). Lastly, we will explore **Individual Conditional Expectation** (**ICE**) plots to explain changes with a prediction when a feature changes.

The following are the main topics we are going to cover in this chapter:

- Measuring the impact of a feature on the outcome
- Practicing PFI
- Interpreting PDPs
- Explaining ICE plots

Technical requirements

This chapter's example uses the `mldatasets`, `pandas`, `numpy`, `sklearn`, `matplotlib`, and `PDPbox` libraries. Instructions on how to install all of these libraries are in the *Preface* of the book. The code for this chapter is located here:

```
https://github.com/PacktPublishing/Interpretable-Machine-
Learning-with-Python/tree/master/Chapter04
```

The mission

We've all heard the stereotypes: firstborns are very responsible and bossy; the youngest is spoiled and carefree; and the middle child is a jealous introvert! It turns out prominent psychology researchers have reached out to your data science consultancy firm and have conducted several small empirical studies on how birth order affects personality. But they just got a hold of a dataset of over 40,000 online quiz entries from the *Open-Source Psychometrics Project*. They are skeptical because it was submitted online and they have never conducted a study of that magnitude, so it's uncharted territory. For these reasons, they would like a third party who is well versed in machine learning to approach the problem with fresh eyes. What they hope to learn is about any relation between the quiz answers and the birth order, and also to determine if there are any questions they could use in their empirical studies, or even if online quizzes are a reliable method to begin with. Your firm has agreed to shed some light on these questions.

Personality and birth order

For well over a century, theories have circulated about how sibling dynamics—and, to some extent, parenting styles, which in themselves are largely defined by birth order—influence different personality traits. Most of these theories have been formulated and studied in "Western" countries, starting from Englishman Francis Galton (1874) linking firstborns with greater intelligence, to Dutchman Bram Buunk's (1997) research associating laterborns with greater jealousy. More recently, more nuanced studies factor gender, age gaps, and socioeconomic status into personality differences. Even then, these theories seldom have widespread consensus. Also, it is known that culture has an effect on parenting styles and sibling dynamics, so the Western theories don't translate well across other cultures.

On the other hand, there have been a series of *psychometric* methodologies that are used to assess personalities, using questionnaires to group individuals into discrete categories and scales. The dataset includes answers to one of these methodologies, the **International Personality Item Pool** (**IPIP**) "Big Five" test. The "Big Five" test is a widely accepted model for personality assessment in academic psychology. The dataset also includes 26 questions specifically designed to find traits associated with different birth orders, and although they have the exact birth orders, researchers are only interested in the following three categories:

- **Firstborn**: The participant is the first of more than one child.

- **Middle child**: The participant is neither the first nor the last of more than one child.

- **Lastborn**: The participant is the last of more than one child.

The original dataset includes entries from all over the world, which is why the researchers asked to focus specifically on majority-English-speaking countries because the questions are in English. They cannot verify that the questions aren't culturally biased.

The approach

The task at hand is to find which features—whether quiz answers, technical, and demographic details—signal birth order the most, and if they are reliable to use for this purpose. One way to do this is by creating classification models to predict birth order, and then doing the following:

- Using the model's intrinsic parameters to discover which features impact the model the most. This concept is called **feature importance**, and it's a **global modular interpretation method**. This was explained in *Chapter 2, Key Concepts of Interpretability*, but we will go into more detail in this chapter.

- Exploring feature importance further with a more reliable permutation-based method called **PFI**.

- Examining the marginal impact to the outcome of the most important features with **PDPs**. That way, we can tell which feature values correlate the most with the predictions.

- Getting a more granular visualization of how individual features impact the models' predictions with ICE plots.

Let's get started!

The preparations

You will find the code for this example here:

https://github.com/PacktPublishing/Interpretable-Machine-Learning-with-Python/blob/master/Chapter04/BirthOrder.ipynb

Loading the libraries

To run this example, you need to install the following libraries:

- `mldatasets` to load the dataset

- `pandas` and `numpy` to manipulate it

- `sklearn` (scikit-learn) to split the data and fit the models

- `matplotlib` and `pdpbox` to visualize the interpretations

You should load all of them first, using the following code:

```
import math
import mldatasets
import pandas as pd
import numpy as np
from sklearn.pipeline import make_pipeline
from sklearn.preprocessing import StandardScaler
from sklearn.model_selection import train_test_split
from sklearn import metrics, linear_model, tree,\
        discriminant_analysis, ensemble, neural_network,
inspection
```

```
import matplotlib.pyplot as plt
from pdpbox import pdp
```

Now, we can continue with data preparation and understanding the steps.

Understanding and preparing the data

We load the data into a dataframe we call `birthorder_df`, like this:

```
birthorder_df = mldatasets.load("personality-birthorder",\
                                prepare=True)
```

`prepare=True` ensures that some data preparation, such as filtering by majority-English-speaking nations and categorical encoding, is performed. This setting will save us some time. There should be nearly 26,000 records and 97 columns. We can verify this was the case with `print(birthorder_df.shape`, which should return `(25813, 97)`, corresponding to what we were expecting.

The data dictionary

We won't describe every column of the data dictionary here because there are so many, mostly pertaining to specific personality questions. Still, if you are curious about these particular questions, you can find them in a file called `FBPS-ValidationData-Codebook.txt`, located here:

`https://www.kaggle.com/lucasgreenwell/firstborn-personality-scale-responses`

However, we will provide a brief overview of the 76 psychological questions, six demographics, features and five technical features of the data dictionary.

The psychological features (quiz answers) of the data dictionary are outlined as follows:

- Q1, Q2, .. Q26: Ordinal; answers to 26 birth-order research questions (based on a five-point Likert scale from 1=Disagree to 3=Neutral to 5=Agree, as well as 0=No answer).

- EXT1, EXT2,... EXT10; EST1, EST2,... EST10; AGR1, AGR2,... AGR10; CSN1, CSN2,... CSN10; OPN1, OPN2,... OPN10: Ordinal; the IPIP "Big Five" questionnaire. It's made up of 50 questions (answers also in a five-point Likert scale from 1=Disagree to 3=Neutral to 5=Agree, as well as 0=No answer).

The demographic features of the data dictionary are outlined as follows:

- `age`: Ordinal; participant's age in years
- `engnat`: Binary; whether English is their native language (1=yes, 2=no)
- `gender`: Categorical; gender (male, female, other, undefined)
- `birthn`: Ordinal; total number of children had by parents from 1 to 10, 11 (for other)
- `country`: Categorical; country of the participant (by two-letter code)
- `birthorder`: Ordinal; target birth order (1: firstborn, 2: middle child, and 3: lastborn)

The technical features of the data dictionary are outlined as follows:

- `source`: Categorical; how the user got to the personality test based on a **HyperText Transfer Protocol** (**HTTP**) referrer (1=Directly from Google, 2=Front page of website, 3=Any other)
- `screensize`: Ordinal; size of screen used to take the test (2=greater than 600 **pixels** (**px**) each side, 1=smaller than that)
- `introelapse`: Continuous; time spent on the personality test landing page (in seconds)
- `testelapse`: Continuous; time spent on the personality test main body (in seconds)
- `endelapse`: Continuous; time spent on the personality test exit page (in seconds)

If you just realized that the features in the data dictionary (87) don't add up to the total amount of columns (97) in the dataset, it's because the three categorical features were already **categorically encoded** using **one-hot encoding**. This process creates individual features for each category so that they are represented in the machine learning model, adding expressiveness and Accuracy. Encoding them as such also means you can interpret them independently.

Data preparation

Since most of the data preparation was done automatically, all we have to do now is train/test split the data. But first, we initialize `rand`, a constant to serve as our `random_state` throughout this exercise. Then, we define y as the `birthorder` column and X as everything else, followed by splitting these two into train and test datasets with `train_test_split`, as illustrated in the following code snippet:

```
rand = 9
y = birthorder_df['birthorder']
X = birthorder_df.drop(['birthorder'], axis=1).copy()
X_train, X_test, y_train, y_test = train_test_split(X, y,\
                                  test_size=0.33, random_
state=rand)
```

We have completed all the data understanding and preparation steps, so we can now move on to the topics mentioned in the overview.

Measuring the impact of a feature on the outcome

For this exercise, we are fitting the training data to six different models' classes: decision trees, gradient boosting trees, random forest, logistic regression, multi-layer perceptron, and **Linear Discriminant Analysis (LDA)**. We learned about the first five in *Chapter 3, Interpretation Challenges*, so we will take a moment to familiarize ourselves with the last one, detailed here:

- `lda`: LDA is a very versatile method. It makes some of the same assumptions that linear regression has about normality and homoscedasticity; however, it stems from dimensionality reduction and is closely related to the **Principal Component Analysis (PCA)** unsupervised method. What it does is compute the distance between the mean of different classes, called **between-class variance**, and the variance within each class, called **within-class variance**. Then, it projects the data to a lower-dimensional space in such a way that it maximizes the distances between classes and minimizes the distance within classes. If you have more than three features, it's hard to imagine the concept of class separability, but say that you took all your data points and reduced them to only two dimensions. Then, there is a way to project them to this lower-dimensional space where you have your data points organized in such a way that you have enough separation between classes. You can draw a line between them (by maximizing between-class variance) and do this while bringing the points of each class closer together (by minimizing within-class variance). Besides classification, LDA can be used for dimensionality reduction and visualizing class separation.

Now, we are placing the scikit-learn models in a Python dictionary (`class_models`) so that we can iterate through them, train, evaluate, and save our results in the very same dictionary structure, as follows:

```
class_models = {
  'decision_tree':{'model': tree.\
        DecisionTreeClassifier(max_depth=6, random_state=rand,\
            class_weight='balanced')},
  'gradient_boosting':{'model':ensemble.\
        GradientBoostingClassifier(n_estimators=200,\
            max_depth=4, subsample=0.5,\
            learning_rate=0.05)},
  'random_forest':{'model':ensemble.\
        RandomForestClassifier(max_depth=11, n_estimators=300,\
            max_features='sqrt', random_state=rand)},
  'logistic':{'model': linear_model.\
        LogisticRegression(multi_class='ovr', solver='lbfgs',\
            class_weight='balanced', max_iter=500)},
  'lda':{'model':discriminant_analysis.\
        LinearDiscriminantAnalysis(n_components=2)},
  'mlp':{'model':make_pipeline(StandardScaler(), neural_
network.\
        MLPClassifier(hidden_layer_sizes=(11,),\
            early_stopping=True, random_state=rand,\
            validation_fraction=0.25, max_iter=500))}
}
```

Each of the models have hyperparameters that have been already tuned for specific reasons. For instance, LDA is performing dimensionality reduction on two dimensions (`n_components=2`) because there are three classes and it shouldn't exceed or equal the number of classes, and one is not enough to capture the variance in the 96 features.

Speaking of classes, these aren't equally distributed, which is why some of them have `class_weight='balanced'` applied to weight classes inversely proportional to their frequencies during training. Balancing helps improve **Precision** and **Recall** for less represented classes.

Logistic Regression comes with five different **solvers**. Each solver approaches finding parameter weights to minimize the cost function (**negative log likelihood**) differently. The one in use is called **Limited-memory Broyden–Fletcher–Goldfarb–Shanno (L-BFGS)** (`solver='lbfgs'`). It was chosen because it's efficient, and for no other reason. Almost all of the rest of the parameters were chosen to prevent overfitting, such as `max_depth`, `n_estimators`, `subsample`, `learning_rate`, and `max_features`.

Next, we iterate every model in the `class_models` dictionary. We `fit` the training data to the model and use `predict` to make predictions for both train and test datasets. We can then save the fitted model in the dataset and use several performance metrics such as Accuracy, Recall, Precision, F1 score, and the **Matthews correlation coefficient** (**MCC**). We covered these metrics in *Chapter 3*, *Interpretation Challenges*, but this time, since it's a multiclass classification problem, we are using `average='weighted'` to weight the metric according to class frequencies. For instance, there's not one `Recall_score` metric but three (one for each class), so what it does is perform a weighted average.

The code is illustrated in the following snippet:

```python
for model_name in class_models.keys():
    fitted_model = class_models[model_name]['model'].\
                                                fit(X_train, y_
train)
    y_train_pred = fitted_model.predict(X_train)
    y_test_pred = fitted_model.predict(X_test)
    class_models[model_name]['fitted'] = fitted_model
    class_models[model_name]['preds'] = y_test_pred
    class_models[model_name]['Accuracy_train'] =\
      metrics.Accuracy_score(y_train, y_train_pred)
    class_models[model_name]['Accuracy_test'] =\
      metrics.Accuracy_score(y_test, y_test_pred)
    class_models[model_name]['Recall_train'] =\
      metrics.Recall_score(y_train, y_train_pred,
  average='weighted')
    class_models[model_name]['Recall_test'] =\
      metrics.Recall_score(y_test, y_test_pred, average='weighted')
    class_models[model_name]['Precision_train'] =\
      metrics.Precision_score(y_train, y_train_pred,\
  average='weighted')
    class_models[model_name]['Precision_test'] =\
      metrics.Precision_score(y_test, y_test_pred,
```

```
average='weighted')
  class_models[model_name]['F1_test'] =\
    metrics.f1_score(y_test, y_test_pred, average='weighted')
  class_models[model_name]['MCC_test'] =\
    metrics.matthews_corrcoef(y_test, y_test_pred)
```

Once we have all of our metrics in the `class_models` dictionary, we can convert this dictionary to a `DataFrame` using `from_dict`. We can sort this `DataFrame` through MCC, using `sort_values` and color-coding all of the rest, and then using `style.background_gradient`, with the following code:

```
class_metrics = pd.DataFrame.\
  from_dict(class_models, 'index')[['Accuracy_train',\
              'Accuracy_test', 'Recall_train', 'Recall_test',
  'Precision_train', 'Precision_test', 'F1_test',\
              'MCC_test']]
with pd.option_context('display.Precision', 3):
  html = class_metrics.sort_values(by='MCC_test',
ascending=False).style. background_gradient(\
cmap='plasma', low=0.43, high=0.63,\
      subset=['Accuracy_train', 'Accuracy_test']).\
  background_gradient(cmap='viridis', low=0.63, high=0.43,\
      subset=['F1_test'])
html
```

The preceding code generates the table shown here in *Figure 4.1*:

	Accuracy_train	Accuracy_test	Recall_train	Recall_test	Precision_train	Precision_test	F1_test	MCC_test
decision_tree	0.497	0.464	0.497	0.464	0.541	0.494	0.441	0.246
gradient_boosting	0.625	0.496	0.625	0.496	0.637	0.490	0.482	0.232
logistic	0.496	0.493	0.496	0.493	0.498	0.494	0.491	0.231
mlp	0.522	0.494	0.522	0.494	0.517	0.485	0.480	0.223
lda	0.501	0.492	0.501	0.492	0.500	0.489	0.477	0.201
random_forest	0.912	0.484	0.912	0.484	0.921	0.478	0.447	0.198

Figure 4.1 – Classification model performance metrics

In *Figure 4.1*, test Accuracy doesn't seem all that impressive, but please note that to interpret Accuracy properly we ought to look at the **No Information Rate (NIR)**, also known as the **null error rate**.

To put the NIR into a concrete example, let's say that we are dealing with an image classification problem, and 85% of our dataset comprises images of dogs, while 15% is of cats. Dogs are, therefore, the majority class. If we were lazy about it, we could predict that all of the images are of dogs and still achieve a rate of 85% Accuracy. The NIR is the Accuracy we would get if we lazily predicted that all of the observations belong to the majority class. To calculate the NIR, all we have to do is divide the number of observations in the majority class (`y_train[y_train==1].shape[0]`) by the total amount of observations (`y_train.shape[0]`), as illustrated in the following code snippet:

```
print('NIR: %.4f' %\
                            (y_train[y_train==1].shape[0]/y_train.
shape[0]))
```

The preceding code should output the following:

```
NIR: 0.4215
```

We should strive to achieve accuracies above this number, and they all are, but not by a huge margin. Given that the models were tuned for increased predictive performance, this is disappointing, but it wasn't the focus of this exercise. It was important to surpass the NIR because otherwise, models are no better than our best "lazy" guess. Otherwise, it means that we ought to question the complexity of our models, regularization methods chosen, and feature selection, not to mention even the quality of our data and the validity of our hypothesis. However, what we are trying to do here is **leverage the model's capacity to unearth latent relationships** between variables to help us connect the dots between quiz answers and birth order, if they can be connected at all.

In any case, Accuracy is not the only metric that matters. We also have weighted Recall, Precision, and F1 score. They are not particularly impressive, but since we have no preference for false positives over false negatives, both Precision and Recall are of equal value to us, so it's good that they are more or less equal. Only Decision Trees have a higher margin between them. For the rest of the models, since the F1 score is the harmonic mean of Precision and Recall, it is—not surprisingly—a similar number. On the other hand, MCC depicts our predictive performance very well because it says our models sit approximately 20% in the interval between as-good-as-random and perfect prediction. Remember that MCC ranges between -1 if every one of our predictions were wrong to 1 if they were all right, and it's 0 if they were as good as random.

Another thing to note is that the larger size of train compared to test for each of these metrics tells us how much our model is overfitting. It's often hard to find the sweet spot where you are maximizing test Accuracy while not overfitting too much, like `gradient_boosting` and `random_forest` are. If we intended to productionize these models, we would need to pay close attention to this, but this is not the goal of this exercise. Our goal is to leverage these models as knowledge-discovery tools.

Feature importance for tree-based models

Three of our models have it easiest. For all tree-based models (even ensembled ones), feature importance has already been calculated using a weighted sum of decreases in node impurity. **Node impurity** is one of the metrics used to decide how to split a branch. It tells you how much of a node belongs to a single class, ranging from 100% impure when it is split evenly to 0% impure when it all belongs to a single class. To get the feature importance of all three models, all we have to do is reference the `feature_importances_` attribute in the fitted model. We will take these importances and save them along with the names of their features in a `DataFrame` for each other model: Decision Tree (`dt_imp_df`), Gradient Boosted Trees (`gb_imp_df`), and Random Forest (`rf_imp_df`), as follows:

```
dt_imp_df = pd.DataFrame({ 'name': X_train.columns,\
    'dt_imp': class_models['decision_tree']['fitted'].\
        feature_importances_ })
gb_imp_df = pd.DataFrame({ 'name': X_train.columns,\
    'gb_imp': class_models['gradient_boosting']['fitted'].\
        feature_importances_ })
rf_imp_df = pd.DataFrame({ 'name': X_train.columns,\
    'rf_imp': class_models['random_forest']['fitted'].\
        feature_importances_ })
```

There are 96 features, and feature importance for all three models is not on the same scale because of differences in the tree structures. It's best to interpret feature importance as a *relative* measure, to compare one feature with others but not across different models. Therefore, instead of comparing these measures, we can compare their rank. We can use the pandas `rank` function to calculate the rank for the importance measures in each model for each feature and save these as a `DataFrame`. It does this without changing the order of the features, since they come unsorted.

The code is illustrated in the following snippet:

```
dt_rank_df = pd.DataFrame({'dt_rank': dt_imp_df['dt_imp'].\
        rank(method='first', ascending=False).astype(int)})
gb_rank_df = pd.DataFrame({'gb_rank': gb_imp_df['gb_imp'].\
        rank(method='first', ascending=False).astype(int)})
rf_rank_df = pd.DataFrame({'rf_rank': rf_imp_df['rf_imp'].\
        rank(method='first', ascending=False).astype(int)})
```

Let's now concatenate each feature importance `DataFrame` with its corresponding rank `DataFrame` and merge all of them into a dataframe called `tree_ranks_df`, which has the feature importance measure and rank of that importance for each model. We can average all of the ranks (`avg_rank`) and then sort them by this so that we can see the features that are most important, on average, first.

The code is illustrated in the following snippet:

```
tree_ranks_df = pd.merge(\
    pd.merge(\
    pd.concat((dt_imp_df, dt_rank_df), axis=1),\
    pd.concat((gb_imp_df, gb_rank_df), axis=1), 'left'),\
    pd.concat((rf_imp_df, rf_rank_df), axis=1), 'left')
tree_ranks_df['avg_rank'] = (tree_ranks_df['dt_rank'] +\
        tree_ranks_df['gb_rank'] +\
        tree_ranks_df['rf_rank'])/3
tree_ranks_df.sort_values(by='avg_rank')
```

The preceding code will produce the data frame shown here in *Figure 4.2*:

	name	dt_imp	dt_rank	gb_imp	gb_rank	rf_imp	rf_rank	avg_rank
28	birthn	0.851533	1	0.371305	1	0.198748	1	1
82	testelapse	0.0137081	3	0.0335579	2	0.0275725	2	2.33333
26	age	0.00667898	7	0.030532	3	0.0248301	3	4.33333
0	Q1	0.0253401	2	0.0236222	6	0.0159306	6	4.66667
81	introelapse	0.00505607	9	0.0297233	4	0.0224896	5	6
12	Q13	0.0080825	4	0.014516	7	0.0113429	8	6.33333
	:	:	:	:	:	:	:	:
90	country_GB	0	91	0.000755431	91	0.00194744	90	90.6667
92	country_NZ	0	93	0.00103713	90	0.000736748	91	91.3333
84	gender_undefined	0	87	0.000316311	94	0.000302447	94	91.6667
91	country_IE	0	92	0.000596172	92	0.000499432	93	92.3333

Figure 4.2 – Feature importance for tree-based models

As you can tell by *Figure 4.2*, there are some similarities between the Decision Tree (dt_rank), Gradient Boosted Trees (dt_rank), and Random Forest (rf_rank) ranks, especially for the last two. Indeed, importance measures don't appear to be on the same scale, so we have used the comparing-ranks approach instead. Another approach would have been to min-max scale the importance measures so that their lowest values are 0 and the highest are 1, yet this would reveal more about the relative distance in importance between features and less about the order. Right now, we are more interested in the order.

In addition to being model-specific, the tree-based models' feature importance methods are **impurity-based**. This is also a disadvantage because impurity makes them inherently biased toward **higher-cardinality features**. Features that are of a higher cardinality are those that have more unique values. For instance, in this example, there are 72 different ages represented in our dataset, while every question has five or six unique values, and all the country and gender ones such as county_GB and gender_undefined are binary—so, two unique values. You have to wonder if the age reason is more important, according to the average rank, than any question, and every question is more important than the binary features are because of this bias.

Feature importance for Logistic Regression

We have already covered feature importance for Logistic Regression in the previous two chapters. You have learned that a fitted Logistic Regression model has coefficients, and these coefficients can be useful clues as to which feature is more important. However, this time there's a twist. Let's print out the `shape` of the `coef_` property for the fitted model, as follows:

```
print(class_models['logistic']['fitted'].coef_.shape)
```

The preceding code will output the following:

```
(3, 96)
```

It turns out there are three sets of coefficients! But why?!

There are three sets because this model is not one but three classifiers in one. If you go back to the model definition, you can see where it says `multi_class='ovr'`. **OvR** stands for **One-vs-Rest**, and what it's doing behind the scenes is predicting firstborns', middle children's, and lastborns' classes independently. In other words, each has its own binary classification problem. Then, it compares the predicted probabilities for each class for each observation, and the one with the highest possibility is the predicted class. OvR is how you end up with three sets of coefficients, and these coefficients can only tell you the most important features to predict each class.

As explained in *Chapter 2, Key Concepts of Interpretability*, the coefficients are the log-odds increased by each additional unit of a feature that a class is a positive match, should all the other features stay the same. In this example, we have three sets of coefficients corresponding to predictions for each class. Hence, the first set of coefficients tells you through the increase of log-odds for each additional unit for every feature that the participant is a firstborn. If it's negative, it signals a decrease in the log-odds for *each additional unit*.

Since we didn't fit our model to normalized data, all our features have different scales, and this is why, to account for this, we can multiply each coefficient by its standard deviation to approximate feature importance. *Chapter 3, Interpretation Challenges*, discussed why this is only an approximation, and there's no consensus on the best method to obtain feature importance for Logistic Regression. Knowing this, we can first compute the standard deviations (`stdv`) and create a new `DataFrame`, `lr_imp_df`, where we place the coefficients for each class multiplied by the standard deviations next to the `name` of the feature.

The code is illustrated in the following snippet:

```
stdv = np.std(X_train, 0)
lr_imp_df = pd.DataFrame({\
    'name': X_train.columns,\
    'first_coef_norm':
            class_models['logistic']['fitted'].coef_[0] *
stdv,\
    'middle_coef_norm':
            class_models['logistic']['fitted'].coef_[1] *
stdv,\
    'last_coef_norm':
            class_models['logistic']['fitted'].coef_[2] *
stdv}).\
    reset_index(drop=True)
```

To approximate how much each feature impacts the model, we can weigh them with the *priors*, which is how much each class is represented in the dataset. Fortunately, the fitted model for LDA saves this as a `priors_` attribute. We can save this into our own `class_priors` variable, like this:

```
class_priors = class_models['lda']['fitted'].priors_
print(class_priors)
```

As appreciated by the `class_priors` array, firstborns comprise 42% of all participants, middle children 24%, and lastborns the remaining 34%. We can use this array to create a weighted average, using the absolute value of the coefficients called `coef_weighted_avg`. In the following code snippet, we are using the absolute value for this weighted average because we aren't interested in whether it increases or decreases log-odds, only in the degree to which it does:

```
lr_imp_df['coef_weighted_avg'] =\
    (abs(lr_imp_df['first_coef_norm']) * class_priors[0]) +\
    (abs(lr_imp_df['middle_coef_norm']) * class_priors[1]) +\
    (abs(lr_imp_df['last_coef_norm']) * class_priors[2])
```

The weighted average we just produced is only an approximation of feature importance so that we can sort features from highest to lowest importance. We will do that next with `sort_values`, and color-code the coefficient columns with `background_gradient` to make it easier to appreciate the differences in values within each column, as follows:

```
lr_imp_df.\
    sort_values(by='coef_weighted_avg', ascending=False).style.\
    background_gradient(cmap='viridis', low=-0.1, high=0.1,\
    subset=['first_coef_norm', 'middle_coef_norm', 'last_coef_
norm'])
```

The preceding code will produce the data frame shown here in *Figure 4.3*:

	name	first_coef_norm	middle_coef_norm	last_coef_norm	coef_weighted_avg
28	birthn	-0.412945	1.3538	-0.0132044	0.499431
26	age	0.0552764	-0.0265002	-0.149019	0.0804694
0	Q1	0.110523	0.0224566	-0.00631052	0.0540604
12	Q13	0.0793163	-0.0382582	-0.000743793	0.0427518
15	Q16	0.0604051	-0.0542339	-0.000581668	0.0385124
19	Q20	-0.0609848	0.0508594	0.0015853	0.0382996
39	EST1	0.0498431	-0.0622704	0.00411372	0.0371717
3	Q4	0.044028	-0.0576418	-0.000594055	0.0324218
59	CSN1	0.0316447	-0.0699186	0.00127486	0.0303448
⋮	⋮	⋮	⋮	⋮	⋮
90	country_GB	-2.218e-05	-0.00138172	4.47252e-05	0.000352116
91	country_IE	-0.00014727	0.000314903	7.59173e-07	0.000136968
92	country_NZ	7.70629e-05	-0.000394417	5.52904e-06	0.000127852
87	gender_other	7.0736e-05	0.000394679	-8.67944e-06	0.000126324
84	gender_undefined	5.65254e-05	-9.94834e-05	-3.80303e-07	4.75334e-05

Figure 4.3 – Feature importance for the Logistic Regression model

In *Figure 4.3*, the exact order doesn't always matter as much as which features are at the top (very relevant), which ones are at the very bottom (irrelevant), and which lie somewhere in between (somewhat relevant). As for each class's coefficients, we can interpret them by which ones are positive or negative, and by more or less what magnitude—for instance, we know that `birthn` negatively correlates with a positive match for firstborn. This insight intuitively makes sense. The higher the number of children a family has, the less likely it is that one of them is the firstborn. The same goes for lastborns—only the odds of a middle child increase as the number of children increases. As `age` increases, the odds of being a lastborn decrease. This conclusion also makes sense because families used to be larger, but it's not clear why it increases for firstborns. However, we would need a different tool to examine this better.

We can also tell that agreement with the statement in Question 1 (`Q1`), which says "*I have read an absurd number of books*" and Question 13 (`Q13`), which says "*I boss people around*" increases the odds that the participant is the firstborn. Also, Question 20 (`Q20`), which says "*I do not need others' praise*", increases the odds of this being a middle child. You can tell the classes are mostly oppositional to each other despite having being fitted separately, and, naturally, there are very few cases in which coefficients for all three classes for a feature are all positive or all negative.

This model-specific feature importance method is not very reliable for assessing the importance of all features holistically, for all classes. Also, since the model is Logistic Regression, it is making a few assumptions about the data that might not hold true, such as little or no multicollinearity between the features, and a linear relationship with the *log-odds*. However, if these assumptions are more or less correct, the advantage for OvR Logistic Regression lies in the separation between classes. You can examine how each feature relates to each class independently.

Feature importance for LDA

As with OvR Logistic Regression, we can extract three sets of coefficients for every feature for LDA as well. To verify, examine the `shape`, like this:

```
print(class_models['lda']['fitted'].coef_.shape)
```

It should output (3, 96). The difference lies in the meaning of these coefficients. They tell us how much each feature weighs in the **separability** of the class. The higher the absolute value of the coefficient, the more that feature assists in separating that class. On the other hand, a lower absolute value of the coefficient indicates that the feature doesn't contribute toward class separability. After all, LDA is like PCA, but it decomposes features into separateness and not correlatedness.

To take a look at these coefficients, we can create a new DataFrame, lda_imp_df, where we place the coefficients for each class multiplied by the standard deviation next to the name of the feature, as follows:

```
lda_imp_df = pd.DataFrame({\
'name': X_train.columns,\
'first_coef_norm': class_models['lda']['fitted'].coef_[0] *
stdv,\
'middle_coef_norm': class_models['lda']['fitted'].coef_[1] *
stdv,\
'last_coef_norm': class_models['lda']['fitted'].coef_[2] *
stdv}).\
reset_index(drop=True)
```

We can now do the same as we did with Logistic Regression and create a weighted average of the absolute value of coefficients (coef_weighted_avg), using the class_priors variable. We do this for the sole purpose of being able to sort the table and get an approximate understanding of which features matter most, while recognizing that this is not an exact science.

The code is illustrated in the following snippet:

```
lda_imp_df['coef_weighted_avg'] =\
        (abs(lda_imp_df['first_coef_norm']) * class_priors[0]) +\
        (abs(lda_imp_df['middle_coef_norm']) * class_priors[1])
+\
        (abs(lda_imp_df['last_coef_norm']) * class_priors[2])
```

We can now use the weighted average (coef_weighted_avg) to sort the features and color-code them in the same way as we did for Logistic Regression, as follows:

```
lda_imp_df.\
  sort_values(by='coef_weighted_avg', ascending=False).style.\
  background_gradient(cmap='viridis', low=-0.1, high=0.1,\
   subset=['first_coef_norm', 'middle_coef_norm', 'last_coef_
norm'])
```

In *Figure 4.4*, generated by the preceding code, you can appreciate that many of the same features that were in the top 10 for Logistic Regression are also in the top 10 for LDA. You can also see similar patterns between classes, such as the middle child being much more aligned with birthn than anything else, while the other two classes have more balance in the features that help predict them.

The output can be viewed here:

	name	first_coef_norm	middle_coef_norm	last_coef_norm	coef_weighted_avg
28	birthn	-0.315215	1.00305	-0.307128	0.475483
0	Q1	0.0899109	-0.0122606	-0.102456	0.0757905
12	Q13	0.0564803	-0.0337293	-0.0462968	0.0476102
51	AGR3	-0.0392475	-0.00558213	0.0523123	0.0357299
15	Q16	0.0395618	-0.0363935	-0.0235674	0.0333487
6	Q7	-0.00407858	0.0644172	-0.0396745	0.0305362
24	Q25	-0.0350918	0.0343628	0.01946	0.0295807
16	Q17	0.034915	-0.00978912	-0.036297	0.0294317
77	OPN9	-0.0326552	0.0447374	0.00925253	0.0275268
33	EXT5	-0.000968246	0.0064997	-0.00331607	0.0030811
85	gender_male	0.00272646	-0.00239968	-0.00169943	0.00229827
81	introelapse	-0.00168655	0.00484121	-0.00127851	0.00229491
36	EXT8	-0.000826513	-0.00324433	0.00327175	0.00223465
7	Q8	-0.000763955	0.0039999	-0.00183324	0.0018961

Figure 4.4 – Feature importance for the LDA model

Similar to OvR Logistic Regression, LDA feature importance has the disadvantages of being model-specific and the assumptions made by the LDA model. LDA assumes little or no multicollinearity between the features and **multivariate normality**—that is, the features are distributed normally for each class. It also shares the same main advantage of OvR Logistic Regression, of being able to observe how each feature relates to each class. However, LDA is more robust to assumption violations and, thus, may be used with noisier data. That being said, **Quadratic Discriminant Analysis (QDA)** is even better in such cases. QDA is like LDA, but makes no normality assumption and splits the classes with a quadratic decision boundary rather than a linear one.

Feature importance for the Multi-layer Perceptron

Neural networks lack intrinsic attributes that can effortlessly help in determining feature importance, as in other model classes. It gets more complicated, even for this single hidden layer example, because there are two sets of weight matrices corresponding to each layer, as illustrated in the following code snippet:

```
print(class_models['mlp']['fitted'][1].coefs_[0].shape)
print(class_models['mlp']['fitted'][1].coefs_[1].shape)
```

The shapes of the two arrays are outputted as follows:

```
(96, 11)
(11, 3)
```

Weights in each matrix can be misleading since they can be amplified or attenuated by each other. If you dot-product these two matrices together and transpose them, you'll get one with the familiar (96, 3) shape, with cells corresponding to each feature and class combination, which we used for Logistic Regression and LDA. However, this is not precisely how the weights are used to predict during forward propagation. For starters, there are non-linear activation functions such as relu and softmax in between and after these matrix operations. Assuming training has been done with normalized data, there have been proposals to take the sum of the absolute products of the weights and the sum of the products of the weights without the absolute values. There are more elaborate schemes involving weighting and normalizing the weights, but these ignore the effect of the hidden layer activation function.

The conclusion is that there's no consensus on how to extract feature importance from the intrinsic parameters of a neural network. As we will learn later in this book, there are other intrinsically interpretable aspects of a neural network—for instance, saliency maps in *Chapter 8, Visualizing Convolutional Neural Networks,* and integrated gradients in *Chapter 9, Interpretation Methods for Multivariate Forecasting and Sensitivity Analysis.*

Although we were able to leverage the intrinsic parameters to get feature importance for all other models, the methods used were inconsistent. Therefore, the results weren't only different because of differences in the models but also because of differences in the methods. So, what would be a reliable method to calculate feature importance for any model? It's called PFI, and we will cover this next.

Practicing PFI

The concept of PFI is much easier to explain than any model-specific feature importance method! It merely measures the increase in prediction error once the values of each feature have been shuffled. The theory for PFI is based on the logic that if the feature has a relationship with the target variable, shuffling will disrupt it and increase the error. On the other hand, if the feature doesn't have a strong relationship with the target variable, the prediction error won't increase by much, if at all. Then, if you rank features by those whose shuffling increases the error the most, you'll appreciate which ones are most important to the model.

In addition to being a **model-agnostic** method, PFI can be used with unseen data such as the test dataset, which is a massive advantage. In this case, because it is overfitting with Random Forest and Gradient Boosting Trees, how reliable can feature importance derived from intrinsic parameters be? It tells you what the model thinks is important according to what was learned from the training data, but it can't tell you what is most important once you introduce unseen data.

In his book *Interpretable Machine Learning*, Christoph Molnar makes arguments in favor of leveraging the training data instead, which can tell you more about the reliance on each feature in the trained model rather than on its individual contribution to the generalizable predictive performance. We are more interested in the latter, so this is why we are using the test dataset.

To compute permutation importance on all of our models, we can leverage our `class_models` dictionary again by iterating each one of them and then calling scikit-learn's `permutation_importance` function to compute the PFIs. The main parameters for the `permutation_importance` function are the fitted model (`fitted_model`), and the features (`X_test`) and labels (`y_test`) of our dataset. We are also defining Accuracy as the prediction-error metric or scorer we want to use (`scoring='Accuracy'`) to compare a decrease in Accuracy after features have been permuted.

The code is illustrated in the following snippet:

```python
for model_name in class_models.keys():
    fitted_model = class_models[model_name]['fitted']
    permutation_imp = inspection.permutation_importance(\
        fitted_model, X_test, y_test, n_jobs=-1,\
        scoring='Accuracy', n_repeats=8, random_state=rand)
    class_models[model_name]['importances_mean'] =\
        permutation_imp.importances_mean
```

PFI shuffles features more than once and then averages prediction errors, which is why it's essential to define the amount of times it should shuffle the feature (n_repeats=8), as well as random_state for reproducibility. PFI can be performed in parallel, leveraging all the processors of your system (n_jobs=-1). Lastly, once PFI has been performed for each model, it saves the averages of the prediction errors (importances_mean).

We can now take the average importances computed for each one of our models and put them in separate columns of a new DataFrame, perm_imp_df, alongside the name of each feature, as illustrated in the following code snippet:

```
perm_imp_df = pd.DataFrame({\
    'name': X_train.columns,\
    'dt_imp': class_models['decision_tree']['importances_mean'],\
    'gb_imp': class_models['gradient_boosting']['importances_
mean'],\
    'rf_imp': class_models['random_forest']['importances_mean'],\
    'log_imp': class_models['logistic']['importances_mean'],\
    'lda_imp': class_models['lda']['importances_mean'],\
    'mlp_imp': class_models['mlp']['importances_mean']}).\
reset_index(drop=True)
```

Solely for sorting the perm_imp_df DataFrame by something, let's average the importances of all six models into a new column, which we call avg_imp, as follows:

```
perm_imp_df['avg_imp'] = (perm_imp_df['dt_imp'] +
                    perm_imp_df['gb_imp'] + perm_imp_df['rf_imp']
+ perm_imp_df['log_imp'] + perm_imp_df['lda_
imp'] + perm_imp_df['mlp_imp'])/6
```

Now, we can round, sort by avg_imp, and save perm_imp_df into a new dataframe called perm_imp_sorted_df. Then, we output it color-coded, like this:

```
perm_imp_sorted_df = perm_imp_df.round(5).\
                    sort_values(by='avg_imp', ascending=False)
perm_imp_sorted_df.style.\
            background_gradient(cmap='viridis_r', low=0,
high=0.2, subset=['dt_imp', 'gb_imp', 'rf_
imp', 'log_imp', 'lda_imp', 'mlp_imp'])
```

The preceding code yields the data frame shown here in *Figure 4.5*:

	name	dt_imp	gb_imp	rf_imp	log_imp	lda_imp	mlp_imp	avg_imp
28	birthn	0.1385	0.10735	0.07604	0.11818	0.08199	0.11172	0.10563
0	Q1	0.00832	0.00688	0.00428	0.00509	0.01103	0.0093	0.00749
26	age	0.00107	0.00327	0.00496	0.00713	-0.00122	0.00183	0.00284
12	Q13	0.00098	-0.00252	-6e-05	0.00428	0.00235	0.00499	0.00167
3	Q4	0	0.00274	0.00163	0.00178	0.0006	0.00214	0.00148
16	Q17	0.00119	-0.00201	0.00255	0.00122	0.00179	0.00273	0.00124
51	AGR3	0.00032	-7e-05	-0.00156	0.00109	0.00339	0.0039	0.00118
24	Q25	0	-6e-05	-0.00087	0.00106	0.00112	0.00465	0.00098
30	EXT2	0	0.00073	0.00161	0.00075	-0.00076	0.00348	0.00097
		⋮	⋮	⋮	⋮	⋮	⋮	⋮
69	OPN1	0.00015	-0.00035	-0.00175	-0.00062	-0.00018	0.00088	-0.00031
21	Q22	0	-0.00279	-0.00025	0.00019	-0.00207	0.00242	-0.00042
79	source	0	-0.00048	6e-05	0.00094	-0.00135	-0.0017	-0.00042
25	Q26	0.00126	-0.00144	-0.00216	0.00015	-0.00211	0.0007	-0.0006
22	Q23	0	-0.00169	-0.00012	-7e-05	-0.0017	-0.00028	-0.00064

Figure 4.5 – Test PFI for all models

Figure 4.5 shows the PFI for the test dataset for all the models fitted in this chapter. It confirms that the models intrinsically have a heavy reliance on `birthn`, but also that it is by far more important than the next most important feature. In fact, `birthn` is so important to the models that if we deducted the average increase in prediction error— which, in this case, corresponds to a decrease in Accuracy—from the test Accuracy of each of the models, they would dip below the no-information rate! This is easy enough to prove by taking the `Accuracy_test` attribute from the `class_models` dictionary, which stores all the test accuracies for every model, and deducting the first six values (`1:7`) from the first row in (`0`) in the sorted importances `DataFrame` (`perm_imp_sorted_df`), as illustrated in the following code snippet:

```
pd.DataFrame.\
    from_dict(class_models, 'index')[['Accuracy_test']] -\
    perm_imp_sorted_df.iloc[0,1:7].to_numpy().reshape((6,1))
```

As you can see here in *Figure 4.6*, generated by the preceding code, not a single model has an Accuracy rate above the NIR (0.4215) once you deduct the PFI of birthn:

	Accuracy_test
decision_tree	0.325639
gradient_boosting	0.388483
random_forest	0.40958
logistic	0.383053
lda	0.409265
mlp	0.37977

Figure 4.6 – Test Accuracy for all models once you deduct the PFI of birthn

Assuming no meaningful level of **multicollinearity**, the overwhelming impact of that single feature means that all the psychological questions combined are not enough to predict birth order. Sadly, it's one of the demographic questions that makes the models somewhat performant, which is certainly not what the researchers would have expected to find. However, this conclusion doesn't mean that there's nothing to learn from this exercise. There's more to model interpretation than understanding which features make a model work or not. But why? So that even when a model is working for the wrong reasons, we can still learn from it. To that end, we ought to dig deeper into why birthn does so well and what can be learned from the rest of the features. The methods we will study next, such as PDPs and ICE plots, will help shed some light on specific features and their relationship with the target and with each other.

Disadvantages of PFI

The main disadvantage of PFI, which is not uncommon among model interpretation techniques, is that the method won't pick up on the impact of features correlated with each other. In other words, **multicollinearity** will trump feature importances. When you shuffle one feature, its correlated feature(s) will remain unshuffled, keeping error rates relatively unaltered, which means clusters of correlated features will have lower importances than they should. There's a strategy to handle this problem, which we will discuss in *Chapter 12, Monotonic Constraints and Model Tuning for Interpretability*.

Interpreting PDPs

A PDP conveys the marginal effect of a feature on the prediction throughout all (or interpolated) possible values for that feature. It's a global model interpretation method that can visually demonstrate the impact of a feature and the nature of the relationship with the target (linear, exponential, monotonic, and so on).

It can also be extended to include two features, to illustrate the effect of their interaction on the model. One feature plot shows in the *y* axis the predicted outcome or relative change in this outcome, and the *x* axis shows all possible values of the feature. The plotted line is calculated by changing the value of the feature to the one in the *x* axis for all the observations and averaging the predictions if this single feature were to change, to get the *y* axis coordinate.

One variation of the PDP deducts the expected value for all observations from the *y* axis, thus centering the marginal effect to the expected value. Another PDP variation will show the distribution of the feature with a histogram or rug plot. Since the PDP line is computed with an average, this matters because, as in areas of the plot where the feature is more sparsely distributed, an average is not as reliable.

Firstly, let's create two lists of the names of the features we wish to interpret (feature_names) and their respective labels (feature_labels), to show in the *x* axis labels and title, as follows:

```
feature_names = ['birthn', 'Q1', 'Q13', 'age']
feature_labels = ['# of Births', 'Question #1', 'Question #13',
 'Age']
```

Now, we can iterate each feature name and use PDPbox's pdp_isolate function to compute a dataframe with all the PDP averages (pdp_feat_df), using the fitted model (model), the dataset (dataset), the names of all the feature columns (model_features), and the feature you want in the *x* axis (feature).

For the fitted model, we are using Gradient Boosting Trees because no model is closest to the average PFI for the first four important features. However, you can change this to see how features on average have a different relationship to the target depending on the model. You will find some are jagged, some are smooth, some are linear, and so on.

For the `dataset`, we will use the test dataset for the very same reason we used it for PFI. One thing to note is that `dataset` expects the entire dataset (features and labels), and because we have them split as `X_test` and `y_test`, we have to concatenate them using the pandas `concat` function. Once we have the dataframe, all we have to do is plot it, and PDPbox has a function that generates the Matplotlib plots, called `pdp_plot`. It takes the previously generated dataframe (`pdp_isolate_out`) and several optional graphical parameters, detailed as follows:

- `center=True` makes the *y* axis relative to the highest or lowest value.

- `x_quantile=True` makes the spacing of *x* axis ticks correspond to quantiles. PDPbox doesn't include a histogram or rug plot to show distribution of features, so this is a good way of overcoming interpretation challenges related to having a sparse or uneven distribution.

- `ncols=3` places all three classes in a single row.

- `plot_lines=True` will plot lines corresponding to a sample of observations.

- `frac_to_plot=100` tells it to plot 100 sampled observations.

- `feature_name` is the label of the feature in the *x* axis.

The following code iterates all four features, generating the `pdp_isolate` dataframe and then plotting the PDPs with it:

```
for i in range(len(feature_names)):
  pdp_feat_df = pdp.pdp_isolate(\
            model=class_models['gradient_boosting']['fitted'],\
            dataset=pd.concat((X_test, y_test), axis=1),
            model_features=X_test.columns, feature=feature_
names[i])
  fig, axes = pdp.pdp_plot(\
            pdp_isolate_out=pdp_feat_df, center=True, x_
quantile=True,\
            ncols=3, plot_lines=True, frac_to_plot=100,
figsize=(15,6), feature_name=feature_labels[i])
```

The preceding code produces the plots shown in *Figures 4.7-4.10*. You can view *Figure 4.7* here:

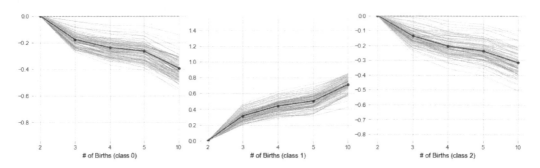

Figure 4.7 – PDP for birthn

Figure 4.7 conveys something we had previously noticed with Logistic Regression feature importance, but now we have a visual representation. The probability of a firstborn (class 0) and a lastborn (class 2) consistently drops as the number of births (birthn) increases. Middle-child (class 1) probabilities go in the opposite direction, starting at almost 0% because there can't be a middle child with two children! This all makes sense. You can also tell from how consistently close the thinner lines are to the thicker one (the average) that this is a strong feature, with little variation across all class predictions.

Figure 4.8 can be viewed here:

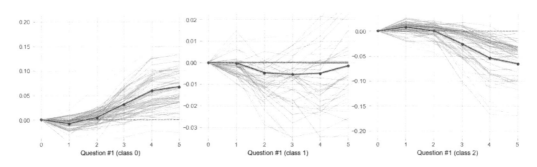

Figure 4.8 – PDP for Q1

Figure 4.8 corresponds to the Likert scale for Q1, "*I have read an absurd number of books*", so for firstborns the probability decreases between N/A (0) and disagree (1) but the climb afterward surpasses the zero mark (no change) and is decidedly increasing by the time it's past neutral (3). Q1 for lastborns has the exact opposite effect. The middle-child result is more interesting because you can see the sampled observations (thin lines) are all over the place, so take this with a grain of salt, but their average suggests what appears to be a mix between firstborns after 3 and lastborns before it. In other words, both total disagreement and agreement with Q1 suggest a higher probability of middle children dipping in between these two extremes.

Figure 4.9 can be viewed here:

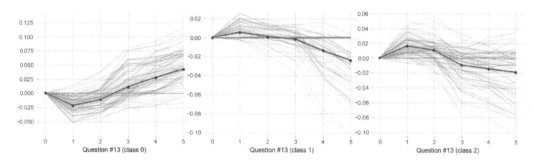

Figure 4.9 – PDP for Q13

The PDP for Q13 ("*I boss people around*") in *Figure 4.9* has similar relationships with the target for firstborns and lastborns to Q1 but is more pronounced at the disagreement end of the Likert scale and slightly less pronounced at the other end. There's much less ambivalence with middle children in Q13 than Q1, this class being less likely as the agreement level increases.

Figure 4.10 can be viewed here:

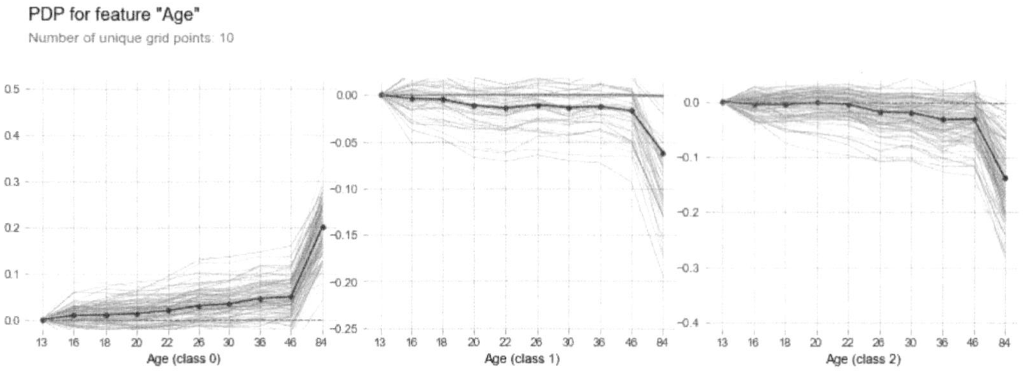

PDP for feature "Age"
Number of unique grid points: 10

Figure 4.10 – PDP for age

Figure 4.10 involves the PDP of the age feature. We can tell that the probability of being a firstborn slowly and consistently increases, on average, as age increases. Although we can interpret this, it's hard to find a logical explanation because families used to be larger, so we perhaps expect the probability to decrease with age. Thankfully, the quantiles can provide clues. Notice that tick marks for ages 16-22 are only 2 years apart, but then this spacing increases to 4, 6, 10, and—finally—38. This means the age distribution is right-skewed, which is not necessarily a bad thing, but a distribution could be also uneven with the classes among each age group.

To prove this hypothesis, let's first put age and birthorder in their own dataframe (birthorder_abbrev_df). Then, we leverage the pandas cut function to set the index to be the same age groups in the quantiles. Now, we first save a series (agegroup_birthorder_counts_s) grouped by this age group index and birthorder, and another one (agegroup_counts_s) just grouped by the index. You can now divide the total age group and birth order tallies by the age group tallies, yielding a series with the percentages (agegroup_pct_birthorder_s). Finally, you can use unstack() to convert the series to a dataframe, and a pandas plot.bar function to turn it to a stacked bar chart, as illustrated in the following code snippet:

```
birthorder_abbrev_df = birthorder_df[['age', 'birthorder']]
birthorder_abbrev_df.set_index(pd.cut(birthorder_abbrev_
df['age'],\
        [12, 16, 18, 20, 22, 26, 30, 36, 46, 88]), inplace=True)
agegroup_birthorder_counts_s = birthorder_abbrev_df.\
        groupby([birthorder_abbrev_df.index, 'birthorder']).size()
agegroup_counts_s =\
```

```
        birthorder_abbrev_df.groupby(\
birthorder_abbrev_df.index) ['birthorder'].count()
agegroup_pct_birthorder_s =\
        agegroup_birthorder_counts_s.div(agegroup_
counts_s, axis=0,level=0)
agegroup_pct_birthorder_s.unstack().plot.bar(stacked=True,\
figsize=(15,8))
```

The preceding code produces the plot shown in *Figure 4.11*:

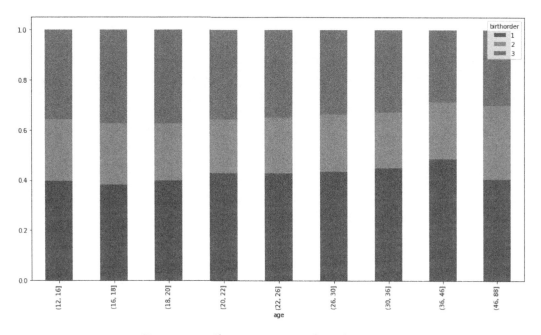

Figure 4.11 – Class priors per equal-sized age groups

Figure 4.11 shows how each class (`birthorder`) is represented in the different age groupings. It may not seem like a lot, but from ages of 16 to 46 the representation of firstborns (class 1) jumped from 38% to nearly 49%, while lastborns (class 3) dipped from 38% to 29%. Meanwhile, middle children (class 2) fluctuated by only 3%. All this is counter-intuitive from what we know about demographics because we know in the 75 years spanning these age groups that average children per family decreased by at least two children in the countries represented and by almost one child in the last 50 of those 75 years. In theory, this means that the likelihood of being a firstborn or lastborn should have decreased as the age increases, while the likelihood of being a middle child increases.

A plausible hypothesis would be that firstborns are overrepresented in older age groups because they are increasingly more likely to participate in these online quizzes to begin with, and the model picked up on this bias. Regardless of whether there's a bias or not, we should deal with relevant class imbalances. We will cover biases in greater depth in *Chapter 11, Bias Mitigation and Causal Inference Methods*, when we learn how to leverage demographic data to reduce class imbalance, and thus the model biases caused by them.

Interaction PDPs

PDP can also be applied to multiple features at once, which can be useful in examining how the interaction of two features relates to the target variable.

We can use PDPbox to generate a PDP interaction plot too. Its pdp_interact function is very similar to pdp_interact and has all the same parameters, except that feature is a list of features. In addition to choosing birthn and Q1 as our features, we have the n_jobs=-1 parameter, which leverages all of our processors for computating in parallel. pdp_interact will output a pdp_birthn_Q1_df dataframe. Now, we ought to plot it with pdp_interact_plot. For pdp_interact_plot, you'll see similar parameters to pdp_plot. For instance, pdp_interact_out is analogous to pdp_isolate_out, taking the dataframe produced from the previous step; and feature_names is like feature_name but takes a list of feature labels, not a single label. plot_type='grid' tells it to generate a grid, which is great for low-cardinality or ordinal features such as birthn and Q1.

The code is illustrated in the following snippet:

```
pdp_birthn_Q1_df = pdp.pdp_interact(\
                model=class_models['random_forest']['fitted'],\
                dataset=pd.concat((X_test, y_test), axis=1),\
                model_features=X_test.columns,
                features=['birthn','Q1'],\
                n_jobs=-1)
fig, axes = pdp.pdp_interact_plot(\
                pdp_interact_out=pdp_birthn_Q1_df,\
                plot_type='grid',\
                x_quantile=True, ncols=2, figsize=(15,15),\
                feature_names=['# of Births','Question #1'])
```

In *Figure 4.12*, outputted as a result of the preceding code, you can tell by the color-coded grid that the average probability of firstborns (class 0) increases as the number of births (birthn) decreases and agreement with Q1 increases. For lastborns (class 2), it's the same for birthn, but exactly the opposite for Q1. So far, these interactions shouldn't be surprising because it is as if you had combined the individual PDPs for each of these features. However, with middle children (class 1) the Q1 chart was a bit ambivalent, but it's important to note how one feature can counteract the average effect of another. Once you see it interact with birthn, the probability mostly moves in one direction, increasing with the birthn feature.

Figure 4.12 can be viewed here:

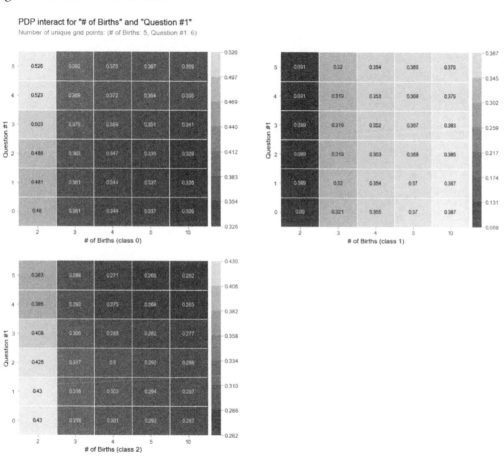

Figure 4.12 – Grid-interaction PDP for birthn and Q1

PDPbox has another type of PDP interaction plot called `contour`, and this is more suited to higher-cardinality or continuous features, so this time we will use `age` and `testelapse` (time-taking test). The code to output the plot is exactly the same as for the previous one except for the different `features`, `feature_names`, and `plot_type`.

The code is illustrated in the following snippet:

```python
pdp_age_testelapse_df = pdp.pdp_interact(\
    model=class_models['random_forest']['fitted'],\
    dataset=pd.concat((X_test, y_test), axis=1),\
    model_features=X_test.columns,\
    features=['age','testelapse'],\
    n_jobs=-1)
fig, axes = pdp.pdp_interact_plot(\
    pdp_interact_out=pdp_age_testelapse_df,\
    plot_type='contour', x_quantile=True, ncols=2,\
    figsize=(15,15),\
    feature_names=['Age','Time taking test (minutes)'])
```

The preceding code yields the output shown here in *Figure 4.13*:

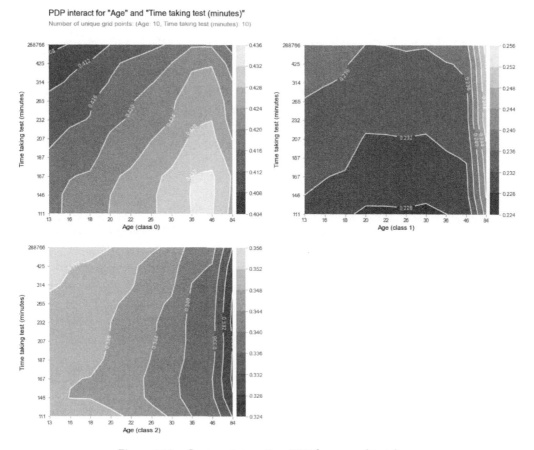

Figure 4.13 – Contour-interaction PDP for age and testelapse

Figure 4.13 conveys that the probability of firstborns (class 0) increases as the time spent taking the test decreases and age increases, so if you are older and quicker at taking the test, there is a higher chance you are a firstborn. Lastborns (class 2) are more or less the opposite: if you are slower while you are younger, the greater chance you have of being a lastborn. Middle children (class 1) increase more in one direction, becoming slightly more probable as testelapse increases, except when age is above 46 and probability quickly increases with age.

Disadvantages of PDP

PDP's main disadvantages are that it can only display up to two features at a time and it assumes independence of features when they might be correlated with each other. To solve the issue of independence, we will cover **Accumulated Local Effect** (**ALE**) plots in the next chapter.

As we have come to learn in this section, PDPs are great to see how, on average, the features relate to the target, but what if we want to visualize the relationship disaggregated (in other words, each individual observation rather than an average)? This aggregation is another disadvantage and is precisely what ICE plots are for, and we will briefly cover these next.

Explaining ICE plots

ICE plots are the answer to the question: *What if my PDP plots obscure the variance in my feature-target relationships?* Indeed, when you are trying to understand how a feature relates to the prediction of a model, a lot can be lost by averaging it out. If you take a close look at the PDP plots for individual features, many of them have thin lines that are not only distant from the average thick line but don't even follow its general direction. These variations can provide additional insight—and, by the way, the thin lines are essentially what ICE plots are about, except you can do much more with them.

ICE plots can include all of your datasets, but having many lines in your plots can be computationally expensive and—more importantly—difficult to appreciate. This is why it's recommended to either sample your dataset or plot the lines with transparency.

We will use both approaches, but let's first sample the dataset. We first set the random seed with np.random.seed for reproducibility and then we set sample_size at 10% of the dataset, and use sample_idx to select randomly the 10% of indexes that will be represented in our ICE plots. Then, we save the sampled observations in a new dataframe (X_test_samp).

The code is illustrated in the following snippet:

```
np.random.seed(rand)
sample_size = 0.1
sample_idx = np.random.choice(\
            X_test.shape[0],
math.ceil(X_test.shape[0]*sample_size),\
            replace=False)
X_test_samp = X_test.iloc[sample_idx,:]
```

The Python ICE implementation we use by default uses the `predict` function, which is great for regression problems. Still, for classification, you end up with straight lines on top of each other, going toward one of the three possible classes. To fix this, you can use `predict_proba` instead, which returns the predicted probabilities. However, this returns three sets of predicted probabilities, and the implementation can't understand this. To fix this, we can create our `predict` functions, one per class, as follows:

```
def predict_prob_first_born(test_df):
  return class_models['random_forest']['fitted'].\
                                      predict_proba(test_df)
  [:,0]
def predict_prob_middle_child(test_df):
  return class_models['random_forest']['fitted'].\
                                      predict_proba(test_df)
  [:,1]
def predict_prob_last_born(test_df):
  return class_models['random_forest']['fitted'].\
                                      predict_proba(test_df)
  [:,2]
```

As you can tell by looking at the three `predict_prob` functions, we are using the `fitted` model for `random_forest` and the test dataset to illustrate ICE. Now, we can use a `mldatasets` function (`plot_data_vs_ice`) that can compute and plot ICE plots beneath one with the data used to generate the plots. On the *x* axis, we can use our `birthn` top feature. To make this a more fun exercise, we will even color-code the lines in accordance with the answers to Q1.

To this end, let's first create a dictionary with the Likert scale (`legend_key`), which we will use as the legend for Q1, as follows:

```
legend_key = {0:'N/A', 1:'Disagree', 2:'Somewhat Disagree',
              3:'Neutral', 4:'Somewhat Agree', 5:'Agree'}
```

Then, we use the `plot_data_vs_ice` function to generate the plots. If you are curious, under the hood it uses the `pycebox` library to plot the ICE plot. We won't get into the details of how to leverage this library directly because our focus is on interpretation, but you can check out the tutorial here:

`https://github.com/AustinRochford/PyCEbox/`

The first two arguments required by the plot_data_vs_ice function are the prediction function and a label to put in the *y* axis. The label relates to what is being predicted with the predict function. It also requires the X data used for predictions, the name of the feature to plot on the *x* axis (feature_name), and its label (feature_label). Optionally, we can specify a feature to use for color-coding (color_by) and our legend for this feature (legend_key).

We will first generate a plot of predicted probability for firstborns, as follows:

```
mldatasets.plot_data_vs_ice(predict_prob_first_born,\
                            'Probability of Firstborn',\
                            X=X_test_samp,\
                            feature_name='birthn',\
                            feature_label='# of Births',\
                            color_by='Q1', legend_key=legend_
key)
```

The preceding code generates the plots shown in *Figure 4.14* and *Figure 4.15*.

The first plot can be viewed here:

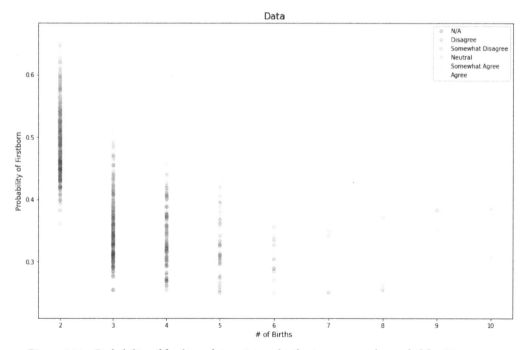

Figure 4.14 – Probability of firstborn data points as birthn increases, color-coded for Q1 answers

You can tell that *Figure 4.15* connects the dots in *Figure 4.14* by modifying the values for `birthn` to each observation so that they match the values in the *x* axis. Also, the ICE plot lines illustrate a sample of the variation there is in the relationship between `birthn` and `birthorder` for firstborns. The color-coding visible once you run the code enriches the interpretation. You can tell that many of the purple and blue lines are erratic, even non-monotonic, and tend to have lower probabilities overall, while yellows and greens are more consistent and higher. It seems that the more you disagree with the statement in `Q1` ("*I have read an absurd number of books*"), the less reliable `birthn` is in predicting a firstborn.

Figure 4.15 can be viewed here:

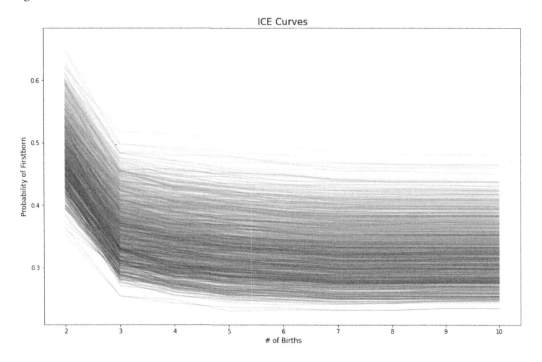

Figure 4.15 – Firstborn ICE plot as birthn increases, color-coded for Q1 answers

We can now do the same for `middle_child` with the same code, except we replace the first two arguments in the `plot_data_vs_ice` function, as follows:

```
mldatasets.plot_data_vs_ice(predict_prob_middle_child,\
                            'Probability of Middle Child',\
                            X=X_test_samp,\
                            feature_name='birthn',\
```

```
                                  feature_label='# of Births',\
                                  color_by='Q1', legend_key=legend_
key)
```

The preceding code generates two plots, just as we did with *Figure 4.14* and *Figure 4.15*. The second one is shown here in *Figure 4.16*:

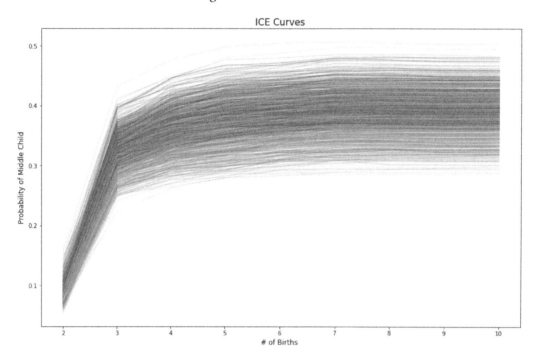

Figure 4.16 – Probability of middle-child ICE plot as birthn increases, color-coded for Q1 answers

The ICE plot lines for the middle child in *Figure 4.16* are more consistent than those for firstborns. All lines increase abruptly from 2 to 3, then smoothly from 3 to 6, and then plateau. The color-coding suggests that the more they agree with the statement in Q1, the less likely it is that they are middle children, no matter what age they are.

Lastly, let's try doing the same for lastborns as we did for the other two classes, as follows:

```
mldatasets.plot_data_vs_ice(predict_prob_last_born,\
                            'Probability of Lastborn',\
                            X=X_test_samp,\
                            feature_name='birthn',\
                            feature_label='# of Births',\
                            color_by='Q1', legend_key=legend_
key)
```

Figure 4.17, shown here, was outputted as a result of the preceding code:

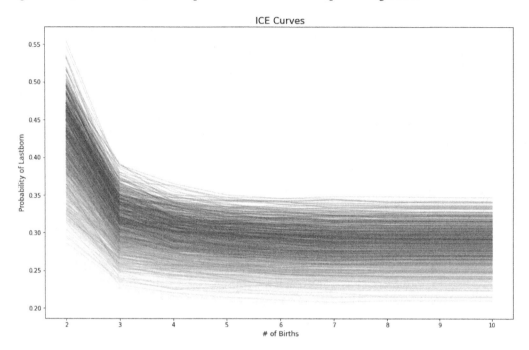

Figure 4.17 – Probability of lastborn ICE plot as birthn increases, color-coded for Q1 answers

The ICE plot for the probability of lastborns in *Figure 4.17* has even more variation than for firstborns. However, as with firstborns, the less in agreement with Q1 the more erratic the lines can be, but, unlike firstborns, agreement with Q1 coincides with less probability, no matter how much `birthn`.

Disadvantages of ICE

ICE curves, like PDPs, assume the independence of features, so they share the same disadvantages. In addition to that, with ICE you can't interact with two continuous or high-cardinality features. For instance, we were able to color-code for Q1 but only because there are six possible values for Q1. Another disadvantage is that it's hard to ascertain the average relationship between a feature and a target, but that's what PDP plots are for.

Ultimately, what ICE plots excel at is looking for clues in the variation of this relationship, and not on its aggregate.

Mission accomplished

The mission was to determine what machine learning could discover from a dataset of 40,000 quiz entries. The psychology researchers wanted to know if they could trust using this data to provide a path forward for their research. They also wanted to know if machine learning interpretation would show them which features and feature values impact the outcome the most.

Using PDPs, we discovered that there were some discrepancies with the distribution of age and birth order, since the proportion of middle children must increase with age. If any modeling exercise is to work in real-world scenarios, the training data **must match real-world distributions**. All is not all lost, though. You can take corrective measures by balancing these distributions. Significant changes likely have to be made to the data to make it more reliable for research purposes. That being said, since it's an online quiz made anonymously, you can expect lying to be commonplace, so the margin of error has to be set accordingly.

As for questions of transparency, according to PFI the number of births (`birthn`) was the most important feature by far. However, the exercise was successful in identifying questions such as `Q1` ("*I have read an absurd number of books*") and `Q13` ("*I boss people around*") that consistently correlate with birth order, and in validating their impact with **ICE plots**. We also uncovered some exciting interactions between age and the amount of time spent taking the test (`testelapse`), using PDPs. Once distribution issues are fixed with age, perhaps this will become more evident.

Summary

After reading this chapter, you should grasp the disadvantages of using the intrinsic parameters of a model to examine the importance of features. We have also answered the question: *What are some useful model-agnostic alternatives to rank features by importance and visualize their predictive impact?* In the next chapter, we will study even more robust global model-agnostic methods that overcome some of the challenges faced by those seen in this one.

Dataset sources

- *Open-Source Psychometrics Project*. (2019). Raw data from online personality tests. `https://openpsychometrics.org/_rawdata/`

Further reading

- Klecka, W. R. (1980). *Discriminant Analysis.* Quantitative Applications in the Social Sciences Series, No. 19. Thousand Oaks, CA: Sage Publications.

- Cardell, N. S., Joerding, W. and Li, Y. (1994). *Why some feedforward networks cannot learn some polynomials.* Neural Computation, 6, 763-768. `https://doi.org/10.1162/neco.1994.6.4.761`

- Boger, Z. and Guterman, H. (1997). *Knowledge extraction from artificial neural network models,* IEEE Systems, Man, and Cybernetics Conference, Orlando, FL. `https://doi.org/10.1109/ICSMC.1997.633051`

- Molnar, C. (2019). *Interpretable Machine Learning. A Guide for Making Black Box Models Explainable.* `https://christophm.github.io/interpretable-ml-book/`

5
Global Model-Agnostic Interpretation Methods

In the previous chapter, *Chapter 4, Fundamentals of Feature Importance and Impact*, we demonstrated how permutation feature importance was a better alternative to leveraging intrinsic model parameters for ranking features by their impact on model outcomes. We also learned how to employ partial dependence plots and individual conditional expectation plots to examine how model outcomes change across feature values and interactions. However, even though all these global model-agnostic methods are exceedingly popular, they have something in common – they are sensitive to collinear features.

This chapter will continue looking at global model-agnostic methods, two of which were designed to mostly mitigate multicollinearity's impact with a very robust statistical foundation. The first is **SHapley Additive exPlanations (SHAP)**, which, mostly, adheres to Shapley values' mathematical principles derived from coalitional game theory. The second is using **Accumulated Local Effects (ALE)** plots, which, by using conditional marginal distributions, provides a better alternative to **Partial Dependence Plots (PDPs)**. Lastly, another common way of explaining black-box models is through white-box models that approximate them, so we will broach the broad subject of **global surrogates**, which can be very accurate and efficient interpretation tools when chosen correctly.

These are the main topics we are going to cover in this chapter:

- Learning about Shapley values
- Interpreting SHAP summary and dependence plots
- Exploring **ALE** plots
- Explaining black-box models with global surrogates

Technical requirements

This chapter's example uses the `mldatasets`, `pandas`, `numpy`, `sklearn`, `tensorflow`, `xgboost`, `rulefit`, `matplotlib`, `seaborn`, `scipy`, `shap`, and `alepython` libraries. Instructions on how to install all of these libraries are in the preface. The code for this chapter is located here: `https://github.com/PacktPublishing/Interpretable-Machine-Learning-with-Python/tree/master/Chapter05`.

The mission

Energy efficiency is a significant concern to consumers that want to spend or pollute less. Therefore, it is in the purview of policymakers, regulators, environmental activists, public health officials, and manufacturers of energy-consuming technologies. In the United States alone, the transportation sector accounted for 28% (`https://www.eia.gov/energyexplained/use-of-energy/transportation.php`) of total energy consumption in 2019, of which more than half is consumed by light-duty passenger vehicles. And even though there has been an increase in the USA's electric car fleet over the last decade, most of their electricity still comes from fossil fuel power plants. Ultimately, this means that all passenger vehicles have a carbon footprint regardless of their fuel type.

For this exercise, let's say the US-based consumer advocacy non-profit that you work for has traditionally focused on car safety, and fraudulent sales practices are shifting their attention to energy efficiency. Safety laws enacted over the last few decades have dramatically reduced manufacturer liability by improving quality control and regulations. While safety is still a concern, it's mostly due to reckless driving and poor atmospheric conditions. Mechanical failure is the reason for only 2-3% of all car crashes. Only very occasionally can this be attributed to a vehicle or parts manufacturers such as brakes, suspension, transmission, or tires. The non-profit boasts that it has also been very successful in curbing fraud and discriminatory practices by car dealerships. Realizing that younger generations are both environmentally and resource-conscious, they want to remain relevant by advocating for fuel efficiency, which can be measured in **miles per gallon** (**MPG**). The higher this number, the more efficient. Fortunately, the U.S. Department of Energy (`https://www.fueleconomy.gov/feg/ws/`) has been recording this number for all vehicles in the country since 1984. The non-profit wants to explain how all the different variables have impacted MPG over the last few decades in their brochures. As their resident data scientist, they'd like you to find the most significant fuel efficiency predictors and possibly illustrate them in a human-interpretable manner.

The approach

You have been provided a dataset with thousands of vehicle models. It includes general, engine, pollution, drivetrain, chassis, and technical details for each model. To find the predictors for MPG, you could leverage tried and proven statistical methods such as hypothesis testing, correlation analysis, and intrinsically interpretable models such as GLMs to gain a solid data understanding. However, you would have to make sure you are using the right statistical methods on a case-by-case basis and check that your data meets their underlying assumptions. And even after all of that, your intrinsic models will lack sufficient predictive accuracy to underpin any findings. Many practitioners trust this classical approach. However, this book favors the view that black-box models can extract more knowledge from data and more reliably and efficiently than with the classical approach. Interpretable machine learning provides the toolset to do so.

To that end, let's take a seven-point shortcut that is not taught in applied statistics class!

1. Prepare all the features just so that they have no nulls and are all numerical.

2. Make sure that with these features, you can predict MPG well using black-box models. We will use neural networks and XGBoost for this example.

3. Evaluate on the test dataset to make sure it is not overfitting too much.

4. Use SHAP to understand how they reached their conclusions.

5. Perform some statistical tests to examine bivariate associations further and rule out any spurious correlations and systematic bias.

6. Explore feature effects on models more with ALE plots.

7. Gain further understanding of the underlying rules of the model with global surrogates.

Let's get started!

The preparations

You will find the code for this example here: `https://github.com/PacktPublishing/Interpretable-Machine-Learning-with-Python/blob/master/Chapter05/FuelEfficiency.ipynb`.

Loading the libraries

To follow this example, you need to install the following libraries:

- `mldatasets` to load the dataset

- `pandas` and `numpy` to manipulate it

- `sklearn` (scikit-learn), `tensorflow`, `xgboost`, and `rulefit` to split the data and fit the models

- `scipy` to perform statistical testing

- `matplotlib`, `seaborn`, `shap`, and `alepython` to visualize the interpretations

You should load all of them first:

```
import math
import os
import mldatasets
import pandas as pd
import numpy as np
from sklearn.model_selection import train_test_split
from sklearn import metrics, tree
import as tf
import tensorflow_docs as tfdocs
import tensorflow_docs.plots
import xgboost as xgb
```

```
from rulefit import RuleFit
from scipy import stats
import matplotlib.pyplot as plt
import seaborn as sns
import shap
from alepython import ale_plot
```

Let's check that TensorFlow has loaded the right version with the `print(tf.__version__)` command. It should be 2.0 or higher.

Understanding and preparing the data

Now, we load the data into a dataframe we will call `fueleconomy_df`. Please note that we are using `prepare=True`, which automatically prepares the features for you so you don't have to:

```
fueleconomy_df = mldatasets.load("vehicle-
fueleconomy",prepare=True)
```

There should be over 43,000 records and 84 columns. We can verify that this is the case with `info()`:

```
fueleconomy_df.info()
```

The output should check out. All features are numeric with no missing values, and categorical features have been already one-hot encoded for us because we used `prepare=True`.

The data dictionary

There are only 25 features, but they become 84 columns because of the categorical encoding, of which 3 are general, 6 engine, 3 pollution, 3 drivetrain, 7 chassis, 2 electronic, and one target feature in the dataset. We can outline the data dictionary broken down by those categories.

Here is a list of features from the **general** category:

- `make`: Categorical – the brand or manufacturer of the vehicle (out of almost 140 different ones)
- `model`: Categorical – the model of the vehicle (out of over $4,000$ different ones)
- `year`: Ordinal – year of the model (from $1984 - 2021$)

The following features are **engine** features:

- `fuelType`: Categorical – the primary type of fuel used by the engine.
- `cylinders`: Ordinal – the number of cylinders of the engine (from $2 - 16$). Generally, the more cylinders, the higher the horsepower.
- `displ`: Continuous – the engine displacement (in liters from $0.6 - 8.4$).
- `eng_dscr`: Text – a description of the engine made up of one or more codes concatenated together (codes found here: `https://www.fueleconomy.gov/feg/findacarhelp.shtml#engine`).
- `phevBlended`: Binary – **PHEV** stands for **Plug-In-Hybrid Vehicle** and `Blended` means that the vehicle will be powered by the battery and only supplemented by fuel. If true, it's using this mode of operation, called charge depleting mode.
- `atvType`: Categorical – alternative fuel types or technologies in use in the engine (out of 8 different ones).

The following are the **pollution** features in the dataset:

- `co2TailpipeGpm`: Continuous – tailpipe CO_2 in grams/mile.
- `co2`: Continuous – tailpipe CO_2 in grams/mile. For models after 2013, it is based on EPA tests. For previous years, CO_2 is estimated using an EPA emission factor (-1 =Not Available).
- `ghgScore`: Ordinal – EPA GHG score (from $0 - 10$, -1=Not available).

We have the following **drivetrain** features:

- `drive`: Categorical – drive axle type of vehicle (from 7 different ones)
- `trany`: Categorical – transmission descriptor mostly in the form "{type}, {speed}-spd," where the type only can be `Manual` or `Automatic`
- `trans_dscr`: Text – a more detailed description of transmission made up of one or more codes concatenated together (codes found here: `https://www.fueleconomy.gov/feg/findacarhelp.shtml#trany`)

Here's a list of **chassis** features:

- `VClass`: Categorical – type of vehicle (out of 34 different ones)
- `pv4`: Continuous – 4-door passenger volume (in cubic feet)
- `lv4`: Continuous – 4-door luggage volume (in cubic feet)
- `lv2`: Continuous – 2-door luggage volume (in cubic feet)

- `pv2`: Continuous – 2-door passenger volume (in cubic feet)
- `hlv`: Continuous – hatchback passenger volume (in cubic feet)
- `hpv`: Continuous – hatchback luggage volume (in cubic feet)

The following are **electronics** features:

- `startStop`: Categorical – start-stop technology included in the vehicle (Y:=yes, N=no, blank=older vehicles)
- `tCharger`: Categorical – vehicle is turbocharged (T=yes, blank=otherwise)

The following is the **target** feature:

- `comb08`: Continuous – combined MPG. For electric and CNG vehicles, this number is **MPGe (gasoline-equivalent miles per gallon)**.

Now that we have taken a peek at the data, we can briefly prepare the data for modeling, and then fit some models!

Data preparation

As you could tell by the `info()` summary, there were no nulls left; we have many categorical encoded columns and all columns are either numeric or boolean, except for `make` and `model`, which we will drop. The dataset is almost ready. All we need to do now is split the dataset into train, test, and validation datasets. To accomplish this, we first put our target feature alone in `y`, everything else except `make` and `model` in `X`, then split `X` and `y` into train (85%) and test (15%) and then `X_train` and `Y_train` into train (80%) and validation (20%). As usual, it's essential to define a seed that we call `rand` for our `random_state` to ensure reproducibility:

```
rand = 9
y = fueleconomy_df['comb08']
X = fueleconomy_df.drop(['comb08','make','model'], axis=1).
copy()
X_train, X_test, y_train, y_test =\
        train_test_split(X, y, test_size=0.15, random_
state=rand)
X_train, X_val, y_train, y_val =\
        train_test_split(X_train, y_train,          test_
size=0.2, random_state=rand)
```

OK! We are now good to go with the modeling and evaluation steps!

Modeling and performance evaluation for deep neural networks

Inconsistencies in model outcomes are compounded by interpretation difficulties, which is why reproducibility is paramount. However, neural network reproducibility can be notoriously difficult to ensure, and given their stochastic nature, it is even more critical to set the seed to have somewhat consistent results. The following code tends to work for TensorFlow 2.0+:

```
os.environ['PYTHONHASHSEED']=str(rand)
tf.random.set_seed(rand)
np.random.seed(rand)
```

We will create a feedforward (`Sequential`) neural network with two hidden layers with 64 hidden nodes each. In Keras, this can be achieved by adding the `Input`, hidden (`Dense(64)`), and output (`Dense(1)`) layers. In between the `Input` and first hidden layer, we are also adding a `Normalization` layer. This layer normalizes all features to have a mean of 0 and a standard deviation of 1. This step is usually done in a separate pre-processing stage, but there are many benefits to have a model pipeline or model itself take care of this step, including cleaner code and increased reliability. After we build our model (`fitted_nn_model`), we can compile using the **mean squared error (MSE)** as our loss and only metric (`metrics=['mse']`). We will use the Adam optimizer with a very low learning rate (`lr = 0.0005`). This will make the training slower but it has converged at a lower MSE with this hyperparameter value. You can use `summary()` to print all the layers with shapes, and parameters for each:

```
fitted_nn_model = tf.keras.Sequential([
    tf.keras.Input(shape=[len(X_train.keys())]),
    tf.keras.layers.experimental.preprocessing.Normalization(),
    tf.keras.layers.Dense(64, activation='relu'),
    tf.keras.layers.Dense(64, activation='relu'),
    tf.keras.layers.Dense(1)
  ])
fitted_nn_model.compile(loss='mean_squared_error',\
                optimizer=tf.keras.optimizers.Adam(lr =
0.0005), metrics=['mse'])
fitted_nn_model.summary()
```

The network should converge somewhere between the 700th and 1,300th epochs. Rather than aiming for a fixed amount of epochs, we can set it at 3,000 and implement early stopping as a callback in the `fit` function. This `EarlyStopping` callback will monitor the validation loss and see if it hasn't improved in the last 200 epochs (`patience`) with an exceedingly low minimum to qualify as an improvement (`min_delta=0.0001`). We also make sure to restore the weights of the epoch with the best validation loss (`restore_best_weights=True`). When we fit the model, we can store the training history (`nn_history`):

```
Model: "sequential"
_____

Layer (type)                    Output Shape                  Param #
========================================================================
normalization (Normalization (None, 81)                       163
_____

dense (Dense)                   (None, 64)                     5248
_____

dense_1 (Dense)                 (None, 64)                     4160
_____

dense_2 (Dense)                 (None, 1)                      65
========================================================================
Total params: 9,636
Trainable params: 9,473
Non-trainable params: 163
_____
```

The network should converge somewhere between the 700th and 1,300th epoch. Rather than aiming for a fixed amount of epochs, we can set it at 3,000 and implement early stopping as a callback in the `fit` function. This `EarlyStopping` callback will monitor the validation loss and see if it hasn't improved in the last 200 epochs (`patience`) with an exceedingly low minimum to qualify as an improvement (`min_delta=0.0001`). We also make sure to restore the weights of the epoch with the best validation loss (`restore_best_weights=True`). When we fit the model, we can store the training history (`nn_history`):

```python
es = \
tf.keras.callbacks.EarlyStopping(monitor='val_loss',mode='min',
                                 verbose=1, patience=200,\
                                 min_delta=0.0001,\
                                 restore_best_weights=\
                                 True)
nn_history = fitted_nn_model.fit(\
                  X_train.astype(float), y_train.
                  astype(float),\
                  epochs=3000, batch_size=128,\
                  validation_data=(X_val.astype(float),\
                  y_val.astype(float)), verbose=1,\
                  callbacks=[es])
```

The `tensorflow_docs` library comes with a plotter specifically designed for the training history (`HistoryPlotter`), which is fantastic because you can plot the history in one or two lines of code:

```python
nn_plotter = tfdocs.plots.HistoryPlotter(smoothing_std=2)
nn_plotter.plot({'Early Stopping': nn_history}, metric
"mse")
plt.show()
```

The preceding code produced *Figure 5.1*. It depicts how after 750 epochs, the validation MSE hovers around 0.75 at its minimum, so the early stopping is triggered:

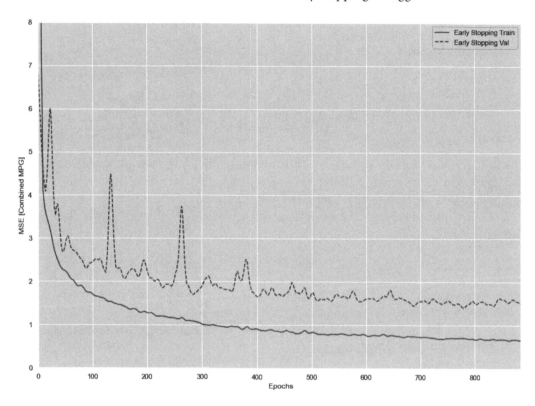

Figure 5.1 – The neural network training history for train and validation MSE

Now let's evaluate the predictive performance. You could always use the Model. evaluate function to see how well the fitted model predicts the test dataset, but it will do it with the loss function and metrics, both **MSE**. We rather use the RMSE instead, which is easier to interpret. To compute the RMSE, we have to run the Model.predict function to get the predictions on both train and test datasets, and then by using scikit-learn's mean_squared_error with squared=False, you can get the RMSE for both. We will also use R-squared, which is a goodness-of-fit measure that tells you what percentage of variability is explained by the model:

```
y_train_nn_pred =\
fitted_nn_model.predict(X_train.astype(float))
y_test_nn_pred =\
fitted_nn_model.predict(X_test.astype(float))
RMSE_nn_train = metrics.mean_squared_error(y_train,\
```

```
                                    y_train_nn_pred, \
                                    squared=False)
RMSE_nn_test = metrics.mean_squared_error(y_test,\
                                    y_test_nn_pred,\
squared=False)
R2_nn_test = metrics.r2_score(y_test, y_test_nn_pred)
print('RMSE_train: %.4f_test: %.4f: %.4f' %
                (RMSE_nn_train, RMSE_nn_test,
                R2_nn_test))
```

The RMSE scores for train and test are close enough, which suggests minimal overfitting, and any RMSE under one is excellent because it means that, on average, the predicted combined MPG is no more than 1 MPG from the observed combined MPG. Also, an R-squared of 99% means that the model explains an overwhelming majority of the variability:

```
RMSE_train: 0.7012   RMSE_test: 0.7878    r2: 0.9907
```

We can also visualize how well the model fits by plotting the observed versus predicted y (combined MPG) with a regression line. We can use the regplot function of seaborn for this, which can deliver this plot in one line. We will customize the scatter plot to make each data point appear as 30% transparent ('alpha':0.3) and green (color="g"), axis labels, and font sizes:

```
plt.ylabel('Predicted Combined MPG', fontsize=14)
sns.regplot(x=y_test, y=y_test_nn_pred, color="g",\
        scatter_kws={'alpha':0.3})
plt.xlabel('Observed Combined MPG (comb08)', fontsize=14)
```

The preceding code outputs *Figure 5.2*:

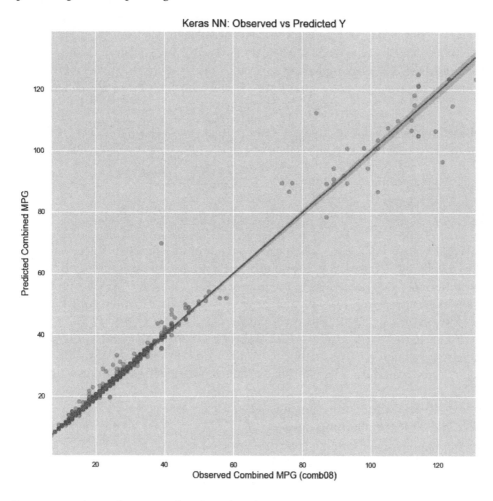

Figure 5.2 – Observed versus predicted combined MPG plot with a regression line for the neural network model

The plot in *Figure 5.2* conveys how well the model is predicting the actual combined MPG. The points are closest to the regression line in the bottom-left quadrant, suggesting that the lower the value is, the better the model is at predicting it, which is not surprising considering how many more points are in the bottom-left quadrant than in the top-right one. We can proceed with training an XGBoost model!

Modeling and performance evaluation for XGBoost

XGBoost is a library that implements gradient boosted decision trees much like scikit-learn's `GradientBoostingRegressor`, an ensemble method we have used in previous chapters. However, while scikit-learn follows the original gradient boosting algorithm to a tee, XGBoost implemented several optimizations that make it faster and more scalable, increase predictive performance, and potentially make it even less prone to overfitting.

The official implementation of XGBoost requires that you store your data in DMatrix objects to increase efficiency even further, like this:

```
dtrain = xgb.DMatrix(X_train, label=y_train)
dval = xgb.DMatrix(X_val, label=y_val)
dtest = xgb.DMatrix(X_test, label=y_test)
```

For this exercise, we will use the scikit-learn wrapper of XGBoost, which converts data to DMatrix objects automatically. The reason for this is that many model-agnostic interpretation methods expect you to use functions that follow the template popularized by scikit-learn, such as `fit(X, y)` and `predict(X)`, where X and y are arrays or sparse matrices, usually NumPy arrays or pandas DataFrames. However, XGBoost doesn't conform to this expectation because DMatrix is an entirely different data type. Nonetheless, the interpretation methods are still technically model-agnostic because they don't depend on the model's intrinsic parameters. Yet, in practice, you would have to write a class that acted as an intermediate, much like the scikit-learn wrapper is doing in this case. The only drawback is that the XGBoost library has many parameters not available in the wrapper. Fortunately, we didn't need to use many of them in this case. We only need to set the maximum tree depth to 7 (`max_depth`), the learning rate to 0.6 (`learning_rate`), and our objective as regression minimizing the squared error (`reg:squarederror`), and then run 4 jobs in parallel (`n_jobs`). It's easy to fit the model while evaluating the RMSE using both the training and validation datasets:

```
fitted_xgb_model = xgb.XGBRegressor(max_depth=7,\
learning_rate=0.6,\
                    n_jobs=4, objective='reg:squarederror',
                    random_state=rand, n_estimators=50).\
            fit(X_train, y_train, eval_metric='rmse',\
            eval_set=[(X_train, y_train),(X_val, y_val)])
```

Once the model has been fitted, we can plot the training history with `matplotlib`. This history can be retrieved from the fitted XGBoost model using the `evals_result()` function, which returns a dictionary. Since we placed two validation datasets in `eval_set`, this dictionary has two items named `validation_0` and `validation_1`. The first one corresponds to the training evaluation, and the second to the validation:

```
plt.plot(fitted_xgb_model.evals_result()['validation_0']
['rmse'])
```

```
plt.plot(fitted_xgb_model.evals_result()['validation_1']
['rmse'])
```

```
plt.ylabel('RMSE [Combined MPG]', fontsize=14)
```

```
plt.xlabel('Round', fontsize=14)
```

```
plt.legend(['Train', 'Val'], loc='upper right')
```

As you can appreciate in *Figure 5.3*, the model converges quickly at close to 0.75 validation RMSE. Although the gap between training and validation RMSE could be potentially narrowed by adjusting hyperparameters, it still indicates relatively minor overfitting. Not a primary concern for a model we don't plan to productionize, and the error remains low with unseen data:

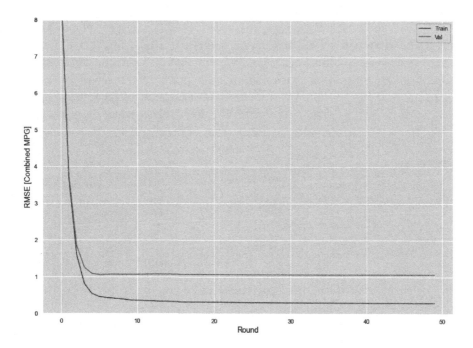

Figure 5.3 – The XGBoost training history for the train and validation RMSE

Let's evaluate against the test dataset to see if this holds true as we did with the neural network:

```
y_train_xgb_pred = fitted_xgb_model.predict(X_train)
y_test_xgb_pred = fitted_xgb_model.predict(X_test)
RMSE_xgb_train = metrics.mean_squared_error(y_train,\
                                            y_train_xgb_pred,
                                            squared=False)
RMSE_xgb_test = metrics.mean_squared_error(y_test,\
                    y_test_xgb_pred, squared=False)
R2_xgb_test = metrics.r2_score(y_test, y_test_xgb_pred)
print('RMSE_train: %.4f_test: %.4f: %.4f' %\
                (RMSE_xgb_train, RMSE_xgb_test,\
                R2_xgb_test))
```

Both the test and train RMSE are even lower now, and the R-square even higher, than with the neural network, which was already pretty good. The predictive performance for this model is also sufficient to be useful for global modular interpretation purposes:

```
RMSE_train: 0.2974   RMSE_test: 0.6809    r2: 0.9930
```

Regarding interpretation, like most tree-based models, XGBoost comes with feature importance capabilities. XGBoost has three different algorithms to compute feature importance: how often the feature appears in the tree (`weight`), the average reduction in error due to a feature (`gain`), and the number of observations affected by a split involving a feature (`cover`). The default is `importance_type="weight"`. Using the following code for `plot_importance`, you can try all three of them and see how much they vary:

```
sns.set()
fig, ax = plt.subplots(figsize=(12, 8))
xgb.plot_importance(fitted_xgb_model, max_num_features=12,\
ax=ax, importance_type="weight")
plt.show()
```

The previous code generates *Figure 5.4*, which depicts one of the many ways of calculating feature importance for XGBoost, but which one should you trust? If you take the top features for all of these ways into consideration, you will find features in common, and it's highly likely that these represent the features that are truly making the most difference in the model:

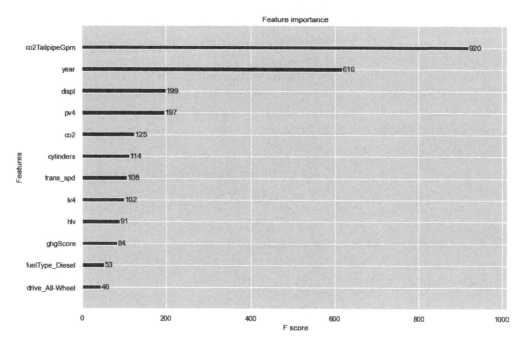

Figure 5.4 – Feature importance as calculated by the XGBoost library using weight

However, we still would like to quantify how much difference is being made and under what circumstances it is being made, and ideally by using a dependable method that is statistically grounded and model-agnostic… meet Shapley values!

Learning about Shapley values

Several chapters in this book will revisit one method in particular: **SHAP**. So, it's best that we get an overview now of the mathematical foundation and the properties behind it. We will do this through a basketball analogy.

Imagine you are blindfolded at a basketball game where a loudspeaker announces whenever a player for your team enters or exits the court or the team scores. The loudspeaker won't tell you who scored and you are blindfolded, so you don't know who scored or who even assisted! They only refer to players by number, and you don't know who they are anyway. They could be good players or bad players. At any given time, your best guess would be that whoever last joined had something to do with the latest outcome, whether good or bad. Therefore, over time you start getting a sense of which players correlate the most with the better results and which have the opposite effect or none at all.

What if we were able to simulate this game with every possible combination of players arriving in different orders many times and average all the differences in scores when each player joined? Then, even if it wasn't precise for one game, for many games we would get a better idea of who were the most valuable players. At a high level, in **coalitional game theory**, also known as **cooperative game theory**, the different combinations of players are **coalitions**, the differences in scores are **marginal contributions**, and the **Shapley value** is the average of these contributions over many simulations. For a model, the features are the players, different subsets of features are the coalitions of players, differences in predictive error are marginal contributions, and you are blindfolded because, of course, the model is a black box or is at least treated as such!

The math involved in calculating Shapley values for a model gets more complicated than the basketball analogy may suggest because it involves sets and factorials, and we won't get into all the algorithmic details described in the papers that adapted Shapley values to machine learning. However, it can be explained simply and intuitively. You have a full coalition with all your features, and you have all the possible subsets of the features minus the feature you are evaluating. The contribution of a feature, also known as the payoff, is a reduction in predictive error, for regression, or an increase in probability for classification. So, to calculate the Shapley value for a feature and a specific subset, you calculate the contribution when you add that feature to that subset. All this is weighted by the probability of randomly drawing that subset of features over all possible subsets. And these weighted contributions are added up across all possible subsets, and voilá! You have your Shapley value. Essentially, it's an *average marginal contribution by a feature across all possible subsets*.

In practice, though, the computation time for Shapley values must invariably grow exponentially as features increase, so a brute-force approach would be very resource-intensive. There are several strategies to minimize computation. The most common one is sampling only some of the possible subsets of features using a method called **Monte Carlo sampling**, which randomly samples from a probability distribution. Also, you can remove a player from a game but you cannot remove a feature from a trained model, so how do you represent how the model performs with and without a feature? Permutation importance does this by shuffling features, but Shapley's algorithm calculates the features' *expected value* over the entire dataset instead. This makes sense because this would be the *best guess* of the value of a feature, and it's a reasonable assumption. It may not be perfect, but it only serves as a baseline to compare the contributions of the feature. Consistency is key.

Speaking of consistency, Shapley values have several properties derived from coalitional game theory that make it ideal as a feature importance method:

- **Dummy**: If a feature i never contributes any marginal value, $Shapley_i = 0$.

- **Substitutability**: If two given features i and j contribute equally to all their possible subsets, $Shapley_i = Shapley_j$.

- **Additivity**: If a model p is an ensemble of k submodels, the contributions of a feature i in the submodels should add up; $Shapley_i^p = \sum_{n=1}^{k} Shapley_j^n$.

- **Efficiency**: Likewise, all Shapley values must add up as the difference between predictions and expected values.

At the time of writing, there are no "pure" Shapley value implementations for Python. Even R implementations use sampling to cut computation time. However, Python's most popular implementation, SHAP, takes even more shortcuts by leveraging some model classes' intrinsic parameters, namely, tree-based and deep learning models, as well as linear surrogate models for the model-agnostic approach.

Interpreting SHAP summary and dependence plots

SHapley Additive exPlanations (SHAP) is a collection of methods, or explainers, that approximate Shapley values while adhering to its mathematical properties, for the most part. The paper calls these values SHAP values, but SHAP will be used interchangeably with Shapley in this book. However, it must be noted that the authors of SHAP took a few liberties with the properties. For instance, some explainers don't comply with the dummy property and leverage reference background data to simulate missing values. Despite these issues, because of SHAP being grounded in other solid properties, it's still better than alternatives studied in *Chapter 4, Fundamentals of Feature Importance and Impact*.

It has three properties that are loosely based on Shapley's:

- **Local accuracy**: Equivalent to Shapley's efficiency property.

- **Consistency**: Encompasses additivity and substitutability axioms, and, in theory, dummy as well.

- **Missingness**: This means that if a feature is missing, its Shapley value is zero. It's a sanity-check property that, in practice, is only needed when features are constant.

Many of the explainers unify other interpretation methods to perform approximation efficiently. For this reason, four of the explainers aren't model-agnostic (see *Figure 5.5*) because the methods unified call into leveraging the model's structure or parameters. The particulars of these algorithms are discussed in the main SHAP paper, "*A Unified Approach to Interpreting Model Predictions*," as well as being discussed in a paper written for tree-based models, TreeSHAP, which was later renamed as TreeExplainer. In addition to this one, two methods work exclusively with the deep learning frameworks TensorFlow/ Keras and PyTorch, which are based on the **DeepLift** and **Expected Gradients** methods, respectively. And there is one that will only work with scikit-learn's linear models. Besides those model-specific explainers, the KernelExplainer, SamplingExplainer, and various other ones are model-agnostic, with some caveats:

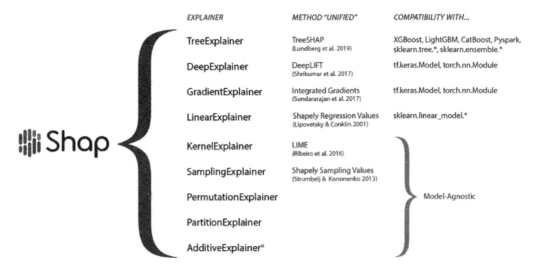

Figure 5.5 – Summary of SHAP explainers

We will now briefly introduce each one of the core SHAP explainers in *Figure 5.5*:

- **TreeExplainer** was specifically designed to efficiently approximate SHAP values for tree-based models such as tree ensembles like XGBoost or Random Forest or CART Decision Trees. Because it uses the conditional expectation value function instead of marginal expectation, it can assign values different from zero to uninfluential features, thus violating the Shapley dummy property. As discussed in *Chapter 4, Fundamentals of Feature Importance and Impact*, this has ramifications when features are collinear.

- **DeepExplainer** works only with deep learning models, and the method unified was **DeepLIFT**. This method has a simple premise, which is that the importance of a feature can be attributed to the difference in the output when provided a reference "neutral" input or baseline. This baseline input could be anything, but it signifies the absence of a feature. A safe route and one chosen by the SHAP library is to use the dataset's feature-wise mean. It then defines the multiplier for each layer as inputs over outputs once the baseline has been deducted ($y - y_{baseline} / x - x_{baseline}$) during backpropagation. The chain rule is applied to the multipliers just as it would be applied to the gradients. The feature importance for a specific instance is the difference between the input and the baseline multiplied by partial "slope" produced during backpropagation for the multipliers. SHAP then takes these outputs and adapts them to comply with SHAP properties.

- **GradientExplainer** has several unified methods under a single umbrella, but the primary one is **Expected Gradients**, an offshoot of **Integrated Gradients** and **SmoothGrad**. We won't explain these here in detail because we will do so in *Chapter 8, Visualizing Convolutional Neural Networks*. As we will learn then, like **DeepLIFT**, Integrated Gradients uses a baseline that represents the absence of the features, and it integrates from the baseline between the output and the input. The SHAP library uses a similar concept called Expected Gradients, which reformulates the integral as an expectation. It then uses the background dataset as a sampling reference values for this expectation, leading to a combined expectation of gradients that converge as attributions that add up much like SHAP values are supposed to do.

- **LinearExplainer** is a very basic explainer inspired solely by one of the first papers about Shapley in the context of supervised learning models. It is limited to only scikit-learn linear models.

- **KernelExplainer** is the most popular model-agnostic method, and it's based on **LIME**, which we will discuss further in *Chapter 6, Local Model-Agnostic Interpretation Methods*. It follows the same steps as LIME, such as fitted weighted linear models, but it uses Shapley sample coalitions and uses a different Kernel, which returns SHAP values as the coefficients. Also, because it replaces absent features with random data while making sample coalitions, it has problems with the dummy property and thus collinear features. We will also discuss this further in *Chapter 6, Local Model-Agnostic Interpretation Methods*.

- **SamplingExpainer** is solely based on the first paper that introduced a sampling approach to approximate Shapley values and is also model-agnostic, but it assumes feature independence. It's a fairly good alternative to KernelExplainer when you have an extensive background dataset, which would be needed for sparse data, for instance.

- **PermutationExplainer** is the closest you can get to brute-force Shapley value approximation. It operates by permutating all the features in both forward and backward directions. If it's done once, it captures SHAP values for up to second-order interactions but can be run more times to achieve even higher fidelity.

- **PartitionExplainer** computes SHAP values on a tree that defines a hierarchy of features. This is recommended when many of your features belong to a group or category or have highly correlated features.

- **AdditiveExplainer** will accept any arbitrary predict function, so it's model-agnostic but will fail if the model is not a **Generalized Additive Model (GAM)**.

In this chapter, we will use GradientExplainer for the Keras model and TreeExplainer for the XGBoost model. But these aren't model-agnostic explainers. Why would we use them in a chapter called *Global Model-Agnostic Interpretation Methods*? Because SHAP as a whole is model-agnostic, because all explainers can collectively cover any model class and use case, be it for tabular, image, or text datasets. More importantly, they can be initialized more or less in the same way and have a consistent set of plots that can be used for interpretation. We will learn how to interpret three of these plots in this chapter. And in subsequent chapters, we will employ KernelExplainer and DeepExplainer and extend to other SHAP plots.

Before we get on with interpretation, we must first perform two simple steps – these can be tricky in some cases, so we will walk through them:

1. **Initializing explainers**: The first step for any SHAP explainer is to initialize it. `TreeExplainer` only requires the fitted tree-based model (`fitted_xgb_model`):

```
shap_xgb_explainer = shap.TreeExplainer(fitted_xgb_model)
```

On the other hand, GradientExplainer requires a background dataset. We can either take a sample or summarize it using `shap.kmeans(data, K)`. We will do a sample of 150 using `np.choice`. Now, `print(background.shape)` should confirm that we have selected 150 samples of the test dataset and, naturally, it has 81 features. Then, to initialize the explainer, we plug in our model (`fitted_nn_model`) and the `background` data. Please note that we are converting the pandas DataFrame to a NumPy array of floats to have it work with TensorFlow:

```
background = \
X_train.iloc[np.random.choice(X_train.shape[0], 150,\
                              replace=False)]
print(background.shape)
shap_nn_explainer =
shap.GradientExplainer(fitted_nn_model,\
                       background.astype(float).
values)
```

Once we have initialized the SHAP explainers, we can use them to calculate SHAP values.

2. **Computing SHAP values**: All explainers have a shap_values function, which takes any amount of observations as long as they match the features' dimensions and compute the SHAP values for them. We will do this for the train and test datasets of the XGBoost model. As discussed in *Chapter 4, Fundamentals of Feature Importance and Impact*, interpreting how a model performs against training data and test data can have different benefits. And even though we are interested in understanding what the model finds in previously unseen data, it's a good sanity check to compare both to ensure that they are almost entirely consistent:

```
shap_xgb_values_train = \
shap_xgb_explainer.shap_values(X_train)
print(shap_xgb_values_train.shape)
shap_xgb_values_test =
shap_xgb_explainer.shap_values(X_test)
print(shap_xgb_values_test.shape)
```

The preceding code should output tuples that match the dimensions of the training ((29389, 81)) and test datasets ((6484, 81)). There should be one SHAP value for each feature for each observation. Unlike other model interpretation methods, the values derived by SHAP are granular enough to be used for all kinds of global and local interpretation, without subsequent fitting or postprocessing.

Now, let's compute the neural network SHAP values for the test dataset and output the type of the object returned by `shap_values`. Note that it's a list and not an array. In theory, only multiple-output models, such as classifiers, produce a list, but single-output regression neural network models also return a list. In this case, the SHAP values you are looking for are the first item on the list (`shap_nn_values_test[0]`):

```
shap_nn_values_test =\
          shap_nn_explainer.shap_values(X_test.astype(float).
values)
print(type(shap_nn_values_test))
print(shap_nn_values_test[0].shape)
```

The preceding snippet should output the SHAP values' dimensions for the neural network model and the test dataset (`(6484, 81)`).

Generating SHAP summary plots

The first thing you can do with SHAP values is generate a `summary_plot` instance. The first parameter is the values followed by the data used to produce them and, optionally, the type of plot (`plot_type`). We will plot the XGBoost summary plot for train and test so we can compare them:

```
shap.summary_plot(shap_xgb_values_train, X_train,
plot_type="dot")
shap.summary_plot(shap_xgb_values_test, X_test,
plot_type="dot")
```

The preceding code produced the plots in *Figure 5.6*. You can tell that they are very similar and more or less consistent up to the ninth feature from top to bottom. The features are ranked by importance from top to bottom. And a line divides the impact of these features, separating the negative and the positive. There are dots on both sides for all features, and the amount of dots indicates how much a feature impacts the model negatively (left) or positively (right):

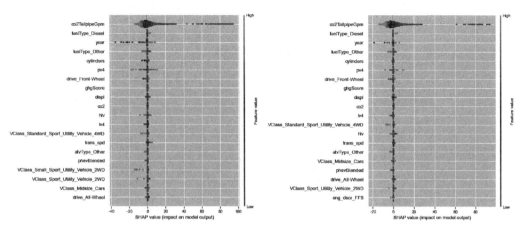

Figure 5.6 – SHAP's summary plot for the XGBoost model for both training and test data

We can tell that the leftmost dots belong to `year`, so they correlate the most with a lower combined MPG. However, they are also outliers, because most of the dots for `year` are concentrated around the middle area. The dots are color-coded, so you can attribute them to high, middle, or low feature values. For instance, we can tell that the outliers are all middle-value years. In other words, in the 37 years spanning between 1984 and 2021, those in the middle are 1996-2009. Those years make sense because they correspond with some of the years with the cheapest oil and the boom of the US economy ending with a financial crisis and the highest oil prices ever. Big gas-guzzling sport utility vehicles were common in this era.

Next, we can output `summary_plot` for the neural network SHAP values and compare it to XGBoost:

```
shap.summary_plot(shap_nn_values_test[0], X_test,\
plot_type="dot")
```

The preceding snippet outputs *Figure 5.7*. The first feature, `co2TailpipeGpm`, is consistent with XGBoost's. High values correlate negatively and low values correlate positively, producing an almost perfect gradient between both extremes. Most values are distributed in the middle. Besides that, it shouldn't be surprising that none of the other features matches the same order. Even `year` is not only less important than for the XGBoost model, overall, but no predictions seem to be very negatively impacted by `year`:

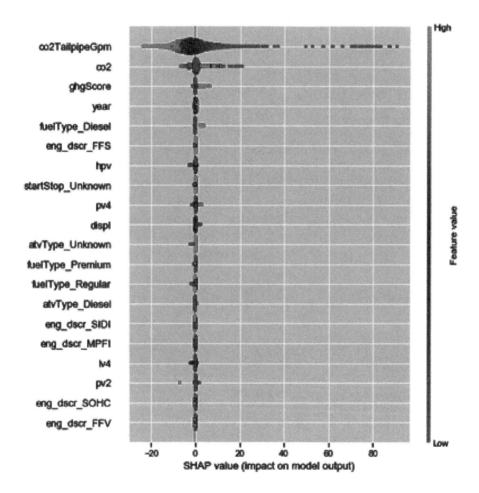

Figure 5.7 – SHAP's summary plot for the neural network model for the test data only

The differences between *Figure 5.6* and *Figure 5.7* can be attributed to the models learning different things about the predictor variables to predict the outcome. It's like asking two students that went to the same class to explain the answer to a question based on what they learned in that class. Assuming they are good students, their explanations will make sense in terms of connecting the question to the answer. They will include many of the same elements in their reasoning, but they will be prioritized and interconnected differently. After all, these students reason differently because they are different people. We are using two models in this exercise precisely because it's better to learn from two students than one!

Understanding interactions

Feature interactions in black-box models are a messy business, but if you dig deep enough, you can find some answers as to how and why they are interacting. Since we are learning from two machine learning models, it makes sense to derive insights from both. And there are a few thousand possible bivariate interactions between our 81 features. However, the vast majority of the average impact on the model output lies in the first feature. Trailing far behind are the other top four or five features. And if you change summary_plot to plot_type="bar", you can observe this more easily. It is very likely that we will find the most salient interactions among this top tier of features.

To this end, let's look into the interactions between the top five features for XGBoost (co2TailpipeGpm, fuelType_Diesel, year, cylinders, and ghgScore) and one that is the second most important for the neural network (co2) but the seventh most important for XGBoost. We create a list (top_features_1) with these features and append the comb08 response variable to it. Then, we subset the train data frame by these features and save it as top_df:

```
top_features_1 = ['comb08'] + ['co2TailpipeGpm',\
 'fuelType_Diesel','co2', 'year', 'ghgScore', 'cylinders']
top_df = fueleconomy_df.loc[X_train.index, top_features_1]
```

Next, we can visualize the **Spearman correlation coefficients** of the features represented in this data frame (`top_df`) with a heatmap. This method measures the **monotonicity** between two features. It outputs a number between -1 and 1, indicating both the strength and direction of the relationship. Values closest to both extremes are the strongest, either negatively or positively, while values nearer zero are the least strong. Spearman coefficients can depict nonlinear relationships as long as they are monotonic. Although this method is a good starting point to prioritize which interactions to examine further, it must be cautioned that a nonlinear relationship that is not monotonic won't be considered strong by this method. A parabolic curve will have a zero Spearman coefficient because it's symmetrically non-monotonic despite there clearly being a significant relationship:

```
corrs = stats.spearmanr(top_df).correlation
mask = np.zeros_like(corrs)
mask[np.triu_indices_from(mask)] = True
ax = sns.heatmap(
corrs, vmin=-1, vmax=1, center=0, mask=mask, square=True,\
    cmap=sns.diverging_palette(20, 220, n=200),\
xticklabels=top_df.columns, yticklabels=top_df.columns
)
```

The preceding snippet produces the plot depicted in *Figure 5.8*. You can tell that `cylinders` and `co2TailpipeGpm` have the largest monotonic correlation with the response variable (`comb08`) and that they are both negative. The rest of the features have a weaker positive monotonic correlation:

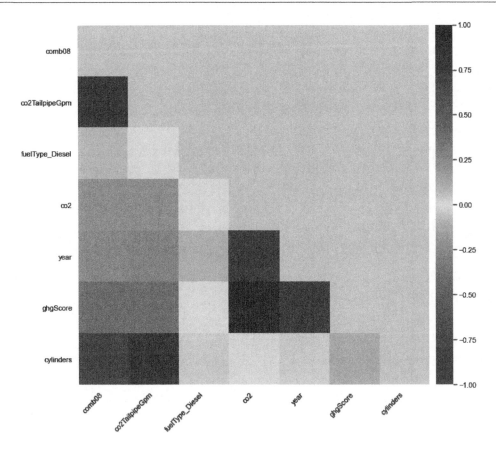

Figure 5.8 – Spearman's correlation plot for top features for both models

Using `spearmanr`, we can also extract the p-values of the hypothesis test that validates the correlation. To be statistically rigorous, you can use point-biserial instead of `fuelType_Diesel` because it's a dichotomous feature. The point-biserial correlation coefficient is like Spearman but between a dichotomous and a continuous variable. It doesn't assume monotonicity, but it makes other assumptions that can be tested for. We won't get into the details here, but it's usually a more robust indicator for this kind of relationship:

```
print('spearman2TailpipeGpm→comb08: %.3f-val: %.4f' %\
        (stats.spearmanr(X_train.co2TailpipeGpm.values,\
        top_df.comb08.values)))
print('point-biserial_Diesel→comb08: %.3f-val: %.4f' %\
        (stats.pointbiserialr(top_df.fuelType_Diesel.
values, top_df.comb08.values)))
```

```
print('spearman→comb08: %.3f-val: %.4f' %\
     (stats.spearmanr(X_train.co2.values,\
top_df.comb08.values)))
print('spearman→comb08: %.3f-val: %.4f' %\
     (stats.spearmanr(X_train.year.values,
top_df.comb08.values)))
print('spearman→comb08: %.3f-val: %.4f' %\
  (stats.spearmanr(top_df.ghgScore.values,
top_df.comb08.values)))
print('spearman→comb08: %.3f-val: %.4f' %
           (stats.spearmanr(X_train.cylinders.values,\
           top_df.comb08.values)))
```

The previous code outputs the following. The p-values below 0.05 validate the correlation hypothesis for all:

```
spearman      co2TailpipeGpm→comb08    corr: -0.994      p-val:
0.0000
point-biserial   fuelType_Diesel→comb08   corr: 0.062 p-val:
0.0000
spearman      co2→comb08         corr: 0.223 p-val: 0.0000
spearman      year→comb08        corr: 0.255 p-val: 0.0000
spearman      ghgScore→comb08        corr: 0.374 p-val: 0.0000

spearman      cylinders→comb08     corr: -0.785      p-val: 0.0000
```

The Spearman heatmap has helped point us in a few interesting directions:

- According to XGBoost's SHAP values, `cylinders` is only the fourth most important feature, yet it appears to be highly monotonically correlated with the target variable and `co2TailpipeGpm`, and to a lesser extent with `ghgScore`.

- According to the neural network's SHAP values, the `co2` feature is only in the top five, yet it has a higher Spearman's than `fuelType_Diesel`. Why is that?

- The neural network also seemed to value `ghgScore` more, and in the correlation heatmap, it has high values for `co2` and `year`. There appears to be something going on between these three features.

An excellent way to examine these feature interactions is with SHAP dependence plots while measuring correlations with `scipy`. We will also plot some scatter plots to compare our findings with the underlying data.

SHAP dependence plots

A SHAP dependence plot is between the SHAP value for a feature on the y-axis and the feature values on the x-axis. Essentially, it shows how over the values represented in the x-axis, the impact on the outcome changes on the y-axis.

A single function (`dependence_plot`) will plot the dependence plot. It just requires the name (`co2TailpipeGpm`) or index of the feature, followed by the SHAP values (`shap_xgb_values_test`) and their corresponding data (`X_test`). Optionally, you can specify an interaction term (`interaction_index`). We are not showing the plot immediately (`show=False`) because we want to make it bigger (`fig.set_size_inches(12,8)`) and then use `plt.show()` to show it. We are also making the dots translucent (`alpha=0.3`) so that areas with fewer points are easier to identify. After that, we can print Spearman's for the interaction as we did before and then plot another dependence plot, but this time for `cylinders` with `ghgScore`. Please note that `cylinders` is an ordinal feature, so `x_jitter=0.4` helps appreciate the distribution better because, for instance, without jitter, all six-cylinder vehicles with a SHAP value of zero would appear as a single dot:

```
shap.dependence_plot("co2TailpipeGpm",shap_xgb_values_test,
                     X_test,interaction_index="cylinders",\
                     alpha=0.3)
print('spearman→co2TailpipeGpm: %.3f-val: %.4f' %
          (stats.spearmanr(X_train.cylinders.values,\
          X_train.co2TailpipeGpm.values)))
shap.dependence_plot("cylinders", shap_xgb_values_train,\
X_train, interaction_index="ghgScore", alpha=0.3,\
```

```
                    x_jitter=0.4)
print('spearman→cylinders: %.3f-val: %.4f' %\
            (stats.spearmanr(top_df.ghgScore.values,\
                top_df.cylinders.values)))
```

The preceding code generates the output in *Figure 5.9* and *Figure 5.10*. The color-coding on the right relates to the values for the interaction term. The first plot tells us that an increase of cylinders correlates with an increase in co2TailpipeGpm, and, in turn, higher values of co2TailpipeGpm correlate with lower SHAP values. Spearman confirms the monotonic nature of this interaction. The second plot is harder to interpret, but it shows that a higher ghgScore correlates with fewer cylinders and slightly higher SHAP values:

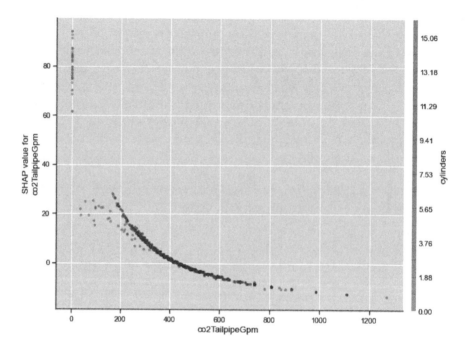

```
spearman    cylinders→co2TailpipeGpm    corr: 0.787 p-val:
0.0000
```

Figure 5.9 – SHAP dependence plots for the XGBoost model and statistics depicting co2TailpipeGpm interactions with cylinders

The plot in *Figure 5.9* suggests that `cylinders` aligns so perfectly with `co2TailpipeGpm` that it's not needed by the model despite its strong correlations. In other words, it's for the most part redundant, except it's likely being used as an interactive term by `ghgScore`:

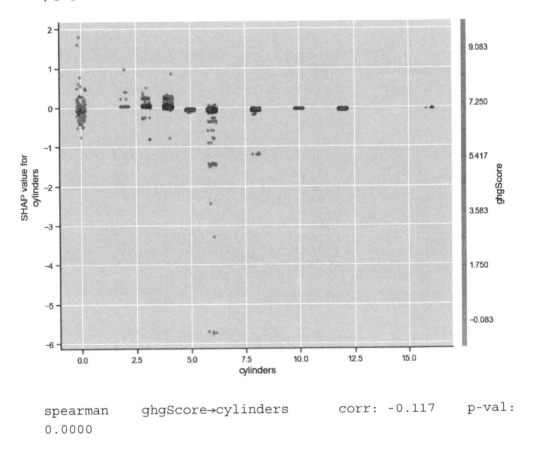

spearman   ghgScore→cylinders   corr: -0.117   p-val:
0.0000

Figure 5.10 – SHAP dependence plots for the XGBoost model and statistics depicting cylinders interactions with ghgScore

Note that there are outliers in *Figure 5.10* where SHAP values are very low or very high when `ghgScore` is high. These outliers are located when `cylinders` has specific values. For example, the model might have learned that when `cylinders` is zero and `ghgScore` is over five, the impact on the outcome should be higher.

SHAP's plots are a visual representation of what the model has learned from our data. However, if we have any doubts, we can always go directly to the source: the data. In *Chapter 4*, *Fundamentals of Feature Importance and Impact*, we generated ICE plots and scatter plots side by side. In that example, we could tell that the model "connected the dots" in the scatter plot by visually representing what it learned with ICE plots.

We can do the same now by scatter plotting `cylinders` against `co2TailpipeGpm` and the target `comb08`. These plots might tell us something that the model isn't telling us or confirm its story. The following code creates two subplots with `regplot` scatter plots. Seaborn's `regplot` is intended for plotting data with a linear regression line. Even though we don't expect linearity, it's often useful to plot the line to show a direction or trend:

```
fig, axs = plt.subplots(1, 2, figsize = (13,6))
sns.regplot(x=X_train.cylinders, y=X_train.co2TailpipeGpm, \
            ax=axs[0], scatter_kws={'alpha':0.3}, \
            line_kws={'color':'g'})
axs[0].set_ylabel('Tailpipe CO2 in grams/mile',
fontsize=13)
axs[0].set_xlabel('Cylinders', fontsize=13)
sns.regplot(x=X_train.cylinders, y=y_train, ax=axs[1], \
marker="+", \
        scatter_kws={'alpha':0.3}, line_kws={'color':'g'})
axs[1].set_ylabel('Combined MPG (comb08)', fontsize=13)
\axs[1].set_xlabel('Cylinders', fontsize=13)
```

The preceding code produced *Figure 5.11*. It confirms that `cylinders` and `co2TailpipeGpm` are positively correlated, while `cylinders` and `comb08` are negatively correlated:

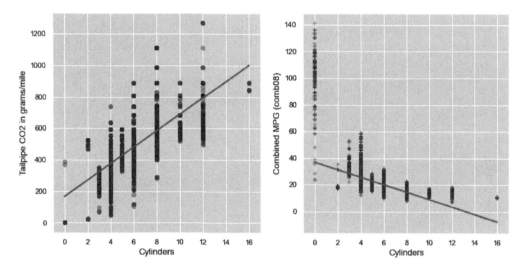

Figure 5.11 – Scatter plots showing the relationship between cylinders and both co2TailpipeGpm and target

Let's now plot `dependence_plot` for `co2TailpipeGpm` interacting with `co2` as we did for `cylinders`:

```
shap.dependence_plot("co2TailpipeGpm",
shap_nn_values_test[0],\
            X_test, alpha=0.3, interaction_index="co2")
print('spearman→co2TailpipeGpm: %.3f-val: %.4f' %\
                    (stats.spearmanr(X_train.co2.values,\
                        X_train.co2TailpipeGpm.values)))
```

The previous code outputs in *Figure 5.12* demonstrate how mid to high values of co2 have a positive monotonic relationship with co2TailpipeGpm but, strangely, low values of co2 have no connection. They are all over the place! Spearman's coefficient indicates a negative monotonic correlation because of this:

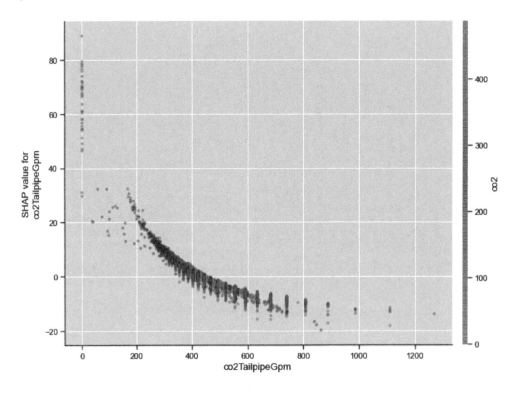

```
spearman    co2→co2TailpipeGpm    corr:  -0.222       p-val:
0.0000
```

Figure 5.12 – SHAP dependence plots for the neural network model and statistics depicting co2TailpipeGpm interactions with co2

Again, plotting the data with `regplot` can shed light on what is going on with the interactions. We will plot `co2` against `co2TailpipeGpm` and `comb08`:

```
fig, axs = plt.subplots(1, 2, figsize = (13,6))
sns.regplot(x=X_train.co2, y=X_train.co2TailpipeGpm, \
ax=axs[0], \
        scatter_kws={'alpha':0.3}, line_kws={'color':'g'})
axs[0].set_ylabel('Tailpipe CO2 in grams/mile
(co2TailpipeGpm)', fontsize=13)
axs[0].set_xlabel('Tailpipe CO2 in grams/mile (co2)', \
fontsize=13)
sns.regplot(x=X_train.co2, y=y_train, ax=axs[1],
marker="+", \
        scatter_kws={'alpha':0.3}, line_kws={'color':'g'})
axs[1].set_ylabel('Combined MPG (comb08)', fontsize=13)
axs[1].set_xlabel('Tailpipe CO2 in grams/mile (co2)',
fontsize=13)
```

The preceding snippet outputs *Figure 5.13*. It depicts how, for the most part, `co2` and `co2TailpipeGpm` are equal, except when `co2=-1`. If you want to confirm this, run a cell with `X_train[X_train.co2TailpipeGpm != X_train.co2].co2`, which will output a pandas series of `co2` when they are not equal. If you dig deeper, you'll realize that all of the -1s are for years prior to 2013. This finding shouldn't be surprising considering what's written in the data dictionary! Indeed, `co2` is `co2TailpipeGpm` but with missing information. It shouldn't be relevant, yet the neural network seemed to have found it important because it correlates strongly with the target – that is, when it is available. In other words, imagine what would happen to the regression line in both plots in *Figure 5.13* if you removed the -1s:

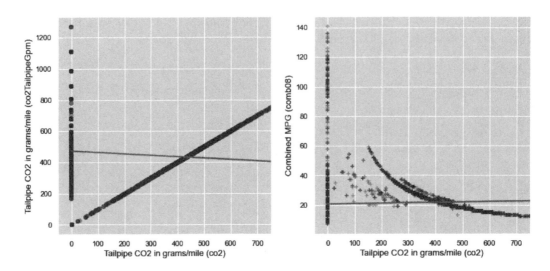

Figure 5.13 – Scatter plots showing the relationship between co2 and both co2TailpipeGpm and target

But if `co2` is `co2TailpipeGpm` but with missing values, shouldn't the neural network have deemed it irrelevant?

Maybe `ghgScore` and `year` hold some answers to this question, so let's plot a couple of `dependence_plot` instances between these features as we've done before:

```
shap.dependence_plot("co2", shap_nn_values_test[0], X_test,\
                     alpha=0.3, interaction_index="ghgScore",\
          x_jitter=10)
print('spearman→co2: %.3f-val: %.4f' %\
     (stats.spearmanr(top_df.ghgScore.values,
top_df.co2.values)))
shap.dependence_plot("ghgScore", shap_nn_values_test[0],\
X_test, alpha=0.3, interaction_index="year",\
          x_jitter=0.4)
print('spearman→year: %.3f-val: %.4f' %
     (stats.spearmanr(top_df.ghgScore.values,\
top_df.year.values)))
```

The preceding snippet outputs *Figure 5.14* and *Figure 5.15*. In the first plot, you can tell that as co2 increases, ghgScore tends to decrease, and the SHAP value increases. As with cylinders, there are outliers, so co2 becomes relevant as an interaction feature when co2=-1:

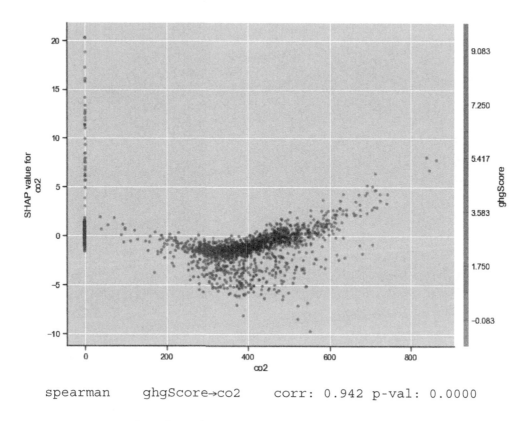

```
spearman       ghgScore→co2      corr: 0.942 p-val: 0.0000
```

Figure 5.14 – SHAP dependence plots for the neural network model and statistics depicting co2 interactions with ghgScore

On the other hand, *Figure 5.15* shows that all the low to mid values for `year` have a `ghgScore` value of -1. This feature seems to be riddled with "not available" values, like `co2`. Besides that, as it increases, the SHAP value slightly decreases, but so does its variance, dramatically:

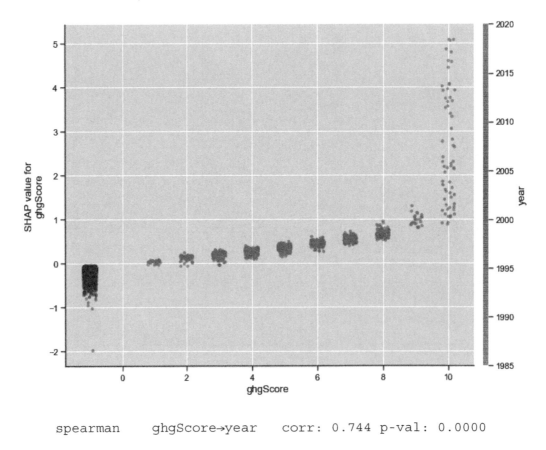

```
spearman    ghgScore→year    corr: 0.744 p-val: 0.0000
```

Figure 5.15 – SHAP dependence plots for the neural network model and statistics depicting ghgScore interactions with year

We can plot `ghgScore` against the most important feature (`co2TailpipeGpm`) and the target to better understand what's going on:

```
fig, axs = plt.subplots(1, 2, figsize = (13,6))
sns.regplot(x=X_train.ghgScore, y=X_train.co2TailpipeGpm,
ax=axs[0],
            scatter_kws={'alpha':0.3}, line_kws={'color':'g'})
axs[0].set_ylabel('Tailpipe CO2 in grams/mile
(co2TailpipeGpm)', fontsize=13)
axs[0].set_xlabel('EPA GHG Score (ghgScore)', fontsize=13)
sns.regplot(x=X_train.ghgScore, y=y_train, ax=axs[1],
marker="+",\
            scatter_kws={'alpha':0.3}, line_kws={'color':'g'})
axs[1].set_ylabel('Combined MPG (comb08)', fontsize=13)
axs[1].set_xlabel('EPA GHG Score (ghgScore)', fontsize=13)
```

The preceding code outputs the pair of plots in *Figure 5.16*, which shows how `ghgScore` aligns so perfectly with `co2TailpipeGpm`, except when it's -1. This score is likely a formula derived from the tailpipe emissions, except before 2013 when it wasn't available – and this translates to it having some visible correlation with the target. However, the only purpose of `ghgScore` in the model is as an interaction feature:

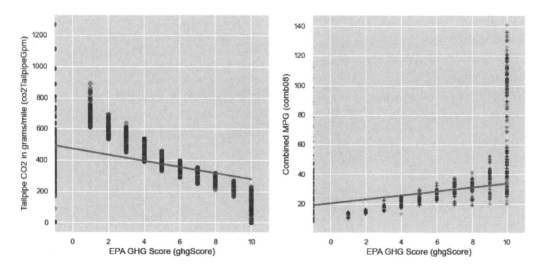

Figure 5.16 – Scatter plots showing the relationship between ghgScore and both co2TailpipeGpm and target

Next, we will study another plot that can be useful to examine the interaction effects between features.

SHAP force plots

In the next chapter, *Chapter 6, Local Model-Agnostic Interpretation Methods*, we will look into this further, but for now it's enough to know that force plots are usually used to explain a single prediction. Force plots depict a continuum, where blue features represent forces pushing predictions in a negative direction and red ones represent forces pushing predictions in a positive direction. In this case, the positive forces represent higher combined MPG (comb08) and negative forces lower.

If we stack the local interpretations vertically side by side, we can use this concept for global interpretation. SHAP's force plot does precisely this when you provide more than one SHAP value and observation to force_plot. It is slower to render this plot, because it more than one plot but a dynamic dashboard. One thing you can do to generate it more quickly is to use your test dataset sample. We will only select 5% (sample_test_size) of the indexes (sample_test_idx) in the test dataset. And since it's a dynamic dashboard, you will need to initialize the JavaScript with the shap.initjs() command before you run force_plot. The force plot requires expected_value, which, in this case, is the mean of the target variable followed by the SHAP values and test data:

```
sample_test_size = 0.05
sample_test_idx = np.random.choice(X_test.shape[0],
            math.ceil(X_test.shape[0]*sample_test_size),\
            replace=False)
shap.initjs()
shap.force_plot(shap_xgb_explainer.expected_value,\
            shap_xgb_values_test[sample_test_idx],\
            X_test.iloc[sample_test_idx])
```

The preceding snippet generates a dashboard. The initial screen clusters all observations clustered by similarity and centered at the expected value (about 21 MPG). Blue forces are pushing MPG downward and pushing red forces upward. The forces, of course, are specific feature values. And if you hover over the chart, it will tell you what these are. In *Figure 5.17*, you can see this in the first screenshot. However, this initial screen is often too busy to be useful, so you'll want to filter and sort the mean effects by feature (with the top dropdown) and maybe see how they interact with other features (with the left dropdown). The second screenshot in *Figure 5.17* shows how after 2013, the mean effects on co2TailpipeGpm tend to be higher. There were also two years in which there were increases, which were 2001 and 2012:

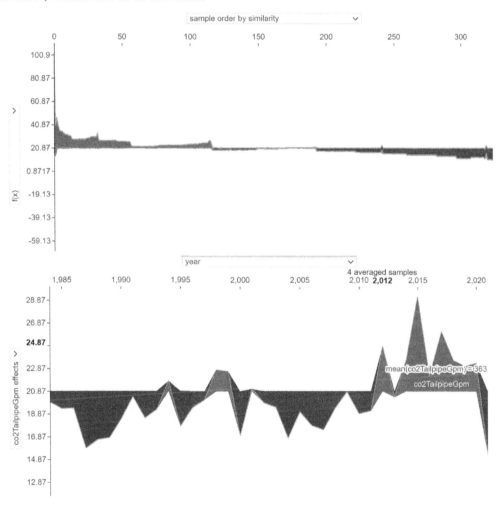

Figure 5.17 – SHAP force plots for all features clustered by explanation similarity followed by results filtered on and ordered by year versus co2TailpipeGpm effects

As beautiful as SHAP dependence plots and interaction visualizations are, they can be harder to interpret than other less-detailed plots. And sometimes, all you want to do is capture the essence of something by showing the general direction of how one feature or two features together interact with the target. That's where we can employ ALE plots.

Accumulated Local Effects (ALE) plots

ALE plots are like the PDPs we studied in *Chapter 4, Fundamentals of Feature Importance and Impact*, except they are unbiased and much faster. By unbiased, we mean they don't have an assumption that seldomly holds true: features are uncorrelated. As we've noticed already, `co2` and `ghgScore` have been derived from `co2TailPipeGpm`. Therefore, they are mostly redundant – except when they are -1 ("Not Available"). So, how can we rely on an interpretation method that confounds their effects?

Thanks to its properties, there's a lot of consistency in SHAP's attributions because it makes simulations based on reasonable expectations – even accounting, for the most part, for colinear features. PDPs make averages of predictions across all feature values (and interpolations) regardless of whether they make sense while assuming independence of the features.

On the other hand, ALE plots take a reasonable approach by factoring data distributions when calculating the *effects* of a feature. They do this by splitting the feature into equally sized intervals (typically, quantiles). Then, they compute how much the predictions change, on average, in each of these intervals – hence *local*. They sum these effects across all intervals – in other words, they are *accumulated*. The effects are relative to an average, so they are then centered on zero. Their simplicity obscures their genius. The averages of interval differences are derivatives, and the accumulation is an integral hidden in plain sight. We won't get into the mathematical details here, but this results in isolating one feature's effect from others!

At the time of writing, the package we will use to produce ALE plots (`https://github.com/blent-ai/ALEPython`) requires data in pandas format. This requirement makes it incompatible with the neural network model. We will use the XGBoost model anyway. But if you wanted to use the neural network model, you could overcome this problem by creating a wrapper class that abstracts the model and converts the pandas DataFrame to NumPy for it. Many of the model-agnostic interpretation libraries struggle to make them compatible with every model class, so you have to resort to tricks to make them "fit." And there's a lack of standardization, which we will discuss in *Chapter 14, What's Next for Machine Learning Interpretability?*, which impedes easier implementation and widespread adoption.

We will now use a `for` loop `for` the top continuous features and plot the ALE plots for each one. The `ale_plot` function is very straightforward. The first argument is the model (`fitted_xgb_model`). Then comes the pandas DataFrame (`X_test`), followed by an array of the features to plot. Optionally, you can set `bins`, which is how many quartiles to use as intervals. There is also another option that is recommended but slows down the process, which is to use **Monte Carlo samples** (`monte_carlo`). If you set this to true, it will create many replica simulations (`monte_carlo_rep`), where it takes a proportion of randomly drawn samples from the data and computes ALE on them (`monte_carlo_ratio`). You end up with thin blue lines representing each replica. The idea behind this is to see how much your ALE plot could vary in a validation dataset drawn from a similar distribution as the test dataset:

```
for feature_name in ['co2TailpipeGpm', 'co2', 'ghgScore',\
                'year', 'cylinders']:
ale_plot(
fitted_xgb_model, X_test, [feature_name], bins=10,\
monte_carlo=True, monte_carlo_rep=50, monte_carlo_ratio=0.4
)
plt.show()
```

The preceding snippet generates five ALE plots. *Figure 5.18* is one of them. It represents how `co2` impacts the XGBoost model according to the test dataset. Completely isolated, it has a tiny impact ranging from -0.05 and 0.30 MPG. Please note that the value for -1 is not even represented in the plot because ALE recognizes that, on its own, it carries no information:

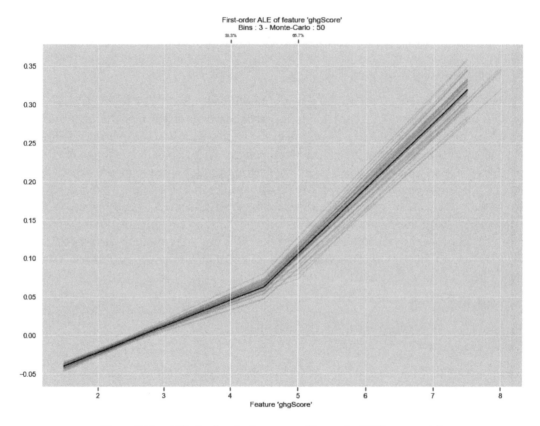

Figure 5.18 – ALE plot for ghgScore according to the XGBoost model

Next, we will generate ALE plots for two features at a time. This is computed the same way, except the quantiles operate in two dimensions, and it accumulates effects in these two dimensions, resulting in a color-coded contour plot. We will iterate again, but this time against pairs of features. `ale_plot` can take two features in the third argument, but Monte Carlo simulations aren't available for two:

```
for interaction in [['co2TailpipeGpm', 'co2'],\
                    ['co2TailpipeGpm', 'ghgScore'],\
                    ['cylinders', 'co2TailpipeGpm'],\
                    ['year', 'co2TailpipeGpm']]:
```

```
ale_plot(fitted_xgb_model, X_test, interaction,\
bins=[10,10])
plt.show()
```

The preceding code outputs four ALE interaction plots. The first three demonstrate negligible interaction effects (of less than 1 MPG). The last one is depicted in *Figure 5.19*. It shows a sizable interaction effect between `year` and `co2TailpipeGpm` especially negatively for years between 1985 and 2004, combined with tailpipe CO2 (`co2TailpipeGpm`) below 300. But wait, isn't lower tailpipe CO2 indicative of higher MPG?

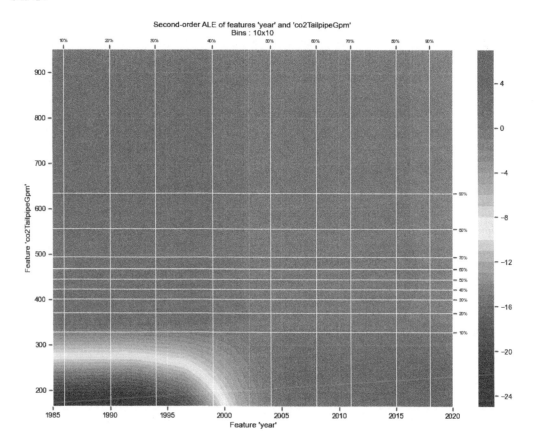

Figure 5.19 – ALE interaction plot between year and co2TailpipeGpm

It turns out that the model has learned that it mustn't trust `co2TailpipeGpm` for these years and tends to penalize the lowest values. It is likely the case that there are either data quality issues or the way `co2TailpipeGpm` was calculated changed over the years, making it uneven.

What if you want to distill some insights about your machine learning model that are too difficult to interpret by other means, such as, for instance, some rules that explain the underlying decision-making logic? Or coefficients that capture the magnitude and direction of a feature for the model? Intrinsically interpretable models have these elements built in, but we prefer black-box models because they perform better. There is a compromise, and it's to use global surrogate models, which we will learn about next!

Global surrogates

Surrogate model is an overloaded term. It is used in engineering, statistics, economics, and physics, to name a few, often in the context of metamodels, mathematical optimizations, or simulations.

In the context of machine learning interpretation methods, **global surrogate model** usually refers to a white-box model that you train with the black-box models' predictions. We do this to extract insights from the white-box model's intrinsic parameters, much like we did in *Chapter 3, Interpretation Challenges*. There is also another way to use surrogate models: to use a black-box model to approximate and evaluate another model that you don't have access to, but you have its predictions. We will do just this in *Chapter 7, Anchor and Counterfactual Explanations*, but we prefer the term **proxy model** for this kind of surrogate.

You don't need any fancy libraries to create a global surrogate. You can use any of the white-box models we discussed in *Chapter 3, Interpretation Challenges*. That being said, there are some models that were designed to be used as surrogates, such as TREPAN. The Skater library has an implementation (`https://oracle.github.io/Skater/reference/interpretation.html#tree-surrogates-using-decision-trees`) you can use and one for **Bayesian Rule List Classifier** (**BRLC**), which is very similar to RuleFit from *Chapter 3, Interpretation Challenges*, except it only works with classification tasks.

We want to extract some rules and a hierarchy for this exercise from our neural network models for this exercise. Therefore, it makes sense to use decision trees and RuleFit. Decision trees help us understand the hierarchy and RuleFit helps us understand the rules.

Fitting surrogates

The first step is to fit the surrogates; the only difference is that training data has the neural network model's predictions as y. Once we fit `DecisionTreeRegressor`, we run `predict` to get the predictions for train and test:

```
fitted_dt_surrogate =\
tree.DecisionTreeRegressor(max_depth=7, random_state=rand).\
                    fit(X_train, y_train_nn_pred)
y_train_dt_pred = fitted_dt_surrogate.predict(X_train)
y_test_dt_pred = fitted_dt_surrogate.predict(X_test)
```

We can do the same for `RuleFit`. Note that RuleFit's `fit` function requires the data in NumPy float format:

```
fitted_rf_surrogate = RuleFit(max_rules=150,\
rfmode='regress', random_state=rand, tree_size=8).\
              fit(X_train.astype(float).values,\
                            np.array(y_train_nn_pred).
squeeze(), X_train.columns)
y_train_rf_pred =\
        fitted_rf_surrogate.predict(X_train.astype(float).
values)
y_test_rf_pred =\
        fitted_rf_surrogate.predict(X_test.astype(float).
values)
```

We are getting the predictions of the surrogate to measure how well each surrogate model fits the neural network model, and how much overfitting there is.

Evaluating surrogates

If the surrogate model's predictions are too far off from the neural network model's prediction, any interpretations won't be useful. Also, if it's overfitting too much, it means the neural network model is only approximated well with training data but not with test data, and when this happens you should not use the surrogate either.

First, let's evaluate the decision tree by computing the RMSE and R-squared value:

```
#Measure how well Decision Tree replicates Neural Network's
# predictions
RMSE_dt_nn_train =\
metrics.mean_squared_error(y_train_nn_pred,\
                  y_train_dt_pred, squared=False)
RMSE_dt_nn_test =\
metrics.mean_squared_error(y_test_nn_pred,\
```

```
                    y_test_dt_pred, squared=False)
R2_dt_nn_test = metrics.r2_score(y_test_nn_pred,\
y_test_dt_pred)
#Print all metrics
print('RMSE_train: %.4f_test: %.4f: %.4f' %\
         (RMSE_dt_nn_train, RMSE_dt_nn_test,\
R2_dt_nn_test))
```

The previous code outputs the following:

```
RMSE_train: 0.5036  RMSE_test: 0.5518   r2: 0.9952
```

The R-squared is high, and the difference in RMSEs does not indicate overfitting at all. Now let's do RuleFit:

```
#Measure how well Rule Fit replicates Neural Network's
predictions
RMSE_rf_nn_train =\
metrics.mean_squared_error(y_train_nn_pred,\
                    y_train_rf_pred, squared=False)
RMSE_rf_nn_test =\
metrics.mean_squared_error(y_test_nn_pred,\
                    y_test_rf_pred, squared=False)
R2_rf_nn_test = metrics.r2_score(y_test_nn_pred,\
y_test_rf_pred)
#Print all metrics
print('RMSE_train: %.4f_test: %.4f: %.4f' %\
         (RMSE_rf_nn_train, RMSE_rf_nn_test,\
R2_rf_nn_test))
```

The preceding code outputs the following results:

```
RMSE_train: 0.8211  RMSE_test: 0.6416   r2: 0.9935
```

RuleFit passes the test. It has worse metrics than the decision tree, but it is still very good. Next, let's use global surrogates for interpretation.

Interpreting surrogates

We can plot the tree for the decision tree to visualize the hierarchy, as we learned to do in *Chapter 3*:

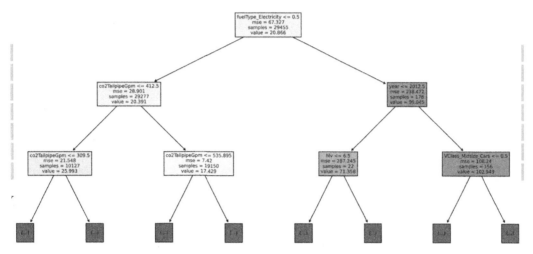

Figure 5.20 – Decision tree surrogate structure up to a depth of 2

The neural network model doesn't have an analogous structure. Nevertheless, if we can replicate the predictions to a high degree with it, then it means that even though `fuelType_Electricity` is not one of the most important features, in aggregate, it's critical as a starting point. And indeed, a decision tree could be useful to understand how to best approach the problem. For instance, it may make sense to make two models: one for electric cars and one for fossil fuel cars. To dig deeper, we can use `tree.export_tree` as we covered in *Chapter 3, Interpretation Challenges,* or explore the tree with scikit-learn's API.

For RuleFit, we can use `get_rules()` to extract the rules, filter out those with a coefficient of zero, and then sort them by `importance`:

```
rulefit_df = fitted_rf_surrogate.get_rules()
rulefit_df = rulefit_df[rulefit_df.coef != 0]
rulefit_df.sort_values(by="importance", ascending=False)
```

The preceding code produces the dataframe in *Figure 5.21*. It shows that linear co2TailPipeGpm is the most important feature, while the `fuelType_Electricity > 0.5` rule is second, followed by a longer rule that also includes `fuelType_ Electricity > 0.5`! So, why didn't we pick up on the importance of `fuelType_ Electricity` before?

	rule	type	coef	support	importance
4	co2TailpipeGpm	linear	-0.034222	1.000000	3.865460
90	fuelType_Electricity > 0.5	rule	18.393562	0.006206	1.444470
104	co2TailpipeGpm <= 367.0 & fuelType_Electricity > 0.5 & ghgScore > 4.5	rule	20.776127	0.003546	1.235005
148	atvType_EV > 0.5 & pv4 > 42.0	rule	15.512440	0.003546	0.922113
193	eng_dscr_PFI > 0.5 & displ <= 0.30000001192092896	rule	12.607181	0.005319	0.917024
14	fuelType_Diesel	linear	2.967849	1.000000	0.488102
95	hpv > 45.0 & co2TailpipeGpm <= 28.5	rule	7.200693	0.003546	0.428034
127	co2TailpipeGpm > 124.0 & trans_spd > 0.5 & atvType_Other > 0.5 & cylinders > 1.5 & co2TailpipeGpm <= 408.5 & co2TailpipeGpm <= 302.5	rule	-7.168212	0.003546	0.426103
216	co2TailpipeGpm <= 250.53571319580078 & co2TailpipeGpm <= 320.5 & co2TailpipeGpm <= 410.5 & co2TailpipeGpm > 40.5	rule	3.457322	0.015071	0.421223
146	VClass_Small_Sport_Utility_Vehicle_2WD <= 0.5 & co2TailpipeGpm <= 45.5	rule	7.574405	0.002660	0.390100

Figure 5.21 – RuleFit surrogate top 10 rules

The SHAP and ALE plots showed us some interesting insights about the features and how they relate to the target and each other. However, given the complexity of XGBoost and neural networks, they conceal simpler truths that can be best distilled in other terms, which only white-box models can demonstrate via the black-box model's predictions.

> **Note**
> A surrogate model's findings can only be conclusive about the original model, and not about the data used to train the model.

There's a lot more to learn about the data from the models themselves and their surrogates. For instance, you can examine every interaction in the top rules of the RuleList using ALE plots or explore the decision tree while looking at the corresponding dependence plots for each feature, especially `fuelType_Electricity`, which seems promising.

Mission accomplished

The mission was to understand how fuel efficiency was impacted over the years by the potential predictors in the dataset. We determined that the most significant fuel efficiency predictors, by far, are pollution-related, and that tailpipe CO_2 in grams/mile (`co2TailpipeGpm`) is the one that stands out. Both pollution and fuel inefficiency decrease with every year. Likewise, they increase with the number of cylinders and when it's a diesel engine (`fuelType_Diesel`). None of this should be surprising to anybody who knows about cars' evolution over the past few decades.

However, there were some revealing insights. For instance, SHAP dependence plots (*Figures 5.12 and 5.14*) helped us understand why the `co2` and `ghgScore` features are redundant. And as depicted by an interaction ALE plot (*Figure 5.19*) there might be some data quality issues with `co2TailpipeGpm` before 2004, which should be investigated further. Global surrogates distilled a sense of hierarchy not visible in other interpretation methods. Even though, in aggregate, electric engine features (`fuelType_Electricity`, `atvType_EV`) and transmission features (`trany_Manual`, `trans_spd`) don't appear to be important, they appear high up in the decision tree (*Figure 5.20*) and in RuleFit's rules (*Figure 5.21*). The hierarchy reveals that they are good initial splitting points to predict MPG.

We have some excellent findings and exciting plots. We can call this a mission accomplished. Nevertheless, in interpretation, with good answers, you often get good questions too! We can continue down the rabbit hole and see where it may lead. For instance, once you remove redundant features, a next step could be training a separate model for fossil fuel and electric vehicles to learn what factors impact MPG and MPGe (gasoline-equivalent miles per gallon) separately. You could generate SHAP plots for both, juxtaposing their top features, and maybe that will help create a more compelling story for your organization!

Summary

After reading this chapter, you should understand Shapley values and how they connect to the SHAP library. You also learned about ALE plots and how they are a better alternative to PDPs. Lastly, you should understand how to leverage global surrogates to learn more about your models.

In the next chapter, we will study local interpretation methods using a **Local Surrogate Model (LIME)** and SHAP.

Further reading

- Shapley, Lloyd S. (1953). "A value for n-person Games". In Kuhn, H. W.; Tucker, A. W. (eds.). Contributions to the Theory of Games. Annals of Mathematical Studies. 28. Princeton University Press. pp. 307–317. `https://doi.org/10.1515/9781400881970-018`

- Lundberg, S., & Lee, S. (2017). A Unified Approach to Interpreting Model Predictions. Advances in Neural Information Processing Systems, 30. `https://arxiv.org/abs/1705.07874` (documentation for SHAP: `https://github.com/slundberg/shap`)

- Lundberg, S.M., Erion, G., & Lee, S. (2018). Consistent Individualized Feature Attribution for Tree Ensembles. ICML Workshop. `https://arxiv.org/abs/1802.03888`

- Shrikumar, A., Greenside, P., & Kundaje, A. (2017). Learning Important Features Through Propagating Activation Differences. `https://arxiv.org/abs/1704.02685`

- Sturmfels, P., Lundberg, S., & Lee, S. (2020). Visualizing the Impact of Feature Attribution Baselines. Distill. `https://www.doi.org/10.23915/distill.00022`

- Apley, D.W. & Zhu, J. (2019). Visualizing the Effects of Predictor Variables in Black Box Supervised Learning Models. arXiv: Methodology. `https://arxiv.org/abs/1612.08468.`

6
Local Model-Agnostic Interpretation Methods

In the previous two chapters, we dealt exclusively with global interpretation methods. This chapter will foray into local interpretation methods, which are there to explain why a single prediction or a group of predictions was made. It will cover how to leverage **SHapley Additive exPlanations' (SHAP's)** `KernelExplainer` and also, another method called **Local Interpretable Model-agnostic Explanations (LIME)** for local interpretations. We will also explore how to use these methods with both tabular and text data.

These are the main topics we are going to cover in this chapter:

- Leveraging SHAP's `KernelExplainer` for local interpretations with SHAP values
- Employing LIME
- Using LIME for **natural language processing (NLP)**

- Trying SHAP for NLP
- Comparing SHAP with LIME

Technical requirements

This chapter's example uses the `mldatasets`, `pandas`, `numpy`, `sklearn`, `nltk`, `lightgbm`, `rulefit`, `matplotlib`, `seaborn`, `shap`, and `lime` libraries. Instructions on how to install all of these libraries are in the *preface* of the book. The code for this chapter is located here:

```
https://github.com/PacktPublishing/Interpretable-Machine-
Learning-with-Python/tree/master/Chapter06
```

The mission

Who doesn't love chocolate?! It's a global favorite, with around nine out of ten people loving it and about a billion people eating it every day. One popular form in which it is consumed is as a chocolate bar. However, even universally beloved ingredients can be used in ways that aren't universally appealing—so, chocolate bars can range from the sublime to the mediocre, to downright unpleasant. Often, this is solely determined by the quality of the cocoa or additional ingredients, and sometimes it becomes an acquired taste once it's combined with exotic flavors.

A French chocolate manufacturer who is obsessed with excellence has reached out to you. They have a problem. All of their bars have been highly rated by critics, yet critics have very particular taste buds. And some bars they love have inexplicably mediocre sales, but non-critics seem to like them in focus groups and tastings, so they are puzzled why sales don't coincide with their market research. They have found a dataset of chocolate bars rated by knowledgeable lovers of chocolate, and these ratings happen to coincide with their sales. To get an unbiased opinion, they have sought your expertise.

As for the dataset, members of the *Manhattan Chocolate Society* have been meeting since 2007 for the sole purpose of tasting and judging fine chocolate, to educate consumers and inspire chocolate makers to produce higher-quality chocolate. Since then, they have compiled a dataset of over 2,200 chocolate bars, rated by their members with the following scale:

- 4.0 - 5.00 = Outstanding
- 3.5 - 3.99 = Highly Recommended
- 3.0 - 3.49 = Recommended

- 2.0 - 2.99 = Disappointing
- 1.0 - 1.90 = Unpleasant

These ratings are derived from a rubric that factors in aroma, appearance, texture, flavor, aftertaste, and overall opinion, and the bars rated are mostly darker chocolate bars since the aim is to appreciate the flavors of cacao. In addition to the ratings, the *Manhattan Chocolate Society* dataset includes many characteristics, such as the country where the cocoa bean was farmed, how many ingredients the bar has, whether it includes salt, and the words used to describe it.

The goal is to understand why one of the chocolate manufacturers' bars is rated Outstanding yet sells poorly, while another one, whose sales are impressive, is rated as *Disappointing*.

The approach

You have decided to use local model interpretation to explain why each bar is rated as it is. To that end, you will prepare the dataset and then train classification models to predict if chocolate-bar ratings are above or equal to *Highly Recommended*, because the client would like all their bars to fall above this threshold. You will need to train two models: one for tabular data, and another NLP one for the words used to describe the chocolate bars. We will employ **support vector machines (SVMs)** and **Light Gradient Boosting Machine (LightGBM)**, respectively, for these tasks. If you haven't used these black-box models, no worries—we will briefly explain them. Once you train the models, then comes the fun part: leverage two local model-agnostic interpretation methods to understand what makes a specific chocolate bar less than *Highly Recommended* or not. These methods are SHAP and LIME, which when combined will provide a richer explanation to convey back to your client. Then, we will compare both methods to understand their strengths and limitations.

The preparations

You will find the code for this example here:

```
https://github.com/PacktPublishing/Interpretable-Machine-
Learning-with-Python/blob/master/Chapter06/ChocoRatings.ipynb
```

Loading the libraries

To run this example, you need to install the following libraries:

- `mldatasets` to load the dataset
- `pandas`, `numpy`, and `nltk` to manipulate it
- `sklearn` (scikit-learn) and `lightgbm` to split the data and fit the models
- `matplotlib`, `seaborn`, `shap`, and `lime` to visualize the interpretations

You should load all of them first, as follows:

```
import math
import mldatasets
import pandas as pd
import numpy as np
import re
import nltk
from nltk.probability import FreqDist
from sklearn.model_selection import train_test_split
from sklearn.pipeline import make_pipeline
from sklearn import metrics, svm
from sklearn.feature_extraction.text import TfidfVectorizer
import lightgbm as lgb
import matplotlib.pyplot as plt
import seaborn as sns
import shap
import lime
import lime.lime_tabular
from lime.lime_text import LimeTextExplainer
```

You will also need to make sure `stopwords` and the `punkt` tokenizer are downloaded prior to loading them, like this:

```
nltk.download('stopwords')
nltk.download('punkt')
from nltk.corpus import stopwords
from nltk.tokenize import word_tokenize
```

Understanding and preparing the data

We load the data into a dataframe we call `chocolateratings_df`, like this:

```
chocolateratings_df = mldatasets.load("chocolate-bar-ratings")
```

There should be over 2,200 records and 18 columns. We can verify this was the case simply by inspecting the contents of the dataframe, like this:

```
chocolateratings_df
```

The output shown here in *Figure 6.1* corresponds to what we were expecting:

	company	company_location	review_date	country_of_bean_origin	cocoa_percent	rating	counts_of_ingredients	beans	cocoa_butter	va
0	5150	U.S.A	2019	Madagascar	76.000000	3.750000	3	have_bean	have_cocoa_butter	have_not_va
1	5150	U.S.A	2019	Dominican republic	76.000000	3.500000	3	have_bean	have_cocoa_butter	have_not_va
2	5150	U.S.A	2019	Tanzania	76.000000	3.250000	3	have_bean	have_cocoa_butter	have_not_va
3	A. Morin	France	2012	Peru	63.000000	3.750000	4	have_bean	have_cocoa_butter	have_not_va
4	A. Morin	France	2012	Bolivia	70.000000	3.500000	4	have_bean	have_cocoa_butter	have_not_va
...	...	...	...	...	...	...	...	...	...	...
2219	Zotter	Austria	2014	Blend	80.000000	2.750000	4	have_bean	have_cocoa_butter	have_not_va
2220	Zotter	Austria	2017	Colombia	75.000000	3.750000	3	have_bean	have_cocoa_butter	have_not_va
2221	Zotter	Austria	2018	Belize	72.000000	3.500000	3	have_bean	have_cocoa_butter	have_not_va
2222	Zotter	Austria	2018	Congo	70.000000	3.250000	3	have_bean	have_cocoa_butter	have_not_va
2223	Zotter	Austria	2018	Blend	75.000000	3.000000	3	have_bean	have_cocoa_butter	have_not_va

2224 rows × 14 columns

Figure 6.1 – Contents of chocolate-bar dataset

The data dictionary

The data dictionary comprises the following:

- `company`: Categorical; the manufacturer of the chocolate bar (out of over 500 different ones)

- `company_location`: Categorical; country of the manufacturer (66 different countries)

- `review_date`: Continuous; year in which the bar was reviewed (from 2006 to 2020)

- `country_of_bean_origin`: Categorical; country where the cocoa beans were harvested (62 different countries)

- `cocoa_percent`: Categorical; what percentage of the bar is cocoa
- `rating`: Continuous; rating given by the *Manhattan Chocolate Society* (possible values: 1-5)
- `counts_of_ingredients`: Continuous; amount of ingredients in the bar
- `beans`: Binary; was it made with cocoa beans? (`have_bean` or `have_not_bean`)
- `cocoa_butter`: Binary; was it made with cocoa butter? (`have_cocoa_butter` or `have_not_cocoa_butter`)
- `vanilla`: Binary; was it made with vanilla? (`have_vanilla` or `have_not_vanilla`)
- `lecithin`: Binary; was it made with lecithin? (`have_lecithin` or `have_not_lecithin`)
- `salt`: Binary; was it made with salt? (`have_salt` or `have_not_salt`)
- `sugar`: Binary; was it made with sugar? (`have_sugar` or `have_not_sugar`)
- `sweetener_without_sugar`: Binary; was it made with sweetener without sugar? (`have_sweetener_without_sugar` or `have_not_sweetener_without_sugar`)
- `first_taste`: Text; word(s) used to describe the first taste
- `second_taste`: Text; word(s) used to describe the second taste
- `third_taste`: Text; word(s) used to describe the third taste
- `fourth_taste`: Text; word(s) used to describe the fourth taste

Now that we have taken a peek at the data, we can quickly prepare this and then work on the modeling and interpretation!

Data preparation

The first thing we ought to do is set aside the text features so that we can process them separately. We can start by creating a dataframe called `tastes_df` with them and then drop them from `chocolateratings_df`. We can then take a look at `tastes_df` using `head` and `tail`, as illustrated in the following code snippet:

```
tastes_df = chocolateratings_df[['first_taste', 'second_taste',
'third_taste', 'fourth_taste']]
chocolateratings_df = chocolateratings_df.\
```

```
    drop(['first_taste', 'second_taste', 'third_taste',
'fourth_taste'], axis=1)
tastes_df.head(90).tail(10)
```

The preceding code produces the dataframe shown here in *Figure 6.2*:

	first_taste	second_taste	third_taste	fourth_taste
80	oily	vegetal	nutty	cocoa
81	oily	vanilla	melon	cocoa
82	rich	sour	mild smoke	nan
83	fruity	sour	nan	nan
84	high roast	high astringnet	nan	nan
85	smokey	savory	nan	nan
86	sandy	roasty	nutty	nan
87	roasty	brownie	nutty	nan
88	red wine	rich cocoa	long	nan
89	creamy	fruit	cocoa	nan

Figure 6.2 – Tastes columns have quite a few null values

Now, let's categorically encode the categorical features. There are too many countries in `company_location` and `country_of_bean_origin`, so let's establish a threshold. Say, if there are fewer than 3.333% (or 74 rows) for any country, let's bucket it into an `Other` category and then encode the categories. We can easily do this with the `make_dummies_with_limits` function we used in the previous chapter and the process is shown again in the following code snippet:

```
chocolateratings_df =\
    mldatasets.make_dummies_with_limits(chocolateratings_df,
        'company_location', 0.03333)
chocolateratings_df =\
    mldatasets.make_dummies_with_limits(chocolateratings_df,
        'country_of_bean_origin', 0.03333)
```

All the binary features have to be turned into 1s and 0s except for `beans`, which is always the same value (`have_bean`), using the following code:

```
chocolateratings_df = chocolateratings_df.\
                    drop(['beans'], axis=1)
binary_features = ['cocoa_butter', 'vanilla', 'lecithin',
'salt',
                   'sugar', 'sweetener_without_sugar']
chocolateratings_df[binary_features] =\
    chocolateratings_df[binary_features].\
        apply(lambda x: np.where(x.str.contains('not'), 0, 1))
```

Now, to process the contents of `tastes_df`, we ought to note that what we would ideally like to see is mostly adjectives that mean—or at least evoke—a taste. Therefore, stop words—which are common words such as and, `of`, and `with`—can be safely discarded, so we would need to load a list of `english` stop words from `nltk`, as follows:

```
stop = stopwords.words('english')
```

If you examine the contents of `tastes_df`, you'll find other elements that can add noise to a model in addition to stop words. You'll find punctuation such as &, adverbs such as `overly`, misspellings such as `astringnet`, and even adjective-noun combinations such as `full body`. These can be removed or replaced with a single adjective. We can use regular expressions to do this, all in one swoop. To this end, let's first create a dictionary (`trans_dict`) with our replacements and `compile` them into a regular expression, as follows:

```
trans_dict = {'?':'','&':'', 'overly intense':'intensest',
    'overly sweet':'sweetest', 'overly tart':'tartest',
    'sl. bitter':'bitterness', 'sl. burnt':'burntness',
    'sl. sweet':'sweetness', 'sl. dry':'dryness',
    'sl. chalky':'chalkiness', 'sl. Burnt':'burntness',
    'hints fruit':'fruitiness', 'hint fruit':'fruitiness',
    'high acid':'acidic', 'high acidity':'acidic',
    'moderate acidity':'acid', 'high roast':'roast',
    'astringcy':'astringent', 'astringnet':'astringent',
    'full body':'robust', 'astringency':'astringent',
    'high astringent':'acidic', 'rich cocoa':'rich',
    'mild bitter':'bitterish', 'fruit long':'fruit',
    'base cocoa':'basic', 'basic cocoa':'basic', '-like':'',
```

```
        'smomkey':'smokey', 'true':'real', '(n)':'','/':' ',
        '-':' ',' +':' ' }
trans_regex = re.\
        compile("|".join(map(re.escape, trans_dict.keys( ))))
```

The following code replaces all the null values with empty strings, then joins all the columns in `tastes_df` together, forming a single series. Then, it strips leading and trailing whitespace and converts all text to lowercase. It has two instances of `apply`—the first doing all the regular expression replacements, and the second one removing the stop words. The code is illustrated in the following snippet:

```
tastes_s = tastes_df.replace(np.nan, '', regex=True).\
        agg(' '.join, axis=1).str.strip().str.lower().\
        apply(lambda s: trans_regex.sub(lambda match:
            trans_dict[match.group(0)], s)).\
        apply(lambda s: ' '.join([word for word in s.split()
            if word not in (stop)]))
```

And voilà! You can verify that the result is a pandas series (`tastes_s`) with (mostly) taste-related adjectives, like this:

```
print(tastes_s)
```

As expected, this series is the same length as the `chocolateratings_df` dataframe, as illustrated in the following code snippet:

```
0                cocoa blackberry robust
1                  cocoa vegetal savory
2                     rich fatty bready
3                  fruity melon roasty
4                       vegetal nutty
                       . . .
2221            muted roasty accessible
2222        fatty mild nuts mild fruit
2223              fatty earthy cocoa
Length: 2224, dtype: object
```

But let's find out how many of its phrases are unique, with the following code:

```
print(np.unique(tastes_s).shape)
```

We can tell from the following output that fewer than 50 phrases are duplicated, so tokenizing by phrases would be a bad idea:

```
(2178,)
```

There are many approaches you could take here, such as tokenizing by bi-grams (sequences of two words) or even subwords (dividing words into logical parts). However, even though order matters slightly (because the first words had to do with the first taste, and so on), our dataset is too small and had too many nulls (especially in `third taste` and `fourth taste`) to derive meaning from the order. This is why it was a good choice to concatenate all the "tastes" together, thus removing their discernible division.

Another thing to note is that our words are (mostly) adjectives. We made a small effort to remove adverbs, but there are still some nouns present, such as "fruit" and "nuts", versus adjectives such as "fruity" and "nutty". We can't be sure if the chocolate connoisseurs who judged the bars meant something different by using "fruit" rather than "fruity". However, if we were sure of this, we could have performed **stemming** or **lemmatization** to turn all instances of "fruit", "fruity", and "fruitiness" to a consistent "fru" (*stem*) or "fruiti" (*lemma*). We won't concern ourselves with this because many of our adjectives' variations are not as common in the phrases anyway.

Let's find out the most common words by first tokenizing them with `word_tokenize` and using `FreqDist` to count their frequency. We can then place the resulting `tastewords_fdist` dictionary into a dataframe (`tastewords_df`). We can save only those words with more than 74 instances as a list (`commontastes_l`). The code is illustrated in the following snippet:

```
tastewords_fdist = FreqDist(word for word in
              word_tokenize(tastes_s.str.cat(sep=' ')))
tastewords_df = pd.DataFrame.from_dict(tastewords_fdist,\
              orient='index').rename(columns={0:'freq'})
commontastes_l = tastewords_df[tastewords_df.freq > 74].\
              index.to_list()
print(commontastes_l)
```

As you can tell from the following output for `commontastes_l`, the most common words are mostly different (except for `spice` and `spicy`):

```
['cocoa', 'rich', 'fatty', 'roasty', 'nutty', 'sweet', 'sandy',
 'sour', 'intense', 'mild', 'fruit', 'sticky', 'earthy',
 'spice', 'molasses', 'floral', 'spicy', 'woody', 'coffee',
 'berry', 'vanilla', 'creamy']
```

Something we can do with this list to enhance our tabular dataset is to turn these common words into binary features. In other words, there would be a column for each one of these "common tastes" (`commontastes_l`), and if the "tastes" for the chocolate bar include it, the column would have a 1, otherwise a 0. Fortunately, we can easily do this with two lines of code. First, we create a new column with our text-tastes series (`tastes_s`). Then, we use the `make_dummies_from_dict` function we used in the last chapter to generate the dummy features by looking for each "common taste" in the contents of our new column, as follows:

```
chocolateratings_df['tastes'] = tastes_s
chocolateratings_df =\
        mldatasets.make_dummies_from_dict(chocolateratings_df,
                        'tastes', commontastes_l)
```

Now that we are done with our feature engineering, we can use `info()` to examine our dataframe, like this:

```
chocolateratings_df.info()
```

The output has all numeric non-null features except for `company`. There are over 500 companies, so **categorical encoding** of this feature would be complicated and, because it would be advisable to bucket most companies as `Other`, it would likely introduce bias toward the few companies that are most represented. Therefore, it's better to remove this column altogether. The output is shown here:

```
<class 'pandas.core.frame.DataFrame'>
RangeIndex: 2224 entries, 0 to 2223
Data columns (total 46 columns):
 #   Column                Non-Null Count    Dtype
---  ------                --------------    -----
 0   company               2224 non-null     object
 1   review_date           2224 non-null     int64
 2   cocoa_percent         2224 non-null     float64
```

3	rating	2224 non-null	float64
4	counts_of_ingredients	2224 non-null	int64
:	:	:	:	:
43	tastes_berry	2224 non-null	int64
44	tastes_vanilla	2224 non-null	int64
45	tastes_creamy	2224 non-null	int64

```
dtypes: float64(2), int64(30), object(1), uint8(13)
memory usage: 601.7+ KB
```

Our last step to prepare the data for modeling starts with initializing `rand`, a constant to serve as our "random state" throughout this exercise. Then, we define y as the `rating` column converted to 1s if greater than or equal to 3.5, and 0 otherwise. X is everything else (excluding `company`). Then, we split X and y into train and test datasets with `train_test_split`, as illustrated in the following code snippet:

```
rand = 9
y = chocolateratings_df['rating'].\
        apply(lambda x: 1 if x >= 3.5 else 0)
X = chocolateratings_df.drop(['rating','company'], axis=1).
copy()
X_train, X_test, y_train, y_test = train_test_split(X, y,\
                test_size=0.33, random_state=rand)
```

In addition to the tabular test and train datasets, for our NLP models we will need text-only feature datasets that are consistent with our `train_test_split` so that we can use the same y labels. To this end, we can do this by subsetting our tastes series (`tastes_s`), using the `index` of our `X_train` and `X_test` sets to yield NLP specific versions of the series, as follows:

```
X_train_nlp = tastes_s[X_train.index]
X_test_nlp = tastes_s[X_test.index]
```

OK! We are all set now. Let's start modeling and interpreting our models!

Leveraging SHAP's KernelExplainer for local interpretations with SHAP values

For this section, and for subsequent use, we will train a **Support Vector Classifier** (**SVC**) model first.

Training a C-SVC model

SVM is a family of model classes that operate in high-dimensional space to find an optimal hyperplane, where they attempt to separate the classes with the maximum margin between them. Support vectors are the points closest to the decision boundary (the dividing hyperplane) that would change it if were removed. To find the best hyperplane, they use a cost function called **hinge loss** and a computationally cheap method to operate in high-dimensional space, called the **kernel trick**, and even though a hyperplane suggests linear separability, it's not always limited to a linear kernel.

The scikit-learn implementation we will use is called C-SVC. SVC uses an L2 regularization parameter called C and, by default, uses a kernel called the **radial basis function** (**RBF**), which is decidedly non-linear. For an RBF, a **gamma** hyperparameter defines the radius of influence of each training example in the kernel, but in an inversely proportional fashion. Hence, a low value increases the radius, while a high value decreases it.

The SVM family includes several variations for classification and even regression classes through **support vector regression** (**SVR**). The most significant advantage of SVM models is that they tend to work effectively and efficiently when there are many features compared to the observations, and even when the features exceed the observations! It also tends to find latent non-linear relationships in the data, without overfitting or becoming unstable. However, SVM is not as scalable to larger datasets, and it's hard to tune its hyperparameters.

Since we will use `seaborn` plot styling, which is activated with `set()`, for some of this chapter's plots, we will first save the original `matplotlib` settings (`rcParams`) so that we can restore them later. One thing to note about `SVC` is that it doesn't natively produce probabilities since it's linear algebra. However, if `probability=True`, the scikit-learn implementation uses cross-validation and then fits a logistic regression model to the SVC's scores to produce the probabilities. We are also using `gamma=auto`, which means it is set to 1/# features—so, 1/44. As always, it is recommended to set your `random_state` parameter for reproducibility. Once we fit the model to the training data, we can use `evaluate_class_mdl` to evaluate our model's predictive performance, as illustrated in the following code snippet:

```
orig_plt_params = plt.rcParams
sns.set()
svm_mdl = svm.SVC(probability=True, gamma='auto', random_
state=rand)
fitted_svm_mdl = svm_mdl.fit(X_train, y_train)
y_train_svc_pred, y_test_svc_prob, y_test_svc_pred =\
```

```
mldatasets.evaluate_class_mdl(fitted_svm_mdl, X_train,\
                    X_test, y_train, y_test)
```

The preceding code produces the output shown here in *Figure 6.3*:

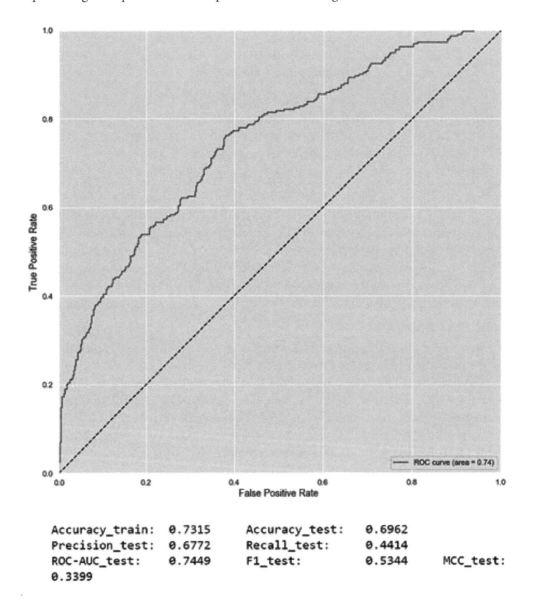

```
Accuracy_train:    0.7315      Accuracy_test:    0.6962
Precision_test:    0.6772      Recall_test:      0.4414
ROC-AUC_test:      0.7449      F1_test:          0.5344      MCC_test:
0.3399
```

Figure 6.3 – Predictive performance of our SVC model

The performance achieved (see *Figure 6.3*) is not bad, considering this is a small imbalanced dataset in an already challenging domain for machine learning models' user ratings. In any case, the **Area Under the Curve** (**AUC**) curve is above the dotted coin toss line, and the **Matthews correlation coefficient** (**MCC**) is safely above 0. More importantly, precision is substantially higher than recall, and this is very good given the hypothetical cost of misclassifying a lousy chocolate bar as *Highly Recommended*. We favor precision over recall because we would prefer to have fewer false positives than false negatives.

Computing SHAP values using KernelExplainer

Given how computationally intensive calculating SHAP values by brute force can be, the SHAP library takes many statistically valid shortcuts. As we learned in *Chapter 5, Global Model-Agnostic Interpretation Methods*, these shortcuts range from leveraging a decision tree's structure (`TreeExplainer`) to the difference in a neural network's activations, and a baseline (`DeepExplainer`) to a neural network's gradient (`GradientExplainer`). These shortcuts make the explainers significantly less model-agnostic since they are limited to a family of model classes. However, there is a truly model-agnostic explainer in SHAP, called the `KernelExplainer`.

`KernelExplainer` has two shortcuts: it samples a subset of all feature permutations for coalitions and uses a weighting scheme according to the size of the coalition to compute SHAP values. The first shortcut is a recommended technique to reduce computation time. The second one is drawn from LIME's weighting scheme, which we will cover next in this chapter, and the authors of SHAP did this so that it remains compliant to Shapley. However, for "missing" features in the coalition, it randomly samples from the features' values in a background training dataset, which violates the **dummy** property of Shapley values. More importantly, as with **permutation feature importance**, if there's multicollinearity, it puts too much weight on unlikely instances. Despite this near-fatal flaw, `KernelExplainer` has all the other benefits of Shapley values and is one of LIME's main advantages.

Before we engage with the `KernelExplainer`, it's important to note that for classification models, it yields a list of multiple SHAP values. You access these for each class with an index. Confusion may arise if this index is not in the order you expect because it's in the order provided by the model. So, it is essential to make sure of the order of the classes in your model by running the following command:

```
svm_mdl.classes_
```

The output tells you that *Not Highly Recommended* has an index of 0, as you would expect, and *Highly Recommended* has an index of 1. We are interested in the SHAP values for the latter because this is what we are trying to predict. The code is shown here:

```
array([0, 1])
```

KernelExplainer takes a predict function for a model (fitted_svm_mdl. predict_proba) and some background training data (X_train_summary). KernelExplainer strongly suggests other measures to minimize computation. One of these is using **k-means** to summarize the background training data instead of using it whole. Another method could be using a sample of the training data. In this case, we opted for k-means clustering into 10 centroids. Once we have initialized our explainer, we can use samples of our test dataset (nsamples=200) to come up with the SHAP values. It uses L1 regularization (l1_reg) during the fitting process. What we are telling it here is to regularize to a point where it only has 20 relevant features. Lastly, we can use a summary_plot to plot our SHAP values for class 1. The code is illustrated in the following snippet:

```
np.random.seed(rand)
X_train_summary = shap.kmeans(X_train, 10)
shap_svm_explainer =\
        shap.KernelExplainer(fitted_svm_mdl.predict_proba,
                        X_train_summary)
shap_svm_values_test = shap_svm_explainer.shap_values(X_test,
                nsamples=200, l1_reg="num_features(20)")
shap.summary_plot(shap_svm_values_test[1], X_test, plot_
type="dot")
```

The preceding code produces the output shown in *Figure 6.4*. Even though the point of this chapter is local model interpretation, it's important to start with the global form of this to make sure outcomes are intuitive. If they aren't, perhaps something is amiss.

The output can be seen here:

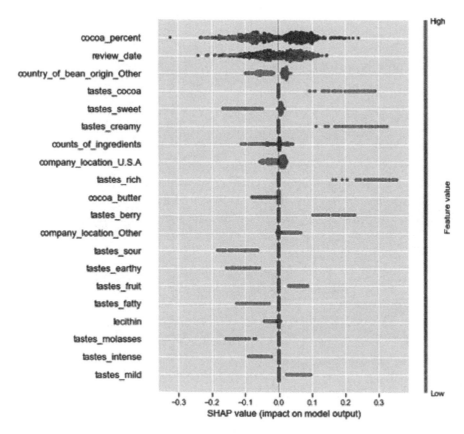

Figure 6.4 – Global model interpretation with SHAP using a summary plot

In *Figure 6.4*, we can tell that the highest (red) cocoa percentages (`cocoa_percent`) tend to correlate with a decrease in the likelihood of *Highly Recommended*, but the middle values (purple) tend to increase it. This finding makes intuitive sense because the darkest chocolates are more of an acquired taste than less-dark chocolates. The low values (blue) are scattered throughout so they show no trend, but this could be because there aren't many. On the other hand, `review date` suggests that it was likely to be *Highly Recommended* in earlier years. There are significant shades of red and purple on both sides of 0, so it's hard to identify a trend here. A dependence plot, such as those used in *Chapter 5, Global Model-Agnostic Interpretation Methods*, would be better for this purpose. However, it's very easy for binary features to visualize how high and low values, ones and zeros, impact the model. For instance, we can tell that the presence of cocoa, creamy, rich, and berry tastes increases the likelihood of the chocolate being recommended, while sweet, earthy, sour, and fatty tastes do the opposite. Likewise, the odds for *Highly Recommended* decrease if the chocolate was manufactured in the US! Sorry, US.

Local interpretation for a group of predictions using decision plots

For local interpretation, you don't have to visualize one point at a time—you can instead interpret several at a time. The key is providing some context to compare the points adequately, and there can't be so many that you can't distinguish them. Usually, you would find outliers or only those that meet specific criteria. For this exercise, we will select only those bars that were produced by your client, as follows:

```
sample_test_idx = X_test.index.\
                get_indexer_for([5,6,7,18,19,21,24,25,27])
```

One great thing about Shapley is its additivity property, which can be easily demonstrated. If you add all the SHAP values to the expected value used to compute them, you get a prediction. Of course, this is a classification problem, so the prediction is a probability; so, to get a Boolean array instead, we have to check if the probability is greater than 0.5. We can check if this Boolean array matches our model's test dataset predictions (y_test_svc_pred) by running the following code:

```
expected_value = shap_svm_explainer.expected_value[1]
y_test_shap_pred =\
            (shap_svm_values_test[1].sum(1) + expected_value) >
0.5
print(np.array_equal(y_test_shap_pred, y_test_svc_pred))
```

It should, and it does! You can see the confirmation here:

```
True
```

SHAP's decision plot comes with a highlight feature that we can use to make false negatives (FN) stand out. Now, let's figure out which of our sample observations are FN, as follows:

```
FN = (~y_test_shap_pred[sample_test_idx]) &
      (y_test.iloc[sample_test_idx] == 1).to_numpy()
```

We can now quickly reset our plotting style back to the default matplotlib style, and plot a decision_plot. It takes the expected_value, the SHAP values, and actual values of those items we wish to plot. Optionally, we can provide a Boolean array of the items we want to highlight, with dotted lines—in this case, the false negatives (FN), as illustrated in the following code snippet:

```
sns.reset_orig()
plt.rcParams.update(orig_plt_params)
```

```
shap.decision_plot(expected_value,\
                shap_svm_values_test[1][sample_test_idx],\
                X_test.iloc[sample_test_idx], highlight=FN)
```

The plot produced in *Figure 6.5* has a single color-coded line for each observation. The color of each line represents not the value of any feature, but the model output. Since we used `predict_proba` in `KernelExplainer` this is a probability, but otherwise it would have displayed SHAP values, and the value they have when they strike the top *x* axis is the predicted value. The features are sorted in terms of importance but only among the observations plotted, and you can tell that the lines increase and decrease horizontally depending on each feature. How much they vary and toward which direction depends on the feature's contribution to the outcome. The gray line represents the class's expected value, which is like the intercept in a linear model. In fact, similarly, all lines start at this value, making it best to read the plot from bottom to top.

You can view the output here:

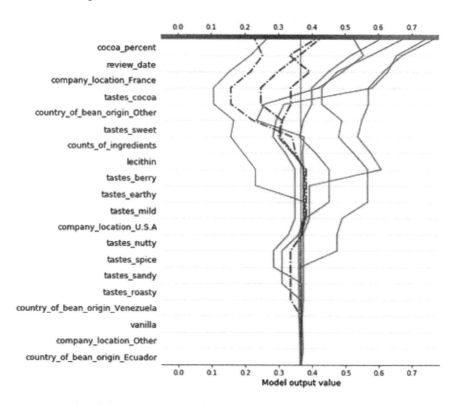

Figure 6.5 – Local model interpretation with SHAP for a sample of predictions, highlighting false negatives

You can tell that there are three false negatives plotted in *Figure 6.5* because they have dotted lines. Using this plot, we can easily visualize which features made them veer toward the left the most because this is what made them negative predictions. For instance, we know that the leftmost false negative was to the right of the expected value line until `lecithin` and then continued decreasing till `company_location_France`, and `review_date` increased its likelihood of *Highly Recommended*, but it wasn't enough. You can tell that `county_of_bean_origin_Other` decreased the likelihood of two of the misclassifications. This decision could be unfair because the country could be one of over 50 countries that didn't get their own feature. Quite possibly, there's a lot of variation between the beans of these countries grouped together.

Decision plots can also isolate a single observation. When it does this, it prints the value of each feature next to the dotted line. Let's plot one for a decision plot of the same company (true-positive observation #696), as follows:

```
shap.decision_plot(expected_value, shap_svm_values_test[1]
[696], X_test.iloc[696], highlight=0)
```

Figure 6.6 here was outputted by the preceding code:

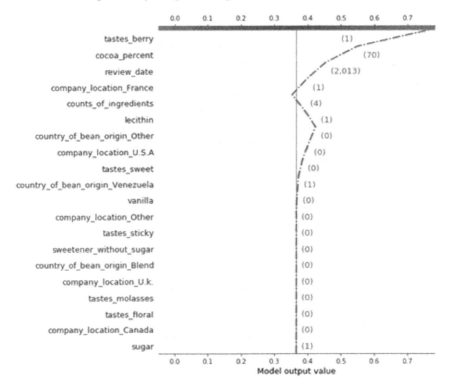

Figure 6.6 – Local model interpretation with SHAP for a single true positive in the sample of predictions

In *Figure 6.6*, you can see that `lecithin` and `counts_of_ingredients` decreased the *Highly Recommended* likelihood to a point where it could have jeopardized it. Fortunately, all features above those veered the line decidedly rightward because `company_location_France=1`, `cocoa_percent=70`, and `tastes_berry=1` are all favorable.

Local interpretation for a single prediction at a time using a force plot

Your client, the chocolate manufacturer, has two bars they want you to compare. Bar #5 is *Outstanding* and #24 is *Disappointing*. They are both in your test dataset. One way of comparing them is to place their values side by side in a dataframe to understand how exactly they differ. We will concatenate the rating, the actual label `y`, and the `y_pred` predicted label to these observations' values, as follows:

```
eval_idxs = (X_test.index==5) | (X_test.index==24)
X_test_eval = X_test[eval_idxs]
eval_compare_df = pd.concat([\
    chocolateratings_df.iloc[X_test[eval_idxs].index].rating,\
    pd.DataFrame({'y':y_test[eval_idxs]}, index=[5,24]),\
    pd.DataFrame({'y_pred':y_test_svc_pred[eval_idxs]},\
    index=[24,5]),\
    X_test_eval], axis=1).transpose()
eval_compare_df
```

The preceding code produces the dataframe shown in *Figure 6.7*. With this dataframe, you can confirm that they aren't misclassifications because `y=y_pred`. A misclassification could make model interpretations unreliable to understand why people tend to like one chocolate bar more than another. Then, you can examine the features to spot the differences—for instance, you can tell that the `review_date` is 2 years apart. Also, the beans for the *Outstanding* bar were from Venezuela, and the *Disappointing* beans came from another, lesser-represented country. The *Outstanding* one had a berry taste, and the *Disappointing* one was earthy.

You can see the observations here:

	5	24
rating	4.00	2.75
y	1.00	0.00
y_pred	1.00	0.00
review_date	2013.00	2015.00
cocoa_percent	70.00	70.00
counts_of_ingredients	4.00	4.00
cocoa_butter	1.00	1.00
vanilla	0.00	0.00
lecithin	1.00	1.00
salt	0.00	0.00
sugar	1.00	1.00
sweetener_without_sugar	0.00	0.00
company_location_Canada	0.00	0.00
company_location_France	1.00	1.00
:	:	:
country_of_bean_origin_Other	0.00	1.00
country_of_bean_origin_Peru	0.00	0.00
country_of_bean_origin_Venezuela	1.00	0.00
:	:	:
tastes_earthy	0.00	1.00
:	:	:
tastes_berry	1.00	0.00
tastes_vanilla	0.00	0.00
tastes_creamy	0.00	0.00

Figure 6.7 – Observations #5 and #24 side by side, with feature differences highlighted in yellow

The force plot can tell us a complete story of what weighed in the model's decisions (and, presumably, the reviewers'), and gives us clues as to what consumers might prefer. Plotting a force_plot requires the expected value for the class of your interest (expected_value), the SHAP values for the observation of your interest, and this observation's actual values. We will start with observation #5, as illustrated in the following code snippet:

```
shap.force_plot(expected_value,\
        shap_svm_values_test[1][X_test.index==5],\
        X_test[X_test.index==5], matplotlib=True)
```

The preceding code produces the plot shown in *Figure 6.8*. This force plot depicts how much `review_date`, `cocoa_percent`, and `tastes_berry` weigh in the prediction, while the only feature that seems to be weighing in the opposite direction is `counts_of_ingredients`.

The output can be seen here:

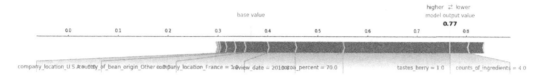

Figure 6.8 – Force plot for observation #5 (Outstanding)

Let's compare it with a force plot of observation #24, as follows:

```
shap.force_plot(expected_value,\
        shap_svm_values_test[1][X_test.index==24],\
        X_test[X_test.index==24], matplotlib=True)
```

The preceding code produces the plot shown in *Figure 6.9*. We can easily tell that `tastes_earthy` and `country_of_bean_origin_Other` are considered highly negative attributes by our model. The outcome could be mostly explained by the difference in the chocolate tasting of "berry" versus "earthy". Despite our findings, the beans' origin country needs further investigation. After all, it is possible that the actual country of origin doesn't correlate with poor ratings.

The output can be seen here:

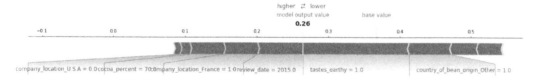

Figure 6.9 – Force plot for observation #24 (Disappointing)

In this section, we covered the `KernelExplainer`, which uses some tricks it learned from LIME. But what is LIME? We will find that out next!

Employing LIME

Until now, the model-agnostic interpretation methods we've covered attempt to reconcile the totality of outputs of a model with its inputs. For these methods to get a good idea of how and why X becomes `y_pred`, they need some data first. Then, they perform simulations with this data, pushing variations of it in and evaluating what comes out of the model. Sometimes, they even leverage a global surrogate to connect the dots. By using what they learned in this process, they yield importances, scores, rules, or values that quantify a feature's impact, interactions, or decisions on a global level. For many methods such as SHAP, these can be observed locally too. However, even when it can be observed locally, what was quantified globally may not apply locally. For this reason, there should be another approach that quantifies the local effects of features solely for local interpretation—one such as LIME!

What is LIME?

LIME trains local surrogates to explain a single prediction. To this end, it starts by asking you which *data point* you want to interpret. You also provide it with your black-box model and a sample dataset. It then makes predictions on a *perturbed* version of the dataset with the model, creating a scheme whereby it samples and *weighs* points higher if they are *closer* to your chosen data point. This area around your point is called a neighborhood. Then, using the sampled points and black-box predictions in this neighborhood, it trains a weighted *intrinsically interpretable surrogate model*. Lastly, it interprets the surrogate model.

There are lots of keywords to unpack here so let's define them, as follows:

- **Chosen data point**: LIME calls the data point, row, or observation you want to interpret an *instance*. It's just another word for this concept.

- **Perturbation**: LIME simulates new samples by perturbing each feature drawing from its training-dataset distribution for categorical features and normal distribution for continuous features.

- **Weighting scheme**: LIME uses an exponential smoothing kernel to both define the neighborhood radius and determine how to weigh the points farthest versus those closest.

- **Closer**: LIME uses Euclidean distance for tabular and image data, and cosine similarity for text. This is hard to imagine in high-dimensional feature spaces, but you can calculate the distance between points for any number of dimensions and find which points are closest to the one of interest.

- **Intrinsically interpretable surrogate model**: LIME uses a sparse linear model with weighted ridge regularization. However, it could use any intrinsically interpretable model as long as the data points can be weighted. The idea behind this is twofold. It needs a model that can yield reliable intrinsic parameters such as coefficients that tell it how much each feature impacts the prediction. It also needs to consider data points closest to the chosen point more because these are more relevant.

Much like with **k-Nearest Neighbors (k-NN)**, the intuition behind LIME is that points in a neighborhood have commonality because you could expect points close to each other to have similar, if not the same, labels. There are decision boundaries for classifiers, so this could be a very naive assumption to make when close points are divided by one.

Similar to another model class in the Nearest Neighbors family, **Radius Nearest Neighbors**, LIME factors in distance along a radius and weighs points accordingly, although it does this exponentially. However, LIME is not a model class but an interpretation method, so the similarities stop there. Instead of "voting" for predictions among neighbors, it fits a weighted surrogate sparse linear model because it assumes that every complex model is linear locally, and because it's not a model class, the predictions the surrogate model makes don't matter. In fact, the surrogate model doesn't even have to fit the data like a glove because all you need from it is the coefficients. Of course, that being said, it is best if it fits well so that there is higher fidelity in the interpretation.

LIME works for tabular, image, and text data and generally has high local fidelity, meaning that it can approximate the model predictions quite well on a local level. However, this is contingent on the neighborhood being defined correctly, which stems from choosing the right kernel width and the assumption of local linearity holding true.

Local interpretation for a single prediction at a time using LimeTabularExplainer

To explain a single prediction, you first instantiate a `LimeTabularExplainer` by providing it with your sample dataset in a NumPy 2D array (`X_test.values`), a list with the names of the features (`X_test.columns`), a list with the indices of the categorical features (only the first three features aren't categorical), and the class names. Even though only the sample dataset is required, it is recommended that you provide names for your features and classes so that the interpretation makes sense. For tabular data, telling LIME which features are categorical (`categorical_features`) is important because it treats categorical features differently from continuous ones, and not specifying this could potentially make for a poor-fitting local surrogate. Another parameter that can greatly impact the local surrogate is `kernel_width`. This defines the diameter of the neighborhood, thus answering the question of what is considered local. It has a default value, which may or may not yield interpretations that make sense for your instance. You could tune this parameter on an instance-by-instance basis to optimize your explanations. The code can be seen in the following snippet:

```
lime_svm_explainer =\
  lime.lime_tabular.LimeTabularExplainer(X_test.values,\
        feature_names=X_test.columns,\
        categorical_features=list(range(3,44)),\
        class_names=['Not Highly Recomm.', 'Highly Recomm.'])
```

With the instantiated explainer, you can now use `explain_instance` to fit a local surrogate model to observation #5. We also will use our model's classifier function (`predict_proba`) and limit our number of features to eight (`num_features=8`). We can take the "explanation" returned and immediately visualize it with `show_in_notebook`. At the same time, the `predict_proba` parameter makes sure it also includes a plot to show which class is the most probable, according to the local surrogate model. The code is illustrated in the following snippet:

```
lime_svm_explainer.\
  explain_instance(X_test[X_test.index==5].values[0],\
            fitted_svm_mdl.predict_proba,\
            num_features=8). show_in_notebook(predict_
proba=True)
```

The preceding code provides the output shown in *Figure 6.10*. According to the local surrogate, a cocoa_percent value smaller or equal to 70 is a favorable attribute, as is the berry taste. A lack of sour, sweet, and molasses tastes also weighs in favorably in this model. However, a lack of rich, creamy, and cocoa tastes does the opposite, but not enough to push the scales toward *Not Highly Recommended*.

The output can be seen here:

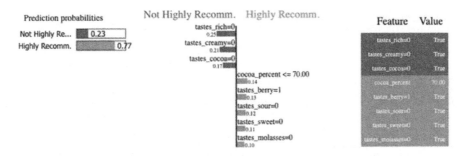

Figure 6.10 – LIME tabular explanation for observation #5 (Outstanding)

With a small adjustment to the code that produced *Figure 6.10*, we can produce the same plot but for observation #24, as follows:

```
lime_svm_explainer.\
  explain_instance(X_test[X_test.index==24].values[0],\
            fitted_svm_mdl.predict_proba,\
            num_features=8).\
  show_in_notebook(predict_proba=True)
```

Here, in *Figure 6.11*, we can clearly see why the local surrogate believes that observation #24 is *Not Highly Recommended*:

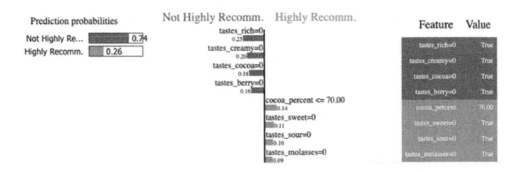

Figure 6.11 – LIME tabular explanation for observation #24 (Disappointing)

Once you compare the explanation of #24 (*Figure 6.11*) with that of #5 (*Figure 6.10*), the problems become evident. A single feature, `tastes_berry`, is what differentiates both explanations. Of course, we have limited it to the top eight features, so there's probably much more to it. However, you would expect the top eight features to include the ones that make the most difference.

According to SHAP, knowing that `tastes_earthy=1` is what globally explains the disappointing nature of the #24 chocolate bar, but this appears to be counterintuitive. So, what happened? It turns out that observations #5 and #24 are relatively similar and, thus, in the same neighborhood. This neighborhood also includes many chocolate bars with berry tastes, and very few with earthy ones. However, there are not enough earthy ones to consider it a salient feature, so it attributes the difference between *Highly Recommended* and *Not Highly Recommended* to other features that seem to differentiate more often, at least locally. The reason for this is twofold: the local neighborhood could be too small, and linear models, given their simplicity, are on the bias end of a *bias-variance trade-off*. This bias is only exacerbated by the fact that some features such as `tastes_berry` can appear relatively more often than `tastes_earthy`. There's an approach we can use to fix this, and we'll cover this in the next section.

Using LIME for NLP

At the beginning of the chapter, we set aside training and test datasets with the cleaned-up contents of all the "tastes" columns for NLP. We can take a peek at the test dataset for NLP, as follows:

```
print(X_test_nlp)
```

This outputs the following:

1194	roasty nutty rich
77	roasty oddly sweet marshmallow
121	balanced cherry choco
411	sweet floral yogurt
1259	creamy burnt nuts woody
	...
327	sweet mild molasses bland
1832	intense fruity mild sour
464	roasty sour milk note
2013	nutty fruit sour floral

1190	rich roasty nutty smoke
Length: 734, dtype: object	

No machine learning model can ingest the data as text, so we need to turn it into a numerical format—in other words, vectorize it. There are many techniques we can use to do this. In our case, we are not interested in the position of words in each phrase, nor the semantics. However, we are interested in their relative occurrence—after all, that was an issue for us in the last section.

For these reasons, **Term Frequency-Inverse Document Frequency (TF-IDF)** is the ideal method because it's meant to evaluate how often a term (each word) appears in a document (each phrase). However, it's weighted according to its frequency in the entire corpus (all phrases). We can easily vectorize our datasets using the TF-IDF method with `TfidfVectorizer` from scikit-learn. However, when you have to make TD-IDF scores, these are fitted to the training dataset only because that way, the transformed train and test datasets have consistent scoring for each term. Have a look at the following code snippet:

```
vectorizer = TfidfVectorizer(lowercase=False)
X_train_nlp_fit = vectorizer.fit_transform(X_train_nlp)
X_test_nlp_fit = vectorizer.transform(X_test_nlp)
```

To get an idea of what the TF-IDF score looks like, we can place all the feature names in one column of a dataframe, and their respective scores for a single observation in another. Note that since the vectorizer produces a `scipy` sparse matrix, we have to convert it into a NumPy matrix with `todense()` and then a NumPy array with `asarray()`. We can sort this dataframe in descending order by TD-IDF scores. The code is shown in the following snippet:

```
pd.DataFrame({'taste':vectorizer.get_feature_names(),\
        'tf-idf': np. asarray(X_test_nlp_fit[X_test_nlp.
index==5]. todense())[0]}).\
  sort_values(by='tf-idf', ascending=False)
```

The preceding code produces the output shown here in *Figure 6.12*:

	taste	tf-idf
305	raspberry	0.59
259	nut	0.49
265	oily	0.46
64	caramel	0.45
274	papaya	0.00
:	:	:
135	edge	0.00
134	easy	0.00
133	easter	0.00
415	yogurt	0.00

416 rows × 2 columns

Figure 6.12 – The TF-IDF scores for words present in observation #5

And as you can tell from *Figure 6.12*, the TD-IDF scores are normalized values between 0 and 1, and those most common in the corpus have a lower value. Interestingly enough, we realize that observation #5 in our tabular dataset had `berry=1` because of **raspberry**. The categorical encoding method we used searched occurrences of `berry` regardless of whether it matched an entire word or not. This isn't a problem because raspberry is a kind of berry, and raspberry wasn't one of our common tastes with its own binary column.

Now that we have vectorized our NLP datasets, we can proceed with the modeling.

Training a LightGBM model

LightGBM, like **XGBoost**, is another very popular and performant gradient-boosting framework that leverages boosted-tree ensembles and histogram-based split finding. The main differences lie in the split method's algorithms, which for LightGBM uses sampling with **Gradient-based One-Side Sampling (GOSS)** and bundling sparse features with **Exclusive Feature Bundling (EFB)** versus XGBoost's more rigorous **Weighted Quantile Sketch** and **Sparsity-aware Split Finding**. Another difference lies in how the trees are built, which is **depth-first** (top-down) for XGBoost and **best-first** (across a tree's leaves) for LightGBM. We won't get into the details of how these algorithms work because that would derail the topic at hand. However, it's important to note that thanks to GOSS, LightGBM is usually even faster than XGBoost, and though it can lose predictive performance due to GOSS split approximations, it gains some of it back with its best-first approach. On the other hand, **Explainable Boosting Machine (EBM)** makes LightGBM ideal for training on sparse features efficiently and effectively, such as those in our X_ train_nlp_fit sparse matrix! That pretty much sums up why we are using LightGBM for this exercise.

To train the LightGBM model, we first initialize the model by setting the maximum tree depth (max_depth), the learning rate (learning_rate), the number of boosted trees to fit (n_estimators), the objective, which is binary classification, and—last but not least—the random_state for reproducibility. With fit, we train the model using our vectorized NLP training dataset (X_train_nlp_fit) and the same labels used for the SVM model (y_train). Once trained, we can evaluate using the evaluate_ class_mdl we used with SVM. The code is illustrated in the following snippet:

```
lgb_mdl = lgb.LGBMClassifier(max_depth=13, learning_rate=0.05,\
    n_estimators=100, objective='binary', random_state=rand)
fitted_lgb_mdl = lgb_mdl.fit(X_train_nlp_fit, y_train)
y_train_lgb_pred, y_test_lgb_prob, y_test_lgb_pred =\
  mldatasets.evaluate_class_mdl(fitted_lgb_mdl, X_train_nlp_fit,
  X_test_nlp_fit, y_train, y_test)
```

The preceding code produces *Figure 6.13*, shown here:

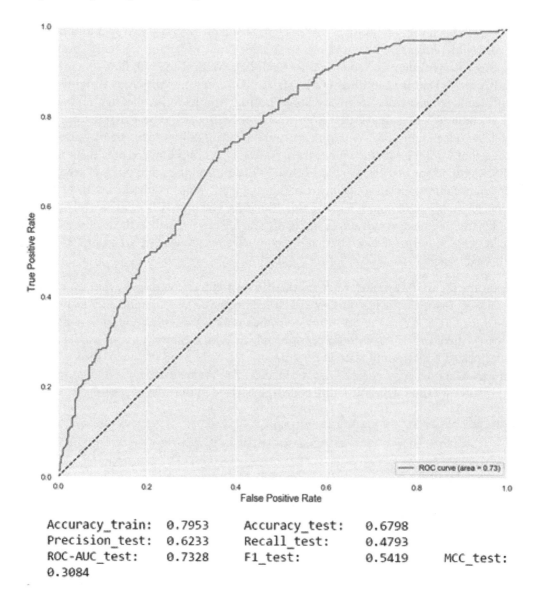

```
Accuracy_train:    0.7953      Accuracy_test:    0.6798
Precision_test:    0.6233      Recall_test:      0.4793
ROC-AUC_test:      0.7328      F1_test:          0.5419      MCC_test:
0.3084
```

Figure 6.13 – Predictive performance of our LightGBM model

The performance achieved by LightGBM (see *Figure 6.13*) is slightly lower than for SVM (*Figure 6.3*) but it's still pretty good, safely above the coin-toss line. The comments for SVM about favoring precision over recall for this model also apply here.

Local interpretation for a single prediction at a time using LimeTextExplainer

To interpret any black-box model prediction with LIME, you need to specify a classifier function such as `predict_proba` for your model, and it will use this function to make predictions with perturbed data in the neighborhood of your instance and then train a linear model with it. The instance must be in its numerical form—in other words, vectorized. However, it would be easier if you could provide any arbitrary text, and it could then vectorize it on the fly. This is precisely what a pipeline can do for you. With the `make_pipeline` function from scikit-learn, you can define a sequence of estimators that transform the data, followed by one that can fit it. In this case, we just need `vectorizer` to transform our data, followed by our LightGBM model (`lgb_mdl`) that takes the transformed data, as illustrated in the following code snippet:

```
lgb_pipeline = make_pipeline(vectorizer, lgb_mdl)
```

Initializing a `LimeTextExplainer` is pretty simple. All parameters are optional, but it's recommended to specify names for your classes. Just as with `LimeTabularExplainer`, a `kernel_width` optional parameter can be critical because it defines the neighborhood's size, and there's a default that may not be optimal but can be tuned on an instance-by-instance basis. The code is illustrated here:

```
lime_lgb_explainer = LimeTextExplainer(class_names=['Not Highly
Recomm.', 'Highly Recomm.'])
```

Explaining an instance with `LimeTextExplainer` is similar to doing it for `LimeTabularExplainer`. The difference is that we are using a pipeline (`lgb_pipeline`), and the data we are providing (first parameter) is text since the pipeline can transform it for us. The code is illustrated in the following snippet:

```
lime_lgb_explainer.\
    explain_instance(X_test_nlp[X_test_nlp.index==5].
values[0],\
                lgb_pipeline.predict_proba, num_features=4).\
    show_in_notebook(text=True)
```

According to the LIME text explainer (see *Figure 6.14*), the LightGBM model predicts *Highly Recommended* for observation #5 because of the word **caramel**. At least according to the local neighborhood, **raspberry** is not a factor.

The output can be seen here:

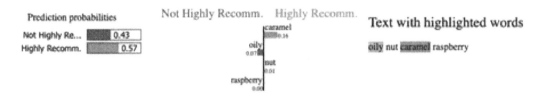

Figure 6.14 – LIME text explanation for observation #5 (Outstanding)

Now, let's contrast the interpretation for observation #5 with that of #24, as we've done before. We can use the same code but simply replace 5 with 24, as follows:

```
lime_lgb_explainer.\
    explain_instance(X_test_nlp[X_test_nlp.index==24].
values[0], \
                lgb_pipeline.predict_proba, num_features=4).
    show_in_notebook(text=True)
```

According to *Figure 6.15*, you can tell that observation #24, described as tasting like **burnt wood earthy choco** is *Not Highly Recommended* because of the words **earthy** and **burnt**.

The output can be seen here:

Figure 6.15 – LIME tabular explanation for observation #24 (Disappointing)

Given that we are using a pipeline that can vectorize any arbitrary text, let's have some fun with that! We will first try a phrase made out of adjectives we suspect that our model favors, then try one with unfavorable adjectives, and lastly try using words that our model shouldn't be familiar with, as follows:

```
lime_lgb_explainer.explain_instance('creamy rich complex
fruity', \
                lgb_pipeline.predict_proba, num_features=4).
    show_in_notebook(text=True)
lime_lgb_explainer.explain_instance('sour bitter roasty
molasses',
```

```
              lgb_pipeline.predict_proba, num_features=4).
    show_in_notebook(text=True)
lime_lgb_explainer.explain_instance('nasty disgusting gross
stuff', \
    lgb_pipeline.predict_proba, num_features=4).
    show_in_notebook(text=True)
```

In *Figure 6.16*, the explanations are spot-on for **creamy rich complex fruity** and **sour bitter roasty molasses** since the model knows these words to be either very favorable or unfavorable. These words are also common enough to be appreciated on a local level.

You can see the output here:

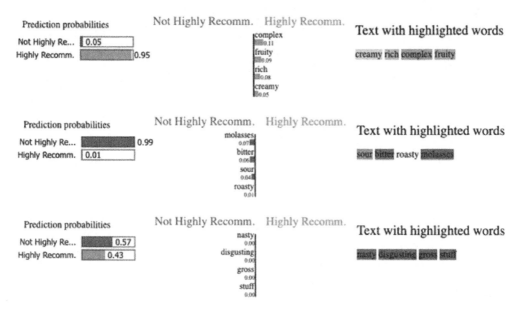

Figure 6.16 – Arbitrary phrases not in the training or test dataset can be effortlessly explained with LIME, as long as words are in the corpus

However, you'd be mistaken to think that the prediction of *Not Highly Recommended* for **nasty disgusting gross stuff** has anything to do with the words. The LightGBM model hasn't seen these words before, so the prediction has more to do with *Not Highly Recommended* being the majority class, which is a good guess, and the sparse matrix for this phrase is all zeros. Therefore, LIME likely found few distant points—if any at all—in its neighborhood, so the zero coefficients of LIME's local surrogate model reflect this.

Trying SHAP for NLP

Most of SHAP's explainers will work with tabular data. `DeepExplainer` can do text but is restricted to deep learning models, and, as we will cover in *Chapter 8, Visualizing Convolutional Neural Networks*, three of them do images, including `KernelExplainer`. In fact, SHAP's `KernelExplainer` was designed to be a general-purpose truly model-agnostic method, but it's not promoted as an option for NLP. It easy to understand why: it's slow, and NLP models tend to be very complex and with hundreds—if not thousands—of features to boot. In cases such as this one, where word order is not a factor and you have a few hundred features, but the top 100 are present in most of your observations, `KernelExplainer` could work.

In addition to overcoming slowness, there are a couple of technical hurdles you would need to overcome. One of them is that `KernelExplainer` is compatible with a pipeline, but it expects a single set of predictions back. But LightGBM returns two sets, one for each class: *Not Highly Recommended* and *Highly Recommended*. To overcome this problem, we can create a `lambda` function (`predict_fn`) that includes a `predict_proba` function, which returns only those predictions for *Highly Recommended*. This is illustrated in the following code snippet:

```
predict_fn = lambda X: lgb_mdl.predict_proba(X)[:,1]
```

The second technical hurdle has to with SHAP's incompatibility with SciPy's sparse matrices, and for our explainer we will need sample vectorized test data, which is in this format. To overcome this issue, can convert our data in SciPy sparse-matrix format to a NumPy matrix and then to a pandas dataframe (`X_test_nlp_samp_df`). To overcome any slowness, we can use the same `kmeans` trick we used last time. Other than the adjustments made to overcome obstacles, the following code is exactly the same as with SHAP performed with the SVM model:

```
X_test_nlp_samp_df = pd.DataFrame(shap.\
                            sample(X_test_nlp_fit, 50).
todense())
shap_lgb_explainer =\
    shap.KernelExplainer(predict_fn,\
                    shap.kmeans(X_train_nlp_fit.todense(),
10))
shap_lgb_values_test =\
    shap_lgb_explainer.shap_values(X_test_nlp_samp_df,\
                        l1_reg="num_features(20)")
shap.summary_plot(shap_lgb_values_test, X_test_nlp_samp_df,\
```

```
          plot_type="dot", feature_names=vectorizer.get_feature_
names())
```

By using SHAP's summary plot in *Figure 6.17*, you can tell that globally the words **creamy**, **rich**, **cocoa**, **fruit**, **spicy**, **nutty**, and **berry** have a positive impact on the model toward predicting *Highly Recommended*. On the other hand, **sweet**, **sour**, **earthy**, **hammy**, **sandy**, and **fatty** have the opposite effect. These results shouldn't be entirely unexpected given what we learned with our prior SVM model with the tabular data and local LIME interpretations. That being said, the SHAP values were derived from samples of a sparse matrix, and they could be missing details and perhaps even be partially incorrect, especially for underrepresented features. Therefore, we should take the conclusions with a grain of salt, especially toward the bottom half of the plot. To increase interpretation fidelity it's best to increase sample size, but given the slowness of `KernelExplainer`, there's a trade-off to consider.

You can view the output here:

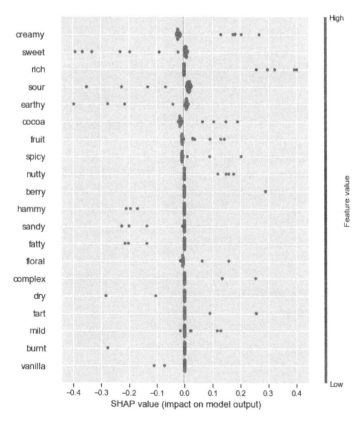

Figure 6.17 – SHAP summary plot for the LightGBM NLP model

Now that we have validated our SHAP values globally, we can use them for local interpretation with a force plot. Unlike LIME, we cannot use arbitrary data for this. With SHAP, we are limited to those data points we have previously generated SHAP values for. For instance, let's take the 18th observation from our test dataset sample, as follows:

```
print(shap.sample(X_test_nlp, 50).to_list()[18])
```

The preceding code outputs this phrase:

```
woody earthy medicinal
```

It's important to note which words are represented in the 18th observation because the X_test_nlp_samp_df dataframe contains the vectorized representation. The 18th observation's row in this dataframe is what you use to generate the force plot, along with the SHAP values for this observation and the expected value for the class, as illustrated in the following code snippet:

```
shap.force_plot(shap_lgb_explainer.expected_value,\
                shap_lgb_values_test[18,:],\
                X_test_nlp_samp_df.iloc[18,:],\
                feature_names=vectorizer.get_feature_names())
```

Figure 6.18 is the force plot for **woody earthy medicinal**. As you can tell, **earthy** and **woody** weigh heavily in a prediction against *Highly Recommended*. The word **medicinal** is not featured in the force plot and instead you get a lack of **creamy** and **cocoa** as negative factors. As you can imagine, *medicinal* is not a word used often to describe chocolate bars, so there was only one observation in the sampled dataset that included it. Therefore, its average marginal contribution across possible coalitions would be greatly diminished.

You can view the output here:

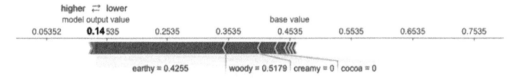

Figure 6.18 – SHAP force plot for the 18th observation of the sampled test dataset

Let's try another one, as follows:

```
print(shap.sample(X_test_nlp, 50).to_list()[9])
```

The 9th observation is the following phrase:

```
intense spicy floral
```

Generating a `force_plot` for this observation is the same as before, except you replace `18` with `9`. If you run this code, you produce the output shown here in *Figure 6.19*:

Figure 6.19 – SHAP force plot for the 9th observation of the sampled test dataset

As you can appreciate in *Figure 6.19*, all words in the phrase are featured in the force plot: **floral** and **spicy** pushing toward *Highly Recommended*, and **intense** toward *Not Highly Recommended*. So, now you know how to perform both tabular and NLP interpretations with SHAP, how does it compare with LIME?

Comparing SHAP with LIME

As you will have noticed by now, both SHAP and LIME have limitations, but they also have strengths. SHAP is grounded in game theory and approximate Shapley values, so its SHAP values mean something. These have great properties such as additivity, efficiency, and substitutability that make it consistent but violate the dummy property. It always adds up and doesn't need parameter tuning to accomplish this. However, it's more suited for global interpretations, and one of its most model-agnostic explainers, `KernelExplainer`, is painfully slow. `KernelExplainer` also deals with missing values by using random ones, which can put too much weight on unlikely observations.

LIME is speedy, very model-agnostic, and adaptable to all kinds of data. However, it's not grounded on strict and consistent principles but has the intuition that neighbors are alike. Because of this, it can require tricky parameter tuning to define the neighborhood size optimally, and even then, it's only suitable for local interpretations.

Mission accomplished

The mission was to understand why one of your client's bars is *Outstanding* while another one is *Disappointing*. Your approach employed the interpretation of machine learning models to arrive at the following conclusions:

- According to SHAP on the tabular model, the *Outstanding* bar owes that rating to its berry taste and its cocoa percentage of 70%. On the other hand, the unfavorable rating for the *Disappointing* bar is due mostly to its earthy flavor and bean country of origin (Other). Review date plays a smaller role, but it seems that chocolate bars reviewed in that period (2013-15) were at an advantage.

- LIME confirms that cocoa_percent<=70 is a desirable property, and that, in addition to **berry**, **creamy**, **cocoa**, and **rich** are favorable tastes, while **sweet**, **sour**, and **molasses** are unfavorable.

- The commonality between both methods using the tabular model is that despite the many non-taste-related attributes, taste features are among the most salient. Therefore, it's only fitting to interpret the words used to describe each chocolate bar via an NLP model.

- The *Outstanding* bar was represented by the phrase **oily nut caramel raspberry**, of which, according to LIMETextExplainer, **caramel** is positive and **oily** is negative. The other two words are neutral. On the other hand, the *Disappointing* bar was represented by **burnt wood earthy choco**, of which **burnt** and **earthy** are unfavorable and the other two are favorable.

- The inconsistencies between the tastes in tabular and NLP interpretations are due to the presence of lesser-represented tastes, including **raspberry**, which is not as common as **berry**.

- According to SHAP's global explanation of the NLP model, **creamy**, **rich**, **cocoa**, **fruit**, **spicy**, **nutty**, and **berry** have a positive impact on the model toward predicting *Highly Recommended*. On the other hand, **sweet**, **sour**, **earthy**, **hammy**, **sandy**, and **fatty** have the opposite effect.

With these notions of which chocolate-bar characteristics and tastes are considered less attractive by *Manhattan Chocolate Society* members, a client can apply changes to their chocolate-bar formulas to appeal to a broader audience—that is, if the assumption is correct about that group being representative of their target audience.

It could be argued that it is pretty apparent that words such as **earthy** and **burnt** are not favorable words to associate with chocolate bars, while **caramel** is. Therefore, we could have reached this conclusion without machine learning! But first of all, a conclusion not informed by data would have been an opinion, and, secondly, context is everything. Furthermore, humans can't always be relied upon to place one point objectively in its context—especially considering it's among thousands of records!

Also, local model interpretation is *not only about the explanation for one prediction* because it's connected to how a model makes all predictions but, more importantly, to how it makes predictions for similar points—in other words, in the local neighborhood! In the next chapter, we will expand on what it means to be in the local neighborhood by looking at the commonalities (*anchors*) and inconsistencies (*counterfactuals*) we can find there.

Summary

After reading this chapter, you should know how to use SHAP's `KernelExplainer`, as well as its decision and force plot to conduct local interpretations. You also should know how to do the same with LIME's instance explainer for both tabular and text data. Lastly, you should understand the strengths and weaknesses of SHAP's `KernelExplainer` and LIME. In the next chapter, we will learn how to create even more human-interpretable explanations of a model's decisions, such as "*if X conditions are met, then Y is the outcome*".

Dataset sources

- Brelinski, Brady (2020). *Manhattan Chocolate Society.* `http://flavorsofcacao.com/mcs_index.html`

Further reading

- Platt, J. C. (1999). *Probabilistic Outputs for Support Vector Machines and Comparisons to Regularized Likelihood Methods.* Advances in Large Margin Classifiers, MIT Press. `https://www.cs.colorado.edu/~mozer/Teaching/syllabi/6622/papers/Platt1999.pdf`
- Lundberg, S. & Lee, S. (2017). *A Unified Approach to Interpreting Model Predictions.* Advances in Neural Information Processing Systems, 30. `https://arxiv.org/abs/1705.07874` (documentation for SHAP: `https://github.com/slundberg/shap`)

- Ribeiro, M. T., Singh, S. & Guestrin, C. (2016). *"Why Should I Trust You?": Explaining the Predictions of Any Classifier*. Proceedings of the 22ⁿᵈ ACM SIGKDD International Conference on Knowledge Discovery and Data Mining. `http://arxiv.org/abs/1602.04938`

- Ke, G., Meng, Q., Finley, T., Wang, T., Chen, W., Ma, W., Ye, Q. & Liu, T. (2017). *LightGBM: A Highly Efficient Gradient Boosting Decision Tree*. Advances in Neural Information Processing Systems vol. 30, pp. 3149-3157. `https://papers.nips.cc/paper/6907-lightgbm-a-highly-efficient-gradient-boosting-decision-tree`

7
Anchor and Counterfactual Explanations

In previous chapters, we have learned how to attribute model decisions to features and their interactions with state-of-the-art global and local model interpretation methods. However, the decision boundaries are not always easy to define nor interpret with these methods. Wouldn't it be nice to be able to derive human-interpretable rules from model interpretation methods? In this chapter, we will cover a few human-interpretable, local, classification-only model interpretation methods. We will first learn how to use scoped rules called **anchors** to explain complex models with statements such as *if X conditions are met, then Y is the outcome*. Then, we will explore **counterfactual** explanations that follow the form *if Z conditions aren't met, then Y is not the outcome*. Lastly, we will explain how **contrastive explanations** combine both anchors and counterfactuals to something such as *Y is the outcome if X conditions are met and Z conditions aren't*.

These are the main topics we are going to cover in this chapter:

- Understanding anchor explanations
- Exploring counterfactual explanations
- Comparing with the contrastive explanation method

Technical requirements

This chapter's example uses the `mldatasets`, `pandas`, `numpy`, `sklearn`, `catboost`, `tensorflow`, `rulefit`, `matplotlib`, `seaborn`, `alibi`, `shap`, and `witwidget` libraries. Instructions on how to install all of these libraries are in the *Preface*. The code for this chapter is located here: `https://github.com/PacktPublishing/Interpretable-Machine-Learning-with-Python/tree/master/Chapter07`.

The mission

In the United States, for the last two decades, private companies and non-profits have been developing criminal risk assessment tools, most of which employ statistical models. As many states can no longer afford their large prison populations, these methods have increased in popularity, *guiding* judges and parole boards through every step of the prison system. However, they often do more than *guide* a decision. They make them for justice system decision-makers because they assume it is correct. Worse of all, they don't exactly know how an assessment was made. The risk is usually calculated with a white-box model, but, in practice, a black-box model is used because it is proprietary. Predictive performance is also relatively low, with median AUC scores for nine tools ranging between 0.57 and 0.74. Still, validity and biases are rarely examined, especially by the criminal justice institutions that purchase them.

Even though traditional statistical methods are still the norm for criminal justice models, to improve performance, some researchers have been proposing leveraging more complex models such as Random Forest with larger datasets. Far from being science fiction drawn from *Minority Report* or *Black Mirror*, in other countries, scoring people based on their likelihood of engaging in antisocial, or even antipatriotic, behavior with big data and machine learning is already a reality.

As more and more AI solutions attempt to make life-changing predictions about us with our data, fairness must be properly assessed, and all its ethical and practical implications must be adequately discussed. *Chapter 1, Interpretation, Interpretability, and Explainability; and Why Does It All Matter?*, covered how fairness is an integral concept for machine learning interpretation. You can evaluate fairness in any model, but fairness is especially tricky when it involves human behavior. The dynamics between human psychological, neurological, and sociological factors are extremely complicated. In the context of predicting criminal behavior, it boils down to what factors are potentially to blame for a crime, because it wouldn't be fair to include anything else in a model, and how these factors interact.

Quantitative criminologists are still debating the best predictors of criminality and their root causes. They're also debating whether it is ethical to *blame* a criminal for these factors to begin with. Thankfully, demographic traits such as race, gender, and nationality are no longer used in criminal risk assessments. But this doesn't mean that these methods are no longer racially biased. Scholars recognize the problem and are proposing solutions.

This chapter will examine racial bias in one of the most widely used risk assessment tools. Given this topic's sensitive and relevant nature, it was essential to provide a modicum of context about criminal risk assessment tools and how machine learning and fairness connects with all of it. We won't go into much more detail, but it can't be understated how vital the context is to appreciate how machine learning could perpetuate structural inequality and unfair biases.

Now, let's introduce you to your mission for this chapter!

Unfair bias in recidivisim risk assessments

An investigative journalist is writing an article on how one particular African American defendant was detained while waiting for trial. A tool called **Correctional Offender Management Profiling for Alternative Sanction (COMPAS)** deemed him as being at risk of recidivism. **Recidivism** is when someone relapses into criminal behavior. And the score convinced the judge that he had to be detained pretrial so much that they didn't even consider any other arguments or testimonies. He was locked up for many months, and, in the trial, was found not guilty. Over 5 years have passed since the trial, and he hasn't been accused of any crime. You could say the prediction for recidivism was a false positive.

The journalist has reached out to you because she would like to ascertain with data science whether there was unfair bias in this particular case. The COMPAS risk assessment is computed using 137 questions (`https://www.documentcloud.org/documents/2702103-Sample-Risk-Assessment-COMPAS-CORE.html`). It includes questions such as the following:

- "Based on the screener's observations, is this person a suspected or admitted gang member?"
- "How often have you moved in the last 12 months?"
- "How often do you have barely enough money to get by?"
- Psychometric LIKERT scale questions such as "I have never felt sad about things in my life," such as those seen in *Chapter 4, Fundamentals of Feature Importance and Impact*.

Even though race is not one of the questions, many of these questions may correlate with race. Not to mention, in some cases, they can be more a question of opinion than fact, and thus be prone to bias.

The journalist cannot provide you with the 137 answered questions or the COMPAS model because this data is not publicly available. However, all defendants' demographic and recidivism data for the same county in Florida is.

The approach

You have decided to do the following:

- **Train proxy models**: You don't have the original features or model, but all is not lost because you have the COMPAS scores – the labels. And we also have relevant features to the problem we can connect to these labels with models. By approximating the COMPAS model via the proxies, you can assess its unfairness of the labels. In this chapter, we will train a CatBoost model and a neural network model.

- **Anchor explanations**: Using this method will unearth insights into why the proxy model makes specific predictions using a series of rules called anchors, which tell you where the decision boundaries lie. The boundaries are relevant for our mission because we want to know why the defendant has been wrongfully predicted to recidivate. It's an approximate boundary to the original model, but there's still some truth to it.

- **Counterfactual explanations**: The opposite concept to anchors is about understanding why similar data points are on the opposite side of the decision boundary, which is particularly notable when discussing topics of unfairness. We will use an unbiased method to find counterfactuals and then use the **What-If Tool (WIT)** to explore counterfactuals and fairness further.

- **Contrastive Explanations Method (CEM)**: To complement anchors and counterfactual methods, you will engage with CEM, which is similar to both and can provide an understanding of the minimum requirements for a defendant to be deemed at high risk for recidivism, shedding some light not only on fairness but also on reliability, which is needed for fairness to be feasible.

The preparations

You will find the code for this example here: `https://github.com/PacktPublishing/Interpretable-Machine-Learning-with-Python/blob/master/Chapter07/Recidivism_part1.ipynb`.

Loading the libraries

To run this example, you need to install the following libraries:

- `mldatasets` to load the dataset
- `pandas` and `numpy` to manipulate the dataset
- `sklearn` (scikit-learn), `catboost`, and `tensorflow` to split the data and fit the models
- `matplotlib`, `seaborn`, `alibi`, `shap`, and `witwidget` to visualize the interpretations

You should load all of them first:

```python
import math
import mldatasets
import pandas as pd
import numpy as np
from sklearn.model_selection import train_test_split
from sklearn import metrics
from catboost import CatBoostClassifier
import tensorflow as tf
from tensorflow import keras
from tensorflow.keras import layers
import matplotlib.pyplot as plt
import seaborn as sns
from alibi.utils.mapping import ohe_to_ord, ord_to_ohe
from alibi.explainers import AnchorTabular
from alibi.explainers import CEM
from alibi.explainers import CounterFactualProto
import shap
import witwidget
from witwidget.notebook.visualization import WitWidget, \
                    WitConfigBuilder
```

Let's check that TensorFlow has loaded the right version with `print(tf.__version__)`. It should be 2.0 or above. We should also disable eager execution and verify that it worked with this command. The output should say that it's `False`:

```
tf.compat.v1.disable_eager_execution()
print('Eager execution enabled:', tf.executing_eagerly())
```

Understanding and preparing the data

We load the data like this into a dataframe we call `recidivism_df`:

```
recidivism_df = mldatasets.load("recidivism-risk",
prepare=True)
```

There should be almost 15,000 records and 23 columns. We can verify this was the case with `info()`:

```
recidivism_df.info()
```

The following output checks out. All features are numeric with no missing values, and categorical features have already been one-hot encoded for us:

```
<class 'pandas.core.frame.DataFrame'>
Int64Index: 14788 entries, 0 to 18315
Data columns (total 23 columns):
 #   Column                Non-Null Count   Dtype
---  ------                --------------   -----
 0   age                   14788 non-null   int8
 1   juv_fel_count         14788 non-null   int8
 2   juv_misd_count        14788 non-null   int8
 3   juv_other_count       14788 non-null   int64
 4   priors_count          14788 non-null   int8
 5   is_recid              14788 non-null   int8
 6   sex_Female            14788 non-null   uint8
 7   sex_Male              14788 non-null   uint8
 8   race_African-American 14788 non-null   uint8
 9   race_Asian            14788 non-null   uint8
 10  race_Caucasian        14788 non-null   uint8
 11  race_Hispanic         14788 non-null   uint8
 12  race_Native American  14788 non-null   uint8
```

13	race_Other	14788 non-null	uint8
14	c_charge_degree_(F1)	14788 non-null	uint8
15	c_charge_degree_(F2)	14788 non-null	uint8
16	c_charge_degree_(F3)	14788 non-null	uint8
17	c_charge_degree_(F7)	14788 non-null	uint8
18	c_charge_degree_(M1)	14788 non-null	uint8
19	c_charge_degree_(M2)	14788 non-null	uint8
20	c_charge_degree_(MO3)	14788 non-null	uint8
21	c_charge_degree_Other	14788 non-null	uint8
22	compas_score	14788 non-null	int64

```
dtypes: int64(2), int8(5), uint8(16)
memory usage: 649.9 KB
```

The data dictionary

There are only nine features, but they become 22 columns because of the categorical encoding:

- age: Continuous, the age of the defendant (between 8 and 9).
- juv_fel_count: Continuous, the number of juvenile felonies (between 0 and 2).
- juv_misd_count: Continuous, the number of juvenile misdemeanors (between 0 and 1).
- juv_other_count: Continuous, the number of juvenile convictions that are neither felonies nor misdemeanors (between 0 and 1).
- priors_count: Continuous, the number of prior crimes committed (between 0 and 13).
- is_recid: Binary, did the defendant recidivate within 2 years (1 for yes, 0 for no)?
- sex: Categorical, the gender of the defendant.
- race: Categorical, the race of the defendant.

- c_charge_degree: Categorical, the degree of what the defendant is currently being charged with. The United States classifies criminal offenses as felonies, misdemeanors, and infractions, ordered from most serious to least. These are subclassified in the form of degrees, which go from 1st (most serious offenses) to 3rd or 5th (least severe). However, even though this is standard for federal offenses, it is tailored to state law on a state level. For felonies, Florida (http://www.dc.state.fl.us/pub/scoresheet/cpc_manual.pdf) has a level system that determines the severity of a crime regardless of the degree, and this goes from 10 (most severe) to 1 (least). The categories of this feature are prefixed with *F* for felonies and *M* for misdemeanors. They are followed by a number, which is a level for felonies and a degree for misdemeanors.

- compas_score: Binary, COMPAS scores defendants as "low," "medium," or "high" risk. In practice, "medium" is often treated as "high" by decision-makers, so this feature has been converted to binary to reflect this behavior: 1: high/medium risk, 0: low risk.

Examining predictive bias with confusion matrices

There are two binary features in the dataset. The first one is the recidivism risk prediction made by COMPAS (compas_score). The second one (is_recid) is the *ground truth* because it's what happened within 2 years of the defendant's arrest. Just as you would with the prediction of any model against its training labels, you can build confusion matrices with these two features. scikit-learn can produce one with the confusion_matrix function (cf_matrix), and we can then create a Seaborn heatmap with it. Instead of plotting the number of **True Negatives (TNs)**, **False Positives (FPs)**, **False Negatives (FNs)**, and **True Positives (TPs)**, we can plot percentages with a simple division (cf_matrix/np.sum(cf_matrix)). The other parameters of heatmap only assist with formatting:

```
cf_matrix = metrics.confusion_matrix(recidivism_df.is_recid,\
                        recidivism_df.compas_score)
sns.heatmap(cf_matrix/np.sum(cf_matrix), annot=True,
    fmt='.2%', cmap='Blues', annot_kws={'size':16})
```

The preceding code outputs *Figure 7.1*. The top-right corner is FPs, which is nearly one-fifth of all predictions, and together with the FNs in the bottom-left corner, they make up over two-thirds:

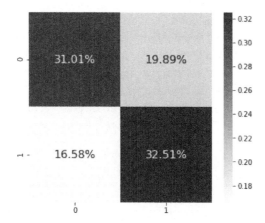

Figure 7.1 – Confusion matrix between the predicted risk of recidivism (compas_score) and the ground truth (is_recid)

Figure 7.1 tells us that the COMPAS model's predictive performance is not very good, especially if we assume that criminal justice decision-makers are taking medium or high risk assessments at face value. It also tells us that FP and FNs occur at a similar rate. Nevertheless, simple visualizations such as the confusion matrix obscure predictive disparities between subgroups of a population. We can quickly compare disparities between two subgroups that historically have been treated differently by the United States criminal justice system. To this end, we first subdivide our data frame into two dataframe: one for Caucasians (`recidivism_c_df`) and another for African Americans (`recidivism_aa_df`). Then we can generate confusion matrices for each data frame and plot them side by side with the following code:

```
recidivism_c_df =\
        recidivism_df[recidivism_df['race_Caucasian'] == 1]
recidivism_aa_df =\
        recidivism_df[recidivism_df['race_African-American'] ==
1]
_ = mldatasets.\
    compare_confusion_matrices(recidivism_c_df.is_recid,\
                               recidivism_c_df.compas_score,\
                               recidivism_aa_df.is_recid,\
                               recidivism_aa_df.compas_
```

```
score, \
                                    'Caucasian', 'African-American', \
                                    compare_fpr=True)
```

The preceding snippet generated *Figure 7.2*. At a glance, you can tell that it's like the confusion matrix for Caucasians has been flipped 90 degrees to form the African American confusion matrix, and even then, it is still less unfair. Pay close attention to the difference between FPs and TNs. As a Caucasian defendant, a result is more than half as likely to be an FP than a TN, but as an African American, it is a few percentage points more likely. In other words, a Black defendant who doesn't recidivate is predicted as at risk of recidivating more than half of the time:

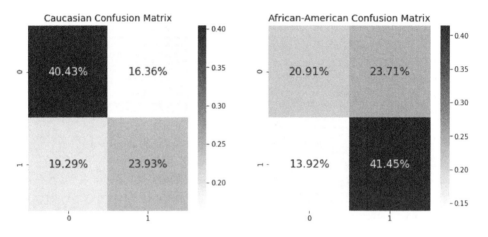

Figure 7.2 – Comparison of the confusion matrices for the predicted risk of recidivism (compas_score) and the ground truth (is_recid) between African Americans and Caucasians in the dataset

Instead of eyeballing it by looking at the plots, we can measure the **False Positive Rate (FPR)**, which is the ratio between these two measures ($FP / (FP + TN)$). Then, we can compare the FPR for both groups and divide between them to examine the relative difference. The higher this ratio between the FPRs, the more unfairness there is, because it means one group is being misclassified to recidivate more often.

Data preparation

Before we move on to the modeling and interpretation, we have one last step.

Since `prepare=True` for the data loading, all we do now is train/test split the data. As usual, it is critical to set your random states so that all your findings are reproducible. We will then set our y to be our target variable (`compas_score`) and set X as every other feature except for `is_recid`, because this is the ground truth. Lastly, we split y and X into train and test datasets as we have before:

```
rand = 9
np.random.seed(rand)
tf.random.set_seed(rand)
y = recidivism_df['compas_score']
X = recidivism_df.drop(['compas_score', 'is_recid'], axis=1).
copy()
X_train, X_test, y_train, y_test = train_test_split(X, y,\
                                    test_size=0.2, random_
state=rand)
```

Now, let's get started!

Modeling

Now, let's quickly train a couple of models we will use throughout this chapter.

Proxy models are a means to emulate output from a black-box model just like **global surrogate models**, which we covered in *Chapter 5, Global Model-Agnostic Interpretation Methods*. So, are they the same thing? In machine learning, surrogate and proxy are terms that are often used interchangeably. However, semantically, surrogacy relates to substitution and proxy relates more to a representation. So, we call these proxy models to distinguish that we don't have the exact training data. Therefore, you only represent the original model because you cannot substitute it. For the same reason, unlike interpretation with surrogates, which is best served by simpler models, a proxy is best suited to complex models that can make up for the difference in training data with complexity.

First, a **CatBoost** classifier. For those of you who aren't familiar with CatBoost, it's an efficient boosted ensembled tree method. It's similar to **LightGBM**, except it uses a new technique called **Minimal Variance Sampling (MVS)** instead of **Gradient-Based One-Side Sampling (GOSS)**. Unlike LightGBM, it grows trees in a balanced fashion. It's called CatBoost because it can automatically encode categorical features, and it's particularly good at tackling overfitting, with unbiased treatment of categorical features and class imbalances. We won't go into a whole lot of detail, but it was chosen for this exercise for those reasons.

As a tree-based model class, you can specify a maximum `depth` value for `CatBoostClassifier`. We are setting a relatively high `learning_rate` value and a lower `iterations` value (the default is 1,000). Once we have used `fit` on the model, we can evaluate the results with `evaluate_class_mdl`:

```
cb_mdl = CatBoostClassifier(iterations=500, learning_rate=0.5,\
                           depth=8)
fitted_cb_mdl = cb_mdl.fit(X_train, y_train, verbose=False) y_
train_cb_pred, y_test_cb_prob, y_test_cb_pred =\
            mldatasets.evaluate_class_mdl(fitted_cb_mdl,\
  X_train, X_test, y_train, y_test)
```

You can appreciate the output of `evaluate_class_mdl` for our CatBoost model in *Figure 7.3*:

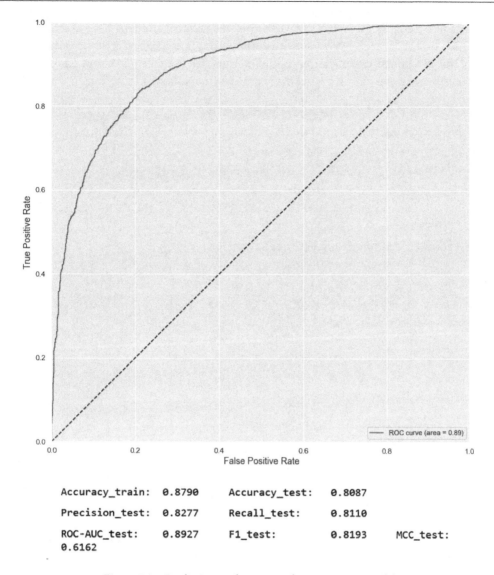

Accuracy_train:	0.8790	Accuracy_test:	0.8087		
Precision_test:	0.8277	Recall_test:	0.8110		
ROC-AUC_test:	0.8927	F1_test:	0.8193	MCC_test:	
0.6162					

Figure 7.3 – Predictive performance of our CatBoost model

From the optics of fairness, we care more about FPs than FNs because it's more unfair to put an *innocent* person in prison than it is to leave a *guilty* person in the streets. Therefore, we should aspire to have higher *precision* than *recall*. *Figure 7.3* confirms this, as well as a healthy ROC curve, ROC-AUC, and MCC.

Next, let's fit a *feedforward neural network*. First, we create it (`keras.Sequential`) with one hidden layer (`layers.Dense`) with seven nodes and `sigmoid` in the output layer, because this is a binary classification problem. Then, we use `compile` and `fit` on the model. Lastly, we use `evaluate_class_mdl` to evaluate the predictions:

```
fitted_nn_mdl = keras.Sequential([
  tf.keras.Input(shape=[len(X_train.keys())]),
  layers.Dense(7, activation='relu'),
  layers.Dense(1, activation='sigmoid')
])
fitted_nn_mdl.compile(loss='mean_squared_error',
optimizer='adam')
nn_history = fitted_nn_mdl.fit(X_train.values, y_train.values,\
         epochs=12, batch_size=32, validation_split=0.2,
verbose=0) y_train_nn_pred, y_test_nn_prob, y_test_nn_pred =\
         mldatasets.evaluate_class_mdl(fitted_nn_mdl,\
X_train, X_test, y_train, y_test)
```

Figure 7.4 depicts the output of the preceding code:

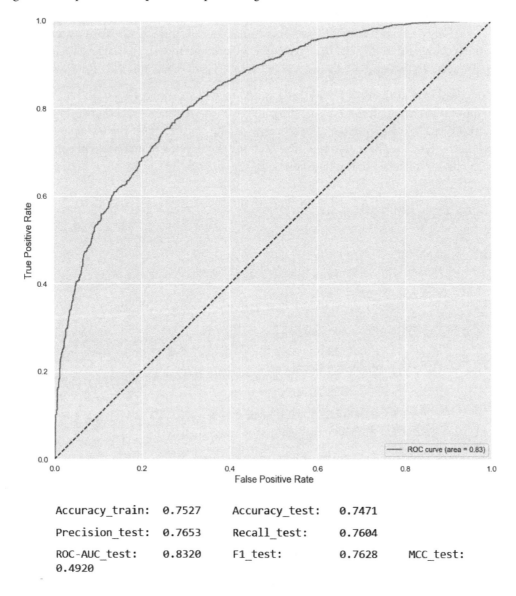

```
Accuracy_train:   0.7527      Accuracy_test:   0.7471

Precision_test:   0.7653      Recall_test:     0.7604

ROC-AUC_test:     0.8320      F1_test:         0.7628      MCC_test:
0.4920
```

Figure 7.4 – Predictive performance of our neural network model

The predictive performance for both models isn't bad considering these are *proxy models* meant to only approximate the real thing with different, yet related, data.

Getting acquainted with our "instance of interest"

The journalist reached out to you with a case in mind: the African American defendant who was falsely predicted to recidivate. This case is #5231 and is your main *instance of interest*. Since our focus is racial bias, we'd like to compare it with similar instances but of different races. To that end, we found case #10127 (Caucasian) and #2726 (Hispanic).

We can take a look at the data for all three. Since we will keep referring to these instances throughout this chapter, let's first save the indexes of the African American (idx1), Hispanic (idx2), and Caucasian (idx3) cases. Then, we can subset the test dataset by these indexes. Since we have to make sure that our predictions match, we will concatenate this subsetted test dataset to the true labels (y_test) and the CatBoost predictions (y_test_cb_pred):

```
idx1 = 5231
idx2 = 2726
idx3 = 10127
eval_idxs = X_test.index.isin([idx1, idx2, idx3])
X_test_evals = X_test[eval_idxs]
eval_compare_df = pd.concat([
    pd.DataFrame({'y':y_test[eval_idxs]},
        index=[idx3, idx2, idx1]),
    pd.DataFrame({'y_pred':y_test_cb_pred[eval_idxs]},
        index=[idx3, idx2, idx1]),
    X_test_evals], axis=1).transpose()
eval_compare_df
```

The preceding code produces the data frame in *Figure 7.5*. You can tell that the predictions match the true labels, and our main *instance of interest* was the only one predicted as a medium or high risk of recidivism. Besides race, the only other differences are with c_charge_degree and one minor age difference:

	10127	2726	5231
y	0	0	1
y_pred	0	0	1
age	24	23	23
:	:	:	:
priors_count	2	2	2
sex_Female	0	0	0
sex_Male	1	1	1
race_African-American	0	0	1
race_Asian	0	0	0
race_Caucasian	1	0	0
race_Hispanic	0	1	0
:	:	:	:
c_charge_degree_(F3)	0	1	0
c_charge_degree_(F7)	0	0	1
c_charge_degree_(M1)	1	0	0
:	:	:	:

Figure 7.5 – Observations #5231, #10127, and #2726 side by side with feature differences highlighted

Throughout this chapter, we will pay close attention to these differences to see whether they played a large role in producing the prediction difference. All the methods we will cover will complete the picture of what can determine or change the proxy model's decision, and, potentially, the COMPAS model by extension. Now that we have completed the setup, we will be moving forward with employing the interpretation methods.

Understanding anchor explanations

In *Chapter 6*, *Local Model-Agnostic Interpretation Methods*, we learned that **LIME** trains a local surrogate model (specifically a **weighted sparse linear model**) on a **perturbed** version of your dataset in the **neighborhood** of your *instance of interest*. The result is that you approximate a **local decision boundary** that can help you interpret the model's prediction for it.

Like LIME, **anchors** are also derived from a model-agnostic perturbation-based strategy. However, they are not about the *decision boundary* but the **decision region**. Anchors are also known as **scoped rules** because they list some **decision rules** that apply to your instance and its *perturbed* neighborhood. This neighborhood is also known as the **perturbation space**. An important detail is to what extent the rules apply to it, known as **precision**.

Imagine the neighborhood around your instance. You would expect the points to have more similar predictions the closer you get to your instance, right? So, if you had decision rules that defined these predictions, the smaller the area surrounding your instance, the more precise your rules. This concept is called **coverage**, which is the percentage of your *perturbation space* that yields a specific *precision*.

Unlike LIME, anchors don't fit a local surrogate model to explain your chosen instance's prediction. Instead, they explore possible candidate decision rules using an algorithm called **Kullback-Leibler divergence Lower and Upper Confidence Bounds** (**KL-LUCB**), which is derived from a **Multi-Armed Bandit** (**MAB**) algorithm.

MABs are a family of *reinforcement learning algorithms* about maximizing payoff when you have limited resources to explore all unknown possibilities. The algorithm originated from understanding how casino slot machine players could maximize their payoff by playing multiple machines. It's called multi-armed bandit because slot machine players are known as one-armed bandits. Yet players don't know which machine will yield the highest payoff, can't try all of them at once, and have finite funds. The trick is to learn how to balance exploration (trying unknown slot machines) with exploitation (using those you already have reasons to prefer).

In the anchors case, each slot machine is a potential decision rule, and the payoff is how much precision it yields. The KL-LUCB algorithm uses confidence regions based on the **Kullback-Leibler divergence** between the distributions to find the decision rule with the highest precision sequentially, yet efficiently.

Preparations for anchor and counterfactual explanations with alibi

Several small steps need to be performed to help the `alibi` library produce human-friendly explanations. The first one pertains to the prediction, since the model may output a 1 or a 0, but it's easier to understand a prediction by its name. To help us with this, we need a list with the class names where the 0 position matches our negative class name and the 1 matches the positive one:

```
class_names = ['Low Risk', 'Medium/High Risk']
```

Next, let's create a numpy array with our main *instance of interest* and print it out. Please note that the single-dimension array needs to be expanded (np.expand_dims) so that it's understood by alibi:

```
X_test_eval = np.expand_dims(X_test.values[X_test.\
            index.get_loc(idx1)], axis=0)
print(X_test_eval)
```

The preceding code outputs an array with the 21 features, of which 12 were the result of **One-Hot Encoding (OHE)**:

```
[[23  0  0  0  2  0  1  1  0  0  0  0  0  0  0  0  1  0  0  0
  0]]
```

A problem with making human-friendly explanations arises when you have OHE categories. To both the machine learning model and the explainer, each OHE feature is separate from the others. Still, to the human interpreting the outcomes, they cluster together as categories of their original features.

The alibi library has several utility functions to deal with this problem, such as ohe_to_ord, which takes a one-hot-encoded instance and puts it in an ordinal format. To use this function, we first define a dictionary (cat_vars_ohe) that tells alibi where the categorical variables are in our features and how many categories each one has. For instance, in our data, gender starts at the 5th index and has two categories, which is why our cat_vars_ohe dictionary begins with 5: 2. Once you have this dictionary, ohe_to_ord can take your instance (X_test_eval) and output it in ordinal format, where each categorical variable takes up a single feature. This utility function will prove useful for Alibi's counterfactual explanations, where the explainer will need this dictionary to map categorical features together:

```
cat_vars_ohe = {5: 2, 7: 6, 13: 8}
print(ohe_to_ord(X_test_eval, cat_vars_ohe)[0])
```

The preceding code outputs the following array:

```
[[23  0  0  0  2  1  0  3]]
```

For when it's in ordinal format, Alibi will need a dictionary that provides names for each category and a list of feature names:

```
category_map = {
 5: ['Female', 'Male'],\
 6: ['African-American', 'Asian', 'Caucasian',\
    'Hispanic', 'Native American', 'Other'],\
 7: ['Felony 1st Degree', 'Felony 2nd Degree',\
    'Felony 3rd Degree', 'Felony 7th Degree',\
    'Misdemeanor 1st Degree', 'Misdemeanor 2nd Degree',\
    'Misdemeanor 3rd Degree', 'Other Charge Degree'] }
feature_names = ['age', 'juv_fel_count', 'juv_misd_count',\
                'juv_other_count', 'priors_count',\
                'sex', 'race', 'c_charge_degree']
```

However, Alibi's anchor explanations use the data as it is provided to our models. We are using OHE data, so we need a category map for that format. Of course, the OHE features are all binary, so they only have two "categories" each:

```
category_map_ohe = {5: ['Not Female', 'Female'],\
  6: ['Not Male', 'Male'],\
  7:['Not African American', 'African American'],\
  8:['Not Asian', 'Asian'], 9:['Not Caucasian', 'Caucasian'],\
  10:['Not Hispanic', 'Hispanic'],\
  11:['Not Native American', 'Native American'],\
  12:['Not Other Race', 'Other Race'],\
  13:['Not Felony 1st Level', 'Felony 1st Level'],\
  14:['Not Felony 2nd Level', 'Felony 2nd Level'],\
  15:['Not Felony 3rd Level', 'Felony 3rd Level'],\
  16:['Not Felony 7th Level', 'Felony 7th Level'],\
  17:['Not Misdemeanor 1st Deg', 'Misdemeanor 1st Deg'],\
  18:['Not Misdemeanor 2nd Deg', 'Misdemeanor 2nd Deg'],\
  19:['Not Misdemeanor 3rd Deg', 'Misdemeanor 3rd Deg'],\
  20:['Not Other Charge Degree', 'Other Charge Degree']}
```

Local interpretations for anchor explanations

All Alibi explainers require a `predict` function, so we create a `lambda` function called `predict_cb_fn` for our CatBoost model. Please note that we are using `predict_proba` for the classifier's probabilities. Then, to initialize `AnchorTabular`, we also provide it with our features' names as they are in our OHE dataset and the category map (`category_map_ohe`). Once it has initialized, we fit it with our training data:

```
predict_cb_fn = lambda x: fitted_cb_mdl.predict_proba(x)
anchor_cb_explainer = AnchorTabular(predict_cb_fn,\
 X_train.columns,\
                                    categorical_
 names=category_map_ohe) anchor_cb_explainer.fit(X_train.values)
```

Before we leverage the explainer, it's good practice to check that the anchor "holds." In other words, we should check that the MAB algorithm found decision rules that help explain the prediction. To verify this, you use the `predictor` function to check that the prediction is the same as the one you expect for this instance. Right now, we are using `idx1`, which is the case of the African American defendant:

```
print('Prediction: %s' %  class_names[anchor_cb_explainer.\
                           predictor(X_test.loc[idx1].values)
 [0]])
```

The preceding code outputs the following:

```
Prediction: Medium/High Risk
```

We can proceed to use the `explain` function to generate an explanation for our instance. We can set our precision threshold to `0.85`, which means we expect the predictions on anchored observations to be the same as our instance at least 85% of the time. Once we have an explanation, we can print the anchors as well as their precision and coverage:

```
anchor_cb_explanation =\
          anchor_cb_explainer.explain(X_test.loc[idx1].values,\
                                      threshold=0.85,
                                      seed=rand)
print('Anchor: %s' % (' AND'.join(anchor_cb_explanation.
anchor)))
print('Precision: %.3f' % anchor_cb_explanation.precision)
print('Coverage: %.3f' % anchor_cb_explanation.coverage)
```

The following output was generated by the preceding code. You can tell that `age`, `priors_count`, and `race_African-American` are factors at 86% precision. Impressively, this rule applies to almost a third of all the perturbation space's instances:

```
Anchor: age <= 25.00 AND
        priors_count > 0.00 AND
        race_African-American = African American
Precision: 0.863
Coverage: 0.290
```

We can try the same code but with a 5% bump in the precision threshold. It produces the same first three anchors it did with a lower precision threshold but now expands it with two more:

```
Anchor: age <= 25.00 AND
        priors_count > 0.00 AND
        race_African-American = African American AND
        c_charge_degree_(M1) = Not Misdemeanor 1st Deg AND
        c_charge_degree_(F3) = Not Felony 3rd Level AND
        race_Caucasian = Not Caucasian
Precision: 0.903
Coverage: 0.290
```

Interestingly enough, although precision did increase by a few percentage points, coverage stayed the same, so the additional anchors apply to a similar subset of perturbations with increased accuracy. At this level of precision, we may confirm that race is a significant factor because being African American is an anchor but so is not being Caucasian. Another factor was `c_charge_degree`. The explanation reveals that being accused of a first-degree misdemeanor or third-level felony would have been better. Understandably, a seventh-level felony is a more serious charge than these two.

Let's now create a black-box anchor explainer for our neural network. One thing to note is that the `lambda` function is different because the network `predict` function outputs a single set of predictions for the positive class, but we need two sets, including one for the negative class. This is simple to overcome because the probabilities for both classes should sum to 100%, hence the negative one should complement the positive one. Everything else about initializing and fitting the explainer is the same:

```
predict_nn_fn = lambda x: np.concatenate((1 -\
        fitted_nn_mdl.predict(x), fitted_nn_mdl.predict(x)),
axis=1)
```

```
anchor_nn_explainer = AnchorTabular(predict_nn_fn, X_train.
columns,\
                        categorical_names=category_map_ohe)
anchor_nn_explainer.fit(X_train.values)
```

Another way of understanding why a model made a specific prediction is looking for a similar data point that had the opposite prediction and figuring out why it made that one. The decision boundary crosses between both points, so it's helpful to contrast decision explanations from both sides of the boundary. This time we will use idx3, which is the case for the Caucasian defendant:

```
anchor_nn_explanation =\
                anchor_nn_explainer.explain(X_test.loc[idx3].
values,\
                                threshold=0.85, seed=rand)
print('Anchor: %s' % (' AND'.join(anchor_nn_explanation.
anchor)))
print('Precision: %.3f' % anchor_nn_explanation.precision)
print('Coverage: %.3f' % anchor_nn_explanation.coverage)
```

The preceding code outputs the anchors as follows:

```
Anchor: priors_count <= 2.00 AND
    race_African-American = Not African American AND
    c_charge_degree_(F3) = Not Felony 3rd Level
Precision: 0.911
Coverage: 0.578
```

The first anchor is `priors_count <= 2.00`, but on the other side of the boundary, the first two anchors were `age <= 25.00` and `priors_count > 0.00`. In other words, for an African American under or equal to the age of 25, any amount of priors is enough to categorize them as having a medium/high risk of recidivism (86% of the time). On the other hand, for a White person, as long as priors don't exceed two and they haven't been accused of a third-level felony, they will be predicted as low risk (91% of the time and with 58% coverage). These decision rules not only suggest racial bias by `race` alone but also by applying **double standards** on other features. A double standard is when different rules are applied when, in principle, the situation is the same. In this case, the different rules for `priors_count` and the absence of `age` as a factor for Caucasian constitutes double standards.

We can now try the Hispanic defendant (`idx2`) to observe whether double standards are also to be found with this instance. We just run the same code as before but replace `idx3` with `idx2`:

```
Anchor: priors_count <= 2.00 AND
        race_African-American = Not African American AND
        race_Hispanic = Hispanic
Precision: 0.908
Coverage: 0.578
```

The explanations for the Hispanic defendant confirm the double standard with `priors_count` and that `race` continues to be a strong factor, since there's one anchor for not being African American and another one for being Hispanic.

For specific model decisions, anchor explanations answer the question *why?*. However, we have crossed the decision boundary looking for answers to why our point wasn't on that side. By doing so, we have dabbled in the question *what if?*. In the next section, we will expand on this question further.

Exploring counterfactual explanations

Counterfactuals are an integral part of human reasoning. How many of us have muttered the words "If I had done X instead, my outcome y would have been different"? There's always one or two things that, if done differently, could lead to the outcomes we prefer!

In machine learning outcomes, you can leverage this way of reasoning to make for extremely human-friendly explanations where we can explain outcomes in terms of what would need to change to get the opposite outcome (the **counterfactual class**). After all, we are often interested in knowing how to make a lousy outcome better. For instance, how do you get your denied loan application approved or decrease your risk of cardiovascular disease from high to low? However, hopefully, answers to those questions aren't a huge list of changes. You expect the smallest amount of changes required to change your outcome.

Regarding fairness, counterfactuals are an important interpretation method, in particular when there are elements involved that *we can't change* or shouldn't have to change. For instance, if you perform exactly the same job and have the same level of experience as your coworker, you expect to have the same salary, right? If you and your spouse share the same assets and credit history but have different credit scores, you have to wonder why. Does it have to do with gender, race, age, or even political affiliations? Whether it's a compensation, credit rating, or recidivism risk model, you'd hope that similar points have similar outcomes.

Finding counterfactuals is not particularly hard. All we have to do is change our *instance of interest* slightly until it changes the outcome. And maybe there's an instance already in the dataset just like that!

In fact, you could say that the three instances we examined with anchors in the previous section are close enough to be counterfactuals of each other, except for the Caucasian and Hispanic cases, which have the same outcome. But the Caucasian and Hispanic instances were "*cherry-picked*" by looking for data points with the same criminal history but different races than the *instance of interest*. Perhaps by comparing similar points, mostly except for race, we limited the scope in such a way that we confirm what we hope to confirm, which is that race matters for the model's decision-making.

This is an example of *selection bias*. After all, counterfactuals are inherently selective because they focus on a few feature changes. And even with a few features, there are so many possible permutations that change the outcome, which means that a single point could have hundreds of counterfactuals. And not all of these will tell a consistent story. This phenomenon is called the **Rashomon effect**. It is named after a famous Japanese movie about a murder mystery. And as we have come to expect from murder mysteries, witnesses have different interpretations of what happened. But in the same way that it's difficult to rely on a single witness, you cannot rely on a single counterfactual. Also, in the same way that great detectives are trained to look for clues everywhere in connection to the scene of a crime (even if it contradicts their instincts), counterfactuals can't be "cherry-picked" because they conveniently tell the story we want them to tell.

Fortunately, there are algorithmic ways of looking for counterfactual instances in an unbiased manner. Typically, these involve finding the closest points with different outcomes, but there are different ways of measuring the distance between points. For starters, there's the **L1** distance (also known as the **Manhattan distance**) and **L2** distance (also known as the **Euclidean distance**), among many others. But there's also the question of normalizing the distances because not all features have the same scale. Otherwise, they would be biased against features with smaller scales, such as one-hot-encoded features. There are many normalization schemes to chose from too. You could use **standard deviation**, **min-max scaling**, or even **median absolute deviation** [9].

In this section, we will explain and use one advanced counterfactual finding method. Then, we will explore Google's WIT. It has a simple L1- and L2-based counterfactual finder, which is limited to the dataset but makes up for it with other useful interpretation features.

Counterfactual explanations guided by prototypes

The most sophisticated counterfactual finding algorithms do the following:

- **Loss**: These leverage a *loss function* that helps optimize to find the counterfactuals closest to our *instance of interest*.

- **Perturbation**: These tend to operate with a *perturbation space* much like anchors do, changing as few features as possible. Please note that counterfactuals don't have to be real points in your dataset. That would be far too limiting. Counterfactuals exist in the realm of the possible, not of the necessarily known.

- **Distribution**: However, they have to be realistic, and therefore, interpretable. For example, a loss function could help determine that age < 0 alone is enough to make any medium-/high-risk instance low-risk. This is why counterfactuals should lie close to the statistical distributions of your data, especially *class-specific distributions*. They also should not be biased against smaller-scale features, namely categorical variables.

- **Speed**: These run fast enough to be useful in real-world scenarios.

Alibi's **Counterfactuals Guided by Prototypes** (*CounterFactualProto*) has all these properties. It has a loss function that includes both L1 (*Lasso*) and L2 (*Ridge*) regularization as a linear combination, just like **Naïve Elastic Net** does (β L1 + L2) but with a weight (β) only on the L1 term. The clever part of this algorithm is that it can (optionally) use an *autoencoder* to understand the distributions. We won't revisit how this works because we covered a **Variational Autoencoder** (**VAE**) in *Chapter 3, Interpretation Challenges*. However, what's important to note here is that autoencoders, in general, are neural networks that learn a compressed representation of your training data. This method incorporates loss terms from the autoencoder, such as one for the nearest prototype. A prototype is the dimensionality-reduced representation of the counterfactual class.

If an autoencoder is not available, the algorithm uses a tree often used for multidimensional search (*k-d trees*) instead. With this tree, the algorithm can efficiently capture the class distributions and also choose the nearest prototype. Once it has the prototype, the perturbations are guided by it. Incorporating a prototype loss term in the loss function ensures that the resulting perturbations will be close enough to the prototype that is in-distribution for the counterfactual class. Many modeling class and interpretation methods overlook the importance of treating continuous and categorical features differently. CounterFactualProto can use two different distance metrics to compute the pairwise distances between categories of a categorical variable: **Modified Value Difference Metric** (**MVDM**) and **Association-Based Distance Metric** (**ABDM**), and can even combine both. Another way in which CounterFactualProto ensures meaningful counterfactuals is by limiting permutated features to predefined ranges. We can use the minimum and maximum values of features to generate a tuple of arrays (feature_range):

```
feature_range =\
    (X_train.values.min(axis=0).reshape(1,21).astype(np.
float32),\
     X_train.values.max(axis=0).reshape(1,21).astype(np.
float32))
print(feature_range)
```

The preceding code outputs two arrays – the first one with the minimum and the second with the maximum of all features:

```
(array([[18.,    0.,    0.,    0.,    0.,    0.,    0.,    0.,    0.,    0.,    0.,
 0.,    0.,
        0.,    0.,    0.,    0.,    0.,    0.,    0.,    0.]],
dtype=float32), array([[96.,   20.,   13.,   11.,   38.,    1.,    1.,    1.,
 1.,   1.,    1.,    1.,    1.,    1.,    1.,    1.,    1.]], dtype=float32))
```

We can now instantiate an explainer with `CounterFactualProto`. As arguments, it requires the black-box model's predict function (`predict_nn_fn`), the shape of the instance you want to explain (`X_test_eval.shape`), the maximum amount of optimization iterations to perform (`max_iterations`), and the feature range for perturbed instances (`feature_range`). Many hyperparameters can be tuned, including the β weight to apply to the L1 loss (`beta`) and the θ weight to apply to the prototype loss (`theta`). Also, you must specify whether to use the k-d tree or not (`use_kdtree`) when the autoencoder model isn't provided. Once the explainer is instantiated, you fit it to the test dataset. We are specifying the distance metric for categorical features (`d_type`) as the combination of ABDM and MVDM:

```
cf_nn_explainer = CounterFactualProto(predict_nn_fn,\
                        X_test_eval.shape, max_iterations=100,\
                        feature_range=feature_range, beta=.1,\
                        theta=5, use_kdtree=True )
cf_nn_explainer.fit(X_test.values, d_type='abdm-mvdm')
```

Creating an explanation with an explainer is similar to how it was with anchors. Just pass the instance (`X_test_eval`) to the `explain` function. However, outputting the results is not as straightforward: mainly because of converting the features between one-hot-encoded and ordinal, and interating among the features. The documentation for Alibi (`https://docs.seldon.io/projects/alibi/`) has a detailed example of how this is done. We will instead use a utility function called `describe_cf_instance` that does this for us using the *instance of interest* (`X_test_eval`), explanation (`cf_nn_explanation`), class names (`class_names`), one-hot.encoded category locations (`cat_vars_ohe`), category map (`category_map`), and feature names (`feature_names`):

```
cf_nn_explanation = cf_nn_explainer.explain(X_test_eval)
mldatasets.describe_cf_instance(X_test_eval, cf_nn_explanation,\
                class_names, cat_vars_ohe, category_map, feature_names)
```

The following output was produced by the preceding code:

```
Instance Outcomes and Probabilities
-------------------------------------------------
        original:   Medium/High Risk
                    [0.46732193 0.53267807]
  counterfactual:   Low Risk
                    [0.50025815 0.49974185]


Categorical Feature Counterfactual Perturbations
-------------------------------------------------
             sex:   Male   -->   Female
            race:   African-American   -->   Asian
 c_charge_degree:   Felony 7th Degree   -->   Felony 1st Degree


Numerical Feature Counterfactual Perturbations
-------------------------------------------------
     priors_count:   2.00   -->   1.90
```

You can appreciate from the output that the *instance of interest* ("original") has a 53.26% probability of being *Medium/High Risk*, but the counterfactual is barely on the *Low Risk* side with 50.03%! A counterfactual that is slightly on the other side is what we would like to see because it likely means that it is as close as possible to our *instance of interest*. There are four feature differences between them, three of which are categorical (sex, race, and c_charge_degree). The fourth difference is with the priors_count numerical feature, which is treated as continuous since the explainer doesn't know it's discrete. In any case, it should be *monotonic*, and therefore fewer priors should always mean lower risk, which means we can interpret the 1.90 as a 1 because if 0.1 fewer priors helped reduce the risk, a whole prior should also do so.

A more powerful insight derived from CounterFactualProto's output is that two demographic features were present in the closest counterfactual to this feature. One was found with a method that is designed to follow our classes' statistical distributions and isn't biased against or in favor of specific types of features. And even though it is surprising to see Asian female in our counterfactual because it doesn't fit the narrative that White males are getting preferential treatment, it is troubling to realize that race appears in the counterfactual at all.

Counterfactual instances and much more with the What-If Tool (WIT)

Google's WIT is a very versatile tool. It requires very little input or preparation and opens up in your Jupyter or Colab notebook as an interactive dashboard with three tabs:

- **Datapoint editor**: To visualize your datapoints, edit them, and explain their predictions.

- **Performance**: To see high-level model performance metrics (for all regression and classification models). For binary classification, this tab is called **Performance and Fairness** because, in addition to high-level metrics, predictive fairness can be compared between your dataset's feature-based slices.

- **Features**: To view general feature statistics.

Given that the **Features** tab doesn't relate to model interpretations, we will explore only the first two in this section.

Configuring WIT

Optionally, we can enrich our interpretations in WIT by creating attributions, which are values that explain how much each feature contributes to each prediction. You could use any method to generate attributions, but we will use SHAP. We covered SHAP first in *Chapter 5, Global Model-Agnostic Interpretation Methods*. Since we will interpret our CatBoost model in the WIT dashboard, the SHAP explainer that is most suitable is TreeExplainer, but DeepExplainer would work for the neural network (and KernelExplainer for both). To initialize TreeExplainer, all we need to pass is the fitted model (fitted_cb_mdl):

```
shap_cb_explainer = shap.TreeExplainer(fitted_cb_mdl)
```

WIT requires all the features in the dataset (including the labels). We will use the test dataset, so you could concatenate `X_test` and `y_test`, but even those two exclude the ground truth feature (`is_recid`). One way of getting all of them is to subset `recidivism_df` with the test dataset indexes (`y_test.index`). WIT also needs your data and your columns in list format so we can save them as variables for later use (`test_np` and `cols_l`). Lastly, for predictions and attributions, we will need to remove our ground truth (`is_recid`) and classification label (`compas_score`), so let's save the index of these columns (`delcol_idx`):

```
test_df = recidivism_df.loc[y_test.index]
test_np = test_df.values
cols_l = test_df.columns
delcol_idx = [cols_l.get_loc("is_recid"),\
              cols_l.get_loc("compas_score")]
```

WIT has several useful functions for customizing the dashboard, such as setting a custom distance metric (`set_custom_distance_fn`), displaying class names instead of numbers (`set_label_vocab`), setting a custom predict function (`set_custom_predict_fn`), and a second predict function to compare two models (`compare_custom_predict_fn`).

In addition to `set_label_vocab`, we are going only to use a custom predict function (`custom_predict_with_shap`). All it needs to function is to take an array with your `examples_np` dataset and produce some predictions (`preds`). However, we first must remove features that we want in the dashboard but weren't used for the training (`delcol_idx`). This function's required output is a dictionary with the predictions stored in a `predictions` key. But we'd also like some attributions too, which is why we need an `attributions` key in that dictionary. Therefore, we take our SHAP explainer and generate `shap_values`, which is a NumPy array. However, attributions need to be a list of dictionaries to be understood by the WIT dashboard. To this end, we iterate `shap_output` and convert each observation's SHAP values array to a dictionary (`attrs`) and then append this to a list (`attributions`):

```
def custom_predict_with_shap(examples_np):
  #For shap values we only need same features
  #that were used for training
  inputs_np = np.delete(np.array(examples_np), delcol_idx, axis=1)
  #Get the model's class predictions
  preds = predict_cb_fn(inputs_np)
  #With test data generate SHAP values which converted
```

```
#to a list of dictionaries format
keepcols_l = [c for i, c in enumerate(cols_l)\
            if i not in delcol_idx]
shap_output = shap_cb_explainer.shap_values(inputs_np)
attributions = []
for shap in shap_output:
  attrs = {}
  for i, col in enumerate(keepcols_l):
    attrs[col] = shap[i]
  attributions.append(attrs)
  #Prediction function must output predictions/attributions
  #in dictionary
  output = {'predictions': preds, 'attributions': attributions}
return output
```

Before we build the WIT dashboard, it's important to note that to find our *instance of interest* in the dashboard, we need to know its position within the NumPy array provided to WIT because these don't have indexes as pandas DataFrames do. To find the position, all we need to do is provide the get_loc function with the index:

```
print(y_test.index.get_loc(5231))
```

The preceding code outputs as 2910, so we can take note of this number. Building the WIT dashboard is fairly straightforward now. We first initialize a config (WitConfigBuilder) with our test dataset in NumPy format (test_np) and our list of features (cols_l). Both are converted to lists with tolist(). Then, we set our custom predict function with set_custom_predict_fn and our target feature (is_recid) and provide our class names. We will use the ground truth this time to evaluate fairness from the perspective of what really happened. Once the config is initializing, the widget (WitWidget) builds the dashboard with it. You can optionally provide a height (default is 1,000 pixels):

```
wit_config_builder = WitConfigBuilder(\
                test_np.tolist(), feature_names=cols_l.
tolist()
  ).set_custom_predict_fn(custom_predict_with_shap).\
  set_target_feature("is_recid").set_label_vocab(class_names)
WitWidget(wit_config_builder, height=800)
```

Datapoint editor

In *Figure 7.6*, you can see the WIT dashboard with its three tabs. We will first explore the first tab (**Datapoint editor**). It has **Visualize** and **Edit** panes on the left, and on the right, it can show you either **Datapoints** or **Partial dependence plots**. When you have **Datapoints** selected, you can visualize the datapoints in many ways using the controls in the upper right (highlighted area *A*). What we have done in *Figure 7.6* is set the following:

- **Binning | X-axis**: c_charge_degree_ (F7).
- **Binning | Y-axis**: compas_score.
- **Color By**: race_African-American.
- Everything else stays the same.

These settings resulted in all our datapoints neatly organized in 2 rows and 2 columns and color-coded by African American or not. The right column is for those with a level 7 charge degree, and the upper row is for those with a *Medium/High Risk* COMPAS score. We can look for datapoint 2910 in this subgroup (*B*) by clicking on the top-rightmost item. It should appear in the **Edit** pane (*C*). Interestingly enough, the SHAP attributions for this datapoint are three times higher for age than they are for race_African-American. But still, race altogether is second to age in importance. Also, notice that in the **Infer** pane, you see the predicted probability for *Medium/High Risk* is approximately 83%:

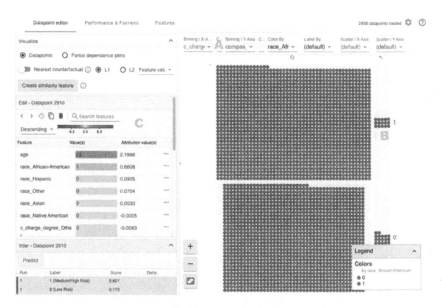

Figure 7.6 – WIT dashboard with our instance of interest

WIT can find the nearest counterfactual using L1 or L2 distances. And it can use either feature values or attributions to calculate the distances. As mentioned earlier, WIT can also include a custom distance finding function if you add it to the configuration. For now, we will select L2 with Feature value. In *Figure 7.7*, these options appear in the highlighted *A* area. Once you choose a distance metric and enable **Nearest counterfactual**, it appears side by side with our *instance of interest* (area *B*), and it compares their predictions as shown in the following figure (*C*). You can sort the features by **Absolute attribution** for a clearer understanding of feature importance on a local level. The counterfactual is only 3 years older but has zero priors instead of two, yet that was enough to reduce the **Medium/High Risk** to nearly 5%:

Figure 7.7 – How to find the nearest counterfactual in WIT

While both our *instance of interest* and counterfactual remain selected, we can visualize them along with all other points. By doing this, you take insights from local interpretations and can create enough context for global understandings. For instance, let's change our visualization settings to the following:

- **Binning | X-axis**: Inference label.
- **Binning | Y-axis**: (none).
- **Scatter | X-axis**: age.
- **Scatter | Y-axis**: priors_count.
- Everything else stays the same.

The result of this visualization is depicted in *Figure 7.8*. You can tell that the **Low Risk** bins' points tend to hover in the lower end of priors_count. Both bins show that prior_count and age have a slight correlation, although this is substantially more pronounced in the **Medium/High Risk** bin. However, what is most interesting is the sheer density of African American data points deemed **Medium/High Risk** in age ranging 18-25 and with prior_count below three compared to those in the **Low Risk** bin. It suggests that both lower age and higher priors_count increases risk more for African Americans than others:

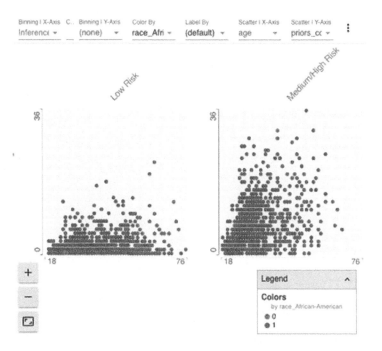

Figure 7.8 – Visualizing age versus priors_count in WIT

We can try creating our own counterfactuals by editing the datapoint. What happens when we reduce `priors_count` to one? The answer to this question is depicted in *Figure 7.9*. Once you make the change and click on the **Predict** button in the **Infer** pane, it adds an entry to the prediction history last in the **Infer** pane. You can tell in **Run #2** that the risk reduces nearly to 33.5%, down nearly 50%!

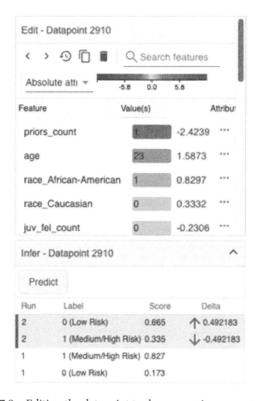

Figure 7.9 – Editing the datapoint to decrease priors_count in WIT

Now, what happens if age is only 2 years older but there are two priors? In *Figure 7.10*, **Run #3** tells you that it barely made it inside the **Low Risk** score:

Figure 7.10 – Editing the datapoint to increase the age in WIT

Another feature that the **Datapoint editor** tab has is **partial dependence plots**, which we covered in *Chapter 4, Fundamentals of Feature Importance and Impact*. If you click on this radio button, it will modify the right pane to look like *Figure 7.11*. By default, if a data point is selected, the PDPs are local, meaning they pertain to the chosen datapoint. But you can switch to global. In any case, it's best to sort plots by variation as done for *Figure 7.11*, where age and priors_count have the highest variation. Interestingly, neither of them is monotonic, which doesn't make sense. The model should be learning that an increase in priors_count should consistently increase risk. It should be the same with a decrease in age. After all, academic research shows that crime tends to peak in the mid-20s and that higher priors increase the likelihood of recidivism. The relationship between these two variables is also well understood, so perhaps some data engineering and monotonic constraints could make sure a model is consistent with known phenomena rather than learning the inconsistencies in the data that lead to unfairness. We will cover this in *Chapter 12, Monotonic Constraints and Model Tuning for Interpretability*:

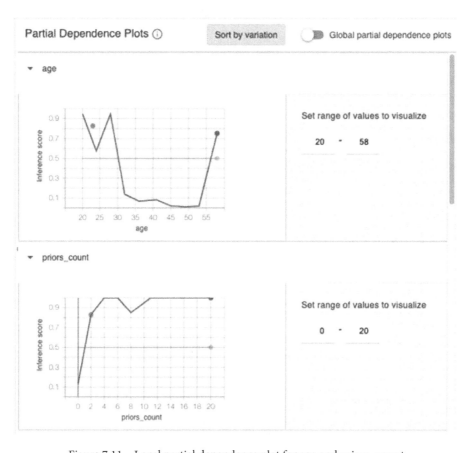

Figure 7.11 – Local partial dependence plot for age and priors_count

Is there something that can be done to improve fairness in a model that has already been trained? Indeed, there is. The **Performance & Fairness** tab can help with that.

Performance & Fairness

When you click on the **Performance & Fairness** tab, you will see that it has **Configure** and **Fairness** panes on the left. And on the right, you can explore the overall performance of the model (see *Figure 7.12*). In the upper part of this pane, it has **False Positives (%)**, **False Negatives (%)**, **Accuracy (%)**, and **F1** fields. If you expand the pane, it shows the ROC curve, PR curve, confusion matrix, and mean attributions – the average Shapley values. We have covered all of these previously in this book either directly or indirectly, except for the PR curve. The **Precision-Recall (PR)** is very much like the ROC curve, except it plots precision against recall instead of TPR versus FPR. In this plot, precision is expected to decrease as recall decreases. Unlike ROC, it's considered worse than a coin toss when the line is close to the *x* axis, and it's best suited to imbalanced classification problems:

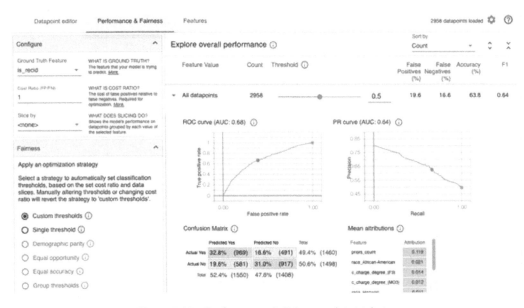

Figure 7.12 – Performance & Fairness tab initial view

A classification model will output probabilities that an observation is in one class or another. We usually take every observation above or equal to 0.5 to belong to the positive class. Otherwise, we predict it to belong to the negative class. This threshold is called the **classification threshold**, and you don't always have to use the standard 0.5.

There are many cases in which it is appropriate to perform **threshold tuning**. One of the most compelling reasons is imbalanced classification problems because often models optimize performance on accuracy alone but end up with bad recall or precision. Adjusting the threshold will improve the metric you most care about:

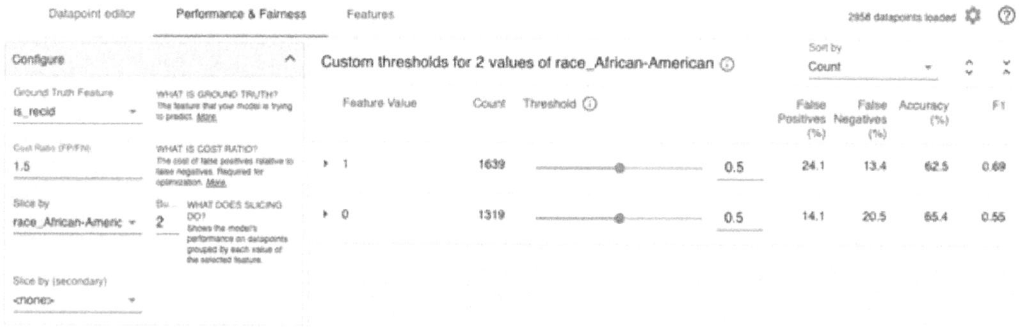

Figure 7.13 – Slicing performance metrics by race_African-American

Another primary reason to adjust thresholds is for fairness. To this end, you need to examine the metric you most care about across different slices of your data. In our case, **False Positives (%)** is where we can appreciate unfairness the most. For instance, take a look at *Figure 7.13*. With the **Configure** pane, we can slice the data by race_African-American, and to the right of it, we can see what we observed at the beginning of this chapter, which is that FPs for African Americans are substantially higher than for other segments. One way to fix this is through an automatic optimization method such as **Demographic parity** or **Equal opportunity**. If you are to use one of these, it's best to adjust **Cost Ratio** (FP/FN) to tell the optimizer that FPs are worth more than FNs:

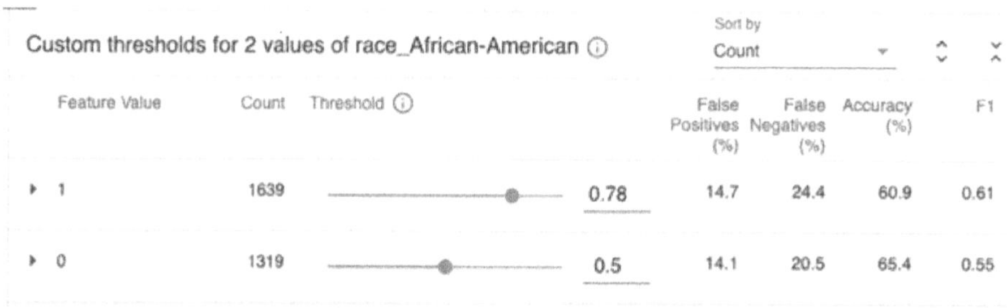

Figure 7.14 – Adjusting the classification threshold for the dataset sliced by race_African-American

We can also adjust thresholds manually using the default **Custom Thresholds** setting (see *Figure 7.14*). For these slices, if we want approximate parity with our FPs, we should use 0.78 as our threshold for when `race_African-American=1`. The drawback is that FNs will increase for this group, not achieving parity on that end. A cost ratio would help determine whether 14.7% in FPs justifies 24.4% in FNs, but to do this we would have to understand the average costs involved. We will examine odds calibration methods further in *Chapter 11, Bias Mitigation and Causal Inference Methods*.

Now that we have a grasp on how anchors and counterfactuals can be used to explain prediction, let's try a method that combines elements from both.

Comparing with CEM

The **Contrastive Explanation Method** (**CEM**) is similar to both anchors and counterfactuals since it explains predictions using what is present (such as anchors) and absent (such as counterfactuals). It calls what is present **Pertinent Positives** (**PPs**) and what is absent **Pertinent Negatives** (**PNs**). However, the difference is that PPs are qualified as being minimally and sufficiently present to predict the same class. Likewise, PNs are minimally and necessarily absent to predict the opposite class. Therefore, CEM works best with continuous and ordinal features because it expects to subtract from features until it reaches the desired outcome. For this reason, it doesn't know how to deal with non-monotonic continuous, non-ordinal, categorical, or even binary, features, for that matter, and our recidivism dataset only has this kind of feature! Admittedly, this chapter's example doesn't make for an ideal CEM use case. We will touch on CEM in subsequent chapters. For now, what matters is to connect it to anchors and counterfactuals and briefly explain how to use the method.

CEM has a perturbation-based strategy, an **Elastic Net** regularizer, and an optional autoencoder to help guide the loss function. Sound familiar? The creators of `CounterFactualProto` based it on the CEM paper. However, CEM doesn't fall back on **k-d trees**, so the optional **autoencoder** is highly recommended to make explanations more realistic when the dataset is relatively small or noisy. Our dataset is, by no means, large or clear as day. Therefore, guiding could be helpful, so we will create a simple autoencoder.

If you haven't done it before, training an *autoencoder* is not as daunting as it may sound. All it is is a neural network shaped like an hourglass, where the objective is to make `input_layer` and `output_layer` match. In between these layers, there's `encoder` and `decoder`, which converge in a layer we call `bottleneck`. This layer is both the encoder's output and the decoder's input. The whole point is to compress the data into the dimensionality-reduced `bottleneck` so that the reconstruction error between `input_layer` and `output_layer` is reduced:

```
input_layer = tf.keras.Input(shape=(21))
encoder = tf.keras.layers.Dense(10, activation='relu')(input_layer)
bottleneck = tf.keras.layers.Dense(3, activation='relu')(encoder)
decoder = tf.keras.layers.Dense(10, activation='relu')(bottleneck)
output_layer = tf.keras.layers.Dense(21,\
                        activation='linear')(decoder)
autoencoder_mdl = tf.keras.Model(input_layer, output_layer)
autoencoder_mdl.summary()
```

The preceding code builds an autoencoder model layer by layer so that it's easier to understand. If you look at `summary()` for it, you can see how the dimensions go from 21 to 10 to 3 in the encoding process. Naturally, in decoding, they go back from 3 to 10 to 21:

Layer (type)	Output Shape	Param #
input_29 (InputLayer)	[(None, 21)]	0
dense_81 (Dense)	(None, 10)	220
dense_82 (Dense)	(None, 3)	33
dense_83 (Dense)	(None, 10)	40

```
dense_84 (Dense)                    (None, 21)                    231
=================================================================
===
Total params: 524
Trainable params: 524
Non-trainable params: 0
```

Then, compiling and fitting the autoencoder is done as you would for any neural network model, except that the first argument in the `fit` function (`X`) and the second argument (`y`) are the same: `X_train`. What you expect the network to produce is something that's as close as possible to what went in:

```
autoencoder_mdl.compile(loss='mean_squared_error',
optimizer='adam')
autoencoder_history = autoencoder_mdl.fit(X_train.values,\
                        X_train.values, epochs=16,\
                        batch_size=32,\
                        validation_split=0.2, verbose=0)
```

To generate a PN, we run the CEM function with the following required arguments:

- The predict function (`predict_nn_fn`)
- The mode (`'PN'`)
- The shape we expect back (`X_test_eval.shape`)

In addition to these arguments, we specify the feature range and the maximum number of iterations as we did with `CounterFactualProto`. But since this time we are using an autoencoder (`ae_model`), we also include `gamma`, which is a hyperparameter that magnifies the reconstruction error loss. Once the explainer has been initialized, you fit it to the training data and create an explanation with `explain` for our *instance of interest* (`X_test_eval`). We then output the original instance and the PN class, followed by the feature values and prediction probabilities for the PN:

```
cem_nn_explainer_pn = CEM(predict_nn_fn, 'PN',\
    X_test_eval.shape, feature_range=feature_range,\
    gamma=100,\
    max_iterations=100, ae_model=autoencoder_mdl)
```

```
cem_nn_explainer_pn.fit(X_train.values, no_info_type='median')
```
```
cem_nn_explanation_pn = cem_nn_explainer_pn.explain(X_test_
eval, verbose=False)
```
```
print("%s -> %s" % (class_names[cem_nn_explanation_pn.X_pred],\
                class_names[cem_nn_explanation_pn.PN_pred]))
print("Probabilities: %s" %\
```
```
                predict_nn_fn(cem_nn_explanation_pn.PN)[0])
print("Values: %s" % cem_nn_explanation_pn.PN[0])
```

The following output was produced by the preceding code. You can tell that the PN for the *instance of interest* is classified as Low Risk. PNs are similar to counterfactuals, so you would expect this to be the case. The output also includes the PN's feature values, and the probabilities show that the PN barely made it as Low Risk with a 50.11% probability:

```
Medium/High Risk -> Low Risk
```
```
Probabilities: [0.50112426 0.49887577]
```
```
Values: [23.     0.    ...    0.45720586    ...    0.  ]
```

PPs are generated exactly like PNs, so we can take the same code and just replace all instances of PN with PP:

```
cem_nn_explainer_pp = CEM(predict_nn_fn, 'PP',
        X_test_eval.shape, feature_range=feature_range,\
        gamma=100,\
        max_iterations=100, ae_model=autoencoder_mdl)
```
```
cem_nn_explainer_pp.fit(X_train.values, no_info_type='median')
```
```
cem_nn_explanation_pp = cem_nn_explainer_pp.explain(X_test_eva
l,\
```
```
                                        verbose=False)
```
```
print("%s -> %s" % (class_names[cem_nn_explanation_pp.X_pred],\
                class_names[cem_nn_explanation_pp.PP_pred]))
print("Probabilities: %s" %\
```
```
                predict_nn_fn(cem_nn_explanation_pp.PP)[0])
print("Values: %s" % cem_nn_explanation_pp.PP[0])
```

The preceding code produced the following output:

```
Medium/High Risk -> Medium/High Risk
Probabilities: [0.29793483 0.70206517]
Values: [0. 0. 0 ... 0. 0. 0.]
```

As you can tell from the output, the PP is classified as Medium/High Risk as you would expect. And it does so with a 70.2% probability. However, the feature values for the PP are all zeros. It turns out that PP looks for what is *minimally and sufficiently present* and finds that all zeros will still produce a Medium/High Risk classification. The PP values are not very intuitive for this use case.

To put it all in context, let's create a data frame (salients_df) with feature values for our *instance of interest* (x), the PN, what's *absent* from the PN (PN-x), and then the PP. We then make sure only features that don't have zeros in PP and PN show up:

```
salients_df = pd.DataFrame({'Feature': X_test.columns,\
        'x': cem_nn_explanation_pn.X[0],\
      'PN': cem_nn_explanation_pn.PN[0],\
    'PN-x': cem_nn_explanation_pn.PN[0]-\
            cem_nn_explanation_pn.X[0],\
      'PP': cem_nn_explanation_pp.PP[0]})
salients_df = salients_df[(salients_df.PP != 0) |\
                (salients_df.PN != 0)]
salients_df
```

The preceding code produced *Figure 7.15*:

	Feature	x	PN	PN-x	PP
0	age	23	23.000000	0.000000	0.000000
4	priors_count	2	2.000000	0.000000	0.000000
5	sex_Female	0	0.397589	0.397589	0.000000
6	sex_Male	1	1.000000	0.000000	0.000000
7	race_African-American	1	0.457206	-0.542794	0.000000
16	c_charge_degree_(F7)	1	1.000000	0.000000	0.000000

Figure 7.15 – Data frame comparing PN, PP, and the instance of interest

In *Figure 7.15*, PN can be interpreted as you would a counterfactual, but the attention is given to what's missing. The PN-x column shows precisely that: more sex_Female and less race_African-American. CEM has no concept of one-hot-encoded features, so it doesn't realize that sex_Male and sex_Female are mutually exclusive, or that they are binary, for that matter. Nevertheless, according to the PN, what can be understood by this is that race and gender determine the decision for our *instance of interest*.

CEM is contrastive because you would usually contrast what needs to be absent by stating what needs to be sufficiently present. But our PP all-zeros column makes no sense. It's like stating that an empty canvas is at least what should be present for a painting to be a painting! Speaking of paintings, because of the continuously subtractive nature of PP, our use case doesn't lend itself to CEM. However, images are the perfect use case. Each feature is a continuous value, a pixel, which can be interpreted as the absence or presence of light or a primary color. In *Chapter 8, Visualizing Convolutional Neural Networks*, we will learn how to interpret neural networks trained with images.

Mission accomplished

This chapter's mission was to see whether there was unfair bias in predicting whether a particular defendant would recidivate. We demonstrated that the FPR for African American defendants is 1.87 times higher than for Caucasian defendants. This disparity was confirmed with WIT, indicating that the model in question is much more likely to misclassify the positive class on the basis of race. However, this is a global interpretation method, so it doesn't answer our question regarding a specific defendant. Incidentally, in *Chapter 11, Bias Mitigation and Causal Inference Methods*, we will cover other global interpretation methods for unfairness.

To ascertain whether the model was racially biased toward the defendant in question, we leveraged anchor and counterfactual explanations – they both output race as a primary feature in their explanations. The anchor did it with relatively high precision and coverage, and *Counterfactuals Guided by Prototypes* found that the closest one has a different race. That being said, in both cases, race wasn't the only feature in the explanations. The features usually included any or all of the following: `priors_count`, `age`, `charge_degree`, and `sex`. The inconsistent rules involving the first three regarding `race` suggest double standards and the involvement of `sex` suggests intersectionality. **Double standards** are when rules are applied unfairly to different groups. **Intersectionality** is to do with how overlapping identities create different systems of interconnected modes of discrimination. However, we know that females of all races are less likely to recidivate according to academic research. Still, we have to ask ourselves whether they have a structural advantage that makes them necessarily privileged in this context. There's a more elaborate dynamic going on than meets the eye. The bottom line is that despite all the other factors that interplay with race, and provided that there's no relevant criminological information that we are missing, yes, there's racial bias involved in this particular prediction.

Summary

After reading this chapter, you should know how to leverage anchors, to understand the decision rules that impact a classification, and counterfactuals, to grasp what needs to change for the predicted class to change. You also learned how to assess fairness using confusion matrices and Google's WIT. Lastly, we covered CEM to explain a decision by what is minimally present and absent. In the next chapter, we will study interpretation methods for **Convolutional Neural Networks (CNNs)**.

Dataset sources

ProPublica Data Store. (2019). COMPAS Recidivism Risk Score Data and Analysis. Originally retrieved from `https://www.propublica.org/datastore/dataset/compas-recidivism-risk-score-data-and-analysisv`

Further reading

- Desmarais, S.L., Johnson, K.L., & Singh, J.P. (2016). Performance of recidivism risk assessment instruments in U.S. correctional settings. Psychol Serv;13(3):206-222. `https://doi.org/10.1037/ser0000075`

- Berk, R., Heidari, H., Jabbari, S., Kearns, M., & Roth, A. (2017). Fairness in Criminal Justice Risk Assessments: The State of the Art. Sociological Methods & Research.

- Angwin, J., Larson, J., Mattu, S., & Kirchner, L. (2016). Machine Bias. There is software that is used across the county to predict future criminals. `https://www.propublica.org/article/machine-bias-risk-assessments-in-criminal-sentencing`

- Ribeiro, M.T., Singh, S., & Guestrin, C. (2018). Anchors: High-Precision Model-Agnostic Explanations. Proceedings of the AAAI/ACM Conference on AI, Ethics, and Society. `https://doi.org/10.1145/3375627.3375830`

- Rocque, M., Posick, C., & Hoyle, J. (2015). Age and Crime. The encyclopedia of crime and punishment, 1-8. `https://doi.org/10.1002/9781118519639.wbecpx275`

- Dhurandhar, A., Chen, P., Luss, R., Tu, C., Ting, P., Shanmugam, K., & Das, P. (2018). Explanations based on the Missing: Towards Contrastive Explanations with Pertinent Negatives. NeurIPS. `https://arxiv.org/abs/1802.07623`

8
Visualizing Convolutional Neural Networks

Up to this point, we have only dealt with tabular data and, briefly, text data in *Chapter 6, Local Model-Agnostic Interpretation Methods*. This chapter will exclusively explore interpretation methods that work with images and, in particular, with the **Convolutional Neural Network** (**CNN**) models that train image classifiers. Typically, deep learning models are regarded as the epitome of black box models. However, one of the benefits of a CNN is how easily it lends itself to visualization, so we can not only visualize outcomes, but every step of the learning process with **activations**. The possibility of interpreting these steps is rare among so-called black box models. Once we have grasped how the CNN is learning, we will study how to use state-of-the-art gradient-based attribution methods such as *Saliency Maps* and *Grad-CAM* to debug class attribution. Lastly, we will extend our attribution debugging know-how with perturbation-based attribution methods such as *Occlusion Sensitivity*, *LIME*, and the *Contrastive Explanation Method*.

These are the main topics we are going to cover:

- Assessing the CNN classifier with traditional interpretation methods
- Visualizing the learning process with activation-based methods
- Evaluating misclassifications with gradient-based attribution methods
- Understanding classifications with perturbation-based attribution methods

Technical requirements

This chapter's example uses the `mldatasets`, `pandas`, `numpy`, `sklearn`, `skimage`, `tensorflow`, `matplotlib`, `seaborn`, `cv2`, `tf-explain`, `tf-keras-vis`, `lime`, `alibi`, and `shap` libraries. Instructions on how to install all of these libraries are in the preface. The code for this chapter is located here: `https://github.com/PacktPublishing/Interpretable-Machine-Learning-with-Python/tree/master/Chapter08`.

The mission

Self-checkout machines that allow customers to process their purchases were invented in 1984, but didn't start to appear in most supermarket chains until the turn of the century. However, despite the many advantages these machines generate for retailers and customers alike, they are far from perfect – they are prone to shoplifting, mechanical failures, lack of accessibility, and an inadequate customer service experience.

In the last decade, a lot of companies have been scrambling to fix these problems with deep learning. For instance, cameras can monitor body pose, product movement, and facial gestures. They can detect shoplifting events or even automatically lower the checkout to be more wheelchair accessible with trained deep learning models.

Another recent trend is that convenience store chains are experiencing a rapid growth phase in most developed countries. However, they struggle to keep up with demand and pay the low wages that allow them to be open when most stores are closed. Japan is ahead of the curve in this trend since convenience stores have long dominated retail, and salaries are relatively high, so they have adapted to keep things convenient. Customers don't only expect 24/7 availability, but very speedy checkouts in this form of retail. Self-checkout can be slower, which is why it hasn't been adopted worldwide in convenience stores. However, it is already available in some Japanese chains with a high degree of success.

Outside of Asia, a large chain of convenience stores bought a self-checkout system from Japan to replicate this success. The executives in this company were thrilled, but they quickly realized that all items must be barcoded in order for this system to work, which is a problem for only one type of item. Unlike Japanese consumers, who don't mind buying plastic-wrapped fruits, in the markets where this chain operates, consumers don't trust whole fruits if they are packaged. Unfortunately, the plastic would be necessary to ensure that the barcode sticker didn't peel off or get damaged, and customers don't trust large barcode stickers directly on their fruit with ample adhesive either. There is an option of entering the fruit name manually, as it is done in supermarkets (see *Figure 8.1*), but it slows down the process by at least 15 seconds per item, which is unacceptable in a "convenience" setting:

Figure 8.1 – Japanese self-checkout with the "Fruit" button highlighted (for illustration purposes only)

The executives decided to leverage the cameras in the self-checkout system to automatically detect the fruits so that customers wouldn't have to enter them. To this end, they identified 16 fruits and vegetables that cannot be sold in packaging and paid an AI consultancy company to develop a model to classify them. This company came back with the most promising results: a whopping 99.9% accuracy, which was surprising considering they asked for no domain knowledge nor data. However, once the retailer tested it with their self-checkout machines, they realized that only somewhere between a fifth and a third of fruits and vegetables were classified correctly. When the executives discussed this with the consultants, they were adamant that their model was nearly perfect, and it was the cameras of the self-checkout system that required calibration.

To seek out a second opinion and an honest evaluation of the model, the convenience store chain has approached another AI consultancy firm – yours!

The approach

No single interpretation method is perfect, and even in the best scenario can only tell you one part of the story. Therefore, you have decided to first assess the model's predictive performance using traditional interpretation methods including the following:

- ROC curves and ROC-AUC
- Confusion matrices and all metrics derived from them (accuracy, precision, recall, F1).

Then, you'll examine the model using two activation-based methods:

- Intermediate activation
- Activation maximization

This is followed by evaluating decisions with three gradient-based methods:

- Saliency maps
- Grad-CAM
- Integrated gradients

This is followed by three perturbation-based methods:

- Occlusion sensitivity
- LIME
- CEM

And, lastly, a bonus backpropagation-based method:

- SHAP's DeepExplainer

I hope that you understand why the model is not performing as it should and how to fix it by the end of this process. You can also leverage the many plots and visualizations you will produce to communicate this story to the convenience store company's executives.

Preparations

You will find most of the code for this example here: `https://github.com/PacktPublishing/Interpretable-Machine-Learning-with-Python/blob/master/Chapter08/FruitClassifier_part1.ipynb`, up to the *Exploring Classifications with Pertubation-Based Attribution Methods* section. That section alone is located here: `https://github.com/PacktPublishing/Interpretable-Machine-Learning-with-Python/blob/master/Chapter08/FruitClassifier_part2.ipynb`.

Loading the libraries

To run this example, you need to install the following libraries:

- `mldatasets` to load the dataset
- `pandas`, `numpy`, and `sklearn` (Scikit-learn) to manipulate it
- `tensorflow` to fit and predict with the models
- `matplotlib`, `seaborn`, `cv2`, `skimage`, `tf-explain`, `tf-keras-vis`, `lime`, `alibi`, and `shap` to visualize the interpretations

You should load all of them first:

```
import math
import os
import mldatasets
import pandas as pd
import numpy as np
from sklearn import preprocessing, metrics
import tensorflow as tf
from tensorflow import keras
from keras.utils.data_utils import get_file
import matplotlib.pyplot as plt
```

```
from matplotlib import cm
import seaborn as sns
import cv2
#PART 1 only
from tf_explain.core.activations import ExtractActivations
from tf_keras_vis.activation_maximization import\

ActivationMaximization
from tf_keras_vis.saliency import Saliency
from tf_keras_vis.utils import normalize
from tf_keras_vis.gradcam import GradcamPlusPlus
from tf_explain.core.integrated_gradients import
IntegratedGradients
#PART 2 only
from skimage.segmentation import mark_boundaries
from tf_explain.core.occlusion_sensitivity import\

OcclusionSensitivity
import lime
from lime import lime_image
from alibi.explainers import CEM
import shap
```

Let's check that TensorFlow has loaded the correct version with this command. It should be version 2.0 or above:

```
print(tf.__version__)
```

Understanding and preparing the data

The data used to train the model was created in academic research and is publicly available at Kaggle (https://www.kaggle.com/moltean/fruits). It's called "Fruit 360" because a motor rotated the fruits as a camera took pictures from every angle and on more than one axis. Pictures were taken with consistent lighting on a white sheet of paper, but the background was replaced with white using an algorithm, so images lack shadows. The Fruit 360 dataset has over 100 classes of fruits and vegetables. The data you will load is the same dataet, except it only has 16 classes corresponding to those the convenience store chain executives wanted to classify. It also includes a small validation set with some pictures they tested the model with and agree that look like the fruits and vegetables they carry in their stores. They have provided the validation images in the dimensions required for the model and in a higher resolution (original) size.

We load the data like this into four datasets corresponding to training, test, validation, and original validation:

```
X_train, X_test, X_val, X_val_orig, y_train, y_test,\
y_val, y_val_orig =\
        mldatasets.load("fruits-360", prepare=True)
```

We can verify that the shapes of the numpy arrays match our expectations with the following code:

```
print('X_train:%s' % (X_train.shape,))
print('X_test:%s' % (X_test.shape,))
print('X_val:%s' % (X_val.shape,))
print('X_val_orig:%s' % (X_val_orig.shape,))
print('y_train:%s' % (y_train.shape,))
print('y_test:%s' % (y_test.shape,))
print('y_val:%s' % (y_val.shape,))
print('y_val_orig:%s' % (y_val_orig.shape,))
```

The preceding code outputs the dimensions of each array. You can tell that the first number in each X tuple matches its corresponding y tuple. The second number in the y tuple indicates that the labels are not already one-hot encoded, but in their text or ordinal form because otherwise there would be 16 instead of 1. You can also tell that all X arrays have equal dimensions of 100 width, 100 height, and 3 channels, except for the original validation (X_val_orig), which is expected to be a higher resolution. We won't need the original validation dataset for inference, so it's OK that it doesn't meet the model's dimension requirements:

```
X_train:     (7872, 100, 100, 3)
X_test:      (2633, 100, 100, 3)
X_val:       (64, 100, 100, 3)
X_val_orig:  (64, 400, 400, 3)
y_train:     (7872, 1)
y_test:      (2633, 1)
y_val:       (64, 1)
y_val_orig:  (64, 1)
```

If you print(X_train[0]), you'll notice that there is a bunch of 255s, which is the maximum number used to express the red, green, and blue in the image. However, for the sake of efficiency and reliability, a CNN is usually trained with each value as float numbers between zero and one. To this end, we will have to normalize the X_train, X_test, and X_val arrays like this:

```
X_train = X_train.astype('float32')/255
X_test = X_test.astype('float32')/255
X_val = X_val.astype('float32')/255
```

Another preprocessing step we will need to perform is to **one-hot encode (OHE)** the y labels because we will need the OHE form to evaluate the model's predictive performance. Once we initialize the OneHotEncoder, we will need to fit it to the training data (X_train). We can also extract the categories from the encoder into a list (fruits_l) to verify that it has all 16:

```
ohe = preprocessing.OneHotEncoder(sparse=False)
ohe.fit(y_train)
fruits_l = ohe.categories_[0].tolist()
print(fruits_l)
```

The preceding code should output the following list. It should be in alphabetical order since the folders with the images are in this order. It is usually safe to assume that the encoder used this order. However, if this assumption is incorrect, we can tell when we assess model performance. For instance, if the encoding was done with the categories in reverse alphabetical order, the class predictions would also be in reverse:

```
['Apple Golden', 'Apple Granny Smith', 'Apple Red', 'Avocado',
'Banana', 'Clementine', 'Grapefruit Pink', 'Mango Red',
'Nectarine', 'Onion Red', 'Onion White', 'Orange', 'Peach',
'Pear', 'Pomegranate', 'Tomato']
```

For the sake of reproducibility, always initialize your random seeds like this:

```
rand = 9
os.environ['PYTHONHASHSEED']=str(rand)
np.random.seed(rand)
tf.random.set_seed(rand)
```

It is acknowledged that determinism is very difficult with deep learning and is often session-, platform-, and architecture-dependent. If you are using an **NVIDIA GPU**, you can install a library called `tensorflow-determinism`, which you can find at `https://github.com/NVIDIA/framework-determinism`.

Now, let's take a peek at what images are in our datasets. We know that the training and test datasets are very similar, so we will start with the test dataset. We can iterate every class in `fruits_l` and randomly select a single one from the test dataset with `np.random.choice`. We place each image on a 4 × 4 grid with the class label above it:

```
plt.subplots(figsize=(10,10))
for f, fruit in zip([*range(len(fruits_l))], fruits_l):
 plt.subplot(4, 4, f+1)
 plt.title(fruits_l[f], fontsize=12)
 idx = np.random.choice(np.where(y_test[:,0] == fruit)[0], 1)
[0]
 plt.imshow(X_test[idx], interpolation='spline16')
 plt.axis("off")
plt.show()
```

The preceding code generates *Figure 8.2*. You can tell that there is significant pixelation around the edges of the fruits; some fruits appear darker than others, and some of the pictures are from odd angles:

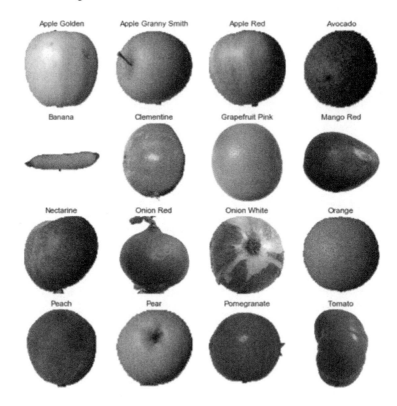

Figure 8.2 – A random sample of the test dataset

Let's now do the same for the validation dataset to compare it to the test/training datasets. We can use the same code as before, except we replace `y_test` with `yval`:

```
plt.subplots(figsize=(10,10))
for f, fruit in zip([*range(len(fruits_l))], fruits_l):
  plt.subplot(4, 4, f+1)
  plt.title(fruits_l[f], fontsize=12)
  idx = np.random.choice(np.where(y_val[:,0] == fruit)[0], 1)[0]
  plt.imshow(X_val[idx], interpolation='spline16')
  plt.axis("off")
plt.show()
```

The preceding code generates *Figure 8.3*. You can tell that the validation set has less pixelated and better-lit fruits and vegetables mostly from the top- and side-facing angles:

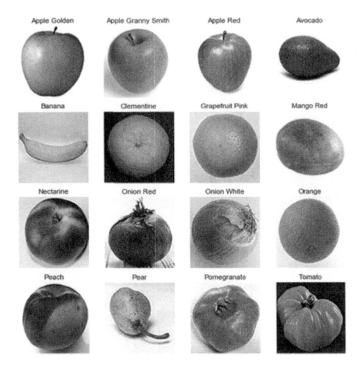

Figure 8.3 – A random sample of the validation dataset

We won't need to train a CNN in this chapter. Thankfully, it has been provided to us by the client.

Loading the CNN model

We can quickly load the model and output its summary like this:

```
model_path = get_file('CNN_fruits_final.hdf5',    'https://
github.com/PacktPublishing/Interpretable-Machine-Learning-with-
Python/blob/master/models/CNN_fruits_final.hdf5?raw=true')
```

```
cnn_fruits_mdl = keras.models.load_model(model_path)
```

```
cnn_fruits_mdl.summary()
```

The preceding snippet outputs the following summary. It has pretty much everything we need to know about the model. It has four convolutional layers (`Conv2D`), each followed by a max pool layer (`MaxPooling2D`). It then has a first `Dropout` layer for regularization, followed by a `Flatten` layer and a fully connected layer (`Dense`). Then, there is one more `Dropout` before the output. Naturally, 16 neurons are in this final layer corresponding to each class:

```
Model: "CNN_fruits"
_____

Layer (type)                    Output Shape              Param #
=================================================================

conv2d_1 (Conv2D)               (None, 99, 99, 16)        208
_____

maxpool2d_1 (MaxPooling2D)      (None, 49, 49, 16)        0
_____

conv2d_2 (Conv2D)               (None, 48, 48, 32)        2080
_____

maxpool2d_2 (MaxPooling2D)      (None, 24, 24, 32)        0
_____

conv2d_3 (Conv2D)               (None, 23, 23, 64)        8256
_____

maxpool2d_3 (MaxPooling2D)      (None, 11, 11, 64)        0
_____

conv2d_4 (Conv2D)               (None, 10, 10, 128)       32896
_____

maxpool2d_4 (MaxPooling2D)      (None, 5, 5, 128)         0
_____

dropout_1 (Dropout)             (None, 5, 5, 128)         0
_____
```

```
flatten (Flatten)              (None, 3200)                    0


dense_1 (Dense)                (None, 150)                480150


dropout_2 (Dropout)            (None, 150)                     0


dense_2 (Dense)                (None, 16)                   2416
===============================================================
===
Total params: 526,006
Trainable params: 526,006
Non-trainable params: 0
```

Assessing the CNN classifier with traditional interpretation methods

We can easily derive accuracies for all three datasets using the model's own `evaluate` function like this:

```
train_score = cnn_fruits_mdl.evaluate(X_train,\
                              ohe.transform(y_train),
verbose=0)
test_score = cnn_fruits_mdl.evaluate(X_test,\
                              ohe.transform(y_test),
verbose=0)
val_score = cnn_fruits_mdl.evaluate(X_val,\
                              ohe.transform(y_val),
verbose=0)
print('Train accuracy:\t{:.1%}'.format(train_score[1]))
print('Test accuracy:\t{:.1%}'.format(test_score[1]))
print('Val accuracy:\t{:.1%}'.format(val_score[1]))
```

The preceding snippet outputted the following figures:

```
Train accuracy: 100.0%
Test accuracy:   99.9%
Val accuracy:    31.2%
```

Indeed, you can expect a model to always reach `100%` training accuracy if you train it for enough epochs using optimal hyperparameters. A near-perfect test accuracy is harder to achieve, depending on how different these two are. We know that the test dataset is simply a sample of images from the same collection, so it's not particularly surprising that such high accuracy (`99.9%`) was achieved.

When classification models are discussed in a business setting, often layman stakeholders are only interested in one number: accuracy. It's easy to let this drive the discussion, but there's much more nuance to it. For instance, the disappointing validation accuracy (`31.2%`) could mean many things. It could mean that five classes are getting perfect classification, and all others are not, or that 10 classes are getting only half misclassified. There are many possibilities of what could be going on.

In any case, when dealing with a multiclass classification problem, an accuracy below 50% might not be as bad as it seems. With 16 classes more or less evenly split, we have to take note that the **No Information Rate** is likely to be around 7%, so 31.2% is still orders of magnitude higher than that. In fact, there is less of a leap to 100%! To a machine learner practitioner, this means that if we judge solely based on validation accuracy results, the model is still learning something of value that can be improved upon.

We will first evaluate the model using the test dataset with the `evaluate_multiclass_mdl` function. The arguments include the model (`cnn_fruits_mdl`), our test data (`X_test`), and corresponding labels (`y_test`), as well as the class names (`fruits_l`) and the encoder (`ohe`). Lastly, we don't need it to plot the ROC curves since they will be perfect (`plot_roc=False`). This function returns the predicted labels and probabilities, which we can store in variables for later use:

```
y_test_pred, y_test_prob =\
    mldatasets.evaluate_multiclass_mdl(cnn_fruits_mdl, X_test,\
                            y_test, fruits_l, ohe, plot_
roc=False)
```

The preceding code generates both *Figure 8.4* with a confusion matrix and *Figure 8.5* with performance metrics for each class:

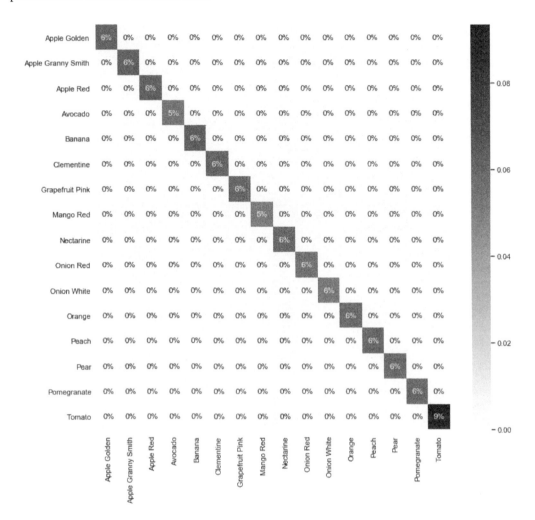

Figure 8.4 – The confusion matrix for the test dataset

Even though the confusion matrix in *Figure 8.4* seems to suggest a perfect classification, once you see the precision and recall breakdown in *Figure 8.5*, you can tell that the model had issues with two varieties of apples, nectarines, and pears:

	precision	recall	f1-score	support
Apple Golden	1.000	1.000	1.000	164
Apple Granny Smith	0.994	1.000	0.997	164
Apple Red	0.994	1.000	0.997	164
Avocado	1.000	1.000	1.000	143
Banana	1.000	1.000	1.000	166
Clementine	1.000	1.000	1.000	166
Grapefruit Pink	1.000	1.000	1.000	166
Mango Red	1.000	1.000	1.000	142
Nectarine	1.000	0.994	0.997	164
Onion Red	1.000	1.000	1.000	150
Onion White	1.000	1.000	1.000	146
Orange	1.000	1.000	1.000	160
Peach	1.000	1.000	1.000	164
Pear	1.000	0.994	0.997	164
Pomegranate	1.000	1.000	1.000	164
Tomato	1.000	1.000	1.000	246
accuracy			0.999	2633
macro avg	0.999	0.999	0.999	2633
weighted avg	0.999	0.999	0.999	2633

Figure 8.5 – The near-perfect predictive performance metrics for the test dataset

Now, let's repeat the same code snippet, but for the validation dataset. This time, we want to see the ROC curves (`plot_roc=True`) but only the averages, and not on a class-by-class basis (`plot_roc_class=False`) because there are only four pictures per class. Given the small number of samples, we can display the numbers in the confusion matrix rather than percentages (`pct_matrix=False`):

```
y_val_pred, y_val_prob =\
    mldatasets.evaluate_multiclass_mdl(cnn_fruits_mdl, X_val,\
                            y_val, fruits_l, ohe, plot
                            _roc=True,\
                            plot_roc_class=False, pct_
                            matrix=False)
```

The preceding code snippet generated the ROC curve in *Figure 8.6*, the confusion matrix in *Figure 8.7*, and the classification table in *Figure 8.8*:

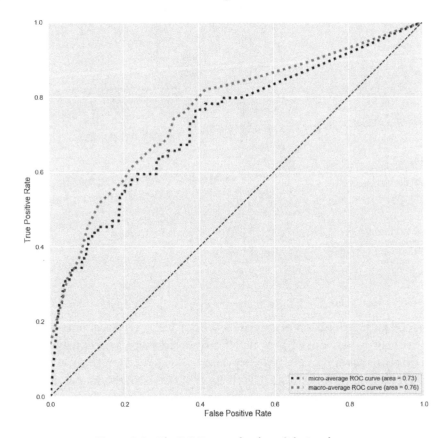

Figure 8.6 – The ROC curve for the validation dataset

The validation ROC plot (*Figure 8.6*) shows the macro-average and micro-average ROC curves. The difference in both of these is in how they are calculated. Macro metrics are computed for each class independently and then averaged, treating each differently. Whereas micro-averages factor in the contribution or representation of each class, generally, micro-averages are more reliable:

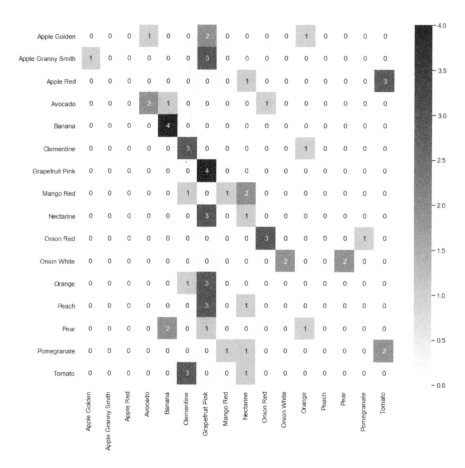

Figure 8.7 – The confusion matrix for the test dataset

If we take a look at the confusion matrix in *Figure 8.7*, we can tell that only bananas and grapefruits are getting four-out-of-four classification. However, a lot of fruits are being misclassified as bananas and grapefruits, especially grapefruits! On the other hand, many fruits are never classified properly, such as all apple varieties and tomatoes. Many of them are similar in shape or color to other fruits, so you could understand how that would happen, but how does an avocado get misclassified as a banana or red onion?

	precision	recall	f1-score	support
Apple Golden	0.000	0.000	0.000	4
Apple Granny Smith	0.000	0.000	0.000	4
Apple Red	0.000	0.000	0.000	4
Avocado	0.667	0.500	0.571	4
Banana	0.571	1.000	0.727	4
Clementine	0.375	0.750	0.500	4
Grapefruit Pink	0.211	1.000	0.348	4
Mango Red	0.500	0.250	0.333	4
Nectarine	0.143	0.250	0.182	4
Onion Red	0.750	0.750	0.750	4
Onion White	1.000	0.500	0.667	4
Orange	0.000	0.000	0.000	4
Peach	0.000	0.000	0.000	4
Pear	0.000	0.000	0.000	4
Pomegranate	0.000	0.000	0.000	4
Tomato	0.000	0.000	0.000	4
accuracy			0.312	64
macro avg	0.264	0.312	0.255	64
weighted avg	0.264	0.312	0.255	64

Figure 8.8 – The predictive performance metrics for the test dataset

The predictive performance metrics in *Figure 8.8* for the validation dataset are consistent with what we saw in the confusion matrix. Grapefruits and bananas have a high recall, but low precision, and half the classes have 0% for both.

Determining what misclassifications to focus on

We have already noticed some exciting misclassifications we can focus on:

- **Grapefruits False Positives**: 15 out of the 64 samples in the validation dataset were misclassified as grapefruits. That's nearly one quarter! What is it about a grapefruit that renders it so easily confused with other fruits according to the model?

- **Avocado False Negatives**: Avocados have a pear shape but have a darker color and a skin with a unique alligator texture. It's not easy to fathom how this fruit could possibly be misclassified.

And to understand these misclassifications, we ought to also examine true positives for those same fruits.

To visualize the tasks ahead, we can create a `DataFrame` (`preds_df`) with the true labels (`y_true`) in one column and predicted labels in another (`y_pred`). And to understand how certain the models are of these predictions, we can create another data frame with the probabilities (`probs_df`). We can generate column totals for these probabilities to sort the columns according to which fruit the model is most certain about across all samples. Then, we can concatenate our predictions data frame with the first eight columns from our probabilities data frame since we know only half the fruits are being classified at all:

```
preds_df = pd.DataFrame({'y_true':y_val[:,0], 'y_pred':y_val_
pred})
probs_df = pd.DataFrame(y_val_prob*100).round(1)
probs_df.loc['Total']= probs_df.sum().round(1)
probs_df.columns = fruits_l
probs_df = probs_df.sort_values('Total', axis=1,
ascending=False)
probs_df.drop(['Total'], axis=0, inplace=True)
probs_final_df = probs_df.iloc[:,0:8]
preds_probs_df = pd.concat([preds_df, probs_final_df], axis=1)
```

Let's now output the data frame with color coding for the prediction instances we are interested in assessing. On one hand, we have the grapefruit false positives and, on the other, the avocado false negatives. But we also have the true positives. We have highlighted all of them but are only interested in those that pertain to our misclassifications. Lastly, we have bolded all probabilities over 50% and hidden all probabilities of 0% so that it's easier to spot any higher probability:

```
pd.set_option('precision', 1)
preds_probs_df.style.apply(lambda x: ['background: lightgreen'\
                if (x[0] == x[1]) else '' for i in x],
axis=1).\
        apply(lambda x: ['background: orange' if (x[0] !=
x[1] and\
        x[1] == 'Grapefruit Pink') else '' for i in x],
axis=1).\


        apply(lambda x: ['background: yellow' if (x[0] !=
x[1] and\
        x[0] == 'Avocado') else '' for i in x], axis=1).\
        apply(lambda x: ['font-weight: bold' if
isinstance(i, float)\
        and i >= 50 else '' for i in x], axis=1).\
      apply(lambda x: ['color:transparent' if i == 0.0 else
''\
        for i in x], axis=1)
```

The preceding code snippet produces *Figure 8.9*. You can tell by the highlights which are the grapefruit false positives and the avocado false negatives , as well as which would be the true positives for these fruits: #36-39 for grapefruit, and #5 and #7 for avocado:

	y_true	y_pred	Grapefruit Pink	Clementine	Banana	Nectarine	Tomato	Onion Red	Avocado	Orange
0	Pear	Banana			100.0					
1	Pear	Banana			100.0					
2	Pear	Orange	5.2							94.8
3	Pear	Grapefruit Pink	96.5		3.5					
4	Avocado	Onion Red						100.0		
5	Avocado	Avocado							0.1	99.9
6	Avocado	Banana			100.0					
7	Avocado	Avocado							100.0	
8	Pomegranate	Tomato					100.0			
:	:	:	:	:	:	:	:	:	:	:
16	Apple Golden	Avocado							99.8	0.2
17	Apple Golden	Grapefruit Pink	100.0							
18	Apple Golden	Orange								100.0
19	Apple Golden	Grapefruit Pink	100.0							
20	Nectarine	Grapefruit Pink	100.0							
21	Nectarine	Nectarine					100.0			
22	Nectarine	Grapefruit Pink	100.0							
23	Nectarine	Grapefruit Pink	100.0							
24	Clementine	Clementine		100.0						
25	Clementine	Clementine	1.9	98.1						
26	Clementine	Clementine		100.0						
27	Clementine	Orange								100.0
28	Onion White	Pear								
29	Onion White	Pear								
30	Onion White	Onion White								
31	Onion White	Onion White	8.2		0.6					
32	Apple Granny Smith	Grapefruit Pink	100.0							
33	Apple Granny Smith	Apple Golden								
34	Apple Granny Smith	Grapefruit Pink	100.0							
35	Apple Granny Smith	Grapefruit Pink	92.7		7.2				0.1	
36	Grapefruit Pink	Grapefruit Pink	100.0							
37	Grapefruit Pink	Grapefruit Pink	100.0							
:	:	:	:	:	:	:	:	:	:	:
56	Orange	Clementine	38.7	61.3						
57	Orange	Grapefruit Pink	100.0							
58	Orange	Grapefruit Pink	51.8	48.2						
59	Orange	Grapefruit Pink	91.6	8.4						
60	Peach	Grapefruit Pink	100.0							
61	Peach	Grapefruit Pink	100.0							
62	Peach	Nectarine		0.1		99.9				
63	Peach	Grapefruit Pink	87.7			11.9				

Figure 8.9 – Table with all 64 samples in the validation dataset and their true and predicted labels, as well as their predicted probabilities

We can easily store the indexes for these instances in lists with the following code. That way, for future reference, we can iterate through these lists to assess individual predictions or subset arrays with them to perform interpretation tasks for the entire group. As you can tell, we have lists for all four groups:

```
avocado_FN_idxs = preds_df[(preds_df['y_true'] !=\
        preds_df['y_pred']) & (preds_df['y_true'] ==
'Avocado')].\
        index.to_list()
avocado_TP_idxs = preds_df[(preds_df['y_true'] ==\
        preds_df['y_pred']) & (preds_df['y_true'] ==
'Avocado')].\
        index.to_list()
grapefruit_FP_idxs = preds_df[(preds_df['y_true'] !=\
        preds_df['y_pred']) & (preds_df['y_pred'] ==\
        'Grapefruit Pink')].index.to_list()
grapefruit_TP_idxs = preds_df[(preds_df['y_true'] ==\
        preds_df['y_pred']) & (preds_df['y_pred'] ==\
        'Grapefruit Pink')].index.to_list()
```

Now that we have all our data preprocessed, the model is fully loaded and lists with the groups of predictions to debug. Now we can move forward. Let the interpretation begin!

Visualizing the learning process with activation-based methods

Before we get into discussing activations, layers, filters, neurons, gradients, convolutions, kernels, and all the fantastic elements that make up a CNN, let's first briefly revisit the mechanics of a CNN and this one in particular.

The convolution layer is the essential building block of a CNN. It convolves the input with **learnable filters**, which are relatively small but are applied across the entire width, height, and depth at specific distances or **strides**. See *Figure 8.10*. In the fruit CNN case, the first convolutional layer has 16 filters with a 2 × 2 kernel, the default 1 × 1 stride, and no zero padding (`valid`). Each filter produces a two-dimensional **activation map** (also known as a **feature map**). It's called an activation map because it denotes positions of activations in the images – in other words, where specific "features" are located. In this context, a feature is an abstract spatial representation that, downstream in the process, is reflected in the learned weights of fully connected (`dense`) layers. Filters are template matching because they end up activating areas of the activation map when certain patterns are found in the input image.

But before we get to our dense layers, we have to reduce the dimensions of our filters until they have a workable size. For instance, if we flatten the output of our first convolution (99 × 99 × 16), we would have nearly 157,000 features. I think we can all agree that that would be too much to feed into a fully connected layer. Even if we use enough neurons to handle this workload, we probably wouldn't have captured enough spatial representations for the neural network to make sense of the images.

For this reason, convolutional layers are often paired with pooling layers, which downsample the input, in this case, **max pooling**, which takes the maximum value in a window or kernel. The kernel size is 2 × 2 in this case, which means that it takes one value from each cluster of four, essentially halving the output's width and height. See *Figure 8.10* next for a visual representation of the layers:

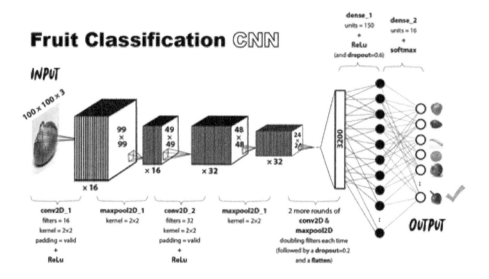

Figure 8.10 – The fruit CNN's architecture

We also stack additional convolution layers to capture successively larger representations. As the filters become smaller in width and height, the learned representations will be larger. In other words, the first convolutional layer may be about details such as texture, the following one about edges, and the last one about shapes. We must then flatten the convolutional layers' output to feed it to the multilayer perceptron that takes over from then on.

Thankfully, the flattened output is of a more workable size: 3,200 features. There are only two **dense** or **fully connected** layers in this CNN. The first one has 150 neurons, and the last one has 16, which, leveraging **softmax** activation, outputs probabilities between 0 and 1 for each of the classes. In the fruit CNN, there were some **dropout** layers involved to help regularize the training. We can ignore these entirely because, for inference, they are ignored.

If this wasn't entirely clear, don't fret! The sections that follow will demonstrate visually through activations, gradients, and perturbations how the network probably learned or did not learn image representations.

Intermediate activations

For inference, the image goes through the network's input and prediction comes out through the output traversing every single layer. However, one of the advantages of having a sequential and layered architecture is that we can extract any layer's output and not just the final layer. The **intermediate activations** are simply the outputs of any of the convolution or pooling layers. They are activation maps because, after an activation function has been applied, the brighter spots map to the image's features. In this case, the model used ReLu on all convolutional layers, so that is what activates the spots. We are only interested in the convolutional layers' intermediate activations because the pooling layers are simply downsampled versions of these ones. Why not see the higher resolution version instead?

What we will do now is iterate across all convolutional layers and extract activations for each one. To this end, we will create a list with convolutional layer names (`target_layers`) and initialize a `tf_explain` explainer with `ExtractActivations()` like this:

```
target_layers = ['conv2d_1', 'conv2d_2', 'conv2d_3',
'conv2d_4']
explainer = ExtractActivations()
```

We can iterate all target layers and all avocado true positive validation samples and generate activation maps for each layer and sample combination. We do this with the `explain` function. It takes the sample image in a very specific format, that is, with an extra dimension (`1, 100, 100, 3`) inside a tuple with `None` as the second element. It also requires the model (`cnn_fruits_mdl`) and layer name (`target_layer`). It outputs the activation maps for every filter in the layer (`viz_img`). To visualize this, we can use a function called `compare_img_pred_viz`, which places the original sample image (`orig_img`) side by side with an image produced by an interpretation method (`viz_img`). It also takes the sample's actual label (`y_true`) and predicted label (`y_pred`). Optionally, we can provide a pandas series with the probabilities for this prediction (`probs_s`) and a `title`:

```
for target_layer in target_layers:
  for idx in avocado_TP_idxs:
   orig_img = X_val_orig[idx]
   viz_img = explainer.explain((np.array([X_val[idx]]), None),\
          cnn_fruits_mdl, target_layer)
   y_true = y_val[idx,0]
   y_pred = y_val_pred[idx]
   probs_s = probs_df.loc[idx]
   title = '{} Activations for Avocado #{}'.\
           format(target_layer, idx)
   mldatasets.compare_img_pred_viz(orig_img, viz_img,\
                      y_true, y_pred, probs_s,
 title=title)
```

The preceding code generates eight images in total, including *Figure 8.11* and *Figure 8.12*. As you can tell by *Figure 8.11*, the first convolutional layer seems to be picking up on the avocado's prickly skin texture as well as its contours:

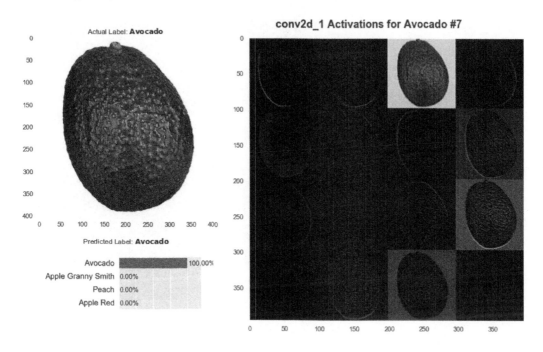

Figure 8.11 – Intermediate activations for the first convolutional layer for avocado #7

Figure 8.12 shows how, by the second convolutional layer, the network is understanding an avocado's contours better and bright areas suggest more depth and convexity:

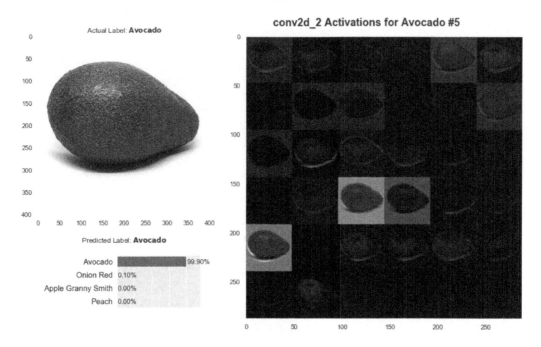

Figure 8.12 – Intermediate activations for the second convolutional layer for avocado #5

To mix things up, let's interpret the intermediate activations of the last two convolution layers with grapefruits. To do that, we simply repeat the same code, but replace `avocado` with `grapefruit`. There are 4 true positives for this fruit, so we will end up with 16 explanations. This modified code snippet will produce *Figure 8.13* and *Figure 8.14*. The third convolutional layer in *Figure 8.13* appears to be picking up on the hollowed-out shape of the grapefruit as well as specular highlights:

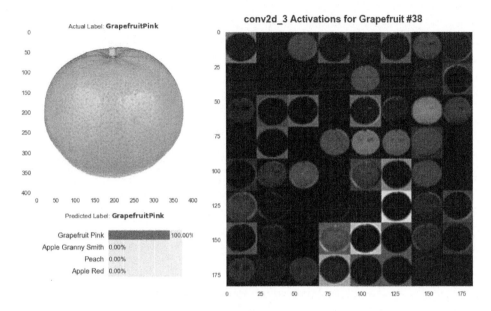

Figure 8.13 – Intermediate activations for the third convolutional layer for grapefruit #38

You can observe in *Figure 8.14* how, by the fourth convolutional layer, there is no other detail in the activation maps other than the grapefruit's roundness:

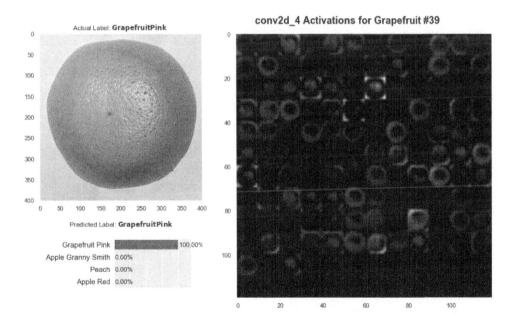

Figure 8.14 – Intermediate activations for the fourth convolutional layer for grapefruit #39

Extracting intermediate activations can provide you with some insight on a sample-by-sample basis. In other words, it's a **local model interpretation method**. But what if we wanted to learn how activations operate globally? That's what activation maximization can do for us.

Activation maximization

For a global interpretation per filter per convolutional layer, we can perform **activation maximization**. As the name suggests, we are maximizing the activation. We do this with **gradient ascent**. If you recall, gradient descent is leveraged during training to find the weights that achieve the lowest loss so that the input matches the desired label as much as possible. With activation maximization, we do the opposite – hence gradient ascent. We keep the weights constant, and we modify the input image until we find the one each filter is maximally responsive to.

We will first need to define two simple functions—one to modify the model, and another to return a custom loss. We need to modify the model because, just like with the intermediate activations method, we need to pretend that the model ends at the chosen target layer. Unlike with intermediate activation, we make target layer activations linear. Note that we would expect convolutional layers to have non-linear activation functions (ReLu, for instance). As for the loss function, we need it to return the loss for a single filter:

```python
def model_modifier(mdl):
  global target_layer
  target = mdl.get_layer(name=target_layer)
  new_mdl = tf.keras.Model(inputs=mdl.inputs, outputs=target.output)
  new_mdl.layers[-1].activation = tf.keras.activations.linear
  return new_mdl
def loss(output):
  global filter_num
  return output[…, filter_num]
```

Now that we have the required functions defined, we can iterate all 4 convolutional target layers and produce a grid with 16 filters for each one. The first layer has 16 filters, but for all others, they are randomly selected with np.random.choice. Then, it iterates every filter and computes the image that maximizes each filter. It does this by first instantiating ActivationMaximization with the model (cnn_fruits_mdl), the model-modifying function (model_modifier), and the instruction to clone the model rather than modify the original (clone=True). Then, you pass the loss function to the instantiated ActivationMaximization, which produces the image:

```
#How many filters to plot Activation Maximization for in each
layer
num_filters = 16
#Compute size (width or height) of image size based on num_
filters
gridsize = math.ceil(math.sqrt(num_filters))
#Iterate each target layer and..
for target_layer in target_layers:
  #Randomly select index of filters from total amount in layer
  for layer in cnn_fruits_mdl.layers:
    if layer.name == target_layer:
      total_filters = layer.filters
  if total_filters == num_filters or total_filters < num_
filters:
    filter_num_l = [*range(num_filters)]
  else:
    filter_num_l = list(np.random.choice([*range(total_
filters)],\
              num_filters))
  #Compute and Plot Activation Maximization for each random
filter
  fig = plt.figure(figsize=(10,10))
  for f, filter_num in zip([*range(len(filter_num_l))],\
                                              filter_
num_l):
    plt.subplot(gridsize, gridsize, f+1)
    plt.title('Filter #{}'.format(filter_num), fontsize=12)
    activation_maximization = ActivationMaximization(cnn_fruits_
mdl,\
                              model_modifier, clone=True)
```

```
   activation = activation_maximization(loss)
   plt.imshow(activation[0].astype(np.uint8),\
 interpolation='spline16')
   plt.axis("off")
   fig.suptitle('{} Layer'.format(target_layer), fontsize=18,\
 weight='bold')
   plt.subplots_adjust(bottom=0, top=0.92)
   plt.show()
```

The preceding code snippet generates 4 images, including *Figure 8.15* and *Figure 8.16*. The first convolutional layer in *Figure 8.15* doesn't appear to be maximally responsive to any pattern in particular other than colors. Mind you, this is a general template and since there are only 16 of them, they can't be very specific:

Figure 8.15 – Activation maximization for the model's first convolutional layer

By the time the network reaches the fourth convolutional layer, the filters appear to be maximally responsive to all kinds of polka dot patterns. They can be much more specific because there are 128 filters in this layer:

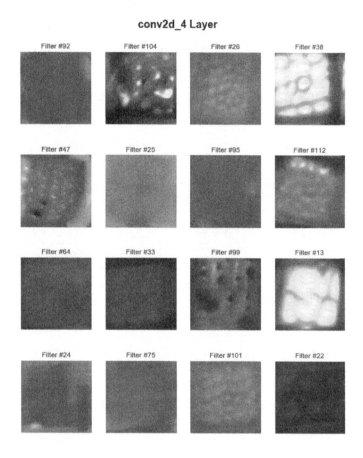

Figure 8.16 – Activation maximization for the model's fourth convolutional layer

For fruits and vegetables, activation maximization is not particularly useful because many fruits share the same shapes and patterns. However, if it were a cat and dog classifier, you would be able to distinguish clearly some patterns belonging to either class. However, the point was to provide an understanding of the role of filters in a CNN.

Next, we will leverage gradients to understand why the model is misclassifying.

Evaluating misclassifications with gradient-based attribution methods

Gradient-based methods calculate **attribution maps** for each classification with both forward and background passes through the CNN. As the name suggests, these methods leverage the gradients in the backward pass to compute the attribution maps. All of these methods are local interpretation methods because they only derive a single interpretation per sample. Incidentally, attributions in this context means that we are attributing the predicted labels to areas of an image. They are often called **sensitivity maps** in academic literature, too.

To get started, we will first need to create an array with all of our misclassification samples (X_misclass) from the validation dataset (X_val). Many of these methods can compute the attribution maps in batch, so this facilitates the process. We can then print the shape of our misclassifications array to ensure that all 17 samples are there:

```
idxs = avocado_FN_idxs + grapefruit_FP_idxs
X_misclass = X_val[idxs]
print(X_misclass.shape)
```

These methods traverse forward in the network to the last fully connected layer. Recall that this layer outputs a probability for each class. We know which of these probabilities is the highest for each sample, which corresponds to the predicted class. However, these methods will turn around into a backward pass before they get to predict the class. Therefore, we will need to tell them which one of the 16 outputs to calculate the loss with. To this end, we will need the sample's label to be ordinal encoded, which we can do with Scikit-Learn's OrdinalEncoder. First we must make sure the labels are in the right format with np.expand_dims, and once all the labels are encoded, we subset those from our samples and convert them into a list that we can easily print:

```
enc = preprocessing.OrdinalEncoder()
enc.fit(y_train)
y_val_pred_exp = np.expand_dims(np.array(y_val_pred),axis=1)
y_val_pred_enc = enc.transform(y_val_pred_exp)
labels_l = y_val_pred_enc[idxs].squeeze().astype(int).tolist()
print(labels_l)
```

The preceding code outputs the following list:

```
[9, 4, 6, 6, 6, 6, 6, 6, 6, 6, 6, 6, 6, 6, 6, 6, 6]
```

As you can tell, there are many sixes in the list (`labels_l`) corresponding to the seventh class, which is a grapefruit. Indeed, 15 out of the 17 examples are of grapefruit false positives.

Next, we define our `model_modifier` function. The only modification we need to perform is to turn the last fully connected layer's activation function to linear. We aren't interested in the probabilities produced by the softmax activation because it potentially deflates the output so that the output for all classes adds up to one. However, we are not interested in the remainder of the classes, just the predicted class. These methods then perform backpropagation to trace this linearly activated output to parts of the image that contributed to it:

```
def model_modifier(mdl):
    mdl.layers[-1].activation = tf.keras.activations.linear
    return mdl
def loss(output):
    global labels_l
    pos_l = [*range(len(labels_l))]
    output_l = []
    for p, l in zip(pos_l, labels_l):
        output_l.append(output[p][l])
    return tuple(output_l)
```

As for the `loss` function in the preceding code snippet, we need it to return a tuple with losses for every sample and predicted class combination. All it does is transform the model's original output to produce only the losses we are interested in. Next, we will study our first gradient-based method.

Saliency maps

"Vanilla" saliency maps rely on the absolute value of gradients. The intuition is that it will find the pixels in the image that can be perturbed the least so that the output changes the most with these values. It doesn't perform perturbations, so it doesn't validate the hypothesis, and the use of absolute values prevents it from finding other evidence to the contrary.

This first saliency map method was groundbreaking at the time and has inspired a bunch of different methods. It's typically nicknamed "vanilla" to distinguish it from other saliency maps, notably **SmoothGrad** saliency, which performs small random perturbations to the sample image – in other words, adds noise. It creates different noisy versions of the same sample image multiple times and then computes the gradients. It then averages these gradients, which is what makes the saliency maps much smoother.

But wait, you may ask: shouldn't it be a perturbation-based method then?! We've already dealt with several perturbation-based methods before in this book, from SHAP to Anchors, and something they have in common is that they perturb the input to measure the effect on the output. SmoothGrad doesn't measure the impact on the output, but focuses its attention on the gradients.

Generating both vanilla and SmoothGrad saliency maps for all of our misclassified samples is relatively simple. You first initialize a `Saliency` object instance by providing your model (`cnn_fruits_mdl`), the model-modifying function (`model_modifier`), and make a copy of the model (`clone=True`). Then you can produce both vanilla and SmoothGrad saliency maps with the same instance. All the instance requires in order to produce a map is the `loss` function and samples (`X_misclass`), and then it normalizes the map so that the output is between 0 and 1. For SmoothGrad you do the same, except that you provide a number of sample variations to produce (`smooth_samples=20`) and an amount of random noise to add to each one (`smooth_noise=0.20`):

```
saliency = Saliency(cnn_fruits_mdl, model_modifier=model_
modifier, clone=True)
saliency_maps = saliency(loss, X_misclass)
saliency_maps = normalize(saliency_maps)
smoothgrad_saliency_maps = saliency(loss, X_misclass,
                            smooth_samples=20,\
                            smooth_noise=0.20)
smoothgrad_saliency_maps = normalize(smoothgrad_saliency_maps)
```

We can plot the output of these saliency maps side by side with the sample image to provide context. Matplotlib can do this easily with a `subplot` grid. We will make a 1 × 3 grid and place sample image #0 in the first spot, its vanilla saliency map in the second, and its SmoothGrad map in the third. The saliency maps produced are grayscale, but we will apply a color map (`cmap='jet'`) to make the salient areas appear more striking:

```
plt.subplots(figsize=(15,5))
plt.subplot(1, 3, 1)
plt.imshow(X_misclass[0])
```

```
plt.grid(b=None)
plt.title("Original Image")
plt.subplot(1, 3, 2)
plt.imshow(saliency_maps[0], cmap='jet')
plt.grid(b=None)
plt.title("Vanilla Saliency Map")
plt.subplot(1, 3, 3)
plt.imshow(smoothgrad_saliency_maps[0], cmap='jet')
plt.grid(b=None)
plt.title("SmoothGrad Saliency Map")
```

The preceding code generates the plots in *Figure 8.17*:

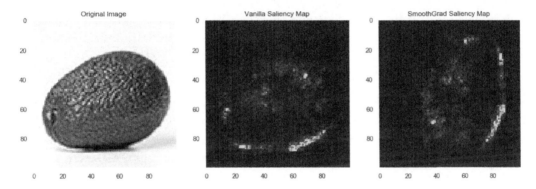

Figure 8.17 – Saliency maps for an avocado misclassified as a red onion

The sample image in *Figure 8.17* is clearly an avocado, but if you run `print(y_val_pred[idxs[0]])`, this will tell you that the prediction is for a red onion. The vanilla saliency map attributes that prediction mostly to the smoother areas caused by the photograph's depth-of-field blur, especially near the fruit's edge. These areas also have a reddish hue, coinciding with the light blue areas in the vanilla saliency map. Some spots around the stem are salient, suggesting that the model thinks that this is also onion-like – perhaps because of the yellow.

As for SmoothGrad, it is striking how different this map is compared to the vanilla. This is not always the case; often, it's just a smoother version. What likely happened was that the 20% noise distorted the attributions, or that 20 smooth samples weren't enough. However, it's tough to tell because it's also possible that SmoothGrad more accurately depicts the real story.

We won't do this now, but you can visually "tune" the smooth_noise and smooth_ samples parameters. You can try it with less noise and more samples, using a series of combinations, such as 5% and 80, and 10% and 40%, trying to figure out whether you see a commonality between them. The one you go with is the one that most clearly depicts this consistent story. One of the shortcomings of SmoothGrad is having to define optimal parameters.

In any case, if you were to take the SmoothGrad saliency map in *Figure 8.17* at face value, the spots that coincide with the reddish areas of the avocado are consistent with the vanilla map. However, instead of heavily marking the fruit's bottom edge, it highlights the right edge, which also has a significant blur. In addition to this, it finds salient areas outside of the fruit. The light gray background is confusing the model since the training data only had white backgrounds.

So, if you were to sum up an interpretation, it would be that the lack of riper avocados with reddish skin, depth-of-field blur, and non-white backgrounds in the training data are the root causes of this misclassification. Now, let's see what we learn from another method.

Grad-CAM

To discuss **Grad-CAM**, we first ought to discuss **CAM**, which stands for **Class Activation Map**. The way CAM works is that it removes all but the last fully connected layers, and it replaces the last **MaxPooling** layer with a **Global Average Pooling (GAP)** layer. For instance, in this case:

1. The last convolutional layer outputs a tensor that is $10 \times 10 \times 128$.

2. GAP reduces dimensions by merely averaging the first two dimensions of this tensor, producing a $1 \times 1 \times 128$ tensor.

3. It then feeds this to a fully connected layer with 16 neurons corresponding to each class.

4. Once you retrain a CAM model and pass a sample image through the CAM model, it takes the weights from the last layer (a 128×16 tensor) and extracts the values corresponding to the predicted class (a 128×1 tensor).

5. Then, you dot product the last convolutional layer's output ($10 \times 10 \times 128$) with the weight tensor (128×1).

6. This weighted sum will end with a $10 \times 10 \times 1$ tensor.

7. With bilinear interpolation to stretch it out to $100 \times 100 \times 1$, this becomes an upsampled class activation map.

The intuition behind CAM is that CNNs inherently retain spatial details in convolutional layers but they are, sadly, lost in fully connected layers. In fact, each filter in the last convolutional layer represents visual patterns at different spatial locations. Once weighted, they represent the most salient regions in the entire image. However, to apply CAM, you must radically modify a model and retrain it, and some models don't lend themselves easily to this.

As the name suggests, Grad-CAM is a similar concept, but lacks the modifying and retraining hassle, and uses gradients instead, specifically, those of the class score (prior to softmax) concerning the convolutional layer's activation maps. Global average pooling is performed on these gradients to obtain **neuron importance weights**. Then, we compute a weighted linear combination of activation maps with these weights, followed by a ReLu. The ReLu is very important because it ensures locating features that only positively influence the outcome. Like CAM, it is upsampled, with bilinear interpolation to match the dimensions of the image.

Grad-CAM does have some shortcomings too, such as failing to identify multiple occurrences or the entirety of the object represented by the predicted class. Like CAM, the resolution of the activation maps may be limited by the final convolutional layer's dimensions, hence the upsampling. For these reasons, we are using **Grad-CAM++** instead, which addresses these issues by computing weighted averages of pixel-wise gradients. It, therefore, produces activation maps that require no upsampling.

There is still a lot of debate ongoing in the CNN interpretation domain. And researchers are still coming up with new and better methods, and even techniques that are nearly perfect for most use cases still have flaws. Regarding CAM-like methods, there are many newer ones, such as **Score-CAM** and **Eigen-CAM**, which provide similar functionality but don't rely on gradients, which can be unstable and, therefore, occasionally unreliable. We won't discuss them here because, of course, they aren't gradient-based! But it's essential to note that it doesn't hurt to try different methods to see what works for your use case.

Creating GradCam++ maps

Now, let's create some Grad-CAM++ maps! It's similar code to saliency maps. We first instantiate the `GradCamPlusPlus` object instance with all the same parameters. Once it's instantiated, you create Grad-CAM++ heatmaps with the same parameters as you did with the saliency map, except you tell it which layer is the penultimate layer (`penultimate_layer=-1`). Then, you normalize the maps, as you've done previously:

```
gradcam = GradcamPlusPlus(cnn_fruits_mdl,\
                    model_modifier, clone=True)
gradcam_maps = gradcam(loss, X_misclass,\
```

```
                    penultimate_layer=-1)
gradcam_maps = normalize(gradcam_maps)
```

With Grad-CAM++ heatmaps now generated for all the validation misclassification samples, let's plot the first one side by side with its heatmaps, both by itself as well as overlaying the sample image. Please note that we are using Matplotlib's colormap function (cm.jet) to convert the original grayscale attribution map to a more expressive heatmap:

```
plt.subplots(figsize=(15,5))
plt.subplot(1, 3, 1)
plt.imshow(X_misclass[0])
plt.grid(b=None)
plt.title("Original Image")
plt.subplot(1, 3, 2)
heatmap = np.uint8(cm.jet(gradcam_maps[0])[..., :3] * 255)
plt.imshow(heatmap)
plt.grid(b=None)
plt.title("Grad-CAM++")
plt.subplot(1, 3, 3)
plt.imshow(X_misclass[0])
plt.imshow(heatmap, alpha=0.5)
plt.grid(b=None)
plt.title("Grad-CAM++ Overlayed")
```

The preceding code generates *Figure 8.18*, which highlights almost the entire upper background more strongly and, to a lesser degree, a belt between the top-left area of the avocado to the bottom blurry area excluding the stem. The only region that coincides a bit with both saliency maps is this bottom tip of the Avocado. However, there were indications that the background was confusing the model in the SmoothGrad saliency, and this heatmap appears to confirm this:

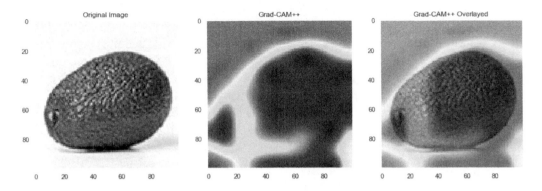

Figure 8.18 – Grad-CAM++ heatmaps for an avocado misclassified as a red onion

Integrated gradients

Integrated gradients (**IG**), also known as **Path-Integrated Gradients**, is a technique that is not exclusive to CNNs. You can apply it to any neural network architecture because it computes the gradients of the output with respect to the inputs averaged all along a path between a **baseline** and the actual input. It is agnostic to the presence of convolutional layers. However, it requires the definition of a baseline, which is supposed to convey a lack of signal, like a uniformly colored image. In practice, for CNNs in particular, this is what a zero baseline represents, which, for every pixel, would mean a completely black image. Also, although the name suggests the use of **path integrals**, integrals aren't computed but approximated, with summation in sufficiently small intervals for a certain number of steps. For a CNN, this means it makes variations of the input image progressively darker until it becomes a black image (the baseline) corresponding to the predefined number of steps. It then feeds these variations to the CNN, computes the gradients for each one, and averages them. The IG is the dot product of the image times the gradient averages.

Like Shapely Values, IG is grounded in solid mathematical theory. In this case, it's the **Fundamental Theorem of Calculus for Line Integrals**. The mathematical proof ensures that attributions add up. In other words, the attributions produced by IG sum to the difference between the prediction between that of the input and of the baseline. In addition to this property, which they call **completeness**, there is linearity preservation, symmetry preservation, and sensitivity. We won't describe each of these properties here. However, it's important to note that some interpretation methods satisfy notable mathematical properties, while others demonstrate their effectiveness in practical terms.

Using the explainer

For IG, we will use a different library called `tf-explain`. As with the others, you first instantiate the explainer object, `IntegratedGradients()`. However, it doesn't batch process every explanation, so instead, we will iterate across all of our misclassification samples and produce each IG heatmap independently with `explain`. Notice that we don't need to modify our model, but we need to define a specific number of steps (`n_steps=25`). In every iteration, we append the map to a list (`ig_maps`) we can reference later:

```
explainer = IntegratedGradients()
ig_maps = []
for i in range(len(labels_1)):
  img = ([X_misclass[i]], None)
  label = labels_1[i]
  ig_map = explainer.explain(img, cnn_fruits_mdl, label, n_
steps=25)
  ig_maps.append(ig_map)
```

As we've done with Grad-CAM++, we can plot our first sample image side by side with the IG map, as well as this map overlayed on top of the image with the following code:

```
plt.subplots(figsize=(15,5))
plt.subplot(1, 3, 1)
plt.imshow(X_misclass[0])
plt.grid(b=None)
plt.title("Original Image")
plt.subplot(1, 3, 2)
heatmap = np.uint8(cm.jet(ig_maps[0])[…, :3] * 255)
plt.imshow(heatmap)
plt.grid(b=None)
plt.title("Integrated Gradients Heatmap")
plt.subplot(1, 3, 3)
plt.imshow(X_misclass[0])
plt.imshow(heatmap, alpha=0.5)
plt.grid(b=None)
plt.title("Integrated Gradients Overlayed")
```

The preceding code outputs *Figure 8.19*:

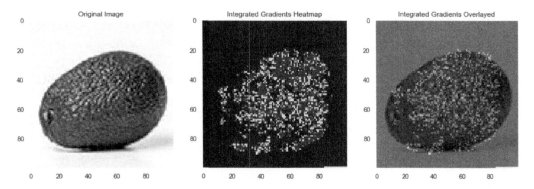

Figure 8.19 – Integrated gradient heatmaps for an avocado misclassified as a red onion

The area in *Figure 8.19* coincides with many of the regions spotted by the vanilla saliency map, in particular, the avocado parts that are reddish or appear to be smoother because of the depth-of-field blur. This further confirms the hypothesis that since the model was trained with green-brown unripe Hass avocados and not the redder, riper kind, it mistakes it for a red onion. The blurry areas suggest smoothness, which is uncharacteristic of an avocado, thus confusing it more. The jury is still out as far as the non-white background being a decisive factor is concerned because only Grad-CAM seemed to think so.

IG, such as Grad-CAM, has its detractors, who have made similar methods that avoid using gradients such as **DeepLift** and offshoots of **Layer-wise Relevance Propagation (LRP)**. Again, we won't discuss these here because they aren't gradient-based! Still, they have many advantages, especially considering zero-valued gradients and discontinuities with gradients, which can lead to misleading attributions. But these point to general disadvantages shared by all gradient-based methods. Specifically, the `tf-explain` library we are using defines the baseline as zero, which can be a problem when using very dark sample images. It should include a parameter to allow for tuning of the baseline. Thankfully, the number of steps can always be increased. The IG paper authors suggest that anywhere between 20 and 300 steps will approximate the integral within 5%.

Tying it all together

Now, we will take everything that we have learned about gradient-based attribution methods and use it to understand the reasons for all the chosen misclassifications (the avocado false negatives and grapefruit false positives). As we did with intermediate activation maps, we can leverage the `compare_img_pred_viz` function to place the higher resolution sample image side by side with the four attribution maps: vanilla saliency, SmoothGrad saliency, Grad-CAM++, and IG. To this end, we first have to iterate all the misclassifications' positions and indexes and extract all the maps. Note that we are using `heatmap_overlay` to produce a new image overlaying the original image with the heatmap for Grad-CAM++ (`map3`) and IG (`map4`). Lastly, we concatenate the four attribution outputs into a single image (`viz_img`). Just as we have done before, we extract the actual label (`y_true`), predicted label (`y_pred`), and pandas series with the probabilities (`probs_s`) to add some context to the plot we will produce. The `for` loop will produce 17 plots, but we are only going to discuss three of them:

```
for pos, idx in zip([*range(len(idxs))], idxs):
 orig_img = X_val_orig[idx]
 map1 = np.uint8(cm.jet(saliency_maps[pos])[..., :3] * 255)
 map2 = np.uint8(cm.jet(smoothgrad_saliency_maps[pos])\
                                            [..., :3] * 255)
 map3 = mldatasets.heatmap_overlay(X_misclass[pos],\
                                    gradcam_maps[pos])
 map4 = mldatasets.heatmap_overlay(X_misclass[pos], ig_maps[pos])
 viz_img = cv2.vconcat([
   cv2.hconcat([map1, map2]),
```

```
    cv2.hconcat([map3, map4])
  ])
  y_true = y_val[idx,0]
  y_pred = y_val_pred[idx]
  probs_s = probs_df.loc[idx]
  title = 'Gradient-Based Attributions for Misclassification
#{}'.\
  format(pos+1)
  mldatasets.compare_img_pred_viz(orig_img, viz_img, y_true,\
                              y_pred, probs_s, title=title)
```

The preceding code generates *Figure 8.20*, *Figure 8.21*, and *Figure 8.22*:

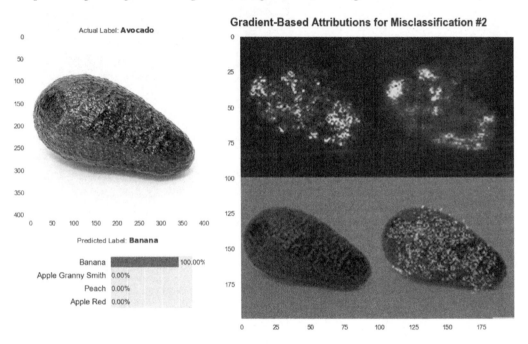

Figure 8.20 – Gradient-based attributions for avocado misclassification #2

The saliency attribution maps in the second misclassified avocado in *Figure 8.20* point to shiny darker regions in the avocado being what caused the misclassification. The banana images in the training data had dark spots with a sheen, specially toward the tips, while the avocado images were duller and darker green with brown spots. As for IG, the dark spots are mostly covered, but there are also many green areas. Grad-CAM++ didn't work in this case, which can happen due to the instability of gradients and the heavy reliance of this method on them:

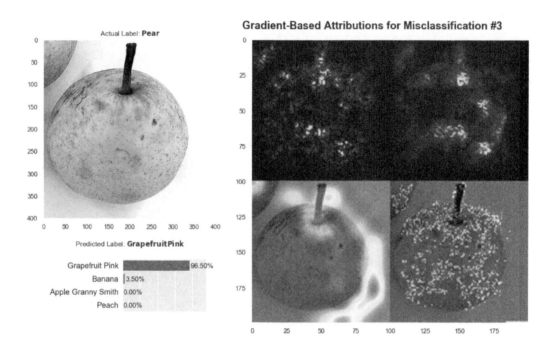

Figure 8.21 – Gradient-based attributions for pear misclassification #3

In *Figure 8.21*, the stem is clearly confusing the model. This makes sense considering the pears in the training data lacked such a dark, prominent stem. They are also a different purer tone of green, with less of a yellow hue, and the spots are more uniformly distributed. For this reason, it's not surprising that according to the model, there was a 3.5% probability it was a banana, which also has random dark spots and a prominent dark stem. IG yields an attribution map that weighs the spots more heavily, but it is somewhat consistent with the saliency maps. On the other hand, Grad-CAM is, once again, confused by the background, but does successfully identify the stem as an area of interest:

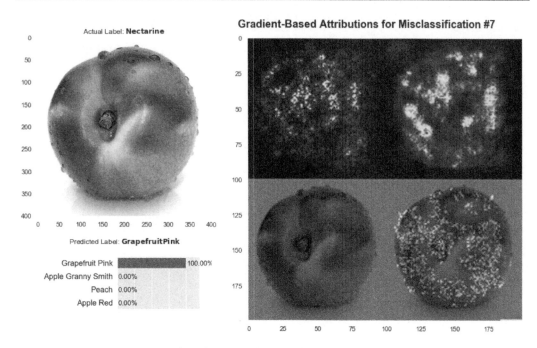

Figure 8.22 – Gradient-based attributions for nectarine misclassification #7

Lastly, *Figure 8.22* is a very interesting one because the nectarine is wet. According to the convenience store executives, many fruits are kept in open refrigerated display cases, which causes condensed water droplets to gather on the fruits' surface. Therefore, a wet fruit is representative of real-world conditions. Unfortunately, the training data didn't account for this, so all fruits were dry. As with previous examples, the stem is a source of confusion, but you can tell that all three attribution methods identify the regions with some droplets or sheen produced by wetness.

Also, IG points to the stem as well. However, you also must wonder why it is so confident that it's a grapefruit? In other words, what are the attributes the model thinks a grapefruit includes or excludes that are depicted in the nectarine (*Figure 8.22*) and pear (*Figure 8.21*) images alike, not to mention all the different samples. We will next try to discover what the model learned about avocados and grapefruits through perturbation-based attribution methods.

Understanding classifications with perturbation-based attribution methods

The code for this section alone can be found here: `https://github.com/PacktPublishing/Interpretable-Machine-Learning-with-Python/blob/master/Chapter08/FruitClassifier_part2.ipynb`. All the preparation steps are repeated from the beginning. However, it has disabled TensorFlow 2 behavior (`tf.compat.v1.disable_v2_behavior()`) because, at the time of writing, the `alibi` library, which we will use for the contrastive explanation method, still relies on TensorFlow 1 constructs.

Perturbation-based methods have already been covered to a great extent in this book so far. So many of the methods we have covered, including SHAP, LIME, Anchors, and even Permutation Feature Importance, employ perturbation-based strategies. The intuition behind them is that if you remove, alter, or mask features in your input data and then make predictions with them, you'll be able to attribute the difference between the new predictions and the original predictions to the changes you made in the input. These strategies can be leveraged in both global and local interpretation methods.

We will now do the same as we did with the misclassification samples, but to the chosen true positives, and gather all of them in a single array (`X_tp`). Printing this array's dimensions should confirm that there are six sample images with the standard width, height, and channels ($100 \times 100 \times 3$):

```
idxs = avocado_TP_idxs + grapefruit_TP_idxs
X_tp = X_val[idxs]
print(X_tp.shape)
```

Likewise, we can do the same as we did with the misclassifications for obtaining the labels from the ordinal encoded array:

```
labels_l = y_val_pred_enc[idxs].squeeze().\
                                    astype(int).tolist()
print(labels_l)
```

The preceding code outputs the following list:

```
[3, 3, 6, 6, 6, 6]
```

As expected, the first two are avocados (class #3) and the last four are grapefruits (class #6).

Occlusion sensitivity

Occlusion sensitivity is a relatively simple method. What it does is occlude portions of the sample input image by incorporating a gray patch. A sensitivity map is produced with the difference in the probability for the target class at every point where this patch is placed. The sensitivity map is interpolated to have the same dimensions as the sample image.

To create the maps, you first initialize the occlusion sensitivity explainer (`OcclusionSensitivity()`) and then iterate each sample image and produce a map for each one with `explain`. All it requires is the image, model (`cnn_fruits_mdl`), label, and patch size. We have defined here a 3 × 3 patch that defines the area that is occluded at a time. Larger patches may impact the classification probability much more, but smaller patches may pinpoint specific areas with the greatest impact:

```python
explainer = OcclusionSensitivity()
os_maps = []
for i in range(len(labels_l)):
  img = ([X_tp[i]], None)
  label = labels_l[i]
  os_map = explainer.explain(img, cnn_fruits_mdl, label, 3)
  os_maps.append(os_map)
```

With the occlusion sensitivity maps all appended into a list (`os_maps`), we can now visualize them quickly as we have before with all the previous methods:

```python
plt.subplots(figsize=(15,5))
plt.subplot(1, 3, 1)
plt.imshow(X_tp[2])
plt.grid(b=None)
plt.title("Original Image")
plt.subplot(1, 3, 2)
plt.imshow(os_maps[2])
plt.grid(b=None)
plt.title("Occlusion Sensitivity")
plt.subplot(1, 3, 3)
plt.imshow(X_tp[2])
plt.imshow(os_maps[2], alpha=0.5)
plt.grid(b=None)
plt.title("Occlusion Sensitivity Overlayed")
```

The preceding code generates *Figure 8.23*. It appears to depict that smooth and less illuminated areas at the top left of the grapefruit have the most impact on its positive classification. What is the significance of these patches?

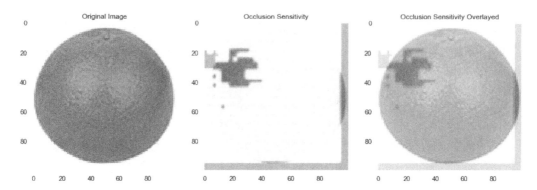

Figure 8.23 – Occlusion sensitivity maps for a grapefruit true positive validation dataset

Let's try a simple experiment with the following code that selects a random grapefruit from the training dataset and generates an occlusion sensitivity map as we did for the validation ones:

```
idx = np.random.choice(np.where(y_train[:,0] ==\
                  'Grapefruit Pink')[0], 1)[0]
os_map_train = explainer.explain(([X_train[idx]], None),\
                  cnn_fruits_mdl, label, 5)
plt.subplots(figsize=(15,5))
plt.subplot(1, 3, 1)
plt.imshow(X_train[idx])
plt.grid(b=None)
plt.title("Original Image")
plt.subplot(1, 3, 2)
plt.imshow(os_map_train)
plt.grid(b=None)
plt.title("Occlusion Sensitivity")
plt.subplot(1, 3, 3)
plt.imshow(X_train[idx])
plt.imshow(os_map_train, alpha=0.5)
plt.grid(b=None)
plt.title("Occlusion Sensitivity Overlayed")
```

If you were to plot the maps, we get *Figure 8.24*. We can try many random training images, and they'll confirm that more or less the same top-left patch is critical in terms of a grapefruit prediction. It helps that the grapefruit is a spherical fruit, and the lighting was consistent in every picture, so the specular highlight is always in the center slightly shifted toward the top left. This lighting produces a gray shadow in the bottom and right surfaces of the fruits. The bar on both these sides denotes how the model responds to a gray block here, which is confusing considering how close this color is to the shadow color:

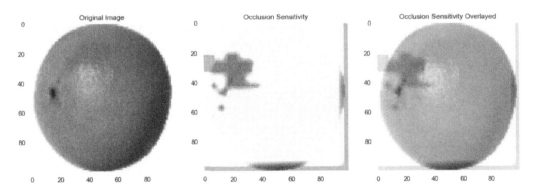

Figure 8.24 – Occlusion sensitivity maps for a grapefruit true positive training dataset

The gray square patch employed in occlusion sensitivity is arbitrary because the building blocks of images aren't necessarily square, and gray may not be the best color to contrast the image's contents. Let's look at another method that segments the image differently but retains the graying-out strategy.

LIME's ImageExplainer

Local interpretable model-agnostic explanations (LIME) were already covered in *Chapter 6, Local Model-Agnostic Interpretation Methods*, but we only explained the tabular and text explainer. Now, we will address the image explainer. The principle is very much the same. It still uses a perturbation strategy and a sparse linear model to identify which features are the most important.

However, in this case, features aren't columns as they are in the tabular explainer, nor words as they are in the text explainer, but **superpixels**! Superpixels aren't literal pixels, but entire segments of the image, which may or may not be grayed out. These segments are computed algorithmically. By default, the `lime` package uses an algorithm called **Quickshift**, but you may use any of Scikit-Learn's image segmentation methods (`skimage.segmentation`).

An advantage of LIME is that it derives linear coefficients that can tell us which features are positively or negatively correlated with the predicted class. In this case, you may have segments that are either, as well as some that are more in a neutral zone, because the coefficients aren't statistically significant.

1) Initializing and creating explanations

We can instantiate a `LimeImageExplainer` very easily. Then we iterate among our samples and produce explanations for each one using the `explain_instance` function. Its parameters include the sample image (`X_tp[i]`) and the predict function for our model (`cnn_fruits_mdl.predict`). There are many other optional parameters, but the defaults are fine for this particular use case:

```
explainer = lime_image.LimeImageExplainer()
lime_expl = []
for i in range(len(labels_l)):
  explanation = explainer.\
      explain_instance(X_tp[i].astype('double'),
                      cnn_fruits_mdl.predict)
  lime_expl.append(explanation)
```

2) Extracting an image and mask from the explanation

We will have to extract the image and its mask from it with `get_image_and_mask` to appreciate a single explanation. We will do this twice, once with `hide_rest=True` and `positive_only=True`, which means it will gray out the portions of the image that don't positively explain the prediction (`img_hide`), and another time with `positive_only=False`, which means it will return the entire image and highlight both positive and negative regions (`img_show`). Lastly, we will extract a dictionary with the coefficients for each segment (`dict_heatmap`) using the `top_labels` attribute in the explanation and apply these coefficients to `segments`, which is a `100 × 100` NumPy array with the segment indexes. The result of this operation is a LIME coefficient heatmap:

```
#Explanation with irrelevant segments hidden
img_hide, mask_hide = lime_expl[2].\
      get_image_and_mask(lime_expl[2].top_labels[0],\
                      positive_only=True, num_features=10,\
                      hide_rest=True)
img_hide = mark_boundaries(img_hide / 2 + 0.5, mask_hide)
#Explanation with all segments marked for positive/negative
```

```
prediction
img_show, mask_show = lime_expl[2].\
        get_image_and_mask(lime_expl[2].top_labels[0],\
                            positive_only=False, num_features=10)
img_show = mark_boundaries(img_show / 2 + 0.5, mask_show)
#Heatmap explanation by segment
dict_heatmap =\
        dict(lime_expl[2].local_exp[lime_expl[2].top_
labels[0]])
heatmap = np.vectorize(dict_heatmap.get)(lime_expl[2].segments)
```

3) Plotting explanations

We can now make a 1×3 subplot grid comparing all three visualization options: the graying out of irrelevant portions, the identifying positive and negative segments, and the heatmap:

```
plt.subplots(figsize=(15,5))
plt.subplot(1, 3, 1)
plt.imshow(img_hide)
plt.grid(b=None)
plt.title("Irrelevant Segments Hidden")
plt.subplot(1, 3, 2)
plt.imshow(img_show)
plt.grid(b=None)
plt.title("Positive/Negative Overlayed")
plt.subplot(1, 3, 3)
plt.imshow(heatmap, alpha=0.5, cmap='RdBu')
plt.grid(b=None)
plt.title("LIME Heatmap")
```

The preceding code plots *Figure 8.25*:

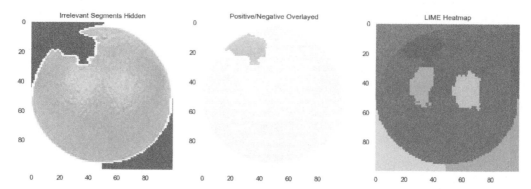

Figure 8.25 – Different ways of visualizing LIME explanations for a grapefruit classification

In *Figure 8.25*, you can tell that the bottom-right and top-left portions (including a segment of the fruit) are not significant in terms of the positive classification as a grapefruit. However, since the second image didn't even highlight these areas as red, we also know that they aren't even that negatively significant. However, almost the entirety of the fruit is highlighted in green, which suggests that these segments positively correlate with the classification. Lastly, you can tell that these green areas aren't equally important in the heatmap, where you notice that the two specular highlights are less important than the bottom half of the fruit. Then, the top-left area of the grapefruit that was grayed out in the first visualization (for `img_hide`) is indeed negatively correlated along with the adjacent corner and the bottom-right corner, but to a lesser degree. This heatmap can be a little misleading as to how much because dark red tones may suggest more negativity than they actually represent. If you print the coefficients in `dict_heatmap`, you will realize that the largest negative coefficient is -0.04, but the highest positive coefficients are about 0.17. This difference explains why there is no area highlighted in red in the second visualization (for `img_show`).

CEM

Contrastive Explanation Method (CEM) was already covered in *Chapter 7, Anchors and Counterfactual Explanations*. However, it's not always useful with tabular data, but it's particularly well-suited for image classification problems where features, in other words, pixels are always continuous, and the low and high values represent the absence and presence of something such as light or primary color.

We won't explain how CEM works again here, but what is important to recall is that you can generate a **Pertinent Negative (PN)**, which is what is minimally and sufficiently absent to predict a different class. On the other hand, you can generate a **Pertinent Positive (PP)**, which is what is minimally and sufficiently present to predict the same class. With that in mind, we will jump right in!

The first optional, but highly recommended, step for CEM is to train an **autoencoder** to guide the loss function, as we did in *Chapter 7, Anchors and Counterfactual Explanations*. We have an `encoder`, `decoder`, and the `bottleneck` in between. However, now we will use convolutional, pooling, and upsampling layers exclusively. The bottleneck reduces dimensionality to one twenty-fourth of the input's dimensions, and the idea is to train this model so that the output matches the input as much as possible:

```
input_layer = tf.keras.layers.Input(shape=(100, 100, 3))
encoder = tf.keras.layers.Conv2D(16, (3, 3), activation='relu',
padding='same')(input_layer)
encoder = tf.keras.layers.Conv2D(16, (3, 3), activation='relu',
padding='same')(encoder)
encoder = tf.keras.layers.MaxPooling2D((2, 2),\
                                padding='same')(encoder)
bottleneck = tf.keras.layers.Conv2D(1, (3, 3), activation=None,
padding='same')(encoder)
decoder = tf.keras.layers.Conv2D(16, (3, 3), activation='relu',
padding='same')(bottleneck)
decoder = tf.keras.layers.UpSampling2D((2, 2))(decoder)
decoder = tf.keras.layers.Conv2D(16, (3, 3), activation='relu',
padding='same')(decoder)
output_layer = tf.keras.layers.Conv2D(3, (3, 3),
activation=None, padding='same')(decoder)
autoencoder_mdl = tf.keras.Model(input_layer, output_layer)
autoencoder_mdl.summary()
```

The preceding code builds an autoencoder model layer by layer so that it's easier to understand. If you look at the summary() for it, you can see how the dimensions go from 100 × 100 × 3 to 50 × 50 × 16 to 50 × 50 × 1 in the encoding process. Naturally, in decoding, they go back from 50 × 50 × 1 to 50 × 50 × 16 to 100 × 100 × 3:

```
Model: "model"
_____
Layer (type)                 Output Shape              Param #
=================================================================
input_1 (InputLayer)         [(None, 100, 100, 3)]     0
_____
conv2d (Conv2D)              (None, 100, 100, 16)      448
_____
conv2d_1 (Conv2D)            (None, 100, 100, 16)      2320
_____
max_pooling2d (MaxPooling2D) (None, 50, 50, 16)        0
_____
conv2d_2 (Conv2D)            (None, 50, 50, 1)         145
_____
conv2d_3 (Conv2D)            (None, 50, 50, 16)        160
_____
up_sampling2d (UpSampling2D) (None, 100, 100, 16)      0
_____
conv2d_4 (Conv2D)            (None, 100, 100, 16)      2320
_____
conv2d_5 (Conv2D)            (None, 100, 100, 3)       435
=================================================================
```

```
Total params: 5,828
Trainable params: 5,828
Non-trainable params: 0
```

Then, compiling and fitting the autoencoder is the same process as with any neural network model, except that the first argument in the fit function (X) and the second argument (y) is the same: X_train. What you expect the network to produce is something as close as possible to what went in:

```
autoencoder_mdl.compile(loss='mse', optimizer='adam')
autoencoder_history = autoencoder_mdl.fit(X_train, X_train,\
                             epochs=5, batch_size=32,\
                             verbose=1,\
                             validation_data=(X_test, X_
test))
```

Let's now see how well our model reproduces our training data by randomly selecting seven of the training images and plotting them against the decoded versions of those very same images. To produce decoded versions, all we need to do is feed the sample training images to the autoencoder's predict function:

```
n = 7
rand_idxs = np.random.choice([*range(len(y_test))], n)
decoded_imgs = autoencoder_mdl.predict(X_test[rand_idxs])
plt.figure(figsize=(14, 4))
for i in range(n):
 ax = plt.subplot(2, n, i + 1)
 plt.imshow(X_test[rand_idxs[i]])
 ax.get_xaxis().set_visible(False)
 ax.get_yaxis().set_visible(False)
 ax = plt.subplot(2, n, i + n + 1)
 plt.imshow(decoded_imgs[i])
 ax.get_xaxis().set_visible(False)
 ax.get_yaxis().set_visible(False)
```

The preceding code generates *Figure 8.26*. As you can tell, the decoded versions are simply blurrier and duller-toned versions of the originals. The overall fidelity is quite good:

Figure 8.26 – Original training images versus the decoded images from the trained autoencoder

We will do just as we did in *Chapter 7, Anchors and Counterfactual Explanations*, and instantiate a CEM explainer object once for PN and another time for PP. This time, we will use our model instead of a predict function and define the input shape as (1, 100, 100, 3) and the feature range as (0.0, 1.0) since the model expects only inputs with float numbers in this range. Aside from this, everything else is the same as before:

```
cem_pn = CEM(cnn_fruits_mdl, 'PN', (1,) + X_train.shape[1:],\
            feature_range=(0.0, 1.0), max_iterations=100,\
            ae_model=autoencoder_mdl, gamma=100, c_init=1.)
cem_pn.fit(X_train, no_info_type='median')
cem_pp = CEM(cnn_fruits_mdl, 'PP', (1,) + X_train.shape[1:],\
            feature_range=(0.0, 1.0), max_iterations=100,\
            ae_model=autoencoder_mdl, gamma=100, c_init=0.5,\
            beta=0.1)
cem_pp.fit(X_train, no_info_type='median')
```

Now that the explainer objects have been instantiated, we can for loop each sample and explain them one by one with both explainers. In both cases, it may generate an image and a prediction. Note that it might not find a PP or PN, so when the prediction is None, there will be no image. In this case, we will create a blank image to represent the lack of PP or PN with np.ones and an empty string to represent the predicted class. And while it's iterating, we will append the predictions and corresponding images to lists:

```
cem_pn_preds = []
cem_pn_imgs = []
cem_pp_preds = []
cem_pp_imgs = []
```

```
for i in range(len(labels_l)):
 pn_explanation = cem_pn.explain(np.array([X_tp[i]]))
 if pn_explanation.PN_pred is not None:
  cem_pn_preds.append(fruits_l[pn_explanation.PN_pred])
  cem_pn_imgs.append(pn_explanation.PN[0])
 else:
  cem_pn_preds.append("")
  cem_pn_imgs.append(np.ones(X_train.shape[1:4]))
 pp_explanation = cem_pp.explain(np.array([X_tp[i]]))
 if pp_explanation.PP_pred is not None:
  cem_pp_preds.append(fruits_l[pp_explanation.PP_pred])
  norm_img = (pp_explanation.PP[0] - pp_explanation.PP[0].
min()) /\
        (pp_explanation.PP[0].max() - pp_explanation.PP[0].
min())
  cem_pp_imgs.append(norm_img)
 else:
  cem_pp_preds.append("")
  cem_pp_imgs.append(np.ones(X_train.shape[1:4]))
```

As we have before, we will take a sample true positive validation image and compare it to its explanations. This time, it will be beside its PN and PP explanations:

```
plt.subplots(figsize=(15,5))
plt.subplot(1, 3, 1)
plt.imshow(X_tp[0])
plt.grid(b=None)
plt.title('Original:'+fruits_l[labels_l[0]])
plt.subplot(1, 3, 2)
plt.imshow(cem_pn_imgs[0])
plt.grid(b=None)
plt.title('PN:'+cem_pn_preds[0])
plt.subplot(1, 3, 3)
plt.imshow(cem_pp_imgs[0])
plt.grid(b=None)
plt.title('PP:'+cem_pp_preds[0])
```

The preceding code produced the image grid in *Figure 8.27*:

Figure 8.27 – CEM pertinent negatives and positives for an avocado true positive validation dataset

The CEM method found both a PN and PP for this one, which isn't always the case. As for the PN, some red pixels sprinkled all over the green avocado was all it took to switch the classification to a red onion. And according to the PP explanation, a pitch-black image with some green dots qualifies as an avocado. These bizarre results call into question the model's predictive capacity and reliability. If you have any doubts that the model determined that the PN image was a red onion or the PP image was an avocado, all we need to do is feed these images back into the models `predict` function and print out the probability and predicted class for each one:

```
pp_pred = cnn_fruits_mdl.predict(np.array([cem_pn_imgs[0]]))[0]
print('PP Probs:%s' % pp_pred)
print('PP Pred:%s' % fruits_l[pp_pred.argmax()])
pn_pred = cnn_fruits_mdl.predict(np.array([cem_pp_imgs[0]]))[0]
print('PN Probs:%s' % pn_pred)
print('PN Pred:%s' % fruits_l[pn_pred.argmax()])
```

The preceding code snippet produces the following output:

```
PP Probs:    [0. 0. 0. 0.155 0. 0. 0. 0. 0. 0.845 0. 0. 0. 0. 0.
0.]
PP Pred:     Onion Red
PN Probs:    [0. 0. 0. 1. 0. 0. 0. 0. 0. 0. 0. 0. 0. 0. 0. 0.]
PN Pred:     Avocado
```

Indeed, not only did an avocado with red sprinkles depicted in the PN qualify as a red onion, but with an 84.5% certainty from the model. And not only did the black canvas with some green and purple spots qualify as an avocado, but with 100% certainty. We will get into this problem in greater depth in *Chapter 13*, *Adversarial Robustness*, but this points not only to a lack of model reliability, but **Adversarial Robustness**, because this classifier is very easily fooled by perturbations, even unintentionally. With its minimal, sufficient, and intentional perturbations, CEM brought to our attention the extent to which the model can be fooled!

Tying it all together

Now, we will take everything that we have learned about perturbation-based attribution methods and use it to understand the reasons for all the chosen true positive classifications (for both avocados and grapefruits). As we did before, we can leverage the `compare_img_pred_viz` function to place the higher-resolution sample image side by side with the four attribution maps: occlusion sensitivity, LIME, PN, and PP. First, we have to iterate all the classifications' positions and indexes and extract all the maps. Note that we are using `heatmap_overlay` to produce a new image overlaying the original image with the heatmap for occlusion (`map1`). Lastly, we concatenate the four attribution outputs into a single image (`viz_img`). Just as we have done before, we extract the actual label (`y_true`), predicted label (`y_pred`), and pandas series with the probabilities (`probs_s`) to add some context to the plot we will produce. The `for` loop will produce six plots, but we will only discuss two of them:

```python
for pos, idx in zip([*range(len(idxs))], idxs):
    orig_img = X_val_orig[idx]
    map1 = mldatasets.heatmap_overlay(X_tp[pos], os_maps[pos]/255)
    img_show, mask_show = lime_expl[pos].\
            get_image_and_mask(lime_expl[pos].top_labels[0],\
            positive_only=False, num_features=10)
    map2 = np.uint8(mark_boundaries(img_show / 2 + 0.5, mask_show)\
                                                          [..., :3] *
255)
    map3 = np.uint8(cem_pn_imgs[pos][..., :3] * 255)
    map4 = np.uint8(cem_pp_imgs[pos][..., :3] * 255)
    viz_img = cv2.vconcat([
        cv2.hconcat([map1, map2]),
        cv2.hconcat([map3, map4])
    ])
```

```
y_true = y_val[idx,0]
y_pred = y_val_pred[idx]
probs_s = probs_df.loc[idx]
title = 'Perturbation-Based Attributions #{} (PN:{}, PP:{})'.
format(pos+1, cem_pn_preds[pos], cem_pp_preds[pos])
mldatasets.compare_img_pred_viz(orig_img, viz_img, y_true,\
                                y_pred, probs_s, title=title)
```

The preceding code snippet generates several explanations, including *Figure 8.28* and *Figure 8.29*. According to occlusion sensitivity, in *Figure 8.28*, you see how a small patch in the top of the fruit and the slightly shadowed bottom tip appear to be most responsible for the prediction. However, LIME highlights most of the avocado in green, but highlights the top-right corner in red. If you look at the avocados in the training data, it becomes clearer why a well-lit, top-right corner is uncharacteristic of an avocado according to the model. In these images, the lighting made this side always so much darker. It also becomes evident how consistently well-lit and green the top-center portions were in these same training images. The bottom tip was still significantly darker, as it is in the validation sample. Lastly, PP returns a gray background with two opposing rings of scattered green and purple dots. There's no point in deriving too much meaning from this besides the fact that the model can be so easily fooled. A robust model would return something that resembled an avocado much more:

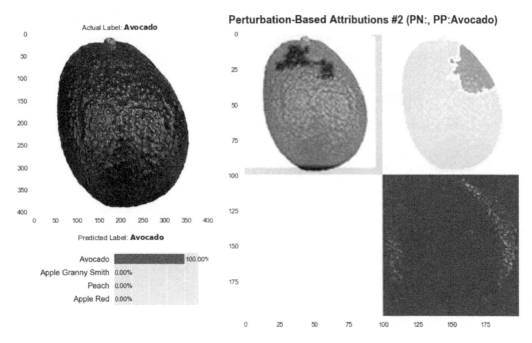

Figure 8.28 – Perturbation-based attributions for avocado classification #2

Occlusion sensitivity for *Figure 8.29* shows a similar patch as it does in all the other grapefruits. The same conclusion applies as before, which is that the model learned that bright yellowish surfaces with some slightly darker dots, no shadows, and no specular highlights are characteristic of grapefruits, and grapefruits alone. If you look at training images for other fruits, such as oranges, apples, peaches, and nectarines, they are less reflective, so appear much duller than they should. Inconsistent lighting and more varied fruit would have been a better strategy in the training dataset to produce a robust model:

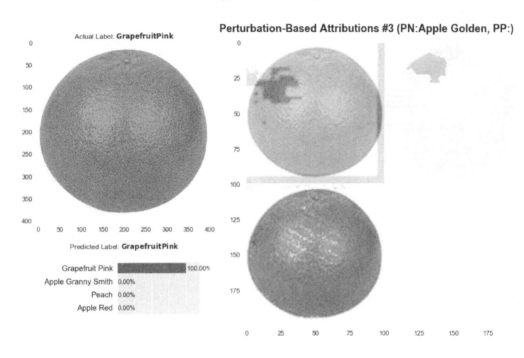

Figure 8.29 – Perturbation-based attributions for grapefruit classification #6

As for LIME in *Figure 8.29*, most of the image is highlighted green, thereby positively correlating with the predicted class. However, the top-right background corner is highlighted in red. LIME created this segment using the Quickshift segmentation algorithm, but the model doesn't necessarily identify entire segments as being characteristic of a class. You can tell which portion is likely the negative correlation culprit once you compare this segment with the occlusion sensitivity patch. This portion of the patch that overlaps the background is the culprit. The hypothesis here would be that it would be uncharacteristic for a spherical fruit to have a gray block attached to its smoothest and well-lit region. As for the PN, you can tell how confused the model is regarding the background because there's noise nearly everywhere. If you can note one trend with PNs, it would be that the whiter and cleaner the background is, the more the noise is concentrated on the fruit. This trend suggests that the model does not understand where the fruit begins and ends because the model was trained with images with only white backgrounds.

Bonus method: SHAP's DeepExplainer

There is one more important method applicable to CNNs, which we haven't discussed: SHAP. We first learned about SHAP in *Chapter 5, Global Model-Agnostic Interpretation Methods*, and then have leveraged it a little bit in every chapter since. We would be remiss not to include it in this chapter because each interpretation method tells you one side of the story, and SHAP is an incredibly useful tool. It wasn't included with the rest of the perturbation methods because although Shapely Values is perturbation-based, SHAP's DeepExplainer, which we will use now, is based on the **Deep Learning Important FeaTures** algorithm (**DeepLIFT**), and DeepLIFT is neither a gradient-based nor a perturbation-based method. It's a backpropagation-based approach! We won't re-explain it here, but suffice to say, like IG and Shapely Values, DeepLIFT was designed for **completeness**, and as such, complies with remarkable mathematical properties. The shap library simply adapts the DeepLIFT output so that it approximates Shapely Values.

It is precisely background samples that help make the approximation to reconcile DeepLIFT with Shapely Values. To that end, the first thing we do is gather 100 random sample images for the training data. We can then print the shape of this `background` array to ensure that it is `(100, 100, 100, 3)`:

```
background = X_train[np.random.choice(X_train.shape[0], 100,\
                     replace=False)]
print(background.shape)
```

Then, we initialize our `DeepExplainer` with the model (`cnn_fruits_mdl`) and the background samples. Then, we extract the `shap_values` for our true positives (`X_tp`) from the explainer:

```
explainer = shap.DeepExplainer(cnn_fruits_mdl, background)
shap_values = explainer.shap_values(X_tp)
```

Once the SHAP values have been computed, we can plot them with `shap.image_plot(shap_values, X_tp)`. However, this would produce a grid of images 6 samples high and 16 classes wide. It's hard to tell what areas of an image are most indicative of one class or another with such a large grid. In this case, we know that only the first seven classes are of any importance, so we could plot `shap.image_plot(shap_values[0:7], X_tp)` instead or, better yet, since we know that the model doesn't confuse avocados and grapefruits, we can simply add the values like this so they appear in a single column:

```
shap.image_plot(shap_values[3] + shap_values[6], X_tp)
```

The preceding code snippet generates *Figure 8.30*. The results should surprise us. In general, the model seems to identify areas in the fruit's periphery as being characteristic of the fruit. However, some darker or brighter areas are highlighted in blue, especially the shadow in the avocado and the right specular highlight in the first grapefruit:

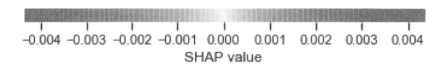

Figure 8.30 – SHAP values for all of the true positive validation samples

Mission accomplished

The mission was to provide an objective evaluation of the fruit classification model for the convenience store chain. The predictive performance on out-of-sample validation images was dismal! You could have stopped there, but then you would not have known how to make a better model.

However, the predictive performance evaluation was instrumental in deriving specific misclassifications, as well as correct classifications, to assess using other interpretation methods. To this end, you ran a comprehensive suite of interpretation methods, including activation, gradient, perturbation, and backpropagation-based methods. The consensus between all the methods was that the model was having the following issues:

- Differentiating between the background and the fruit

- Understanding that different fruit classes share some color hues

- Confounding lighting conditions such as specular highlights and shadows as specific fruit characteristics

- Being confused by moisture conditions such as water droplets

- An inability to identify unique features of each fruit as stems, skin textures, and spots

Furthermore, the **Contrastive Explanation Method (CEM)** indicated that the model is not at all robust to adversarial attacks.

To address these problems, the model needed to be trained from scratch with a more varied dataset, hopefully, one that reflects the real-world conditions of convenience stores; for instance, many backgrounds, different lighting conditions, wet fruit, and even fruit partially occluded by hands, gloves, bags, and so on. Also, the fruit varieties and level of maturity must reflect what is consistently carried in these stores. Once this dataset has been compiled, it is essential to leverage data augmentation to make the model even more robust to all sorts of variations: angle, brightness, contrast, saturation, and hue variants. And in order to address the problems the CEM identified, there's much more that we can do to stress test the model. We cover this in *Chapter 13, Adversarial Robustness*.

Summary

After reading this chapter, you should understand how to leverage traditional interpretation methods to more thoroughly assess predictive performance on a CNN classifier and visualize the learning process of CNNs with activation-based methods. You should also understand how to compare and contrast misclassifications and true positives with gradient-based and perturbation-based attribution methods. In the next chapter, we will study interpretation methods for multivariate time series and sensitivity analysis.

Dataset and image sources

- Baron, Karl (photographer). (2003, March 26). Local Daiei got a self-checkout [digital image]. CC 2.0 License: `https://www.flickr.com/photos/82365211@N00/9244253015`.

- Muresan, H., and Oltean, M. (2017). *Fruit recognition from images using deep learning*. Acta Universitatis Sapientiae, Informatica, 10, 26 – 42: `https://arxiv.org/abs/1712.00580`.

- Oltean, M. (2020). *Fruits 360*: `https://www.kaggle.com/moltean/fruits` (CC BY-SA 4.0).

Further reading

- Smilkov, D., Thorat, N., Kim, B., Viégas, F., and Wattenberg, M. (2017). *SmoothGrad: Removing noise by adding noise*. ArXiv, abs/1706.03825: `https://arxiv.org/abs/1706.03825`.

- Chattopadhyay, A., Sarkar, A., Howlader, P., and Balasubramanian, V. (2018). *Grad-CAM++: Generalized Gradient-Based Visual Explanations for Deep Convolutional Networks*. 2018 IEEE Winter Conference on Applications of Computer Vision (WACV), 839-847: `https://arxiv.org/abs/1710.11063`.

- Sundararajan, M., Taly, A., and Yan, Q. (2017). *Axiomatic Attribution for Deep Networks*. Proceedings of Machine Learning Research, pp. 3319–3328, International Convention Centre, Sydney, Australia: `https://arxiv.org/abs/1703.01365`.

- Zeiler, M.D., and Fergus, R. (2014). *Visualizing and Understanding Convolutional Networks*. In European conference on computer vision, pp. 818–833: `https://arxiv.org/abs/1311.2901`.

- Shrikumar, A., Greenside, P., and Kundaje, A. (2017). *Learning Important Features Through Propagating Activation Differences*: `https://arxiv.org/abs/1704.02685`.

9

Interpretation Methods for Multivariate Forecasting and Sensitivity Analysis

Throughout this book, we have learned about various methods we can use to interpret supervised learning models. They can be quite effective at assessing models while also uncovering their most influential predictors and their hidden interactions. But as the term supervised learning suggests, these methods can only leverage known samples and permutations based on these known samples' distributions. However, when these samples represent the past, things can get tricky! As the Nobel laureate in Physics Niels Bohr famously quipped, *"Prediction is very difficult, especially if it's about the future."*

Indeed, when you see datapoints fluctuating in a time series, they may appear to be rhythmically dancing in a predictable pattern – at least in the best-case scenarios. Like a dancer moving to a beat, every repetitive movement (or frequency) can be attributed to seasonal patterns, while a gradual change in volume (or amplitude) is attributed to an equally predictable trend. The dance is inevitably misleading because there are always missing pieces of the puzzle that slightly shift the data points, such as a delay in a supplier's supply chain causing an unexpected dent in today's sales figures. To make matters worse, there's also unforeseen catastrophic once-in-a-decade, once-in-a-generation, or, simply, once-ever events that can radically make the somewhat understood movement of a time series unrecognizable, similar to a ballroom dancer having a seizure. For instance, in 2020, sales forecasts everywhere, either for better or worse, were rendered useless by COVID-19!

We could call this an extreme outlier event, but we must recognize that models weren't built to predict these momentous events because they were trained on almost entirely likely occurrences. Not predicting these unlikely yet most consequential events is why we shouldn't place so much trust in forecasting models to begin with, especially without discussing certainty or confidence bounds.

This chapter will examine a multivariate forecasting problem with **Long Short-Term Memory (LSTM)** models. We will first assess the models with traditional interpretation methods, followed by the **Integrated Gradient** method we learned about in *Chapter 8, Visualizing Convolutional Neural Networks*, to generate our model's local attributions. But more importantly, we will understand the LSTM's learning process and limitations better. We will then employ a prediction approximator method and SHAP's KernelExplainer for both global and local interpretation. Lastly, *forecasting and uncertainty are intrinsically linked*, and *Sensitivity Analysis* is a family of methods designed to measure the uncertainty of the model's output in relation to its input, so it's very useful in forecasting scenarios. We will also study two such methods: **Morris** for *factor prioritization* and **Sobol** for *factor fixing*, which involves cost sensitivity.

The following are the main topics we are going to cover:

- Assessing time series models with traditional interpretation methods
- Generating LSTM attributions with integrated gradients
- Computing global and local attributions with SHAP's KernelExplainer
- Identifying influential features with factor prioritization
- Quantifying uncertainty and cost sensitivity with factor fixing

Technical requirements

This chapter's example uses the `mldatasets`, `pandas`, `numpy`, `sklearn`, `statsmodels`, `tensorflow`, `matplotlib`, `seaborn`, `alibi`, `distython`, `shap`, and `SALib` libraries. Instructions on how to install all these libraries can be found in this book's preface. The code for this chapter is located here: `https://github.com/PacktPublishing/Interpretable-Machine-Learning-with-Python/tree/master/Chapter09`.

The mission

Highway traffic congestion is a problem that's affecting cities across the world. As vehicle per capita steadily increases across the developing world with not enough road and parking infrastructure to keep up with it, congestion has been increasing at alarming levels. In the United States, the vehicle per capita statistic is among the highest in the world (838 per 1,000 people for 2019). For this reason, US cities represent 62 out of the 381 cities worldwide. with at least a 15% congestion level.

Minneapolis is one such city (see the following screenshot) where that threshold was recently surpassed and keeps rising. To put this metropolitan area into context, congestion levels are extremely severe above 50%, but moderate level congestion (15-25%) is already a warning sign of bad congestion to come. It's challenging to reverse congestion once it reaches 25% because any infrastructure improvement will be costly to implement without disrupting traffic even further. One of the worst congestion points is between the twin cities of Minneapolis and St. Paul throughout the Interstate 94 (I-94) highway, which congests alternate routes as commuters try to cut on travel time. Knowing this, the mayors of both cities have obtained some federal funding to expand the highway:

RANK BY FILTER	WORLD RANK	CITY		COUNTRY	CONGESTION LEVEL			CONGESTION LEVEL	
								Clear all	
1	31	Los Angeles		United States of America	42%	↑ 1%	>	☑ ● > 50%	
2	52	New York		United States of America	37%	↑ 1%	>	☑ ● 25%-50%	
3	59	San Francisco		United States of America	36%	↑ 2%	>	☑ ● 15%-25%	
:	:	:		: :	:	:		● < 15%	
39	333	Minneapolis		United States of America	17%	↑ 1%	>		

Figure 9.1 – TomTom's 2019 traffic index for Minneapolis

The mayors want to be able to tout a completed expansion as a joint accomplishment to get reelected for a second term. However, they are well aware that a noisy, dirty, and obstructive expansion can be a big nuisance for commuters, so the construction project could backfire politically if it's not made nearly invisible. Therefore, they have stipulated that the construction company prefabricate as much as possible elsewhere and assemble only during low-volume hours. These hours have less than 1,500 vehicles per hour. They can also only work on one direction of the highway at a time and only block no more than half of its lanes when they are working on it. To ensure compliance with these stipulations, they will fine the company if they are blocking no more than a quarter of the highway any time that volume is above this threshold, at a rate of $15 per vehicle.

In addition to that, if the highway exceeds half-capacity while the construction crew are on-site, it will cost them $5,000 a day. To put this into perspective, blocking during a typical peak hour could cost them $67,000 per hour, plus the $5,000 daily fee! The local authorities will use **Automated Traffic Recorder (ATR)** stations along the route to monitor traffic volume, as well as local traffic police to register when lanes are getting blocked for construction.

It's been planned as a 2-year construction project; the first year will expand the westbound lanes on the I-94 route, while the second will expand the eastbound lanes. The on-site portion of the construction will only occur from May through October because snow is less likely to delay construction during these months. Throughout the rest of the year, they will focus on pre-fabrication. They will attempt to work weekdays only because the workers union negotiated generous overtime pay for weekends. Therefore, weekend construction will happen only if there are significant delays. However, the union agreed to work holidays May through October for the same rate.

The construction company doesn't want to take any risks! Therefore, they need a model to predict traffic for the I-94 route and, more importantly, to understand what factors create uncertainty and possibly increase costs. They have hired a machine learning expert to do this: you!

The ATR data provided by the construction company includes hourly traffic volumes up to September 2018, as well as weather data at the same timescale. It only consists of the westbound lanes because that expansion will come first. Also, since 2015, congestion has become considerably worse during peak hours, which has become the new normal for commuters. Therefore, they are only interested in training the model with 3 years' worth of data.

The approach

You have trained a **Bidirectional LSTM** model with almost 2 and a half years' worth of data (October 2015 – March 2018). You reserved the last 13 weeks for testing (July – September 2018) and the prior 13 weeks to that for validation (April – June 2018). This made sense because the combined testing and validation datasets align well with the highway expansion project's expected conditions (May – October). You wondered about using other splitting schemes that leveraged only the data representative of these conditions, but you didn't want to reduce the training data so drastically, and maybe they might need it for winter predictions after all. A look-back window defines how much past data a time series model has access to. You chose 672 hours (4 weeks) as the look-back window size because as the model moves forward, it can learn daily and weekly seasonality, as well as some trends and patterns that can only be observed across several weeks. You also trained another model with a lookback of 168 hours (1 week) as a backup. You have outlined the following steps to meet the client's expectations:

1. With *RMSE, regression plots, confusion matrices*, and much more, you will access the models' predictive performance and, more importantly, how the error is distributed.

2. With *Integrated Gradients*, you will understand if you took the best modeling strategy since it can help you visualize each of the model's pathways to a decision, and help you choose a model based on that.

3. With *SHAP's KernelExplainer* and a prediction approximation method, you will derive both a global and local understanding of what features matter to the chosen model.

4. With *Morris Sensitivity Analysis*, you will identify *Factor Prioritization*, which ranks factors (in other words, features) by how much they can drive output variability.

5. With *Sobol Sensitivity Analysis*, you will compute *Factor Fixing*, which helps determine what factors aren't influential. It does this by quantifying the input factors' contributions and interactions to the output's variability. With this, you can understand what uncertain factors may have the most effect on potential fines and costs, thus producing a variance-based cost-sensitivity analysis.

The preparation

You can find the code for this example here: `https://github.com/PacktPublishing/Interpretable-Machine-Learning-with-Python/blob/master/Chapter09/Traffic.ipynb`.

Loading the libraries

To run this example, you will need to install the following libraries:

- `mldatasets` to load the dataset
- `pandas` and `numpy` to manipulate the dataset
- `tensorflow` to load the model
- `statsmodels`, `sklearn` (scikit-learn), `matplotlib`, `seaborn`, `alibi`, `distython`, `shap`, and `SALib` to create and visualize the interpretations

You should load all of them first:

```python
import math
import os
import mldatasets
import pandas as pd
import numpy as np
import tensorflow as tf
from tensorflow import keras
from tensorflow.keras.preprocessing.sequence import
TimeseriesGenerator
from keras.utils.data_utils import get_file
from sklearn.preprocessing import MinMaxScaler
from sklearn import metrics
from statsmodels.tsa.seasonal import seasonal_decompose
from statsmodels.tsa.stattools import acf
import matplotlib.pyplot as plt
import seaborn as sns
from alibi.explainers import IntegratedGradients
from distython import HEOM
import shap
from SALib.sample import morris as ms
from SALib.analyze import morris as ma
from SALib.plotting import morris as mp
from SALib.sample.saltelli import sample as ss
from SALib.analyze.sobol import analyze as sa
from SALib.plotting.bar import plot as barplot
```

Let's check that TensorFlow has loaded the right version by using the `print(tf.__version__)` command. It should be 2.0 or above.

Understanding and preparing the data

In the following snippet, we are loading the data into a DataFrame called `traffic_df`. Please note that the `prepare=True` parameter is important because it performs necessary tasks such as subsetting it to the required timeframe since October 2015, some interpolation, correcting holidays, and performing one-hot encoding:

```
traffic_df = mldatasets.load("traffic-volume", prepare=True)
```

There should be over 25,000 records and 15 columns. We can verify this with `traffic_df.info()`:

```
<class 'pandas.core.frame.DataFrame'>
DatetimeIndex: 25656 entries, 2015-10-28 00:00:00 to 2018-09-30
23:00:00
Data columns (total 15 columns):
 #   Column          Non-Null Count   Dtype
---  ------          --------------   -----
 0   dow             25656 non-null   int64
 1   hr              25656 non-null   int64
 2   temp            25656 non-null   float64
 3   rain_1h         25656 non-null   float64
 4   cloud_coverage  25656 non-null   float64
 5   is_holiday      25656 non-null   int64
 6   traffic_volume  25656 non-null   float64
 7   weather_Clear   25656 non-null   uint8
 8   weather_Clouds  25656 non-null   uint8
 9   weather_Haze    25656 non-null   uint8
 10  weather_Mist    25656 non-null   uint8
 11  weather_Other   25656 non-null   uint8
 12  weather_Rain    25656 non-null   uint8
 13  weather_Snow    25656 non-null   uint8
 14  weather_Unknown 25656 non-null   uint8
dtypes: float64(4), int64(3), uint8(8)
memory usage: 1.8 MB
```

The preceding output checks out. All the features are numeric and have no missing values, and the categorical features have already been one-hot encoded for us.

The data dictionary

There are only eight features, but they become 15 columns because of categorical encoding:

- dow: Ordinal; day of week starting with Monday (between $0 - 6$)
- hr: Ordinal; hour of day (between $0 - 23$)
- temp: Continuous; average temperature in Celsius (between -30 and 37)
- rain_1h: Continuous; mm of rainfall occurred in the hour (between $0 - 31$)
- cloud_coverage: Continuous; percentage of cloud coverage (between $0 - 100$)
- is_holiday: Binary; is the day a national or state holiday when it occurs Monday – Friday (1 for yes, 0 for no)?
- traffic_volume: Continuous, target, traffic volume
- weather: Categorical; a short description of the weather during that hour (Clear | Clouds | Haze | Mist | Rain | Snow | Unknown | Other)

Understanding the data

The first step in understanding a time series problem is understanding the target variable. This is because it determines how you approach everything else, from data preparation to modeling. The target variable is likely to have a special relationship with time, such as a seasonal movement or a trend.

Understanding weeks

First, we can sample one 168-hour period from every season to understand the variance a bit better between days of the week, and then get an idea of how they could vary across seasons and holidays:

```
fig, (ax0,ax1,ax2,ax3) = plt.subplots(4,1, figsize=(15,8))
plt.subplots_adjust(top = 0.99, bottom=0.01, hspace=0.4)
traffic_df[:168].traffic_volume.plot(ax=ax0)
traffic_df[(168*13):(168*14)].traffic_volume.plot(ax=ax1)
traffic_df[(168*26):(168*27)].traffic_volume.plot(ax=ax2)
traffic_df[(168*39):(168*40)].traffic_volume.plot(ax=ax3)
```

The preceding code generates the plots shown in the following image. If you read them from left to right, you'll see that they all start with Wednesday and end with Tuesday of the following week. Every day of the week starts and ends at a low point, with a high point in-between. Weekdays tend to have two peaks corresponding to morning and afternoon rush hour, while weekends only have one mid-afternoon bump:

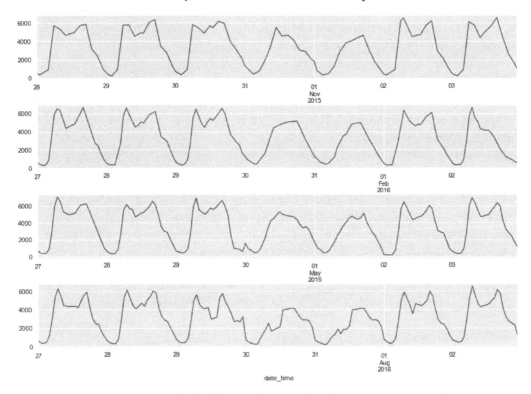

Figure 9.2 – Several sample weekly periods for traffic_volume representing each season

There are some major inconsistencies, such as Saturday October 31, which is basically Halloween and is not an official holiday. Also, February 2 (a Tuesday) was the beginning of a severe snowstorm, and the period of the August 27 through to September 2 is much more chaotic than the other sample weeks. It turns out that in that year, the State Fair occurred. Like Halloween, it's not a federal nor regional holiday either, but it's important to note that the fairgrounds are located halfway between Minneapolis and St. Paul. You'll also notice that on Friday 29, there's a midnight bump in traffic, which can be attributed to this being a big day for Minneapolis concerts.

Trying to explain these inconsistencies while comparing periods in your time series is a good exercise as it helps you figure out what variables to add to your model, or at least know what is missing. In our case, we know our `is_holiday` variable doesn't include days such as Halloween or the entire State Fair week, nor do we have a variable for big music or sporting events. The original dataset has a `snow_1h` variable, but it was removed because it wasn't reliable. To produce a more robust model, it would be advisable to look for reliable external data sources and add more features that cover all these possibilities, not to mention validate the existing variables. For now, we will work with what we've got.

Understanding days

It is crucial for the highway expansion project to understand what traffic looks like for the average workday. The construction crew will be working on weekdays only (Monday – Friday) unless they experience delays, in which case they will also work weekends. We must also make a distinction between holidays and other weekdays because these are likely to be different.

To this end, we will create a DataFrame (`weekend_df`) and engineer a new column (`type_of_day`) that codes hours as being part of a "Holiday," "Weekday," or "Weekend." Then, we can group by this column and the `hr` column, and aggregate with `mean` and standard deviation (`std`). We can then `pivot` so that we have one column with the average and standard deviations traffic volumes for every `type_of_day` category, where the rows represent the hours of the day (`hr`). Then, we can plot the resulting DataFrame. We can create intervals with the standard deviations:

```python
weekend_df =\
    traffic_df[['hr', 'dow', 'is_holiday', 'traffic_volume']].copy()
weekend_df['type_of_day'] = np.where(weekend_df.is_holiday == 1,\
    'Holiday', np.where(weekend_df.dow >= 5, 'Weekend',
'Weekday'))
weekend_df = weekend_df.groupby(['type_of_day','hr'])\
            ['traffic_volume'].agg(['mean','std']).\
            reset_index().pivot(index='hr', columns='type_of_day',\
                                values=['mean', 'std'])
weekend_df.columns = [''.join(col).strip().replace('mean','')
                    for col in weekend_df.columns.values]
fig, ax = plt.subplots(figsize=(15,8))
weekend_df[['Holiday','Weekday','Weekend']].plot(ax=ax)
```

```
plt.fill_between(weekend_df.index,\
  np.maximum(weekend_df.Weekday - 2 * weekend_df.std_Weekday,
0),\
      weekend_df.Weekday + 2 * weekend_df.std_Weekday,\
      color='darkorange', alpha=0.2)
plt.fill_between(weekend_df.index,\
  np.maximum(weekend_df.Weekend - 2 * weekend_df.std_Weekend,
0),\
      weekend_df.Weekend + 2 * weekend_df.std_Weekend,
      color='green', alpha=0.1)
plt.fill_between(weekend_df.index,\
    np.maximum(weekend_df.Holiday - 2 * weekend_df.std_Holiday,
0),\
      weekend_df.Holiday + 2 * weekend_df.std_Holiday,
      color='cornflowerblue', alpha=0.1)
ax.axhline(y=5300, linewidth=3, color='red', dashes=(2,2))
ax.axhline(y=2650, linewidth=2, color='darkviolet',
dashes=(2,2))
ax.axhline(y=1500, linewidth=2, color='teal', dashes=(2,2))
```

The preceding snippet results in the following plot. It represents the hourly average, but there's quite a bit of variation, which is why the construction company is proceeding with caution. There are horizontal lines that have been plotted representing each of the thresholds:

- 5,300 for full capacity.

- 2,650 for half-capacity, after which the construction company will get fined the daily amount specified.

- 1,500 is the no-construction threshold, after which the construction company will get fined the hourly amount specified.

They only want to work Monday – Friday during the hours that are typically below the 1,500 threshold. These five hours would be 11 p.m. (the day before) to 4 a.m. If they had to work weekends, this schedule would typically be delayed until 1 a.m. and end at 6 a.m. There's considerably less variance during weekdays, so it's understandable why the construction company is adamant about only working weekdays. During these hours, holidays appear to be similar to weekends, but holidays tend to vary even more than weekends, which is potentially even more problematic:

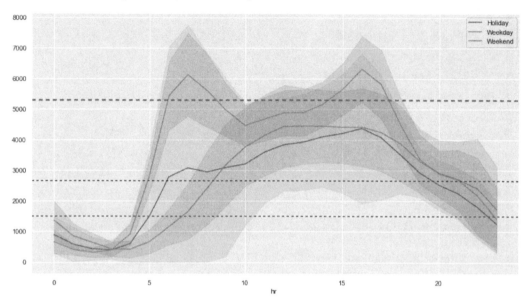

Figure 9.3 – The average hourly traffic volume for holidays, weekdays, and weekends, with intervals

Usually, for a project like this, you would explore the predictor variables to the extent we have done with the target. This book is about model interpretation, so we will learn about the predictors by interpreting the models. But before we get to the models, we must prepare the data for them.

Data preparation

The first data preparation step is to split it into train, validation, and test sets. Please note that the test dataset comprises the last 13 weeks (2184 hours), while the validation dataset comprises the 13 weeks before that, so it starts at 4368 and ends 2184 hours before the last row of the DataFrame:

```
train = traffic_df[:-4368]
valid = traffic_df[-4368:-2184]
test = traffic_df[-2184:]
```

Now that the DataFrame has been split, we can plot it to ensure that its parts are split as intended. We can do so with the following code:

```
plt.plot(train.index.values, train.traffic_volume.values,
        label='train')
plt.plot(valid.index.values, valid.traffic_volume.values,
        label='validation')
plt.plot(test.index.values, test.traffic_volume.values,
        label='test')
plt.ylabel('Traffic Volume')
plt.legend()
```

The preceding code produces the following plot. It shows that almost 2½ years of data was allocated for the training dataset, and about a quarter of a year to validation and test each. We won't reference the validation dataset from this point on during this exercise because it was only instrumental during training to assess the model's predictive performance after every epoch:

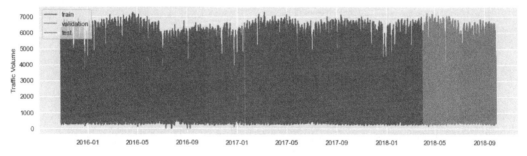

Figure 9.4 – Time series split into train, validation, and test sets

The next step is to min-max normalize the data. We are doing this because larger values lead to slower learning for all neural networks in general and LSTMs are very prone to **exploding and vanishing gradients**. Relatively uniform and small numbers can help counter these problems. We will discuss this later in this chapter, but basically, the network becomes either numerically unstable or ineffective at reaching a global minimum.

We can min-max normalize with `MinMaxScaler` from the `scikit` package. For now, all we will do is `fit` the scaler so that we can use them whenever we need them. We will create a scaler for our target (`traffic_volume`) called `y_scaler` and another for the rest of the variables (`X_scaler`) with the entire dataset, so that transformations are consistent no matter what part you are using, be it `train`, `valid`, or `test`. All the `fit` process does is save the formula to make each variable fit between zero and one:

```
y_scaler = MinMaxScaler()
y_scaler.fit(traffic_df[['traffic_volume']])
X_scaler = MinMaxScaler()
X_scaler.fit(traffic_df.drop(['traffic_volume'], axis=1))
```

Now, we will `transform` both our train and test datasets with our scaler, creating *y* and *X* pairs for each:

```
y_train = y_scaler.transform(train[['traffic_volume']])
X_train = X_scaler.transform(train.drop(['traffic_volume'],
axis=1))
y_test = y_scaler.transform(test[['traffic_volume']])
X_test = X_scaler.transform(test.drop(['traffic_volume'],
axis=1))
```

However, for a time series model, the *y* and *X* pairs we created aren't useful because each observation is a timestep. And each timestep is more than the variables for that timestep, but the previous timesteps are going a certain amount of lag backward. Therefore, you have to generate an array for every timestep, as well as its lags. Fortunately, `keras` has a function called `TimeseriesGenerator` that takes your *X* and *y* and produces a generator that feeds the data to your model. You must specify a certain `length`, which is the number of lagging timesteps (also known as the **lookback window**). The default `batch_size` is one, but we are using 24 because the client prefers to get forecasts 24 hours at a time, and also training and inference are much faster with a larger batch size.

Naturally, when you need to forecast tomorrow, you will need tomorrow's weather, but you can complete the timesteps with weather forecasts:

```
gen_train_672 = TimeseriesGenerator(X_train, y_train,\
                                    length=672,\
                                    batch_size=24)
gen_test_672 = TimeseriesGenerator(X_test, y_test, length=672,
                                   batch_size=24)
print("gen_train_672:%sx%s→%s" % (len(gen_train_672),
```

```
            gen_train_672[0][0].shape,
            gen_train_672[0][1].shape))
print("gen_test_672:%sx%s→%s" % (len(gen_test_672),
            gen_test_672[0][0].shape,
            gen_test_672[0][1].shape))
```

The preceding snippet outputs the dimensions of the training generator (gen_train_672) and the testing generator (gen_test_672), which use a length of 672 and a batch size of 24:

```
gen_train_672:    859 ×    (24, 672, 14)    →    (24, 1)
gen_test_672:     63 ×    (24, 672, 14)    →    (24, 1)
```

The model that was trained with a 1-month look-back window will need this generator. Each generator is a list of tuples corresponding to each batch. Index 0 of this tuple is the X feature array, while index 1 is the y label array. Therefore, the first number output is the length of the list, which is the number of batches. The dimensions of the X and y array follow. For instance, gen_train_672 has 859 batches, and each batch has 24 timesteps, with a length of 672 and 14 features. The shape of the predicted labels expected from these 24 timesteps is (24,1).

Now, we must do the same to prepare generators for our 1-week look-back window model, which should have a length of 168 hours and the same batch_size:

```
gen_train_168 = TimeseriesGenerator(X_train, y_train,\
                            length=168,
                            batch_size=24)
gen_test_168 = TimeseriesGenerator(X_test, y_test, length=168,
                            batch_size=24)
```

The preceding code creates the generators for our 1-week lookback model. Lastly, before moving forward with handling models and stochastic interpretation methods, let's attempt to make things more reproducible by initializing our random seeds:

```
rand = 9
os.environ['PYTHONHASHSEED']=str(rand)
tf.random.set_seed(rand)
np.random.seed(rand)
```

Loading the LSTM models

We can quickly load the first model and output its summary like this:

```
model_path = get_file('LSTM_traffic_672_final.hdf5',
    'https://github.com/PacktPublishing/Interpretable-Machine-
Learning-with-Python/blob/master/models/LSTM_traffic_672_final.
hdf5?raw=true')
lstm_traffic_672_mdl = keras.models.load_model(model_path)
lstm_traffic_672_mdl.summary()
```

As you can tell by the summary that's produced by the preceding snippet, the model starts with a **Bidirectional LSTM** layer with an output of (24, 672). 24 corresponds to the batch size, while 672 means that there's not one but two 336-unit LSTMs going in opposite directions and meeting in the middle. It has a dropout of 10%, and then a dense layer with a single ReLu activated unit. The ReLu ensures that all the predictions are over zero since negative traffic volume makes no sense:

```
Model: "Traffic_Bidirectional_LSTM_672"


_____
____
Layer (type)                  Output Shape              Param #
=================================================================
===
Bidir_LSTM (Bidirectional)    (24, 672)                 943488


_____
____
Dropout (Dropout)             (24, 672)                 0


_____
____
Dense (Dense)                 (24, 1)                   673
=================================================================
===
Total params: 944,161
Trainable params: 944,161
Non-trainable params: 0


_____
____
```

Then, you can load the second model in the same fashion and print its `summary()`:

```
model_path = get_file('LSTM_traffic_168_final.hdf5',
    'https://github.com/PacktPublishing/Interpretable-Machine-
Learning-with-Python/blob/master/models/LSTM_traffic_168_final.
hdf5?raw=true')
lstm_traffic_168_mdl = keras.models.load_model(model_path)
lstm_traffic_168_mdl.summary()
```

The summary produced by the preceding code is for a unidirectional LSTM model with 168 units in the LSTM layer corresponding to the lookback window of 168 hours. It has a 15% dropout and a `dense` layer with a single ReLu activated unit. Note that this model is nearly 8 times smaller than the bidirectional one, which makes sense because it has almost 8 times fewer parameters:

```
Model: "Traffic_LSTM_168"
_____

Layer (type)                    Output Shape                 Param #
=================================================================

LSTM (LSTM)                     (24, 168)                    122976


Dropout (Dropout)               (24, 168)                    0


Dense (Dense)                   (24, 1)                      169
=================================================================
Total params: 123,145
Trainable params: 123,145
Non-trainable params: 0
_____
```

For the sake of simplicity, from this point forward, we will refer to the bidirectional LSTM trained on a 4-week look-back window as the "672 model." On the other hand, the unidirectional LSTM with the 1-week window will be the "168 model." Now, let's assess both models using traditional interpretation methods.

Assessing time series models with traditional interpretation methods

A time series regressor model can be evaluated as you would evaluate any regression model; that is, using metrics derived from **mean square error** or the **r-squared** score. There are, of course, cases in which you will need to use a metric with medians, logs, deviances, or absolute values. These models don't require any of this.

Using standard regression metrics

The `evaluate_reg_mdl` function can evaluate the model, output some standard regression metrics, and plot them. The parameters for this model are the fitted model (`lstm_traffic_672_mdl`), X_train (`gen_train_672`), X_test (`gen_test_672`), y_train, and y_test.

Optionally, we can specify a `y_scaler` so that the model is evaluated with the labels inverse transformed, which makes the plot and **root mean square error** (**RMSE**) much easier to interpret. Another optional parameter that is very much necessary, in this case, is `y_truncate=True` because our `y_train` and `y_test` are of larger dimensions than the predicted labels. This discrepancy happens because the first prediction occurs several timesteps after the first timestep in the dataset due to the look-back window. Therefore, we would need to deduct these timesteps from `y_train` in order to match the length of `gen_train_672`.

We will now evaluate both models with the following code. To observe the prediction's progress as it happens, we will use `predopts={"verbose":1}`. Please note how much longer inference takes for the first model (`lstm_traffic_672_mdl`):

```
print(lstm_traffic_672_mdl.name)
y_train_pred_672, y_test_pred_672, y_train_672, y_test_672 =\
  mldatasets.evaluate_reg_mdl(lstm_traffic_672_mdl, gen_
train_672,\
            gen_test_672, y_train, y_test, scaler=y_scaler,\
            y_truncate=True,  predopts={"verbose":1})
print(lstm_traffic_168_mdl.name)
y_train_pred_168, y_test_pred_168, y_train_168, y_test_168 =\
```

```
mldatasets.evaluate_reg_mdl(lstm_traffic_168_mdl, gen_
train_168,\
                gen_test_168, y_train, y_test, scaler=y_scaler,
                y_truncate=True, predopts={"verbose":1})
```

The preceding snippet produced the plots and metrics shown in the following image. They both have similar performance metrics, except that model 168 is overfitting much more since the training RMSE is significantly better. The "regression plots" are, essentially, scatter plots of the observed versus predicted traffic volumes, fitted to a linear regression model to show how well they match. These plots show that model 672 has a tendency to predict zero traffic when it's substantially higher. Besides that, there are more extreme outlier points for model 168, but model 672 tends to diverge a bit more toward the highest traffic volumes:

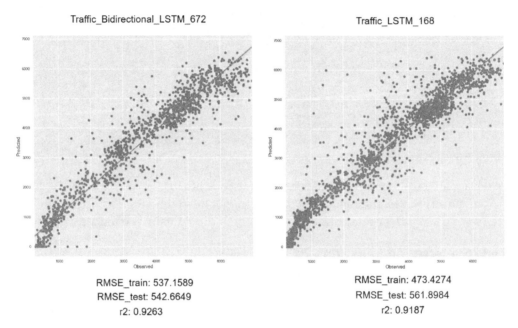

Figure 9.5 – Predictive performance evaluations for both models

We can also evaluate our models by comparing observed versus predicted traffic for both. It would be helpful to break down the error by the hour and type of day too. To this end, we can create DataFrames with these values – one for each model. But first, we must truncate the DataFrame (-y_test_pred_672.shape[0]) so that it matches the length of the predictions array, and we won't need all the columns, so we are providing indexes for only those we are interested in: traffic_volume is #6 but we also will want dow (#0), hr (#1), and is_holiday (#5). We will rename traffic_volume to actual_traffic and create a new column called predicted_traffic with our predictions. Then, we will engineer a type_of_day column, as we did previously, which tells us if it's a holiday, weekday, or weekend. Finally, we can drop the dow and is_holiday columns since we won't need them:

```
evaluate_672_df = test.iloc[-y_test_pred_672.
shape[0]:, [0,1,5,6]].\
            rename(columns={'traffic_volume':'actual_traffic'})
evaluate_672_df['predicted_traffic'] = y_test_pred_672
evaluate_672_df['type_of_day'] =\
        np.where(evaluate_672_df.is_holiday == 1, 'Holiday',\
        np.where(evaluate_672_df.dow >= 5, 'Weekend',
'Weekday'))
evaluate_672_df.drop(['dow','is_holiday'], axis=1,
inplace=True)
```

We replace all the 672s for 168s and run the same code but for the other model. You can quickly review the contents of the dataframes by simply running a cell with evaluate_672_df or evaluate_168_df. Both should have 4 columns.

Predictive error aggregations

It may be that some days and times of day are more prone to predictive errors. To get a better sense of how these errors are distributed across time, we can plot RMSE on an hourly basis segmented by type_of_day. To do this, we must first define an rmse function and then group each of the models' evaluated DataFrames by type_of_day and hr and use the apply function to aggregate using the rmse function. We can then pivot to ensure that each type_of_day has a column with the RMSEs on an hourly basis. We can then average these columns and store them in a Series:

```
def rmse(g):
  rmse = np.sqrt(metrics.\
      mean_squared_error(g['actual_traffic'],
                  g['predicted_traffic']))
```

```
    return pd.Series({'rmse': rmse})|
evaluate_by_hr_672_df = evaluate_672_df.\
        groupby(['type_of_day', 'hr']).apply(rmse).reset_
index().\
        pivot(index='hr', columns='type_of_day', values='rmse')
evaluate_by_hr_168_df = evaluate_168_df.\
        groupby(['type_of_day', 'hr']).apply(rmse).reset_
index().\
        pivot(index='hr', columns='type_of_day', values='rmse')
mean_by_daytype_672_s = evaluate_by_hr_672_df.mean(axis=0)
mean_by_daytype_168_s = evaluate_by_hr_168_df.mean(axis=0)
```

Now that we have DataFrames with the hourly RMSEs for holidays, weekdays, and weekends, as well as the average for these "types" of day, we can plot them. We will create two subplots: one for model 672 and another for 168. We will then plot the evaluate_by_hr DataFrames on these subplots. We will also create dotted horizontal lines with the averages for each type_of_day from the mean_by_daytype pandas series:

```
fig, (ax0,ax1) = plt.subplots(2, 1, figsize=(15,10))
plt.subplots_adjust(top = 0.99, bottom=0.01, hspace=0.2)
evaluate_by_hr_672_df.plot(ax=ax0)
ax0.set_title('672 model: Hourly RMSE distribution',
fontsize=16)
ax0.set_ylim([0,2500])
ax0.axhline(y=mean_by_daytype_672_s.Holiday, linewidth=2,
        color='cornflowerblue', dashes=(2,2))
ax0.axhline(y=mean_by_daytype_672_s.Weekday, linewidth=2,
        color='darkorange', dashes=(2,2))
ax0.axhline(y=mean_by_daytype_672_s.Weekend, linewidth=2,
        color='green', dashes=(2,2))
evaluate_by_hr_168_df.plot(ax=ax1)
ax1.set_title('168 model: Hourly RMSE distribution',
fontsize=16)
ax1.set_ylim([0,2500])
ax1.axhline(y=mean_by_daytype_168_s.Holiday, linewidth=2,
    color='cornflowerblue', dashes=(2,2))
ax1.axhline(y=mean_by_daytype_168_s.Weekday, linewidth=2,
```

```
    color='darkorange', dashes=(2,2))
ax1.axhline(y=mean_by_daytype_168_s.Weekend, linewidth=2,
    color='green', dashes=(2,2))
```

The preceding code generated the plots shown in the following image. As we can see, model 168 has a consistently lower RMSE for all types of day and hours of day – at least for the time of year represented by the test dataset. However, this could mean one model is overestimating the traffic volume, and overestimating is not as bad as underestimating:

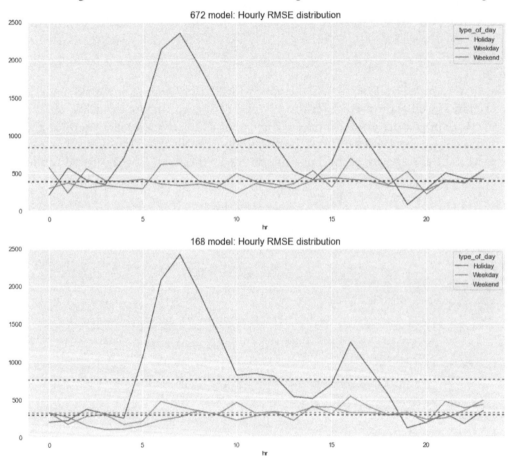

Figure 9.6 – Hourly RMSE segmented by type_of_day for both models

Evaluating it like a classification problem

Indeed, just like classification problems can have false positives and false negatives, and also realize that one is more costly than another, you can frame any regression problem with concepts such as underestimation and overestimation. This framing is especially useful when one is more costly than the other. If you have clearly defined thresholds, as we have for this project, you can evaluate any regression problem as you would a classification one. We will assess both models with a confusion matrix with the half capacity and no-construction thresholds. To accomplish this, we can `for` loop both model evaluation DataFrames and use `np.where` to get binary arrays for when the actuals and predictions surpassed each threshold. We can then use the `compare_confusion_matrices` function to compare the confusion matrices for each model:

```python
evaluate_dfs = [evaluate_672_df, evaluate_168_df]
lookbacks = [672, 168]
for e in range(2):
  evaluate_df = evaluate_dfs[e]
  lb = lookbacks[e]
  actual_over_half_cap = np.where(evaluate_df['actual_traffic'] >\
          2650, 1, 0)
  pred_over_half_cap = np.where(evaluate_df['predicted_traffic'] >\
          2650, 1, 0)
  actual_over_nc_thresh = np.where(evaluate_df['actual_traffic'] >\
          1500, 1, 0)
  pred_over_nc_thresh = np.where(evaluate_df['predicted_traffic'] >\
          1500, 1, 0)
  mldatasets.\
    compare_confusion_matrices(actual_over_half_cap,\
      pred_over_half_cap, actual_over_nc_thresh, pred_over_nc_thresh,
      str(lb)+' model: Over Half-Capacity',\
    str(lb)+' model: Over No-Construction Threshold')
```

The preceding snippet produced the confusion matrices shown in the following image. We are most interested in the percentage of false negatives because predicting no traffic beyond the threshold when, in fact, it did rise above it, will lead to a steep fine. On the other hand, the cost of false positives is in preemptively leaving the construction site when traffic didn't rise above the threshold after all. It's better to be safe than sorry, though! If you compare false negatives for the "no-construction" threshold, the 672 model (1.32%) is twice as high as that of the 168 model (0.64%). For the half-capacity threshold, the 672 model's false negative percentage is lower than the 162 model's. Ultimately, what matters most is the no-construction threshold:

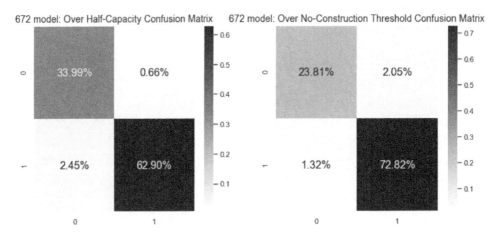

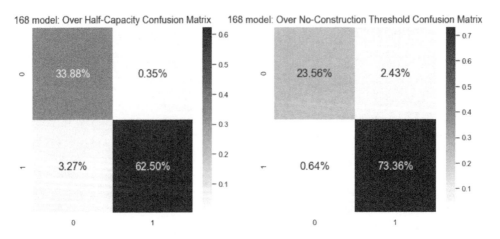

Figure 9.7 – Confusion matrices for going over half and the no-construction threshold for both models

Now that we have leveraged traditional methods to understand the model's decisions, let's move on to some more advanced model-agnostic methods.

Generating LSTM attributions with integrated gradients

We first learned about **integrated gradients** (**IG**) in *Chapter 8, Visualizing Convolutional Neural Networks*. Unlike the other gradient-based attribution methods studied in that chapter, path-integrated gradients is not contingent on convolutional layers, nor is it limited to classification problems. In fact, since it computes the gradients of the output concerning the inputs averaged along the path, the input and output could be anything! It is common to use integrated gradients with CNNs and **Recurrent Neural Networks** (**RNNs**), like the one we are interpreting in this chapter. Frankly, when you see an IG LSTM example online, it has an embedding layer and is an NLP classifier, but IG could be used very effectively for LSTMs that even process sounds or genetic data!

The integrated gradient explainer and the explainers that we will use moving forward can access any part of the traffic dataset. First, let's create a generator for all of it and for both models:

```
y_all = y_scaler.transform(traffic_df[['traffic_volume']])
X_all = X_scaler.transform(traffic_df.drop(['traffic_volume'],\
                           axis=1))
gen_all_672 = TimeseriesGenerator(X_all, y_all, length=672,\
                                  batch_size=24)
gen_all_168 = TimeseriesGenerator(X_all, y_all, length=168,\
                                  batch_size=24)
```

Integrated gradients is a local interpretation method. so let's get a few sample "instances of interest" we can interpret. We know holidays are a concern, so let's see if our models pick up on the importance of `is_holiday` for one example (`holiday_afternoon_s`). Also, mornings are a concern, especially mornings with a larger than average rush hour because of weather conditions, so we have one example for that (`peak_morning_s`). Lastly, a hot day might have more traffic, especially on a weekend (`hot_saturday_s`):

```
X_df = traffic_df.drop(['traffic_volume'], axis=1).\
                                          reset_
index(drop=True)
holiday_afternoon_s = X_df[(X_df.index >= 23471) & (X_
df.dow==0) &\
        (X_df.hr==16) & (X_df.is_holiday==1)]
peak_morning_s = X_df[(X_df.index >= 23471) & (X_df.dow==2) &\
        (X_df.hr==8) & (X_df.weather_Clouds==1) &\
```

```
        (X_df.temp<20)]
hot_saturday_s = X_df[(X_df.index >= 23471) & (X_df.dow==5) &\
        (X_df.hr==12) & (X_df.temp>29)]
```

Now that we have created some instances, let's instantiate our explainers.
`IntegratedGradients` from the `alibi` package only requires a deep learning model,
but it is recommended to set a number of steps (`n_steps`) for the integral approximation
and `internal_batch_size`. We will instantiate one explainer for each model:

```
ig_672 = IntegratedGradients(lstm_traffic_672_mdl,
                    n_steps=25, internal_batch_size=24)
ig_168 = IntegratedGradients(lstm_traffic_168_mdl,
                    n_steps=25, internal_batch_size=24)
```

Before we iterate our samples and the explainers, it is important to realize how we need
to input the sample to the explainer because it will need a batch of 24. To this end, we will
have to get the index of the sample once we've deducted the lookback window (`nidx`).
Then, you can obtain the batch for this sample from the generator (`gen_all_672`).
Each batch includes 24 timesteps, so you floor `nidx` by 24 (`nidx//24`) to get the batch's
position for that sample. Once you've got the batch for the sample (`batch_X`) and printed
the shape (`24, 672, 14`), it shouldn't surprise you that the first number is 24. Of
course, we will need to get the index of the sample within the batch (`nidx%24`) to obtain
the data for that sample:

```
nidx = holiday_afternoon_s.index.tolist()[0] - 672
batch_X = gen_all_672[nidx//24][0]
print(batch_X.shape)
```

The IG process is pretty slow, so we are only going to iterate the first two sample instances.
The `for` loop will use the previously explained method to locate the batch for the sample
(`batch_X`).This `batch_X` is inputted into the `explain` function. This is because this
is a regression problem and there's no target class; that is, `target=None`. Once the
explanation is produced, the `attributions` property will have the attributions for
the entire batch. We can only obtain this for the sample and `transpose` it to produce
an image that has this shape: (`14, lb`). The rest of the code in the `for` loop simply
obtains the labels to use in the tick marks and then plots an image stretched out to fit the
dimensions of our `figure`, along with its labels:

```
samples = [holiday_afternoon_s, peak_morning_s]
sample_names = ['Holiday Afternoon', 'Peak Morning']
igs = [ig_672, ig_168]
```

```python
lbs = [672, 168]
for s in range(len(samples)):
 for i in range(len(igs)):
  nidx = samples[s].index.tolist()[0] - lb
  lb = lbs[i]
  if lb == 672:
   batch_X = gen_all_672[nidx//24][0]
   p = 5 #Create 5 tick marks…
   f = '7D' #seperated by 1 week periods
  else:
   batch_X = gen_all_168[nidx//24][0]
   p = 8 #Create 8 tick marks…
   f = '1D' #seperated by 1 day periods
  explanation = igs[i].explain(batch_X, target=None)
  attributions = explanation.attributions
  attribution_img = np.transpose(attributions[nidx%24,:,:])
  end_date = traffic_df.iloc[samples[s].index].\
        index.to_pydatetime()[0]
  date_range = pd.date_range(end=end_date, periods=p,\
                   freq=f).to_pydatetime().tolist()
  columns = samples[s].columns.tolist()
  plt.title('Integrated Gradient Attribution Map for {} for the
{} model'.\
     format(sample_names[s], lb), fontsize=16)
  plt.imshow(attribution_img, interpolation='nearest',\
        aspect='auto', cmap='plasma')
  plt.xticks(np.linspace(0,672,p).astype(int), labels=date_
range)
  plt.yticks([*range(14)], labels=columns)
  plt.colorbar(pad=0.01,fraction=0.02,anchor=(1.0,0.0))
  plt.show()
```

The preceding code will generate the plots shown in *Figure 9.8* and *Figure 9.9*. On the y-axis, you can see the variable names, while on the x-axis, you can see the dates corresponding to the lookback window for the sample in question. The rightmost part of the x-axis is the sample's date, and as you move left, you go backward in time. For instance, the holiday afternoon sample was 4 p.m. September 3 and for the 672 model, there is 4 weeks' worth of lookback, so each tick mark backward is a week before that date. The 168 model only has a week of lookback, so each tick mark represents a day:

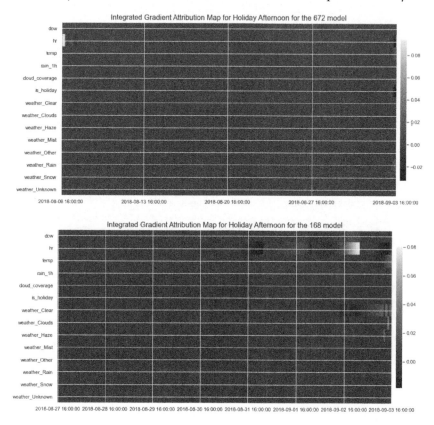

Figure 9.8 – Annotated integrated gradients attribution map for a holiday afternoon for both models

You can tell by the intensity in the attribution maps in *Figure 9.8* which hour/variables mattered for the prediction. The colorbar to the right of each attribution map can serve as a key. Negative numbers correspond to a darker color and negative correlation, while positive numbers correspond to a lighter color and positive correlation. However, something that is pretty evident is the tendency for intensities to fade as it goes backward in time. You can tell that the 672 model, which is bidirectional, has this happen from both ends, which makes sense because it's bidirectional. What is surprising is how fast this happens.

As for "Peak Morning" in *Figure 9.9*, attributions make sense since both models realize that it is clear after it had been previously rainy and cloudy, which caused the rush hour to peak quickly rather than increase slowly. To a certain degree, the LSTM has learned that only recent weather matters – no more than 2 or 3 days' worth. However, that is not the only reason the integrated gradients fade. They also fade because of the **vanishing gradient problem**. This problem occurs during backpropagation because the gradient values are multiplied by the weight matrices in each step, so gradients can exponentially decrease to zero:

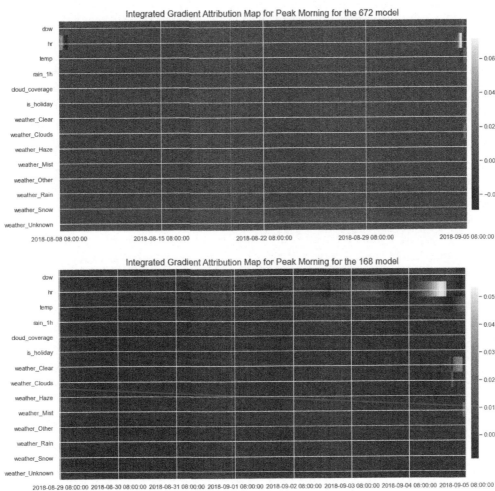

Figure 9.9 – Annotated integrated gradients attribution map for a peak morning for both models

Our LSTMs are organized in a very long sequence, making the network ever-more ineffective at capturing dependencies long-term. Fortunately, these LSTMs are **stateful**, which means they string batches in a sequence by leveraging states from the previous batch. **Statefulness** ensures learning from a long sequence, despite vanishing gradients. However, if we observe the attribution maps for "Holiday Afternoon," there seem to be no attributions for `is_holiday` for either model. It turns out September 3 (Labor Day) in *Figure 9.9* is nearly 2 months after the previous holiday (Independence Day), which is a more festive holiday. Is it possible that the model is not picking up on these patterns?

We could try subcategorizing holidays by their traffic patterns to see if that helps the model identify them. We could also make rolling aggregations of previous weather conditions to make it easier for the model to pick up on recent weather patterns. Weather patterns span hours, so it is intuitive to aggregate, not to mention easier to interpret. Interpretation methods can point us in the right direction as to how to improve models, and there's certainly a lot of room for improvement.

Given what we learned with the hourly RMSE distribution, confusion matrices, and the IG attribution maps, there's no doubt that the 168 model is the better model. It has lower RMSEs during the working hours and a lower false-negative rate for going over the no-construction threshold. As for IG attribution maps, they show that a week lookback is not too short because the 672 model has nothing but null attributions for over 3 weeks. That being said, we will move forward with the 672 model instead because since it's more flawed, it makes for a more interesting use case! The following code will ensure that we are using model 672, but you can always rerun all the code moving forward with 168 and do a comparison:

```
lookback = 672
gen_all = gen_all_672
lstm_traffic_mdl = lstm_traffic_672_mdl
```

Next, we will have a stab at a permutation-based method!

Computing global and local attributions with SHAP's KernelExplainer

Permutation methods make changes to the input to assess how much difference they will produce to a model's output. We first discussed this in *Chapter 4, Fundamentals of Feature Importance and Impact*, but if you recall, there's a coalitional framework to perform these permutations that will produce the average marginal contribution for each feature across different coalitions of features. This process's outcome is **Shapely Values**, which have essential mathematical properties such as additivity and symmetry. Unfortunately, shapely values are costly to compute for datasets that aren't small, so the SHAP library has approximation methods. One of these methods is the **KernelExplainer**, which we used in *Chapter 5, Global Model-Agnostic Interpretation Methods*. It approximates the Shapely Values with a weighted local linear regression, just like LIME does.

Why use the KernelExplainer?

We have a deep learning model, so why aren't we using SHAP's **DeepExplainer** as we did with the CNN in *Chapter 8, Visualizing Convolutional Neural Networks*? DeepExplainer adapted the DeepLIFT algorithm to approximate the Shapely Values. It works very well with any forward feed network that's used for tabular data, CNNs, and RNNs with an embedding layer, such as those used for an NLP classifier, or even to detect genomic sequences. It gets trickier for multivariate time series because DeepExplainer doesn't know what to do with the input's three-dimensional array. Even if it did, it includes data for previous timesteps, so you cannot permute one timestep without considering the previous ones. For instance, if the permutation dictates that the temperature is 5 degrees lower, shouldn't that affect all the previous timestep's temperatures up to a certain amount of hours? And what if it's 20 degrees lower? Doesn't that mean it's likely in a different season with entirely different weather – perhaps more clouds and snow as well?

SHAP's KernelExplainer can receive any arbitrary black box predict function. It also makes assumptions about the input dimensions. Fortunately, we can change the input data before it permutes it, making it seem to the KernelExplainer like it's dealing with a tabular dataset. The arbitrary predict function doesn't have to simply call the model's predict function – it can change data both on the way in and on the way out!

Defining a strategy to get it to work with a multivariate time series model

To mimic likely past weather patterns based on the permutated input data, we could create a generative model or something to that effect. This strategy will help us generate a variety of past timesteps that fit the permutated timestep, as well as generate images for a specific class. Although this would likely lead to more accurate predictions, we won't use this strategy because it's incredibly time-consuming.

Instead, we will find the time series data that best suits the permutated input with existing examples from our `gen_all` generator. There are distance metrics we can use to find the one that is closest to the permutated input. However, we must place some guardrails because if the permutation is for a Saturday at 5 a.m. with a temperature of 27 degrees Celsius and 90 percent cloud coverage, the closest observation to this one could be on a Friday at 7a.m., but regardless of the weather traffic, it would be completely different. Therefore, we can implement a filter function that ensures that it only finds closest observations for the same `dow`, `is_holiday`, and `hr`. The filter function can also clean up the permutated sample to remove or modify anything nonsensical for the model, such as a continuous value for a categorical feature:

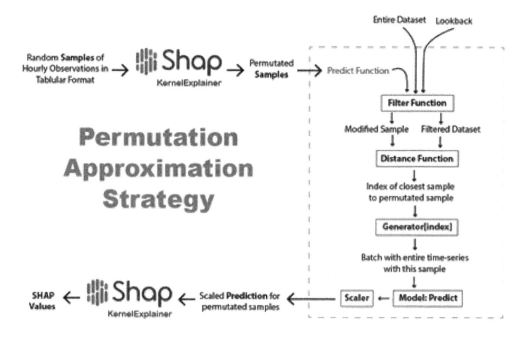

Figure 9.10 – Permutation approximation strategy

The preceding diagram depicts the rest of the process where it uses a distance function to find the closest observation to the modified permutated sample. This function returns the closest observation index, but the model can't predict on singular observations (or timesteps), so it requires its past hourly history up to the lookback window. For this reason, it retrieves the right batch from the generator and makes a prediction on that, but the predictions will be on a different scale, so they need to be inverse transformed with `y_scaler`. Once the predict function has iterated through all the samples and made predictions for it and rescaled them, it sends them back to the KernelExplainer, which outputs their SHAP values.

Laying the groundwork for the permutation approximation strategy

You can define a custom filter function (`filt_fn`). It takes a `pandas` DataFrame with the entire dataset (`X_df`) you want to filter from, as well as the permutated sample (`x`) for filtering and the length of the `lookback` window. The function can also modify the permutated sample. In this case, we have to do this because so many features of the model are discrete, but the permutation process makes them continuous. As we mentioned previously, all the filtering does is protect the distance function from finding a nonsensical closest sample to the permutated sample by limiting the options:

```python
def filt_fn(X_df, x, lookback):
    x_ = x.copy()
    x_[0] = round(x_[0])
    x_[1] = round(x_[1])
    x_[4] = round(x_[4])
    x_[5] = round(x_[5])
    if x_[1] < 0:
        x_[1] = 24 + x_[1]
        x_[0] = x_[0] - 1
    if x_[0] < 0:
        x_[0] = 7 + x_[0]
    X_filt_df = X_df[(X_df.index >= lookback) & (X_df.dow==x_[0]) & (X_df.hr==x_[1]) &
        (X_df.is_holiday==x_[5]) & (X_df.temp-5<=x_[2]) & (X_df.temp+5>=x_[2])]
    return X_filt_df, x_
```

If you refer to *Figure 9.10*, after the filter function, the next thing we ought to define is the distance function. We could use any standard distance function accepted by `scipy.spatial.distance.cdist`, such as "Euclidean," "cosine," or "Hamming." The problem with these standard distance functions is that they either work well with continuous or discrete variables but not both. We have both in this dataset!

Fortunately, some alternatives exist that can handle both, such as **Heterogeneous Euclidean-Overlap Metric (HEOM)** and **Heterogeneous Value Difference Metric (HVDM)**. Both methods apply different distance metrics, depending on the nature of the variable. HEOM uses a normalized Euclidean ($\sqrt{(a-b)^2}$) for continuous and, for discrete, "overlap" distance; that is, a distance of zero if the same and one otherwise.

HVDM is more complicated because, for continuous variables, it's the absolute distance between both values, divided by the standard deviation of the feature in question times four ($|a - b| / 4$), which is a great distance metric for handling outliers. For discrete variables, it uses a normalized **Value Difference Metric**, which is based on the difference between the conditional probability of both values.

Even though HVDM is better than HEOM for datasets with many continuous values, it is overkill in this case. Once the dataset has been filtered by day of week (dow) and hour (hr), the remaining discrete features are all binary, so "overlap" distance is ideal, and for the three remaining continuous features (temp, rain_1h, and cloud_coverage), Euclidean distance should suffice. distython has an HEOM distance method, and all it requires is a background dataset (X_df.values) and the indexes of the categorical features (cat_idxs). We can programmatically identify these features with an np.where command. If you want to verify that these are the right ones, run print(cat_idxs) in a cell. Only indexes 2, 3, and 4 should be omitted:

```
cat_idxs = np.where(traffic_df.drop(['traffic_volume'],\
                                      axis=1).dtypes !=
np.float64)[0]
heom_dist = HEOM(X_df.values, cat_idxs)
print(cat_idxs)
```

Now, we can create a lambda function that takes puts everything depicted in *Figure 9.10* together. It leverages a function called approx_predict_ts that takes care of the entire pipeline. It takes our filter function (filt_fn), distance function (heom_dist.heom), generator (gen_all), and fitted model (lstm_traffic_mdl), and chains them together, as described in *Figure 9.10*. It also scales the data with our scalers (X_scaler and y_scaler). Distance is computed on transformed features for higher accuracy, and the predictions are reversed transformed on the way out:

```
predict_fn = lambda X: mldatasets.\
    approx_predict_ts(X, X_df, gen_all, lstm_traffic_mdl,\
        dist_metric=heom_dist.heom, lookback=lookback,\
        filt_fn=filt_fn, X_scaler=X_scaler, y_scaler=y_scaler)
```

We can now use the prediction function with `KernelExplainer`, but it should be done on samples that are most representative of the construction crew's expected working conditions; that is, they plan to work May through October only, preferably on weekdays and low-traffic hours. To this end, let's create a DataFrame (`working_season_df`) that only includes these months and initializes a `KernelExplainer` with `predict_fn` and the k-means of the DataFrame as background data:

```
working_season_df =\
        traffic_df[lookback:].drop(['traffic_volume'], axis=1).
copy()
working_season_df =\
        working_season_df[(working_season_df.index.month >= 5)
&\
                (working_season_df.index.month <= 10)]
explainer = shap.KernelExplainer(predict_fn,\
                shap.kmeans(working_season_df.values, 10))
```

We can now produce SHAP values for a random set of observations of the `working_season_df` dataframe.

Computing the SHAP values

We will `sample` 48 observations from it. `KernelExplainer` is rather slow, especially when it's using our approximation method. To get an optimal global interpretation, it is best to use a high number of observations but also a high `nsamples`, which is the number of times we need to reevaluate the model when explaining each prediction. Unfortunately, having 50 of each would cause the explainer to take many hours to run, depending on your available compute, so we will use `nsamples=5`. You can look at SHAP's progress bar and adjust it accordingly. Once it's done, it will produce a feature importance `summary_plot` containing the SHAP values:

```
X_samp_df = working_season_df.sample(48, random_state=rand)
shap_values = explainer.shap_values(X_samp_df, nsamples=5)
shap.summary_plot(shap_values, X_samp_df)
```

The preceding code plots the summary shown in the following graph. Not surprisingly, `hr` and `dow` are the most important features, followed by some weather features. Strangely enough, temperature and rain don't seem to weigh in on the predictions, but late Spring through Fall may not be a significant factor. Or maybe more observations and a higher `nsample` will yield a better global interpretation:

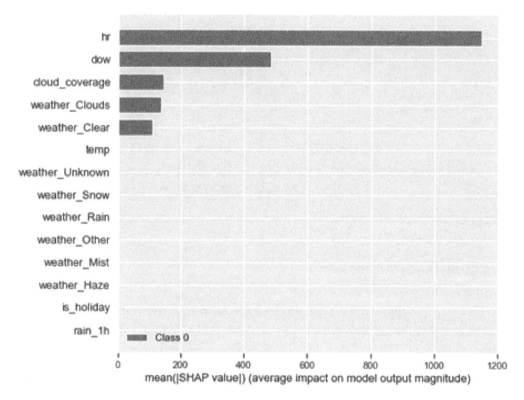

Figure 9.11 – SHAP summary plot based on the SHAP values produced by 48 sampled observations

We can do the same with the instances of interest we chose in the previous section for local interpretations. Let's iterate through all these datapoints. Then, we can produce a single `shap_values` but this time with `nsamples=60`, and then generate a `force_plot` for each one:

```
datapoints = [holiday_afternoon_s, peak_morning_s, hot_
saturday_s]
datapoint_labels = ['Holiday Afternoon', 'Peak Morning',\
                    'Hot Saturday']
for i in range(len(datapoints)):
  print(datapoint_labels[i])
```

```
shap_values_single = explainer.shap_values(datapoints[i],\
                                             nsamples=60)
shap.force_plot(explainer.expected_value, shap_values_
single[0],\
                datapoints[i], matplotlib=True)
plt.show()
```

The preceding code generates the plots shown in the following image. "Holiday afternoon" has the hour (hr=16) pushing toward a higher prediction, while the fact that it's a Monday (dow=0) and a holiday (is_holiday=1) is a driving force in the opposite direction. On the other hand, "Peak Morning" is mostly peak due to the hour (hr=8.0), but it has a high cloud_coverage, affirmative weather_Clouds, and yet no rain (rain_1h=0.0). Lastly, "Hot Saturday" has the day of week (dow=5) pushing for a lower value, but the abnormally high value is mostly due to it being midday and it having a collection of weather features, the most important of which is temp=29.42... (85°F):

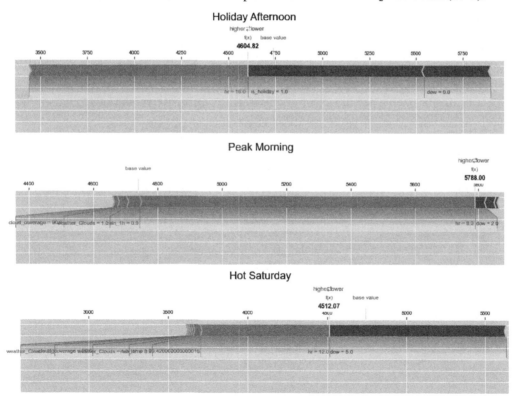

Figure 9.12 – Force plots generated with SHAP values using nsamples=60 for a Holiday Afternoon, Peak Morning, and Hot Saturday

With SHAP's game theory-based approach, we can gauge how many permutations for the existing observations marginally vary the predicted outcome across many possible coalitions of features. However, this approach can be very limiting because our background data's existing variance shapes our understanding of outcome variance.

In the real world, *variability is often determined by what is NOT represented in your data – but infinitesimally plausible.* For instance, reaching 25°C (77°F) before 5 a.m. in a Minneapolis summer is not a common occurrence, but with global warming, it could become frequent, so we would want to simulate how it could impact traffic patterns. Forecasting models are particularly prone to risk, so simulating is a crucial interpretation component to assess this uncertainty. A better understanding of uncertainty can yield more robust models or directly inform decisions. Next, we will discuss how we can produce simulations with sensitivity analysis methods.

Identifying influential features with factor prioritization

The **Morris Method** is one of several global sensitivity analysis methods that range from simpler **Fractional Factorial** to complicated **Monte Carlo Filtering**. Morris is somewhere in-between this spectrum, falling into two categories. It uses **one-at-a-time sampling**, which means that only one value changes between consecutive simulations. It's also **elementary effects** (**EE**), which means that it doesn't quantify the exact effect of a factor in a model but rather gauges its importance and relationship with other factors. By the way, **factor** is just another word for a feature or variable that's commonly used in applied statistics. To be consistent with the related theory, we will use this word in this and the next section.

Another property of Morris is that it's less computationally expensive than the variance-based methods we will study next. It can provide more insights than simpler and less costly methods such as regression-, derivative-, or factorial-based ones. It can't quantify effects precisely but can identify those with negligible or interaction effects, making it an ideal method for screening factors when the number of factors is low. Screening is also known as **factor prioritization** because it can prioritize your factors by how they are classified.

Computing Morris sensitivity indices

The Morris method derives a distribution of elementary effects that it associates with an individual factor. Each EE distribution has a mean (μ) and a standard deviation (σ). These two statistics are what helps map the factors into different classifications. The mean could be negative when the model is non-monotonic, so a Morris method variation adjusts for this with absolute values (μ *) so that it is more manageable to interpret. We will use this variation here.

Now, let's limit the scope of this problem to make it more manageable. The traffic uncertainties the construction crew will face will be ongoing from May to October, Monday to Friday, from 11 p.m. to 4 a.m. Therefore, we can take the working_season_df DataFrame and subset it further to produce a working hours one (working_hrs_df) that we can describe. We will include the 2.5%, 50%, and 97.5% percentiles to understand where the median and outliers lie:

```
working_hrs_df = working_season_df[(working_season_df.dow < 5)
& ((working_season_df.hr < 5) | (working_season_df.hr > 22))]
working_hrs_df.describe(percentiles=[.025,.5,.975]).transpose()
```

The preceding code produced the following table. We can use this table to extract the ranges we will use for our features in the simulation. Typically, we would use plausible values that have exceeded the existing maximums or minimums. For most models, any feature value can be increased or decreased beyond its known limits, and since the model learned a monotonic relationship, it can infer a realistic outcome. For instance, it might learn that rain beyond a certain point will increasingly diminish traffic. Then, say you want to simulate a severe flood with, say, 30 mm of rain per hour; it can accurately predict no traffic:

	count	mean	std	min	2.5%	50%	97.5%	max
dow	2232.000000	1.991935	1.415458	0.000000	0.000000	2.000000	4.000000	4.000000
hr	2232.000000	5.500000	7.933780	0.000000	0.000000	2.500000	23.000000	23.000000
temp	2232.000000	16.026438	5.380406	-2.570000	3.178750	16.935000	24.476750	30.458000
rain_1h	2232.000000	0.099628	0.603634	0.000000	0.000000	0.000000	1.451250	10.920000
cloud_coverage	2232.000000	29.178763	36.701417	0.000000	0.000000	1.000000	90.000000	100.000000
is_holiday	2232.000000	0.037634	0.190353	0.000000	0.000000	0.000000	1.000000	1.000000
weather_Clear	2232.000000	0.432348	0.495513	0.000000	0.000000	0.000000	1.000000	1.000000
weather_Clouds	2232.000000	0.207885	0.405885	0.000000	0.000000	0.000000	1.000000	1.000000
weather_Haze	2232.000000	0.010753	0.103159	0.000000	0.000000	0.000000	0.000000	1.000000
weather_Mist	2232.000000	0.104391	0.305835	0.000000	0.000000	0.000000	1.000000	1.000000
weather_Other	2232.000000	0.058244	0.234256	0.000000	0.000000	0.000000	1.000000	1.000000
weather_Rain	2232.000000	0.181452	0.385478	0.000000	0.000000	0.000000	1.000000	1.000000
weather_Snow	2232.000000	0.002240	0.047288	0.000000	0.000000	0.000000	0.000000	1.000000
weather_Unknown	2232.000000	0.002688	0.051789	0.000000	0.000000	0.000000	0.000000	1.000000

Figure 9.13 – Summary statistics for the period that the construction crew plans to work through

However, because we are using a prediction approximation method that samples from historical values, we are limited to how far we can push the boundaries outside of the known. For this reason, we will use the 2.5% and 97.5% percentile values as our limits. We should note that this is an important caveat for any findings, especially for features that could plausibly extend beyond these limits, such as temp, rain_1h, and cloud_coverage.

Another thing to note from the summary of *Figure 9.13* is that many weather-related binary features are very sparse. You can tell by their extremely low mean. Each factor that's added to the sensitivity analysis simulation slows it down, so we will only take the top three; that is, `weather_Clear`, `weather_Clouds`, and `weather_Rain`. These factors are specified along with the other six factors into a "problem" dictionary (`morris_problem`), which has their corresponding `names`, `bounds`, and `groups`. Now, `bounds` is critical because it denotes what ranges of values will be simulated for each factor. We will use $[0,4]$ (Monday – Friday) for dow and $[-1,4]$ (11p.m. – 4a.m.) for hr. The filter function automatically translates negative hours into hours from the day before so that -1 on a Tuesday is equivalent to 23 on a Monday. The rest of the bounds were informed by the percentiles. Note that `groups` all have factors in the same group, except for the three weather ones:

```python
morris_problem = {
  # There are nine variables
  'num_vars': 9,
  # These are their names
  'names': ['dow', 'hr', 'temp', 'rain_1h', 'cloud_coverage',\
            'is_holiday', 'weather_Clear', 'weather_Clouds',\
            'weather_Rain'],
  # Plausible ranges over which we'll move the variables
  'bounds': [[0, 4], # dow
             [-1, 4], # hr
             [3., 25.], # temp (C)
             [0., 1.5], # rain_1h
             [0., 90.], # cloud_coverage
             [0, 1], # is_holiday
             [0, 1], # weather_Clear
             [0, 1], # weather_Clouds
             [0, 1] # weather_Rain
            ],
  # Only weather is grouped together
  'groups': ['dow', 'hr', 'temp', 'rain_1h', 'cloud_coverage',\
             'is_holiday', 'weather', 'weather', 'weather']
}
```

Once the dictionary has been defined, we can generate Morris method samples with SALib's `sample` method. In addition to the dictionary, it takes a number of trajectories (`300`) and levels (`num_levels=4`). The method uses a grid with factors and levels to construct the trajectories for which inputs are randomly moved **one-at-a-time (OAT)**. What is important to heed here is that more levels add more resolution to this grid, potentially making for a better analysis. However, this can be very time-consuming. It's better to start with a ratio between the number of trajectories and levels of $25:1$ or higher. Then, you can decrease this ratio progressively. In other words, if you have enough compute, you can make `num_levels` match the number of trajectories, but if you have this much compute available, you could try `optimal_trajectories=True`. However, given that we have groups, `local_optimization` would have to be `False`. The output of `sample` is an array that is one column for each factor and $(G + 1) \times T$ rows (where G is the number of groups and T is the number of trajectories). We have seven groups and 300 trajectories, so `print` should output a shape of 2,400 rows and 9 columns:

```
morris_sample = ms.sample(morris_problem, 300,\
                          num_levels=4, seed=rand)
print(morris_sample.shape)
```

Given that the predict function will only work with 14 factors, we should modify the samples to fill the remaining five factors with zeroes. We use zeroes because that is the median value for these features. Medians are least likely to increase traffic, but you ought to tailor your default values on a case-by-case basis. If you recall our **Cardiovascular Disease (CVD)** example from *Chapter 2, Key Concepts of Interpretability*, the feature value that would increase CVD risk was sometimes the minimum or maximum.

The `np.hstack` function can concatenate the array horizontally so that three zero factors follow the samples for the first eight factors. Then, there's a lonely ninth sample factor corresponding to `weather_Rain`, followed by two zero factors. The resulting array should have the same numbers of rows as before but 14 columns:

```
morris_sample_mod = np.hstack((morris_sample[:,0:8],\
                     np.zeros((morris_sample.
shape[0],3)),\
                     morris_sample[:,8:9],\
                     np.zeros((morris_sample.
shape[0],2))))
print(morris_sample_mod.shape)
```

The numpy array known as `morris_sample_mod` now has the Morris samples in a shape that can be understood by our predict function. If this was a model that had been trained on a tabular dataset, we could just leverage the model's predict function. However, just as we did with SHAP, we have to use the approximation method. This time, we won't use `predict_fn` because we want to set one additional option, `progress_bar=True`, in `approx_predict_ts`. Everything else will remain the same. The progress bar will come in handy because this should take a while. Run the cell and take a coffee break:

```
morris_preds = mldatasets.\
    approx_predict_ts(morris_sample_mod, X_df, gen_all,\
                      lstm_traffic_mdl, filt_fn=filt_fn,\
                      dist_metric=heom_dist.heom,\
                      lookback=lookback,\
                      X_scaler=X_scaler, y_scaler=y_scaler,\
                      progress_bar=True)
```

To produce a sensitivity analysis with SALib's `analyze` function, all you need is your problem dictionary (`morris_problem`), the original Morris samples (`morris_sample`), and the predictions we just produced with those samples (`morris_preds`). There's an optional confidence interval level argument (`conf_level`), but the default of 95 is good. It uses resamples to compute this confidence level, which is 1,000 by default. This setting can also be changed with an optional `num_resamples` argument:

```
morris_sensitivities = ma.analyze(morris_problem,\
morris_sample,\
                         morris_preds, print_to_console=False)
```

Analyzing the elementary effects

`analyze` will return a dictionary with the Morris sensitivity indices, including the mean (μ) and standard deviation (σ) elementary effect, as well as the absolute value of the mean ($\mu *$). It's easier to appreciate these values in a tabular format so that we can place them into a DataFrame and sort and color-code them according to $\mu *$, which can be interpreted as the overall importance of the factor. σ, on the other hand, is how much the factor interacts with other ones:

```
morris_df = pd.DataFrame({'features':morris_
sensitivities['names'],\
                        'μ':morris_sensitivities['mu'],\
                        'μ*':morris_sensitivities['mu_star'],\
                        'σ':morris_sensitivities['sigma']})
```

```
morris_df.sort_values('µ*', ascending=False).style.\
                    background_gradient(cmap='plasma',
subset=['µ*'])
```

The preceding code outputs the DataFrame depicted in the following image. You can tell that `is_holiday` surprisingly becomes the second-most important factor although not by a huge margin, at least during the bounds specified in the problem definition (`morris_problem`). Another thing to note is that `weather` does have an absolute mean elementary effect but inconclusive interaction effects. Groups are challenging to assess, especially when they are sparse binary factors:

	features	µ	µ*	σ
1	hr	-429.300110	1455.506958	1544.544312
5	is_holiday	-345.794861	379.520477	588.769897
0	dow	130.311508	336.568451	554.439819
2	temp	62.087799	202.984299	422.309845
6	weather	nan	75.732839	nan
3	rain_1h	-2.807377	30.730101	113.262093
4	cloud_coverage	9.897467	17.152805	74.319984

Figure 9.14 – The Elementary Effects (EE) decomposition of the factors

The DataFrame in the preceding figure is not the best way to visualize the elementary effects. When there are not too many factors, it's easier to plot them. SALib comes with two plotting methods. The horizontal bar plot (`horizontal_bar_plot`) and covariance plot (`covariance_plot`) can be placed side by side. The covariance plot is excellent, but it doesn't annotate the areas it delineates. We will learn about these next. So, solely for instructional purposes, we will use `text` to place the annotations:

```
fig, (ax0, ax1) = plt.subplots(1,2, figsize=(12,8))
mp.horizontal_bar_plot(ax0, morris_sensitivities, {})
mp.covariance_plot(ax1, morris_sensitivities, {})
ax1.text(ax1.get_xlim()[1] * 0.45, ax1.get_ylim()[1] * 0.75,\
    'Non-linear and/or-monotonic',\
    horizontalalignment='center', color='gray')
ax1.text(ax1.get_xlim()[1] * 0.75, ax1.get_ylim()[1] * 0.5,\
                'Almost', horizontalalignment='center', color='gray')
ax1.text(ax1.get_xlim()[1] * 0.83, ax1.get_ylim()[1] * 0.2,\
    'Monotonic', horizontalalignment='center', color='gray')
```

```
ax1.text(ax1.get_xlim()[1] * 0.9, ax1.get_ylim()[1] * 0.025,
    'Linear', horizontalalignment='center', color='gray')
```

The preceding code produces the plots shown in the following figure. The bar plot on the left ranks the factors by μ *, while the lines sticking out of each bar signify their corresponding confidence bands. The covariance plot to the right is a scatter plot with μ * on the x-axis and σ on the y-axis. Therefore, the farther right the point is, the more important it is, while the further up it is in the plot, the more it interacts with other factors and becomes increasingly less monotonic. Naturally, this means that factors that don't interact much and are mostly monotonic ones comply with linear regression assumptions, such as linearity and multicollinearity. However, the spectrum between linear and non-linear or non-monotonic is determined diagonally by the ratio between σ and μ *:

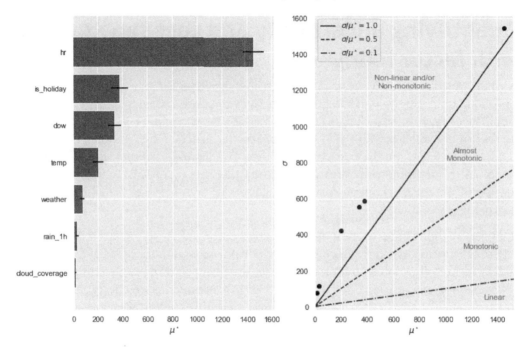

Figure 9.15 – A bar and covariance plot depicting the Elementary Effects (EE)

You can tell by the preceding covariance plot that all the factors are non-linear or non-monotonic. `hr` is by far the most important, with the following three (`is_holiday`, `dow`, and `temp`) clustered relatively nearby. The `weather` group is not on the plot because interactivity was inconclusive, yet `rain_1h` and `cloud_coverage` are more interactive than important on their own.

Elementary effects help us understand how to classify our factors in accordance with their effects on model outcomes. However, it's not a robust method to properly quantify their effects or those derived from factor interactions. For that, we would have to turn to a variance-based global method that uses a probabilistic framework to decompose the output's variance and trace it back to the inputs. Those methods include **Fourier Amplitude Sensitivity Test** (**FAST**) and Sobol. We will study the latter approach next.

Quantifying uncertainty and cost sensitivity with factor fixing

With the Morris indices, it became evident that all the factors are non-linear or non-monotonic. There's a high degree of interactivity between them – as expected! It should be no surprise that climate factors (`temp`, `rain_1h`, and `cloud_coverage`) are likely multicollinear with `hr`. There are also patterns to be found between `hr`, `is_holiday`, and `dow` and the target. Many of these factors most definitely don't have a monotonic relationship with the target. We know this already. For instance, traffic doesn't consistently increase as hours increase throughout the day. That's not the case between days of the week either!

However, we didn't know to what degree `is_holiday` and `temp` impacted the model, particularly during the crew's working hours, which was an important insight. That being said, factor prioritization with Morris indices is usually to be taken as a starting point or "first setting" because once you ascertain that there are interaction effects, it's best if you disentangle them. To this end, there's a "second setting" called **factor fixing**. We can quantify the variance and, by doing so, the uncertainty brought on by all the factors.

Only **variance-based methods** can quantify these effects in a statistically rigorous fashion. **Sobol Sensitivity Analysis** is one of these methods, which means that it decomposes the model's output variance into percentages and attributes it to the model's inputs and interactions. Like Morris, it has a sampling step, as well as a sensitivity index estimation step.

Unlike Morris, the sampling doesn't follow a series of levels but the input data's distribution. It uses a **quasi-Monte Carlo method**, where it samples points in hyperspace that follow the inputs' probability distributions. **Monte Carlo** methods are a family of algorithms that perform random sampling, often for optimization or simulation. They seek to cut corners on problems that would be impossible to solve with brute force or entirely deterministic approaches. Monte Carlo methods are common in sensitivity analysis precisely for this reason. Quasi-Monte Carlo methods have the same goal. However, they converge faster because they use a deterministic low-discrepancy sequence instead of using a pseudorandom one. The Sobol method uses the **Sobol sequence**, devised by the same mathematician. We will use another sampling scheme derived from Sobol's, called Saltelli's.

Once the samples have been produced, Monte Carlo estimators compute the variance-based sensitivity indices. These indices are capable of quantifying non-linear non-additive effects and second-order indices, which relate to the interaction between two factors. Morris can reveal interactivity in your model, but not precisely how it is manifested. Sobol can tell you what factors are interacting and to what degree.

Generating and predicting on Salteli samples

To begin a Sobol sensitivity analysis with `SALib`, we must first define a problem. We'll do the same as what we did with Morris. This time, we will reduce the factors because we realized that the `weather` grouping led to inconclusive results. We should include the least sparse of all weather factors; that is, `weather_Clear`. And since Sobol uses a probabilistic framework, there's no harm in expanding the bounds to their minimum and maximum values for `temp`,`rain_1h`, and `cloud_coverage`, as seen in *Figure 9.13*:

```
sobol_problem = {
  'num_vars': 7,
  'names': ['dow', 'hr', 'temp', 'rain_1h', 'cloud_coverage',\
            'is_holiday', 'weather_Clear'],
  'bounds': [[0, 4], # dow
            [-1, 4], # hr
            [-3., 31.], # temp (C)
            [0., 11.], # rain_1h
            [0., 100.], # cloud_coverage
            [0, 1], # is_holiday
            [0, 1] # weather_Clear
```

```
            ],
    'groups': None
  }
```

Generating the samples should look familiar too. The Saltelli `sample` function requires the following:

- A problem statement (`sobol_problem`)
- A number of samples to produce per factor (`300`)
- Second-order indices to compute (`calc_second_order=True`)

Given that we want the interactions, the output of `sample` is an array that has one column for each factor and $N \times (2F + 2)$ rows (where N is the number of samples and F is the number of factors). We have seven factors and 300 samples per factor, so `print` should output a shape of 4,800 rows and 7 columns. First, we will modify it, as we did previously, with `hstack` to add the 7 empty factors needed to make the predictions, resulting in 14 columns instead:

```
saltelli_sample = ss.sample(sobol_problem, 300,\
                        calc_second_order=True, seed=rand)
saltelli_sample_mod = np.hstack((saltelli_sample,\
                        np.zeros((saltelli_sample.
shape[0],7))))
print(saltelli_sample_mod.shape)
```

Now, let's predict on these samples. This should take a while, so it's coffee time once more:

```
saltelli_preds = mldatasets.\
    approx_predict_ts(saltelli_sample_mod, X_df, gen_all,\
                lstm_traffic_mdl, filt_fn=filt_fn,\
                dist_metric=heom_dist.heom, lookback=lookback,\
                X_scaler=X_scaler, y_scaler=y_scaler,\
                progress_bar=True)
```

Performing Sobol sensitivity analysis

For Sobol sensitivity analysis (`analyze`), all you need is a problem statement (`sobol_problem`) and the model outputs (`saltelli_preds`). But the predictions don't tell the story of uncertainty. Sure, there's variance in the predicted traffic, but that traffic is only a problem once it exceeds 1,500. Uncertainty is something you want to relate to risk or reward, costs or revenue, loss or profit – something tangible you can connect to your problem.

First, we must assess if there's any risk at all. To get an idea of whether the predicted traffic in the samples exceeded the no-construction threshold during the working hours, we can use `print(max(saltelli_preds[:,0]))`. The maximum traffic level should be somewhere in the neighborhood of 1,800-1,900, which means that there's at least some risk that the construction company will pay a fine. Instead of using the predictions (`saltelli_preds`) as the model's output, we can create a simple binary array with ones when it exceeded 1,500 and zero otherwise. We will call this `costs`, and then run the `analyze` function with it. Note that `calc_second_order=True` is also set here too. It will throw an error if `sample` and `analyze` don't have a consistent setting. Like with Morris, there's an optional confidence interval level argument (`conf_level`), but the default of 95 is good:

```
costs = np.where(saltelli_preds > 1500, 1,0)[:,0]
factor_fixing_sa = sa.analyze(sobol_problem, costs,\
                    calc_second_order=True, print_to_
console=False)
```

`analyze` will return a dictionary with the Sobol sensitivity indices, including the first-order (`S1`), second-order (`S2`), and total-order (`ST`) indices, as well as the total confidence bounds (`ST_conf`). The indices correspond to percentages, but the totals won't necessarily add up unless the model is additive. It's easier to appreciate these values in a tabular format so that we can place them into a DataFrame and sort and color-code them according to the total, which can be interpreted as the overall importance of the factor. However, we will leave the second-order indices out because they are two-dimensional and akin to a correlation plot:

```
sobol_df = pd.DataFrame({'features':sobol_problem['names'],\
                    '1st':factor_fixing_sa['S1'],\
                    'Total':factor_fixing_sa['ST'],\
                    'Total Conf':factor_fixing_sa['ST_conf'],\
                    'Mean of Input':saltelli_sample.mean(axis=0)
    [0:7]})
sobol_df.sort_values('Total', ascending=False).style.\
```

```
                    background_gradient(cmap='plasma',
    subset=['Total'])
```

The preceding code outputs the DataFrame depicted in the following image. You can tell that `temp` and `is_holiday` are in the top four, at least during the bounds specified in the problem definition (`sobol_problem`). Another thing to note is that `weather_Clear` does have more of an effect on its own, but `rain_1h` and `cloud_coverage` seem to have no effect on the potential cost:

	features	1st	Total	Total Conf	Mean of Input
1	hr	0.009185	0.886824	0.912979	1.495931
2	temp	0.006123	0.506757	0.660847	14.059766
0	dow	0.009185	0.380068	0.366337	1.995599
5	is_holiday	0.003062	0.380068	0.479628	0.498047
6	weather_Clear	-0.003062	0.126689	0.314201	0.499023
3	rain_1h	0.000000	0.000000	0.000000	5.511458
4	cloud_coverage	0.000000	0.000000	0.000000	50.024740

Figure 9.16 – Sobol global sensitivity indices for the seven factors

Something interesting about the first-order values is how low they are, suggesting that interactions account for most of the model output variance. We can easily produce a heatmap with second-order indices to corroborate this. It's the combination of these indices and the first-order ones that add up to the totals:

```
sns.heatmap(factor_fixing_sa['S2'], cmap='Blues',\
            xticklabels=sobol_problem['names'],\
            yticklabels=sobol_problem['names'])
```

The preceding code outputs the following heatmap:

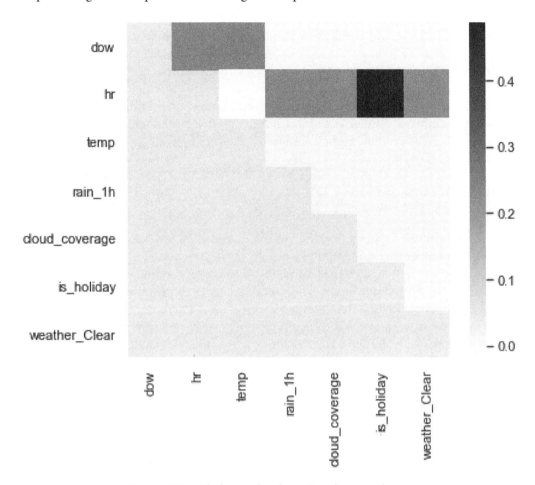

Figure 9.17 – Sobol second-order indices for seven factors

Here, you can tell that is_holiday and hr are the two factors that contribute the most to the output variance. hr has sizable interactions with all the factors except temp, but dow does so with hr and temp.

Incorporating a realistic cost function

Now, we can create a cost function that takes our inputs (`saltelli_sample`) and outputs (`saltelli_preds`) and computes how much the twin cities would fine the construction company, plus any additional costs the additional traffic could produce. It is better to do this if both the input and outputs are in the same array because we will need details from both to calculate the costs. We can use `hstack` to join the samples and their corresponding predictions, producing an array with eight columns (`saltelli_sample_preds`). We can then define a cost function that can compute the costs (`cost_fn`), given an array with these eight columns:

```
#Join input and outputs into a sample+prediction array
saltelli_sample_preds = np.hstack((saltelli_sample, saltelli_preds))
```

We know that the half-capacity threshold wasn't exceeded for any sample predictions, so we won't even bother to include the daily penalty in the function. Besides that, the fines are $15 per vehicle that exceeds the hourly no-construction threshold. In addition to these fines, to be able to leave on time, the construction company estimates additional costs: $1,500 in extra wages if the threshold is exceeded at 4 a.m. and $4,500 more on Fridays to speed up the move of their equipment because it can't stay on the highway shoulder during weekends. Once we have the cost function, we can iterate through the combined array (`saltelli_sample_preds`), calculating costs for each sample. List comprehension can do this efficiently:

```
#Define cost function
def cost_fn(x):
  cost = 0
  if x[7] > 1500:
    cost = (x[7] - 1500) * 15
    if round(x[1]) == 4:
      cost = cost + 1500
      if round(x[0]) == 4:
        cost = cost + 4500
  return cost
#Use list comprehension to compute costs for sample+prediction
array
costs2 = np.array([cost_fn(xi) for xi in saltelli_sample_preds])
```

```
#Print total fines for entire sample predictions
print(sum(costs2))
```

The `print` statement should output a cost somewhere between $110-130 thousand. But not to worry! The construction crew only plans to work about 180 days on-site per year and 5 hours each day, for a total of 900 hours. However, there are 4,800 samples, which means that there's over 5 years' worth of predicted costs due to excess traffic. In any case, the point of calculating these costs is to figure out how they relate to the model's inputs. More years' worth of samples means tighter confidence intervals.

We can now perform the analysis again but with `costs2`, and we can save the analysis into a `factor_fixing2_sa` dictionary. Lastly, we can produce a new sorted and color-coded DataFrame with this dictionary's values, as we did previously for *Figure 9.16*, which generates the output shown in the following figure:

```
factor_fixing2_sa = sa.analyze(sobol_problem, costs2,\
                   calc_second_order=True, print_to_
console=False)
```

As you can tell by the following image, once the actual costs have been factored in, `is_holiday` becomes the riskiest factor and `dow` becomes more important too, while the last three factors retain their positions from *Figure 9.16*:

	features	1st	Total	Total Conf	Mean of Input
5	is_holiday	0.000852	0.953684	3.509326	0.498047
1	hr	0.010101	0.748595	1.132665	1.495931
2	temp	0.000677	0.552892	0.843215	14.059766
0	dow	0.009874	0.514826	0.452778	1.995599
6	weather_Clear	-0.002776	0.121222	0.404481	0.499023
4	cloud_coverage	-0.000000	0.000000	0.000000	50.024740
3	rain_1h	-0.000000	0.000000	0.000000	5.511458

Figure 9.18 – Sobol global sensitivity indices for the seven factors using the realistic cost function

One thing that is hard to appreciate with a table is the confidence intervals of the sensitivity indices. For that, we can use a bar plot, but first, we must convert the entire dictionary into a DataFrame so that SALib's plotting function can plot it:

```
factor_fixing2_df = factor_fixing2_sa.to_df()
fig, (ax) = plt.subplots(1,1, figsize=(15, 7))
sp.plot(factor_fixing2_df[0], ax=ax)
```

The preceding code generates the following bar plot. The 95% confidence interval for is_holiday is much larger than for other important factors, which shouldn't be surprising considering that the model was trained with fewer instances of holidays (only 3% of days are holidays). Another interesting insight is how weather_Clear has negative first-order effects, so the positive total-order indices are entirely attributed to second-order ones, which expand the confidence interval:

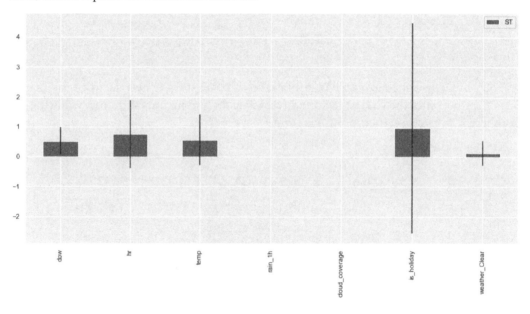

Figure 9.19 – Bar plot with the Sobol sensitivity total-order indices and their confidence intervals using a realistic cost function

To understand how, let's plot the heatmap shown in *Figure 9.17* again but this time using factor_fixing2_sa instead of factor_fixing_sa. The following heatmap should depict how the realistic costs reflect the interactions in the model:

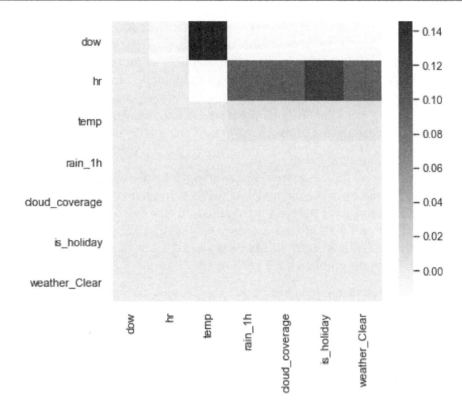

Figure 9.20 – Sobol second-order indices for seven factors while factoring a more realistic cost function

The preceding heatmap shows similar salient interactions to those in *Figure 9.17* but they're much more nuanced since there are more shades. It becomes evident that there's negligible interaction between `hr` and `temp`, and that there are smaller second-order effects between `dow` and `hr` than between `dow` and `temp`. Meanwhile, `hr` still interacts with every other factor except `temp`, but effects are less stark between `is_holiday` and the others.

Mission accomplished

The mission was to train a traffic prediction model and understand what factors create uncertainty and possibly increase costs for the construction company. We can conclude that a large portion of the potential $20,000/year in fines can be attributed to the `is_holiday` factor. Therefore, the construction company should rethink working holidays. There are only five or six holidays between May and October, and they could cost more because of the fines than working on a few Sundays instead. Of course, these conclusions are for the chosen model – which we can compare with other, better models. With this caveat, the mission was successful, but there's still a lot of room for improvement.

For instance, one thing that could be covered in further depth is the true impact of `temp` and `rain_1h`, and features for snow. Our prediction approximation method precluded Sobol from testing the effect of extreme weather events. If we modified the model to train on aggregated weather features at single timesteps and built in some guardrails, we could simulate weather extremes with Sobol. And the "third setting" of sensitivity analysis, known as factor mapping, could help pinpoint how exactly some factor values affect the predicted outcome, leading to a sturdier cost-benefit analysis, but we won't cover this in this chapter.

Throughout Part Two of this book, we explored an ecosystem of interpretation methods: global and local; model-specific and model-agnostic; permutation-based and sensitivity-based. There's no shortage of interpretation methods to choose from for any machine learning use case. However, it cannot be stressed enough that *NO method is perfect*. Still, they can complement each other to approximate a better understanding of your machine learning solution and the problem it aims to solve.

This chapter's focus on certainty in forecasting was designed to shed light on a particular problem in the machine learning community: overconfidence. *Chapter 1, Interpretation, Interpretability, Explainability, and Why It All Matters,* in the *Recognizing the business importance of interpretability* section, described the many biases that infest human decision-making. These biases are often fueled by overconfidence in domain knowledge or our models' impressive results. And these impressive results cloud us from grasping the limitations of our models as the public distrust of AI increases.

As we discussed in *Chapter 1, Interpretation, Interpretability, Explainability, and Why It All Matters,* machine learning is only meant to tackle *incomplete problems*. Otherwise, we might as well use deterministic and procedural programming like those found in closed-loop systems. An incomplete problem requires an incomplete solution, which should be optimized to solve as much of it as possible. Whether through gradient descent, least-squares estimation, or splitting and pruning a decision tree, machine learning doesn't produce a model that generalizes perfectly. That lack of completeness in machine learning is precisely why we need interpretation methods. In a nutshell: models learn from our data, and we can learn a lot from our models, but only if we interpret them!

Interpretability doesn't stop there, though. Model interpretations can drive decisions and help us understand model strengths and weaknesses. However, often, there are problems in the data or models themselves that can make them less interpretable. In Part Three of this book, we'll learn how to tune models and the training data for interpretability by reducing complexity, mitigating bias, placing guardrails, and enhancing reliability.

Statistician George E.P. Box famously quipped that *"all models are wrong, but some are useful."* Perhaps they aren't always wrong, but humility is required from machine learning practitioners to accept that even high-performance models should be subject to scrutiny and our assumptions about them. Uncertainty with machine learning models is expected and shouldn't be a source of shame or embarrassment. This leads us to another takeaway from this chapter: that uncertainty comes with ramifications, be it costs or profit lift, and that we can gauge these with sensitivity analysis.

Summary

After reading this chapter, you should understand how to assess a time series model's predictive performance, know how to perform local interpretations for them with integrated gradients, and know how to produce both local and global attributions with SHAP. You should also know how to leverage sensitivity analysis factor prioritization and factor fixing for any model.

In the next chapter, we will learn how to reduce complexity in a model and make it more interpretable with feature selection and engineering.

Dataset and image sources

- TomTom. (2019). Traffic Index: `https://www.tomtom.com/en_gb/traffic-index/ranking/?congestion=WORST,BAD,MODERATE`

- UCI Machine Learning Repository (2019). Metro Interstate Traffic Volume Data Set:`https://archive.ics.uci.edu/ml/datasets/Metro+Interstate+Traffic+Volume`

References

- Wilson, D.R., & Martinez, T. (1997). Improved Heterogeneous Distance Functions. J. Artif. Int. Res. `6-1. pp.1-34. https://arxiv.org/abs/cs/9701101`

- Morris, M. (1991). Factorial sampling plans for preliminary computational experiments. Quality Engineering, 37, 307-310. `https://doi.org/10.2307%2F1269043`

- Saltelli, A., Tarantola, S., Campolongo, F., & Ratto, M. (2007). Sensitivity analysis in practice: A guide to assessing scientific models. Chichester: John Wiley & Sons.

- Sobol, I.M. (2001), Global sensitivity indices for nonlinear mathematical models and their Monte Carlo estimates. MATH COMPUT SIMULAT,55(1–3),271-280 https://doi.org/10.1016/S0378-4754(00)00270-6

- Saltelli, A., P. Annoni, I. Azzini, F. Campolongo, M. Ratto, and S. Tarantola (2010). "Variance based sensitivity analysis of model output. Design and estimator for the total sensitivity index." Computer Physics Communications, 181(2):259-270. https://doi.org/10.1016/j.cpc.2009.09.018

Section 3: Tuning for Interpretability

In this section, you will comprehend how to mitigate the influence of bias in datasets and discover how to tune models for interpretability.

This section includes the following chapters:

- *Chapter 10, Feature Selection and Engineering for Interpretability*
- *Chapter 11, Bias Mitigation and Causal Inference Methods*
- *Chapter 12, Monotonic Constraints and Model Tuning for Interpretability*
- *Chapter 13, Adversarial Robustness*
- *Chapter 14, What's Next for Machine Learning Interpretability?*

10
Feature Selection and Engineering for Interpretability

In the first three chapters, we discussed how complexity hinders **machine learning** (**ML**) interpretability. There's a trade-off because you want some complexity to maximize predictive performance, yet not to the extent that you cannot rely on the model to satisfy the tenets of interpretability: fairness, accountability, and transparency. This chapter is the first of four focused on how to tune for interpretability. One of the easiest ways to improve interpretability is through feature selection. It has many benefits, such as faster training and making the model easier to interpret. But if these two reasons don't convince you, perhaps another one will.

A common misunderstanding is that complex models can self-select features and perform well nonetheless, so why even bother to select features? Yes, many model classes have mechanisms that can take care of useless features, but they aren't perfect. And the potential for overfitting increases with each one that remains. Overfitted models aren't reliable, even if they are more accurate. So, while employing model mechanisms such as regularization is still highly recommended to avoid overfitting, feature selection is the first step.

In this chapter, you will comprehend how irrelevant features adversely weigh on the outcome of a model and, thus, the importance of feature selection for model interpretability. Then, we will review filter-based feature selection methods such as **Spearman's correlation**, and learn about embedded methods such as **LASSO and Ridge regression**. Then, you will discover wrapper methods such as **sequential feature selection** and hybrid ones such as **recursive feature elimination** (**RFE**), as well as more advanced ones, such as **genetic algorithms** (**GAs**). Lastly, even though feature engineering is typically conducted before selection, there's value in exploring feature engineering for many reasons after the dust has settled and features have been selected.

These are the main topics we are going to cover in this chapter:

- Understanding the effect of irrelevant features
- Reviewing filter-based feature selection methods
- Exploring embedded feature selection methods
- Discovering wrapper, hybrid, and advanced feature selection methods
- Considering feature engineering

Technical requirements

This chapter's example uses the `mldatasets`, `pandas`, `numpy`, `scipy`, `mlxtend`, `genetic_selection`, `xgboost`, `sklearn`, `matplotlib`, and `seaborn` libraries. Instructions on how to install all of these libraries are in the *Preface*.

The GitHub code for this chapter is located here: `https://github.com/PacktPublishing/Interpretable-Machine-Learning-with-Python/tree/master/Chapter10/`.

The mission

It has been estimated that there are over 10 million non-profits worldwide, and while a large portion of them have public funding, most of them depend mostly on private donors, both corporate and individual, to continue operations. As such, fundraising is mission-critical and carried out throughout the year.

Year over year, donation revenue has grown but there are several problems non-profits face: donor interests evolve, so a charity popular one year might be forgotten the next; competition is fierce between non-profits; and demographics are shifting. In the United States, the average donor only gives two charitable gifts per year and is over 64 years old. Identifying potential donors is challenging and campaigns to reach them can be expensive.

A National Veterans Organization non-profit arm has a large mailing list of about 190,000 past donors and would like to send a special mailer to ask for donations. However, even with a special bulk discount rate, it costs them $0.68 per address. This adds up to over $130,000. They only have a marketing budget of $35,000. Given that they have made this a high priority, they are willing to extend the budget but only if the **return on investment (ROI)** is high enough to justify the additional cost.

To minimize the use of their limited budget, instead of mass mailing, they'd like to try direct mailing, which aims to identify potential donors using what is already known, such as past donations, geographic location, and demographic data. They will reach other donors via email instead, which is much cheaper, costing no more than $1,000/month for their entire list. They hope this hybrid marketing plan will yield better results. They also recognize that high-value donors respond better to personalized paper mailers, while smaller donors respond better to email anyway.

No more than six percent of the mailing list donates at any given campaign. Using ML to predict human behavior is by no means an easy task, especially when it's so imbalanced. Nevertheless, success is not measured by the highest predictive accuracy but by profit lift. In other words, the direct mailing model evaluated on the test dataset should produce more profit than if they mass-mailed the entire dataset.

They have sought your assistance to use ML to produce a model that identifies the most probable donors, but also in a way that *guarantees* an ROI. Note that the model must be reliable in producing an ROI.

You received the dataset from the non-profit, which is more or less evenly split between train and test. If you send the mailer to absolutely everybody in the test dataset, you make a profit of $11,173, but if you manage somehow to identify only those that will donate, the maximum yield of $73,136 will be attained. Your goal is to achieve a high-profit lift and reasonable ROI. When the campaign runs, it will identify most probably donors for the entire mailing list, and they hope to spend not much more than $35,000 in total. However, the dataset has 435 columns, and some simple statistical tests and modeling exercises show that the data is too noisy to identify the potential donors' reliability because of overfitting.

The approach

You've decided to first fit a base model with all the features and assess it at different levels of complexity to understand how having more features increases the propensity to overfit. Then, you employ a series of feature selection methods ranging from simple filter-based methods to the most advanced ones to determine which one achieves the profitability and reliability goals sought after by the client. Lastly, once a list of final features has been selected, at this stage, feature engineering can be considered to enhance model interpretability.

Given the cost-sensitive nature of the problem, thresholds are important to optimize the profit lift. We will get into the role of thresholds later on, but one significant effect is that even though this is a classification problem, it is best to use regression models, and then use predictions to classify so that there's only one threshold to tune. That is, for classification models, you would need a threshold for the label, say those that donated over $1, and then another one for probabilities predicted. On the other hand, regression predicts the donation, and the threshold can be optimized based on that.

The preparations

You will find the code for this example here: `https://github.com/PacktPublishing/Interpretable-Machine-Learning-with-Python/tree/master/Chapter10/Mailer.ipynb`.

Loading the libraries

To run this example, you need to install the following libraries:

- `mldatasets` to load the dataset
- `pandas`, `numpy`, and `scipy` to manipulate it
- `mlxtend`, `genetic_selection`, `xgboost`, and `sklearn` (scikit-learn) to fit the models
- `matplotlib` and `seaborn` to create and visualize the interpretations

To load the libraries, use the following code block:

```
import math
import os
import mldatasets
import pandas as pd
import numpy as np
```

```
import timeit
from tqdm.notebook import tqdm
from sklearn.feature_selection import VarianceThreshold,\
                                      mutual_info_classif,
SelectKBest
from sklearn.feature_selection import SelectFromModel
from sklearn.linear_model import LogisticRegression,
LassoCV, LassoLarsCV, LassoLarsIC
from mlxtend.feature_selection import SequentialFeatureSelector
from sklearn.feature_selection import RFECV
from sklearn.decomposition import PCA import shap
from genetic_selection import GeneticSelectionCV
from scipy.stats import rankdata
from sklearn.discriminant_analysis import
LinearDiscriminantAnalysis
from sklearn.ensemble import ExtraTreesRegressor,\
RandomForestRegressor
import xgboost as xgb
import matplotlib.pyplot as plt
import seaborn as sns
```

Next, we will load and prepare the dataset.

Understanding and preparing the data

We load the data like this into two dataframes (X_train, X_test) with the features and two NumPy arrays with corresponding labels (y_train, y_test). Please note that these dataframes have already been previously prepared for us to remove sparse or unnecessary features, treat missing values, and encode categorical features:

```
X_train, X_test, y_train, y_test =\
                    mldatasets.load("nonprofit-mailer",\
prepare=True)
y_train = y_train.squeeze()
y_test = y_test.squeeze()
```

All features are numeric with no missing values and categorical features have already been one-hot encoded for us. Between both train and test mailing lists, there should be over 191,500 records and 435 features. You can check this is the case like this:

```
print(X_train.shape)
print(y_train.shape)
print(X_test.shape)
print(y_test.shape)
```

The preceding code should output the following:

```
(95485, 435)
(95485,)
(96017, 435)
(96017,)
```

Next we can verify that the test labels have the right amount of donators (test_donators), donations (test_donations), and profit ranges (test_min_profit, test_max_profit). We can print these, and then do the same for the training dataset:

```
var_cost = 0.68
y_test_donators = y_test[y_test > 0]
test_donators = len(y_test_donators)
test_donations = sum(y_test_donators)
test_min_profit = test_donations - (len(y_test)*var_cost)
test_max_profit = test_donations - (test_donators*var_cost)
print('%s test donators totaling $%.0f (min profit: $%.0f,
max profit: $%.0f)' %\
    (test_donators, test_donations, test_min_profit,\
    test_max_profit))
y_train_donators = y_train[y_train > 0]
train_donators = len(y_train_donators)
train_donations = sum(y_train_donators)
train_min_profit = train_donations -
(len(y_train)*var_cost)
train_max_profit = train_donations -
(train_donators*var_cost)
print('%s train donators totaling $%.0f (min profit: $%.0f,
max profit: $%.0f)' %\
```

```
    (train_donators, train_donations, train_min_profit, \
    train_max_profit))
```

The preceding code should output the following:

```
4894 test donators totaling $76464 (min profit: $11173,
maxprofit: $73136)
```

```
4812 train donators totaling $75113 (min profit: $10183, max
profit: $71841)
```

Indeed, if the non-profit mass-mailed to everyone on the test mailing list, they'd make about $11,000 profit but would have to go grossly over budget to achieve this. The non-profit recognizes that making the max profit by identifying and targetting only donors is nearly an impossible feat. Therefore, they would be content with producing a model that reliably can yield more than the min profit but with a smaller cost, preferably under budget.

Understanding the effect of irrelevant features

Feature selection is also known as **variable or attribute selection**. It is the method by which you can automatically or manually select a subset of specific features useful to the construction of ML models.

It's not necessarily true that more features lead to better models. Irrelevant features can impact the learning process, leading to overfitting. Therefore, we need some strategies to remove any features that might adversely affect learning. Some of the advantages of selecting a smaller subset of features include the following:

- *It's easier to understand simpler models*: For instance, feature importance for a model that uses 15 variables is much easier to grasp than one that uses 150 variables.

- *Shorter training time*: Reducing the number of variables decreases the cost of computing, speeds up model training, and perhaps most notably, simpler models have quicker inference times.

- *Improved generalization by reducing overfitting*: Sometimes, with little prediction value, many of the variables are just noise. The ML model, however, learns from this noise and triggers overfitting while minimizing generalization simultaneously. We may significantly enhance the generalization of ML models by removing these irrelevant noisy features.

- *Variable redundancy*: It is common for datasets to have collinear features, which could mean they are redundant. In cases like these, as long as no significant information is lost, we can retain only one variable and delete others.

Now, we will fit some models to demonstrate the effect of too many features.

Creating a base model

Let's create a base model for our mailing list dataset to see how this plays out. But first, let's set our random numbers for reproducibility:

```
rand = 9
os.environ['PYTHONHASHSEED']=str(rand)
np.random.seed(rand)
```

We will use XGBoost's **Random Forest (RF)** regressor (XGBRFRegressor) throughout this chapter. It's just like scikit-learn's but faster because it uses second-order approximations of the objective function. It also has more options, such as setting the learning rate and monotonic constraints, examined in *Chapter 12, Monotonic Constraints and Model Tuning for Interpretability*. We initialize XGBRFRegressor with a max_depth value of 4 and always use 200 estimators for consistency. Then, we fit it with our training data. We will use timeit to measure how long it takes, which we save in a variable (baseline_time) for later reference:

```
stime = timeit.default_timer()
reg_mdl = xgb.XGBRFRegressor(max_depth=4,\
n_estimators=200, seed=rand)
fitted_mdl = reg_mdl.fit(X_train, y_train)
etime = timeit.default_timer()
baseline_time = etime-stime
```

Now that we have a base model, let's evaluate it.

Evaluating the model

Next, let's create a dictionary (`reg_mdls`) to house all the models we will fit in this chapter to test which feature subsets produce the best models. Here, we can evaluate the RF model with all the features and a `max_depth` value of 4 (`rf_4_all`) using `evaluate_reg_mdl`. It will make a summary and a scatter plot with a regression line:

```
reg_mdls = {}
reg_mdls['rf_4_all'] = mldatasets.evaluate_reg_mdl(fitted_mdl,\
                            X_train, X_test, y_train, y_test,
    plot_regplot=True, ret_eval_dict=True)
```

The preceding code produces the metrics and plot shown in *Figure 10.1*:

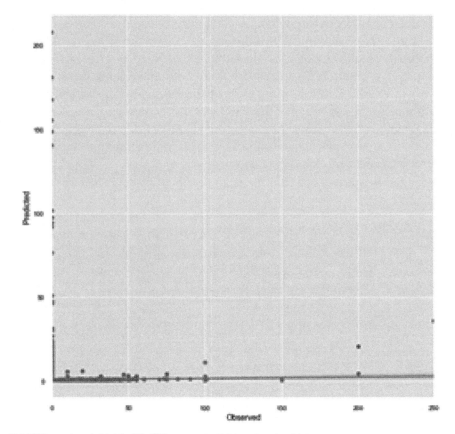

RMSE_train: 4.3210 RMSE_test: 4.6359 r2: -0.1084

Figure 10.1 – Base model predictive performance

For a plot like the one in *Figure 10.1*, usually a diagonal line is expected, so one glance at this plot would tell you that the model is useless. Also, the RMSEs may not seem bad but in the context of such a lopsided problem, they are dismal. Consider this: only 5% of the list makes a donation, and only 20% of those are over $20, so an average error of $4.3 − $4.6 of is enormous.

So, is this model useless? The answer lies in what thresholds we use to classify with it. Let's start by defining an array of thresholds (`threshs`), ranging from $0.40 to $25. We start spacing these out by a cent until it reaches $1, then by 10 cents until it reaches $3, and after that spaced by $1:

```
threshs = np.hstack([np.linspace(0.40,1,61),
np.linspace(1.1,3,20), np.linspace(4,25,22)])
```

There's a function in `mldatasets` that can compute profit at every threshold (`profits_by_thresh`). All it needs is the actual (`y_test`) and predicted labels, followed by the thresholds (`threshs`), the variable cost (`var_costs`), and the `min_profit` required. It produces a `pandas` dataframe with the revenue, costs, profit, and ROI for every threshold, as long as profit is above the `min_profit`. Remember, we had set this minimum at the beginning of the chapter as $11,173 because it makes no sense to target donators under this amount. After we generate these profit dataframes for the test and train datasets, we can place the maximum, and minimum amounts in the model's dictionary for later use. And then, we employ `compare_df_plots` to plot the costs, profits, and ROI ratio for test and train for every threshold where it exceeded the profit minimum:

```
y_formatter = plt.FuncFormatter(lambda x, loc:\
"${:,}K".format(x/1000))
profits_test = mldatasets.profits_by_thresh(y_test,\
                    reg_mdls['rf_4_all']['preds_test'],
threshs, var_costs=var_cost,\
min_profit=test_min_profit)
profits_train = mldatasets.profits_by_thresh(y_train,\
                    reg_mdls['rf_4_all']['preds_train'],
threshs, var_costs=var_cost,\ min_profit=train_min_profit)
```

```
reg_mdls['rf_4_all']['max_profit_train'] =\
                                    profits_train.profit.max()
reg_mdls['rf_4_all']['max_profit_test'] = \
profits_test.profit.max()
reg_mdls['rf_4_all']['max_roi'] = profits_test.roi.max()
reg_mdls['rf_4_all']['min_costs'] = \
profits_test.costs.min()
reg_mdls['rf_4_all']['profits_train'] = profits_train
reg_mdls['rf_4_all']['profits_test'] = profits_test
mldatasets.compare_df_plots(\
                profits_test[['costs', 'profit', 'roi']],\
                profits_train[['costs', 'profit', 'roi']],\
                'Test', 'Train', y_formatter=y_formatter,\
                x_label='Threshold',\
plot_args={'secondary_y':'roi'})
```

The preceding snippet generates the plots in *Figure 10.2*. You can tell that **Test** and **Train** are almost identical. Costs decrease steadily at a high rate and profit at a lower rate, while ROI increases steadily. However, some differences exist, such as ROI, which become a bit higher eventually, and although viable thresholds start at the same point, **Train** does end at a different threshold. It turns out the model can turn a profit, so despite the appearances of the plot in *Figure 10.1*, the model is far from useless:

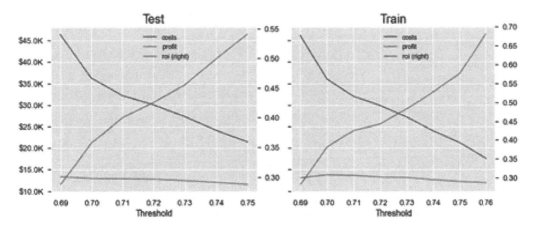

Figure 10.2 – Comparison between profit, costs, and ROI for the test and train datasets for the base
model across thresholds

The difference in RMSEs for the train and test sets didn't lie. The model did not overfit. The main reason for this is that we used relatively shallow trees by setting our `max_depth` value at 4. We can easily see this effect of using shallow trees by computing how many features had a `feature_importances_` value of over 0:

```
reg_mdls['rf_4_all']['num_feat'] =\
        sum(reg_mdls['rf_4_all']['fitted'].feature_importances_
> 0)
print(reg_mdls['rf_4_all']['num_feat'])
```

The preceding code outputs 160. In other words, only 160 were used out of 435—there are only so many features that can be accommodated into such a shallow tree! Naturally, this leads to lowering overfitting, but at the same time, the choice of features with measures of impurity over a random selection of features is not necessarily the most optimal.

Training the base model at different max depths

So, what happens if we make the trees deeper? Let's repeat all the steps we did for the shallow one but for max depths between 5 and 12:

```
for depth in tqdm(range(5, 13)):
  mdlname = 'rf_'+str(depth)+'_all'
  stime = timeit.default_timer()
  reg_mdl = xgb.XGBRFRegressor(max_depth=depth,\
n_estimators=200, seed=rand)
  fitted_mdl = reg_mdl.fit(X_train, y_train)
  etime = timeit.default_timer()
  reg_mdls[mdlname] =\
mldatasets.evaluate_reg_mdl(fitted_mdl,\
                            X_train, X_test, y_train,
y_test, plot_regplot=False, show_summary=False,\
                            ret_eval_dict=True)
  reg_mdls[mdlname]['speed'] = (etime-stime)/baseline_time
  reg_mdls[mdlname]['depth'] = depth
  reg_mdls[mdlname]['fs'] = 'all'
```

```
profits_test = mldatasets.profits_by_thresh(y_test,\
                      reg_mdls[mdlname]['preds_test'],
threshs, var_costs=var_cost,\
min_profit=test_min_profit)
 profits_train = mldatasets.profits_by_thresh(y_train,
                      reg_mdls[mdlname]['preds_train'],\
threshs, var_costs=var_cost,\
min_profit=train_min_profit)
 reg_mdls[mdlname]['max_profit_train'] =\
profits_train.profit.max()
 reg_mdls[mdlname]['max_profit_test'] =\
profits_test.profit.max()
 reg_mdls[mdlname]['max_roi'] = profits_test.roi.max()
 reg_mdls[mdlname]['min_costs'] = profits_test.costs.min()
 reg_mdls[mdlname]['profits_train'] = profits_train
 reg_mdls[mdlname]['profits_test'] = profits_test
 reg_mdls[mdlname]['total_feat'] =\
          reg_mdls[mdlname]['fitted'].feature_importances_.
shape[0]
 reg_mdls[mdlname]['num_feat'] =\
          sum(reg_mdls[mdlname]['fitted'].feature_importances_
> 0)
```

Now, let's plot the details in the profits dataframes for the "deepest" model (with a max depth of 12) as we did before with `compare_df_plots`, producing *Figure 10.3*:

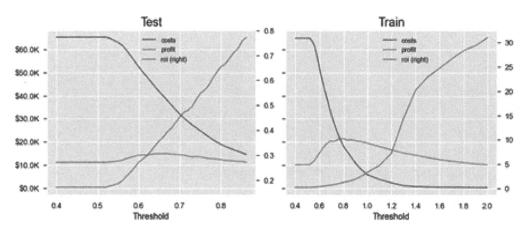

Figure 10.3 – Comparison between profit, costs, and ROI for the test and train datasets for a "deep" base model across thresholds

See how different **Test** and **Train** are this time in *Figure 10.3*. **Test** reaches a max of about $15,000 and **Train** exceeds $20,000. **Train**'s costs dramatically fall, making the ROI orders of magnitude much higher than **Test**. Also, the ranges of thresholds are much different. Why is this a problem, you ask? If we had to guess what threshold to use to pick who to target in the next mailer, the optimal for **Train** is higher than for **Test**—meaning that by using an overfit model, we could miss the mark and underperform in unseen data.

Next, let's convert our model dictionary (`reg_mdls`) into a dataframe and extract some details from it. Then, we can sort it by depth, color-code it, and output it:

```
reg_metrics_df = pd.DataFrame.from_dict(reg_mdls, 'index')\
                  [['depth', 'fs', 'rmse_train',
'rmse_test', 'max_profit_train',\
'max_profit_test', 'max_roi', 'min_costs', 'speed',
'num_feat']]
with pd.option_context('display.precision', 2):
  html = reg_metrics_df.sort_values(by='depth',\
                              ascending=False).style.\
        background_gradient(cmap='plasma', low=0.3,
high=1, subset=['rmse_train', 'rmse_test']).\
```

```
        background_gradient(cmap='viridis', low=1,
high=0.3, subset=['max_profit_train',\
'max_profit_test'])
html
```

The preceding snippet outputs the dataframe shown in *Figure 10.4*. Something that should be immediately visible is how RMSE train and RMSE test are inverses. One decreases dramatically, and another increases slightly as depth increases. The same can be said for profit. ROI tends to increase with depth and training speed and the number of features used as well:

	depth	fs	rmse_train	rmse_test	max_profit_train	max_profit_test	max_roi	min_costs	speed	num_feat
rf_12_all	12	all	3.94	4.69	21521.98	14932.84	0.77	14532.28	2.89	415
rf_11_all	11	all	3.99	4.69	19904.00	15141.86	0.76	14928.04	2.73	398
rf_10_all	10	all	4.05	4.68	18603.92	14987.06	0.78	14396.28	2.43	383
rf_9_all	9	all	4.10	4.68	17453.14	14777.74	0.80	13997.12	2.19	346
rf_8_all	8	all	4.14	4.67	16439.72	14563.04	0.73	15308.84	1.94	315
rf_7_all	7	all	4.18	4.66	15435.32	14187.62	0.66	17164.56	1.71	277
rf_6_all	6	all	4.23	4.65	14651.12	13845.27	0.59	19305.20	1.41	240
rf_5_all	5	all	4.27	4.64	14242.32	13752.13	0.59	19199.12	1.22	201
rf_4_all	4	all	4.32	4.64	13715.90	13261.88	0.53	22392.40	1.00	160

Figure 10.4 – Comparing metrics for all base RF models with different depths

You could be tempted to use `rf_11_all` with the highest profitability, but it will be risky to use it! A common misunderstanding is that black-box models can effectively cut through any amount of irrelevant features. While it will often be able to find something of value and make the most out of it, too many features will hinder its reliability by overfitting with more ease. Fortunately, there is a sweet spot where you can reach high profitability with minimal overfitting, but to get there, you have to reduce the number of features first!

Reviewing filter-based feature selection methods

Filter-based methods independently pick out features from a dataset without employing any ML. These methods depend only on the variables' characteristics and are relatively effective, computationally inexpensive, and quick to perform. Therefore, being the low-hanging fruit of feature selection methods, they are usually the first step in any feature selection pipeline.

Two kinds of filter-based methods exist:

- **Univariate**: Individually and independently of the feature space, they evaluate and rate a single feature at a time. One problem that can occur with univariate methods is that they may filter out too much since they don't take into consideration the relationship between features.

- **Multivariate**: These take into account the entire feature space and how features within interact with each other.

Overall, for the removal of obsolete, redundant, constant, duplicated, and uncorrelated features, filter methods are very strong. However, by not accounting for complex, non-linear, non-monotonic correlations and interactions that only ML models can find, they aren't effective whenever these relationships are prominent in the data.

We will review three categories of filter-based methods:

- Basic
- Correlation
- Ranking

We will explain them further in their own sections.

Basic filter-based methods

We employ **basic filter methods** in the data preparation stage, specifically, the data cleaning stage, before any modeling. The reason for this is there's a low risk of taking feature selection decisions that would adversely impact models. They involve common-sense operations such as removing features that carry no information or duplicate it.

Constant features with a variance threshold

Constant features don't change in the training dataset and, therefore, carry no
information, and the model can't learn from them. We can use a univariate method called
`VarianceThreshold`, which filters out features that are low-variance. We will use
a threshold of zero because we want to filter out only features with **zero variance**—in
other words, constant. It only works with numeric features, so we must first identify which
features are numeric and which are categorical. Once we fit the method on the numeric
columns, `get_support()` returns the list of features that aren't constant, and we can
use set algebra to return only the constant features (`num_const_cols`):

```
num_cols_l = X_train.select_dtypes([np.number]).columns
cat_cols_l = X_train.select_dtypes([np.bool,
np.object]).columns
num_const = VarianceThreshold(threshold=0)
num_const.fit(X_train[num_cols_l])
num_const_cols = list(set(X_train[num_cols_l].columns) -\
                           set(num_cols_l[num_const.get_
support()]))
```

The preceding snippet produced a list of constant numeric features, but how about
categorical features? Categorical features would only have one category or unique value.
You can easily check this by applying the `nunique()` function on categorical features.
It will return a `pandas` Series, and then a lambda function can filter out only those with
one unique value. Then, `.index.tolist()` returns the name of the features as a list.
Now, you just join both lists of constant features and voilá! You have all constants (`all_
const_cols`). You can print them; there should be three:

```
cat_const_cols = X_train[cat_cols_l].nunique()[lambda x:\
                                      x<2].index.
tolist()
all_const_cols = num_const_cols + cat_const_cols
print(all_const_cols)
```

In most cases, removing constant features isn't good enough. A redundant feature might
be almost constant or **quasi-constant**.

Quasi-constant features with Value-Counts

Quasi-constant features are almost entirely the same value. Unlike constant filtering, using a variance threshold won't work because high variance and quasi-constantness aren't mutually exclusive. Instead, we will iterate all features and get `value_counts()`, which returns the number of rows for each value. Then, divide these counts by the total number of rows to get a percentage and sort by the highest. If the top value is higher than the predetermined threshold (`thresh`), we append it to a list of quasi-constant columns (`quasi_const_cols`). Please note that choosing this threshold must be done with a lot of care and understanding of the problem. For instance, in this case, we know that it's lopsided because only 5% donate, most of which donate a low amount, so even a tiny percentage of a feature might make an impact, which is why our threshold is so high at 99.9%:

```
thresh = 0.999
quasi_const_cols = []
num_rows = X_train.shape[0]
for col in tqdm(X_train.columns):
  top_val = (X_train[col].value_counts() /
                  num_rows).sort_values(ascending=False).
values[0]
  if top_val >= thresh:
   quasi_const_cols.append(col)
print(quasi_const_cols)
```

The preceding code should have printed five features, which include the three that were previously obtained. Next, we will deal with another form of irrelevant features: duplicates!

Duplicating features

Usually, when you discuss duplicates with data, you immediately think of duplicate rows, but **duplicate columns** are also problematic. You can find them just as you would find duplicate rows with the pandas `duplicated()` function, except you would transpose the dataframe first inversing columns and rows:

```
X_train_transposed = X_train.T
dup_cols =\
  X_train_transposed[X_train_transposed.duplicated()].index.
tolist()
print(dup_cols)
```

The preceding snippet outputs a list with the two duplicated rows.

Removing unnecessary features

Unlike other feature selection methods, which you should test with models, you can apply basic filter-based feature selection methods right away by removing the features you deemed useless. But just in case, it's good practice to make a copy of the original data. Please note that we don't include constant columns (`all_constant_cols`) in the columns we are to drop (`drop_cols`) because the quasi-constant ones already include them:

```
X_train_orig = X_train.copy()
X_test_orig = X_test.copy()
drop_cols = quasi_const_cols + dup_cols
X_train.drop(labels=drop_cols, axis=1, inplace=True)
X_test.drop(labels=drop_cols, axis=1, inplace=True)
```

Next, we will explore multivariate filter-based methods on the remaining features.

Correlation filter-based methods

Correlation filter-based methods quantify the strength of the relationship between two features. It is useful for feature selection because we might want to filter out extremely correlated features or those that aren't correlated with others at all. Either way, it is a multivariate feature selection method—bivariate to be precise.

But first, we ought to choose a correlation method:

- **Pearson's correlation coefficient**: Measures how linearly correlated two features are between -1 (negative) and 1 (positive) with 0 meaning no linear correlation. Like linear regression, it assumes linearity, normality, and homoscedasticity.

- **Spearman's rank correlation coefficient**: Measures the strength of monotonicity of two features regardless of whether they are linearly related or not. It also measured between -1 and 1 with 0 meaning no monotonic correlation. It makes no distribution assumptions and can work with both continuous and discrete features. However, its weakness is with non-monotonic relationships.

- **Kendall's tau correlation coefficient**: Measures the ordinal association between features. It also ranges between -1 and 1, but they mean low and high, respectively. It's useful with discrete features.

The dataset is a mix of continuous and discrete, and we cannot make any linear assumptions about it, so spearman is the right choice. All three can be used with the pandas corr function though:

```
corrs = X_train.corr(method='spearman')
print(corrs.shape)
```

The preceding code should output the shape of the correlation matrix, which is (428, 428). This dimension makes sense because there are 428 features left, and each feature has a relationship with 428 features, including itself.

We can now look for features to remove in the correlation matrix (corrs). Note that to do so, we must establish thresholds. For instance, we can say that an extremely correlated feature has an absolute value coefficient over 0.99 and less than 0.15 for an uncorrelated feature. With these thresholds in mind, we can find features that are correlated to only one feature and extremely correlated to more than one feature. Why one feature? Because the diagonals in a correlation matrix are always 1 because a feature is always perfectly correlated with itself. The lambda functions in the following code make sure we are accounting for this:

```
extcorr_cols = (abs(corrs) > 0.99).sum(axis=1)[lambda x:\
                                        x>1].index.
tolist()
print(extcorr_cols)
uncorr_cols = (abs(corrs) > 0.15).sum(axis=1)[lambda x:\
                                        x==1].index.
tolist()
print(uncorr_cols)
```

The preceding code outputs the two lists as follows:

```
['MAJOR', 'HHAGE1', 'HHAGE3', 'HHN3', 'HHP1', 'HV1', 'HV2',
'MDMAUD_R', 'MDMAUD_F', 'MDMAUD_A']
['TCODE', 'MAILCODE', 'NOEXCH', 'CHILD03', 'CHILD07',
'CHILD12', 'CHILD18', 'HC15', 'MAXADATE']
```

The first list is one of features that are extremely correlated with ones other than themselves. While this is useful to know, you shouldn't remove features from this list without understanding what features they are correlated with and how, as well as with the target. Then, only if redundancy is found, make sure you only remove one of them. The second one is of uncorrelated features to any others than themself, which in this case is suspicious given the sheer amount of features. That being said, you also should inspect them one by one, especially to measure them against the target to see whether they are redundant. However, we will take a chance and make a feature subset (corr_cols) excluding the uncorrelated ones:

```
corr_cols =\
        X_train.columns[~X_train.columns.isin(uncorr_cols)].
tolist()
print(len(corr_cols))
```

The preceding code should output 419. Let's now fit the RF model with only these features. Given that there are still over 400 features, we will use a max_depth value of 11. Except for that and a different model name (mdlname), it's the same code as before:

```
mdlname = 'rf_11_f-corr'
stime = timeit.default_timer()
reg_mdl = xgb.XGBRFRegressor(max_depth=11,
n_estimators=200, seed=rand)
fitted_mdl = reg_mdl.fit(X_train[corr_cols], y_train)
    :
reg_mdls[mdlname]['num_feat'] =\
        sum(reg_mdls[mdlname]['fitted'].feature_importances_
> 0)
```

Before we compare the results for the preceding model, let's learn about ranking filter methods.

Ranking filter-based methods

Ranking filter-based methods are based on statistical univariate ranking tests, which assess the strength of features against the target. These are some of the most popular methods:

- **ANOVA F-test**: **Analysis of Variance (ANOVA)** F-test measures the linear dependency between features and the target. As the name suggests, it does this by decomposing the variance. It makes similar assumptions to linear regression, such as normality, independence, and homoscedasticity. In scikit-learn, you can use `f_regression` and `f_classification` for regression and classification, respectively, to rank features by the F-score yielded by the F-test.

- **Chi-square test of independence**: This test measures the association between non-negative categorical variables and binary targets, so it's only suitable for classification problems. In scikit-learn, you can use `chi2`.

- **Mutual information (MI)**: Unlike the two previous methods, this one is derived from information theory rather than classical statistical hypothesis testing. It's a different name but a concept we have already discussed in this book as the **Kullback-Leibler (KL) divergence** because it's the KL for feature X and target Y. The Python implementation in scikit-learn uses a numerically stable and symmetric offshoot of KL called **Jensen-Shannon (JS)** divergence instead and leverages k-nearest neighbors to compute distances. Features can be ranked by MI with `mutual_info_regression` and `mutual_info_classif` for regression and classification, respectively.

Of the three options mentioned, the one that is most appropriate for this dataset is MI because we cannot assume linearity among our features, and most of them aren't categorical either. We can try classification with a threshold of $0.68, which at least covers the cost of sending the mailer. To that end, we must first create a binary classification target (`y_train_class`) with that threshold:

```
y_train_class = np.where(y_train > 0.68, 1, 0)
```

Next, we can use `SelectKBest` to get the top-160 features according to **MI classification (MIC)**. We then employ `get_support()` to obtain a Boolean vector (or mask), which tells us which features are in the top 160, and we subset the list of features with this mask:

```
mic_selection = SelectKBest(mutual_info_classif, k=160).fit(X_
train, y_train_class)
```

```
mic_cols =\
X_train.columns[mic_selection.get_support()].tolist()
print(len(mic_cols))
```

The preceding code should confirm that there are 160 features in the mic_cols list. Incidentally, this is an arbitrary number. Ideally, if there was time, we could test different thresholds for the classification target and *ks* for the MI, looking for the model that achieved the highest profit lift while underfitting the least. Next, we can fit the RF model as we've done before with the MIC features. This time, we will use a max depth of 5 because there are significantly fewer features:

```
mdlname = 'rf_5_f-mic'
stime = timeit.default_timer()
reg_mdl = xgb.XGBRFRegressor(max_depth=5, n_estimators=200,\
                            seed=rand)
fitted_mdl = reg_mdl.fit(X_train[mic_cols], y_train)
:
reg_mdls[mdlname]['num_feat'] =\
        sum(reg_mdls[mdlname]['fitted'].feature_importances_
> 0)
```

Now, let's plot the profits for test and train as we did in *Figure 10.3* but for the MIC model. It will produce what's shown in *Figure 10.5*:

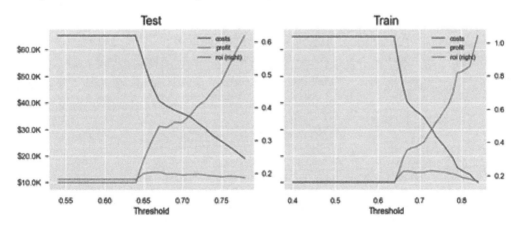

Figure 10.5 – Comparison between profit, costs, and ROI for the test and train datasets for a model with MIC features across thresholds

In *Figure 10.5*, you can tell that there is quite a bit of difference between **Test** and **Train**, yet similarities indicate minimal overfitting. For instance, the highest profitability can be found between 0.65 and 0.7 for **Train**, and while **Test** is mostly between 0.65 and 0.7, it only gradually decreases afterward.

Although we have visually examined the MIC model, it's nice to have some reassurance by looking at raw metrics. Next, we will compare all the models we have trained so far using consistent metrics.

Comparing filter-based methods

We have been saving metrics into a dictionary (`reg_mdls`), which we easily convert to a dataframe and output as we have done before, but this time we sort by `max_profit_test`:

```
reg_metrics_df = pd.DataFrame.from_dict(reg_mdls, 'index')\
                 [['depth', 'fs', 'rmse_train',\
'rmse_test', 'max_profit_train',\ 'max_profit_test',\
                        'max_roi', 'min_costs', 'speed', 'num_
feat']]
with pd.option_context('display.precision', 2):
  html = reg_metrics_df.sort_values(by='max_profit_test',\
                              ascending=False).style.\
        background_gradient(cmap='plasma', low=0.3,\
high=1, subset=['rmse_train',\
  'rmse_test']).background_gradient(cmap='viridis', low=1, \
high=0.3, subset=['max_profit_train', 'max_profit_test'])
html
```

The preceding snippet generated what is shown in *Figure 10.6*. It is evident that the filter MIC model is the least overfitted of all. It ranked higher than more-complex models with more features and took less time to train than any model. Its speed is an advantage for hyperparameter tuning. What if we wanted to find the best classification target thresholds or MIC *k*s? We won't do this now, but we could likely get a better model if we ran every combination but it would take time to do and even more with more features:

	depth	fs	rmse_train	rmse_test	max_profit_train	max_profit_test	max_roi	min_costs	speed	total_feat	num_feat
rf_11_all	11	all	3.99	4.69	19904.00	15141.86	0.76	14928.04	2.73	435	398
rf_10_all	10	all	4.05	4.68	18603.92	14987.06	0.78	14396.28	2.43	435	383
rf_12_all	12	all	3.94	4.69	21521.98	14932.84	0.77	14532.28	2.89	435	415
rf_11_f-corr	11	f-corr	3.98	4.67	19923.84	14894.94	0.77	14592.80	2.47	419	404
rf_9_all	9	all	4.10	4.68	17453.14	14777.74	0.80	13997.12	2.19	435	346
rf_8_all	8	all	4.14	4.67	16439.72	14563.04	0.73	15308.84	1.94	435	315
rf_5_f-mic	5	f-mic	4.31	4.57	14983.34	14481.39	0.62	18971.32	0.39	160	103
rf_7_all	7	all	4.18	4.66	15435.32	14187.62	0.66	17164.56	1.71	435	277
rf_6_all	6	all	4.23	4.65	14651.12	13845.27	0.59	19305.20	1.41	435	240
rf_5_all	5	all	4.27	4.64	14242.32	13752.13	0.59	19199.12	1.22	435	201
rf_4_all	4	all	4.32	4.64	13715.90	13261.88	0.53	22392.40	1.00	435	160

Figure 10.6 – Comparing metrics for all base models and filter-based feature-selected models

In *Figure 10.6*, you can tell that the correlation filter model (f-corr) performs worse than the model with more features and an equal amount of max_depth, which suggests that we must have removed an important feature. As cautioned in that section, the problem with blindly setting thresholds and removing anything above it is that you can inadvertently remove something useful. Not all extremely correlated and uncorrelated features are useless, so further inspection is required. Next, we will explore some embedded methods that when combined with cross-validation, which require less oversight.

Exploring embedded feature selection methods

Embedded methods exist within models themselves by naturally selecting features during training. You can leverage the intrinsic properties of any model that has them to capture the features selected:

- **Tree-based models**: For instance, we have used the following code many times to count the number of features used by the RF models, which is evidence of feature selection naturally occurring in the learning process:

```
sum(reg_mdls[mdlname]['fitted'].feature_importances_ > 0)
```

  XGBoost's RF uses `gain` by default, which is the average decrease in error in all splits where it used the feature to compute feature importance. We can increase the threshold above 0 to select even fewer features according to this relative contribution. However, by constraining the trees' depth, we forced the model to choose even fewer features already.

- **Regularized models with coefficients**: We will study this further in *Chapter 12, Monotonic Constraints and Model Tuning for Interpretability*, but many model classes can incorporate penalty-based regularization, such as L1, L2, and elastic net. However, not all of them have intrinsic parameters such as coefficients that can be extracted to determine which features were penalized.

This section will only cover regularized models given that we are using a tree-based model already. It's best to leverage different model classes to get different perspectives of what features matter the most.

We covered some of these models in *Chapter 3, Interpretation Challenges*, but these are a few model classes that incorporate penalty-based regularization and output feature-specific coefficients:

- **Least absolute shrinkage and selection operator** (**LASSO**): Because it uses L1 penalty in the loss function, LASSO can set coefficients to 0.

- **Least-angle regression** (**LARS**): Similar to LASSO but is vector-based and is more suitable to high-dimensional data. It is also fairer toward equally correlated features.

- **Ridge regression**: Uses L2 penalty in the loss function and because of this can only shrink coefficients of irrelevance close to 0 but not to 0.

- **Elastic net regression**: Uses a mix of both L1 and L2 norms as penalties.

- **Logistic regression**: Contingent on the solver, it can handle L1, L2, or elastic net penalties.

There are also several variations of the preceding models, such as **LASSO LARS**, which is a LASSO fit using the LARS algorithm, or even **LASSO LARS IC**, which is the same but uses AIC or BIC criteria for the model section:

- **Akaike's Information Criteria** (**AIC**): A relative goodness of fit measure founded in information theory

- **Bayesian Information Criteria** (**BIC**): Has a similar formula to AIC but has a different penalty term

OK, now let's use `SelectFromModel` to extract top features from a LASSO model. We will use `LassoCV` because it can automatically cross-validate to find optimal penalty strength. Once you fit it, we can get the feature mask with `get_support()`. We can then print the number of features and list of features:

```
lasso_selection = SelectFromModel(LassoCV(n_jobs=-1,\
                                                            random_
state=rand))
lasso_selection.fit(X_train, y_train)
lasso_cols =\
X_train.columns[lasso_selection.get_support()].tolist()
print(len(lasso_cols))
print(lasso_cols)
```

The preceding code outputs the following:

```
7
['ODATEDW', 'TCODE', 'POP901', 'POP902', 'HV2', 'RAMNTALL',
'MAXRDATE']
```

Now, let's try the same but with `LassoLarsCV`:

```
llars_selection = SelectFromModel(LassoLarsCV(n_jobs=-1))
llars_selection.fit(X_train, y_train)
llars_cols =\
X_train.columns[llars_selection.get_support()].tolist()
print(len(llars_cols))
print(llars_cols)
```

The preceding snippet produces the following output:

```
8
['RECPGVG', 'MDMAUD', 'HVP3', 'RAMNTALL', 'LASTGIFT',
 'AVGGIFT', 'MDMAUD_A', 'DOMAIN_SOCIALCLS']
```

Lasso shrunk coefficients for all but seven features to 0, and Lasso LARS did the same but for eight. However, notice how there's no overlap between both lists! OK, so let's try incorporating AIC model selection into Lasso Lars with `LassoLarsIC`:

```
llarsic_selection = \
SelectFromModel(LassoLarsIC(criterion='aic'))
llarsic_selection.fit(X_train, y_train)
llarsic_cols =\
        X_train.columns[llarsic_selection.get_support()].
tolist()
print(len(llarsic_cols))
print(llarsic_cols)
```

The preceding snippet generates the following output:

```
111
['TCODE', 'STATE', 'MAILCODE', 'RECINHSE', 'RECP3', 'RECPGVG',
 'RECSWEEP',..., 'DOMAIN_URBANICITY', 'DOMAIN_SOCIALCLS', 'ZIP_
LON']
```

It's the same algorithm but with a different method for selecting the value of the regularization parameter. Note how this less-conservative approach expands the number of features to 111. Now, so far, all of the methods we have used have the L1 norm. Let's try one with L2—more specifically, L2-penalized logistic regression. We do exactly what we did before, but this time we fit with the binary classification targets (`y_train_class`):

```
log_selection = SelectFromModel(LogisticRegression(C=0.0001,\
                            solver='sag', penalty='l2', n_
jobs=-1, random_state=rand))
log_selection.fit(X_train, y_train_class)
log_cols =\
X_train.columns[log_selection.get_support()].tolist()
print(len(log_cols))
print(log_cols)
```

The preceding code produces the following output:

```
87
['ODATEDW', 'TCODE', 'STATE', 'POP901', 'POP902', 'POP903',
 'ETH1', 'ETH2', 'ETH5', 'CHIL1', 'HHN2',..., 'AMT_7', 'ZIP_
LON']
```

Now that we have a few feature subsets to test, we can place their names into a list (`fsnames`) and the feature subset lists into another list (`fscols`):

```
fsnames = ['e-lasso', 'e-llars', 'e-llarsic', 'e-logl2']
fscols = [lasso_cols, llars_cols, llarsic_cols, log_cols]
```

We can then iterate across all list names and fit and evaluate our XGBRFRegressor model as we have done before but increasing `max_depth` at every iteration:

```
for i, fsname in tqdm(enumerate(fsnames), total=len(fsnames)):
  depth = i + 3
  cols = fscols[i]
  mdlname = 'rf_'+str(depth)+'_'+fsname
  stime = timeit.default_timer()
  reg_mdl = xgb.XGBRFRegressor(max_depth=depth,\
n_estimators=200, seed=rand)
  fitted_mdl = reg_mdl.fit(X_train[cols], y_train)
  :
  reg_mdls[mdlname]['num_feat'] =\
        sum(reg_mdls[mdlname]['fitted'].feature_importances_
> 0)
```

Now, let's see how our embedded feature-selected models fare in comparison to the filtered ones. We will rerun the code we ran to output what was shown in *Figure 10.6*. This time, we will get what is shown in *Figure 10.7*:

	depth	fs	rmse_train	rmse_test	max_profit_train	max_profit_test	max_roi	min_costs	speed	total_feat	num_feat
rf_11_all	11	all	3.99	4.69	19904.00	15141.86	0.76	14928.04	2.73	435	398
rf_10_all	10	all	4.05	4.68	18603.92	14987.06	0.78	14396.28	2.43	435	383
rf_12_all	12	all	3.94	4.69	21521.98	14932.84	0.77	14532.28	2.89	435	415
rf_11_f-corr	11	f-corr	3.98	4.67	19923.84	14894.94	0.77	14592.80	2.47	419	404
rf_9_all	9	all	4.10	4.68	17453.14	14777.74	0.80	13997.12	2.19	435	346
rf_5_e-llarsic	5	e-llarsic	4.28	4.45	15168.46	14768.37	0.56	20441.48	0.32	111	87
rf_8_all	8	all	4.14	4.67	16439.72	14563.04	0.73	15308.84	1.94	435	315
rf_5_f-mic	5	f-mic	4.31	4.57	14983.34	14481.39	0.62	18971.32	0.39	160	103
rf_6_h-rfe-lda	6	h-rfe-lda	4.25	4.48	15329.72	14351.74	0.71	15824.28	0.61	183	129
rf_6_e-logl2	6	e-logl2	4.28	4.60	15353.44	14199.90	0.67	16904.12	0.32	87	84
rf_7_all	7	all	4.18	4.66	15435.32	14187.62	0.66	17164.56	1.71	435	277
rf_6_all	6	all	4.23	4.65	14651.12	13845.27	0.59	19305.20	1.41	435	240
rf_5_all	5	all	4.27	4.64	14242.32	13752.13	0.59	19199.12	1.22	435	201
rf_4_e-llars	4	e-llars	4.36	4.45	14014.10	13633.19	0.52	22906.48	0.06	8	8
rf_6_h-rfe-rf	6	h-rfe-rf	4.40	4.78	13202.61	13347.15	0.41	28596.04	0.08	1	1
rf_4_all	4	all	4.32	4.64	13715.90	13261.88	0.53	22392.40	1.00	435	160
rf_3_e-lasso	3	e-lasso	4.46	4.49	14166.64	12930.30	0.51	22248.92	0.05	7	7

Figure 10.7 – Comparing metrics for all base models and filter-based and embedded feature-selected models

According to *Figure 10.7*, three out of the four embedded methods we tried produced models with the lowest test RMSE. They also all train much faster than any othesr and are more profitable than any other model of equal complexity. One of them (rf_5_e-llarsic) is even highly profitable. Compare this with rf_9_all with similar test profitability to see how performance diverges with that on the training data.

Discovering wrapper, hybrid, and advanced feature selection methods

The feature selection methods studied so far are computationally inexpensive because they require no model fitting or fitting simpler white-box models. In this section, we will learn about other, more exhaustive methods with many possible tuning options. The categories of methods included here are as follows:

- **Wrapper**: Exhaustively look for the best subset of features by fitting an ML model using a search strategy that measures improvement on a metric.

- **Hybrid**: A method that combines embedded and filter methods with wrapper methods.

- **Advanced**: A method that doesn't fall into any of the previously discussed categories. Examples include dimensionality reduction, model-agnostic feature importance, and GAs.

And now, let's get started with wrapper methods!

Wrapper methods

The concept behind **wrapper methods** is reasonably simple: evaluate different subsets of features on the ML model and choose the one that achieves the best score in a predetermined objective function. What varies here is the search strategy:

- **Sequential forward selection** (**SFS**): This approach begins without a feature and adds one, one at a time.

- **Sequential forward floating selection** (**SFFS**): Same as the previous except for every feature it adds, it can remove one as long as the objective function increases.

- **Sequential backward selection** (**SBS**): This process begins with all features present and eliminates one feature at a time.

- **Sequential floating backward selection** (**SFBS**): Same as the previous except for every feature it removes, it can add one as long as the objective function increases.

- **Exhaustive feature selection** (**EFS**): This approach seeks all possible combinations of features.

- **Bidirectional search** (**BDS**): This last one simultaneously allows both forward and backward function selection to get one unique solution.

These methods are greedy algorithms because they solve the problem piece by piece, choosing pieces based on their immediate benefit. Even though they may arrive at a global maximum, they take an approach more suited for finding local maxima. Depending on the number of features, they might be too computationally expensive to be practical, especially EFS, which grows combinatorially.

To allow for shorter search times, we will do two things:

1. Start our search with the features collectively selected by other methods to have a smaller feature space to chose from. To that end, we combine feature lists from several methods into a single `top_cols` list:

```
top_cols =\
list(set(mic_cols).union(set(llarsic_cols)).\
                union(set(log_cols)))
len(top_cols)
```

2. Sample our datasets so that ML models speed up. We can use `np.random.choice` to do random selection of row indexes without replacement:

```
sample_size = 0.1
sample_train_idx = np.random.choice(X_train.shape[0],\

math.ceil(X_train.shape[0]*sample_size), replace=False)
sample_test_idx = np.random.choice(X_test.shape[0],\
                math.ceil(X_test.shape[0]*sample_size),\
        replace=False)
```

Out of the wrapper methods presented, we will only perform SFS and SBS given how time-consuming they are. Still, with an even smaller dataset, you can try the other options, which the `mlextend` library also supports.

Sequential forward selection (SFS)

The first argument of a wrapper method is an unfitted estimator (a model). In `SequentialFeatureSelector`, we are placing a `LinearDiscriminantAnalysis` model. Other arguments include the direction (`forward=true`), whether it's floating (`floating=False`), the number of features we wish to select (`k_features=27`), the number of cross-validations (`cv=3`), and the loss function to use (`scoring=f1`). Some recommended optional arguments to enter are the verbosity (`verbose=2`) and the number of jobs to run in parallel (`n_jobs=-1`). Since it could take a while, you'll definitely want it to output something and use as many processors as possible:

```
sfs_lda = SequentialFeatureSelector(\
            LinearDiscriminantAnalysis(n_components=1),
            forward=True, floating=False,
            k_features=27, cv=3,\
            scoring='f1', verbose=2, n_jobs=-1)
sfs_lda =\
sfs_lda.fit(X_train.iloc[sample_train_idx][top_cols],\
            y_train_class[sample_train_idx])
sfs_lda_cols =\
            X_train.columns[list(sfs_lda.k_feature_idx_)].
tolist()
```

Once we fit the SFS, it will return the index of features that have been selected with `k_feature_idx_`, and we can use those to subset the columns and obtain the list of feature names.

Sequential Backward Selection (SBS)

For SBS, we will use `ExtraTreesRegressor`, which controls overfitting by training extremely randomized decision trees on sub-samples of the dataset. Because of its wild nature, it might be able to find subsets of features that a model such as LDA will not:

```
sbs_et = SequentialFeatureSelector(\
            ExtraTreesRegressor(max_depth=3,\
            random_state=rand),\
            floating=False, k_features=135,\
            forward=False, cv=2,\
            scoring='neg_root_mean_squared_error',\
            verbose=2,\
```

```
                n_jobs=-1)
sbs_et =\
sbs_et.fit(X_train.iloc[sample_train_idx][top_cols],\
             y_train[sample_train_idx])
sbs_et_cols =\
X_train.columns[list(sbs_et.k_feature_idx_)].tolist()
```

Once SBS is fitted, we will do the same as before, saving the selected features.

Typically, wrapper methods are very effective at finding feature subsets that will reduce overfitting and increase predictive performance because they detect important feature interactions that filter methods cannot. The main limitation has been that we have had to sample the training data to make them viable for this use case.

Hybrid methods

Starting with 435 features, there are over 10^{42} combinations of 27 feature subsets alone! So, you can see how EFS would be impractical on such a large feature space. Therefore, except for EFS on the entire dataset, wrapper methods will invariably take some shortcuts to select the features. Whether you are going forward, backward, or both, as long as you are not assessing every single combination of features, you could easily miss out on the best one.

However, we can leverage the more rigorous, exhaustive search approach of wrapper methods with filter and embedded methods' efficiency. The result of this is **hybrid methods**. For instance, you could employ filter or embedded methods to derive only the top-10 features and perform EFS or SBS on only those.

Recursive feature elimination

Another, more common approach is something such as SBS, but instead of removing features based on improving a metric alone, using the model's intrinsic parameters to rank the features and only removing the least ranked. The name of this approach is **RFE**, and it is a hybrid between embedded and wrapper methods. You can only use models with `feature_importances_` or coefficients (`coef_`) because this is how the method knows what features to remove. Model classes in scikit-learn with these attributes are classified under `linear_model`, `tree`, and `ensemble`. Also, scikit-learn-compatible versions of XGBoost, LightGBM, and CatBoost also have `feature_importances_`.

We will use the cross-validated version of RFE because it's more reliable. RFECV takes the estimator first (`LinearDiscriminantAnalysis`). We can then define `step`, which sets how many features it should remove in every iteration, the number of cross-validations (`cv`), and the metric used for evaluation (`scoring`). Lastly, it is recommended to set the verbosity (`verbose=2`) and leverage as many processors as possible (`n_jobs=-1`). To speed it up, we will use a sample again for the training and start with the 267 for `top_cols`:

```
rfe_lda = RFECV(LinearDiscriminantAnalysis(n_components=1),\
step=2, cv=3, scoring='f1', verbose=2, n_jobs=-1)
rfe_lda.fit(X_train.iloc[sample_train_idx][top_cols],
        y_train_class[sample_train_idx])
rfe_lda_cols =\
 np.array(top_cols)[rfe_lda.support_].tolist()
```

We can try `RandomForestRegressor`, this time with a larger step size of `0.05`, which means that 5% of all the features are to be removed in every iteration:

```
rfe_rf = RFECV(RandomForestRegressor(random_state=rand,\
                                     max_depth=4),\
                  step=0.05, cv=3, verbose=2, n_jobs=-1,\
                  scoring='neg_root_mean_squared_error')
rfe_rf.fit(X_train.iloc[sample_train_idx][top_cols],
        y_train[sample_train_idx])
rfe_rf_cols = np.array(top_cols)[rfe_rf.support_].tolist()
```

Next, we will try different methods that don't relate to the main three feature selection categories: filter, embedded, and wrapper.

Advanced methods

Many methods can be categorized under advanced feature selection methods, including the following subcategories:

- **Dimensionality reduction**: Some dimensionality reduction methods, such as **Principal Component Analysis** (**PCA**), can return explained variance on a feature basis. For others, such as factor analysis, it can be derived from other outputs. Explained variance can be used to rank features.

- **Model-agnostic feature importance**: Any feature importance method covered in *Chapter 4, Fundamentals of Feature Importance and Impact*, and *Chapter 5, Global Model-Agnostic Interpretation Methods*, can be used to obtain the top features of a model for feature selection purposes.

- **GA**: This is a wrapper method in the sense that it "wraps" a model assessing predictive performance across many feature subsets. However, unlike the wrapper methods we examined, it's not greedy, and it's more optimized to work with large feature spaces. It's called genetic because it's inspired by biology—natural selection, specifically.

- **Auto-encoders**: We won't delve into this one, but deep learning can be leveraged for feature selection with auto-encoders.

We will briefly cover the first three in this section so you can understand how they can be implemented. Let's dive right in!

Dimensionality reduction

We covered PCA in *Chapter 3, Interpretation Challenges*, but we didn't extract the explained variance from it, and we actually used it to reduce the dimensions. As seen in the following code, this time we will keep the number of components (n_components) as the number of features, and leverage its ability to decompose the variance through **singular value decomposition (SVD)**:

```
pca = PCA(n_components=X_train.shape[1])
fitted_pca = pca.fit(X_train)
pca_evrs = pd.DataFrame({'col':X_train.columns,\
                    'evr':fitted_pca.explained_variance_
ratio_}).sort_values(by='evr',ascending=False)
pca_cols = pca_evrs.head(150).col.tolist()
```

As you can tell in the preceding snippet, you can fit PCA as you would any model except it doesn't require labels because it's an unsupervised method. Then, we extract explained_variance_ratio_ (the **explained variance ratio**, or **EVR**) and place it in a dataframe that we sort by EVR. Lastly, we take the top-150 features and save them into a list (pca_cols).

Model-agnostic feature importance

A popular model-agnostic feature importance method that we have used throughout this book is SHAP, and it has many properties that make it more reliable than other methods. In the following code, we can take our best model and extract `shap_values` for it using `TreeExplainer`:

```
fitted_rf_mdl = reg_mdls['rf_11_all']['fitted']
shap_rf_explainer = shap.TreeExplainer(fitted_rf_mdl)
shap_rf_values =\
    shap_rf_explainer.shap_values(X_test_orig.iloc[sample_test_
idx])
shap_imps = pd.DataFrame({'col':X_train_orig.columns,\
                          'imp':np.abs(shap_rf_values).
mean(0)}).sort_values(by='imp',ascending=False)
shap_cols = shap_imps.head(150).col.tolist()
```

Then, we average for the absolute value of the SHAP values across the first dimension is what provides us with a ranking for each feature. We put this value in a dataframe and sort it as we did for PCA. Lastly, also take the top 150 and place them in a list (`shap_cols`).

Genetic algorithms

GAs are a stochastic global optimization technique inspired by natural selection, which wrap a model much like wrapper methods do. However, they don't follow a sequence on a step-by-step basis. GAs don't have iterations but generations, which include populations of chromosomes. Each chromosome is a binary representation of your feature space where 1 means to select a feature and 0 to not. Each generation is produced with the following operations:

- **Selection**: Like with natural selection, this is partially random (exploration) and partially based on what has already worked (exploitation). What has worked is its fitness. Fitness is assessed with a "scorer" much like wrapper methods. Poor fitness chromosomes are removed, whereas good ones get to reproduce t hrough "crossover."

- **Crossover**: Randomly, some good bits (or features) of each parent go to a child.

- **Mutation**: Even when a chromosome has proved effective, given a low mutation rate, it will occasionally mutate or flip one of its bits, in other words, features.

The Python implementation we will use has many options. We won't explain all of them here but they are documented well in the code should you be interested. The first attribute is the estimator. We can also define the cross-validation iterations (`cv=3`), `scoring` to determine whether chromosomes are fit, and the maximum number of features it should select in each chromosome (`max_features`). There are some important probabilistic properties, such as probability for a mutated bit (`mutation_independent_proba`) and that bits will get exchanged (`crossover_independent_proba`). Generation-wise, `n_gen_no_change` provides a means for early stopping if generations haven't improved, and `n_generations`, by default, 40, is a hard stopping point. You can fit `GeneticSelectionCV` as you would any model. It can take a while, so it is best to define the verbosity and allow it to use all the processing capacity. Once finished, we can use the Boolean mask (`support_`) to subset the features:

```
ga_rf = GeneticSelectionCV(RandomForestRegressor(random_
state=rand, max_depth=3),\
                cv=3, scoring='neg_root_mean_squared_error',\
                max_features=90, crossover_independent_proba=0.5,\
                n_gen_no_change=5, mutation_independent_proba=0.05,\
                n_jobs=-1, verbose=2)
ga_rf = ga_rf.fit(X_train[top_cols], y_train)
ga_rf_cols = np.array(top_cols)[ga_rf.support_].tolist()
```

OK, now that we have covered a wide variety of wrapper, hybrid, and advanced feature selection methods in this section, let's evaluate all of them at once and compare results.

Evaluating all feature-selected models

As we have done with embedded methods, we can place feature subset names (`fsnames`), lists (`fscols`), and corresponding `depths` in lists:

```
fsnames = ['w-sfs-lda', 'w-sbs-et', 'h-rfe-lda','h-rfe-rf',\
            'a-pca', 'a-shap', 'a-ga-rf']
fscols = [sfs_lda_cols, sbs_et_cols, rfe_lda_cols,\
  rfe_rf_cols, pca_cols, shap_cols, ga_rf_cols]
depths = [5, 6, 6, 6, 6, 6, 5]
```

Then, we can iterate across all feature subsets, training XGBRFRegessor with them and placing the evaluation results in the model dictionary (reg_mdls):

```
for i, fsname in tqdm(enumerate(fsnames), total=len(fsnames)):
  depth = depths[i]
  cols = fscols[i]
  mdlname = 'rf_'+str(depth)+'_'+fsname
  stime = timeit.default_timer()
  reg_mdl = xgb.XGBRFRegressor(max_depth=depth,\
n_estimators=200, seed=rand)
  fitted_mdl = reg_mdl.fit(X_train[cols], y_train)
  etime = timeit.default_timer()
  reg_mdls[mdlname] =\
mldatasets.evaluate_reg_mdl(fitted_mdl,\
                            X_train[cols], X_test[cols], \
                            y_train,\
                            y_test, plot_regplot=False,\
                            show_summary=False, ret_eval_
dict=True)
  :
  reg_mdls[mdlname]['num_feat'] =\
          sum(reg_mdls[mdlname]['fitted'].feature_importances_
> 0)
```

As done throughout this chapter, we can convert `reg_mlds` into a dataframe (`reg_metrics_df`) but this time filter it to only include models with a max depth of less than 7 (`reg_metrics_df = reg_metrics_df[reg_metrics_df.depth < 7']`). Then, we can output the dataframe. The result of this is depicted in *Figure 10.8*:

	depth	fs	rmse_train	rmse_test	max_profit_train	max_profit_test	max_roi	min_costs	speed	total_feat	num_feat
rf_5_e-llarsic	5	e-llarsic	4.28	4.45	15168.46	14768.37	0.56	20441.48	0.32	111	87
rf_5_f-mic	5	f-mic	4.31	4.57	14983.34	14481.39	0.62	18971.32	0.39	160	103
rf_6_h-rfe-lda	6	h-rfe-lda	4.25	4.48	15329.72	14351.74	0.71	15824.28	0.61	183	129
rf_6_a-shap	6	a-shap	4.23	4.52	15263.60	14282.20	0.61	18767.32	0.50	150	135
rf_5_a-ga-rf	5	a-ga-rf	4.39	4.45	14274.52	14220.53	0.69	13237.56	0.07	63	63
rf_6_e-logl2	6	e-logl2	4.28	4.60	15353.44	14199.90	0.67	16904.12	0.32	87	84
rf_6_all	6	all	4.23	4.65	14651.12	13845.27	0.59	19305.20	1.41	435	240
rf_5_w-sfs-lda	5	w-sfs-lda	4.43	4.63	14377.13	13801.55	0.51	22508.95	0.11	27	27
rf_5_all	5	all	4.27	4.64	14242.32	13752.13	0.59	19199.12	1.22	435	201
rf_4_e-llars	4	e-llars	4.36	4.45	14014.10	13633.19	0.52	22906.48	0.06	8	8
rf_6_a-pca	6	a-pca	4.30	4.46	14353.54	13351.57	0.47	23901.32	0.54	150	126
rf_6_h-rfe-rf	6	h-rfe-rf	4.40	4.78	13202.61	13347.15	0.41	28596.04	0.08	1	1
rf_4_all	4	all	4.32	4.64	13715.90	13261.88	0.53	22392.40	1.00	435	160
rf_6_w-sbs-et	6	w-sbs-et	4.34	4.53	14222.49	13119.17	0.71	14711.66	0.45	135	123
rf_3_e-lasso	3	e-lasso	4.46	4.49	14166.64	12930.30	0.51	22248.92	0.05	7	7

Figure 10.8 – Comparing metrics for all feature-selected models

Figure 10.8 shows how feature-selected models are more profitable than ones that include all the features compared at the same depths. Also, the embedded Lasso LARS with AIC (`e-llarsic`) method and the MIC (`f-mic`) filter method outperform all wrapper, hybrid, and advanced methods. Still, we also impeded these methods by using a sample of the training dataset, which was necessary to speed up the process. Maybe they would have outperformed the top ones otherwise. However, the four feature selection methods that follow are pretty competitive:

- RFE with LDA: Hybrid method (`h-rfe-lda`)
- SHAP: Advanced method (`a-shap`)
- GAs with RF: Advanced method (`a-ga-rf`)
- Embedded logistic regression with L2 regularization: Embedded method (`e-logl2`)

It would make sense to spend many days running many variations of the methods reviewed in this book. For instance, perhaps RFE with L1 regularized logistic regression or GA with support vector machines with additional mutation yields the best model. There are so many different possibilities! Nevertheless, if you were forced to make a recommendation based on *Figure 10.8*, by profit alone, the 111-feature e-llarsic is the best option, but it also has higher minimum costs and lower maximum ROI than any of the top models. There's a trade-off. And even though it has among the lowest test RMSEs, the 63-feature GA RF model (a-ga-rf) has the same RMSE and beat it in max ROI and min costs. Therefore, these are the two reasonable options. But before making a final determination, profitability would have to be compared side by side across different thresholds to assess when each model can make the most reliable predictions and at what costs and ROIs.

Considering feature engineering

Let's assume that the non-profit has chosen to use the model whose features were selected with Lasso LARS with AIC (e-llarsic) but would like to evaluate whether you can improve it further. Now that you have removed over 300 features that might have only marginally improved predictive performance but mostly added noise, you are left with more relevant features. However, you also know that 63 features selected by the GAs (a-ga-rf) produced the same amount of RMSE as the 111 features. This means that while there's something in those extra features that improves profitability, it does not improve the RMSE.

From a feature selection standpoint, many things can be done to approach this problem. For instance, examine the overlap and difference of features between e-llarsic and a-ga-rf, and do feature selection variations strictly on those features to see whether the RMSE dips on any combination while keeping or improving on current profitability. However, there's also another possibility, which is feature engineering. There are a few important reasons you would want to perform feature engineering at this stage:

- **Make model interpretation easier to understand**: For instance, sometimes features have a scale that is not intuitive, or the scale is intuitive but the distribution makes it hard to understand. As long as transformations to these features don't worsen model performance, there's value in transforming the features to understand the outputs of interpretation methods better. As you train models on more engineered features, you realize what works and why it does. This will help you understand the model and, more importantly, the data.

- **Place guardrails on individual features**: Sometimes, features have an uneven distribution, and models tend to overfit in sparser areas of the feature's histogram or where influential outliers exist.

- **Clean up counterintuitive interactions**: Some interactions that models find make no sense and only exist because the features correlate, but not for the right reasons. They could be confounding variables or perhaps even redundant ones (such as the one we found in *Chapter 5, Global Model-Agnostic Interpretation Methods*). You could decide to engineer an interaction feature or remove a redundant one.

In reference to the last two reasons, we will examine feature engineering strategies in more detail in *Chapter 12, Monotonic Constraints and Model Tuning for Interpretability*. This section will focus on the first reason, particularly because it's a good place to start since it will allow you to understand the data better until you know it well enough to make more transformational changes.

So, we are left with 111 features but have no idea how they relate to the target or each other. The first thing we ought to do is run a feature importance method. We can use SHAP's `TreeExplainer` on the `e-llarsic` model. An advantage of `TreeExplainer` is that it can compute SHAP interaction values, `shap_interaction_values`, instead of outputting an array of (N, 111) dimensions where *N* is the number of observations as `shap_values` does; it will output (N, 111, 111). You can produce a `summary_plot` graph with it that ranks both individual features and interactions. The only difference for interaction values is you use `plot_type="compact_dot"`:

```
fitted_rf_mdl = reg_mdls['rf_5_e-llarsic']['fitted']
shap_rf_explainer = shap.TreeExplainer(fitted_rf_mdl)
shap_rf_interact_values = shap_rf_explainer.\

shap_interaction_values(X_test.\
                        iloc[sample_test_idx][llarsic_cols])
shap.summary_plot(shap_rf_interact_values,\
            X_test.iloc[sample_test_idx][llarsic_cols],
        plot_type="compact_dot", sort=True)
```

The preceding snippet produces the SHAP interaction summary plot shown in *Figure 10.9*:

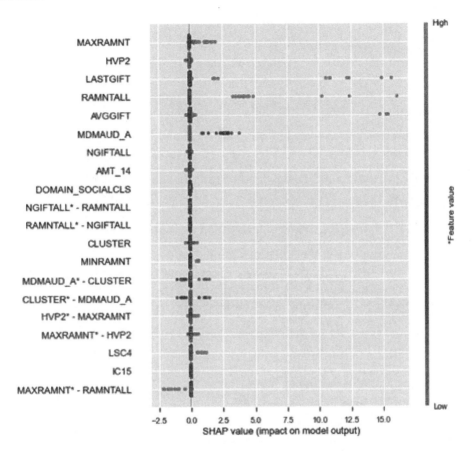

Figure 10.9 – SHAP interaction summary plot

You can read *Figure 10.9* as you would any summary plot except it includes bivariate interactions twice—first with one feature and then with another. For instance, MDMAUD_A* - CLUSTER is the interaction SHAP values for that interaction from MDMAUD_A's perspective, so the feature values correspond to that feature alone, but the SHAP values are for the interaction. Another interesting finding is that high values for most features correspond with higher SHAP values. Precisely, MDMAUD_A and CLUSTER are the exceptions.

Throughout this book, chapters with tabular data have started with a data dictionary. This one was an exception, given that there were 435 features to begin with. Now, it makes sense to at the very least understand what the top features are. The complete data dictionary [1] can be found here, `https://kdd.ics.uci.edu/databases/kddcup98/epsilon_mirror/cup98dic.txt`, but some of the features have already been changed because of categorical encoding, so we will explain them in more detail here:

- **MAXRAMNT**: Continuous, the dollar amount of the largest gift to date

- **HVP2**: Discrete, percentage of homes with a value of >= $150,000 in the neighborhoods of donors (values between 0 and 100)

- **LASTGIFT**: Continuous, the dollar amount of the most recent gift

- **RAMNTALL**: Continuous, the dollar amount of lifetime gifts to date

- **AVGGIFT**: Continuous, the average dollar amount of gifts to date

- **MDMAUD_A**: Ordinal, the donation amount code for donors who have given a $100 + gift at any time in their giving history (values between 0 and 3, -1 for those who have never exceeded $100). The amount code is the third byte of an **RFA (recency/frequency/amount)** major customer matrix code, which is the amount given. The categories are as follows:

  0: Less than $100 (low dollar)

  1: $100 − 499 (core)

  2: $500 − 999 (major)

  3: $1,000 + (zop)

- **NGIFTALL**: Discrete, number of lifetime gifts to date

- **AMT_14**: Ordinal, donation amount code of the RFA for the 14th previous promotion (2 years prior), which corresponds to the last dollar amount given back then:

  0: $0.01 − 1.99

  1: $2.00 − 2.99

  2: $3.00 − 4.99

  3: $5.00 − 9.99

  4: $10.00 − 14.99

5: $15.00 − 24.99

6: $25.00 and above

- **DOMAIN_SOCIALCLS**: Nominal, **socio-economic status (SES)** of the neighborhood, which combines with DOMAIN_URBANICITY (0: Urban, 1: City, 2: Suburban, 3: Town, 4: Rural), meaning the following:

  1: Highest SES

  2: Average SES, except above average for urban communities

  3: Lowest SES, except below average for urban communities

  4: Lowest SES for urban communities only

- **CLUSTER**: Nominal, code indicating which cluster group the donor falls in

- **MINRAMNT**: Continuous, dollar amount of the smallest gift to date

- **LSC2**: Discrete, percent age of Spanish-speaking families in the donor's neighborhood (values between 0 and 100)

- **IC15**: Discrete, percentage of families with an income of < $15,000 in the donor's neighborhood (values between 0 and 100)

The following insights can be distilled by the preceding dictionary and *Figure 10.9*:

- **Gift amounts prevail**: Seven of the top features pertain to gift amounts, whether it's a total, min, max, averagem, or last. If you include the count of gifts (NGIFTALL), there are eight features involving donation history, making complete sense. So, why is this relevant? Because they are likely highly correlated and understanding how could hold the keys on how to improve the model. Perhaps other features can be created that distill these relationships much better.

- **High values of continuous gift amount features have high SHAP values**: Plot a box plot of any of those features like this, plt.boxplot(X_test.MAXRAMNT), and you'll see how right-skewed these features are. Perhaps a transformation such as breaking them into bins—called "discretization"—or using a different scale such as logarithmic (try plt.boxplot(np.log(X_test.MAXRAMNT))) can help interpret these features but also help find the pockets where the likelihood of donation dramatically increases.

- **Relationship with the 14th previous promotion**: What happened 2 years before they made that promotion connect to the one denoted in the dataset labels? Were the promotional materials similar? Is there a seasonality factor occurring at the same time every couple of years? Maybe you can engineer a feature that better identifies this phenomenon.

- **Inconsistent classifications**: DOMAIN_SOCIALCLS has different categories depending on the DOMAIN_URBANICITY value. We can make this consistent by using all five categories in the scale (Highest, Above Average, Average, Below Average, and Lowest) even if this means non-urban donors would be using only three. The advantage to doing this would be easier interpretation, and it's highly unlikely it would adversely impact the model's performance.

The SHAP interaction summary plot is useful for identifying feature and interaction rankings and some commonalities between them. But to dig deeper into interactions, you first need to quantify their impact. To this end, let's create a heatmap with only the top interactions as measured by their mean absolute SHAP value (shap_rf_interact_avgs). We should then set all the diagonal values to 0 (shap_rf_interact_avgs_nodiag) because these aren't interactions but feature SHAP values, and it's easier to observe the interactions without them. We can place this matrix in a dataframe but it's a dataframe of 111 columns and 111 rows, so to filter it by those features with those most interactions, we sum them and rank them with scipy's rankdata. Then, we use the ranking to identify the 12 most interactive features (most_interact_cols) and subset the dataframe by them. Finally, we plot the dataframe as a heatmap:

```
shap_rf_interact_avgs =\
np.abs(shap_rf_interact_values).mean(0)
shap_rf_interact_avgs_nodiag = shap_rf_interact_avgs.copy()
np.fill_diagonal(shap_rf_interact_avgs_nodiag, 0)
shap_rf_interact_df =\
pd.DataFrame(shap_rf_interact_avgs_nodiag)
shap_rf_interact_df.columns = X_test[llarsic_cols].columns
shap_rf_interact_df.index = X_test[llarsic_cols].columns
shap_rf_interact_ranks = 112 -\
            rankdata(np.sum(shap_rf_interact_avgs_nodiag,
axis=0))
most_interact_cols =\
            shap_rf_interact_df.columns[shap_rf_interact_ranks
< 13]
shap_rf_interact_df =\
        shap_rf_interact_df.loc[most_interact_cols,most_interact_
cols]
sns.heatmap(shap_rf_interact_df, cmap='Blues', annot=True,\
            annot_kws={'size':10}, fmt='.3f',\
linewidths=.5)
```

The preceding snippet outputs what is shown in *Figure 10.10*. It depicts the most salient feature interactions according to SHAP interaction absolute mean values. Note that these are averages, so given how right-skewed most of these features are, it is likely much higher for many observations. However, it's still a good indication of relative impact:

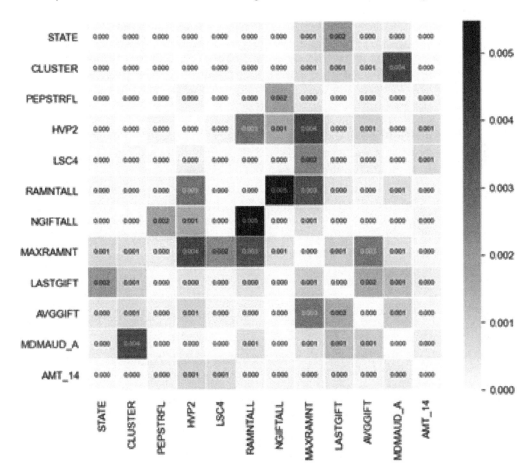

Figure 10.10 – SHAP interactions heatmap

One way in which we can understand feature interactions one by one is with SHAP's `dependence_plot`. For instance, we can take our top feature, `MAXRAMNT`, and plot it with color-coded interactions with features such as `RAMNTALL`, `LSC4`, `HVP2`, and `AVGGIFT`. But first, we will need to compute `shap_values`. There are a couple of problems, though, that need to be addressed, which we mentioned earlier. They have to do with the following:

- **The prevalence of outliers**: We can cut them out of the plot by limiting the *x* and *y* axes using percentiles for the feature and SHAP values, respectively, with `plt.xlim` and `plt.ylim`. This essentially zooms in to cases that lie between the 1st and 99th percentiles.

- **Lopsided distribution of dollar amount features**: It is common in any feature involving money for it to be right-skewed. There are many ways to simplify it, such as using percentiles to bin the feature, but a quick way to make it easier to appreciate is by using a logarithmic scale. In `matplotlib`, you can do this with `plt.xscale('log')` without any need to transform the feature.

The following code accounts for the two issues. You can try commenting out `xlim`, `ylim`, or `xscale` to see the big difference they individually make in understanding `dependence_plot`:

```
shap_rf_values =\
    shap_rf_explainer.shap_values(X_test.iloc[sample_test_idx]\
                                  [llarsic_cols])
maxramt_shap = shap_rf_values[:,llarsic_cols.index("MAXRAMNT")]
shap.dependence_plot("MAXRAMNT", shap_rf_values,\
                     X_test.iloc[sample_test_idx][llarsic_cols],\
                interaction_index="AVGGIFT", show=False,
alpha=0.1)
plt.xlim(xmin=np.percentile(X_test.MAXRAMNT, 1),\
        xmax=np.percentile(X_test.MAXRAMNT, 99))
plt.ylim(ymin=np.percentile(maxramt_shap, 1),\
        ymax=np.percentile(maxramt_shap, 99))
plt.xscale('log')
```

The preceding code generates what is shown in *Figure 10.11*. It shows how there's a tipping point somewhere between 10 and 100 for `MAXRAMNT` where the mean impact on the model output starts to creep out, and these correlate with a higher `AVGGIFT` value:

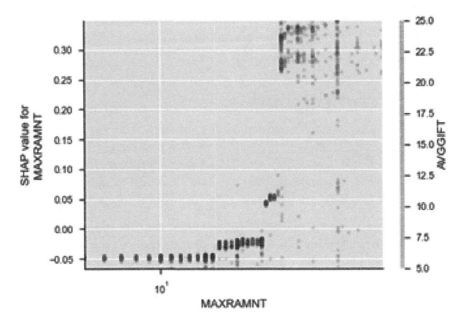

Figure 10.11 – SHAP interaction plot between MAXRAMNT and AVGGIFT

A lesson you could take from *Figure 10.11* is that a cluster is formed by certain values of these features and possibly a few other two that increase the likelihood of a donation. From a feature engineering standpoint, you could take unsupervised methods to create special cluster features solely based on the few features you have identified as related. Or you could take a more manual route, comparing different plots to understand how to best identify clusters. You could derive binary features from this process or even a ratio between features that more clearly depict interactions or cluster belonging.

The idea here is not to reinvent the wheel trying to do what the model already does so well but to, first and foremost, aim for a more straightforward model interpretation. Hopefully, that will even have a positive impact on predictive performance by tidying up the features, because if you understand them better, maybe the model does so too! It's like smoothing a grainy image; it might confuse you less and the model too (see *Chapter 13, Adversarial Robustness*, for more on that)! But understanding the data better through the model has other positive side effects.

In fact, the lessons don't stop with feature engineering or modeling but can be directly applied to promotions. What if tipping points identified could be used to encourage donations? Perhaps get a free mug if you donate over X? Or set up a recurring donation of X and be in the exclusive list of "silver" patrons?

We will end this topic on that curious note, but hopefully, this inspires you to appreciate how we can apply lessons from model interpretation to feature selection, engineering, and much more.

Mission accomplished

To approach this mission, you have reduced overfitting using primarily the toolset of feature selection. The non-profit is pleased with a profit lift of roughly 30%, costing a total of $35,601, which is $30,000 less than it would cost to send everyone in the test dataset the mailer. However, they still want assurance that they can safely employ this model without worries that they'll experience losses.

In this chapter, we've examined how overfitting can cause the profitability curves not to align. Misalignment is critical because it could mean that choosing a threshold based on training data would not be reliable on out-of-sample data. So, you use `compare_df_plots` to compare profitability between the test and train sets as you've done before, but this time for the chosen model (`rf_5_e-llarsic`):

```
profits_test = reg_mdls['rf_5_e-llarsic']['profits_test']
profits_train = reg_mdls['rf_5_e-llarsic']['profits_train']
mldatasets.compare_df_plots(\
            profits_test[['costs', 'profit', 'roi']],\
            profits_train[['costs', 'profit', 'roi']],
            'Test',\
            'Train', x_label='Threshold', \
            y_formatter=y_formatter,\
            plot_args={'secondary_y':'roi'})
```

The preceding code generates what is shown in *Figure 10.12*. You can show this to the non-profit to prove that there's a sweet spot at $0.68 that is the second highest profit attainable in **Test**. It is also within reach of their budget and achieves an ROI of 41%. More importantly, these numbers are not far from what they are for **Train**. Another thing that is great to see is that the profit curve slowly slides down for both **Train** and **Test** instead of dramatically falling off a cliff. The non-profit can be assured that the operation would still be profitable if they choose to increase the threshold. After all, they want to target donors from the entire mailing list, and for that to be financially feasible, they have to be more exclusive. Say they are using a threshold of $0.77 on the entire mailing list; the campaign would cost about $46,000 but return over $24,000 in profit:

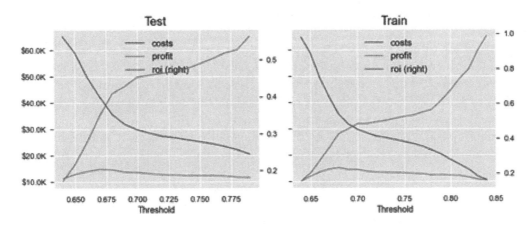

Figure 10.12 – Comparison between profit, costs, and ROI for the test and train datasets for the model
with Lasso Lars via AIC features across different thresholds

Congratulations! You have accomplished this mission!

But there's one crucial detail we'd be remiss if we didn't bring up.

Although we trained this model with the next campaign in mind, the model will likely
be used in future direct marketing campaigns without retraining. This model reusing
presents a problem. There's a concept called **data drift**, also known as **feature drift**, which
is that over time, what the model learned about the features concerning the target variable
no longer holds true. Another, **concept drift**, is about how the definition of the target
feature changes over time. For instance, what constitutes a profitable donor can change.
Both drifts can happen simultaneously, and with problems involving human behavior,
this is to be expected. Behavior is shaped by cultures, habits, attitudes, technologies, and
fashions, which are always evolving. You can caution the non-profit that you can only
assure that the model will be reliable for the next campaign, but they can't afford to hire
you for model retraining every single time!

You can propose to the client to create a script that monitors drift directly on their mailing
list database. If it finds significant changes in the features used by the model, it will alert
both them and you. You could, at this point, trigger automatic retraining of the model.
However, if the drift is due to data corruption, you won't have an opportunity to address
the problem. And even if automatic retraining is done, it can't be deployed if performance
metrics don't meet predetermined standards. Either way, you should keep a close eye on
predictive performance to be able to guarantee reliability. Reliability is an essential theme
in model interpretability because it relates heavily to accountability. We won't cover drift
detection in this book, but future chapters discuss data augmentation (*Chapter 11, Bias
Mitigation and Causal Inference Methods*) and adversarial robustness (*Chapter 13*), which
pertain to reliability.

Summary

In this chapter, we have learned about how irrelevant features impact model outcomes and how feature selection provides a toolset to solve this problem. We then explored many different methods in this toolset, from the most basic filter methods to the most advanced ones. Lastly, we broached the subject of feature engineering for interpretability. Feature engineering can make for a more interpretable model that will perform better. We will cover this topic in more detail in *Chapter 12, Monotonic Constraints and Model Tuning for Interpretability*. In the next chapter, we will discuss methods for bias mitigation and causal inference.

Dataset sources

- Ling, C., & Li, C. (1998). *Data Mining for Direct Marketing: Problems and Solutions.* In Proceedings of the Fourth International Conference on Knowledge Discovery and Data Mining (KDD'98). AAAI Press, 73–79. https://dl.acm.org/doi/10.5555/3000292.3000304

- UCI Machine Learning Repository. (1998). KDD Cup 1998 Data Data Set. https://archive.ics.uci.edu/ml/datasets/KDD+Cup+1998+Data

Further reading

- Ross, B.C. (2014). *Mutual Information between Discrete and Continuous Data Sets.* PLoS ONE, 9. https://journals.plos.org/plosone/article?id=10.1371/journal.pone.0087357

- P. Geurts, D. Ernst., & L. Wehenkel. (2006). *Extremely randomized trees.* Machine Learning, 63(1), 3-42. https://link.springer.com/article/10.1007/s10994-006-6226-1

- Abid, A., Balin, M.F., & Zou, J. (2019). *Concrete Autoencoders for Differentiable Feature Selection and Reconstruction.* ICML. https://arxiv.org/abs/1901.09346

- Tan, F., Fu, X., Zhang, Y., & Bourgeois, A.G. (2008). *A genetic algorithm-based method for feature subset selection.* Soft Computing, 12, 111-120. https://link.springer.com/article/10.1007/s00500-007-0193-8

- Manuel Calzolari. (2020, October 12). manuel-calzolari/sklearn-genetic: sklearn-genetic 0.3.0 (Version 0.3.0). Zenodo. http://doi.org/10.5281/zenodo.4081754

11
Bias Mitigation and Causal Inference Methods

In *Chapter 7, Anchors and Counterfactual Explanations*, we examined fairness and its connection to decision-making but limited to post-hoc model interpretation methods. In *Chapter 10, Feature Selection and Engineering for Interpretability*, we broached the topic of cost-sensitivity, which often relates to balance or fairness. In this chapter, we will engage with methods that will balance data and tune models for fairness.

With a credit card default dataset, we will learn how to leverage target visualizers such as class balance to detect undesired bias, then how to reduce it via preprocessing methods such as reweighting and disparate impact remover for in-processing and equalized odds for post-processing. Extending from the topics of *Chapter 7, Anchors and Counterfactual Explanations,* and *Chapter 10, Feature Selection and Engineering for Interpretability*, we will also study how policy decisions can have unexpected, counterintuitive, or detrimental effects. A decision, in the context of hypothesis testing, is called a **treatment**. For many decision-making scenarios, it is critical to estimate their effect and make sure this estimate is reliable.

Therefore, we will hypothesize treatments for reducing credit card default for the most vulnerable populations and leverage causal modeling to determine its **average treatment effects (ATE)** and **conditional average treatment effects (CATE)**. Finally, we make sure we test causal assumptions and the robustness of estimates using a variety of methods.

These are the main topics we are going to cover:

- Detecting bias
- Mitigating bias
- Creating a causal model
- Understanding heterogeneous treatment effects
- Testing estimate robustness

Technical requirements

This chapter's example uses the `mldatasets`, `pandas`, `numpy`, `sklearn`, `lightgbm`, `xgboost`, `matplotlib`, `seaborn`, `xai`, `aif360`, `econml`, and `dowhy` libraries. Instructions on how to install all of these libraries are in the preface. The code for this chapter is located here:

`https://github.com/PacktPublishing/Interpretable-Machine-Learning-with-Python/tree/master/Chapter11`

The mission

Over 2.8 billion credit cards are circulating worldwide, and they collectively spend over $25 trillion (US) every year (`https://www.ft.com/content/ad826e32-2ee8-11e9-ba00-0251022932c8`). These are astronomic amounts, no doubt, but the credit card industry's size is best measured not by what is spent, but by what is owed. Card issuers such as banks make the bulk of their money from interest. So, the over-$60 trillion owed by consumers, of which credit card debt is a sizable portion, provides a steady income to lenders in the form of interest. It could be argued this is good for business, but it also poses ample risk because if a borrower defaults before the principal plus operation costs have been repaid, the lender could lose, especially once they've exhausted legal avenues to collect the debt.

When there's a credit bubble, this problem is compounded because an unhealthy level of debt can compromise lender finances and take their stakeholders down with them when the bubble collapses. Such was the case with the 2008 housing bubble, also known as the subprime mortgage crisis. These bubbles often begin with speculation on growth and seeking unqualified demand to fuel that growth. In the case of the mortgage crisis, it offered mortgages to people with no proven capacity to repay. It also, sadly, targeted minorities who had their entire net worth wiped out once the bubble burst. Financial crises and depressions, and every calamity in between, tend to affect those that are most vulnerable at much higher rates.

Credit cards have also been involved in catastrophic bubbles, notably South Korea in 2003 (`https://www.bis.org/repofficepubl/arpresearch_fs_200806.10. pdf`) and Taiwan in 2006. This chapter will examine data from 2005, leading to the Taiwanese credit card crisis. By 2006, delinquent credit card debt reached $268 billion owed by over 700,000 people. Just over 3% of the Taiwanese population could not pay even the credit card's minimum balance, and colloquially were known as **credit card slaves**. Significant societal ramifications ensued, such as a sharp increase in homelessness, drug traffic/abuse, and even suicide. In the aftermath of the 1997 Asian financial crisis, suicide steadily increased around the region. A 23% jump between 2005 and 2006 pushed Taiwan's suicide rate to the world's second-highest (`https://www.taiwannews. com.tw/en/news/358044`).

If we trace back the crisis to its root causes, it was about new card-issuing banks having exhausted a saturated real-estate market, slashing requirements to obtain credit cards, which at the time were poorly regulated by authorities. It hit younger people the most because they typically have less income and experience in managing money. In 2005, the Taiwanese Financial Supervisory Commission issued new regulations to raise credit card applicants' requirements, preventing new credit card slaves. However, more policies would be needed to attend to the debt and the debtors already in the system. Authorities started discussing the creation of **asset management corporations** (**AMCs**) to take bad debts from the balance sheet of banks. They also wanted to pass a *debtors' repayment regulation* that would provide a framework to negotiate a reasonable repayment plan. Both of these policies weren't codified into law till 2006.

Hypothetically, let's say it's August 2005, and you have come from the future armed with novel machine learning and causal inference methods! A Taiwanese bank wants to create a classification model to predict customers that will default on their loans. They have provided you with a dataset with 30,000 of their credit card customers. Regulators are still drafting the laws, so there's an opportunity to propose policies that benefit both the bank and the debtors. When the law has passed, using the classification model, they can then anticipate which debts they should sell to the AMC and, with the causal model, estimate which policies would benefit other customers and the bank, but they want to do this fairly and robustly—this is your mission!

The approach

The bank has stressed to you how important it is that there's fairness embedded in your methods because the regulators and the public at large want assurance that banks will not cause any more harm. Their reputation depends on it too, because in the past months, the media has been relentless in blaming them for dishonest and predatory lending practices, causing distrust in consumers. For this reason, they want to use state-of-the-art robustness testing to demonstrate that the prescribed policies will alleviate the problem. Your proposed approach includes the following points:

- Younger lenders have been reported to be more prone to default on repayment, so you expect to find age bias, but you will also *look for bias* with other protected groups such as gender.

- Once you have detected bias, you can *mitigate bias* with preprocessing, in-processing, and post-processing algorithms using the **AI Fairness 360 (AIF360)** library. In this process, you will train different models with each algorithm, assess their fairness, and choose the fairest model.

- To be able to understand the impact of policies, the bank has conducted an experiment on a small portion of customers. With the experimental results, you can fit a *causal model* through the dowhy library that will identify the *causal effect*. These effects were broken down further by the causal model to reveal the heterogeneous treatment effects.

- Then, we can *assess the heterogeneous treatment effects* to understand them and decide which treatment is the most effective.

- Lastly, to *ensure that our conclusions are robust*, you will refute this estimate with several methods to see if the effect holds.

Let's dig in!

The preparations

You will find the code for this example here:

```
https://github.com/PacktPublishing/Interpretable-Machine-
Learning-with-Python/blob/master/Chapter11/CreditCardDefaults.
ipynb
```

Loading the libraries

To run this example, you need to install the following libraries:

- `mldatasets` to load the dataset

- `pandas` and `numpy` to manipulate it

- `sklearn` (scikit-learn), `xgboost`, `aif360`, and `lightgbm` to split the data and fit the models

- `matplotlib`, `seaborn`, and `xai` to visualize the interpretations

- `econml` and `dowhy` for causal inference

You should load all of them first, as follows:

```
import math
import os
import mldatasets
import pandas as pd
import numpy as np
from tqdm.notebook import tqdm
from sklearn import model_selection, tree
import lightgbm as lgb
import xgboost as xgb
from aif360.datasets import BinaryLabelDataset
from aif360.metrics import BinaryLabelDatasetMetric,\
ClassificationMetric
from aif360.algorithms.preprocessing import Reweighing,\
DisparateImpactRemover
from aif360.algorithms.inprocessing import PrejudiceRemover,\
```

```
GerryFairClassifier
from aif360.algorithms.postprocessing.\
                calibrated_eq_odds_postprocessing import\

CalibratedEqOddsPostprocessing
from aif360.algorithms.postprocessing.eq_odds_postprocessing
import EqOddsPostprocessing
from econml.dr import LinearDRLearner
import dowhy
from dowhy import CausalModel
import xai
from networkx.drawing.nx_pydot import to_pydot
from IPython.display import Image, display
import matplotlib.pyplot as plt
import seaborn as sns
```

Understanding and preparing the data

We load the data like this into a dataframe we call `ccdefault_all_df`:

```
ccdefault_all_df = mldatasets.load("cc-default", prepare=True)
```

There should be 30,000 records and 31 columns. We can verify this was the case with `info()`, like this:

```
ccdefault_all_df.info()
```

The preceding code outputs the following:

```
<class 'pandas.core.frame.DataFrame'>
Int64Index: 30000 entries, 1 to 30000
Data columns (total 31 columns):
 #   Column          Non-Null Count   Dtype
---  ------          --------------   -----
 0   CC_LIMIT_CAT    30000 non-null   int8
 1   EDUCATION       30000 non-null   int8
 2   MARITAL_STATUS  30000 non-null   int8
 3   GENDER          30000 non-null   int8
 4   AGE_GROUP       30000 non-null   int8
```

5	pay_status_1	30000 non-null	int8
6	pay_status_2	30000 non-null	int8
7	pay_status_3	30000 non-null	int8
8	pay_status_4	30000 non-null	int8
9	pay_status_5	30000 non-null	int8
10	pay_status_6	30000 non-null	int8
11	paid_pct_1	30000 non-null	float64
12	paid_pct_2	30000 non-null	float64
13	paid_pct_3	30000 non-null	float64
14	paid_pct_4	30000 non-null	float64
15	paid_pct_5	30000 non-null	float64
16	paid_pct_6	30000 non-null	float64
17	bill1_over_limit	30000 non-null	float64
18	IS_DEFAULT	30000 non-null	int8
19	_AGE	30000 non-null	int16
20	_spend	30000 non-null	int32
21	_tpm	30000 non-null	int16
22	_ppm	30000 non-null	int16
23	_RETAIL	30000 non-null	int8
24	_URBAN	30000 non-null	int8
25	_RURAL	30000 non-null	int8
26	_PREMIUM	30000 non-null	int8
27	_TREATMENT	30000 non-null	int8
28	_LTV	30000 non-null	float64
29	_CC_LIMIT	30000 non-null	int32
30	_risk_score	30000 non-null	float64

```
dtypes: float64(9), int16(3), int32(2), int8(17)
memory usage: 3.2 MB
```

The output checks out. All features are numeric with no missing values because we used prepare=True. Categorical features are all int8 because they have been already encoded.

The data dictionary

There are 30 features, but we won't use them together because 18 of them are for the bias mitigation exercise, and the remaining 12 that start with an underscore (_) are for the causal inference exercise. Soon, we will split the data into the corresponding datasets for each exercise. It's important to note that lowercase features have to do with each client's transactional history, whereas client account or target features are uppercase.

We will use the following features in the *bias mitigation exercise*:

- CC_LIMIT_CAT: ordinal; the credit card limit (_CC_LIMIT) separated into eight more or less equally distributed quartiles

- EDUCATION: nominal; the customer's educational attainment level (0: Other, 1: High School, 2: Undergraduate, 3: Graduate)

- MARITAL_STATUS: nominal; the customer's marital status (0: Other, 1: Single, 2: Married)

- GENDER: nominal; the gender of the customer (1: Male, 2: Female)

- AGE GROUP: binary; denoting if the customer belongs to a privileged age group (1: privileged (26-47 years old), 0: underprivileged (every other age))

- pay_status_1... pay_status_6: ordinal; the repayment status for the previous six periods from April, pay_status_6, to August 2005, pay_status_1 (-1: pay duly, 1: payment is 1 month delayed, 2: payment is 2 months delayed... 8: 8 months delayed, 9: 9 months and above)

- paid_pct_1... paid_pct_6: continuous; what percentage of the bill due each month from April, paid_pct_6, to August 2005, paid_pct_1, was paid

- bill1_over_limit: continuous; the last bill's ratio in August 2005 over the corresponding credit limit

- IS_DEFAULT: binary; target; whether the customer defaulted

These are the features we will use only in the *causal inference exercise*:

- _AGE: continuous; the age in years of the customer

- _spend: continuous; how much was spent by each customer in **New Taiwan Dollar (NT$)**

- _tpm: continuous; median transactions per month made by the customer with the credit card over the previous 6 months

- _ppm: continuous; median purchases per month made by the customer with the credit card over the previous 6 months

- _RETAIL: binary; if the customer is retail, instead of a customer obtained through their employer

- _URBAN: binary; if it's an urban customer

- _RURAL: binary; if it's a rural customer

- _PREMIUM: binary; if the customer is "premium". Premium customers get cashback offers and other spending incentives.

- _TREATMENT: nominal; the intervention or policy prescribed to each customer (-1: not part of the experiment, 0: Control group, 1: Lower Credit Limit, 2: Payment Plan, 3: Payment Plan and Credit Limit)

- _LTV: continuous; the outcome of the intervention, which is the lifetime value estimated in *NT$* given the credit payment behavior over the previous 6 months

- _CC_LIMIT: continuous; the original credit card limit in *NT$* that the customer had before the treatment. Bankers expect the outcome of the treatment to be greatly impacted by this feature.

- _risk_score: continuous; the risk score that the bank computed 6 months prior for each customer based on credit card bills' ratio over their credit card limit. It's like bill1_over_limit except it's a weighted average of 6 months of payment history, and it was produced 5 months before to choose the treatment.

We will explain the causal inference features a bit more and their purpose in the corresponding section. Meanwhile, let's break down the _TREATMENT feature by its values with value_counts() to understand how we will split this dataset, as follows:

```
ccdefault_all_df._TREATMENT.value_counts()
```

The preceding code outputs the following:

```
-1     28904
 3       274
 2       274
 1       274
 0       274
Name: _TREATMENT, dtype: int64
```

Most of the observations are treatment -1, so they are not part of the causal inference. The remainder was split evenly between the three treatments (1-3) and the control group (0). Naturally, we will use these four groups for the causal inference exercise. However, since the control group wasn't prescribed treatment, we can use it in our bias mitigation exercise along with the -1 treatments. We have to be careful to exclude customers whose behaviors were manipulated in the bias mitigation exercise. The whole point is to predict which customers are most likely to default under "business as usual" circumstances while attempting to reduce bias.

Data preparation

Our single data preparation step, for now, is to split the datasets, which can be easily done by subsetting the pandas DataFrames using the _TREATMENT column. We will create one DataFrame for each exercise with this subsetting: bias mitigation (ccdefault_ bias_df) and causal inference (ccdefault_causal_df). These can be seen in the following code snippet:

```
ccdefault_bias_df =\
                ccdefault_all_df[ccdefault_all_df._TREATMENT
< 1]
ccdefault_causal_df =\
                ccdefault_all_df[ccdefault_all_df._TREATMENT
>= 0]
```

We will do a few other data preparation steps within the in-depth sections but, for now, we are good to go to get started!

Detecting bias

There are many sources for bias in machine learning. As outlined in *Chapter 1, Interpretation, Interpretability, and Explainability; and Why Does It All Matter?*, there are ample sources of bias. Those rooted in the *truths* that the data is representing, such as systemic and structural ones that lead to prejudice bias in the data. There are also biases rooted in the data itself, such as sample, exclusion, association, and measurement biases. Lastly, there are biases in the insights we derive from data or models we have to be careful with, such as conservatism bias, salience bias, and fundamental attribution error.

For this example, to properly disentangle so many bias levels, we ought to connect our data to census data for Taiwan in 2005 and historical lending data split by demographics. Then, using these external datasets, control for credit card contract conditions, as well as gender, income, and other demographic data to ascertain if young people, in particular, were targeted for high-interest credit cards they shouldn't have qualified for. We would also need to trace the dataset to the authors and consult with them and the domain experts to examine the dataset for bias-related data quality issues. Ideally, these steps would be necessary to validate the hypothesis but would be a monumental task requiring several chapters' worth of explanation.

Therefore, in the spirit of expediency, we take the premise of this chapter at face value. That is, due to predatory lending practices, certain age groups are more vulnerable to credit card default, not through any fault of their own. In the same spirit, we will also take at face value the quality of the dataset. With these caveats in place, it means that if we find disparities between age groups in the data or any model derived from this data, it can be attributed solely to predatory practices.

There are also two kinds of fairness, outlined here:

- **Procedural fairness**: This is about fair or equal treatment. It's hard to define this term legally because it depends so much on the context.
- **Outcome fairness**: This is solely about measuring fair outcomes.

These two concepts aren't mutually exclusive since the procedure may be fair but the outcome unfair, or vice versa. In this example, the unfair *procedure* was the offering of high-interest credit cards to unqualified customers. Nevertheless, we are going to focus on outcome fairness during this chapter.

When we discuss bias in machine learning, it will impact *protected* features, and within these features there will be *privileged* and *underprivileged* groups. The latter is a group that is adversely impacted by the bias. There are also many ways in which the bias is manifested, and thus addressed as follows:

- **Representation**: There can be a lack of representation or an overrepresentation of the underprivileged group. The model will learn either too little or too much about this group, compared to others.
- **Distribution**: Differences in distribution of features between groups can lead the model to make biased associations that can impact model outcomes either directly or indirectly.

- **Probability**: For classification problems, class balance discrepancies between groups such as those discussed in *Chapter 7, Anchor and Counterfactual Explanations,* can lead to the model learning that one group has a higher probability to be part of one class or another. These can be easily observed through confusion matrices or comparing their classification metrics such as false positive or false negative rates.

- **Hybrid**: A combination of any of the preceding manifestations.

Strategies for any bias manifestation are discussed in the bias mitigation section, but the kind we address in the chapter pertains to disparities with probability for our main protected attribute (_AGE). We will observe this through these means:

- **Visualizing dataset bias**: Observing disparities in the data for protected feature through visualizations.

- **Quantifying dataset bias**: Measuring them using fairness metrics.

- **Quantifying model bias**: We will train a classification model and use other fairness metrics designed for models.

Model bias can be visualized, as we have done already in *Chapter 7, Anchors and Counterfactual Explanations,* or as we will do in *Chapter 12, Monotonic Constraints and Model Tuning for Interpretability.* We will quickly explore some other visualizations later in this chapter, in a subsection called *Tying it all together!* Without further ado, let's move on to the practical portion of this section.

Visualizing dataset bias

The data itself tells the story of how probable it is that one group belongs to a positive class versus another. If it's a categorical feature, these probabilities can be obtained by dividing the `value_counts()` function for the positive class over all. For instance, for gender, we could do this:

```
ccdefault_bias_df[ccdefault_bias_df.IS_DEFAULT==1].GENDER.
          value_counts()/ccdefault_bias_df.GENDER.value_
counts()
```

The preceding snippet produces the following output, which shows that males have, on average, a higher probability of defaulting on their credit card:

```
2    0.206529
1    0.241633
Name: GENDER, dtype: float64
```

The code of how to do this for a continuous feature is a bit more complicated. It is recommended that you use pandas' qcut to divide the feature into quartiles first and then use the same approach used for categorical features. Fortunately, the plot_prob_progression function does this for you and plots the progression of probabilities for each quartile. The first attribute is a pandas series, array, or list with the protected feature (_AGE), and the second is the same but for the target feature (IS_DEFAULT). We then choose the amount of intervals (x_intervals) that we are setting as quartiles (use_quartiles=True). The rest of the attributes are aesthetic, such as the label, title, and adding a mean_line. The code can be seen in the following snippet:

```
mldatasets.plot_prob_progression(ccdefault_bias_df._AGE,\
                    ccdefault_bias_df.IS_DEFAULT, x_intervals=8,\
                    use_quartiles=True, xlabel='Age', \
                    mean_line=True,\
                    title='Probability of Default by Age')
```

The preceding code produced the following output, which depicts how the youngest (21-25) and oldest (47-79) are most likely to default. All other groups represent just over one standard deviation from the mean:

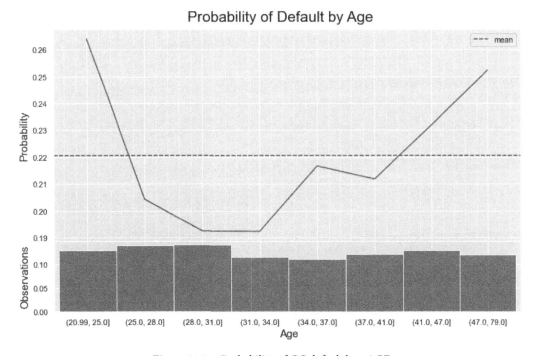

Figure 11.1 – Probability of CC default by _AGE

We can call the youngest and oldest quartiles the underprivileged group and all others the privileged group. In order to detect and mitigate unfairness, it is best to code them as a binary feature—and we have done just that with AGE_GROUP. We can leverage plot_prob_progression again, but this time with AGE_GROUP instead of AGE, and we will replace the numbers with labels we can interpret more easily. The code can be seen in the following snippet:

```
mldatasets.plot_prob_progression(\
    ccdefault_bias_df.AGE_GROUP.
replace({0:'21-25,48+',1:'26-47'}),\
    ccdefault_bias_df.IS_DEFAULT, xlabel='Age Group',\
    title='Probability of Default by Age Group',\
mean_line=True)
```

The preceding snippet produced the following output, in which the disparities between both groups are pretty evident:

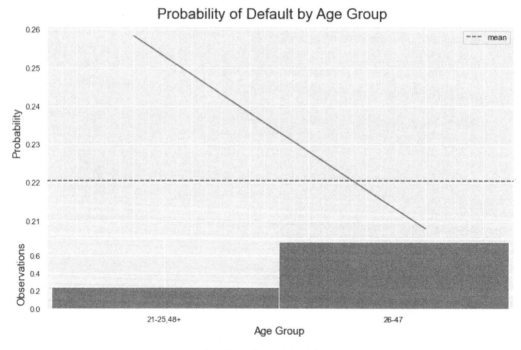

Figure 11.2 – Probability of CC default by AGE_GROUP

Next, let's bring back GENDER into the picture. We can employ plot_prob_contour_
map, which is like plot_prob_progression but in two dimensions, color-coding
the probabilities instead of drawing a line. So, the first two attributes are the features we
want on the *x* axis (GENDER) and *y* axis (AGE_GROUP), and the third is the target (IS_
DEFAULT). Since both our features are binary, it is best to use plot_type='grid' as
opposed to contour. The code can be seen in the following snippet:

```
mldatasets.plot_prob_contour_map(\
  ccdefault_bias_df.GENDER.replace({1:'Male',2:'Female'}),\
  ccdefault_bias_df.AGE_GROUP.
replace({0:'21-25,48+',1:'26-47'}),\
  ccdefault_bias_df.IS_DEFAULT, xlabel='Gender', ylabel='Age
Group',\
  title='Probability of Default by Gender/Age Group',
annotate=True,\
  plot_type='grid')
```

The preceding snippet generates the following output. It is immediately evident how the
most privileged group is 26-47-year-old females, followed by their male counterparts at
about 3-4% apart. The same happens with the underprivileged age group:

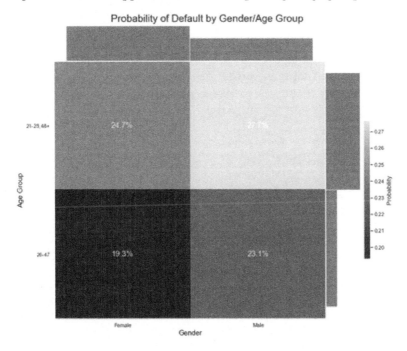

Figure 11.3 – Probability grid of CC default by GENDER and AGE_GROUP

The gender difference is an interesting observation, and we could present a number of hypotheses as to why females are defaulting less. Are they just simply better at managing debt, or do men have other burdens such as family or couples' expenses? Does it have to do with their marital status or education? We won't dig deeper into these questions. Given that we only know of age-based discrimination, we will only use AGE_GROUP in privilege groups but keep GENDER a protected attribute, which will be factored in some fairness metrics we will monitor. Speaking of metrics, we will quantify dataset bias next.

Quantifying dataset bias

There are three kinds of fairness metrics, outlined here:

- **Individual fairness**: How close individual observations are to their peers in the data. Distance metrics such as *Euclidean* and *Manhattan distance* can serve this purpose.

- **Group fairness**: How labels or outcomes between groups are on average distant to each other. These can be measured either in the data or for a model.

- **Both**: A few metrics measure entropy or variance by factoring inequality both in-group and between groups, such as the *Theil index* and the *coefficient of variation*.

We will focus exclusively on group fairness metrics in this chapter.

Before we compute fairness metrics, there are a few pending data preparation steps. Let's make sure the dataset we will use for the bias mitigation exercise (ccdefault_bias_df) only has the pertinent columns, which are those that don't begin with underscore ("_"). On the other hand, the causal inference exercise will include only the underscored columns plus AGE_GROUP and IS_DEFAULT. The code can be seen in the following snippet:

```
cols_bias_l = ccdefault_all_df.\
    columns[~ccdefault_all_df.columns.str.startswith('_')].
tolist()
cols_causal_l =
    ['AGE_GROUP','IS_DEFAULT'] + ccdefault_all_df.\
    columns[ccdefault_all_df.columns.str.startswith('_')].
tolist()
ccdefault_bias_df = ccdefault_bias_df[cols_bias_l]
ccdefault_causal_df = ccdefault_causal_df[cols_causal_l]
```

Also, it's more important to quantify dataset bias on the training data because that is the data the model will learn from, so let's go ahead and split the data into train and test X and y pairs. We do this after we have, of course, initialized the random seed to aim for some reproducibility. The code can be seen in the following snippet:

```
rand = 9
os.environ['PYTHONHASHSEED']=str(rand)
np.random.seed(rand)
y = ccdefault_bias_df['IS_DEFAULT']
X = ccdefault_bias_df.drop(['IS_DEFAULT'], axis=1).copy()
X_train, X_test, y_train, y_test =\
            model_selection.train_test_split(X, y,\
    test_size=0.25,\
                                random_state=rand)
```

Even though we will use the pandas data we just split for training and performance evaluation, the library we will use for this exercise, called AIF360, abstracts datasets into base classes. These classes include the data converted to a NumPy array and store attributes related to fairness. For regression, AIF360 has `RegressionDataset`, but for this binary classification example, we will use the `BinaryLabelDataset`. You can initialize it with the Pandas dataframe with both features and labels (`X_train.join(y_train)`). Then, you specify the name of the label (`label_names`) and protected attributes (`protected_attribute_names`), and it is recommended that you enter a value for `favorable_label` and `unfavorable_label`, which tells AIF360 which label values are preferred so that it factors it into how it assess fairness. As confusing as it may seem, positive and, in contrast, negative in binary classification only pertain to what we are trying to predict—the positive class—and not whether it is a favorable outcome. The code can be seen in the following snippet:

```
train_ds = BinaryLabelDataset(df=X_train.join(y_train),\
            label_names=['IS_DEFAULT'],\
            protected_attribute_names=['AGE_GROUP',\
                                'GENDER'],\
            favorable_label=0, unfavorable_label=1)
test_ds = BinaryLabelDataset(df=X_test.join(y_test),\
            label_names=['IS_DEFAULT'],\
            protected_attribute_names=['AGE_GROUP',\
                                'GENDER'],\
            favorable_label=0, unfavorable_label=1)
```

Next, we create arrays for `unprivileged_groups` and `privileged_groups`. Those in `AGE_GROUP=1` have a lower probability of default so they are privileged, and vice versa. Then, with these and the abstracted dataset for train (`train_ds`), we can initialize a metrics class via `BinaryLabelDatasetMetric`. This class has functions for computing several group fairness metrics, judging the data alone. We will output three of them and then explain what they mean. The code can be seen in the following snippet:

```
unprivileged_groups=[{'AGE_GROUP': 0}]
privileged_groups=[{'AGE_GROUP': 1}]
metrics_train_ds = BinaryLabelDatasetMetric(train_ds,\
                    unprivileged_groups=unprivileged_groups,\
                    privileged_groups=privileged_groups)
print('Statistical Parity Difference (SPD): %.4f' %\
        metrics_train_ds.statistical_parity_difference())
print('Disparate Impact (DI): %.4f' %\
        metrics_train_ds.disparate_impact())
print('Smoothed Empirical Differential Fairness (SEDF): %.4f' %\
        metrics_train_ds.smoothed_empirical_differential_
fairness())
```

The preceding snippet generates the following output:

Statistical Parity Difference (SPD):	-0.0437
Disparate Impact (DI):	0.9447
Smoothed Empirical Differential Fairness (SEDF):	0.3514

Now, let's explain what each metric means, as follows:

- **Statistical parity difference (SPD)**: Also known as the **mean difference**, this is the difference between the mean probability of favorable outcomes between underprivileged and privileged groups. A negative number is bad and a positive number is better, yet a number closer to zero is always preferable. It's computed with the following formula, where f is the value for the favorable class:

$$Pr(Y = f | D = \text{unprivileged}) - Pr(Y = f | D = \text{privileged})$$

- **Disparate impact** (**DI**): DI is exactly like SPD except it's the ratio not the difference. And, as ratios go, the closer to one the better; under one would mean disadvantaged, and over one means advantaged. The formula is shown here:

$$\frac{Pr(Y = f | D = \text{unprivileged})}{Pr(Y = f | D = \text{privileged})}$$

- **Smoothed empirical differential fairness** (**SEDF**): This fairness metric is one of the many newer ones from a paper called *"An Intersectional Definition of Fairness"*. Unlike the previous two metrics, it's not restricted to the predetermined privileges and underprivileged groups, but it's extended to include all the categories in the protected attributes—in this case, the four in *Figure 11.3*. The authors of the paper argue that fairness is particularly tricky when you have a crosstab of protected attributes. This occurs because of **Simpson's paradox**, which is that one group can be advantaged or disadvantaged in aggregate but not when subdivided into crosstabs. We won't get into the math, but their method accounts for this possibility while measuring a sensible level of fairness in intersectional scenarios. To interpret it, zero represents absolute fairness, and the farther from zero, the less fair it is.

Next, we will quantify group fairness metrics for a model.

Quantifying model bias

Before we compute metrics, we will need to train a model. To that end, we will initialize a LightGBM classifier (LGBMClassifier) with optimal hyperparameters (lgb_params). These have already been hyperparameter-tuned for us (more details on how to do this in *Chapter 12, Monotonic Constraints and Model Tuning for Interpretability*). Please note that these parameters include scale_pos_weight, which is for class weighting. Since this is an unbalanced classification task, this is an essential parameter to leverage so that the classifier is cost-sensitive-trained, penalizing one form of misclassification over another. Once the classifier is initialized, it is fit and evaluated with evaluate_class_mdl, which returns a dictionary with predictive performance metrics that we can store in a model dictionary (cls_mdls). The code can be seen in the following snippet:

```
cls_mdls = {}
lgb_params = {'learning_rate': 0.4, 'reg_alpha': 21,\
              'reg_lambda': 1, 'scale_pos_weight': 1.8}
lgb_base_mdl = lgb.LGBMClassifier(random_seed=rand, \
max_depth=6, num_leaves=33,  **lgb_params)
```

```
lgb_base_mdl.fit(X_train, y_train)
cls_mdls['lgb_0_base'] = mldatasets.\
    evaluate_class_mdl(lgb_base_mdl, X_train, X_test,\
            y_train, y_test, plot_roc=False,\
            plot_conf_matrix=True,\
            show_summary=True, ret_eval_dict=True)
```

The preceding snippet of code outputs *Figure 11.4*. The scale_pos_weight parameter ensures a healthier balance between false positives in the top-right corner and false negatives in the bottom left. As a result, precision and recall aren't too far off from each other. We favor high precision for a problem such as this one because we want to maximize true positives; however, not at great expense of recall, so a balance between both is even more critical. While hyperparameter tuning, the F1 score, and the **Matthews correlation coefficient** (MCC) are useful metrics to use to this end. The evaluation of the LightGBM base model is shown here:

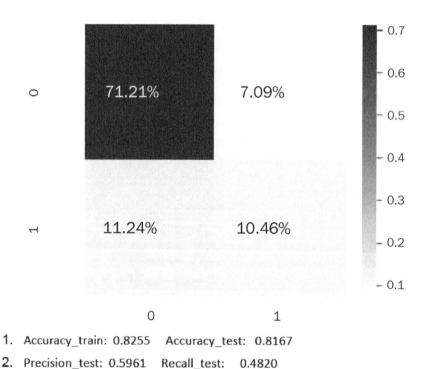

1. Accuracy_train: 0.8255   Accuracy_test: 0.8167

2. Precision_test: 0.5961   Recall_test: 0.4820

3. ROC-AUC_test: 0.7901   F1_test: 0.5330   MCC_test: 0.4243

Figure 11.4 – Evaluation of LightGBM base model

Next, let's compute the fairness metrics for the model. To do this, we need to make a "deep" copy (deepcopy=True) of the AIF360 dataset, but we change the labels and scores to be those predicted by our model. The compute_aif_metrics function employs the ClassificationMetric class of AIF360 to do for the model what BinaryLabelDatasetMetric did for the dataset. However, it doesn't engage with the model directly. It computes fairness using the original dataset (test_ds) and the modified one with the model's predictions (test_pred_ds). The compute_aif_metrics function creates a dictionary with several precalculated metrics (metrics_test_dict) and the metric class (metrics_test_cls), which can be used to obtain metrics one by one. The code can be seen in the following snippet:

```
test_pred_ds = test_ds.copy(deepcopy=True)
test_pred_ds.labels =\
cls_mdls['lgb_0_base']['preds_test'].\
reshape(-1,1)
test_pred_ds.scores = \
cls_mdls['lgb_0_base']['probs_test'].\
reshape(-1,1)
metrics_test_dict, metrics_test_cls = mldatasets.\
                        compute_aif_metrics(test_ds, test_
pred_ds,\
                        unprivileged_groups=unprivileged_
groups,\
                        privileged_groups=privileged_groups)
cls_mdls['lgb_0_base'].update(metrics_test_dict)
print('Statistical Parity Difference (SPD): %.4f' %\
                        metrics_test_cls.statistical_parity_
difference())
print('Disparate Impact (DI): %.4f' %\
                        metrics_test_cls.disparate_impact())
print('Average Odds Difference (AOD): %.4f' %\
                        metrics_test_cls.average_odds_difference())
print('Equal Opportunity Difference (EOD): %.4f' %\
                        metrics_test_cls.equal_opportunity_
difference())
print('Differential Fairness Bias Amplification (DFBA): %.4f'
%\
            metrics_test_cls.differential_fairness_bias_
amplification())
```

The preceding snippet generates the following output:

```
Statistical Parity Difference (SPD):                -0.0679
Disparate Impact (DI):                               0.9193
Average Odds Difference (AOD):                       -0.0550
Equal Opportunity Difference (EOD):                  -0.0265
Differential Fairness Bias Amplification (DFBA):     0.2328
```

Now, putting the metrics we already explained aside, let's explain what the other ones mean, as follows:

- **Average odds difference (AOD)**: The difference between **false-positive rates** **(FPR)** averaged with the difference between **false-negative rates (FNR)** for both privileged and underprivileged groups. Negative means there's a disadvantage for the underprivileged group, and the closer to zero, the better. The formula is shown here:

$$1/2 \left[(FPR_{D=\text{unprivileged}} - FPR_{D=\text{privileged}}) + (TPR_{D=\text{unprivileged}} - TPR_{D=\text{privileged}})) \right]$$

- **Equal opportunity difference (EOD)**: It's only the **true positive rate (TPR)** differences of AOD, so it's only useful to measure the *opportunity* for TPRs. As with AOD, negative confirms a disadvantage for the underprivileged group, and the closer to zero, the better. The formula is shown here:

$$TPR_{D=\text{unprivileged}} - TPR_{D=\text{privileged}}$$

- **Differential fairness bias amplification (DFBA)**: This metric comes from the same paper as SEDF, and like this, it also has zero as baseline of fairness and is also intersectional. However, it only measures the difference in unfairness in proportion between the model and the data in a phenomenon called bias amplification. In other words, the value represents how much more the model increases unfairness over the original data.

If you compare the model's SPD and DI metrics to that of the data, they are indeed worse. No surprise there, because it's to be expected since model-learned representations tend to amplify bias. You can confirm this with the DFBA metrics. As for AOD and EOD, they tend to be in the same neighborhood as the SPD metrics, but ideally, the EOD metric is substantially closer to zero than the AOD metric because we care more about TPRs in this example.

Next, we will go over methods to mitigate bias in the model.

Mitigating bias

We can mitigate bias at three different levels with methods that operate at these individual levels:

- **Preprocessing**: These are interventions to detect and remove bias from the training **data** before training the model. Methods that leverage preprocessing have the advantage that they tackle bias at the source. On the other hand, any undetected bias is still amplified by the model.

- **In-processing**: These methods mitigate bias during the **model training** and are, therefore, highly dependent on the model and tend to not be model-agnostic like the preprocessing and post-processing methods. They also require hyperparameter tuning to calibrate fairness metrics.

- **Post-processing**: These methods mitigate bias during **model inference**. In *Chapter 7, Anchors and Counterfactual Explanations,* we touched on the subject of using the What-If tool to choose the right thresholds (see *Figure 7.14* in that chapter), and we manually adjusted them to achieve parity with false positives. Just as we did then, post-processing methods aim to detect and correct fairness directly in the outcomes, but what adjustments to make will depend on which metrics matter most to your problem. They have the advantage that they can tackle outcome unfairness where it can have the greatest impact, but since it's disconnected from the rest of the model development, it can distort things.

Please note that bias mitigation methods can hurt predictive performance, so there's often a trade-off. They can be opposing goals, especially in cases where the data is reflective of a biased truth. We can choose to aim for a better truth instead: a righteous one—*the one we want, not the one we have.*

This section will explain several methods for each level but will only implement and evaluate two for each. Also, we won't do it in this chapter, but you can combine different kinds of methods to maximize mitigation—for instance, you could use a preprocessing method to de-bias the data then train a model with it, and lastly use a post-processing method to remove bias added by the model.

Pre-processing bias mitigation methods

These are some of the most important preprocessing or data-specific bias mitigation methods:

- **Unawareness**: Also known as **suppression**. The most straightforward way to remove bias is to exclude biased features from the dataset, but it's a naïve approach because you assume that bias is strictly contained in those features.

- **Feature engineering**: Sometimes, continuous features capture bias because there are so many sparse areas where the model can fill voids with assumptions or learn from outliers. It can do the same with interactions. Feature engineering can place guardrails. We will discuss this topic in *Chapter 12, Monotonic Constraints and Model Tuning for Interpretability*.

- **Balancing**: Also known as **resampling**. On their own, representation problems are relatively easy to fix by balancing the dataset. The XAI library (`https://github.com/EthicalML/xai`) has a `balance` function that does this by random downsampling and upsampling of group representations. Downsampling, or under-sampling, is what we typically call sampling, which is just taking a certain percentage of the observations, whereas upsampling, or over-sampling, creates a certain amount of random duplicates. Some strategies synthetically upsample rather than duplicate, such as the **Synthetic Minority Oversampling TEchnique (SMOTE)**. However, we must caution that it's always preferable to downsample than upsample if you have enough data. It's best not to use only the balancing strategy if there are other possible bias problems.

- **Relabeling**: Also known as **massaging**, this is having an algorithm change the labels for observations that appear to be most biased, resulting in *massaged data* by ranking them. Usually, this is performed with a Naïve-Bayes classifier, and to maintain class distribution, it not only promotes some observations but demotes an equal amount.

- **Reweighing**: This method similarly ranks observations as relabeling does, but instead of flipping their labels it derives a weight for each one, which we can then implement in the learning process. Much like class weights are applied to each class, sample weights are applied to each observation or sample. Many regressors and classifiers, `LGBMClassifier` included, support sample weights. Even though technically, reweighting doesn't touch the data and solution applied to the model, it is a preprocessing method because we detected bias in the data.

- **Disparate impact remover**: The authors of this method were very careful to abide by legal definitions of bias and preserve the integrity of the data without changing the labels or the protected attributes. It implements a repair process that attempts to remove bias in the remaining features. It's an excellent process to use whenever we suspect that's where most of the bias is located—that is, the features are highly correlated with the protected attributes but it doesn't address bias elsewhere. In any case, it's a good baseline to use to understand how much of the bias is non-protected features.

- **Learning fair representations**: This leverages an adversarial learning framework. There's a generator (autoencoder) that creates representations of the data excluding the protected attribute, and a critic whose goal is that the learned representations within privileged and underprivileged groups are as close as possible.

- **Optimized preprocessing for discrimination prevention**: This method produces transformations through mathematical optimization to the data in such a way that overall probability distributions are maintained. At the same time, the correlation between protected attributes and the target is nullified. The result of this process is data that is distorted slightly to de-bias it.

Given that there are so many preprocessing methods, we will only employ two of them in this chapter. Still, if you are interested in using ones we won't cover, they are available in the AIF360 library, and you can read about them in their documentation (http://aif360.mybluemix.net/).

Reweighing method

The Reweighing method is fairly simple to implement. You initialize it by specifying the groups, then fit and transform the data as you would with any scikit-learn encoder or scaler. For those that aren't familiar with fit, the algorithm learns how to transform the provided data, and transform uses what was learned to transform it. The code can be seen in the following snippet:

```
reweighter = Reweighing(unprivileged_groups=unprivileged_
groups,\
                        privileged_groups=privileged_groups)
reweighter.fit(train_ds)
train_rw_ds = reweighter.transform(train_ds)
```

The transformation derived from this process doesn't change the data but creates weights for each observation. The AIF360 library is equipped to factor these weights into the calculations of fairness, so we can use `BinaryLabelDatasetMetric`, as we have before, to compute different metrics. The code can be seen in the following snippet:

```
metrics_train_rw_ds =\
BinaryLabelDatasetMetric(train_rw_ds,\
                    unprivileged_groups=unprivileged_groups,\
                    privileged_groups=privileged_groups)
print('Statistical Parity Difference (SPD): %.4f' %\
    metrics_train_rw_ds.statistical_parity_difference())
print('Disparate Impact (DI): %.4f' %\
    metrics_train_rw_ds.disparate_impact())
print('Smoothed Empirical Differential Fairness (SEDF): %.4f'
%\
    metrics_train_rw_ds.smoothed_empirical_differential_
fairness())
```

The preceding code outputs the following:

```
Statistical Parity Difference (SPD):          -0.0000
Disparate Impact (DI):                         1.0000
Smoothed Empirical Differential Fairness (SEDF):   0.1942
```

The weights have a perfect effect on SPD and DI, making them absolutely fair from those metrics' standpoint. However, note that SEDF is better than before, but not zero. This is because privileged and underprivileged groups only pertain to the AGE_GROUP protected attribute, but not GENDER. SEDF is a measure of intersectional fairness that reweighting does not address.

You would think that adding weights to observations would adversely impact predictive performance. However, this method was designed to maintain balance. In an unweighted dataset, all observations have a weight of one, and therefore the average of all the weights is one. While reweighting changes the weights for observations, the mean is still approximately one. You can check this is the case by taking the absolute difference in the mean of `instance_weights` between the original dataset and the reweighted one. It should be infinitesimal. The code can be seen in the following snippet:

```
np.abs(train_ds.instance_weights.mean() -\
        train_rw_ds.instance_weights.mean()) < 1e-6
```

So, how can you apply `instance_weights`?, you ask. Many model classes have a lesser-known attribute in the `fit` method, called `sample_weight`. You simply plug it in there, and while training, it will learn from observations in accordance with the respective weights. This method is shown in the following code snippet:

```
lgb_rw_mdl = lgb.LGBMClassifier(random_seed=rand,\
max_depth=6, num_leaves=33, **lgb_params)
lgb_rw_mdl.fit(X_train, y_train,\
                    sample_weight=train_rw_ds.instance_
weights)
```

We can evaluate this model as we have with the base model, with `evaluate_class_mdl`. However, when we calculate the fairness metrics with `compute_aif_metrics`, we will save them in the model dictionary. Instead of looking at each method's outcomes one by one, we will compare them at the end of the section. Have a look at the following code snippet:

```
cls_mdls['lgb_1_rw'] = mldatasets.\
        evaluate_class_mdl(lgb_rw_mdl, train_rw_ds.features,\
X_test, train_rw_ds.labels, y_test,\
plot_roc=False, plot_conf_matrix=True,\
show_summary=True, ret_eval_dict=True)
test_pred_rw_ds = test_ds.copy(deepcopy=True)
test_pred_rw_ds.labels =\
cls_mdls['lgb_1_rw']['preds_test'].\

reshape(-1,1)
test_pred_rw_ds.scores =\
cls_mdls['lgb_1_rw']['probs_test']. reshape(-1,1)
metrics_test_rw_dict, _ = mldatasets.\
        compute_aif_metrics(test_ds, test_pred_rw_ds,\
                        unprivileged_groups=unprivileged_groups,\
                        privileged_groups=privileged_groups)
cls_mdls['lgb_1_rw'].update(metrics_test_rw_dict)
```

The preceding snippet outputs the confusion matrix and performance metrics, as shown in the following screenshot:

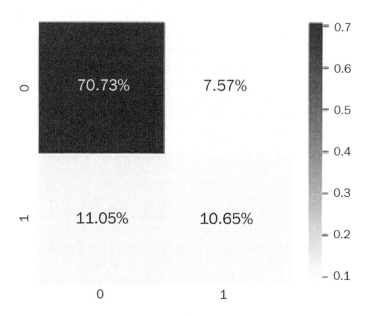

1. Accuracy_train: 0.8240   Accuracy_test: 0.8138
2. Precision_test: 0.5847   Recall_test: 0.4908
3. ROC-AUC_test: 0.7886   F1_test: 0.5337   MCC_test: 0.4210

Figure 11.5 – Evaluation of LightGBM reweighted model

If you compare *Figure 11.5* to *Figure 11.4*, you can conclude that there's not much difference in predictive performance between the reweighted and the base model. This outcome was expected, but it's still good to verify it. Some bias-mitigation methods do adversely impact predictive performance, but reweighing is not one of them. Neither should DI remover, for that matter, which we will discuss next!

Disparate impact remover method

This method focuses on bias not located in the protected attribute (AGE_GROUP), so we will have to delete this feature during the process. To that end, we will need its index— in other words, what position it has within the list of columns. We can save this position (protected_index) as a variable, like this:

```
protected_index = train_ds.feature_names.index('AGE_GROUP')
```

DI remover is not non-parametric. It requires a repair level between zero and one, so we need to find the optimal one. To that end, we can iterate through an array with different values for repair level (levels), initialize DisparateImpactRemover with each level, and fit_transform the data, which will de-bias the data. However, we then train the model without the protected attribute and use BinaryLabelDatasetMetric to assess the disparate_impact. Remember that DI is a ratio, so it's a metric that can be between over or under one, and an optimal DI is closest to one. Therefore, as we iterate across different repair levels, we will continuously save the model whose DI is closest to one. We will also append the DIs into an array for later use. Have a look at the following code snippet:

```
di = np.array([])
train_dir_ds = None
test_dir_ds = None
lgb_dir_mdl = None
X_train_dir = None
X_test_dir = None
levels = np.hstack([np.linspace(0., 0.1, 41),\
                    np.linspace(0.2, 1, 9)])
for level in tqdm(levels):
  di_remover = DisparateImpactRemover(repair_level=level)
  train_dir_ds_i = di_remover.fit_transform(train_ds)
  test_dir_ds_i = di_remover.fit_transform(test_ds)
  X_train_dir_i = np.delete(train_dir_ds_i.features,\
                       protected_index, axis=1)
  X_test_dir_i = np.delete(test_dir_ds_i.features,\
                       protected_index, axis=1)

  lgb_dir_mdl_i = lgb.LGBMClassifier(random_seed=rand,\
max_depth=5, num_leaves=33, **lgb_params)
```

```
lgb_dir_mdl_i.fit(X_train_dir_i, train_dir_ds_i.labels)
test_dir_ds_pred_i = test_dir_ds_i.copy()
test_dir_ds_pred_i.labels = \
lgb_dir_mdl_i.predict(X_test_dir_i)
metrics_test_dir_ds =\
BinaryLabelDatasetMetric(test_dir_ds_pred_i,
                    unprivileged_groups=unprivileged_groups,\
                    privileged_groups=privileged_groups)
di_i = metrics_test_dir_ds.disparate_impact()
if (di.shape[0]==0) or (np.min(np.abs(di-1)) >= abs(di_i-1)):
 print(abs(di_i-1))
 train_dir_ds = train_dir_ds_i
 test_dir_ds = test_dir_ds_i
 X_train_dir = X_train_dir_i
 X_test_dir = X_test_dir_i
 lgb_dir_mdl = lgb_dir_mdl_i
 di = np.append(np.array(di), di_i)
```

To observe DI at different repair levels, we can use the following code, and if you want to zoom in the area where the best DI is located, just uncomment the xlim line:

```
plt.plot(levels, di, marker='o')
plt.ylabel('Disparate Impact (DI)', fontsize=14)
plt.xlabel('Repair Level', fontsize=14)
#plt.xlim(0,0.1)
```

The preceding code generates the following output. As you can tell by this, there's an optimal repair level somewhere between 0 and 0.1 because that's where it gets closest to one:

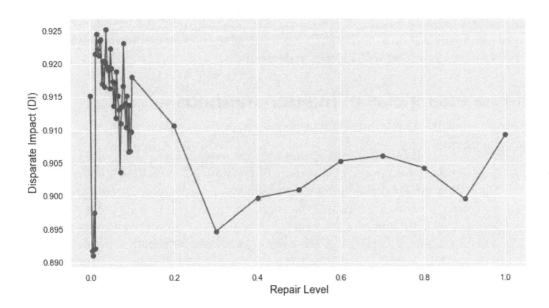

Figure 11.6 – DI at different DI remover repair levels

Now, let's evaluate the best DI repaired model with `evaluate_class_mdl` and compute the fairness metrics (`compute_aif_metrics`). We won't even plot the confusion matrix this time, but we will save all results into the `cls_mdls` dictionary for later inspection. The code can be seen in the following snippet:

```
cls_mdls['lgb_1_dir'] = mldatasets.\
        evaluate_class_mdl(lgb_dir_mdl, X_train_dir,\
X_test_dir, train_dir_ds.labels,\
test_dir_ds.labels, plot_roc=False,\
plot_conf_matrix=False, show_summary=False,\
ret_eval_dict=True)


test_pred_dir_ds = test_ds.copy(deepcopy=True)
test_pred_dir_ds.labels =\
cls_mdls['lgb_1_dir']['preds_test']. reshape(-1,1)
metrics_test_dir_dict, _ =
    mldatasets.compute_aif_metrics(test_ds, test_pred_dir_ds,\
                    unprivileged_groups=unprivileged_
groups,\
                    privileged_groups=privileged_groups)
cls_mdls['lgb_1_dir'].update(metrics_test_dir_dict)
```

The next link in the chain-after data is the model, so even if you de-bias the data, the model introduces bias on its own, thus it makes sense to train models that are equipped to deal with it, which is what we will learn to do next!

In-processing bias mitigation methods

These are some of the most important in-processing or model-specific bias mitigation methods:

- **Cost-sensitive training**: We are already incorporating this method into every LightGBM model trained in this chapter through the `scale_pos_weight` parameter. It's typically used in imbalanced classification problems and is simply seen as a means to improve accuracy for minor classes. However, given that imbalances with classes tend to favor some groups over others, this method also mitigates bias. It can be incorporated as class weights or by creating a custom loss function. The implementation will vary according to the model class and what costs are associated with the bias. If they grow linearly with misclassifications, class weighting will suffice, but otherwise, a custom loss function is recommended.

- **Constraints**: Many model classes support monotonic and interaction constraints, and **TensorFlow Lattice** (**TFL**) offers more advanced custom shape constraints. These ensure that relationships between features and targets are restricted to a certain pattern, placing guardrails at the model level. There are many reasons you would want to employ them, but chief among them is to mitigate bias. We will discuss this topic in *Chapter 12, Monotonic Constraints and Model Tuning for Interpretability*.

- **Prejudice remover regularizer**: This method defines prejudice as the statistical dependence between the sensitive and target variables. However, the aim of this method is to minimize indirect prejudice, which excludes the prejudice that can be avoided by simply removing the sensitive variable. Therefore, the method starts by quantifying it with a **prejudice index** (**PI**), which is the mutual information between the target and sensitive variable. Incidentally, we covered mutual information in *Chapter 10, Feature Selection and Engineering for Interpretability*. Then, along with L2, the PI is incorporated into a custom regularization term. In theory, any model classifier can regularize using the PI-based regularizer, but the only implementation, so far, uses logistic regression.

- **Gerry fair classifier**: This is inspired by the concept of **fairness gerrymandering**, which has the appearance of fairness on one group but lacks fairness when subdivided into subgroups. The algorithm leverages a **fictitious play** game-theory-inspired approach in which you have a zero-sum game between a *learner* and an *auditor*. The learner minimizes the prediction error and aggregate fairness-based penalty term. The auditor takes it one step further by penalizing the learner based on the worse outcomes for the most unfairly treated subgroup. The game's objective is to achieve a **Nash equilibrium**, which is achieved when two non-cooperative players with possibly contradictory aims reach a solution that partially satisfies both. In this case, the learner gets a minimal prediction error and aggregate unfairness, and the auditor gets minimal subgroup unfairness. The implementation of this method is model-agnostic.

- **Adversarial debiasing**: Similar to Gerry fair, adversarial debiasing leverages two opposing actors, but this time it's with two neural networks: a predictor and an adversary. We maximize the predictor's ability to predict the target while minimizing the adversary's ability to predict the protected feature, thus increasing equality of odds between privileged and underprivileged groups.

- **Exponentiated gradient reduction**: This method automates cost-sensitive optimization by reducing it into a sequence of such problems and using fairness constraints concerning protected attributes such as demographic parity or equalized odds. It is model-agnostic but limited only to scikit-learn-compatible binary classifiers.

Given that there are so many in-processing methods, we will only employ two of them in this chapter. Still, if you are interested in using ones we won't cover, they are available in the AIF360 library and documentation.

Prejudice remover method

The `PrejudiceRemover` method is a special implementation of logistic regression. You initialize it with the learning rate (`eta`) and specific the sensitive attribute and class attribute. Then, you `fit` it. The method can be seen in the following code snippet:

```
log_pr_mdl = PrejudiceRemover(eta=1.0,\
sensitive_attr='AGE_GROUP', class_attr='IS_DEFAULT')
log_pr_mdl.fit(train_ds)
```

We can use the `predict` function to get train and test prediction and then employ `evaluate_class_metrics_mdl` and `compute_aif_metrics` to obtain predictive performance and fairness metrics, respectively. We place both into the `cls_mdls` dictionary, as illustrated in the following code snippet:

```
train_pred_pr_ds = log_pr_mdl.predict(train_ds)
test_pred_pr_ds = log_pr_mdl.predict(test_ds)
cls_mdls['log_2_pr'] = mldatasets.\
    evaluate_class_metrics_mdl(log_pr_mdl,\
train_pred_pr_ds.labels,\
        test_pred_pr_ds.scores, test_pred_pr_ds.labels,\
y_train, y_test)
metrics_test_pr_dict, _ = mldatasets.\
    compute_aif_metrics(test_ds, test_pred_pr_ds,\
                        unprivileged_groups=unprivileged_
groups,\
                        privileged_groups=privileged_groups)
cls_mdls['log_2_pr'].update(metrics_test_pr_dict)
```

Next, we will learn about a more model-agnostic in-processing method that takes into account intersectionality.

Gerry fair classifier method

The Gerry fair classifier is partially model-agnostic. It only supports linear models, **support vector machines (SVMs)**, kernel regression, and decision trees. You initialize `GerryFairClassifier` by defining a regularization strength (`C`), a fairness approximation for early stopping (`gamma`), whether to be verbose (`printflag`), the maximum amount of iterations (`max_iters`), the model (`predictor`), and the fairness notion to employ (`fairness_def`). We will use the fairness notion of false-negatives (`"FN"`) to compute the fairness violations' weighted disparity. Once it's been initialized, all we need to do is `fit` it and enable `early_termination` to stop if it hasn't improved in five iterations. The code is shown in the following snippet:

```
dt_gf_mdl = GerryFairClassifier(C=100, gamma=.005,\
max_iters=50, fairness_def='FN', printflag=True,\
predictor=tree.DecisionTreeRegressor(max_depth=3))
dt_gf_mdl.fit(train_ds, early_termination=True)
```

We can use the `predict` function to get train and test prediction and then employ
`evaluate_class_metrics_mdl` and `compute_aif_metrics` to obtain predictive
performance and fairness metrics, respectively. We place both into the `cls_mdls`
dictionary, as illustrated in the following code snippet:

```
train_pred_gf_ds = dt_gf_mdl.predict(train_ds, threshold=False)
test_pred_gf_ds = dt_gf_mdl.predict(test_ds, threshold=False)
cls_mdls['dt_2_gf'] = mldatasets.\
     evaluate_class_metrics_mdl(dt_gf_mdl, train_pred_gf_
ds.labels,\
                    None, test_pred_gf_ds.labels, y_train,
y_test)
metrics_test_gf_dict, _ = mldatasets.\
    compute_aif_metrics(test_ds, test_pred_gf_ds,\
                    unprivileged_groups=unprivileged_
groups,\
                    privileged_groups=privileged_groups)
cls_mdls['dt_2_gf'].update(metrics_test_gf_dict)
```

The next—and last—link in the chain-after model is the inference, so even if you de-bias
the data and the model there might be some bias left, thus it makes sense to deal with it in
this stage too, which is what we will learn to do next!

Post-processing bias mitigation methods

These are some of the most important post-processing or inference-specific bias mitigation methods:

- **Prediction abstention**: This has many potential benefits such as fairness, safety, or controlling costs, but which one will depend on your problem. Typically, a model will return all predictions, even low-confidence ones—that is, predictions that are close to the classification threshold or when the model returns confidence intervals that fall outside of a predetermined threshold. When fairness is involved, if we change predictions to **I don't know** (**IDK**) in low-confidence regions, the model will likely become fairer as a side-effect when we assess fairness metrics only against predictions that were made. It is also possible to make prediction abstention an in-processing method. A paper called *Predict Responsibly: Increasing Fairness by Learning to Defer* discusses two approaches to do this by training a model to either **punt** (learn to predict IDK) or **defer** (predict IDK when the odds of being correct are lower than expert opinion). Another paper called *The Utility of Abstaining in Binary Classification* employs a reinforcement learning framework called **Knows what it knows** (**KWIK**), which has self-awareness of its mistakes but allows for abstentions.

- **Equalized odds postprocessing**: Also known as disparate mistreatment, this ensures that privileged and underprivileged groups have equal treatment for misclassifications, whether false-positive or false-negative. It finds optimal probability thresholds with which changing the labels equalizes the odds between groups.

- **Calibrated equalized odds postprocessing**: Instead of changing the labels, this method modifies the probability estimates so that they are on average equal. It calls this calibration. However, this constraint cannot be satisfied for false-positives and false-negatives concurrently, so you are forced to prefer one over the other. Therefore, it is advantageous in cases where recall is far more important than precision or vice-versa, and there are benefits to calibrating the estimated probabilities.

- **Reject option classification**: This method leverages the intuition that predictions around the decision boundary tend to be the least fair. It then finds an optimal band around the decision boundary for which flipping the labels for unprivileged and privileged groups yields the most equitable outcomes.

We will only employ two of these post-processing methods in this chapter. Reject option classification is available in the AIF360 library and documentation.

Equalized odds post-processing method

The equalized odds post-processing method (`EqOddsPostprocessing`) is initialized with the groups we want to equalize odds for and the random `seed`. Then, we `fit` it. Note that fitting takes two datasets: the original one (`test_ds`) and then the dataset with predictions for our base model (`test_pred_ds`). What `fit` does is compute the optimal probability thresholds. Then, `predict` creates a new dataset where these thresholds have changed the `labels`. The code can be seen in the following snippet:

```
epp = EqOddsPostprocessing(privileged_groups=privileged_
groups,\
                            unprivileged_groups=unprivileged_
groups,\
                            seed=rand)
epp = epp.fit(test_ds, test_pred_ds)
test_pred_epp_ds = epp.predict(test_pred_ds)
```

We can employ `evaluate_class_metrics_mdl` and `compute_aif_metrics` to obtain predictive performance and fairness metrics for **equal-proportion probability** (**EPP**), respectively. We place both into the `cls_mdls` dictionary. The code can be seen in the following snippet:

```
cls_mdls['lgb_3_epp'] = mldatasets.\
    evaluate_class_metrics_mdl(lgb_base_mdl,\
                  cls_mdls['lgb_0_base']['preds_train'],\
test_pred_epp_ds.scores, test_pred_epp_ds.labels,\
                  y_train, y_test)
metrics_test_epp_dict, _ = mldatasets.\
    compute_aif_metrics(test_ds, test_pred_epp_ds,\
                        unprivileged_groups=unprivileged_
groups,\
                        privileged_groups=privileged_groups)
cls_mdls['lgb_3_epp'].update(metrics_test_epp_dict)
```

Next, we will learn another post-processing method. The main difference is that it calibrates the probability scores rather than only change the predicted labels.

Calibrated equalized odds postprocessing method

Calibrated equalized odds (`CalibratedEqOddsPostprocessing`) is implemented exactly like equalized odds, except it has one more crucial attribute (`cost_constraint`). This attribute defines which constraint to satisfy since it cannot make the scores fair for FPRs and FNRs simultaneously. We choose FPR and then, `fit`, `predict`, and `evaluate`, as we did for equalized odds. The code can be seen in the following snippet:

```
cpp = CalibratedEqOddsPostprocessing(\
                                privileged_groups=privileged_groups,
                                unprivileged_groups=unprivileged_
groups,\
                                cost_constraint="fpr", seed=rand)
cpp = cpp.fit(test_ds, test_pred_ds)
test_pred_cpp_ds = cpp.predict(test_pred_ds)
cls_mdls['lgb_3_cpp'] = mldatasets.\
    evaluate_class_metrics_mdl(lgb_base_mdl,\
                cls_mdls['lgb_0_base']['preds_train'],\
                test_pred_cpp_ds.scores,\
                test_pred_cpp_ds.labels,\
                y_train, y_test)
metrics_test_cpp_dict, _ = mldatasets.\
    compute_aif_metrics(test_ds, test_pred_cpp_ds,\
                            unprivileged_groups=unprivileged_
groups,\
                            privileged_groups=privileged_groups)
cls_mdls['lgb_3_cpp'].update(metrics_test_cpp_dict)
```

Now that we have tried six bias mitigation methods, two at every level, we can compare them against each other and the base model!

Tying it all together!

To compare the metrics for all the methods, we can take the dictionary (`cls_mdls`) and place it in the dataframe (`cls_metrics_df`). We are only interested in a few performance metrics and most of the fairness metrics recorded. Then, we output the dataframe sorted by test accuracy and with all the fairness metrics color-coded. The code can be seen in the following snippet:

```
cls_metrics_df = pd.DataFrame.from_dict(cls_mdls, 'index')
        [['accuracy_train', 'accuracy_test', 'f1_test', 'mcc_
test',\
        'SPD', 'DI', 'AOD', 'EOD', 'DFBA']]
with pd.option_context('display.precision', 4):
  html = cls_metrics_df.sort_values(by='accuracy_test',\
                        ascending=False).style.\
        background_gradient(cmap='plasma_r', low=0.3,
high=1,\
                        subset=['SPD', 'AOD', 'EOD']).\
        background_gradient(cmap='viridis_r', low=1,
high=0.3,\
                        subset=['DI', 'DFBA'])
html
```

The preceding snippet outputs the following dataframe:

	accuracy_train	accuracy_test	f1_test	mcc_test	SPD	DI	AOD	EOD	DFBA
dt_2_gf	0.8214	0.8262	0.4812	0.4135	-0.0548	0.9388	-0.0430	-0.0216	0.2521
lgb_0_base	0.8255	0.8167	0.5330	0.4243	-0.0679	0.9193	-0.0550	-0.0265	0.2328
lgb_1_rw	0.8240	0.8138	0.5337	0.4210	-0.0371	0.9552	-0.0171	-0.0018	0.0349
lgb_1_dir	0.8237	0.8129	0.5301	0.4171	-0.0624	0.9252	-0.0493	-0.0214	0.2545
lgb_3_epp	0.8255	0.8101	0.5152	0.4025	-0.0260	0.9688	0.0022	-0.0021	0.0031
lgb_3_cpp	0.8255	0.2622	0.2129	-0.3055	-0.0711	0.7609	-0.0635	-0.1262	0.0432
log_2_pr	0.1912	0.1873	0.2844	-0.3363	0.0520	1.7627	0.0498	0.0235	0.3454

Figure 11.7 – Comparision of all bias mitigation methods with different fairness metrics

Figure 11.7 shows that most methods yielded models that are fairer than the base model for SPD, AOD, and EOD. Calibrated equalized odds post-processing (`lgb_3_cpp`) was the exception, but it had one of the best DFBAs. Note that this method is particularly good at achieving parity for FPR or FNR while calibrating scores, but none of these fairness metrics are useful for picking up on this. Instead, you could create a metric that's the ratio between FPRs, as we did in *Chapter 7, Anchors and Counterfactual Explanations*. Incidentally, this would be the perfect use case for calibrated equalized odds (CPP). As for DI, two methods yielded a suboptimal DI; one is too low and the other is too high. In CPP's case, this is due to the lopsided nature of the calibration, but in the prejudice remover's case (`log_2_pr`), logistic regression wasn't able to obtain good accuracy while constraining the fairness with regularization.

The method that obtained the best SPD, DI, AOD, and DFBA, and the second-best EOD was equalized odds post-processing (`lgb_3_epp`), so let's visualize fairness for it using XAI's plots. To this end, we first create a dataframe with the test examples (`test_df`), and then use `replace` to make an `AGE_GROUP` categorical and obtain the list of categorical columns (`cat_cols_1`). Then, we can compare different metrics (`metrics_plot`) using the true labels (`y_test`), predicted probability scores for the EPP model, the dataframe (`test_df`), the protected attribute (`cross_cols`), and categorical columns. We can do the same for the **receiver operating characteristic (ROC)** plot (`roc_plot`) and the **precision-recall (PR)** plot (`pr_plot`). The code can be seen in the following snippet:

```python
test_df = ccdefault_bias_df.loc[X_test.index]
test_df['AGE_GROUP'] = test_df.AGE_GROUP.\
                        replace({0:'unprivileged',
1:'privileged'})
cat_cols_1 = ccdefault_bias_df.dtypes[lambda x: x==np.int8].\
                                                        index.
tolist()
_ = xai.metrics_plot(y_test, cls_mdls['lgb_3_epp']['probs_
test'],\
                    df=test_df, cross_cols=['AGE_GROUP'],\
                    categorical_cols=cat_cols_1)
_ = xai.roc_plot(y_test, cls_mdls['lgb_3_epp']['probs_test'],\
                df=test_df, cross_cols=['AGE_GROUP'],\
                categorical_cols=cat_cols_1)
_ = xai.pr_plot(y_test, cls_mdls['lgb_3_epp']['probs_test'],\
                df=test_df, cross_cols=['AGE_GROUP'],\
                categorical_cols=cat_cols_1)
```

The preceding snippet outputs the three plots in *Figure 11.8*. The first one shows that even the fairest model still has some disparities between both groups, especially between precision and recall and, by extension, F1 score, which is their average. However, the ROC curve shows how close both groups are from an FPR versus a TPR standpoint. The third plot is where the disparities in precision and recall become even more evident. This all comes to demonstrate how hard it is to keep a fair balance on all fronts! Some methods are best for making one aspect perfect but nothing else, while others are pretty good on a handful but nothing else. Despite the shortcomings of the methods, most of them achieved a sizable improvement. Ultimately, choosing methods will depend on what you most care about, and combining them is also recommended for maximum effect! The output is shown here:

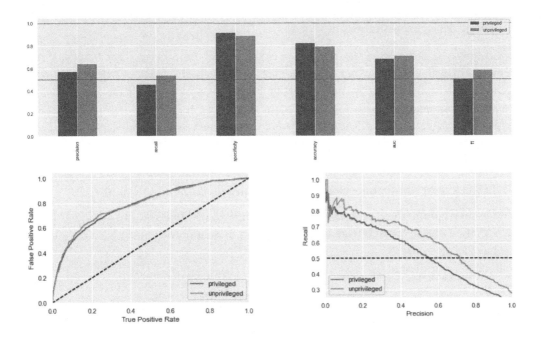

Figure 11.8 – Plots demonstrating fairness for fairest model

We conclude the bias mitigation exercise and will move on to the causal inference exercise, where we will discuss how to ensure fair and robust policies.

Creating a causal model

Decision-making will often involve understanding cause and effect. If the effect is desirable, you can decide to replicate its cause, or otherwise avoid it. You can change something on purpose to observe how it changes outcomes, or to trace back an accidental effect to its cause, or to simulate which change will produce the most beneficial impact. Causal inference can help us do all this by creating causal graphs and models. These tie all variables together and estimate effects to make more principled decisions. However, to properly assess the impact of a cause, whether by design or accident, you'll need to separate its effect from confounding variables.

The reason causal inference is relevant to this chapter is that the bank's policy decisions have the power to impact cardholder livelihoods significantly and, given the rise in suicides, even to the degree of life and death. Therefore, there's a moral imperative to assess policy decisions with the utmost care.

The Taiwanese bank started a lending policy experiment 6 months ago. The bank saw the writing on the wall and knew that the customers with the highest risk of default would somehow be written off their balance sheets in a way that diminished these customers' financial obligations. Therefore, the experiment's focus only involved what the bank considered salvageable, which were low-to-mid risk-of-default customers, and now that the experiment has ended, they want to understand how the following policies have impacted customer behavior:

- **Lower credit limit**: Some customers had their credit limit reduced by 25%.
- **Payment plan**: They were given 6 months to pay back their current credit card debt. In other words, the debt was split up into six parts, and every month they would have to pay one part.
- **Both measures**: A reduction in credit limit and the payment plan.

Also, prevailing credit card interest rates in Taiwan were around 16-20% in 2005, but the bank caught wind that these, in short order, would be capped at 4% by the Taiwanese Financial Supervisory Commission. Therefore, they ensured all customers in the experiment were automatically provided with interest rates at that level. Some bank executives thought this would only aggravate the indebtedness and create more "credit card slaves" in the process. These concerns prompted the proposal to create the experiment with the lower credit card limit as a countermeasure. On the other hand, the payment plan was devised to understand whether debt relief gave customers breathing room to use the card without fear.

On the business side, the rationale was that a healthy level of spending needed to be encouraged because with lower interest rates, the bulk of the profits would come from payment processing, cashback partnerships, and other sources tied to spending and, in turn, increased customer longevity. Yet, this would also be beneficial to customers because if they were more profitable as spenders than debtors, it meant the incentives were in place to keep them from becoming the latter. All this justified the use of estimated lifetime value (_LTV) as a proxy metric for how the experiment's outcome benefited both the bank and its customers. For years, the bank has been using a reasonably accurate calculation to estimate how much value a credit card holder will provide to the bank given their spending and payment history, and parameters such as limits and interest rates.

In the parlance of experimental design, the chosen policy is called a **treatment**, and along with the three treated groups, there's a control group that wasn't prescribed a treatment—that is, no change in policy at all, not even the lower interest rates. Before we move forward, let's first initialize a list with the treatment names (treatment_names) and one that includes even the control group (all_treatment_names), as follows:

```
treatment_names = ['Lower Credit Limit', 'Payment Plan',\
                   'Payment Plan &Credit Limit']
all_treatment_names = np.array(["None"] + treatment_names)
```

Now, let's examine the results of the experiment to help us design an optimal causal model.

Understanding the results of the experiment

A fairly intuitive way of assessing the effectiveness of treatment is by comparing their outcomes. We want to know the answers to the following two simple questions:

- Did the treatments decrease the default rate compared to the control group?

- Were the spending behaviors conducive to an increase in lifetime value estimates?

We can visualize both in a single plot. To this end, we obtain a Pandas series with the percentage for each group that defaulted (pct_s), then another one with the sum of lifetime values for each group (ltv_s) in thousands of NTD (K$). We put both series into a Pandas dataframe and plot it, as illustrated in the following code snippet:

```
pct_s =\
ccdefault_causal_df[ccdefault_causal_df.IS_DEFAULT==1].\
                groupby(['_TREATMENT']).size() /\
                ccdefault_causal_df.groupby(['_TREATMENT']).
size()
```

```
ltv_s =\
ccdefault_causal_df.groupby(['_TREATMENT'])['_LTV'].\
sum()/1000
plot_df = pd.DataFrame({'% Defaulted':pct_s, 'Total LTV,
K$':ltv_s})
plot_df.index = all_treatment_names
ax = plot_df.plot(secondary_y=['Total LTV, K$'], figsize=(8,5))
ax.get_legend().set_bbox_to_anchor((0.7, 0.99))
plt.grid(False)
plt.title("Credit Policy Experiment Outcomes", fontsize=16)
```

The preceding snippet outputs the plot shown in *Figure 11.9*. It can be inferred that all treatments fare better than the control group. The lowering of the credit limit on its own decreases the default rate over 12% and more than doubles the estimated LTV, while the payment plan only decreases the defaults 3% and increases the LTV by about 85%. However, both policies combined quadrupled the control group's LTV and reduced the default rate nearly 15%! The output can be seen here:

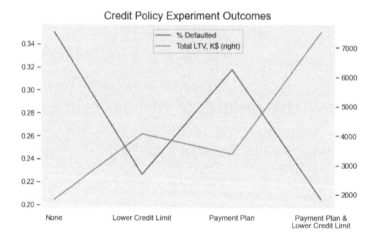

Figure 11.9 – Outcomes for treatment experiment with different credit policies

Before bank executives rejoice that they have found the winning policy, we must examine how they distributed it among the credit cardholders in the experiment. We learned that they chose treatment according to their risk factor, which is measured by the _risk_score variable. However, lifetime value is largely affected by the credit limit available (_CC_LIMIT), so we must take that into account. One way to understand the distribution is by plotting both variables against each other in a scatter plot color-coded by _TREATMENT. The code for this can be seen in the following snippet:

```
sns.scatterplot(\
  x=ccdefault_causal_df['_CC_LIMIT'].values,\
  y=ccdefault_causal_df['_risk_score'].values,\
  hue=all_treatment_names[ccdefault_causal_df['_TREATMENT'].
values],\
  hue_order=all_treatment_names)
plt.title("Chosen Credit Policy ('Treatment') by Customer")
plt.xlabel("Original Credit Limit")
plt.ylabel("Risk Factor")
```

The preceding code generated the plot in *Figure 11.10*. It shows that the three treatments correspond to different risk levels, while the control group (None) is spread out more vertically. The choice to assign treatments based on risk level also meant that they unevenly distributed the treatments based on _CC_LIMIT. We ought to ask ourselves if this experiment's biased conditions make it even viable to interpret the outcomes. Have a look at the following output:

Figure 11.10 – Risk factors versus original credit limit

The scatterplot in *Figure 11.10* demonstrated the stratification of the treatments across risk factors. However, scatter plots can be challenging to interpret for understanding distributions. For that, it's best to use a **kernel density estimate (KDE)** plot. So, let's see how _CC_LIMIT is distributed across all treatments with Seaborn's displot, and also do one for lifetime value (_LTV) while we are it! Have a look at the following code snippet:

```
sns.displot(ccdefault_causal_df, x="_CC_LIMIT",\
            hue="_TREATMENT", kind="kde", fill=True)
sns.displot(ccdefault_causal_df, x="_LTV", hue="_TREATMENT",\
            kind="kde", fill=True)
```

The preceding snippet produced the two KDE plots in *Figure 11.11*. We can easily tell how apart all four distributions are for both plots, mostly regarding treatment #3 ("Payment Plan & Lower Credit Limit"), which tends to be centered significantly more to the right and to have a longer and fatter right tail. You can view the output here:

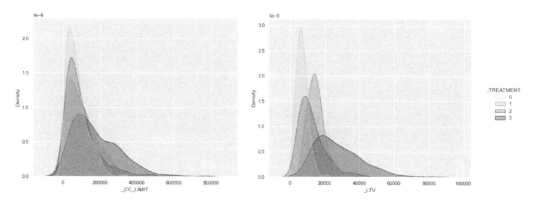

Figure 11.11 – KDE distributions for _CC_LIMIT and _LTV by _TREATMENT

Ideally, when you design an experiment such as this, you should aim for equal distribution among all groups based on any pertinent factors that could alter the outcomes. However, this might not always be feasible, either because of logistical or strategic constraints. In this case, the outcome (_LTV) varies according to customer credit card limits (_CC_LIMIT), the **heterogeneity feature**—in other words, the varying feature that directly impacts the treatment effect, also known as the **heterogeneous treatment effect modifier**. We can create a causal model that includes both the _TREATMENT feature and the effect modifier (_CC_LIMIT).

Understanding causal models

The causal model we will build can be separated into four components, as follows:

- **Outcome** (Y): The outcome variable(s) of the causal model.

- **Treatments** (T): The treatment variable(s) that influences the outcome.

- **Effect modifiers** (X): The variable(s) that influences the effect's heterogeneity conditioning it. It sits in between the treatment and the outcome.

- **Controls** (W): Also known as **common causes** or **confounders**. They are the features that influence both the outcome and the treatment.

We will start by identifying each one of these components in the data as separate pandas dataframes, as follows:

```
W = ccdefault_causal_df[['_spend', '_tpm', '_ppm', '_RETAIL',\
                         '_URBAN', '_RURAL', '_PREMIUM']]
X = ccdefault_causal_df[['_CC_LIMIT']]
T = ccdefault_causal_df[['_TREATMENT']]
Y = ccdefault_causal_df[['_LTV']]
```

We will use the **doubly robust learning** (**DRL**) method to estimate the treatment effects. It's called "doubly" because it leverages two models, as follows:

- It predicts the outcome with a *regression model*, as illustrated here:
$$Y \sim W + X$$

- It predicts the treatment with a *propensity model*, as illustrated here:
$$Y \sim W + X$$

It's also *robust* because of the final stage, which combines both models while maintaining many desirable statistical properties such as confidence intervals and asymptotic normality. More formally, the estimation leverages regression model g and propensity model p conditional on treatment t, like this:

$$Y_t = g_t(W,X) + \epsilon_t$$

It also does this:

$$Pr[T = t|X,W] = p_t(W,X)$$

The goal is to derive the **Conditional Average Treatment Effect (CATE)** denoted as $\theta_t(X)$ associated with each treatment t given heterogeneous effect X. First, the DRL method de-biases the regression model by applying the inverse propensity, like this:

$$Y_{i,t}^{\text{DRL}} = g_t(W_i, X_i) + \frac{Y_i - g_t(W_i, X_i)}{p_t(X_i, W_i)} + 1\{T_i = t\}$$

How exactly to estimate $\theta_t(X)$ from $Y_{i,t}^{\text{DRL}}$ will depend on the DRL variant employed. We will use a linear variant (`LinearDRLearner`) so that it returns coefficients and intercepts, which can be easily interpreted. It derives $\theta_t(X)$ by running **ordinary linear regression (OLS)** for the outcome differences between a treatment t and the control $(Y_{i,t}^{\text{DRL}} - Y_{i,0}^{\text{DRL}})$ on X_t. This intuitively makes sense because the estimated effect of a treatment minus the estimated effect of the absense of a treatment (t = 0) is the *net* effect of said treatment.

Now, with all the theory out of the way, let's dig in!

Initializing the linear doubly robust learner

We can initialize a `LinearDRLearner` from the `econml` library, which we call `drlearner`, by specifying any scikit-learn-compatible regressor (`model_regression`) and classifier (`model_propensity`). We will use XGBoost for both, but note that the classifier has a `objective=multi:softmax` attribute. Remember that we have multiple treatments, so it's a multiclass classification problem. The code can be seen in the following snippet:

```
drlearner = LinearDRLearner(\
        model_regression=xgb.XGBRegressor(learning_rate=0.1),\
        model_propensity=xgb.XGBClassifier(learning_rate=0.1,\
                        max_depth=2,objective="multi:softmax"),\
        random_state=rand)
```

If you want to understand what both the regression and propensity model are doing, you can easily fit `xgb.XGBRegressor().fit(W.join(X), Y)` and `xgb.XGBClassifier(objective="multi:softmax").fit(W.join(X), T)` models. We won't do this now but if you were curious, you could evaluate their performance and even run feature importance methods to understand what impacts their predictions individually. The causal model brings them together with the DRL framework, leading to different conclusions.

Fitting the causal model

We can use `fit` in the `drlearner` to fit the causal model leveraging the dowhy wrapper of `econml`. The first attributes are the Y, T, X, and Y components: pandas dataframes. Optionally, you can provide variable names for each of these components: the column names of each of the pandas dataframes. Lastly, we would like to estimate the treatment effects. Optionally, we can provide the effect modifiers (X) to do this with, and we will use half of this data to do so, as illustrated in the following code snippet:

```
causal_mdl = drlearner.dowhy.fit(Y, T, X, W,\
                             outcome_names=Y.columns.to_
list(),\
                             treatment_names=T.columns.to_
list(),\
                             feature_names=X.columns.to_
list(),\
                             confounder_names=W.columns.to_
list(),\
                             target_units=X.iloc[:550].values)
```

With the causal model initialized, we can visualize it. The `pydot` library with `pygraphviz` can do this for us. Please note that this library is notoriously fickle, so it might fail and show you the much less attractive default graphic instead with `view_model`. Don't worry if this happens. Have a look at the following code snippet:

```
try:
    display(Image(to_pydot(causal_mdl._graph._graph).create_
png()))
except:
    causal_mdl.view_model()
```

The code in the preceding snippet outputs the model diagram shown here. With it, you can appreciate how all the variables connect:

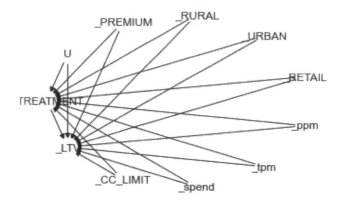

Figure 11.12 – Causal model diagram

The causal model has already been fitted, so let's examine and interpret the results, shall we?

Understanding heterogeneous treatment effects

Firstly, it's important to note how the DoWhy wrapper of econml has cut down on a few steps with the dowhy.fit method. Usually, when you build a CausalModel such as this one directly with DoWhy, it has a method called identify_effect that derives the probability expression for the effect to be estimated (the *identified estimand*). In this case, this is called the **average treatment effect** (**ATE**). Then, another method called estimate_effect takes this expression and the models it's supposed to tie together (regression and propensity). With them, it computes both the ATE, $Y_{i,t}^{DRL}$, and CATE, $\theta_{i,t}(X)$, for every outcome i and treatment t. However, since we used the wrapper to fit the causal model, it automatically takes care of both the identification and estimation steps.

You can access the identified ATE with the identified_estimand_ property and the estimate results with the estimate_ property for the causal model. The code can be seen in the following snippet:

```
identified_ate = causal_mdl.identified_estimand_
print(identified_ate)
drlearner_estimate = causal_mdl.estimate_
print(drlearner_estimate)
```

The code shown in the preceding snippet outputs the **estimand expression** for
`identified_estimand_`, which is a derivation of the expected value for $Y \sim W + X$
$Y \sim W + X$, with some assumptions. Then, the causal-"realized" `estimate_` returns the
ATE for treatment #1, as illustrated in the following code snippet:

```
Estimand type: nonparametric-ate


### Estimand : 1
Estimand name: backdoor1 (Default)
Estimand expression:
      d
──────────────(Expectation(_LTV|_URBAN,_ppm,_CC_LIMIT,_tpm,_
spend,_RETAIL,_PREM
d[_TREATMENT]



IUM,_RURAL))


Estimand assumption 1, Unconfoundedness: If U→{_TREATMENT}
and U→_LTV then P(_LTV|_TREATMENT,_URBAN,_ppm,_CC_LIMIT,_tpm,_
spend,_RETAIL,_PREMIUM,_RURAL,U) = \
P(_LTV|_TREATMENT,_URBAN,_ppm,_CC_LIMIT,_tpm,_spend,_RETAIL,_
PREMIUM,_RURAL)


*** Causal Estimate ***


## Identified estimand
Estimand type: nonparametric-ate


## Realized estimand
b: _LTV~_TREATMENT+_URBAN+_ppm+_CC_LIMIT+_tpm+_spend+_RETAIL+_
PREMIUM+_RURAL | _CC_LIMIT
Target units:
```

```
## Estimate
Mean value: 7221.414390341943
Effect estimates: [6762.97178458 7330.10299182
7355.87769131 ... 7217.74562572 7492.35375285
 7214.96052799]
```

Next, we can iterate across all treatments in the causal model and return a `summary` for each treatment, like this:

```
for i in range(causal_mdl._d_t[0]):
   print("Treatment: %s" % treatment_names[i])
   display(econml_mdl.summary(T=i+1))
```

The preceding code outputs three linear regression summaries. The first one looks like this:

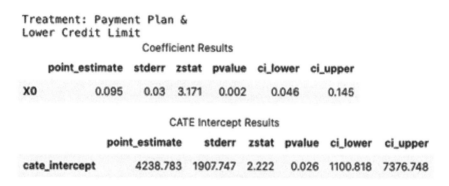

Figure 11.13 – Summary for one of the treatments

To get a better sense of the coefficients and intercepts, we can plot them with their respective confidence intervals. To do this, we first create an index of treatments (`idxs`). There are three treatments, so this is just an array of numbers between 0 and 2. Then, place all the coefficients (`coef_`) and intercepts (`intercept_`) into an array using list comprehension. However, it's a bit more complicated for the 90% confidence intervals for both coefficients and intercepts because `coef[interval[` and `]{custom-style="P - Code"}intercept]{custom-style="P - Italics"}` interval return the lower and upper bounds of these intervals. We need the length of the margin of error in both directions, not the bounds. We deduct the coefficient and intercepts from these bounds to obtain their respective margin of error, as illustrated in the following code snippet:

```
idxs = np.arange(0, causal_mdl._d_t[0])
coefs = np.hstack([causal_mdl.coef_(T=i+1) for i in idxs])
intercepts = np.hstack([causal_mdl.intercept_(T=i+1) for i in
idxs])
coefs_err = np.hstack([causal_mdl.coef__interval(T=i+1) for i
in\
idxs])
coefs_err[0, :] = coefs - coefs_err[0, :]
coefs_err[1, :] = coefs_err[1, :] - coefs
intercepts_err = \
np.vstack([causal_mdl.intercept__interval(T=i+1)\
                                                    for i in
idxs]).T
intercepts_err[0, :] = intercepts - intercepts_err[0, :]
intercepts_err[1, :] = intercepts_err[1, :] - intercepts
```

Next, we plot the coefficients for each treatment and respective errors using `errorbar`. We can do the same with the intercepts as another subplot, as illustrated in the following code snippet:

```
ax1 = plt.subplot(2, 1, 1)
plt.errorbar(idxs, coefs, coefs_err, fmt="o")
plt.xticks(idxs, treatment_names)
plt.setp(ax1.get_xticklabels(), visible=False)
plt.title("Coefficients")
plt.subplot(2, 1, 2)
plt.errorbar(idxs, intercepts, intercepts_err, fmt="o")
plt.xticks(idxs, treatment_names)
plt.title("Intercepts")
```

The preceding snippet outputs the following:

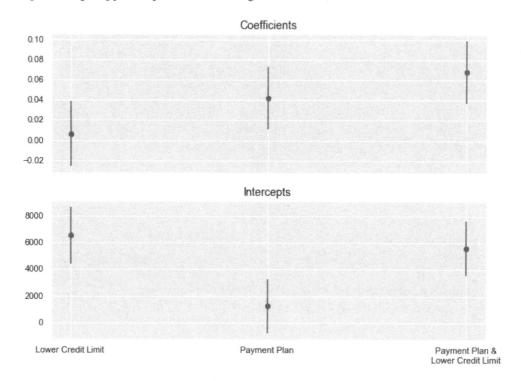

Figure 11.14 – Coefficients and intercepts for all treatments

With *Figure 11.14*, you can appreciate how relatively large the margin of error is for all intercepts and coefficients. Nonetheless, it's pretty clear that on coefficients alone, treatments keep getting marginally better when read from left to right. But before we conclude that **Payment Plan & Lower Credit Limit** is the best policy, we must consider the intercept, which is lower for this treatment than the first one. Essentially, this means that a customer with a minimal credit card limit is likely to improve lifetime value more by the first policy because the coefficients are multiplied by the limit, whereas the intercept is the starting point. Given that there's no one best policy for all customers, let's examine how to choose policies for each, using the causal model.

Choosing policies

We can decide on a credit policy on a customer basis using the `const_marginal_ effect` method, which takes the X effect modifier (`_CC_LIMIT`) and computes the counterfactual CATE, $\theta(X)$. In other words, it returns the estimated `_LTV` for all treatments for all observations in X.

However, they don't all cost the same. Setting up a payment plan requires administrative and legal costs of about *NT*$1,000 per contract, and according to the bank's actuarial department, lowering the credit limit 25 has an opportunity cost estimated at *NT*$72 per average payments per month (_ppm) over the lifetime of the customer. To factor these costs, we can set up a simple `lambda` function that takes the payment plan costs for all treatments and adds them to the variable credit limit costs, which, naturally, is multiplied by _ppm. Given an array with credit card limits of *n* length, the cost function returns an array of $(n, 3)$ dimensions with a cost for each treatment. Then, we obtain the counterfactual CATE and deduct the costs (`treatment_effect_minus_costs`). Then, we expand the array to include a column of zeros representing the "None" treatment and use `argmax` to return each customer's recommended treatment index (`recommended_T`), as illustrated in the following code snippet:

```
cost_fn = lambda X: np.repeat(np.array([[0, 1000, 1000]]),\
                            X.shape[0], axis=0) +\
        (np.repeat(np.array([[72, 0, 72]]), X.shape[0], axis=0) *\
        X._ppm.values.reshape(-1,1))
treatment_effect_minus_costs =\
                        causal_mdl.const_marginal_effect(X=X.
values) -\
                        cost_fn(ccdefault_causal_df)
treatment_effect_minus_costs = np.hstack([np.zeros(X.shape),\
                                        treatment_marginal_
effect])
recommended_T = np.argmax(treatment_effect_minus_costs, axis=1)
```

We can `scatterplot` the _CC_LIMIT and _ppm, color-coded by the recommended treatment to observe the customer's optimal credit policy, as follows:

```
sns.scatterplot(\
                x=ccdefault_causal_df['_CC_LIMIT'].values,\
                y=ccdefault_causal_df['_ppm'].values,\
                hue=all_treatment_names[recommended_T],\
                hue_order=all_treatment_names)
plt.title("Optimal Credit Policy by Customer")
plt.xlabel("Original Credit Limit")
plt.ylabel("Payments/month")
```

The preceding snippet outputs the following scatter plot:

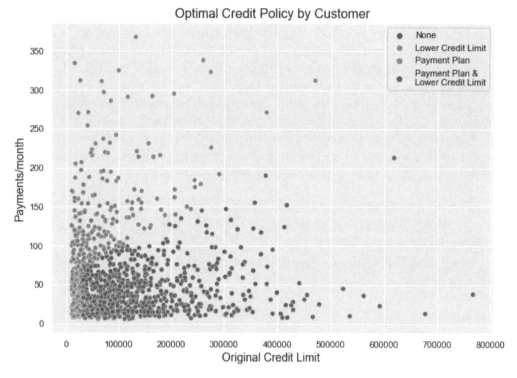

Figure 11.15 – Optimal credit policy by customer depending on original credit limit and card usage

It's evident in *Figure 11.15* that no treatment is ever recommended. This fact holds even when costs aren't deducted—you can remove `cost_fn` and rerun the code that outputs the plot to verify. You can deduce that all treatments are beneficial to customers, some more than others. And, of course, some treatments benefit the bank more than others, depending on the customer. There's a thin line to tread here.

One of the biggest concerns is fairness to customers, especially those that the bank wronged the most: the underprivileged age group. Just because one policy is more costly to the bank than another, it should preclude the opportunity to access other policies. One way to assess this would be with a percentage-stacked bar plot for all recommended policies. That way, we can observe how the recommended policy is split between privileged and underprivileged groups. Have a look at the following code snippet:

```
ccdefault_causal_df['recommended_T'] = recommended_T
plot_df =\
        ccdefault_causal_df.groupby(['recommended_T','AGE_
GROUP']).
                                            size().reset_
index()
plot_df['AGE_GROUP'] = plot_df.AGE_GROUP.
replace({0:'unprivileged',\
1:'privileged'})
plot_df = plot_df.pivot(columns='AGE_GROUP',
index='recommended_T',\
                        values=0)
plot_df.index = treatment_names
plot_df = plot_df.apply(lambda r: r/r.sum()*100, axis=1)

plot_df.plot.bar(stacked=True, rot=0)
plt.xlabel('Optimal Policy')
plt.ylabel('%')
```

The code in the preceding snippet outputs the following:

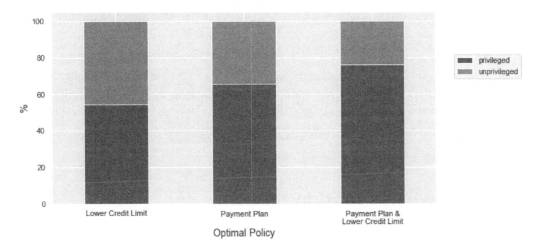

Figure 11.16 – Fairness of optimal policy distributions

Figure 11.16 shows how privileged groups are at a higher proportion assigned one of the policies with the **Payment Plan**. This disparity is primarily due to the bank's costs being a factor, so if the bank were to absorb some of these costs, it could make it fairer. But what would be a fair solution? Choosing credit policies is an example of procedural fairness, and there are many possible definitions. Does equal treatment literally mean equal treatment or proportional treatment? Does it encompass notions of freedom of choice too? What if a customer prefers one policy over another? Should they be allowed to switch? Whatever the definition is, it can be resolved with help from the causal model. We can assign all customers the same policy, or the distribution of recommended policies can be calibrated so that proportions are equal, or every customer can choose between a first and second most optimal policy. There are so many ways to go about it!

Testing estimate robustness

The DoWhy library comes with four methods to test the robustness of the estimated causal effect, outlined as follows:

- **Random common cause**: Adding a randomly generated confounder. If the estimate is robust, the ATE should not change too much.

- **Placebo treatment refuter**: Replacing treatments with random variables (placebos). If the estimate is robust, the ATE should be close to zero.

- **Data subset refuter**: Removing a random subset of the data. If the estimator generalizes well, the ATE should not change too much.

- **Add unobserved common cause**: Adding a unobserved confounder that is associated with both the treatment and the outcome. The estimator assumes some level of unconfoundedness, but adding more should bias the estimates. Depending on the strength of the confounder's effect, it should have an equal impact on the ATE.

We will test robustness with the first two next.

Adding random common cause

This method is the easiest to implement by calling `refute_estimate` with `method_name="random_common_cause"`. This will return a summary that you can print. Have a look at the following code snippet:

```
ref_random = \
causal_mdl.refute_estimate(method_name="random_common_cause")
print(ref_random)
```

The code in the preceding snippet outputs the following:

```
Refute: Add a Random Common Cause
Estimated effect:7221.414390341943
New effect:7546.695920181393
```

The preceding output tells us that a new common cause, or *W* variable, doesn't have a sizable impact on the ATE.

Replacing treatment with a random variable

With this method, we will replace the treatment variable with noise. If the treatment correlates robustly with the outcome, this should bring the average affect to zero. To implement it, we also call the `refute_estimate` function but with `placebo_treatment_refuter` for the method. We must also specify the `placebo_type` and the number of simulations (`num_simulations`). The placebo type we will use is `permute`, and the more simulations the better, but this will also take longer. The code can be seen in the following snippet:

```
ref_placebo = causal_mdl.refute_estimate(\
                        method_name="placebo_treatment_
refuter",\
                        placebo_type="permute", num_
simulations=20)
print(ref_placebo)
```

The preceding code outputs the following:

```
Refute: Use a Placebo Treatment
Estimated effect:7221.414390341943
New effect:132.77295305233164
p value:0.43187234564256083
```

As you can tell by the preceding output, the new effect is close to zero. However, given that the p-value is above 0.05, we cannot reject the null hypothesis that ascertains that the ATE is greater than zero. This tells us that the estimated causal effect is not very robust. We can likely improve it by adding relevant confounders or by using a different causal model, but also, the experimental design had flaws that we cannot fix, such as the biased way the bank prescribed the treatments according to the risk factor.

Mission accomplished

The mission of this chapter was twofold, as outlined here:

- Create a fair predictive model to predict which customers are most likely to default.

- Create a robust causal model to estimate which policies are most beneficial to customers and the bank.

Regarding the first goal, we have produced four models with bias mitigation methods that are objectively fairer than the base model, according to four fairness metrics (SPD, DI, AOD, EOD)—when comparing privileged and underprivileged age groups. However, only two of these models are intersectionally fairer using both age group and gender, according to DFBA (see *Figure 11.7*). We can still improve fairness significantly by combining methods, yet any one of the four models improves the base model.

As for the second goal, the causal inference framework determined that any of the policies tested is better than no policy for both parties. Hooray! However, it yielded estimates that didn't establish a single winning one. Still, as expected, the recommended policy varies according to the customer's credit limit—on the other hand, if we aim to maximize bank profitability, we must factor in the average use of credit cards. The question of profitability presents two goals that we must reconcile: prescribing the recommended policies that benefit either the customer or the bank the most.

For this reason, how to be procedurally fair is a complicated question with many possible answers, and any of the solutions would involve the bank absorbing some of the costs associated with implementing the policies. As for robustness, despite the flawed experiment we can conclude that our estimates have a mediocre level of robustness, passing one robustness test but not the other. That being said, it all depends on what we consider robust enough to validate our findings. Ideally, we would ask the bank to start a new unbiased experiment, but waiting another 6 months might not be feasible. In data science, we often find ourselves working with flawed experiments and biased data and have to make the most of it. Causal inference provides a way to do so by disentangling cause and effect, complete with estimates and their respective confidence intervals. We can then offer findings with all the disclaimers so that decision-makers can make informed decisions. Biased decisions lead to biased outcomes, so the moral imperative of tackling bias can start by shaping decision-making.

Summary

After reading this chapter, you should understand how bias can be detected visually and with metrics, both in data and models—then, mitigated through preprocessing, in-processing, and post-processing methods. We also learned about causal inference by estimating heterogeneous treatment effects, making fair policy decisions with them, and testing robustness for them. In the next chapter, we also discuss bias but learn how to tune models to meet several objectives, including fairness.

Dataset sources

Yeh, I. C., & Lien, C. H. (2009). *The comparisons of data mining techniques for the predictive accuracy of probability of default of credit card clients.* Expert Systems with Applications, 36(2), 2473-2480.

`https://dl.acm.org/doi/abs/10.1016/j.eswa.2007.12.020`

Further reading

1. Chang, C., Chang, H.H., & Tien, J. (2017). *A Study on the Coping Strategy of Financial Supervisory Organization under Information Asymmetry: Case Study of Taiwan's Credit Card Market.* Universal Journal of Management, 5, 429-436. `http://doi.org/10.13189/ujm.2017.050903`

2. Foulds, J., & Pan, S. (2020). *An Intersectional Definition of Fairness.* 2020 IEEE 36th International Conference on Data Engineering (ICDE), 1918-1921. `https://arxiv.org/abs/1807.08362`

3. Kamiran, F., & Calders, T. (2011). *Data preprocessing techniques for classification without discrimination.* Knowledge and Information Systems, 33, 1-33. `https://link.springer.com/article/10.1007/s10115-011-0463-8`

4. Feldman, M., Friedler, S., Moeller, J., Scheidegger, C., & Venkatasubramanian, S. (2015). *Certifying and Removing DI.* Proceedings of the 21st ACM SIGKDD International Conference on Knowledge Discovery and Data Mining. `https://arxiv.org/abs/1412.3756`

5. Kamishima, T., Akaho, S., Asoh, H., & Sakuma, J. (2012). *Fairness-Aware Classifier with Prejudice Remover Regularizer.* ECML/PKDD. `https://dl.acm.org/doi/10.5555/3120007.3120011`

6. Kearns, M., Neel, S., Roth, A., & Wu, Z. (2018). *Preventing Fairness Gerrymandering: Auditing and Learning for Subgroup Fairness.* ICML. `https://arxiv.org/pdf/1711.05144.pdf`

7. Pleiss, G., Raghavan, M., Wu, F., Kleinberg, J., & Weinberger, K.Q. (2017). *On Fairness and Calibration.* NIPS.

    `https://arxiv.org/abs/1709.02012`

8. Foster, D. and Syrgkanis, V. (2019). *Orthogonal Statistical Learning.* ICML. `http://arxiv.org/abs/1901.09036`

12

Monotonic Constraints and Model Tuning for Interpretability

Most model classes have hyperparameters that can be tuned for faster execution speed, increasing predictive performance and reducing overfitting. One way of reducing overfitting is by introducing regularization into the model training. In *Chapter 3, Interpretation Challenges*, we called regularization a remedial interpretability property, which reduces complexity with a penalty or limitation that forces the model to learn sparser representations of the inputs. Regularized models generalize better, which is why it is highly recommended to tune models with this strategy. As a side effect, fewer features and their interactions are essential to the regularized model, making the model easier to interpret—*less noise means a clearer signal*!

And even though there are many hyperparameters, we will only focus on those that improve interpretability by controlling overfitting. Also, to a certain extent, we will revisit bias mitigation through class imbalance-related hyperparameters explored in previous chapters.

Chapter 2, Key Concepts of Interpretability, explained three model properties that impact interpretability: non-linearity, interactivity, and non-monotonicity. Left to its own devices, a model can learn some spurious and counterintuitive non-linearities and interactivities. As discussed in *Chapter 10, Feature Selection and Engineering for Interpretability,* guardrails can be placed to prevent this through careful feature engineering. However, what can we do to place guardrails for monotonicity? In this chapter, we will learn how to do just this with monotonic constraints. And just as monotonic constraints can be the model counterpart to feature engineering, regularization can be the model counterpart to the feature selection methods we covered in *Chapter 10*!

These are the main topics we are going to cover in this chapter:

- Placing guardrails with feature engineering
- Tuning models for interpretability
- Implementing model constraints

Technical requirements

This chapter's example uses the `mldatasets`, `pandas`, `numpy`, `sklearn`, `xgboost`, `lightgbm`, `catboost`, `tensorflow`, `bayes_opt`, `tensorflow_lattice`, `matplotlib`, `seaborn`, `scipy`, `xai`, and `shap` libraries. Instructions on how to install all of these libraries are in the preface. The code for this chapter is located here:

```
https://github.com/PacktPublishing/Interpretable-Machine-
Learning-with-Python/tree/master/Chapter12
```

The mission

The issue of algorithmic fairness is one with massive societal implications, from the allocation of welfare resources, to the prioritization of life-saving surgeries, to screening job applications. These machine learning algorithms can determine a person's livelihood or life, and it's often the most marginalized and vulnerable populations that get the worst treatment from these algorithms because they perpetuate systemic biases learned from the data. Therefore, it's poorer families that get misclassified for child abuse; it's racial-minority people that get underprioritized for medical treatment; and it's women that get screened out of high-paying tech jobs. Even in cases involving less immediate and individualized risks such as online searches, Twitter bots, and social media profiles, societal prejudice such as elitism, racism, sexism, and agism are reinforced.

This chapter will continue on the mission from *Chapter 7, Anchor and Counterfactual Explanations*. If you aren't familiar with this, please go back and just read the first few pages of *Chapter 7* to get a solid understanding of the problem first. The recidivism case from *Chapter 7* is one of algorithmic bias. The co-founder of the company that developed the **COMPAS algorithm** (where **COMPAS** stands for **Correctional Offender Management Profiling Alternative Sanctions**) admitted that it's tough to make a score without questions that are correlated with race. This correlation is one of the main reasons that scores are biased against African Americans. The other reason is the likely overrepresentation of black defendants in the training data. We don't know for sure because we don't have the original training data, but we know that non-white minorities are the majority jailed. We also know that black people are typically overrepresented in arrests because of codified discrimination in terms of minor drug-related offenses and overpolicing in black communities.

So, what can we do to fix it?

In *Chapter 7, Anchor and Counterfactual Explanations*, we managed to demonstrate via a *proxy model* that the COMPAS algorithm was biased. For this chapter, let's say that the journalist published your findings, and an algorithmic justice advocacy group read the article and reached out. Companies that make criminal assessment tools are not taking responsibility for bias, and say that their tools simply reflect the *reality*. The advocacy group has hired you to demonstrate that a machine learning model can be trained to be significantly less biased toward black defendants, while ensuring that the model reflects only proven criminal justice *realities*.

These proven realities include the monotone decrease of recidivism risk with age, and a strong correlation with priors, which increases strongly with age. Another fact supported by the academic literature is how females are significantly less prone to recidivism and criminality in general.

Before we move on, we must recognize that supervised learning models face several impediments in capturing domain knowledge from data. For instance, consider the following:

- **Sample, exclusion, or prejudice bias**: What if your data doesn't truly represent the environment your model intends to generalize? If that's the case, the domain knowledge won't align with what you observe in the data. What if the environment that produced the data has a built-in systemic or institutional bias? Then, the data will reflect these biases.

- **Class imbalance**: As seen in *Chapter 11, Bias Mitigation and Causal Inference Methods*, class imbalance could favor some groups over others. While taking the most effective route toward high accuracy, a model will learn from this imbalance, contradicting domain knowledge.

- **Non-monotonicity**: Sparse areas in a features histogram or high-leverage outliers could cause a model to learn non-monotonicity when domain knowledge calls for otherwise, and any the previously mentioned problems could contribute to this as well.

- **Uninfluential features**: An unregularized model will, by default, try to learn from all features as long as they carry some information, but this stands in the way of learning from relevant features. A more parsimonious model is more likely to prop up features supported by domain knowledge.

- **Counterintuivite interactions**: As mentioned in *Chapter 10, Feature Selection and Engineering for Interpretability*, there could be counterintuitive interactions that a model is favoring over domain knowledge-supported interactions. As a side effect, these could end up favoring some groups that correlate with them. And in *Chapter 7, Anchors and Counterfactual Explanations*, we saw proof of this through an understanding of double standards.

- **Exceptions**: Our domain knowledge facts are based on an aggregate understanding, but when looking for patterns on a more granular scale, models will find exceptions such as pockets where female recidivism is of higher risk than that of males. Known phenomena might not support these models but they could be valid nonetheless, so we must be careful not to erase them with our tuning efforts.

The advocacy group has validated the data as adequately representative of only one county in Florida, and they have provided you with a balanced dataset. The first impediment is a tough one to ascertain and control. The second one had been taken care of. It's now up to you to deal with the remaining four!

The approach

You have decided to take a three-fold approach, as follows:

- **Placing guardrails with feature engineering**: Leveraging lessons learned in *Chapter 7*, as well as the domain knowledge we already have about priors and age, in particular, we will engineer some features.

- **Tuning models for interpretability**: Once the data is ready, we will tune many models with different class weighting and overfitting prevention techniques. These methods will ensure that the models not only generalize better but are easier to interpret.

- **Implementing model constraints**: Last but not least, we will implement monotonic and interaction constraints on the best models to make sure that they don't stray from trusted and fair interactions.

In the last two sections, we will make sure the models perform accurately and fairly. We will also compare recidivism risk distributions between the data and the model to ensure that they align.

The preparations

You will find the code for this example here:

```
https://github.com/PacktPublishing/Interpretable-Machine-
Learning-with-Python/tree/master/Chapter12/Recidivism_part2.
ipynb
```

Loading the libraries

To run this example, you need to install the following libraries:

- `mldatasets` to load the dataset

- `pandas` and `numpy` to manipulate it

- `sklearn` (scikit-learn), `xgboost`, `lightgbm`, `catboost`, `tensorflow`, `bayes_opt`, and `tensorflow_lattice` to split the data and fit the models

- `matplotlib`, `seaborn`, `scipy`, `xai`, and `shap` to visualize the interpretations

You should load all of them first, as follows:

```
import math
import os
import copy
import mldatasets
import pandas as pd
import numpy as np
from sklearn import preprocessing, model_selection, metrics,\
     linear_model, svm, neural_network, ensemble
```

```
import xgboost as xgb
import lightgbm as lgb
import catboost as cb
import tensorflow as tf
from bayes_opt import BayesianOptimization
import tensorflow_lattice as tfl
from tensorflow.keras.wrappers.scikit_learn import
KerasClassifier
import matplotlib.pyplot as plt
import seaborn as sns
import scipy
import xai
import shap
```

Let's check that `tensorflow` has loaded the right version with `print(tf.__version__)`. This should be 2.0 and above.

Understanding and preparing the data

We load the data like this into a DataFrame we call `recidivism_df`:

```
recidivism_df = mldatasets.load("recidivism-risk-balanced")
```

There should be over 11,000 records and 11 columns. We can verify this was the case with `info()`, as follows:

```
recidivism_df.info()
```

The preceding code outputs the following:

```
<class 'pandas.core.frame.DataFrame'>
RangeIndex: 11142 entries, 0 to 11141
Data columns (total 12 columns):
```

#	Column	Non-Null Count	Dtype
0	sex	11142 non-null	object
1	age	11142 non-null	int64
2	race	11142 non-null	object
3	juv_fel_count	11142 non-null	int64
4	juv_misd_count	11142 non-null	int64

5	juv_other_count	11142 non-null	int64
6	priors_count	11142 non-null	int64
7	c_charge_degree	11142 non-null	object
8	days_b_screening_arrest	11142 non-null	float64
9	length_of_stay	11142 non-null	float64
10	compas_score	11142 non-null	int64
11	is_recid	11142 non-null	int64

```
dtypes: float64(2), int64(7), object(3)
memory usage: 1.0+ MB
```

The output checks out. There are no missing values, and all but three features are numeric (sex, race, and charge_degree). This is the same data we used in *Chapter 7, Anchors and Counterfactual Explanations*, so the data dictionary is exactly the same. However, the dataset has been balanced with sampling methods, and this time it hasn't been prepared for us so we will need to do this, but before this, let's gain an understanding of what the balancing did.

Verifying the sampling balance

We can check how race and is_recid are distributed with XAI's imbalance_plot. In other words, it will tally how many records exist for each race-is_recid combination. This plot will allow us to observe if there are imbalances in the number of defendants that recidivated for each race. The code can be seen in the following snippet:

```
categorical_cols_l = ['sex', 'race', 'c_charge_degree',\
        'is_recid', 'compas_score']
xai.imbalance_plot(recidivism_df, 'race', 'is_recid',\
        categorical_cols=categorical_cols_l)
```

The preceding code outputs *Figure 12.1*, which depicts how all races have equal amounts of is_recid=0 and is_recid=1. However, **Other** is not at parity in numbers with the other races. Incidentally, this version of the dataset has bucketed all other races as **Other**, and the choice to not upsample **Other** or downsample the other two races to achieve total parity is made because they are less represented in the defendant population. This balancing choice is one of many that can be done in a situation such as this. Demographically, it all depends on what your data is supposed to represent: Defendants? Inmates? Civilians in the general population? And at what level? Of the county? The state? The country?

The output can be seen here:

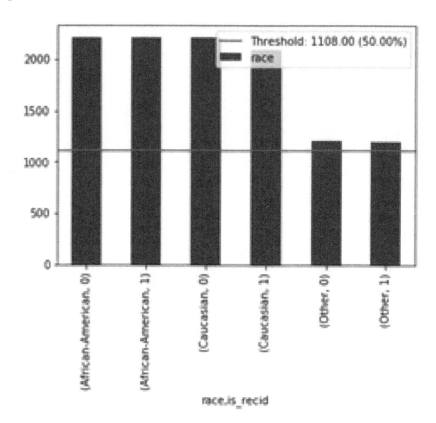

Figure 12.1 – Distribution of 2-year recidivism (is_recid) by race

Next, let's compute how well each of our features monotonically correlates to the target. We learned about Spearman's rank-order correlation in *Chapter 5, Global Model-Agnostic Interpretation Methods,* but it will be instrumental in this chapter because it measures the monotonicity between two features. After all, one of the technical topics of this chapter is monotonic constraints, and the primary mission is to produce a significantly less biased model.

We first create a new `DataFrame` without `compas_score` (`recidivism_corr_df`). Using this dataframe, we output a color-coded dataframe with a `feature` column with the first 10 features' names and another one with the Spearman coefficient (`correlation_to_target`) for all 10 features toward the 11th—the target variable. The code can be seen in the following snippet:

```
recidivism_corr_df = recidivism_df.drop(['compas_score'],\
  axis=1)
```

```
pd.DataFrame({'feature': recidivism_corr_df.columns[:-1],\
    'correlation_to_target':\
        scipy.stats.spearmanr(recidivism_corr_df).
correlation[10,:-1]
}).style.background_gradient(cmap='coolwarm')
```

The preceding code outputs the dataframe shown in *Figure 12.2*. The most correlated features are `priors_count` followed by `age`, the three juvenile counts, and `sex`. The coefficients for `c_charge_degree`, `days_b_screening_arrest`, `length_of_stay`, and `race` are negligible.

The output can be seen here:

	feature	correlation_to_target
0	sex	0.093255
1	age	-0.155838
2	race	-0.004598
3	juv_fel_count	0.082138
4	juv_misd_count	0.117976
5	juv_other_count	0.125797
6	priors_count	0.283640
7	c_charge_degree	-0.037764
8	days_b_screening_arrest	0.032485
9	length_of_stay	0.012530

Figure 12.2 – Spearman coefficients of all features toward the target, prior to feature engineering

Next, we will learn how to use feature engineering to "bake in" some domain knowledge to the features.

Placing guardrails with feature engineering

In *Chapter 7, Anchors and Counterfactual Explanations*, we learned that besides `race`, the features most prominent in our explanations were `age`, `priors_count`, and `c_charge_degree`. Thankfully, the data is now balanced, so the racial bias attributed to this imbalance is now gone. However, through anchor and counterfactual explanations, we found some troubling inconsistencies. In the case of `age` and `priors_count`, these inconsistencies were due to how those features were distributed. We can correct issues with distribution through feature engineering, and that way ensure that a model doesn't learn from uneven distributions. In `c_charge_degree`'s case being categorical, it lacked a discernible order, and this lack of order created unintuitive explanations.

In this section, we will study **ordinalization**, **discretization**, and **interaction terms**, three ways in which you can place guardrails through feature engineering.

Ordinalization

Let's first take a look in the following code snippet at how many observations we have for every `c_charge_degree` category:

```
recidivism_df.c_charge_degree.value_counts()
```

The preceding code produced the following output:

(F3)	6555
(M1)	2632
(F2)	857
(M2)	768
(F1)	131
(F7)	104
(MO3)	76
(F5)	7
(F6)	5
(NI0)	4
(CO3)	2
(TCX)	1
Name: c_charge_degree, dtype: int64	

Each of the charge degrees corresponds to the charge's gravity. There's an order to these gravities, which is lost by using a categorical feature. We can easily fix this by replacing each category with a corresponding order.

We can put a lot of thought into what this order should be. For instance, we could look at sentencing laws or guidelines—there are minimum or maximum years of prison enforced for different degrees. We could also look at statistics on how violent these people are on average and assign this information to the charge degree. There's potential for bias in every decision such as this, and if we don't have substantial evidence to support it, it's best to use a sequence of integers. So, that's what we are going to do now. We will create a dictionary (`charge_degree_code_rank`) that maps the degrees to a number corresponding to a rank of gravity, from low to high. Then, we use the pandas `replace` function to use the dictionary to perform the replacements. The code can be seen in the following snippet:

```
charge_degree_code_rank = {'(F10)': 15, '(F9)':14, '(F8)':13,\
              '(F7)':12, '(TCX)':11, '(F6)':10, '(F5)':9,\
          '(F4)':8, '(F3)':7, '(F2)':6, '(F1)':5, '(M1)':4,\
          '(NI0)':4, '(M2)':3, '(CO3)':2, '(MO3)':1,
 '(X)':0}
recidivism_df.c_charge_degree.replace(charge_degree_code_rank,\
                           inplace=True)
```

One way to assess how this order corresponds to recidivism probability is through a line plot that shows how it changes as the charge degree increases. We can use a function called `plot_prob_progression` for this that takes a continuous feature in the first argument (`c_charge_degree`) to measure against probability for a binary feature in the second (`is_recid`). It can split the continuous feature by intervals (`x_intervals`), and even use quartiles (`use_quartiles`). Lastly, you can define axis labels and titles. The code can be seen in the following snippet:

```
mldatasets.plot_prob_progression(recidivism_df.c_charge_degree,
         recidivism_df.is_recid, x_intervals=12,\
         use_quartiles=False, xlabel='Relative Charge Degree',\
      title='Probability of Recidivism by Relative Charge
 Degree')
```

The preceding code generates the plot in *Figure 12.3*. As the now-ranked charge degree increases, the tendency is that the probability of 2-year recidivism decreases, except for rank 1. Below the probability, there are bar charts that show the distribution of the observations over every rank. Because of it being so unevenly distributed, you should take the tendency with a grain of salt. You'll notice that some ranks such as 0, 8 and 13-15 aren't in the plot because the charge-degree categories existed in the criminal justice system but weren't in the data.

The output can be seen here:

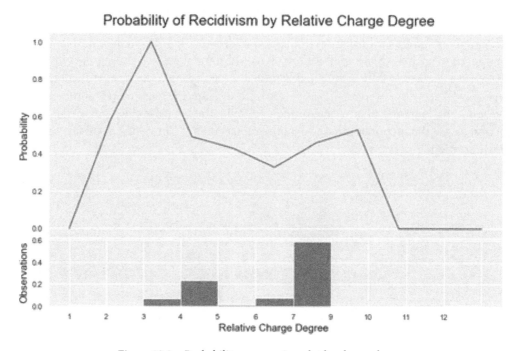

Figure 12.3 – Probability progression plot by charge degree

Feature engineering-wise, we can't do much more to improve `c_charge_degree` because it already represents discrete categories now enhanced with an order. Any further transformations could produce a significant loss of information unless we had evidence to suggest otherwise. On the other hand, continuous features inherently have an order, but a problem may arise from the level of precision they carry because small differences may not be meaningful but the data may tell the model otherwise. Uneven distributions and counterintuitive interactions only exacerbate this problem.

Discretization

To understand how to discretize our `age` continuous feature best, let's try two different approaches. We can use equal-sized discretization, also known as fix-width bins or intervals, which means the size of the bin is determined by $(max(x) - min(x)) / N$, where N is the number of bins. Another way to do this is with equal-frequency discretization, also known as quartiles, which ensures that each bin has more or less the same of observations. Although sometimes, given the histogram's skewed nature, it may be impossible to split them N ways, so you may end up with N-1 or N-2 quartiles.

It is easy to compare both approaches with `plot_prob_progression`, but this time we produce two plots, one with fixed-width bins (`use_quartiles=False`) and another with quartiles (`use_quartiles=True`). The code can be seen in the following snippet:

```
mldatasets.plot_prob_progression(recidivism_df.age,\
        recidivism_df.is_recid, x_intervals=7,\
use_quartiles=False,\
        title='Probability of Recidivism by Age Discretized in
Fix-Width Bins', xlabel='Age')
mldatasets.plot_prob_progression(recidivism_df.age,\
        recidivism_df.is_recid, x_intervals=7,\
use_quartiles=True,\
        title='Probability of Recidivism by Age Discretized\
in Quartiles', xlabel='Age')
```

The preceding snippet outputs *Figure 12.4*. By looking at the **Observations** portion of the fix-width bin plot, you can tell that the histogram for the `age` feature is right-skewed, which causes the probability to shoot up for the last bin. The reason for this is some outliers exist in this bin. On the other hand, the fix-frequency (quartile) plot histogram is more even, and probability consistently decreases. In other words, it's monotonic—as it should be, according to our domain knowledge on the subject.

The output can be seen here:

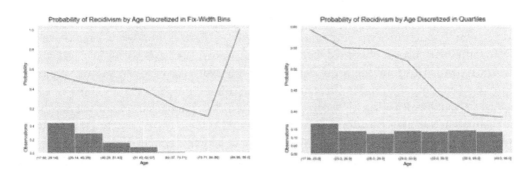

Figure 12.4 – Comparing two discretization approaches for age

It is easy to observe why using quantiles to bin the feature is a better approach. We can take age and engineer a new feature called age_group. The qcut pandas function can perform the quantile-based discretization. The code can be seen in the following snippet:

```
recidivism_df['age_group'] = pd.qcut(recidivism_df.age, 7,\
                                    precision=0).astype(str)
```

So, we now have a discretized age into age_group. However, it must be noted that many model classes discretize automatically, so why bother? Because it allows you to control its effects. Otherwise, the model might decide on bins that don't ensure monotonicity. For instance, maybe the model might always use 10 quartiles whenever possible. Still, if you attempt this level of granularity on age (x_intervals=10), you'll end up with spikes in the probability progression. Our goal was to make sure that the models would learn that age and the incidence of is_recid have a monotonic relationship, and we cannot ascertain this if we allow the model to choose bins that may or may not achieve the same goal.

We will remove age because age_group has everything we need. But wait—you ask—won't we lose some important information by removing this variable? Yes, but only because of its interaction with priors_count. So, before we drop any features, let's examine this relationship and realize how, through creating an interaction term, we can retain some of the information lost through the removal of age, while keeping the interaction.

Interaction terms and non-linear transformations

We already know from *Chapter 7, Anchor and Counterfactual Explanations*, that age and priors_count are two of the most important predictors, and we can easily see how together they impact the incidence of recidivism (is_recid) with plot_prob_contour_map. This function produces contour lines with color-coded contour regions, signifying different magnitudes. They are useful in topography, where they show elevation heights. In machine learning, they can show how a metric changes in regions across two dimensions. In this case, our dimensions are age and priors_count, and the metric is the incidence of recidivism. The arguments received by this function are the same as plot_prob_progression except that it takes two features corresponding to the *x* axis and *y* axis. The code can be seen in the following snippet:

```
mldatasets.plot_prob_contour_map(recidivism_df.age,\
        recidivism_df.priors_count,\
        recidivism_df.is_recid,\
     use_quartiles=True, xlabel='Age', ylabel='Priors Count',\
```

```
            title='Probability of Recidivism by Age/Priors Discretized
in Quartiles')
```

The preceding snippet generated *Figure 12.5*, which shows how, when discretized by quartiles, the probability of 2-year recidivism increases, the lower the `age` and the higher the `priors_count`. It also shows histograms for both features. `priors_count` is very right-skewed, so discretization is challenging, and the contour map does not offer a perfectly diagonal progression between bottom right and top left. And if this plot looks familiar, it's because it's just like the partial dependence interaction plots we produced in *Chapter 4, Fundamentals of Feature Importance and Impact*, except it's not measured against the predictions of a model but the ground truth (`is_recid`). We must distinguish between what the data can tell us directly and what the model has learned from it.

The output can be seen here:

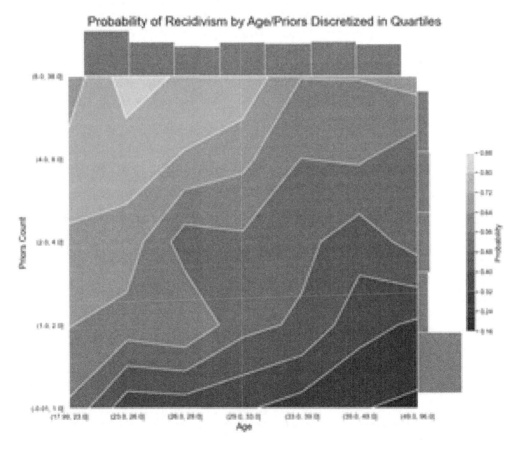

Figure 12.5 – Recidivism probability contour map for age and priors_count

We can now engineer an interaction term that includes both features. Even though the contour map discretized the features to observe a smoother progression, we do not need to discretize this relationship. What makes sense is to make it a ratio of `priors_count` per year. But years since when? Years since defendants were an adult, of course. But to obtain the years, we cannot use `age` - 18 because this would lead to zero division, so we will use 17 instead. There are, of course, many ways to do this. The best way would be if we hypothetically had ages with decimals, and by deducting 18 we could compute a very precise priors-per-year ratio. Still, unfortunately, we don't have that. You can see the code in the following snippet:

```
recidivism_df['priors_per_year'] =\
            recidivism_df['priors_count']/(recidivism_df['age']
 - 17)
```

Black-box models typically find interaction terms automatically. For instance, hidden layers in a neural network have all the first-order interactions, but because of the non-linear activations it is not limited to linear combinations. However, "manually" defining interaction terms and even non-linear transformation allows us to interpret these better once the model has been fitted. Furthermore, we can also use monotonic constraints on them, precisely what we will do later with `priors_per_year`. For now, let's examine if its monotonicity holds with `plot_prob_progression`. Have a look at the following code snippet:

```
mldatasets.plot_prob_progression(recidivism_df.priors_per_year,
    recidivism_df.is_recid, x_intervals=8, xlabel='Priors Per
Year',\
    title='Probability of Recidivism by Priors per Year
(according to data)')
```

The preceding snippet outputs the progression in the following screenshot, which shows how the new feature is almost monotonic:

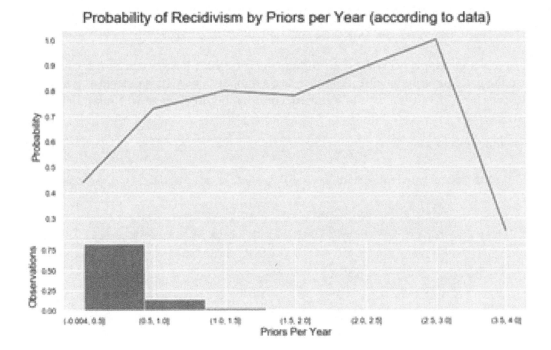

Figure 12.6 – Probability progression for priors_per_year

The reason `priors_per_year` isn't more monotonic is how sparse the over-3.0 priors-per-year interval is. It would be therefore very unfair to these few defendants to enforce monotonicity on this feature because they present a 75% risk dip. One way to tackle this is to shift them over to the left, by setting `priors_per_year=-1` for these observations, as illustrated in the following code snippet:

```
recidivism_df.loc[recidivism_df.priors_per_year > 3,\
                  'priors_per_year'] = -1
```

Of course, this shift changes the interpretation of the feature ever so slightly, knowing that the few values of -1 really mean over 3. Now, let's generate another contour map, but this time between `age_group` and `priors_per_year`. The latter will be discretized in quartiles (`y_intervals=6, use_quartiles=True`) so that the probability of recidivism is more easily observed. The code is shown in the following snippet:

```
mldatasets.plot_prob_contour_map(recidivism_df.age_group,
          recidivism_df.priors_per_year, recidivism_df.is_
recid,\
          y_intervals=6, use_quartiles=True, xlabel='Age
Group',\
```

```
            title='Probability of Recidivism by Age/Priors per
Year Discretized in Quartiles', ylabel='Priors Per Year')
```

The preceding snippet generates the contours in *Figure 12.7*. It shows that, for the most part, the plot moves in one direction. We were hoping to achieve this outcome because it allows us through one interaction feature to control monotonicity on what used to involve two features.

The output can be seen here:

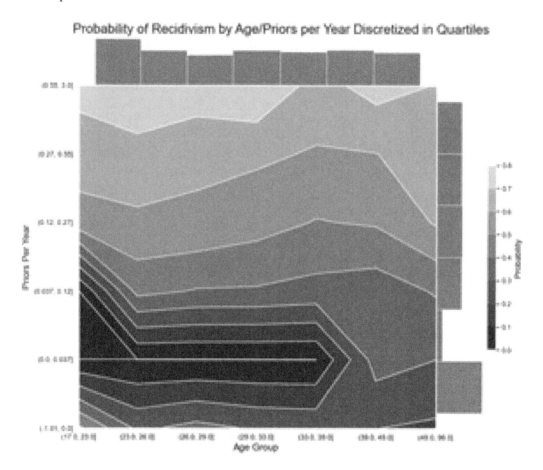

Figure 12.7 – Recidivism probability contour map for age_group and priors_per_year

Almost everything is ready, but `age_group` is still categorical, so we have to encode it to take a numerical form.

Categorical encoding

The best categorical encoding method for `age_group` is **ordinal encoding**, also known as **label encoding**, because it will retain its order. We should also encode the other two categorical features in the dataset, `sex` and `race`. For `sex`, ordinal encoding converts it into binary form—equivalent to **dummy encoding**. On the other hand, `race` is a tougher call because it has three categories, and using ordinal encoding could lead to bias. However, whether to **one-hot-encode** instead depends on which model classes you are using. Tree-based models have no bias issues with ordinal features but other models that operate with weights on a feature-basis, such as neural networks and logistic regression, could learn the wrong thing by virtue of this order. Considering that the dataset has been balanced on `race`, there's a lower risk of this happening and we will remove this feature later anyway, so we will go ahead and ordinal-encode it.

To ordinal-encode the three features, we will use scikit-learn's `OrdinalEncoder`. We can use its `fit_transform` function to fit and transform the features in one fell swoop. Then, we should also delete unnecessary features while we are at it. Have a look at the following code snippet:

```
cat_feat_l = ['sex', 'race', 'age_group']
ordenc = preprocessing.OrdinalEncoder(dtype=np.int8)
recidivism_df[cat_feat_l] =\
                    ordenc.fit_transform(recidivism_df[cat_
feat_l])
recidivism_df.drop(['age', 'priors_count', \
'compas_score'], axis=1,\
                    inplace=True)
```

Now, we aren't entirely done yet. We still ought to initialize our random seeds, and train/test split our data.

Other preparations

The next preparations are fairly straightforward. To ensure reproducibility, let's set a random seed everywhere it is needed, then set our `y` as `is_recid` and `X` as every other feature. We perform `train_test_split` on those two. Lastly, we reconstruct the `recidivism_df` dataframe with the `X` followed by the `y`. The only reason for this is so that `is_recid` is the last column, which will help with the next step. The code can be seen here:

```
rand = 9
os.environ['PYTHONHASHSEED'] = str(rand)
```

```
tf.random.set_seed(rand)
np.random.seed(rand)
y = recidivism_df['is_recid']
X = recidivism_df.drop(['is_recid'], axis=1).copy()
X_train, X_test, y_train, y_test =\
        model_selection.train_test_split(X, y, test_
size=0.2,\
                                         random_
state=rand)
recidivism_df = X.join(y)
```

We will now verify that Spearman's correlations have improved where needed and stay the same, otherwise. Have a look at the following code snippet:

```
pd.DataFrame({'feature': X.columns,\
            'correlation_to_target':\
            scipy.stats.spearmanr(recidivism_df).
correlation[10,:-1]
        }).style.background_gradient(cmap='coolwarm')
```

The preceding code outputs the dataframe shown in *Figure 12.8*. Please compare it with *Figure 12.2*. Note that discretized in quartiles, age is even more monotonically correlated with the target. Once ordinalized, c_charge_degree is also much more correlated, and priors_per_year has also improved over priors_count. No other features should have been affected, including those that have the lowest coefficients.

The output can be seen here:

	feature	correlation_to_target
0	sex	0.093255
1	race	-0.004598
2	juv_fel_count	0.082138
3	juv_misd_count	0.117976
4	juv_other_count	0.125797
5	c_charge_degree	0.069803
6	days_b_screening_arrest	0.032485
7	length_of_stay	0.012530
8	age_group	-0.152131
9	priors_per_year	0.321885

Figure 12.8 – Spearman correlation coefficients of all features toward the target (after feature engineering)

Features with the lowest coefficients are likely also unnecessary in a model, but we will let the model decide if they are useful through regularization. That's what we will do next.

Tuning models for interpretability

Traditionally, regularization was only achieved by imposing penalty terms such as **L1**, **L2**, or **Elastic-net** on the coefficients or weights, which shrink the impact of the least relevant features. As seen in *Embedded methods* section of *Chapter 10, Feature Selection and Engineering for Interpretability*, this form of regularization results in feature selection while also reducing overfitting. And this brings us to another broader definition of regularization, which does not require a penalty term. Often, this comes as imposing a limitation, or a stopping criterion that forces the model to curb its complexity.

In addition to regularization, both in its narrow (penalty-based) and broad sense (*overfitting methods*), there are other methods that tune a model for interpretability—that is, improve the fairness, accountability, and transparency of a model through adjustments to the training process. For instance, the class imbalance hyperparameters we discussed in *Chapter 10, Feature Selection and Engineering for Interpretability* and the adversarial debiasing in *Chapter 11, Bias Mitigation and Causal Inference Methods* enhance fairness. Also, the constraints we will study further in this chapter have potential benefits for fairness, accountability, and transparency.

There are so many different tuning possibilities and in so many model classes. As stated at the beginning of the chapter, we will focus on interpretability-related options, but will also limit the model classes to a popular deep learning library (Keras), a handful of popular tree ensembles (XGBoost, RandomForest, and so on), **support vector machines** (**SVMs**), and logistic regression. Except for the last one, these are all considered black-box models.

Tuning a Keras neural network

For a Keras model, we will choose the best regularization parameters through hyperparameter tuning and **stratified K-fold cross-validation**. We will do this using the following steps:

1. First, we will need to define the model and the parameters to tune.

2. Then, we run the tuning.

3. Next, we examine its results.

4. Finally, we extract the best model and evaluate its predictive performance.

Let's look at each of these steps in detail.

Defining the model and parameters to tune

The first thing we ought to do is create a function (`build_nn_mdl`) to build and compile a regularizable Keras model. The function takes arguments that will help tune it. It takes a tuple with the amount of neurons in hidden layers (`hidden_layer_sizes`), and an amount of L1 (`l1_reg`) and L2 (`l1_reg`) regularization to apply on the layer's kernel. Lastly, it takes an amount of `dropout`, which, unlike L1 and L2 penalties, is a **stochastic regularization method** because it employs random selection. Have a look at the following code snippet:

```
def build_nn_mdl(hidden_layer_sizes, l1_reg=0, l2_reg=0,
dropout=0):
  nn_model = tf.keras.Sequential([
```

```
    tf.keras.Input(shape=[len(X_train.keys())]),
    tf.keras.layers.experimental.preprocessing.Normalization()
])
reg_args = {}
if (l1_reg > 0) or (l2_reg > 0):
 reg_args = {'kernel_regularizer':
    tf.keras.regularizers.l1_l2(l1=l1_reg, l2=l2_reg)}
for hidden_layer_size in hidden_layer_sizes:
 nn_model.add(tf.keras.layers.Dense(hidden_layer_size,
        activation='relu', **reg_args))
 if dropout > 0:
  nn_model.add(tf.keras.layers.Dropout(dropout))
 nn_model.add(tf.keras.layers.Dense(1, \
activation='sigmoid'))
 nn_model.compile(loss='binary_crossentropy',\
        optimizer=tf.keras.optimizers.Adam(lr=0.0004),\
        metrics=['accuracy',tf.keras.metrics.
AUC(name='auc')])
    return nn_model
```

The previous function initializes the model (nn_model) as a Sequential model
with an input layer that corresponds to the number of features in training data, and a
Normalization() layer that standardizes the input. Then, if either penalty term is over
zero, it will set a dictionary (reg_args) with the kernel_regularizer assigned to
tf.keras.regularizers.l1_l2 initialized with these penalties. Once it adds the
hidden (Dense) layers with the corresponding hidden_layer_size, it will pass the
reg_args dictionary as extra arguments to each layer. After all hidden layers have been
added, it will optionally add the Dropout layer and the final Dense layer with sigmoid
activation for the output. The model is then compiled with binary_crossentropy,
and an Adam optimizer with a slow learning rate, and is set to monitor accuracy
and auc metrics.

Running the hyperparameter tuning

Now that we have defined the model and parameters to tune, we initialize the
RepeatedStratifiedKFold cross-validator, which splits (n_splits) the training
data in five a total of three times (n_repeats) using different randomization in each
repetition. We then create a grid (nn_grid) for the grid-search hyperparameter tuning.
It's testing only two possible options for three of the parameters (l1_reg, l2_reg, and
dropout), which will result in $2^3 = 8$ combinations. We will use a scikit-learn wrapper
(KerasClassifier) for our model to be compatible with the scikit-learn grid search.
Speaking of which, we next initialize GridSearchCV, which, using the Keras model
(estimator), performs a cross-validated (cv) grid search (param_grid). We want it to
choose the best parameters based on precision (scoring) and also not raise errors in the
process (error_score=0). Finally, we fit GridSearchCV as we would with any Keras
model, passing X_train, y_train, epochs, and batch_size. The code can be seen
in the following snippet:

```
cv = model_selection.RepeatedStratifiedKFold(n_splits=5,\
                                n_repeats=3, random_
state=rand)
nn_grid = {'hidden_layer_sizes':[(80,)], \
'l1_reg':[0,0.005],\
            'l2_reg':[0,0.01], 'dropout':[0,0.05]}
nn_model = KerasClassifier(build_fn=build_nn_mdl)
nn_grid_search = model_selection.GridSearchCV(estimator=nn_
model,\
                cv=cv, n_jobs=-1, param_grid=nn_grid,\
                scoring='precision', error_score=0,
verbose=0)
nn_grid_result = nn_grid_search.fit(X_train.astype(float),
                        y_train.astype(float),
                        epochs=400,\
                        batch_size=128, verbose=0)
```

Examining the results

Once the grid search has been completed, you can output the best parameters in
a dictionary with this command: print(nn_grid_result.best_params_).
Or, you can place all the results into a DataFrame, sort them by the highest precision
(sort_values), and output as follows:

```
pd.DataFrame(nn_grid_result.cv_results_)
    [['param_hidden_layer_sizes','param_l1_reg', 'param_l2_
reg',\
       'param_dropout', 'mean_test_score', 'std_test_score',\
       'rank_test_score']].\
  sort_values(by='rank_test_score')
```

The preceding snippet output the dataframe shown in *Figure 12.9*. The unregularized model is dead last, showing that all regularized model combinations performed better. One thing to note is that given the approximately 1.5-2% standard deviations (std_test_score) and that the top performer is only 2.2% from the lowest performer, in this case the benefits are marginal from a precision standpoint, but you should use a regularized model nonetheless because of other benefits.

The output can be seen here:

	param_hidden_layer_sizes	param_l1_reg	param_l2_reg	param_dropout	mean_test_score	std_test_score	rank_test_score
7	(80,)	0.005000	0.010000	0.050000	0.677521	0.021471	1
6	(80,)	0.005000	0	0.050000	0.674577	0.016117	2
3	(80,)	0.005000	0.010000	0	0.670866	0.030145	3
5	(80,)	0	0.010000	0.050000	0.670802	0.015510	4
2	(80,)	0.005000	0	0	0.666052	0.027208	5
1	(80,)	0	0.010000	0	0.663211	0.016589	6
4	(80,)	0	0	0.050000	0.663133	0.015309	7
0	(80,)	0	0	0	0.654557	0.017369	8

Figure 12.9 – Results for cross-validated grid search for a NN model

Evaluating the best model

Another important element that the grid search produced is the best-performing model (nn_grid_result.best_estimator_). We can create a dictionary to store all the models we will fit in this chapter (fitted_class_mdls) and then, using evaluate_class_mdl, evaluate this regularized Keras model and keep the evaluation in the dictionary at the same time. Have a look at the following code snippet:

```
fitted_class_mdls = {}
fitted_class_mdls['keras_reg'] =
   mldatasets.evaluate_class_mdl(nn_grid_result.best_
estimator_,\
```

```
        X_train.astype(float), X_test.astype(float),\
        y_train.astype(float), y_test.astype(float),\
    plot_roc=False, plot_conf_matrix=True, ret_eval_
dict=True)
```

The preceding snippet produced the confusion matrix and metrics shown in *Figure 12.10*. The accuracy is a little bit better than the original COMPAS model from *Chapter 7, Anchors and Counterfactual Explanations*, but the strategy to optimize for higher precision while regularizing yielded a model with nearly half as many false positives but 50% more false negatives.

The output can be seen here:

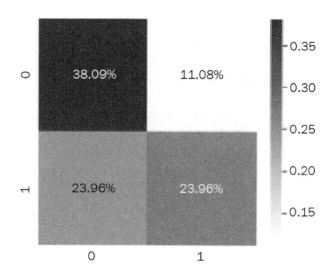

Accuracy_train: 0.6427   Accuracy_test: 0.6496

Precision_test: 0.7080   Recall_test: 0.5287

ROC-AUC_test: 0.6992   F1_test: 0.6054   MCC_test: 0.3125

Figure 12.10 – Evaluation of the regularized Keras model

Calibrating the class balance can be improved even further by employing a custom loss function or class weights, as we will do later. Next, we will cover how to tune other model classes.

Tuning other popular model classes

In this section, we will fit many different models, both unregularized and regularized. To this end, we will pick from a wide selection of parameters that perform penalized regularization, control overfitting through other means, and account for class imbalance.

A quick introduction to relevant model parameters

For your reference, there are two tables with parameters used to tune many popular models. These have been split into two parts. Part A (*Figure 12.11*) has five scikit-learn models with penalty regularization. Part B (*Figure 12.12*) is all tree ensembles, including scikit-learn's RandomForest models and models from the most popular boosted-tree libraries (XGBoost, LightGBM, and CatBoost).

Part A can be seen here:

		LogisticRegression		RidgeClassifier Ridge		SVC SVR		NuSVC NuSVR		MLPClassifier MLPRegressor	
	algorithm	solver	"lbfgs"	solver	"auto"	kernel	"rbf"	kernel	"rbf"	solver	"adam"
	regularization	penalty	"l2"								
		C	+/- 1	alpha	+/- 1	C	+/- 1	nu	+/- 0.5	alpha	+ 0.0001
		l1_ratio	None			gamma	"scale"	gamma	"scale"		
OVERFITTING	iterations	max_iter	+/- 100	max_iter	+ None	max_iter	+ -1	max_iter	+ -1	max_iter	+/- 200
	learning rate									learning_rate_init	0.001
										learning_rate	"adaptive"
	early stopping	tol	- 1e-4	tol	- 1e-3	tol	- 1e-3	tol	- 1e-3	tol	- 1e-4
										n_iter_no_change	- 10
										early_stopping	False
										validation_fraction	0.1
	class imbalance	class_weight	None	class_weight	None	class_weight	None	class_weight	None		
	sample weight	sample_weight*	None	sample_weight*	None	sample_weight*	None	sample_weight*	None		

Figure 12.11 – Tuning parameters for penalty-regularized scikit-learn models

In *Figure 12.11*, you can observe models in the columns and corresponding parameter names in the rows with their default values to the right. In between the parameter name and default value, there's a plus or minus sign indicating whether changing the defaults in one direction or another should make the model more conservative. These parameters are also grouped by the following categories:

- **algorithm**: Some training algorithms are less prone to overfitting, but often this depends on the data.

- **regularization**: Only in the stricter sense. In other words, parameters that control a penalty-based regularization.

- **iterations**: This controls how many training rounds, iterations, or epochs are performed. Adjusting this in one direction or another can impact overfitting. In tree-based models, the number of estimators or trees is what's analogous.

- **learning rate**: This controls how quickly the learning happens. It works in tandem with iterations. The lower the learning rate, the higher the iterations to optimize the objective function. However, you want to cut the training short before it's overfitted, and that why you need early stopping.

- **early stopping**: These parameters control when to stop the training.

- **class imbalance**: For most models, this penalizes misclassifications on smaller classes in the loss function, and for tree-based models, in particular, it is used to reweight the splitting criterion. Either way, it only works with classifiers.

- **sample weight**: We leveraged this one in *Chapter 11, Bias Mitigation and Causal Inference Methods*, to assign weights on a sample basis to mitigate bias.

There are both classification and regression models in the headings, and they share the same parameters. Please note that scikit-learn's `LinearRegression` isn't featured under `LogisticRegression` because it doesn't have built-in regularization. In any case, we will use only classification models in this section.

Part B can be seen here:

	RandomForestClassifier / RandomForestRegressor		XGBRFClassifier / XGBRFRegressor		XGBClassifier / XGBRegressor		LGBMClassifier / LGBMRegressor		CatboostClassifier / CatboostRegressor	
algorithm			booster	"gbtree"	booster	"gbtree"	boosting	"gbdt"		
regularization			reg_lambda	+ 1	reg_lambda	+ 1	lambda_l2	+ 0	l2_leaf_reg	+ 3
			reg_alpha	+ 0	reg_alpha	+ 0	lambda_l1	+ 0		
feature sampling	max_features	+/- "auto"	colsample_bytree	- 1	colsample_bytree	- 1	feature_fraction	- 1		
			colsample_bylevel	- 1	colsample_bylevel	- 1				
			colsample_bynode	- 1	colsample_bynode	- 1				
learning rate			eta	+/- 1	eta	+/- 0.3	learning_rate	+/- 0.1	learning_rate	+/- 0.03
iterations / # trees	n_estimators	+/- 100	n_estimators	+/- 100	num_round	+/- 100	num_iterations	+ 100	iterations	+ 1000
early stopping	oob_score	+ False	early_stopping_rounds*	None	early_stopping_rounds*	None	early_stopping_rounds*	0	early_stopping_rounds*	False
			eval_set*	None	eval_set*	None	eval_set*	None	eval_set*	None
			eval_metric*	None	eval_metric*	None	eval_metric*	None	eval_metric*	None
tree size	max_depth	- None	max_depth	- 6	max_depth	- 6	max_depth	- -1	depth	- 6
	max_leaf_nodes	- None			max_leaves	- 0	num_leaves	- 31		
	min_samples_leaf	+ 1					min_data_in_leaf	- 20		
	min_weight_fraction_leaf	+ 0					min_sum_hessian_in_leaf	+ 1e-3		
splitting	min_samples_split	+ 2	gamma	+ 0	gamma	+ 0	min_split_gain	+ 0	min_data_in_leaf	+ 1
	min_impurity_decrease	+ 0	min_child_weight	+ 1	min_child_weight	+ 1			grow_policy	SymmetricTree
	criterion	"gini"							random_strength	+ 1
bagging	max_samples	None	subsample	+ 1	subsample	+ 1	bagging_fraction	- 1	subsample	+ 0.66-1
	bootstrap	True	sampling_method	"uniform"	sampling_method	"uniform"	bagging_freq	+ 0		
class imbalance (classifiers only)	class_weight	None	scale_pos_weight	+/- 1	scale_pos_weight	+/- 1	class_weight	None	class_weights	None
							scale_pos_weight	+/- 1	scale_pos_weight	+/- 1
							is_unbalance	+ False	auto_class_weights	+ False
sample weight	sample_weight*	None	sample_weight*	None	sample_weight*	None	sample_weight*	None	sample_weight*	None
constraints			monotone_constraints	+ None	monotone_constraints	+ None	monotone_constraints	+ None	monotone_constraints	+ None
			interaction_constraints	+ None	interaction_constraints	+ None	interaction_constraints	+ None		

OVERFITTING

Figure 12.12 – Tuning parameters for tree-ensemble models

Figure 12.12 is very similar to *Figure 12.11* except that it has a few more parameter categories that are only available in tree ensembles, such as the following:

- **feature sampling**: This works by considering fewer features in node splits, nodes, or tree training. It is a stochastic regularization method because features are randomly selected.

- **tree size**: Constraining the tree either by maximum depth or maximum leaves, or some other parameter that restricts its growth which, in turn, curbs overfitting.

- **splitting**: Any parameter that controls how nodes in the tree are split can indirectly impact overfitting.

- **bagging**: Also known as **bootstrap aggregating**, this starts by bootstrapping, which involves randomly taking samples from the training data to fit weak learners. This method reduces variance and helps with overfitting, and by extension, the corresponding sampling parameters are usually prominent in hyperparameter tuning.

- **constraints**: We will explain these in further detail in the next section, but this maps how the features should be constrained to decrease or increase against the output. It can reduce overfitting in areas where data is very sparse. However, reducing overfitting is not usually the main goal, while interaction constraints can limit which features are allowed to interact.

Please note that parameters with an asterisk (*) in *Figure 12.12* denote those set in the `fit` function as opposed to those initialized with the model. Also, except for scikit-learn's `RandomForest` models, all other parameters typically have many aliases. For these, we are using the scikit-learn wrapper functions, but all the parameters also exist in the native versions. We can't possibly explain every model parameter here, but it is recommended that you go directly to the documentation for more insight into what each one does. The point of the section was to serve as a guide or reference.

Next, we will take steps similar to what we did with the Keras model but for many different models at once, and, lastly, we will assess the best model for fairness.

Batch hyperparameter tuning models

OK—so, now that we have taken a quick crash course on which levers we can pull for tuning the models, let's define a dictionary with all the models, as we've done in other chapters. This time, we have included a `grid` with some parameter values for a grid search. Have a look at the following code snippet:

```
class_mdls = {
 'logistic':{
        'model':linear_model.LogisticRegression(random_
state=rand,\
                                                 max_iter=1000),
     'grid':{'C':np.linspace(0.01, 0.49, 25),\
                 'class_weight':[{0:6,1:5}],
             'solver':['lbfgs', 'liblinear', 'newton-cg']}},
 'svc':{'model':svm.SVC(probability=True,\
random_state=rand),
     'grid':{'C':[15,25,40], 'class_weight':[{0:6,1:5}]}},
 'nu-svc':{'model':svm.NuSVC(probability=True,\
random_state=rand),
     'grid':{'nu':[0.2,0.3], 'gamma':[0.6,0.7],\
     'class_weight':[{0:6,1:5}]}},
 'mlp':{'model':neural_network.MLPClassifier(random_
state=rand,\
       hidden_layer_sizes=(80,), early_stopping=True),\
     'grid':{'alpha':np.linspace(0.05, 0.15, 11),
     'activation':['relu','tanh','logistic']}},
 'rf':{'model':ensemble.RandomForestClassifier(random_
state=rand,
                 max_depth=7, oob_score=True,\
bootstrap=True),\
   'grid':{'max_features':[6,7,8],\
'max_samples':[0.75,0.9,1],
         'class_weight':[{0:6,1:5}]}},
 'xgb-rf':{'model':xgb.XGBRFClassifier(seed=rand, eta=1,\
                                        max_depth=7, n_
estimators=200),
     'grid':{'scale_pos_weight':[0.85],\
'reg_lambda':[1,1.5,2],
           'reg_alpha':[0,0.5,0.75,1]}},
 'xgb':{'model':xgb.XGBClassifier(seed=rand, eta=1,\
max_depth=7),\
   'grid':{'scale_pos_weight':[0.7],\
'reg_lambda':[1,1.5,2],\
```

```
              'reg_alpha':[0.5,0.75,1]}},
  'lgbm':{'model':lgb.LGBMClassifier(random_seed=rand,\
                                    learning_rate=0.7, max_
depth=5),
    'grid':{'lambda_l2':[0,0.5,1], 'lambda_l1':[0,0.5,1],\
          'scale_pos_weight':[0.8]}},
  'catboost':{'model':cb.CatBoostClassifier(random_seed=rand,\
                        depth=5, learning_rate=0.5,
verbose=0),
    'grid':{'l2_leaf_reg':[2,2.5,3], 'scale_pos_
weight':[0.65]}}
  }
```

The next step is to add a `for` loop to every model in the dictionary, then `deepcopy` it and `fit` it to produce a "base" unregularized model. Next, we produce an evaluation for it with `evaluate_class_mdl` and save it into the `fitted_class_mdls` dictionary we had previously created for the Keras model. Now, we need to produce the regularized version of the model. So, we do another `deepcopy` and follow the same steps we took with Keras to do the `RepeatedStratifiedKFold` cross-validated grid search with `GridSearchCV`, and we also evaluate in the same way, saving the results in the fitted model dictionary. The code is shown in the following snippet:

```
for mdl_name in class_mdls:
  print(mdl_name)
  base_mdl = copy.deepcopy(class_mdls[mdl_name]['model'])
  base_mdl = base_mdl.fit(X_train, y_train)
  fitted_class_mdls[mdl_name+'_base'] =
    mldatasets.evaluate_class_mdl(base_mdl, X_train, X_test,\
          y_train, y_test, plot_roc=False, plot_conf_
matrix=False,\
          show_summary=False, ret_eval_dict=True)
  reg_mdl = copy.deepcopy(class_mdls[mdl_name]['model'])
  grid = class_mdls[mdl_name]['grid']
  cv = model_selection.RepeatedStratifiedKFold(n_splits=5,\
                        n_repeats=3, random_state=rand)
  grid_search =\
model_selection.GridSearchCV(estimator=reg_mdl,\
                  cv=cv, param_grid=grid,
scoring='precision',\
```

```
                       n_jobs=-1, error_score=0, verbose=0)
grid_result = grid_search.fit(X_train, y_train)
fitted_class_mdls[mdl_name+'_reg'] =\
    mldatasets.evaluate_class_mdl(grid_result.best_estimator_,\
            X_train, X_test, y_train, y_test, plot_roc=False,\
            plot_conf_matrix=False, show_summary=False,\
            ret_eval_dict=True)
fitted_class_mdls[mdl_name+'_reg']['cv_best_params'] =\
                                grid_result.best_params_
```

Once the code has finished, we can rank models by precision.

Evaluating models by precision

We can extract the fitted model dictionary's metrics and place them into a `DataFrame` with `from_dict`. We can then sort the models by their highest test precision and color-code the two columns that matter the most, which are `precision_test` and `recall_test`. The code can be seen in the following snippet:

```
class_metrics = pd.DataFrame.from_dict(fitted_class_mdls,\
                    'index')[['accuracy_train', 'accuracy_test',\
                        'precision_train', 'precision_test',\
                        'recall_train', 'recall_test',\
                        'roc-auc_test', 'f1_test', 'mcc_
test']]
with pd.option_context('display.precision', 3):
  html = class_metrics.sort_values(by='precision_test',\
            ascending=False).\
    style.background_gradient(cmap='plasma',
                        subset=['precision_test']).\
    background_gradient(cmap='viridis', subset=['recall_test'])
html
```

The preceding code will output the dataframe shown in *Figure 12.13*. You can tell that regularized tree-ensemble models rule the ranks, followed by their unregularized counterparts. The one exception is regularized Nu-SVC, which is number two, and its unregularized version dead last!

The output can be seen here:

	accuracy_train	accuracy_test	precision_train	precision_test	recall_train	recall_test	roc-auc_test	f1_test	mcc_test
catboost_reg	0.964	0.820	0.992	0.837	0.935	0.802	0.881	0.819	0.641
nu-svc_reg	0.939	0.807	0.950	0.836	0.925	0.772	0.858	0.803	0.616
xgb_reg	0.966	0.820	0.988	0.828	0.943	0.815	0.877	0.821	0.639
lgbm_reg	0.936	0.797	0.966	0.814	0.903	0.778	0.870	0.796	0.594
xgb_base	0.976	0.823	0.984	0.812	0.967	0.848	0.880	0.830	0.646
catboost_base	0.970	0.817	0.980	0.809	0.958	0.838	0.879	0.823	0.634
lgbm_base	0.935	0.797	0.949	0.802	0.918	0.799	0.861	0.800	0.594
logistic_reg	0.643	0.638	0.721	0.745	0.445	0.437	0.701	0.551	0.309
⋮	⋮	⋮	⋮	⋮	⋮	⋮	⋮	⋮	⋮
keras_reg	0.643	0.650	0.674	0.708	0.527	0.529	0.699	0.605	0.312

Figure 12.13 – Top models according to the cross validated grid-search

The Keras regularized neural network model has lower precision than logistic regression, but higher recall. It's true that we want to optimize for high precision because it impacts false positives, which we want to minimize, but precision can be at 100% and recall at 0%, and if that's the case, your model is no good. At the same time, there's fairness, which is about having a low false-positive rate but being equally distributed across races. So, there's a balancing act, and chasing one metric won't get us there.

Assessing fairness for the highest-performing model

To first determine how to proceed, we must first assess how our highest-performing model does in terms of fairness. We can do this with compare_confusion_matrices. As you would do with scikit-learn's confusion_matrix, the first argument is the ground truth or target values (often known as "y_true"), and the second is the model's predictions (often known as "y_pred"). The difference here is it takes two sets of "y_true" and "y_pred", one corresponding to one segment of the observations and one to another. After these first four arguments, you give each segment a name, so this is what the following two arguments tell you. Lastly, compare_fpr=True ensures that it will compare the **false positive rate** (**FPR**) between both confusion matrices. Have a look at the following code snippet:

```
y_test_pred =\
fitted_class_mdls['catboost_reg']['preds_test']
_ = mldatasets.\
    compare_confusion_matrices(y_test[X_test.race==1],\
        y_test_pred[X_test.race==1], y_test[X_test.race==0],\
```

```
        y_test_pred[X_test.race==0], 'Caucasian', 'African-
American',\
        compare_fpr=True)
y_test_pred = \
fitted_class_mdls['catboost_base']['preds_test']
_ = mldatasets.\
    compare_confusion_matrices(y_test[X_test.race==1],\
        y_test_pred[X_test.race==1], y_test[X_test.race==0],\
        y_test_pred[X_test.race==0], 'Caucasian', 'African-
American',\
        compare_fpr=True)
```

The preceding snippet outputs *Figure 12.14* and *Figure 12.15*, corresponding to the regularized and base models respectively. You can see *Figure 12.14* here:

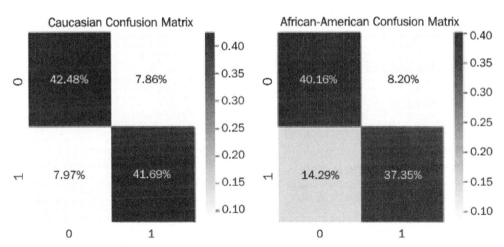

Figure 12.14 – Confusion matrices between races for the regularized CatBoost model

Figure 12.15 tells us that the FPRs are lower for the regularized model. You can see the output here:

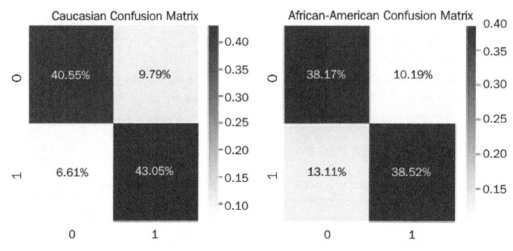

African-American FPR: 21.1%

Caucasian FPR: 19.5%

Ratio FPRs: 1.08 x

Figure 12.15 – Confusion matrices between races for the base CatBoost model

However, the base model in *Figure 12.15* has an FPR ratio of 1.08 compared to 1.09 for the regularized model, which is slightly less fair despite the better overall metrics. This difference is not enough to justify using the base model. But when trying to achieve several goals at once, it's hard to evaluate and compare models in an objective manner, and that's what we will do in the next section.

Optimizing for fairness with Bayesian hyperparameter tuning and custom metrics

Our mission is to produce a model with high precision and a good recall while maintaining fairness across different races. So, keeping true to the entire mission will require a custom metric to be designed.

Designing a custom metric

We could use the F1 score, but it treats precision and recall equally, so we will have to create a weighted metric. While we are at it, we can also factor in how precision and recall are distributed for each race. One way to do this is by using the standard deviation, which quantifies the variation in this distribution. To that end, we will penalize precision with half the intergroup standard deviation for precision, and we can call this penalized precision, for lack of a better term. The formula is shown here:

$$P_{penalized} = P - \frac{1}{2}\sigma_P$$

We can do the same for recall, as illustrated here:

$$R_{penalized} = R - \frac{1}{2}\sigma_R$$

Then, we make a weighted average for penalized precision and recall where precision is worth twice as much as recall, as illustrated here:

$$\text{custom\_metric} = \frac{2 \times P_{penalized} + R_{penalized}}{3}$$

To compute this new metric, we will need to create a function that we can call `weighted_penalized_pr_average`. It takes `y_true` and `y_pred` as the predictive performance metrics. However, it also includes `X_group` with a pandas series or array containing the values for the group, and `group_vals` with a list of values that it will subset the predictions by. In this case, the group is `race`, which can be values from 0 to 2. The function includes a `for` loop that iterates through these possible values, subsetting the predictions by each group. That way, it can compute precision and recall for each group. After this, the rest of the function simply performs the three mathematical operations outlined previously. The code can be seen in the following snippet:

```
def weighted_penalized_pr_average(y_true, y_pred, X_group,\
                    group_vals, penalty_mult=0.5,\
                    precision_mult=2,\
                    recall_mult=1):
    precision_all = metrics.precision_score(y_true, y_pred,\
                                    zero_division=0)
    recall_all = metrics.recall_score(y_true, y_pred,\
    zero_division=0)
```

```
p_by_group = []
r_by_group = []
for group_val in group_vals:
  in_group = X_group==group_val
   p_by_group.append(metrics.precision_score(y_true[in_group],\
                      y_pred[in_group], zero_division=0))
    r_by_group.append(metrics.recall_score(y_true[in_group],\
                      y_pred[in_group], zero_division=0))
  precision_all = precision_all -\
                           (np.array(p_by_group).std()*penalty_
mult)
  recall_all = recall_all -\
                           (np.array(r_by_group).std()*penalty_
mult)
  return ((precision_allprecision_mult)+(recall_allrecall_
mult))/\
        (precision_mult+recall_mult)
```

Now, to put this function to work, we will need to run the tuning.

Running Bayesian hyperparameter tuning

Bayesian optimization is a *global optimization method* that uses the posterior distribution of black-box objective functions and their continuous parameters. In other words, it sequentially searches the best parameters to test next based on past results. Unlike grid search, it doesn't try fixed combinations of parameters on a grid, but exploits what it already knows and explores the unknown.

The bayesian-optimization library is model-agnostic. All it needs is a function and parameters with their bounds. It will explore values for those parameters within those bounds. The function takes those parameters and returns a number. This is the number, or target, the Bayesian optimization algorithm will maximize.

The following code is for the objective function, which initializes a RepeatedStratifiedKFold cross-validation with four splits and three repeats. It then iterates across the splits and fits the CatBoostClassifier with them. Lastly, it computes the weighted_penalized_pr_average custom metric for each model training and appends it to a list. Finally, the function returns the median of the custom metric for all 12 trainings. The code is shown in the following snippet:

```python
def hyp_catboost(l2_leaf_reg, scale_pos_weight):
 cv = model_selection.RepeatedStratifiedKFold(n_splits=4,\
                                    n_repeats=3, random_
state=rand)
 metric_l = []
 for train_index, val_index in cv.split(X_train, y_train):
  X_train_cv, X_val_cv = X_train.iloc[train_index],\
                         X_train.iloc[val_index]
  y_train_cv, y_val_cv = y_train.iloc[train_index],
                         y_train.iloc[val_index]
  mdl = cb.CatBoostClassifier(random_seed=rand,learning_
rate=0.5,\
                  verbose=0, depth=5, l2_leaf_reg=l2_leaf_
reg,\
                 scale_pos_weight=scale_pos_weight)
  mdl = mdl.fit(X_train_cv, y_train_cv)
  y_val_pred = mdl.predict(X_val_cv)
  metric = weighted_penalized_pr_average(y_val_cv, y_val_pred,\
                      X_val_cv['race'], range(3))
  metric_l.append(metric)
 return np.median(np.array(metric_l))
```

Now that the function has been defined, running the Bayesian optimization process is straightforward. First, set the parameter-bounds dictionary (pbounds), initialize BayesianOptimization with the hyp_catboost function, and then run it with maximize. The maximize function takes init_points, which sets how many iterations it should run initially using random exploration. Then, n_iter is the number of optimization iterations it should perform to find the maximum value. We will set init_points and n_iter to 3 and 7, respectively, because it could take a long time, but the larger these numbers, the better. The code can be seen in the following snippet:

```python
pbounds = {
    'l2_leaf_reg': (2,4),
    'scale_pos_weight': (0.55,0.85)
    }
optimizer = BayesianOptimization(hyp_catboost, pbounds,\
                                 random_state=rand)
optimizer.maximize(init_points=3, n_iter=7)
```

Once it's finished, you can access the best parameters, like this:

```
print(optimizer.max['params'])
```

It will return a dictionary with the parameters, as follows:

```
{'l2_leaf_reg': 2.0207483077713997, 'scale_pos_weight':
0.7005623776446217}
```

Now, let's fit a model with these parameters and evaluate it.

Fitting and evaluating a model with the best parameters

Initializing CatBoostClassifier with these parameters is as simple as passing the
best_params dictionary as an argument. Then, all you need to do is fit the model and
evaluate it (evaluate_class_mdl). The code is shown in the following snippet:

```
cb_opt = cb.CatBoostClassifier(random_seed=rand, depth=5,\
              learning_rate=0.5, verbose=0,\
**optimizer.max['params'])
cb_opt = cb_opt.fit(X_train, y_train)
fitted_class_mdls['catboost_opt'] =\
    mldatasets.evaluate_class_mdl(cb_opt, X_train, X_test,\
y_train,\
                  y_test, plot_roc=False, plot_conf_
matrix=True,\
                  ret_eval_dict=True)
```

The preceding snippet outputted the following predictive performance metrics:

```
Accuracy_train:  0.9721   Accuracy_test:   0.8282
Precision_test:  0.8354   Recall_test:     0.8244
ROC-AUC_test:    0.8815   F1_test:         0.8299   MCC_test:
0.6564
```

They are the highest Accuracy_test, Precision_test, and Recall_test metrics
we have achieved so far. Let's now see how the model fares with fairness using compare_
confusion_matrices. Have a look at the following code snippet:

```
y_test_pred = fitted_class_mdls['catboost_opt']['preds_test']
_ = mldatasets.
  compare_confusion_matrices(y_test[X_test.race==1],\
```

```
        y_test_pred[X_test.race==1], y_test[X_test.race==0],\
        y_test_pred[X_test.race==0], 'Caucasian', 'African-
American',\
    compare_fpr=True)
```

The preceding code outputs *Figure 12.16*, which depicts the best fairness metrics we have obtained so far, as you can see here:

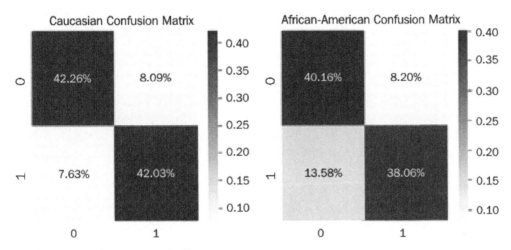

African-American FPR: 16.9%

Caucasian FPR: 16.1%

Ratio FPRs: 1.06 x

Figure 12.16 – Comparison of confusion matrices between races for the optimized CatBoost model

These results are good, but we cannot be completely assured that the model is not racially biased because the feature is still there. One way to measure its impact is through feature importance methods.

Examining racial bias through feature importance

Even though CatBoost is our best performing model, we are moving forward with XGBoost because CatBoost doesn't support interaction constraints, which we will implement in the next section. But first, we will compare them both in terms of what they found important. Also, **SHapley Additive exPlanations** (**SHAP**) values provide a robust means to measure and visualize feature importance, so let's compute them for our optimized CatBoost model and the regularized XGBoost one. To do so, we need to initialize `TreeExplainer` with each model and then use `shap_values` to produce the values for each, as illustrated in the following code snippet:

```
fitted_cb_mdl = fitted_class_mdls['catboost_opt']['fitted']
shap_cb_explainer = shap.TreeExplainer(fitted_cb_mdl)
shap_cb_values = shap_cb_explainer.shap_values(X_test)
fitted_xgb_mdl = fitted_class_mdls['xgb_reg']['fitted']
shap_xgb_explainer = shap.TreeExplainer(fitted_xgb_mdl)
shap_xgb_values = shap_xgb_explainer.shap_values(X_test)
```

Next, we can generate two `summary_plot` plots side by side, using Matplotlib's `subplot`, as follows:

```
ax0 = plt.subplot(1, 2, 1)
shap.summary_plot(shap_xgb_values, X_test,\
plot_type="dot",\
                 plot_size=None, show=False)
ax0.set_title("XGBoost SHAP Summary", fontsize=15)
ax1 = plt.subplot(1, 2, 2)
shap.summary_plot(shap_cb_values, X_test, plot_type="dot",\
                 plot_size=None, show=False)
ax1.set_title("Catboost SHAP Summary", fontsize=15)
```

The preceding snippet generates *Figure 12.17*, which shows how similar CatBoost and XGBoost are. This similarity shouldn't be surprising because, after all, they are both gradient-boosted decision trees. The bad news is that `race` is fourth for both. However, the prevalence of the shade that corresponds to lower feature values on the right suggests that African American (`race=0`) negatively correlates with recidivism.

The output can be seen here:

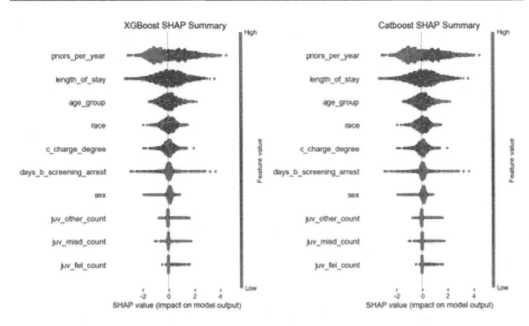

Figure 12.17 – SHAP summary plot for regularized XGBoost and optimized CatBoost model

In any case, it makes sense to remove race from the training data, but we must first ascertain why the model thinks this is a critical feature. Have a look at the following code snippet:

```
shap_xgb_interact_values =\
                shap_xgb_explainer.shap_interaction_values(X_
test)
```

In *Chapter 5, Global Model-Agnostic Interpretation Methods,* we discussed assessing interaction effects. It's time to revisit this topic, but this time we will extract SHAP's interaction values (shap_interaction_values) instead of using SHAP's dependence plots. We can easily rank SHAP interactions with a summary_plot plot. A SHAP summary plot is very informative, but it's not nearly as intuitive as a heatmap for interactions. To generate a heatmap with labels, we must place the shap_ xgb_interact_values summed on the first axis in a DataFrame, then name the columns and rows (index) with the names of the features. The rest is simply using Seaborn's heatmap function to plot the dataframe as a heatmap. The code can be seen in the following snippet:

```
shap_xgb_interact_avgs =\
np.abs(shap_xgb_interact_values).mean(0)
np.fill_diagonal(shap_xgb_interact_avgs, 0)
```

```
shap_xgb_interact_df = pd.DataFrame(shap_xgb_interact_avgs)
shap_xgb_interact_df.columns = X_test.columns
shap_xgb_interact_df.index = X_test.columns
sns.heatmap(shap_xgb_interact_df, cmap='Blues',\
  annot=True,\
            annot_kws={'size':13}, fmt='.2f',\
linewidths=.5)
```

The preceding code produced the heatmap shown in *Figure 12.18*. It demonstrates how `race` is interacting most heavily with `length_of_stay`, `age_group`, and `priors per year`. These interactions would, of course, disappear once we removed `race`. However, given this finding, careful consideration ought to be given if these features don't have racial bias built in. Research supports the need for `age_group` and `priors_per_year`, which leaves `length_of_stay` as a candidate for scrutiny. We won't do this in this chapter, but it's certainly food for thought.

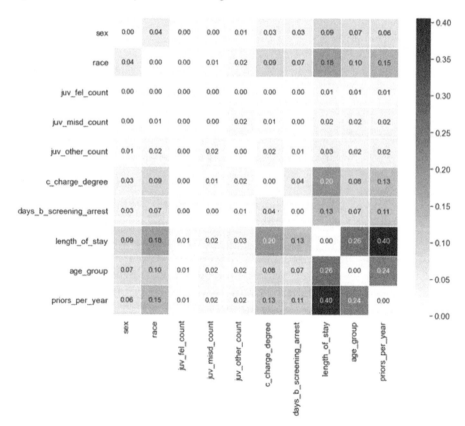

Figure 12.18 – Heatmap with SHAP interaction values for the regularized XGBoost model

Another interesting insight from *Figure 12.18* is how features can be clustered. You can pretty much draw a box around the lower-right quadrant between `c_charge_degree` and `priors_per_year` because once we remove `race`, most of the interaction will be located here. There are many benefits to limit troubling interactions. For instance, why should all the juvenile delinquency features such as `juv_fel_count` interact with `age_group`? Why should `sex` interact with `length_of_stay`? Next, we will learn how to place a fence around the lower-right quadrant, limiting interactions between those features with **interaction constraints**. We will also ensure monotonicity for `priors_per_year` with **monotonic constraints**.

Implementing model constraints

We will discuss next how to implement constraints first with XGBoost and all popular tree ensembles, for that matter, because the parameters are named the same (see *Figure 12.12*). Then, we will do so with TensorFlow Lattice. But before we move forward with any of that, let's remove `race` from the data, as follows:

```
X_train_con = X_train.drop(['race'], axis=1).copy()
X_test_con = X_test.drop(['race'], axis=1).copy()
```

Now, with `race` out of the picture, the model left to its own devices may still have some bias. However, the feature engineering we performed and the constraints we will place can help align the model against them, given the double standards we found in *Chapter 7, Anchor and Counterfactual Explanations*. That being said, the resulting model might perform worse against the test data. There are two reasons for this, outlined here:

- **Loss of information**: Race, especially through interaction with other features, impacted the outcome, so it unfortunately carried some information.

- **Misalignment between reality and policy-driven ideals**: This occurs when the main reason to enforce these constraints is to ensure that the model not only complies with domain knowledge but ideals, and these might not be evident in the data. We must remember that a whole host of institutional racism could have tainted the ground truth. The model reflects the data, but the data reflects reality on the ground, which is itself unfair.

With that in mind, let's get started with constraint implementation!

Constraints for XGBoost

We will take three simple steps in this section. We will first define our training parameters, then train and evaluate a constrained model, and, lastly, examine the effects of the constraints.

Setting regularization and constraint parameters

We take the best parameters for our regularized XGBoost model with `print(fitted_class_mdls['xgb_reg']['cv_best_params'])`. They are in the `best_xgb_params` dictionary, along with `eta` and `max_depth`. Then, to enforce monotonic constraints on `priors_per_year`, we must first know its position and in what direction is the monotonic correlation. From *Figure 12.8*, we know the answers to both of the questions. It is the last feature, and the correlation is positive, so the `mono_con` tuple should have nine items, with the last one being a one and the rest zeros. As for interaction constraints, we will only allow the last five features to interact with each other, and the same goes for the first four. The `interact_con` tuple is a list of lists that reflects these constraints. The code can be seen in the following snippet:

```
best_xgb_params = {'eta': 1.3, 'max_depth': 8, 'reg_alpha':
0.4451,\
                   'reg_lambda': 0.7168, 'scale_pos_weight':
0.9914}
mono_con = (0,0,0,0,0,0,0,0,1)
interact_con = [[4, 5, 6, 7, 8],[0, 1, 2, 3]]
```

Next, we will train and evaluate the XGBoost model with these constraints.

Training and evaluating the constrained model

We will now do training and evaluation in one fell swoop. First, we will initialize the `XGBClassifier` model with our constraint and regularization parameters and then fit it using training data that lacks the `race` feature (`X_train_con`). We then evaluate the predictive performance with `evaluate_class_mdl` and compare fairness with `compare_confusion_matrices`, as we have done before. The code can be seen in the following snippet:

```
xgb_con = xgb.XGBClassifier(seed=rand,monotone_
constraints=mono_con,
        interaction_constraints=interact_con,\
**best_xgb_params)
xgb_con = xgb_con.fit(X_train_con, y_train)
fitted_class_mdls['xgb_con'] =
```

```
mldatasets.evaluate_class_mdl(xgb_con, X_train_con,\
 X_test_con,\
              y_train, y_test, plot_roc=False, ret_eval_dict=True)
y_test_pred = fitted_class_mdls['xgb_con']['preds_test']
_ = mldatasets.\
   compare_confusion_matrices(y_test[X_test.race==1],
                y_test_pred[X_test.race==1],\
 y_test[X_test.race==0],\
                y_test_pred[X_test.race==0], 'Caucasian',\
                'African-American', compare_fpr=True)
```

The preceding snippet produces the confusion matrix pair in *Figure 12.19* and some predictive performance metrics. If we compare the matrices to those in *Figure 12.16*, racial disparities, as measured by our FPR ratio, took a hit. Also, predictive performance is lower than the optimized CatBoost model across the board, by 2-4%. We could likely increase these metrics by a bit by performing the same *Bayesian hyperparameter tuning* on this model.

The confusion matrix output can be seen here:

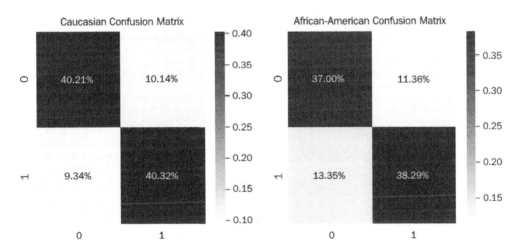

African-American FPR: 23.5%

Caucasian FPR: 20.1%

Ratio FPRs: 1.17 x

Figure 12.19 – Comparison of confusion matrices between races for the constrained XGBoost model

One thing to take in account is that although racial inequity is a primary concern of this chapter, we also want to ensure that the model is optimal in other ways. As stated before, it's a balancing act. For instance, it's only fitting that defendants with most `priors_per_year` are riskier than those with the least, and we ensured this with monotonic constraints. Let's verify these outcomes!

Examining constraints

An easy way to observe the constraints in action is to plot a SHAP `summary_plot`, as we did in *Figure 12.17*, but this time we will only plot one. Have a look at the following code snippet:

```
fitted_xgb_con_mdl = fitted_class_mdls['xgb_con']['fitted']
shap_xgb_con_explainer =\
shap.TreeExplainer(fitted_xgb_con_mdl)
shap_xgb_con_values =\
shap_xgb_con_explainer.shap_values(X_test_con)
shap.summary_plot(shap_xgb_con_values, X_test_con,\
plot_type="dot")
```

The preceding code produces *Figure 12.20*. This demonstrates how `priors_per_year` from left to right is a cleaner gradient, which means that lower values are consistently having a negative impact, and the higher ones a positive one—as they should!

You can see the output here:

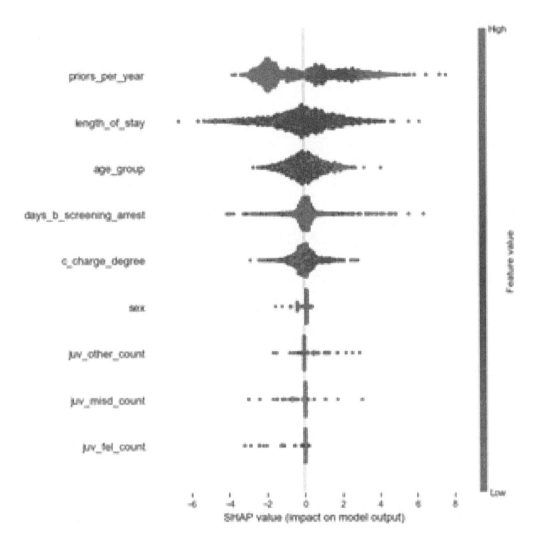

Figure 12.20 – SHAP summary plot for the constrained XGBoost model

Next, let's examine the `age_group` versus `priors_per_year` interaction we saw through the lens of the data in *Figure 12.7*. We can also use `plot_prob_contour_map` for models by adding extra arguments, as follows:

- The fitted model (`fitted_xgb_con_mdl`)
- Dataframe to use for inference with the model (`X_test_con`)
- The names of the two columns in the dataframe to compare on each axis (`x_col`, `y_col`)

The outcome is an interaction partial dependence plot, like those shown in *Chapter 4, Fundamentals of Feature Importance and Impact*, except that it uses the dataset (recidivism_df) to create the histograms for each axis. We will create two such plots right now for comparison—one for the regularized XGBoost model and another for the constrained one. The code for this can be seen in the following snippet:

```
mldatasets.plot_prob_contour_map(recidivism_df.age_group,\
        recidivism_df.priors_per_year,\
recidivism_df.is_recid,\
        x_intervals=ordenc.categories_[2],\
y_intervals=6,\
        use_quartiles=True, xlabel='Age Group',\
        ylabel='Priors Per Year', X_df=X_test,\
x_col='age_group',\
        y_col='priors_per_year', model=fitted_xgb_mdl,\
    title='Probability of Recidivism by Age/Priors per Year
(according to XGBoost Regularized Model)')
mldatasets.plot_prob_contour_map(recidivism_df.age_group,\
        recidivism_df.priors_per_year,\
recidivism_df.is_recid,\
        x_intervals=ordenc.categories_[2], y_intervals=6,\
        use_quartiles=True, xlabel='Age Group',\
        ylabel='Priors Per Year', X_df=X_test_con,\
x_col='age_group',\
        y_col='priors_per_year', model=fitted_xgb_con_mdl,\
    title='Probability of Recidivism by Age/Priors per Year
(according to XGBoost Constrained Model)')
```

The preceding code produces the plots shown in *Figure 12.21*. It shows that the regularized XGBoost model reflects the data (see *Figure 12.7*). On the other hand, the constrained XGBoost model smoothened and simplified the contours, as can be seen here:

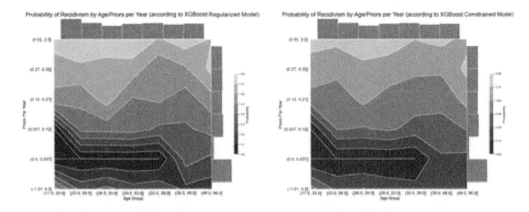

Figure 12.21 – Recidivism probability contour map for age_group and priors_per_year according to
XGBoost regularized and constrained models

Next, we can generate the SHAP interaction values heatmap from *Figure 12.18* but for
the constrained model. The code is the same but uses the shap_xgb_con_explainer
SHAP explainer and X_test_con data. The code can be seen in the following snippet:

```
shap_xgb_interact_values =\
          shap_xgb_con_explainer.shap_interaction_values(X_
test_con)
shap_xgb_interact_df =\
pd.DataFrame(np.sum(shap_xgb_interact_values,
                                      axis=0))
shap_xgb_interact_df.columns = X_test_con.columns
shap_xgb_interact_df.index = X_test_con.columns
sns.heatmap(shap_xgb_interact_df, cmap='RdBu', annot=True,
          annot_kws={'size':13}, fmt='.0f', linewidths=.5)
```

The preceding snippet output the heatmap shown in *Figure 12.22*. It shows how the
interaction constraints were effective because of zeros in the lower-left and lower-right
quadrants, which correspond to interactions between the two groups of features
we separated. If you compare with *Figure 12.18*, you can also tell how the constraints
shifted the most salient interactions, making age_group and length_of_stay by
far the most important ones.

The output can be seen here:

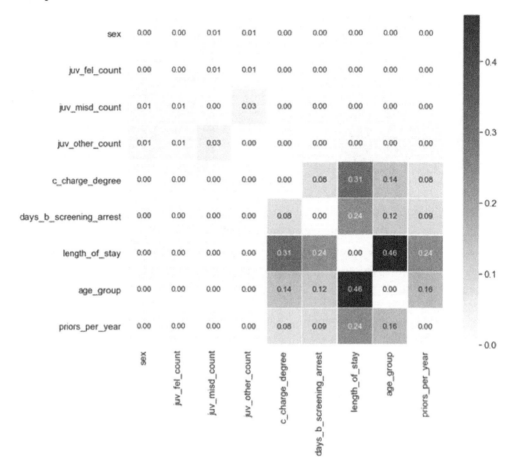

Figure 12.22 – Heatmap with SHAP interaction values for the constrained XGBoost model

Now, let's see how TensorFlow implements monotonicity and other "shape constraints" via TensorFlow Lattice.

Constraints for TensorFlow Lattice

Neural networks can be brutally efficient in finding an optimal for the `loss` function. The loss is tied to a consequence we wish to predict. In this case, that would be 2-year recidivism. In ethics, a *utilitarian* (or *consequentialist*) view of fairness has no problem with this as long as the model's training data isn't biased. Yet a *deontologist* view believes that ethical principles or policies drive ethical questions and supersede consequences. Inspired by this, TensorFlow Lattice can embody ethical principles into models as model shape constraints.

A lattice is an **interpolated lookup table**, which is a grid that approximates inputs to outputs through interpolation. In high-dimensional space, these grids become hypercubes. The mappings of each input to output are constrained through **calibration layers**, and these support many kinds of constraints—not just monotonicity. *Figure 12.23* shows this here:

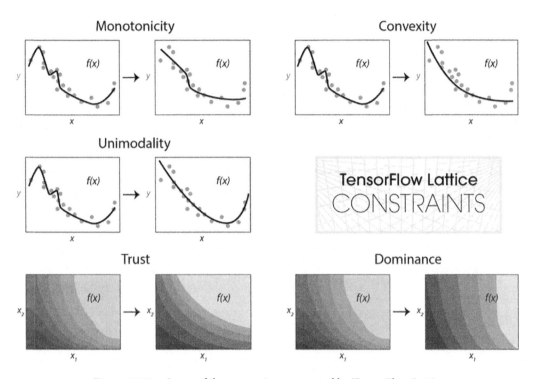

Figure 12.23 – Some of the constraints supported by TensorFlow Lattice

Figure 12.23 shows several shape constraints. The first three are applied to a single feature (x) constraining the $f(x)$ line, representing the output. The last two are applied to a pair of features (x_1, x_2) constraining the color-coded contour map ($f(x)$). A brief explanation for each follows:

- **Monotonicity**: This makes the function ($f(x)$) always increase (1) or decrease (-1) against the input (x).

- **Convexity**: This forces the function ($f(x)$) to be convex (1) or concave (-1) against the input (x). Convexity can be mixed with monotonicity to have an effect like the one in *Figure 12.23*.

- **Unimodality**: This is like monotonicity, except that it goes in both directions allowing the function ($f(x)$) to have a single valley (1) or peak (-1).

- **Trust**: This forces one monotonic feature (x_1) to rely on another one (x_2). The example in *Figure 12.23* is **Edgeworth Trust**, but there's also a **Trapezoid Trust** variation with a different shape constraint.

- **Dominance**: Monotonic dominance constrains one monotonic (x_1) feature to define the direction of the slope or effects when compared to another (x_2). An alternative, range dominance, is similar, except both features are monotonic.

Neural networks are particularly prone to overfitting, and the levers for controlling it are comparably hard to maneuver. For instance, exactly what combination of hidden nodes, dropout, weight regularization, and epochs will lead to an acceptable level of overfitting is challenging to tell. On the other hand, moving a single parameter in a tree-based model, tree depth, in one direction will likely lower overfitting to an acceptable level, albeit it might require many different parameters to make it optimal.

Enforcing shape constraints not only increases interpretability but regularizes the model because it simplifies the function. TensorFlow Lattice also supports different kinds of penalty-based regularization on a per-feature basis or to the calibration layer's kernel, leveraging L1 and L2 penalties via **Laplacian**, **Hessian**, **Torsion**, and **Wrinkle** regularizers. These regularizers have the effect of making functions more flat, linear, or smooth. We won't explain them but suffice to say, there is regularization to cover any use case.

There are also several ways to implement the framework—too many to elaborate here! Yet, it's important to point out that this example is just one of a handful of ways of implementing it. TFL comes with built-in **canned estimators** that abstract some of the configurations. You can also create a **custom estimator** using the TFL layers. For Keras, you can either use **premade models** or build a Keras model with TensorFlow Lattice layers. This last one is what we will do next!

Initializing the model and Lattice inputs

We will now create a series of *input layers*, which each include a single feature. These connect to *calibration layers*, which make each input fit into a **piece-wise linear** (**PWL**) function that complies with individual constraints and regularizations, except for `sex`, which will use categorical calibration. The calibration layers all feed into a multidimensional *Lattice layer*, producing output via a *Dense layer* with *sigmoid* activation. This description can be a lot to take in, so feel free to skip ahead to *Figure 12.24* to get some visual aid.

Incidentally, there are many kinds of layers available, which you can connect to produce a **deep lattice network (DLN)**, including the following:

- **Linear** for linear functions between more than one input, including those with dominance shape constraints.

- **Aggregation** to perform an aggregation function on more than one input.

- **Parallel combination** to place many calibration layers within a single function, making it compatible to Keras `Sequential` layers.

We won't use any of these layers in this example, but perhaps knowing this will further inspire you to explore the TensorFlow Lattice library further. Anyway, back to this example!

The first thing to define is `lattice_sizes`, which is a tuple that corresponds to a number of vertices per dimension. We have one dimension per feature in the chosen architecture, so we need to choose nine numbers greater or equal to two. Features with less cardinality for categorical or inflection points for continuous warrant fewer vertices. However, we might also want to restrict a feature's expressiveness by purposely choosing an even smaller number of vertices. For instance, `juv_fel_count` has 10 unique values, but we will assign only two vertices to it. `lattice_sizes` is shown here:

```
lattice_sizes = [2, 2, 2, 2, 3, 5, 7, 7, 6]
```

Next, we will initialize two lists, one to place all the input layers (`model_inputs`) and another for the calibration layers (`lattice_inputs`). Then, for each feature, one by one, we define an input layer with `tf.keras.layers.Input` and a calibration layer with either categorical calibration (`tfl.layers.CategoricalCalibration`) or PWL calibration (`tfl.layers.PWLCalibration`). Both input and calibration layers will get appended to their respective lists for each feature. What happens inside the calibration layer depends on the feature. All PWL calibrations use `input_keypoints`, which asks where the PWL function should be segmented. Sometimes, this is best answered with fixed widths (`np.linspace`), or other times with fixed frequency (`np.quantile`). Categorical calibration instead uses buckets (`num_buckets`) that correspond to the amount of categories. All calibrators have the following arguments:

- `output_min`: The minimum output for the calibrator

- `output_max`: The maximum output for the calibrator—always has to match the output minimum + lattice size - 1

- `monotonicity`: Whether it should monotonically constrain the PWL function, and if so, how

- `kernel_regularizer`: How to regularize the function

In addition to these arguments, `convexity` and `is_cyclic` (for monotonic unimodal) can modify the constraint shape. Have a look at the following code snippet:

```python
model_inputs = []
lattice_inputs = []


sex_input = tf.keras.layers.Input(shape=[1], name='sex')
lattice_inputs.append(tfl.layers.CategoricalCalibration(
  name='sex_calib', num_buckets=2, output_min=0.0,\
  output_max=lattice_sizes[0] - 1.0,\
  kernel_regularizer=tf.keras.regularizers.l1_l2(l1=0.001),\
  kernel_initializer='constant')(sex_input))
model_inputs.append(sex_input)
juvf_input = tf.keras.layers.Input(shape=[1],\
name='juv_fel_count')
lattice_inputs.append(tfl.layers.PWLCalibration(
  name='juvf_calib', monotonicity='none',\
  input_keypoints=np.linspace(0, 20, num=5,\
dtype=np.float32),\
  output_min=0.0, output_max=lattice_sizes[1] - 1.0,\
  kernel_regularizer=tf.keras.regularizers.l1_l2(l1=0.001),\
  kernel_initializer='equal_slopes')(juvf_input))
model_inputs.append(juvf_input)
:
age_input = tf.keras.layers.Input(shape=[1], name='age_group')
lattice_inputs.append(tfl.layers.PWLCalibration(
  name='age_calib', monotonicity='none',\
  input_keypoints=np.linspace(0, 6, num=7,\
dtype=np.float32),\
  output_min=0.0, output_max=lattice_sizes[7] - 1.0,\
  kernel_regularizer=('hessian', 0.0, 1e-4))(age_input))
model_inputs.append(age_input)
priors_input = tf.keras.layers.Input(shape=[1],\
```

```
                                     name='priors_per_year')
lattice_inputs.append(tfl.layers.PWLCalibration(
    name='priors_calib', monotonicity='increasing',\
    input_keypoints=np.quantile(X_train_con['priors_per_year'],\
                     np.linspace(0, 1, num=7)),
    output_min=0.0, output_max=lattice_sizes[8] - 1.0)(priors_
input)))
model_inputs.append(priors_input)
```

So, we now have a list with `model_inputs` and another with calibration layers, which will be the input to the lattice (`lattice_inputs`). All we need to do now is tie these together to a lattice.

Building a Keras model with TensorFlow Lattice layers

We already have the first two building blocks of this model connected. Now, let's create the last two building blocks, starting with the lattice (`tfl.layers.Lattice`). As arguments, it takes `lattice_sizes`, output minimums and maximums, and `monotonicities` it should enforce. Note that the last item, `priors_per_year`, has monotonicity set as `increasing`. The lattice layer then feeds into the final piece, which is the `Dense` layer with `sigmoid` activation. The code can be seen in the following snippet:

```
lattice = tfl.layers.Lattice(
         name='lattice', lattice_sizes=lattice_sizes,\
         monotonicities=[
             'none', 'none', 'none', 'none', 'none',\
             'none', 'none', 'none', 'increasing'
         ],\
         output_min=0.0, output_max=1.0)(lattice_inputs)
model_output = tf.keras.layers.Dense(1, name='output',
                              activation='sigmoid')(lattice)
```

The two first building blocks as `input` can now get connected with the last two as `outputs` with `tf.keras.models.Model`. And voilà! We now have a fully formed model, with the code shown here:

```
tfl_mdl = tf.keras.models.Model(inputs=model_inputs,
                              outputs=model_output)
```

You can always run `tfl_mdl.summary()` to get an idea of how all the layers connect, but it's not as intuitive as using `tf.keras.utils.plot_model`, which is illustrated in the following code snippet:

```
tf.keras.utils.plot_model(tfl_mdl, rankdir='LR')
```

The preceding code generates the model diagram shown here in *Figure 12.24*:

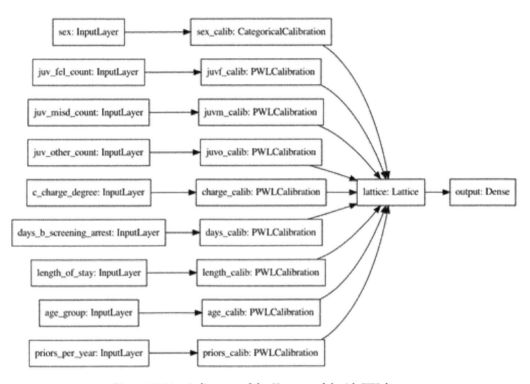

Figure 12.24 – A diagram of the Keras model with TFL layers

Next, we need to compile the model. We will use a `binary_crossentropy` loss function, an `Adam` optimizer, and employ accuracy and **Area Under the Curve** (**AUC**) as metrics, as illustrated in the following code snippet:

```
tfl_mdl.compile(loss='binary_crossentropy',\
                optimizer=tf.keras.optimizers.Adam(lr=0.004),\
                metrics=['accuracy',tf.keras.metrics.
AUC(name='auc')])
```

We are almost ready to go now! What follows next is the very last step.

Training and evaluating the model

If you take one hard look at *Figure 12.24*, you'll notice that the model doesn't have one input layer but nine, so this means that we must split our training and test data into nine parts. We can use np.split to do this, which will yield a list of nine NumPy arrays. As for the labels, TFL doesn't accept arrays with a single dimension. With expand_dims, we convert their shapes from (N,) to (N,1), as illustrated in the following code snippet:

```
X_train_expand = np.split(X_train_con.values.astype(np.
float32),\
                          indices_or_sections=9, axis=1)
y_train_expand = np.expand_dims(y_train.values.astype(np.
float32),\
                                axis=1)
X_test_expand = np.split(X_test_con.values.astype(np.float32),\
                         indices_or_sections=9, axis=1)
y_test_expand = np.expand_dims(y_test.values.astype(np.
float32),\
                               axis=1)
```

Now comes the training! To prevent overfitting, we can use EarlyStopping by monitoring the validation AUC (val_auc). And to account for class imbalance, in the fit function, we use class_weight, as illustrated in the following code snippet:

```
es = tf.keras.callbacks.EarlyStopping(monitor='val_auc',
mode='max',
                     verbose=1, patience=20, restore_best_
weights=True)
tfl_history = tfl_mdl.fit(X_train_expand, y_train_expand,
                 class_weight={0:18, 1:16}, batch_size=128,\
                     epochs=60, validation_split=0.2,
shuffle=False,\
                     callbacks=[es], verbose=1)
```

Once the model has been trained, we can use evaluate_class_mdl to output a quick summary of predictive performance, as we have before, and then compare_confusion_matrices to examine fairness, as we did previously. The code is shown in the following snippet:

```
fitted_class_mdls['tfl_con'] =
  mldatasets.evaluate_class_mdl(tfl_mdl, X_train_expand,
```

```
                    X_test_expand, y_train.values.astype(np.float32),\
                    y_test.values.astype(np.float32), plot_roc=False,\
                    ret_eval_dict=True)
y_test_pred = fitted_class_mdls['tfl_con']['preds_test']
_ = mldatasets.\
    compare_confusion_matrices(y_test[X_test.race==1],\
                    y_test_pred[X_test.race==1], y_test[X_test.
race==0],\
                    y_test_pred[X_test.race==0], 'Caucasian',\
                    'African-American', compare_fpr=True)
```

The preceding snippet produced the confusion matrices in *Figure 12.25*. The TensorFlow Lattice model performs overall much better than the regularized Keras model, yet the FPR ratio is worse than the constrained XGBoost model. It must be noted that XGBoost's parameters were previously tuned. With TensorFlow Lattice, a lot could be done to improve FPR, including using a custom loss function or better early stopping metrics that somehow account for racial disparities.

The output can be seen here:

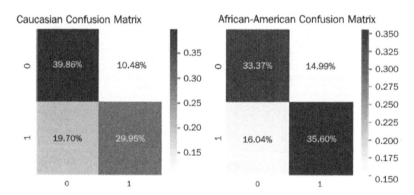

Figure 12.25 – Comparison of confusion matrices between races for the constrained TensorFlow Lattice model

Next, we will make some conclusions based on what was learned in this chapter and determine if we accomplished the mission.

Mission accomplished

It's often the data that takes the blame for a poor-performing, uninterpretable, or biased model, and that can be true, but many different things can be done in the preparation and modeling stages to improve it. To offer an analogy, it's like baking a cake. You need quality ingredients, yes. But seemingly small differences in the preparation of these ingredients and baking itself—such as the baking temperature, the container used, and time—can make a huge difference. Hell! Even things that are out of your control, such as atmospheric pressure or moisture, can impact baking! Even after it's all finished, how many different ways can you assess the quality of a cake?

This chapter is about these many details, and, as with baking, they are **part exact science and part artform**. The concepts discussed in this chapter also have far-reaching consequences, especially regarding how to optimize a problem that doesn't have a single goal and has profound societal implications. One possible approach is to combine metrics and account for imbalances. To that end, we have created a metric: a weighted average of precision recall that penalizes racial inequity, and we can efficiently compute it for all of our models and place it into the model dictionary (`fitted_class_mdls`). Then, as we have done before, we put it into a `DataFrame` and output it but, this time, sort by the custom metric (`wppra_test`). The code can be seen in the following snippet:

```
for mdl_name in fitted_class_mdls:
  fitted_class_mdls[mdl_name]['wppra_test'] =\
    weighted_penalized_pr_average(y_test,\
          fitted_class_mdls[mdl_name]['preds_test'],
          X_test['race'], range(3))
class_metrics = pd.DataFrame.from_dict(fitted_class_mdls,
      'index')[['precision_test', 'recall_test', 'wppra_test']]
with pd.option_context('display.precision', 3):
  html = class_metrics.sort_values(by='wppra_test',\
                            ascending=False).\
        style.background_gradient(cmap='plasma',\
                            subset=['precision_
test']).\
              background_gradient(cmap='viridis',\
                            subset=['recall_test'])
  html
```

The preceding code produced the dataframe shown here in *Figure 12.26*:

	precision_test	recall_test	wppra_test
catboost_opt	0.835	0.824	0.815
catboost_reg	0.837	0.802	0.810
xgb_base	0.812	0.848	0.806
catboost_base	0.809	0.838	0.800
xgb_reg	0.828	0.815	0.797
nu-svc_reg	0.836	0.772	0.791
lgbm_reg	0.814	0.778	0.783
xgb_con	0.800	0.804	0.781
lgbm_base	0.802	0.799	0.774
tfl_con	0.739	0.651	0.693

Figure 12.26 – Top models in this chapter when sorted by weighted penalized precision-recall average custom metric

In *Figure 12.26*, it's tempting to propose one of the models at the very top. However, they were trained with `race` as a feature and didn't account for proven criminal justice *realities*. However, the highest-performing constrained model—the XGBoost one (`xgb_con`)—lacked race, ensured that `priors_per_year` is monotonic, and that with `age_group` isn't allowed to interact with juvenile delinquency features, and it did all this while significantly improving predictive performance when compared to the original model. It is fairer, too, because it reduced the ratio of the FPR between the privileged and underprivileged groups from 1.84x (*Figure 7.2*) to 1.17x (*Figure 12.19*). It's not perfect, but it's a massive improvement!

The mission was to prove that accuracy and domain knowledge could coexist with a boost in fairness, and we have completed it successfully. That being said, there's still room for improvement. Therefore, the plan of action would have to showcase the constrained XGBoost model to your client, and continue improving and building more constrained models. The unconstrained ones should only serve as a benchmark.

You can make substantial fairness improvements, if you combine the methods from this chapter with those learned in *Chapter 11, Bias Mitigation and Causal Inference Methods*. We didn't incorporate them into this chapter, to focus solely on model (or in-processing) methods that are typically not seen as part of the bias-mitigation toolkit, but they very much can assist to that end, not to mention model-tuning methods that serve to make a model more reliable.

Summary

After reading this chapter, you should understand how to leverage data engineering to enhance interpretability, regularization to reduce overfitting, and constraints to comply with policies. The primary end goals are to place guardrails and curb the complexity that hinders interpretability.

In the next chapter, we will look at ways to enhance model reliability through adversarial robustness.

Dataset sources

- ProPublica Data Store (2019). *COMPAS Recidivism Risk Score Data and Analysis*. Originally retrieved from `https://www.propublica.org/datastore/dataset/compas-recidivism-risk-score-data-and-analysis`.

Further reading

- Hastie, T. J., Tibshirani, R. J. and Friedman, J. H. (2001). *The elements of statistical learning*. Springer-Verlag, New York, USA

- Wang, S. & Gupta, M. (2020). *Deontological Ethics By Monotonicity Shape Constraints*. AISTATS. `https://arxiv.org/abs/2001.11990`

- Cotter, A., Gupta, M., Jiang, H., Ilan, E. L., Muller, J., Narayan, T., Wang, S. & Zhu, T. (2019). *Shape Constraints for Set Functions*. ICML. `http://proceedings.mlr.press/v97/cotter19a.html`

- Gupta, M. R., Cotter A., Pfeifer, J., Voevodski, K., Canini, K., Mangylov, A., Moczydlowski, W. and van Esbroeck, A. (2016). *Monotonic Calibrated Interpolated Look-Up Tables. Journal of Machine Learning Research*. 17(109):1–47. `https://arxiv.org/abs/1505.06378`

- Noble, S. (2018). *Algorithms of oppression: data discrimination in the age of Google*. NYU Press.

13
Adversarial Robustness

Machine learning interpretation has many concerns, ranging from knowledge discovery to high-stakes ones with tangible ethical implications, such as the fairness issues examined in the last two chapters. In this chapter, we will direct our attention to concerns involving reliability, safety, and security.

As we realized using the **contrastive explanation method** (**CEM**) in *Chapter 8, Visualizing Convolutional Neural Networks*, we can easily trick an image classifier into making embarrassingly false predictions. This ability can have serious ramifications. For instance, a perpetrator can place a black sticker on a yield sign, and while most drivers would still recognize this as a yield sign, a self-driving car would no longer recognize it and, as a result, crash. A bank robber could wear a cooling suit designed to trick a bank vault's thermal imaging system, and while any human would notice it, the imaging system wouldn't.

It doesn't have to be even a sophisticated image classifier. Any model can be tricked! **The counterfactual examples** produced in *Chapter 7, Anchors and Counterfactual Explanations,* are like adversarial examples, except with the goal of deceiving. An attacker could leverage any misclassification example, straddling the decision boundary adversarially—for instance, a spammer could realize that adjusting some email attributes increases the likelihood of circumventing spam filters.

Complex models are more vulnerable to adversarial attacks, so why would we trust them?! We can certainly make them more foolproof, and that's what adversarial robustness entails. An adversary can purposely thwart a model in many ways, but we will focus on evasion attacks and briefly explain other forms of attacks. Then, we explain two defense methods: spatial smoothing preprocessing, and adversarial training. Lastly, we will demonstrate one robustness evaluation method and one certification method.

These are the main topics we are going to cover in this chapter:

- Learning about evasion attacks
- Defending against targeted attacks with preprocessing
- Shielding against any evasion attack via adversarial training of a robust classifier
- Evaluating and certifying adversarial robustness

Technical requirements

This chapter's example uses the `mldatasets`, `numpy`, `sklearn`, `tensorflow`, `keras`, `adversarial-robustness-toolbox`, `matplotlib`, and `seaborn` libraries. Instructions on how to install all of these libraries are in the preface of this book. The code for this chapter is located here:

```
https://github.com/PacktPublishing/Interpretable-Machine-
Learning-with-Python/tree/master/Chapter13
```

The mission

The privately contracted security-services-industry market worldwide is valued at over 250 billion **United States dollars** (**USD**) and is growing at around 5% annually. However, it faces many challenges, such as a shortage of adequately trained guards and specialized security experts in many jurisdictions, as well as a whole host of unexpected security threats. These threats include widespread coordinated cybersecurity attacks, massive riots, social upheaval, and—last but not least—health risks brought on by pandemics. Indeed, 2020 tested the industry with a wave of ransomware and misinformation attacks, protests, and COVID-19, to boot.

In the wake of this, one of the largest hospital networks in the US asked their contracted security company to monitor the correct use of masks of both visitors and personnel throughout the hospital. The security company struggled with this request because it would divert security personnel from tackling other threats such as intruders, combative patients, and belligerent visitors. It has video surveillance in every hallway, operating room, waiting room, and hospital entrance. It's impossible to have eyes on every camera feed every time, so they thought that they could assist guards with deep learning models.

These models already alert staff to unusual activity, such as running in the hallways and brandishing weapons anywhere on the premises. They have proposed to the hospital network that they would like to add a new model that detects the correct usage of masks. Before COVID-19 there were policies in place for mandatory mask usage in certain areas of each hospital, and during COVID-19 this was required everywhere. Hospital administrators would like to turn on and off this monitoring feature, depending on pandemic risk levels moving forward. They realize that personnel get fatigued and forget to put masks back on, or that they partially slip off at times. Many visitors are also hostile toward using masks and may wear one when entering the hospital, but take it off when no guard is around. This isn't always intentional, so they wouldn't want to send guards on every alert, unlike with other threats. Instead, they'd rather use awareness and a little bit of shame to modify behavior and only intervene with repeat offenders:

Figure 13.1 – Radar speed signs such as this one help curb speeding

Awareness is a very effective method, such as with radar speed signs (see *Figure 13.1*) that make roads safer by making drivers aware that they are driving too fast. It could be equally effective to have a screen at the end of heavily trafficked hallways, showing snapshots of those that have either recently mistakenly or purposely not complied with mandatory mask usage, potentially creating some embarrassment for offenders. The system would log repeat offenders so that security guards could look for them and either make them comply or ask them to vacate the premises.

There's some concern with visitors trying to trick the model into evading compliance, so the security company has hired you to ensure that the model is robust toward this kind of adversarial attack. Security officers have noticed some low-tech trickery before, such as people momentarily covering their face with their hands or a part of their sweater when they realized cameras were monitoring them. And in one disturbing incident, a visitor dimmed the lights and sprayed some gel on a camera, and in another, an individual painted their mouth. However, there are concerns for higher-tech attacks, such as jamming a camera's wireless signal or shining high-powered lasers directly toward cameras. Devices that perform these attacks are increasingly easier to obtain and could impact other surveillance functions on a larger scale, such as theft-prevention functions. The security company hopes this robustness exercise can inform their efforts to improve every surveillance system and model.

Eventually, the security company would like to produce their own dataset with facial images from the hospitals they monitor. Meanwhile, synthetically masked faces from external sources is the best they can do to productionize a model in the short term. To this end, you have been provided a large dataset of synthetically correctly and incorrectly masked faces and their unmasked counterparts. The two datasets were combined into a single one, and the original dimensions of 1024 × 1024 were reduced to a thumbnail size of 124 × 124. Also, for efficiency's sake, 21,000 images were sampled from the nearly 210,000 images found in these datasets.

The approach

You've decided to take a four-fold approach, as follows:

- Exploring several possible evasion attacks to understand how vulnerable the model is to them and how credible they are as threats

- Using a preprocessing method to protect the model against these attacks

- Leveraging adversarial retraining to produce a robust classifier that is intrinsically less prone to many of these attacks

- Evaluating robustness with state-of-the-art methods to be able to assure hospital administrators that the model is adversarially robust

Let's get started!

The preparations

You will find most of the code for this example at `https://github.com/PacktPublishing/Interpretable-Machine-Learning-with-Python/tree/master/Chapter13/Masks_part1.ipynb`, up to the code used in the *Certifying robustness with randomized smoothing* section. The code for that section alone is located at `https://github.com/PacktPublishing/Interpretable-Machine-Learning-with-Python/tree/master/Chapter13/Masks_part2.ipynb`.

Loading the libraries

To run this example, you need to install the following libraries:

- `mldatasets` to load the dataset
- `numpy` and `sklearn` (scikit-learn) to manipulate it
- `tensorflow` to fit the models
- `matplotlib` and `seaborn` to visualize the interpretations

You should load all of them first, as follows:

```
import math
import os
import warnings
warnings.filterwarnings("ignore")
import mldatasets
import numpy as np
from sklearn import preprocessing
import tensorflow as tf
from tensorflow.keras.utils import get_file
import matplotlib.pyplot as plt
import seaborn as sns
#PART 1 only
from sklearn import metrics
from art.estimators.classification import KerasClassifier
from art.attacks.evasion import FastGradientMethod,\
                ProjectedGradientDescent, BasicIterativeMethod
from art.attacks.evasion import CarliniLInfMethod
from art.attacks.evasion import AdversarialPatchNumpy
```

```
from art.defences.preprocessor import SpatialSmoothing
```

```
from art.defences.trainer import AdversarialTrainer
```

```
from tqdm.notebook import tqdm
```

```
#PART 2 only
```

```
from art.estimators.classification import
TensorFlowV2Classifier
```

```
from art.estimators.certification.randomized_smoothing import\
                              TensorFlowV2RandomizedSmoothing
```

```
from art.utils import compute_accuracy
```

Let's check that TensorFlow has loaded the right version, with `print(tf.__version__)`. The version should be 2.0 or above.

We should also disable eager execution and verify that it worked with the following commands. The output should say that it's `False`:

```
tf.compat.v1.disable_eager_execution()
```

```
print('Eager execution enabled:', tf.executing_eagerly())
```

Understanding and preparing the data

We load the data into four NumPy arrays corresponding to the train/test datasets. While we are at it, we divide X face images by 255 because, that way, they will be of values between zero and one, which is better for deep learning models. We will need to record the `min_` and `max_` for the training data because we will need these later.

The code can be seen in the following snippet:

```
X_train, X_test, y_train, y_test =\
  mldatasets.load("maskedface-net_thumbs_sampled", prepare=True)
X_train, X_test = X_train / 255.0, X_test / 255.0
min_ = X_train.min()
max_ = X_train.max()
```

It's always important to verify your data when you load it to make sure it didn't get corrupted. You can do this with the following code:

```
print('X_train dim:\t%s' % (X_train.shape,))
print('X_test dim:\t%s' % (X_test.shape,))
print('y_train dim:\t%s' % (y_train.shape,))
print('y_test dim:\t%s' % (y_test.shape,))
```

```
print('X_train min:\t%s' % (min_))
print('X_train max:\t%s' % (max_))
print('y_train labels:\t%s' % (np.unique(y_train)))
```

The preceding snippet will produce the output shown next, which tells you that the images have dimensions of 128 × 128 pixels and three channels (color). There are 16,800 training images and 4,200 test images. The labels only have a one in the second value, which indicates that it's not one-hot encoded. Indeed, by printing the unique values (np. unique(y_train)), you can tell that the labels are represented as text—Correct for correctly masked, Incorrect for incorrectly masked, and None for no mask. The code is shown in the following snippet:

```
X_train dim:    (16800, 128, 128, 3)
X_test dim: (4200, 128, 128, 3)
y_train dim:    (16800, 1)
y_test dim: (4200, 1)
X_train min:    0.0
X_train max:    1.0
y_train labels: ['Correct' 'Incorrect' 'None']
```

Therefore, a preprocessing step we will need to perform is to **one-hot encode (OHE)** the y labels because we will need the OHE form to evaluate the model's predictive performance. Once we initialize the OneHotEncoder, we will need to fit it to the training data (y_train). We can also extract the categories from the encoder into a list (labels_l) to verify that it has all three.

Have a look at the following code snippet:

```
ohe = preprocessing.OneHotEncoder(sparse=False)
ohe.fit(y_train)
labels_l = ohe.categories_[0].tolist()
print(labels_l)
```

For reproducibility's sake, always initialize your random seeds like this:

```
rand = 9
os.environ['PYTHONHASHSEED'] = str(rand)
tf.random.set_seed(rand)
np.random.seed(rand)
```

Granted, determinism is very difficult with deep learning and often is session-, platform-, and architecture-dependent. If you are using an NVIDIA **graphics processing unit (GPU)**, you can install a library called `tensorflow-determinism`.

Many of the adversarial attack, defense, and evaluation methods we will study in this chapter are very resource-intensive, so if we used the entire test dataset with them, they could likely take many hours on a single method! For efficiency, it is strongly suggested to use samples of the test dataset. Therefore, we will create a medium 200-image sample (X_test_mdsample, y_test_mdsample) and a small 20-image sample (X_test_smsample, y_test_smsample) using np.random.choice. The code is shown in the following snippet:

```
sampl_md_idxs = np.random.choice(X_test.shape[0],
200,replace=False)
X_test_mdsample = X_test[sampl_md_idxs]
y_test_mdsample = y_test[sampl_md_idxs]
sampl_sm_idxs = np.random.choice(X_test.shape[0], 20,
replace=False)
X_test_smsample = X_test[sampl_sm_idxs]
y_test_smsample = y_test[sampl_sm_idxs]
```

Now, let's take a peek at the images in our datasets. In the preceding code, we have taken a medium and a small sample of our test dataset. We place each image of our small sample in a 4 × 5 grid with the class label above it, with the following code:

```
plt.subplots(figsize=(15,12))
for s in range(20):
 plt.subplot(4, 5, s+1)
 plt.title(y_test_smsample[s][0], fontsize=12)
 plt.imshow(X_test_smsample[s], interpolation='spline16')
 plt.axis('off')
```

The preceding code plots the grid of images shown here in *Figure 13.2*:

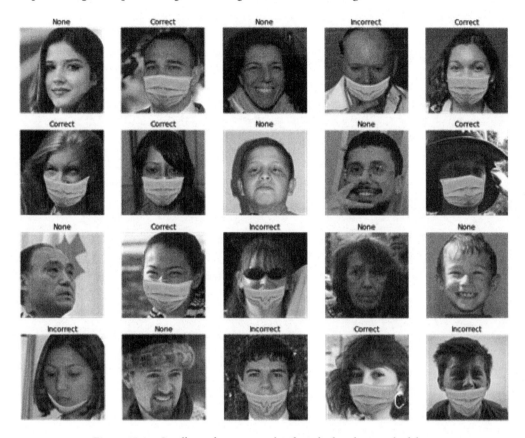

Figure 13.2 – Small test dataset sample of masked and unmasked faces

Figure 13.2 depicts a variety of correctly and incorrectly masked and unmasked faces of all ages, genders, and ethnicities. Despite this variety, one thing to note about this dataset is that it only has light-blue surgical masks represented, and images are mostly at a front-facing angle. Ideally, we would generate an even larger dataset with all colors and types of masks, and augment it further with random rotations, shears, and brightness adjustments, either before or during training. These augmentations would make for a much more robust model. Nevertheless, we must differentiate between this general type of robustness and adversarial robustness, and even though both are essential, spending time on the former would detract from the latter. Thus, let's assume that the dataset has already been augmented.

Loading the CNN base model

You don't have to train the **convolutional neural network** (**CNN**) base model, but the code to do so is provided nonetheless in the GitHub repository. The pre-trained model has also been stored there. We can quickly load the model and output its summary, like this:

```
model_path = get_file('CNN_Base_MaskedFace_Net.hdf5',\
        'https://github.com/PacktPublishing/Interpretable-
Machine-Learning-with-Python/blob/master/models/CNN_Base_
MaskedFace_Net.hdf5?raw=true')
base_model = tf.keras.models.load_model(model_path)
base_model.summary()
```

The preceding snippet outputs the following summary:

```
Model: "CNN_Base_MaskedFaceNet_Model"
```

Layer (type)	Output Shape	Param #
conv2d_1 (Conv2D)	(None, 126, 126, 16)	448
maxpool2d_1 (MaxPooling2D)	(None, 63, 63, 16)	0
conv2d_2 (Conv2D)	(None, 61, 61, 32)	4640
maxpool2d_2 (MaxPooling2D)	(None, 30, 30, 32)	0
conv2d_3 (Conv2D)	(None, 28, 28, 64)	18496
maxpool2d_3 (MaxPooling2D)	(None, 14, 14, 64)	0
conv2d_4 (Conv2D)	(None, 12, 12, 128)	73856
maxpool2d_4 (MaxPooling2D)	(None, 6, 6, 128)	0
flatten_6 (Flatten)	(None, 4608)	0
dense_1 (Dense)	(None, 768)	3539712

dropout_6 (Dropout)	(None, 768)	0
dense_2 (Dense)	(None, 3)	2307

```
=================================================================
Total params: 3,639,459
Trainable params: 3,639,459
Non-trainable params: 0
```

The summary has pretty much everything we need to know about the model. It has four convolutional layers (Conv2D), each followed by a max pool layer (MaxPooling2D). It then has a Flatten layer and a fully connected layer (Dense). Then, there's more Dropout before the second Dense layer. Naturally, three neurons are in this final layer, corresponding to each class.

Assessing the CNN base classifier

We can evaluate the model using the test dataset with the evaluate_multiclass_mdl function. The arguments include the model (base_model), our test data (X_test), and corresponding labels (y_test), as well as the class names (labels_l) and the encoder (ohe). Lastly, we don't need it to plot the **receiver operating characteristic** (**ROC**) curves since they will be perfect (plot_roc=False). This function returns the predicted labels and probabilities, which we can store into variables for later use.

The code can be seen in the following snippet:

```
y_test_pred, y_test_prob =\
    mldatasets.evaluate_multiclass_mdl(base_model, X_test, y_
test,\
    labels_l, ohe, plot_conf_matrix=True,
predopts={"verbose":1})
```

The preceding code generates *Figure 13.3*, with a confusion matrix and performance metrics for each class. This can be seen here:

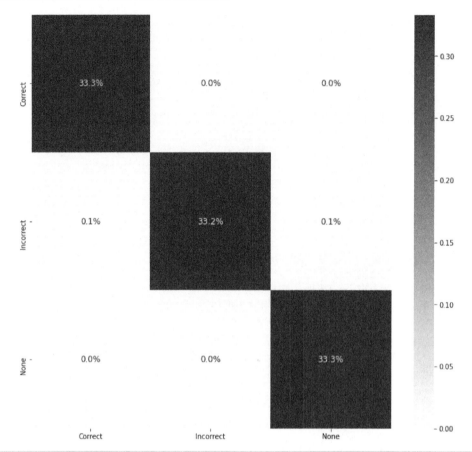

	precision	recall	f1-score	support
Correct	0.998	0.998	0.998	1400
Incorrect	0.999	0.995	0.997	1400
None	0.996	0.999	0.998	1400
accuracy			0.997	4200
macro avg	0.997	0.997	0.997	4200
weighted avg	0.997	0.997	0.997	4200

Figure 13.3 – The confusion matrix and predictive performance metrics for the base classifier evaluated on the test dataset

Even though the confusion matrix in *Figure 13.3* seems to suggest a perfect classification, you can tell that the model had issues with misclassifying as incorrectly masked once you see the precision-and-recall breakdown.

Now, we can start attacking this model to assess how perfect it actually is!

Learning about evasion attacks

There are six broad categories of adversarial attacks, detailed as follows:

- **Evasion**: This means designing an input that can cause a model to incorrectly predict, especially when it wouldn't fool a human observer. It can either be targeted or untargeted, depending on an attacker's intention to fool the model into misclassifying one class toward another, or not. The attack methods can be white-box if the attacker has full access to the model and its training dataset, or black-box with only inference access. Gray-box is in the middle; black-box is always model-agnostic; whereas white- and gray-box methods might be.

- **Poisoning**: Injecting faulty training data or parameters into a model can come in many forms, depending on an attacker's capabilities and access. For instance, for systems with user-generated data, the attacker may be capable of adding faulty data or labels. If they have more access, they could perhaps modify large amounts of data. They could also adjust the learning algorithm, or only the hyperparameters or data augmentation schemes. As with evasion, poisoning can also be targeted or untargeted.

- **Inference**: This means extracting the training dataset through model inference. Inference attacks also come in many forms and can be used for espionage (privacy attacks) through membership inference, which confirms if one example (for instance, a specific person) was in the training dataset. Attribute inference ascertains if an example category (for instance, ethnicity) was represented in the training data. Input inference (also known as model inversion) has attack methods to extract the training dataset from a model rather than guessing and confirming. These have broad privacy and regulatory implications, especially in medical and legal applications, and in jurisdictions with stronger privacy such as the **General Data Protection Regulation** (**GDPR**) in the **European Union** (**EU**), many other industries can be impacted.

- **Trojaning**: Hacking existing models repurposed by others for transfer learning or as part of an ensemble of models to change a model's behaviors.

- **Backdooring**: Similar to Trojans but a backdoor remains, even when retrained from scratch.

- **Reprogramming**: Remote sabotaging of a model during training by sneaking in examples that are specifically designed to produce specific outputs. For instance, if you provide enough examples labeled as tiger shark, where four small black squares are always in the same place, the model will learn that this is a tiger shark, regardless of what it is.

The first three methods are the most widespread forms of adversarial attacks. Attacks can be further subcategorized once we split them by stage and goal (see *Figure 13.4*). The stage refers to when an attack is perpetrated because it can impact the model training or its inference, and the goal is what the attacker hopes to gain from it. This chapter will only deal with evasion sabotage attacks because we expect hospital visitors, patients, and personnel to occasionally sabotage the production model.

The following table provides an overview of adversarial attack category methods by stage and goal:

		Goal		
		Espionage	Sabotage	Fraud
Stage	Training	Inference (by poisoning)	Trojaning	
			Poisoning	
			Backdooring	
	Production	Inference	Reprogramming	
			Evasion	

Figure 13.4 – Table of adversarial attack category methods by stage and goal

Even though we use white-box methods to attack, defend, and evaluate a model's robustness, we don't expect attackers to have this level of access. We will only use white-box methods because we have full access to the model, and it's not worth the trouble to try black- or gray-box methods. In other circumstances, such as a bank surveillance system with a thermal imaging system and a corresponding model to detect perpetrators, you could expect professional attackers to use black-box methods to find vulnerabilities! So, as defenders of this system, we would be wise to try the very same attack methods.

The library we will use for adversarial robustness is called the **Adversarial Robustness Toolbox (ART)**, and it's supported by the **LF AI & Data Foundation**, the same folks that support other open source projects such as **AI Explainability 360 (AIX360)** and the **AI Fairness 360 (AIF360)** project, which was explored in *Chapter 11, Bias Mitigation and Causal Inference Methods*. ART requires that attacked models are abstracted in an estimator or classifier, even if it's a black-box one. We will use `KerasClassifier` for most of this chapter except for the last section, in which we use `TensorFlowV2Classifier`. Initializing an ART classifier is fairly simple. You must specify the `model` attribute, and sometimes there are other required attributes. For `KerasClassifier` all remaining attributes are optional, but it is recommended you use `clip_values` to specify the range of the features. Many attacks are input permutations, so knowing which input values are allowed or feasible is essential.

Have a look at the following code snippet:

```
base_classifier = KerasClassifier(model=base_model,\
                                  clip_values=(min_, max_))
y_test_mdsample_prob = np.max(y_test_prob[sampl_md_idxs],
axis=1)
y_test_smsample_prob = np.max(y_test_prob[sampl_sm_idxs],
axis=1)
```

In the preceding code, we will also prepare two arrays with probabilities for the predicted class for the medium and small samples, while we are at it. It is entirely optional, but these assist in placing the predicted probability next to the predicted label when plotting some examples.

Fast Gradient Sign Method attack

One of the most popular attack methods is the **Fast Gradient Sign Method (FGSM or FGM)**. As the name implies, this leverages a deep learning model's gradient to find adversarial examples. It performs small perturbations on the pixels of the input image, either additions or subtractions, and which one to use depends on the gradient's sign, which indicates the direction in which the loss would increase or decrease, according to the pixel's intensity.

As with all ART attack methods, you first initialize it by providing the ART estimator or classifier. `FastGradientMethod` also requires an `eps` attack step size, which will condition the attack strength. Incidentally, `eps` stands for epsilon (ϵ), which in math usually represents error margins or infinitesimal approximation errors. A low step size will cause pixel-intensity changes to be less visible, but it will also misclassify fewer examples. A larger step size will cause more examples to be misclassified, with more visible changes.

The code for this can be seen here:

```
attack_fgsm = FastGradientMethod(base_classifier, eps=0.1)
```

After initializing, the next step is to `generate` the adversarial examples. The only required attribute is original examples (`X_test_mdsample`). Please note that FGSM can be targeted, so there's an optional `targeted` attribute in the initialization, but you would also need to provide corresponding labels in the generation. This attack is untargeted because the attacker's intent is to sabotage the model.

The code for this can be seen here:

```
X_test_fgsm = attack_fgsm.generate(X_test_mdsample)
```

Generating the adversarial examples with FGSM is quick, unlike other methods, hence the "Fast" in the name!

Now, we are going to do two things in one swoop. First, we'll evaluate the adversarial examples (`X_test_fgsm`) against our base classifier's model (`base_classifier. model`) with `evaluate_multiclass_mdl`. Then, we can employ `compare_image_ predictions` to plot a grid of images, contrasting the randomly selected adversarial examples (`X_test_fgsm`) against the original ones (`X_test_mdsample`), and their corresponding predicted labels (`y_test_fgsm_pred, y_test_mdsample`) and probabilities (`y_test_fgsm_prob, y_test_mdsample_prob`). We are customizing the titles and limiting the grid to 4 examples (`num_samples`). By default, `compare_ image_predictions` only compares misclassifications, but the `use_misclass` optional attribute can be set to `false` to compare correct classifications.

The code can be seen in the following snippet:

```
y_test_fgsm_pred, y_test_fgsm_prob =\
        mldatasets.evaluate_multiclass_mdl(base_classifier.
model,\
                                X_test_fgsm, y_test_mdsample,\
                        labels_l, ohe, plot_conf_matrix=False,\
                        plot_roc=False)
y_test_fgsm_prob = np.max(y_test_fgsm_prob, axis=1)
mldatasets.compare_image_predictions(X_test_fgsm, X_test_
mdsample,\
    y_test_fgsm_pred, y_test_mdsample.flatten(), y_test_fgsm_
prob,\
    y_test_mdsample_prob, title_mod_prefix="Attacked:",\
```

```
    title_difference_prefix="FSGM Attack Average
Perturbation:",\
    num_samples=4)
```

The preceding code outputs this table first, which shows that the model has only 44% accuracy with FGSM-attacked examples! And even though it wasn't a targeted attack, it was most effective toward correctly masked faces. So, hypothetically, if perpetrators managed to cause this level of signal distortion or interference, they would severely undermine the security company's ability to monitor mask compliance.

The code also outputs *Figure 13.5*, which shows some misclassifications caused by the FGSM attack. The attack pretty much evenly distributed noise throughout the images. It also shows that the image was only modified by a mean absolute error of 0.092, and since pixel values range between 0 and 1, this means 9.2%. If you were to calibrate attacks so that they are less detectable but still impactful, you must note that an eps value of 0.1 causes a 9.2% mean absolute perturbation, which reduces accuracy to 44%:

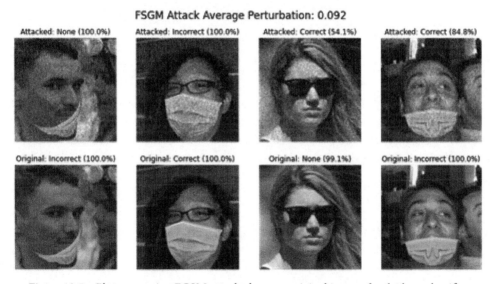

Figure 13.5 – Plot comparing FGSM-attacked versus original images for the base classifier

Speaking of less detectable attacks, we will now learn about **Carlini & Wagner (C&W)** attacks.

C&W infinity-norm attack

In 2017, C&W employed three *norm-based distance metrics*: L_0, L_2, and L_∞, measuring the differences between the original and adversarial example. In other papers these metrics had already been discussed, including the FGSM one. The innovation introduced by C&W was how these metrics were leveraged, using a gradient-descent-based optimization algorithm designed to approximate a loss function minima. Specifically, to avoid getting stuck, they use multiple starting points in the gradient descent, and so that the process "yields a valid image", it evaluates three methods to box-constrain the optimization problem. In this case, we want to find an adversarial example where the distances between that example and the original image are minimal while also remaining realistic.

All three C&W attacks (L_0, L_2, and L_∞) use the Adam optimizer to quickly converge. Their main difference is the distance metric, of which L_∞ is arguably the best one. It's defined as such:

$$L_\infty = ||x - x'||_\infty = max(|x_1 - x'_1|, \ldots, |x_n - x'_n|)$$

And, because it's the maximum distance to any coordinate, you make sure that the adversarial example is not just "on average" minimally different but not too different anywhere in the feature space. That's what would make an attack less detectable!

Initializing C&W infinity-norm attacks and generating adversarial examples with it is similar to FGSM. To initialize `CarliniLInfMethod`, we define an `eps` and, optionally, a `batch_size` (default is 128). Then, to `generate` an untargeted adversarial attack, the same applies as with FGSM—Only `X` is needed when untargeted, but `y` is needed when targeted.

The code is shown in the following snippet:

```
attack_cw = CarliniLInfMethod(base_classifier, eps=0.3,\
                              batch_size=40)
X_test_cw = attack_cw.generate(X_test_mdsample)
```

We will now evaluate the C&W adversarial examples (`X_test_cw`), just as we did with FGSM. It's exactly the same code but with `fsgm` replaced with `cw`, and different titles in `compare_image_predictions`. Just as with FGSM, the following code will yield a classification report and a grid of images (shown in *Figure 13.6*):

```
y_test_cw_pred, y_test_cw_prob =\
    mldatasets.evaluate_multiclass_mdl(base_classifier.model,\
              X_test_cw, y_test_mdsample, labels_l, ohe,\
```

```
                          plot_conf_matrix=False, plot_roc=False)
y_test_cw_prob = np.max(y_test_cw_prob, axis=1)
mldatasets.compare_image_predictions(X_test_cw, X_test_
mdsample,\
    y_test_cw_pred, y_test_mdsample.flatten(), y_test_cw_prob,\
    y_test_mdsample_prob, title_mod_prefix="Attacked:",\
    title_difference_prefix="C&W Inf Attack Average
Perturbation:",\
    num_samples=4)
```

As outputted by the preceding code, the C&W adversarial examples have 92% accuracy with our base model. It is sufficient a drop to render the model useless for its intended purpose. If the attacker disturbed a camera's signal just enough, they could achieve the same results. And, as you can tell from *Figure 13.6* here, the perturbation of 0.3% is tiny compared to FGSM, but it was sufficient to misclassify 8%, including the four in the grid that seem apparent to the naked eye:

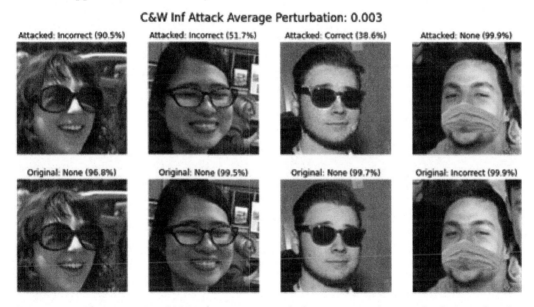

Figure 13.6 – Plot comparing C&W infinity norm-attacked versus original images for the base classifier

Sometimes, it doesn't matter if an attack goes undetected or not. The point of it is to make a statement, and that's what **adversarial patches (APs)** can do.

Targeted AP attack

An AP is a robust, universal, and targeted method. You generate a patch that you can either superimpose on an image or print and physically place in a scene, to trick a classifier into ignoring everything else in the scene. It is designed to work under a wide variety of conditions and transformations. Unlike other adversarial-example-generation approaches, there's no intention of camouflaging the attack because, essentially, you are replacing a detectable portion of the scene with the patch. The method works by leveraging a variant of **Expectation over Transformation (EOT)**, which trains images over transformations of a given patch on different locations of an image. What it learns is the patch that fools the classifier the most, given the training examples.

This method requires more parameters and steps than FGSM and C&W. For starters, we will use AdversarialPatchNumpy, which is a variant that works with any neural network image or video classifier. There's also one for TensorFlow v2, but our base classifier is KerasClassifier. The first argument is the classifier (base_classifier), and the other ones we will define are optional but highly recommended. The scale_min and scale_max scaling ranges are particularly important because they define how big patches can be in relation to the images—in this case, we want to test no smaller than 40% and no larger than 70%. Besides that, it makes sense to define a target class (target). In this case, we want the patch to target the "Correct" class. For the learning_rate and max iterations (max_iter) we are using the defaults, but note that these can be tuned to improve patch adversarial effectiveness.

The code for this can be seen in the following snippet:

```
attack_ap = AdversarialPatchNumpy(base_classifier, scale_
min=0.4,\
                    scale_max=0.7, learning_rate=5., max_
iter=500,\
                    batch_size=40, target=0)
```

We don't want the patch-generation algorithm to waste time testing patches everywhere in images, so we can direct this effort by using a Boolean mask. This mask tells it where it can center the patch. To make the mask, we start by creating an array of 0s of size 128 × 128. Then, we place 1s in the rectangular area between pixels 80-93 and 45-84, which loosely corresponds to covering the center of the mouth area in most of the images. Lastly, we expand the array's dimensions so that it's (1, W, H) and convert it to a Boolean. Then, we can proceed to generate patches using the small-size test dataset samples and the mask.

The code for this is shown in the following snippet:

```
placement_mask = np.zeros((128,128))
placement_mask[80:93,45:83] = 1
placement_mask = np.expand_dims(placement_mask, axis=0).
astype(bool)
patch, patch_mask = attack_ap.generate(x=X_test_smsample,\
        y=ohe.transform(y_test_smsample), mask=placement_mask)
```

We can now plot the patch with the following code:

```
plt.imshow(patch * patch_mask)
```

The preceding code produced the image shown here in *Figure 13.7*. As expected, it has plenty of shades of blue found in masks. It also has bright red and yellow hues, mostly missing from training examples, which confuses the classifier:

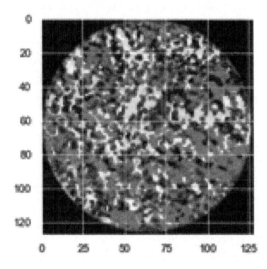

Figure 13.7 – AP generated to misclassify as correctly masked

Unlike other methods, `generate` didn't produce adversarial examples but a single patch, which is an image we can then place on top of images to create adversarial examples. This task is performed with `apply_patch`, which takes the original `X_test_smsample` examples and a scale—we are using 55%. It is also recommended to use a `mask`, which will make sure the patch is applied where it makes more sense—in this case, in the area around the mouth.

The code for this is shown in the following snippet:

```
X_test_ap = attack_ap.apply_patch(X_test_smsample, scale=0.55,\
                                    mask=placement_mask)
```

Now, it's time to evaluate our attack and examine some misclassifications. We will do exactly as before, reusing the code that produced *Figure 13.5* and *Figure 13.7*, except that we replace the variables so that they have ap and a corresponding title.

The code is shown in the following snippet:

```
y_test_ap_pred, y_test_ap_prob =\
        mldatasets.evaluate_multiclass_mdl(base_classifier.
model,\
                            X_test_ap, y_test_smsample, labels_l, ohe,\
                            plot_conf_matrix=False, plot_roc=False)
y_test_ap_prob = np.max(y_test_ap_prob, axis=1)
mldatasets.compare_image_predictions(X_test_ap, X_test_
smsample,\
        y_test_ap_pred, y_test_smsample.flatten(), y_test_ap_
prob,\
        y_test_smsample_prob, title_mod_prefix="Attacked:",\
        title_difference_prefix="AP Attack Average
Perturbation:",\
        num_samples=4)
```

The preceding code yields the accuracy result of our attack at 65%, which is quite good considering how few examples it was trained on. The AP needs more than the other method. Targeted attacks, in general, need more examples to understand how to best target one class. The preceding code also produced the grid of images shown here in *Figure 13.8*, which demonstrates how, hypothetically, if people walked around holding a cardboard patch in front of their face, they could easily fool the model:

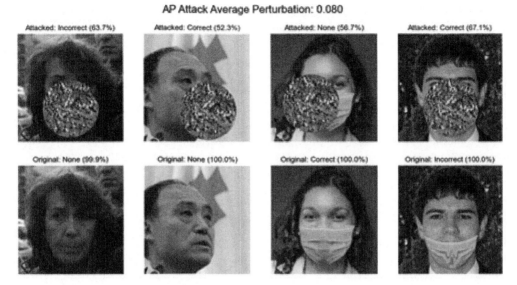

Figure 13.8 – Plot comparing AP-attacked versus original images for the base classifier

So far, we have studied three attack methods but haven't yet tackled how to defend against these attacks. We will explore a couple of solutions for this next.

Defending against targeted attacks with preprocessing

There are five broad categories for adversarial defenses, detailed as follows:

- **Preprocessing**: Changing a model's inputs so that they are harder to attack.

- **Adversarial training**: Training a new robust model that is designed to overcome attacks.

- **Detection**: Detecting attacks—for instance, you can train a model to detect adversarial examples.

- **Transformer**: Modifying the model architecture and training so that it's more robust—this may include techniques such as distillation, input filters, neuron pruning, and unlearning.

- **Postprocessing**: Changing model outputs to overcome production-inference or model-extraction attacks.

Only the first four defenses work with evasion attacks, and in this chapter we will only cover the first two: **preprocessing** and **adversarial training**. FGSM and C&W can be defended easily with either of these, but AP is tougher to defend against, so it might require a stronger **detection** or **transformer** method.

Before we defend, we must create a targeted attack. We will employ **Projected Gradient Descent (PGD)**, which is a strong attack very similar in output to FGSM—that is, it produces noisy images. We won't explain PGD in detail here, but what is important to note is, as with FGSM, it is regarded as a *first-order adversary* because it leverages first-order information about a network (due to gradient descent). Also, PGD in experiments proves that robustness against PGD ensures robustness against any first-order adversary. Precisely, PGD is a strong attack, so it makes for conclusive benchmarks.

To create a targeted attack against the correctly masked class, it's best that we only select examples that aren't correctly masked (`y_test_notmasked`), with their corresponding labels (`y_test_notmasked`) and predicted probabilities (`y_test_notmasked_prob`). Then, we want to create an array with the class (`Correct`) for which we want to generate adversarial examples (`y_test_masked`).

The code for this is shown in the following snippet:

```
not_masked_idxs = np.where(y_test_smsample != 'Correct')[0]
X_test_notmasked = X_test_smsample[not_masked_idxs]
y_test_notmasked = y_test_smsample[not_masked_idxs]
y_test_notmasked_prob = y_test_smsample_prob[not_masked_idxs]
y_test_masked = np.array(['Correct'] *\
                    X_test_notmasked.shape[0]).reshape(-1,1)
```

We initialize `ProjectedGradientDescent` as we did FGSM, except we are going to set the maximum perturbation (`eps`), attack step size (`eps_step`), maximum iterations (`max_iter`), and `targeted=True`. Precisely because it is targeted, we are going to set both `X` and `y`.

The code for this is shown in the following snippet:

```
attack_pgd = ProjectedGradientDescent(base_classifier,
eps=0.3,\
                            eps_step=0.01, max_iter=40,
targeted=True)
X_test_pgd = attack_pgd.generate(X_test_notmasked,\
                            y=ohe.transform(y_test_masked))
```

Now, let's evaluate the PGD attack as we have done before, but this time let's plot the confusion matrix (`plot_conf_matrix=True`), as follows:

```
y_test_pgd_pred, y_test_pgd_prob =\
        mldatasets.evaluate_multiclass_mdl(base_classifier.
model,\
                X_test_pgd, y_test_notmasked, labels_l,
ohe,\
                plot_conf_matrix=True, plot_roc=False)
y_test_pgd_prob = np.max(y_test_pgd_prob, axis=1)
```

The preceding snippet produces the confusion matrix shown in *Figure 13.9*. The PGD attack was so effective that it produced an accuracy rate of 0%, making all unmasked and incorrectly masked examples appear to be masked.

The output can be seen here:

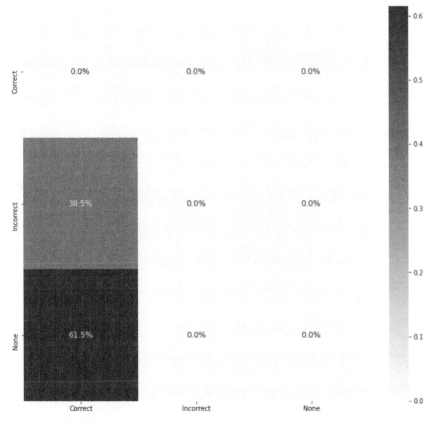

Figure 13.9 – Confusion matrix for PGD-attacked examples evaluated against the base classifier

Next, let's run `compare_image_prediction` to see some random misclassifications, as follows:

```
mldatasets.compare_image_predictions(X_test_pgd, X_test_
notmasked, \
        y_test_pgd_pred, y_test_notmasked.flatten(), y_test_pgd_
prob, \
        y_test_smsample_prob, title_mod_prefix="Attacked:", \
        title_difference_prefix="PGD Attack Average
Perturbation:", \
        num_samples=4)
```

The preceding code plots the grid of images shown in *Figure 13.10*. The mean absolute perturbation is the highest we've seen so far at 14.7%, and all unmasked faces in the grid are classified as correctly masked.

The output can be seen here:

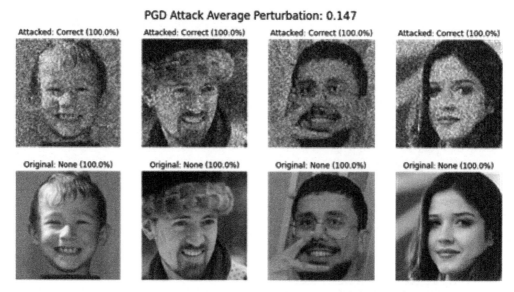

Figure 13.10 – Plot comparing PGD-attacked versus original images for the base classifier

The accuracy cannot get worse, and the images are grainy beyond repair. So, how can we combat noise? If you recall, we have dealt with this problem before. In *Chapter 8, Visualizing Convolutional Neural Networks*, **SmoothGrad** improved saliency maps by averaging the gradients. It's a different application but the same principle—just as for a human, a noisy saliency map is more challenging to interpret than a smooth one, and a grainy image is much more challenging for a model to interpret than a smooth one.

Spatial smoothing is just a fancy way of saying *blur*! However, what's novel about it being introduced as an adversarial defence method is that the proposed implementation (SpatialSmoothing) calls for using the median and not the mean in a sliding window. The window_size value is configurable, and it is recommended to adjust it where it is most useful as a defense. Once the defence has been initialized, you plug in the adversarial examples (X_test_pgd). This will output spatially smoothed adversarial examples (X_test_pgd_ss).

The code for this can be seen in the following snippet:

```
defence_ss = SpatialSmoothing(window_size=11)
X_test_pgd_ss, _ = defence_ss(X_test_pgd)
```

Now, we can take the blurred adversarial examples produced and evaluate them as we did before, first with evaluate_multiclass_mdl to get predicted labels (y_test_pgd_ss_pred) and probabilities (y_test_pgd_ss_prob), as well as the output of some predictive performance metrics. With compare_image_predictions to plot a grid of images, let's use use_misclass=False to compare properly classified images—in other words, the adversarial examples that were defended successfully.

The code for this can be seen in the following snippet:

```
y_test_pgd_ss_pred, y_test_pgd_ss_prob =\
        mldatasets.evaluate_multiclass_mdl(base_classifier.
model,\
                X_test_pgd_ss, y_test_notmasked, labels_l,
ohe,\
                plot_conf_matrix=False, plot_roc=False)
y_test_pgd_ss_prob = np.max(y_test_pgd_ss_prob, axis=1)


mldatasets.compare_image_predictions(X_test_pgd_ss,\
   X_test_notmasked, y_test_pgd_ss_pred, y_test_notmasked.
flatten(),\
   y_test_pgd_ss_prob, y_test_notmasked_prob, use_
misclass=False,\
   title_mod_prefix="Attacked+Defended:", num_samples=4,\
   title_difference_prefix="PGD Attack & Defended Average
Perturbation:")
```

The preceding code yields an accuracy rate of 54%, which is much better than 0% before the spatial smoothing defense. It also produces *Figure 13.11*, which demonstrates how blur effectively thwarted the PGD attack. It even halved the mean absolute perturbation!

The output can be seen here:

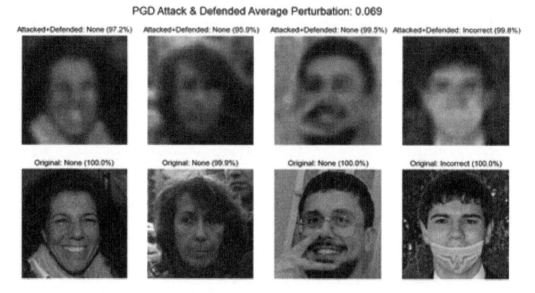

Figure 13.11 – Plot comparing spatially smoothed PGD-attacked images versus the original images for the base classifier

Next, we will try another defence method in our toolbox: adversarial training!

Shielding against any evasion attack via adversarial training of a robust classifier

In *Chapter 8, Visualizing Convolutional Neural Networks*, we faced a fruit image classifier that would likely perform poorly in the intended environment of a convenience store self-serve checkout. The abysmal performance on out-of-sample data was due to the classifier being trained on many images of one or two fruits per class, taken from entirely different angles with consistent illumination. It turns out that the variety of angles wasn't as important as the variety of fruit and illumination! The chapter's conclusion called for the training of a network with images representing their intended environment, to make for a more robust model.

For model robustness, training data variety is critical, but only if it represents the intended environment. In statistical terms, it's a question of using samples for training that accurately depict the population so that the model learns to classify them correctly. For adversarial robustness, the same principles apply. If you augment the data to include plausible examples of adversarial attacks, the model will learn to classify them. In a nutshell: that's what adversarial training is.

Machine learning researchers suggest this form of defense as very effective to any kind of evasion attack, essentially shielding it. That being said, it's not impervious. Its effectiveness is contingent on using the right kind of adversarial examples in training and using the optimal hyperparameters, and so forth. There are some guidelines outlined by researchers, such as increasing the number of neurons in the hidden layers, and using PGD or the **Basic Iterative Method** (**BIM**) method to produce adversarial examples for the training. BIM is like FGSM but not as fast, because it iterates to approximate the best adversarial example within a ϵ-neighborhood for the original image. The eps attribute bounds this neighborhood.

Training a robust model can be very resource-intensive. It is not required because you can download one already trained for you, but it's important to understand how you can perform this with ART. We will explain these steps, and if you want you to complete the model training with ART, you can. Otherwise, just skip the steps and download the trained model. robust_model is very much like base_model, except that we are using equal-sized filters in the four convolutional (Conv2D) layers. We do this to decrease complexity, to counter the complexity we are adding by quadrupling the neurons in the first hidden (Dense) layer, as suggested by machine learning researchers.

The code for this can be seen in the following snippet:

```
robust_model = tf.keras.models.Sequential([
  tf.keras.layers.InputLayer(input_shape=X_train.shape[1:]),
  tf.keras.layers.Conv2D(32, kernel_size=(3, 3),
activation='relu'),
  tf.keras.layers.MaxPooling2D(pool_size=(2, 2)),
  tf.keras.layers.Conv2D(32, kernel_size=(3, 3),
activation='relu'),
  tf.keras.layers.MaxPooling2D(pool_size=(2, 2)),
  tf.keras.layers.Conv2D(32, kernel_size=(3, 3),
activation='relu'),
  tf.keras.layers.MaxPooling2D(pool_size=(2, 2)),
  tf.keras.layers.Conv2D(32, kernel_size=(3, 3),
activation='relu'),
```

```
    tf.keras.layers.MaxPooling2D(pool_size=(2, 2)),
    tf.keras.layers.Flatten(),
    tf.keras.layers.Dense(3072, activation='relu'),
    tf.keras.layers.Dropout(0.2),
    tf.keras.layers.Dense(3, activation='softmax')
], name='CNN_Robust_MaskedFaceNet_Model')
robust_model.compile(optimizer=tf.keras.optimizers.
Adam(lr=0.001),\
        loss='categorical_crossentropy', metrics=['accuracy'])
robust_model.summary()
```

The summary() command in the preceding code snippet outputs the following code. You can see that the trainable parameters total around 3.6 million—similar to the base model:

```
Model: "CNN_Robust_MaskedFaceNet_Model"


Layer (type)                    Output Shape                 Param #
=====================================================================
conv2d_1 (Conv2D)               (None, 126, 126, 32)         896


maxpool2d_1 (MaxPooling2D)      (None, 63, 63, 32)           0


conv2d_2 (Conv2D)               (None, 61, 61, 32)           9248


maxpool2d_2 (MaxPooling2D)      (None, 30, 30, 32)           0


conv2d_3 (Conv2D)               (None, 28, 28, 32)           9248


maxpool2d_3 (MaxPooling2D)      (None, 14, 14, 32)           0


conv2d_4 (Conv2D)               (None, 12, 12, 32)           9248


maxpool2d_4 (MaxPooling2D)      (None, 6, 6, 32)             0


flatten (Flatten)               (None, 1152)                 0


dense_1 (Dense)                 (None, 3072)                 3542016
```

dropout (Dropout)	(None, 3072)	0
dense_2 (Dense)	(None, 3)	9219

```
=================================================================
Total params: 3,579,875
Trainable params: 3,579,875
Non-trainable params: 0
```

Next, we can adversarially train the model by first initializing a new `KerasClassifier` classifier with the `robust_model`. Then, we initialize a `BasicIterativeMethod` attack on this classifier. Lastly, we initialize `AdversarialTrainer` with `robust_classifier` and the BIM attack, and `fit` it. Please note that we saved the BIM attack into a variable called `attacks` because this could be a list of ART attacks instead of a single one. Also, note that `AdversarialTrainer` has an attribute called `ratio`. This attribute determines what percentage of the training examples are adversarial examples. This percentage dramatically impacts the effectiveness of adversarial attacks. If it's too low, it might not perform well with adversarial examples and, if it's too high, it might perform less effectively with non-adversarial examples. If you run the `trainer`, it will likely take many hours to complete, so don't get alarmed.

The code is shown in the following snippet:

```
robust_classifier = KerasClassifier(model=robust_model,\
                                clip_values=(min_, max_))
attacks = BasicIterativeMethod(robust_classifier, eps=0.3,\
                        eps_step=0.01, max_iter=20)
trainer = AdversarialTrainer(robust_classifier, attacks,
ratio=0.5)
trainer.fit(X_train, ohe.transform(y_train), nb_epochs=30,\
            batch_size=128)
```

If you didn't train the `robust_classifier`, we can download a pre-trained `robust_model` and initialize the `robust_classifier` with it, like this:

```
model_path = get_file('CNN_Robust_MaskedFace_Net.hdf5',
        'https://github.com/PacktPublishing/Interpretable-
Machine-Learning-with-Python/blob/master/models/CNN_Robust_
MaskedFace_Net.hdf5?raw=true')
robust_model = tf.keras.models.load_model(model_path)
robust_classifier = KerasClassifier(model=robust_model,\
                                    clip_values=(min_, max_))
```

Now, let's evaluate the `robust_classifier` against the original test dataset, using `evaluate_multiclass_mdl`. We set `plot_conf_matrix=True` to see the confusion matrix, as follows:

```
y_test_robust_pred, y_test_robust_prob =\
        mldatasets.evaluate_multiclass_mdl(robust_classifier.
model,\
            X_test, y_test, labels_l, ohe, plot_conf_
matrix=True,\
                predopts={"verbose":1})
```

The preceding code outputs the confusion matrix and performance metrics shown in *Figure 13.12*. It's 1.8% less accurate than the base classifier. Most of the misclassifications are with correctly masked faces getting classified as incorrectly masked. There's certainly a trade-off when choosing a 50% adversarial example ratio, or perhaps we can do some tuning to the hyperparameters or the model architecture to improve this.

The output can be seen here:

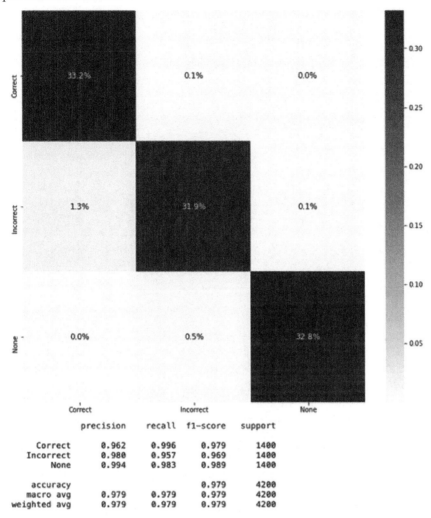

```
              precision    recall  f1-score   support

     Correct      0.962     0.996     0.979      1400
   Incorrect      0.980     0.957     0.969      1400
        None      0.994     0.983     0.989      1400

    accuracy                          0.979      4200
   macro avg      0.979     0.979     0.979      4200
weighted avg      0.979     0.979     0.979      4200
```

Figure 13.12 – Robust classifier confusion metrics and performance metrics

Let's see how the robust model fares against adversarial attacks. Let's use the FastGradientMethod again, but this time replace base_classifier with robust_classifier, as follows:

```
attack_fgsm_robust = FastGradientMethod(robust_classifier,
eps=0.1)
```

```
X_test_fgsm_robust = attack_fgsm_robust.generate(X_test_
mdsample)
```

Next, we can employ `evaluate_multiclass_mdl` and `compare_image_predictions` to measure and observe the effectiveness of our attack, but this time against the `robust_classifier`, as follows:

```
y_test_fgsm_robust_pred, y_test_fgsm_robust_prob =\
        mldatasets.evaluate_multiclass_mdl(robust_classifier.
model,\
            X_test_fgsm_robust, y_test_mdsample, labels_l, ohe,\
                plot_conf_matrix=False, plot_roc=False)
y_test_fgsm_robust_prob = np.max(y_test_fgsm_robust_prob,
axis=1)
mldatasets.compare_image_predictions(X_test_fgsm_robust,\
        X_test_mdsample, y_test_fgsm_robust_pred, num_
samples=4,\
        y_test_mdsample.flatten(), y_test_fgsm_robust_prob,\
        y_test_mdsample_prob, title_mod_prefix="Attacked:",\
        title_difference_prefix="FSGM Attack Average
Perturbation:")
```

The preceding snippet outputs some performance metrics, which evidenced an accuracy rate of 95.5%. If you compare how an equally strengthened FGSM attack fared against the `base_classifier`, it yielded 44% accuracy. That was quite an improvement! The preceding code also produces the image grid shown in *Figure 13.13*. You can tell how the FGSM attack against the robust model makes less grainy and more patchy images. On average, they are overall less perturbed than they were against the base model because so few of them were successful, but those that were, were significantly degraded. It appears as if it reduced their color depth from millions of possible colors (24+ bits) to 256 (8-bit) or 16 (4-bit) colors. Of course, an evasion attack can't actually do that, but what happened was the FGSM algorithm converged at the same shades of blue, brown, red, and orange as ones that could fool the classifier! Other shades remain unaltered.

The output can be seen here:

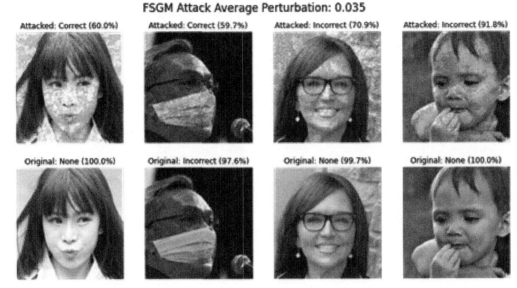

Figure 13.13 – Plot comparing FGSM-attacked versus original images for the robust classifier

So far, we have evaluated the robustness of models but only against one attack strength, not factoring in possible defenses in a rigorous cross-validated manner, thus certifying its robustness. In the next section, we will study two methods that do this.

Evaluating and certifying adversarial robustness

It's necessary to test your systems in any engineering endeavor to see how vulnerable they are to attacks or accidental failures. However, security is a domain where you must stress-test your system to ascertain what level of attack is needed to make your system break down beyond an acceptable threshold. Furthermore, figuring out what level of defense is needed to curtail an attack is useful information too.

Comparing model robustness with attack strength

We now have two classifiers we can compare against an equally strengthed attack, and we can try different attack strengths to see how they fare across all of them. We will use FGSM because it's fast, but you could use any method!

The first attack strength we can assess is no attack strength. In other words, what is the classification accuracy against the test dataset with no attack? We had already stored the predicted labels for both the base (`y_test_pred`) and robust (`y_test_robust_pred`) models, so this is easy to obtain with the `accuracy_score` metric from scikit-learn, as illustrated in the following code snippet:

```
accuracy_base_0 = metrics.accuracy_score(y_test, y_test_pred)
accuracy_robust_0 = metrics.accuracy_score(y_test, \
                                           y_test_robust_pred)
```

We can now iterate across a range of attack strengths (`eps_range`) between 0.01 and 0.9. Using `linspace`, we can generate 9 values between 0.01 and 0.09 and 9 values between 0.1 and 0.9, and `concatenate` them into a single array. We will test attacks for these 18 eps values by `for` looping through all of them, and then attacking each model and retrieving the post-attack accuracies with `evaluate`. The respective accuracies are appended to two lists (`accuracy_base` and `accuracy_robust`), and after the `for` loop, we prepend zero to `eps_range` to account for the accuracies prior to any attacks, as illustrated in the following code snippet:

```
eps_range = np.concatenate((np.linspace(0.01, 0.09, 9),\
                    np.linspace(0.1, 0.9, 9)), axis=0).tolist()
accuracy_base = [accuracy_base_0]
accuracy_robust = [accuracy_robust_0]
for eps in tqdm(eps_range, desc='EPS'):
 attack_fgsm.set_params(**{'eps': eps})
 X_test_fgsm_base_i = attack_fgsm.generate(X_test_mdsample)
 _, accuracy_base_i =\
     base_classifier.model.evaluate(X_test_fgsm_base_i,\
                                    ohe.transform(y_test_
mdsample))
 attack_fgsm_robust.set_params(**{'eps': eps})
 X_test_fgsm_robust_i =attack_fgsm_robust.generate(X_test_
mdsample) _, accuracy_robust_i =\
     robust_classifier.model.evaluate(X_test_fgsm_robust_i,\
                                    ohe.transform(y_test_
mdsample))
 accuracy_base.append(accuracy_base_i)
 accuracy_robust.append(accuracy_robust_i)
eps_range = [0] + eps_range
```

Now, we can plot the accuracies for both classifiers across all attack strengths with the following code:

```
fig, ax = plt.subplots(figsize=(14,7))
ax.plot(np.array(eps_range), np.array(accuracy_base), 'b-',\
        label='Base classifier')
ax.plot(np.array(eps_range), np.array(accuracy_robust), 'r-',
        label='Robust classifier')
legend = ax.legend(loc='upper center', shadow=True,
fontsize=15)
plt.xlabel('Attack strength (eps)', fontsize=17)
plt.ylabel('Accuracy', fontsize=17)
```

The preceding code generates *Figure 13.14*, which demonstrates that the robust model performs better between attack strengths of 0.02 and 0.3 but then consistently does about 10% worse.

The output can be seen here:

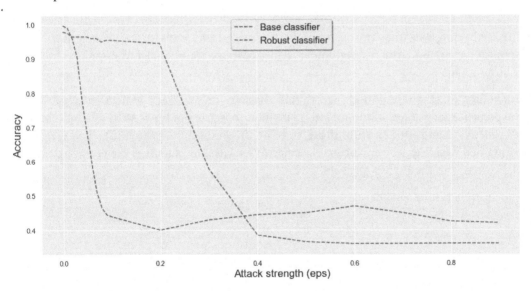

Figure 13.14 – Accuracy measured for the robust and base classifiers at different FGSM-attack strengths

One thing that *Figure 13.14* fails to account for is defenses. If, say, hospital cameras were constantly jammed or tampered with, the security company would be remiss not to defend its models. The easiest way to do that for this kind of attack is with some sort of smoothing.

Adversarial training also produces an empirically robust classifier that you cannot guarantee will work under certain pre-defined circumstances, which is why there's a need for certifiable defenses. And how about building these defenses into the model itself and certifying robustness while we're at it? Indeed, that's what we will cover next – certifying robustness with randomized smoothing!

Certifying robustness with randomized smoothing

The code for this section alone can be found at `https://github.com/ PacktPublishing/Interpretable-Machine-Learning-with-Python/ tree/master/Chapter12/Masks_part2.ipynb`. All the preparation steps are repeated from the beginning. However, unlike the rest, it uses a TensorFlow v2 ART estimator and not a Keras ART estimator because, at the time of this writing, ART's Randomized Smoothing is not available for Keras, and many of the previously explained methods aren't available for Tensorflow v2. For this reason, we don't disable eager execution (`tf.compat.v1.disable_eager_execution()`) in this notebook as we did before. Also, the default float type is set to 32 (`tf.keras.backend.set_ floatx('float32')`) because the implementation of this method can be unstable with 64 float types.

The method we will study now is more than an evaluation method; it's a robustness certification method. But it's even more than that too, because it also trains a robust model.

Previously, we saw how smoothing can foil adversarial noise, but you have to apply this in the preprocessing stage, not to mention you have to figure out how much to apply so that it's effective. **Randomized Smoothing** employs this smoothing principle by constructing a "smoothed" classifier g from a base classifier f. As with any classifier, the predicted class c is the class with the highest probability $\mathbb{P}$.

The formula can be seen here:

$$g(x) = \underset{c \in Y}{\arg\max} \, \mathbb{P}(f(x + \epsilon) = c)$$

The difference is that it's applying random *Gaussian noise* ϵ to copies of the input. It's Gaussian because it follows a normal $\mathcal{N}$ distribution and is bounded by a variance of σ^2.

The formula can be seen here:

$$\epsilon \sim \mathcal{N}(0, \sigma^2 I)$$

The certification process guarantees this result by proving that the smoothed classifier g is robust for x within an L_2 radius R, as illustrated here:

$$R = \frac{\sigma}{2}(\phi^{-1}(p_a) - \phi^{-1}(p_b))$$

Here, ϕ^{-1} is the **cumulative distribution function** (CDF) for the Gaussian function, and p_a and p_b represent the probabilities for the most probable and second-most probable class respectively. What is important to take away from this is that class predictions operate in decision boundaries, and the role of the radius is to act as a threshold for abstaining from certifying robustness of the smoothed classifier g for x.

Indeed, an appealing property of a smoothed classifier is that it can abstain from both predicting and certifying. For prediction, it might be "too close to call" if it fails a binomial hypothesis test wherein an α parameter is the threshold, making it provably vulnerable to adversarial attacks. However, Randomized Smoothing implementations can opt not to enforce prediction abstention, but they will fail to certify the prediction.

To train a smoothed classifier, we must first define a base classifier and all its training parameters. To that end, we need to initialize some standard parameters such as the number of epochs (nb_epochs), batch_size, the gradient descent optimization algorithm (optimizer), and the loss function (loss_object). Randomized smoothing also needs to know the number of classes (nb_classes) and the sample size (sample_size), which is how many perturbed instances it should create per example. We next have to change our training and test datasets to be float32 instead of float64. It will also be useful to make a one-hot encoded version of our labels so that it's easier to plug them into training (y_train_ohe) and evaluation (y_test_mdsample_ohe) functions without having to transform them every time.

The code can be seen in the following snippet:

```
nb_epochs = 10
batch_size = 128
optimizer = tf.keras.optimizers.Adam(lr=0.001)
loss_object = tf.keras.losses.CategoricalCrossentropy()
nb_classes = len(np.unique(y_train))
sample_size = 100
X_train, X_test_mdsample = X_train.astype(np.float32),\
                           X_test_mdsample.astype(np.float32)
y_train_ohe = ohe.transform(y_train).astype(np.float32)
y_test_mdsample_ohe =\
                ohe.transform(y_test_mdsample).astype(np.float32)
```

Let's now make a simple function, `get_model`, which returns an untrained base model. It has the same architecture of the previously used base model.

The code can be seen here:

```
def get_model(input_shape, min_, max_):
  test_model = Sequential([
   Conv2D(16, (3, 3), activation='relu', input_shape=input_
shape),
    MaxPooling2D(pool_size=(2, 2)),
    Conv2D(32, (3, 3), activation='relu'),
    MaxPooling2D(pool_size=(2, 2)),
    Conv2D(64, (3, 3), activation='relu'),
    MaxPooling2D(pool_size=(2, 2)),
    Conv2D(128, (3, 3), activation='relu'),
    MaxPooling2D(pool_size=(2, 2)),
    Flatten(),
    Dense(768, activation='relu'),
    Dropout(0.35),
    Dense(3, activation='softmax')
  ])
  return test_model
```

Next, we define a `train_step` function that applies gradient updates to `trainable_variables` given the `model`, `images`, and `labels`. It leverages the previously defined `loss_object` function to compute the loss, and `optimizer` to apply the gradients, as illustrated in the following code snippet:

```
def train_step(model, images, labels):
  with tf.GradientTape() as tape:
   predictions = model(images, training=True)
   loss = loss_object(labels, predictions)
  gradients = tape.gradient(loss, model.trainable_variables)
  optimizer.apply_gradients(zip(gradients,\
                        model.trainable_variables))
```

The following function, `train_rs_classifier`, initializes and trains a smooth classifier using ART's `TensorFlowV2RandomizedSmoothing` estimator. If `sigma` (σ) is zero, which means there's no variance in the intended Gaussian noise, it also can construct an unsmoothed classifier with `TensorFlowV2Classifier` and place it in `TensorFlowV2RandomizedSmoothing` so that it can be certified with `sigma_cert`. The function takes training data (`X_train`, `y_train`) and all the parameters we had previously initialized. It also defaults the α threshold for abstaining predictions at 0.001.

The code can be seen here:

```python
def train_rs_classifier(X_train, y_train, nb_epochs, batch_\
size,\
                        min_, max_, nb_classes, sample_size,\
                        loss_object, train_step, sigma=0,\
                        sigma_cert=0.5, alpha=0.001):
    input_shape = X_train.shape[1:]
    if sigma > 0:
        rs_classifier = TensorFlowV2RandomizedSmoothing(model=\
                        get_model(input_shape, min_, max_),\
                        input_shape=input_shape,\
                        clip_values=(min_, max_),\
                        nb_classes=nb_classes,\
                        sample_size=sample_size,\
                        loss_object=loss_object,\
                        train_step=train_step,\
                        scale=sigma, alpha=alpha,\
                        channels_first=False)
        rs_classifier.fit(X_train, y_train, nb_epochs=nb_epochs,|
                        batch_size=batch_size)
        return rs_classifier
    else:
        classifier = TensorFlowV2Classifier(model=\
                        get_model(input_shape, min_, max_),\
                        input_shape=input_shape,\
                        clip_values=(min_, max_),\
                        nb_classes=nb_classes,\
                        loss_object=loss_object,\
                        train_step=train_step,\
```

```
                                channels_first=False)
    classifier.fit(X_train, y_train, nb_epochs=nb_epochs,\
                    batch_size=batch_size)
    rs_classifier = TensorFlowV2RandomizedSmoothing(model=\
                                classifier.model,\
                        input_shape=input_shape,\
                        clip_values=(min_, max_),\
                        nb_classes=nb_classes,\
                        sample_size=sample_size,\
                        loss_object=loss_object,\
                        train_step=train_step,\
                        scale=sigma_cert, alpha=alpha,\
                        channels_first=False)
    return classifier, rs_classifier
```

Now, let's train three classifiers, as follows:

- `classifier_0`: An unsmoothed classifier. Please note that when $\sigma = 0$, the `train_rs_classifier` function also returns `rs_classifier_0`, which is not a smoothed classifier but the trained unsmoothed certifiable classifier.

- `rs_classifier_1`: A certifiably smoothed classifier, with $\sigma = 0.25$.

- `rs_classifier_2`: A certifiably smoothed classifier, with $\sigma = 0.5$.

The following snippet trains the three classifiers listed previously, using the `train_rs_classifier` function:

```
sigma_0 = 0
classifier_0, rs_classifier_0 = train_rs_classifier(X_train,\
        y_train_ohe, nb_epochs, batch_size, min_, max_, nb_
classes,\
        sample_size, loss_object, train_step, sigma_0)
sigma_1 = 0.25
rs_classifier_1 = train_rs_classifier(X_train, y_train_ohe,\
        nb_epochs, batch_size, min_, max_, nb_classes, sample_
size,\
        loss_object, train_step, sigma_1)
sigma_2 = 0.5
rs_classifier_2 = train_rs_classifier(X_train, y_train_ohe,\
```

```
          nb_epochs, batch_size, min_, max_, nb_classes, sample_
size,\
          loss_object, train_step, sigma_2)
```

Once we have trained our three classifiers, we can `predict` on test samples (`X_test_mdsample`) for all of them. This will take more time than usual because it needs to make sure the predictions are robust.

The code for this can be seen here:

```
y_preds_0 = classifier_0.predict(X_test_mdsample)
y_preds_rs_1 = rs_classifier_1.predict(X_test_mdsample)
y_preds_rs_2 = rs_classifier_2.predict(X_test_mdsample)
```

With the predictions, we can now gauge predictive performance for all three classifiers, with `compute_accuracy`. A useful feature of this function is that it returns accuracy and coverage. Coverage is what percentage of the predictions were made—in other words, what percentage it didn't abstain—and accuracy is computed only over predictions it did make.

Have a look at the following code snippet:

```
acc_0, cov_0 = compute_accuracy(y_preds_0, y_test_mdsample_ohe)
acc_rs_1, cov_rs_1 = compute_accuracy(y_preds_rs_1,\
                                      y_test_mdsample_ohe)
acc_rs_2, cov_rs_2 = compute_accuracy(y_preds_rs_2,\
                                      y_test_mdsample_ohe)
print("Original Classifier")
print(": %.2f%%: %.2f%%" % (acc_0, cov_0))
print("Classifier (σ=%.2f)" % (sigma_1))
print(": %.2f%%: %.2f%%" % (acc_rs_1, cov_rs_1))
print("Classifier (σ=%.2f)" % (sigma_2))
print(": %.2f%%: %.2f%%" % (acc_rs_2, cov_rs_2))
```

The preceding code outputs the following:

```
Original Classifier
      Accuracy: 99.50%    Coverage: 100.00%


Smoothed Classifier (σ=0.25)
      Accuracy: 100.00%    Coverage: 99.50%
```

```
Smoothed Classifier (σ=0.50)
    Accuracy: 98.99%    Coverage: 99.50%
```

With only 100 samples and evaluated against 200 images, all three classifiers aren't too far off from each other. The $\sigma = 0.25$ smoothed classifier reports a 100% accuracy but with 99.5%, which suggests one image is particularly hard to classify. It's likely the same one the unsmoothed classifier misclassified. The $\sigma = 0.5$ smoothed classifier reduces accuracy, suggesting that an increase in σ noise pushed another image into being misclassified.

These results seem very promising, but we haven't actually stress-tested the classifiers. We do this with `certify`, except this time we increase the number of samples to 500 (n). This function returns predictions and corresponding radiuses for each prediction, as illustrated in the following code snippet:

```
predictions_0, radiuses_0 = rs_classifier_0.certify(X_test_
mdsample,
                                                     n=500)
predictions_1, radiuses_1 = rs_classifier_1.certify(X_test_
mdsample,
                                                     n=500)
predictions_2, radiuses_2 = rs_classifier_2.certify(X_test_
mdsample,
                                                     n=500)
```

How do we leverage the radiuses to certify accuracy? We must use the radiuses as thresholds, measuring the percentage of predictions above a radius threshold that remain correct. We can create a function to this effect (`calc_cert_accuracy`). This takes a list of radius thresholds to test (`radius_list`), the results of a model certification process (`predictions`, `radiuses`), and labels (`y_test`) to test the prediction against.

The code for this can be seen in the following snippet:

```
def calc_cert_accuracy(radius_list, predictions, radiuses, y_
test):
  cert_accuracy = []
  nb_certs = len(radiuses)
  for r in radius_list:
    r_idx = np.where(radiuses >= r)[0]
    y_test_subset = y_test[r_idx]
    cert_accuracy_r = np.sum(predictions[r_idx] ==\
                      np.argmax(y_test_subset, axis=1)) /
```

```
nb_certs
    cert_accuracy.append(cert_accuracy_r)
  return cert_accuracy
```

We will now plot a line chart with radius thresholds to test in the *x* axis and corresponding certified accuracy in the *y* axis for all three classifiers. We will test 151 radiuses (`radius_list`) between 0 and 1.5 (spaced evenly at 0.01), and then use `calc_cert_accuracy` to calculate the certified accuracy for the three classifiers. The rest of the code is simply plotting these against the `radius_list` function, as illustrated in the following code snippet:

```
radius_list = np.linspace(0, 1.5, 151)
cert_accuracy_0 = calc_cert_accuracy(radius_list,
predictions_0,\
                            radiuses_0, y_test_mdsample_ohe)
cert_accuracy_1 = calc_cert_accuracy(radius_list,
predictions_1,\
                            radiuses_1, y_test_mdsample_ohe)
cert_accuracy_2 = calc_cert_accuracy(radius_list,
predictions_2,\
                            radiuses_2, y_test_mdsample_ohe)
plt.figure(figsize=(14,9))
plt.plot(radius_list, cert_accuracy_0, 'r-', label='original')
plt.plot(radius_list, cert_accuracy_1, '-', color='green',\
        label='smoothed, σ=' + str(sigma_1))
plt.plot(radius_list, cert_accuracy_2, '-', color='blue',\
        label='smoothed, σ=' + str(sigma_2))
plt.xlabel('Radius', fontsize=14)
plt.ylabel('Certified Accuracy', fontsize=14)
plt.legend()
plt.show()
```

The preceding code produces the plot shown here in *Figure 13.15*:

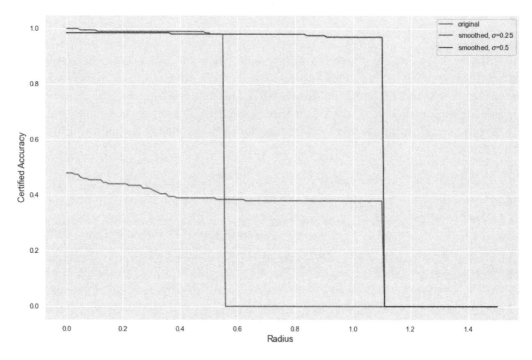

Figure 13.15 – Certified accuracy for original unsmoothed classifier and both smoothed classifiers

Figure 13.15 demonstrates that both smoothed models are initially more robust than the unsmoothed one, but smooth with $\sigma = 0.5$ is always certifiably more robust, while $\sigma = 0.25$ is not past a radius of about 0.5. Of course, we would have had even more conclusive results if we had evaluated against more than 200 test images, but the superiority of smoothed classifiers would probably hold.

Mission accomplished

The mission was to perform some adversarial robustness tests on the face-mask model to determine if hospital visitors and staff can evade mandatory mask compliance. The base model performed very poorly on many evasion attacks, from the most aggressive to the most subtle.

You also looked at possible defenses to these attacks, such as spatial smoothing and adversarial retraining, and then explored ways to evaluate and certify the robustness of your proposed defenses. You can now provide an end-to-end framework for defending against this kind of attack. That being said, what you did was only a **proof of concept** (**POC**).

Next, you can propose training a certifiably robust model against attacks the hospital expects to encounter the most, but first you need the ingredients for a generally robust model. To this end, you will need to take all 210,000 images in the original dataset, make many variations on mask colors and types with them, and augment them even further with reasonable brightness, shear, and rotation transformations. Lastly, the robust model needs to be trained with several kinds of attacks, including several kinds of APs. These are important because they mimic the most common compliance evasion behavior of concealing faces with body parts or clothing items.

Summary

After reading this chapter, you should understand how attacks can be perpetrated on machine learning models and through evasion attacks in particular. You should know how to perform FGSM, BIM, PGD, C&W, and AP attacks and defend against them with spatial smoothing, adversarial training, and randomized smoothing. Last but not least, you should know how to evaluate and certify adversarial robustness. The next chapter is the last one, and it outlines some ideas on what's next for machine learning interpretation.

Dataset sources

- Cabani, A., Hammoudi, K., Benhabiles, H. and Melkemi, M. *"MaskedFace-Net - A dataset of correctly/incorrectly masked face images in the context of COVID-19"*, Smart Health, ISSN 2352-6483, Elsevier, 2020. https://doi.org/10.1016/j.smhl.2020.100144 (Creative Commons BY-NC-SA 4.0 license by NVIDIA Corporation)

- Karras, T., Laine, S. and Aila, T. (2019). *A Style-Based Generator Architecture for Generative Adversarial Networks*. 2019 IEEE/CVF Conference on Computer Vision and Pattern Recognition (CVPR), 4396-4405. https://arxiv.org/abs/1812.04948 (Creative Commons BY-NC-SA 4.0 license by NVIDIA Corporation)

Further reading

- Polyakov, A. (2019, Aug 6). *How to attack Machine Learning* (Evasion, Poisoning, Inference, Trojans, Backdoors) [Blog Post]. `https://towardsdatascience.com/how-to-attack-machine-learning-evasion-poisoning-inference-trojans-backdoors-a7cb5832595c`

- Carlini, N. and Wagner, D. (2017). *Towards Evaluating the Robustness of Neural Networks*. 2017 IEEE Symposium on Security and Privacy (SP), 39-57. `https://arxiv.org/abs/1608.04644`

- Brown, T., Mané, D., Roy, A., Abadi, M. and Gilmer, J. (2017). *Adversarial Patch*. ArXiv. `https://arxiv.org/abs/1712.09665`

- Cohen, J. M., Rosenfeld, E. and Kolter, J. Z. (2019). *Certified Adversarial Robustness via Randomized Smoothing*. ICML. `https://arxiv.org/abs/1902.02918`

14
What's Next for Machine Learning Interpretability?

Over the last thirteen chapters, we have explored the field of **Machine Learning** (**ML**) interpretability. As stated in the preface, it's a broad area of research, most of which hasn't even left the lab and become widely used yet, and this book has no intention of covering absolutely all of it. Instead, the objective is to present various interpretability tools in sufficient depth to be useful as a starting point for beginners and even complement the knowledge of more advanced readers. This chapter will summarize what we've learned in the context of the ecosystem of ML interpretability methods, and then speculate on what's to come next!

These are the main topics we are going to cover in this chapter:

- Understanding the current landscape of ML interpretability
- Speculating on the future of ML interpretability

Understanding the current landscape of ML interpretability

First, we will provide some context on how the book relates to the main goals of ML interpretability and how practitioners can start applying the methods to achieve those broad goals. Then, we'll discuss what the current areas of growth in research are.

Tying everything together!

As discussed in *Chapter 1, Interpretation, Interpretability, and Explainability; and Why Does It All Matter?*, there are three main themes when talking about ML interpretability: **Fairness, Accountability, and Transparency** (**FAT**), and each of these presents a series of concerns (see *Figure 14.1*). I think we can all agree these are all desirable properties for a model! Indeed, these concerns all present opportunities for the improvement of **Artificial Intelligence** (**AI**) systems. These improvements start by leveraging model interpretation methods to evaluate models, confirm or dispute assumptions, and find problems.

What your aim is will depend on what stage you are at in the ML workflow. If the model is already in production, the objective might be to evaluate it with a whole suite of metrics, but if the model is still in early development, the aim may be to find deeper problems that a metric won't discover. Perhaps you are also just using black-box models for knowledge discovery as we did in *Chapters 4, 5,* and *6*; in other words, leveraging the models to learn from the data with no plan to take it into production. If this is the case, you might confirm or dispute the assumptions you had about the data, and by extension, the model.

In any case, none of these aims are mutually exclusive, and you should probably always be looking for problems and disputing assumptions, even when the model appears to be performing well!

And regardless of the aim and primary concern, it is recommended that you use many interpretation methods, not only because no technique is perfect, but also because all problems and aims are interrelated. In other words, there's no justice without consistency and no reliability without transparency. In fact, you can read *Figure 14.1* from bottom to top as if it were a pyramid, because transparency is foundational, followed by accountability in the second tier, and, ultimately, fairness as the cherry on top. Therefore, even when the goal is to assess model fairness, the model should be stress-tested for robustness. All feature importances and interactions should be understood. Otherwise, it won't matter if predictions aren't robust and transparent:

DIAGNOSTICS **aim:**
EVALUTING MODEL / CHECKING ASSUMPTIONS / DETECTING PROBLEMS / UNDERSTANDING DATA

	Concerns	Interpretation Methods
FAIRNESS	Equity Justice Diversity Inclusion	• Class Balance [3] [4] [7] [10] [11] [12] • Comparing Metrics [7] [11] [12] (FPR, FNR) • Comparing Plots [7] [11] [12] (Confusion Matrix, ROC Curve, PR Curve) • Group Fairness Metrics / *Individual Fairness Metrics* [11] (SPD, DI, AOD, EOD, DFBA, *CDD*) • Contour / Heat Probability Maps [12] • *Sampling Bias Evaluations*
ACCOUNTABILITY	Reliability Certainty Security Safety Robustness *Privacy*	• Out-of-sample Evaluations [8] • Sensitivity Analysis [9] (Sobol, Morris, *FAST*) • Causal Inference Methods [11] (DRL, *DML*, *Forest Based*, *Meta-Learners*) • Evasion Adversarial Robustness Evaluations [13] (FSGM, PGD, C&W, Adversarial Patches, *Boundary*, *PDG*, *B&B*, *DeepFool*..) • *Inference, Extraction & Poisoning Adversarial Robustness Evaluations* • *Anomaly Detection / Metrics* • *Privacy Metrics*
TRANSPARENCY	Interpretability Explainability Consistency Credibility Clarity	• Feature Importance Methods [1] [2] [3] [4] [5] [8] [9] [10] [12] (SHAP, Permutation, Model-specific) • Dimensionality Reduction Methods [3] [10] (PCA, t-SNE, VAE, *DIP-VAE*) • Glass-box Models [3] (EBM, Skoped-Rules) • Partial Dependence Plots & similar [4] [5] [7] [9] [11] [12] (ICE, ALE, SHAP Dependence) • White-box Surrogates [5] [10] [12] (Logistic Regression, Linear Regression, Rule Models, CART, KNN, *ProfWeight*) • Confirming with Statistical Tests & Correlations [5] [10] [12] (Spearman, Point-biserial, Cramér's V, Z-test) • Local Interpretation [6] [7] [9] (Decision Regions, ICE, Anchors, Counterfactuals, WIT, CEM, SHAP) • Deep Learning-specific [8] [9] (IG, Saliency Maps, Grad-CAM, SmoothGrad, *Semantic Segmentation*) • *Explainability Metrics*

Figure 14.1 – ML interpretation methods

There are many interpretation methods covered in *Figure 14.1*, and these are by no means every interpretation method available. They represent the most popular methods with well-maintained open source libraries behind them. In this book, we have touched on most of them, albeit some of them only briefly. Those that weren't discussed are in *italics* and those that were have the relevant chapter numbers provided next to them. There's been a focus on **model-agnostic** methods for **black-box supervised learning models**. Still, outside of this realm, there are also many other interpretation methods, such as those found in reinforcement learning, generative models, or the many statistical methods used strictly for linear regression. And even within the supervised learning black-box model realm, there are hundreds of application-specific model interpretation methods used for applications ranging from chemistry graph CNNs to transformer networks.

That being said, many of the methods discussed in this book can be tailored to a wide variety of applications. Integrated gradients can be used to interpret audio classifiers, hydrological forecasting models, and NLP sentiment classifiers. Sensitivity analysis can be employed in financial modeling and infectious disease risk models. Causal inference methods can be leveraged to improve user experience and drug trials.

Improve is the operative word here, because interpretation methods have a flip side!

In this book, that flip side has been referred to as *tuning for interpretability,* which means creating solutions to problems with FAT. Those solutions can be appreciated in *Figure 14.2*:

TREATMENT aim: FIXING & ANTICIPATING F.A.T PROBLEMS ("TUNING FOR INTERPRETABILITY")

	APPROACH	DATA	MODEL	PREDICTION
FAIRNESS	Mitigating Bias	Reweighting / DIR [11] LFR / DIR / Unawareness [12]	Cost-sensitive Learning [10][11][12] Prejudice Regul. / GerryFair [11]	Calibrating/Equalizing Odds [7][11] Reject Option Classification
	Placing Guardrails	Feature Engineering [10][12]	Monotonic Constraints [12]	Prediction Abstention [11][13]
	Enhancing Reliability	Data Augmentation [8][11][13]	Adversarial Debiasing [11]	*Fairness Model Certification*
	Reducing Complexity	Feature Selection [10]	Regularization [3][12]	
ACCOUNTABILITY	Enhancing Reliability	*Drift Detection* Data Augmentation [9][11][13]	Adversarial Training [13] *Adv. Transformer Defenses* Adversarial Robustness Certified Training & Inference [13]	*Adv. Postprocessing Defenses* *Adv. Detection Defenses* *Prediction Confidence Intervals*
	Reducing Complexity	Feature Selection [10] *Adv. Preprocessing Defenses* [13]	Regularization [3][12]	
	Mitigating Bias	Feature Engineering [10][12]	Monotonic Constraints [12] (+ interaction/bi-variate constraints)	Calibrating/Equalizing Odds [7][11]
	Ensuring Privacy	*Data Anonymization* *Differential Privacy*	*Federated Learning* *All Inference-attack Adversarial Defenses*	*Privacy-Preserving Inference*
TRANSPARENCY	Reducing Complexity	Feature Selection [10]	Regularization [3][12]	
	Enhancing Reliability	Feature Engineering [10][12]	Monotonic Constraints [12]	Local Interpretation [6][7][8][9]

Figure 14.2 – Toolset to treat FAT issues

I have observed five approaches to interpretability solutions:

- **Mitigating Bias**: Any corrective measure taken to account for bias. Please note that this bias refers to the sampling, exclusion, prejudice, and measurement biases in the data, along with any other bias introduced in the ML workflow.

- **Placing Guardrails**: Any solution that ensures that the model doesn't contradict domain knowledge and predict without confidence.

- **Enhancing Reliability**: Any fix that increases the confidence and consistency of predictions, excluding those that do so by reducing complexity.

- **Reducing Complexity**: Any means by which sparsity is introduced. As a side effect, this generally enhances reliability by generalizing better.

- **Ensuring Privacy**: Any effort to secure private data and model architecture from third parties. We didn't cover this approach in this book.

There are also three areas in which these approaches can be applied:

- **Data ("pre-processing")**: By modifying the training data

- **Model ("in-processing")**: By modifying the model, its parameters, or training procedure

- **Prediction ("post-processing")**: By intervening in the inference of the model

There's a fourth area that can impact the other three; namely, data and algorithmic governance. This includes regulations and standards that dictate a certain methodology or framework. It's a missing column because very few industries and jurisdictions have laws dictating what methods and approaches should be applied to comply with FAT. For instance, governance could impose a standard for explaining algorithmic decisions, data provenance, or a robustness certification threshold. We will discuss this further in the next section.

You can tell in *Figure 14.2* that many of the methods repeat themselves for FAT. **Feature Selection and Engineering**, **Monotonic Constraints**, and **Regularization** benefit all three but are not always leveraged by the same approach. **Data Augmentation** also can enhance reliability for fairness and accountability. As with *Figure 14.1*, the items in italics were not covered in the book, of which two topics stand out: **Adversarial Robustness** and **Privacy Preservation** are fascinating topics and deserve books of their own.

Current trends

One of the most significant deterrents of AI adoption is a lack of interpretability, which is partially the reason why 50-90% of AI projects never take off, and the other is the ethical transgressions that happen as a result of not complying with FAT. In this aspect, **Interpretable Machine Learning (iML)** has the power to lead ML as a whole because it can help with both goals with the corresponding methods in *Figure 14.1* and *Figure 14.2*.

Thankfully, we are witnessing an increase in interest and production in iML, mostly under **Explainable Artificial Intelligence (XAI)** — see *Figure 14.3*. In the scientific community, iML is still the most popular term, but XAI dominates in public settings:

XAI versus iML – which one to use?

My take: Although they are understood as synonyms and *iML* is regarded as more of an academic term, ML practitioners, even those in industry, should be wary about using the term *XAI*. Words can have outsized suggestive power. *Explainable* presumes full understanding but *interpretable* leaves room for error, as there always should be when talking about models, and extraordinarily complex black-box ones at that. Furthermore, AI has captured the public imagination as a panacea or has been vilified as dangerous. Either way, along with the term *explainable*, it serves to make it even more filled with hubris for those who think it's a panacea, and perhaps calm some concerns for those who think it's dangerous. XAI as a marketing term might be serving a purpose. However, for those that build models, the suggestive power of the word *explainable* can make us overconfident of our interpretations. That being said, this is just an opinion.

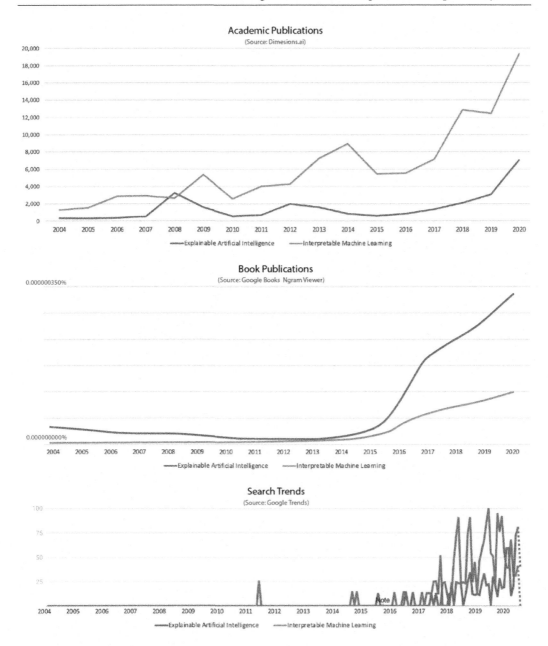

Figure 14.3 – Publication and search trends for iML and XAI

This means that just as ML is starting to get standardized, regulated, consolidated, and integrated into a whole host of other disciplines, interpretation will soon get a seat at the table.

ML is replacing software in all industries. And as more is getting automated, more models are deployed to the cloud. And it will get worse with the **Artificial Intelligence of Things (AIoT)**. Deployment is not traditionally in the ML practitioner's wheelhouse. That is why ML increasingly depends on **Machine Learning Operations (MLOps)**. And the pace of automation means more tools are needed to build, test, deploy, and monitor these models. At the same time, there's a need for the standardization of tools, methods, and metrics. Slowly but surely, this is happening. Since 2017, we have had the **Open Neural Network Exchange (ONNX)**, an open standard for interoperability. And at the time of the writing, the **International Organization for Standardization (ISO)** has over two dozen AI standards being written (and one published), several of which involve interpretability. Naturally, some things will get standardized because of common use, due to the consolidation of ML model classes, methods, libraries, service providers, and practices. Over time one or a few in each area will become the victors. Lastly, given ML's outsized role in algorithmic decision-making, it's only a matter of time before they get regulated. Only some financial markets regulate trading algorithms, such as the **Securities and Exchange Commission (SEC)** in the United States and the **Financial Conduct Authority (FCA)** in the UK. Besides that, only data privacy and provenance regulations are widely enforced, such as HIPAA in the US and LGPD in Brazil. The GDPR in the European Union takes this a bit further with the "right to an explanation" for algorithmic decisions but the intended scope and methodology are still unclear.

ML interpretability is growing quickly but is lagging behind ML. Some interpretation tools have been integrated into the cloud ecosystem, from SageMaker to DataRobot. They are yet to be fully automated, standardized, consolidated, and regulated, but there's no doubt that this will happen.

Speculating on the future of ML interpretability

I'm used to hearing the metaphor of this period being the "Wild West of AI", or worse, an "AI Gold Rush"! It conjures images of unexplored and untamed territory being eagerly conquered, or worse, civilized. Yet, in the 19th century, the United States' western areas were not too different from other regions on the planet and had already been inhabited by Native Americans for millennia, so the metaphor doesn't quite work. Predicting with the accuracy and confidence that we can achieve with ML would spook our ancestors and is not a "natural" position for us humans. It's more akin to flying than exploring unknown land.

The article *Toward the Jet Age of machine learning* (linked in the *Further reading* section at the end of this chapter) presents a much more fitting metaphor of AI being like the dawn of aviation. It's new and exciting, and people still marvel at what we can do from down below (see *Figure 14.4*)!

However, it yet had to fulfill its potential. Decades after the barnstorming era, aviation matured into the safe, reliable, and efficient Jet Age of **commercial aviation**. In the case of aviation, the promise was that it could reliably take goods and people halfway around the world in less than a day. In AI's case, the promise is that it can make fair, accountable, and transparent decisions — maybe not for any decision, but at least those it was designed to make, unless it's an example of **Artificial General Intelligence (AGI)**:

Figure 14.4 – Barnstorming during the 1920s (United States Library of Congress's Prints and Photographs Division)

So how do we get there? The following are a few ideas I anticipate will occur in the pursuit of reaching the Jet Age of ML.

A new vision for ML

As we intend to go farther with AI than we have ever gone before, the ML practitioners of tomorrow have to be more aware of the dangers of the sky. And by the sky, I mean the new frontiers of predictive and prescriptive analytics. The risks are numerous and involve all kinds of biases and assumptions, problems with data both known and potential, and our models' mathematical properties and limitations. It's easy to be deceived by ML models thinking they are software. Still, in this analogy, software is completely deterministic in nature – it's solidly anchored to the ground, not hovering in the sky!

For civil aviation to become safe, it required a new mindset — a new culture. The fighter pilots of WWII, as capable they were, had to be retrained to work in civil aviation. It's not the same mission because when you know that you are carrying passengers on board, and the stakes are high, everything changes. Ethical AI, and by extension, iML, ultimately require this awareness that models directly or indirectly carry passengers "on board." And that models aren't as robust as they seem. A robust model must be able to reliably withstand almost any condition over and over again in the same way the planes of today do. To that end, we need to be using more instruments, and those instruments come in the form of interpretation methods.

A multidisciplinary approach

Tighter integration with many disciplines is needed for models that comply with the principles of FAT. This means more significant involvement of AI ethicists, lawyers, sociologists, psychologists, human-centered designers, and countless other professions. Along with AI technologists and software engineers, they will help code best practices into standards and regulations.

Adequate standardization

New standards will be needed not only for code, metrics, and methodologies, but also for language. The language behind data has mostly been derived from statistics, math, computer science, and econometrics, which leads to a lot of confusion.

Enforcing regulation

It will likely be required that all production models fulfill the following specifications:

- Are certifiably robust and fair
- Are capable of explaining their reasoning behind one prediction with a TRACE command and, in some cases, are required to deliver the reasoning with the prediction

- Can abstain from a prediction they aren't confident about

- Yield confidence levels for all predictions

- Have metadata with training data provenance (even if anonymized) and authorship and, when needed, regulatory compliance certificates and metadata tied to a public ledger – possibly a blockchain

- Have security certificates much like websites do to ensure a certain level of trust

- Expire, and stop working upon expiration, until they are retrained with new data

- Be taken offline automatically when they fail model diagnostics and only put online again when they pass

- Have **Continuous Training/Continuous training (CT/CI)** pipelines that help retrain the model and perform the model diagnostics at regular intervals to avoid any model downtime

- Are diagnosed by a certified AI auditor when they fail catastrophically and cause public damage

New regulations will likely create new professions such as AI auditors and model diagnostics engineers. But they will also prop up MLOps engineers and ML automation tools.

Seamless machine learning automation with built-in interpretation

In the future, we won't program an ML pipeline; it will mostly be a drag-and-drop affair with a dashboard offering all kinds of metrics. It will evolve to be mostly automated. Automation shouldn't come as a surprise because some existing libraries perform automated feature-selection model training. Some interpretability-enhancing procedures may be done automatically, but most of them should require human discretion. However, interpretation ought to be injected throughout the process, much like planes that mostly fly themselves have instruments that alert pilots of issues; the value is in informing the ML practitioner of potential problems and improvements at every step. Did it find a feature to recommend for monotonic constraints? Did it find some imbalances that might need adjusting? Did it find anomalies in the data that might need some correction? Show the practitioner what needs to be seen to make an informed decision and let them make it.

Tighter integration with MLOps engineers

Certifiably robust models trained, validated, and deployed at a click of a button require more than just cloud infrastructure – the orchestration of tools, configurations, and people trained in MLOps to monitor them and perform maintenance at regular intervals.

Much like aviation took a few decades to become the safest mode of transportation, it will take AI a few decades to become the safest mode of decision-making. It will take a global village to get us there, but it will be an exciting journey! And remember, *the best way to predict the future is to create it.*

Further reading

- O'Neil, C. (2017). Weapons of Math Destruction. Penguin Books.

- Talwalkar, A. (2018, April 25). Toward the Jet Age of machine learning. O'Reilly. https://www.oreilly.com/content/toward-the-jet-age-of-machine-learning/

Packt.com

Subscribe to our online digital library for full access to over 7,000 books and videos, as well as industry leading tools to help you plan your personal development and advance your career. For more information, please visit our website.

Why subscribe?

- Spend less time learning and more time coding with practical eBooks and Videos from over 4,000 industry professionals

- Improve your learning with Skill Plans built especially for you

- Get a free eBook or video every month

- Fully searchable for easy access to vital information

- Copy and paste, print, and bookmark content

Did you know that Packt offers eBook versions of every book published, with PDF and ePub files available? You can upgrade to the eBook version at packt.com and as a print book customer, you are entitled to a discount on the eBook copy. Get in touch with us at customercare@packtpub.com for more details.

At www.packt.com, you can also read a collection of free technical articles, sign up for a range of free newsletters, and receive exclusive discounts and offers on Packt books and eBooks.

Other Books You May Enjoy

If you enjoyed this book, you may be interested in these other books by Packt:

Automated Machine Learning

Adnan Masood

ISBN: 978-1-80056-768-9

- Explore AutoML fundamentals, underlying methods, and techniques
- Assess AutoML aspects such as algorithm selection, auto featurization, and hyperparameter tuning in an applied scenario
- Find out the difference between cloud and operations support systems (OSS)
- Implement AutoML in enterprise cloud to deploy ML models and pipelines
- Build explainable AutoML pipelines with transparency

Hands-On Machine Learning with scikit-learn and Scientific Python Toolkits

Tarek Amr

ISBN: 978-1-83882-604-8

- Understand when to use supervised, unsupervised, or reinforcement learning algorithms

- Find out how to collect and prepare your data for machine learning tasks

- Tackle imbalanced data and optimize your algorithm for a bias or variance tradeoff

- Apply supervised and unsupervised algorithms to overcome various machine learning challenges

- Employ best practices for tuning your algorithm's hyper parameters

- Discover how to use neural networks for classification and regression

Packt is searching for authors like you

If you're interested in becoming an author for Packt, please visit `authors.packtpub.com` and apply today. We have worked with thousands of developers and tech professionals, just like you, to help them share their insight with the global tech community. You can make a general application, apply for a specific hot topic that we are recruiting an author for, or submit your own idea.

Leave a review - let other readers know what you think

Please share your thoughts on this book with others by leaving a review on the site that you bought it from. If you purchased the book from Amazon, please leave us an honest review on this book's Amazon page. This is vital so that other potential readers can see and use your unbiased opinion to make purchasing decisions, we can understand what our customers think about our products, and our authors can see your feedback on the title that they have worked with Packt to create. It will only take a few minutes of your time, but is valuable to other potential customers, our authors, and Packt. Thank you!

Index

T

Printed in Great Britain
by Amazon

76291086R00418